Medieval Kingship

Medieval Kingship

by **Henry A. Myers**
Professor of Political Science and History
James Madison University

in cooperation with
Herwig Wolfram
Universitätsprofessor
Institut für österreichische
Geschichtsforschung
University of Vienna

Nelson-Hall nh **Chicago**

The author acknowledges permission given by the following sources to reproduce or cite material indicated:

James Madison University Journal, revised version of an article by the author, "National Identity and the Promotion of Medieval Kingship," Vol. XXXVI (1978), pp. 41-48, given in this volume as a section of chapter 5, "Kingship and Early National Identity."

Professor Boyd H. Hill, Jr., and George Allen and Unwin, Ltd., excerpts from the translation of Emperor Henry IV's 1074 grant of privileges to the town of Worms in *Medieval Monarchy in Action*, © 1972.

Rowman and Littlefield, publishers, citations from *Henry Plantagenet* by Richard Barber, © 1964.

New York University Press, citations from *The Rise of the Aragonese-Catalan Empire, 1200-1300,* © 1971 by New York University.

Library of Congress Cataloging in Publication Data

Myers, Henry Allen, 1934-
  Medieval kingship.

  Bibliography: p.
  Includes index.
  1. Monarchy—History. 2. Kings and rulers,
Medieval. 3. Feudalism—Europe. I. Wolfram,
Herwig. II. Title.
JC375.M9   321.3 094   81-11050
ISBN 0-88229-633-7 (cloth)   AACR2
ISBN 0-88229-782-1 (paper)

Copyright © 1982 by Henry Allen Myers

Manufactured in the United States of America.

10   9   8   7   6   5   4   3   2   1

CONTENTS

PREFACE

IN SPITE OF ALL the current interest in individual kings and queens, medieval and modern, evidenced by the fact that their stories continue to make good movie, television and paperback fare, no previous book has fit together the basic pieces of kingship's origins and development. The purpose of this book is to show how and why kingship came upon the scene of Western civilization to dominate political reality and popular imagination for well over a thousand years.

The scope of this undertaking has made it an inherently immodest one for Professor Wolfram and me on several counts: we have sought not only to offer a lucid account of a very broad and involved subject but to hold the interest of different types of readers with it. We hope that the book will appeal at least to those of the general public who enjoy stories of kings and queens and that many medievalists will also find items in it which are new and of interest to them, particularly in the sections dealing with the early Middle Ages. We have further had in mind teachers and students in courses in Western civilization who might find a book useful or interesting which expands upon such figures as Constantine, Theoderic, Clovis, Charlemagne, Thomas à Becket and Joan of Arc as these relate to the unfolding of medieval kingship. Our aim, in short, has been to illustrate the development of kingship in the West in both fact and theory, while giving people a readable book of reasonable length at the same time. We did not want to compile a catalog of names and events which could easily have taken twice the space of the present volume and still not accomplished our purpose. This intent has dictated our principles of selection from the vast amount of biographical and documentary material available about the topic — principles which we have necessarily applied subjectively although, we hope, not capriciously. We have dwelt at some length on personages and happenings without respect to their relative familiarity when they have appeared to us to illustrate something significant in the development of kingship. We have (needless to say) omitted many, perhaps equally pertinent illustrations. Although we have avoided such phrases as: "Space does not allow . . ." and ". . . would go beyond the scope of this book," the reader may safely assume that much would have been included if space or our intended readership did not require limitations.

Our method of cooperation has been this: following an outline of essential points to be covered which we agreed on at the University of California, Los Angeles, when Professor Wolfram held a guest professorship there in 1968–1969, I have drafted the chapters, section by section, from a working base at James Madison University in Harrisonburg, Virginia, while he, using the incomparable facilities for medievalists of the Institute für osterreichische Geschichtsforschung in Vienna, has suggested appropriate additions and revisions along the way. While we generally had no trouble agreeing either on material to be included or interpretations of it, new studies deserving at least some consideration kept appearing on many of our subtopics. This has prolonged the gestation period of the book with the result that it has taken many more years to complete than we foresaw at the outset.

On the scholarly side, we have tried as much as possible to give credit where credit is due in the footnotes. Beyond that, we both owe a considerable debt to Professor Heinrich Fichtenau of the University of Vienna for answers to several specific questions of fact and interpretation concerning kingship in the Merovingian and Carolingian periods which only his expertise could provide. Some of the first part of chapter 2 was organized along lines derived from the studies of Professor David S. Berkowitz of Brandeis University. I also received very welcome encouragement and direction in the early stages of the project from my former advisor at Brandeis and later good friend, Professor Edgar N. Johnson. Although he did not live to see any part of the book completed in final form, some of his insights, particularly concerning the relation of the medieval Church-state controversy to kingship, are reflected in chapters 5 and 7. A considerable amount of the basic research on Spanish kingship was done at James Madison University by Ms. Sarah M. Vorhies, and I am indebted for help in running down some of the sources dealing with Roman law to my former graduate assistant, Mr. Wilbert Mahoney. On the theory that source citations in footnotes should allow the reader to follow up on them with as much ease as possible, I have generally cited the more readily available editions of late-ancient and medieval writing as long as they are sound. This has occasionally meant citing good editions enjoying somewhat less scholarly repute in preference to those editions considered nearly definitive in the field but which are so jealously guarded by the few libraries owning them that their use is difficult.

On the logistic side, constant and cheerful assistance far beyond the line of duty was provided by Ms. Janis Pivarnik, Ms. Marcia E. Grimes, and Mr. Thomas McLaughlin, James Madison University librarians, who tirelessly procured books and articles for the work through interlibrary loan year after year. In fact, general acknowledgment is also due librarians at many institutions and to the interlibrary-loan system in general. While I was able to do some of the underlying research in Vienna and Boston, where access to medieval sources is fairly easy, the bulk of it still had to be done in the Shenandoah Valley at a considerable remove from libraries geared to medieval studies. The books and photocopied material received through interlibrary loan were indispensable for proceeding.

The considerable task of typing and retyping the manuscript (some parts numerous times) was divided among many hands, but in this regard I would like to acknowledge the particularly careful work done by Ms. Belinda Babb, Ms. Elizabeth Beveridge, Ms. Shirley Black, Ms. Carolyn Dickenson, Ms. Janice Haynes, and Ms. Theresa Baker. James Madison University professors Carolyn Marshall and Dorothy Rush read parts of the manuscript and made many useful editorial suggestions. My wife, Nancy, proofread many of the sections and alerted me from time to time to problems in clarity and consistency.

Some of the background research was facilitated by a sabbatical leave from Lowell Technological Institute in 1966–1967, and some financial aid for the project was provided by the James Madison University Office of Sponsored Research during the academic year 1973–1974. An early version of the section from chapter 5, "National Identity and the Promotion of Medieval Kingship," appeared in Volume 36 (1978) of the *James Madison Journal,* pp. 41–48.

Henry A. Myers
James Madison University
September 1981

Chapter 1

The Dual Origin of Medieval Kingship

KINGSHIP AND MONARCHY

"Kingship" and "monarchy" are concepts which overlap; both today and in some earlier periods of history they have been used nearly interchangeably. Yet the stories of their development as terms for political ideas and institutions are certainly not identical.

Monarchy is the more rational of the two concepts and is easier both to define and to identify. Monarchy is simply the rule, whole or partial, of one person over a political unit. Limited within a framework of previously existing constitutional arrangements, it can be a part of a government which coexists with others. Not limited by a constitution of any sort nor forced to share sovereignty with another branch of government, it is then "absolute monarchy" or "despotism." Any number of intermediary gradations are possible.

Kingship is both the rule of one person over a political unit, as at least its nominal head, and the art or science by which such a ruler governs well. Like monarchy, kingship may also be exercised under a constitution or in the absence of one; a king may rule as the sole governmental authority or in conjunction with other institutions. The problematic thing about kingship, from the standpoint of isolating it for a moment from monarchy, is that both more and less are expected of the kingly officeholder than simply ruling as one man: more, in the sense that the king must possess a certain mystique or charisma in order to fulfill his role adequately; less, in the sense that a role of embodying and symbolizing the people may actually be his main function, while major political decisions can be made by others without necessarily drawing into question the worth of the office or its holder.

Another way of distinguishing the pair of concepts is in the historical justifications for them. Monarchy has been justified in terms of the straightforward, political need of having all or an important part of gov-

1

ernmental decisions made by one man. Kingship has been justified by a tribe's or nation's need for a figure who has more to offer than the common run of humanity in the way of being able to bring fortune in the form of victory and prosperity through his own person to the people; such a figure may even be necessary to give them their unity as tribe or nation in the first place.

Kingship, except as an art and science, is not based particularly on logic or rationality. It is consequently foreign to rationalistic periods of intellectual history, while monarchy remains a constant element. To John Adams, who during the Enlightenment pursued the struggle for an American republic with great fervor, the United States Constitution had a strong element of monarchy in it and rightly so (in fact, he felt it could well be stronger), for it allowed the elected president to make and enforce such decisions as one man that ". . . his power during those four years is much greater than that of an avoyer, a consul, a podesta, a doge, a stadtholder; nay than a king of Poland; nay than a king of Sparta."[1] Monarchy, then, as the plain political power position of a king or single executive, presented various useful models for comparing the American presidency with reasonable counterparts. Kingship, however, with its aura of mystery and irrationality in the relations it presupposes between kings and peoples, was as obviously foreign to an intelligent discussion of the Constitution for Adams as monarchy was necessary.

All this notwithstanding, more often than not, attributes of monarchy and kingship were used in the Middle Ages with reference to the same individuals and institutions. Medieval kingship had its origins in the royal tradition of the Germanic tribes of northern Europe, but it owed much of its development to the largely rational concept of monarchy derived from later Roman civilization. It makes most sense to proceed by describing first what Germanic kingship was like, apart from Roman influences, and then to bring in the monarchical tradition of Rome.

GERMANIC KINGSHIP

The essence of Germanic kingship was "doing well" for the people; a king was supposed to be able to assure his people victory in war and prosperity in peace. To this end he had to function as an effective intermediary between his people and the gods. It was a great help—in fact, a necessity—if his people could feel that he stood rather well with the gods to begin with. The Germanic peoples expected their king to have *Heil,* a concept sometimes given in English as "luck" or "fortune," but for the Germanic peoples a thing quite unrelated to chance or accident. A king who had *Heil* did well for his people, not because things happened to go surprisingly well for him but instead because in his person he subdued or eliminated elements of chance.

The English term "king" (Old English *cyning*) derives, as do its cognates in other Germanic languages, from "kin" (*cyn*). The king was the man whose *Heil* was sufficiently impressive to a group who considered themselves kin to each other that they saw him as mediating for all of them with the powers of light and darkness. In this sense, he represented the kinship, but the word "represent" is too weak as currently used to convey his function. "Represent" must be thought of much more literally: re-present, to take and present again. The king was the man who took the tribe's identity in his own person and presented it, suffused with his own *Heil*, before the gods of war and harvest.

A Germanic king had less actual power of command than rulers of Greek and Italian city states during ancient times, and he often had less to decide about the conduct of battles than Roman or Hellenistic military commanders. And yet he seems to have been so important that when he was killed, the battle and quite probably the whole war was lost. Why? The answer is comprehensible only in terms of his subsuming the identity of the tribe and assuring its success with his *Heil*. If the person who guaranteed the well-being of the tribe showed by being killed that he did not have enough *Heil* to come out of battle alive, he was obviously weighed in the balance and found wanting as far as being a guarantor of anyone's welfare was concerned. A tribe who had entrusted not only their confidence but their very identity to the man with the most *Heil* among them, and who then saw him so utterly devoid of *Heil* as to be killed, could only run for it.

Unlike the modern idea of "fortune," *Heil* was not separable from personal ability. A king won his battles through his *Heil*, but his *Heil* gave him special abilities; it did not compensate for the lack of them. The Germanic king was expected to look and act his part. He was supposed to be the best fighter and athlete among his men and to overawe strangers with his very presence. Drawing on centuries of ideal depictions of kings in Scandinavian literature, Vilhelm Grønbech distilled the following set of attributes for the king as he should be:

> . . . ambitious and always on the lookout, lest someone surpass him in any respect; never satisfied with the amount of honor attained as long as there was more to be won; deep and far-sighted in his plans; one who makes use of all means that could lead to the goal; possessed of great speaking ability and convincing to the point that men desire just what he has suggested to them; full of life and joy, generous to his men; so full of personal appeal that all the bold young men are attracted to him; a good adviser and a faithful friend; ferocious to his enemies and the enemies of his friends.[2]

The dreams of kings foretold the future more clearly than those of others. Kings were held to be more perceptive, more able to balance courage and caution, in a word, more intelligent than others, or, at the very least, better able than others to tell good advice from bad and to pick wise counselors who would plot the best course of action for attack, retreat, or negotiation.

The idea of *Heil* lives on in its English cognates, "health" and "healing." Kings were not only supposed to have better physical constitutions than others, manifested by longevity and the fact that their wounds healed more quickly than those of ordinary men, but they were also expected to be able to impart health and healing. Touching a king was good for a variety of ailments, according to a belief which lasted well into historical times. Objects belonging to a king were endowed with curative powers. For example, a drink of water in which Magnus II, king of Norway, had washed his royal hands and a chance to sleep on the king's bed are recorded in the eleventh century as curing a boy of amnesia.[3]

Altogether convinced of the value of heredity, as men of ancient and medieval times were, it was only natural that they should see kingly attributes flowing from *Heil* as hereditary. While the king started off as embodying the kin in the sense of all the tribe, and the tribe continued to rely on him to "represent" them in the sense noted, the royal family was distinguished for being a kinship within the larger tribal kinship. To have enough *Heil* to be a king presupposed coming from ancestors with the same attribute. "Royal blood" was necessary for kingship. The lineage of a king whom the gods treated well was comprehensible to the early Teutons necessarily as divine in one sense or another. In pre-Christian times, Anglo-Saxon kings were apt to trace their descent from Wotan.[4] After all, if the gods showed favor to a king and his heirs, what could be more reasonable than to assume that the gods were favoring a line of men who were more the gods' *own* than the rest of the tribe. Later, with the help of Judaic elements in Christianity, this Germanic kingship notion was to be transformed into the idea that God chose certain royal lines to enjoy His favor.

Far enough back in Germanic history, we find traces of two distinct types of kings. Their differentiation itself reflects something of the kingship-monarchy breakdown in the way their roles justified themselves. One was a tribal embodiment in a sacred person, the other a warrior ruler. The first was needed in order to deal with the gods effectively, the second for the reason of needing one man's leadership in battle. This distinction was clearly remembered as late as the fourth century A.D. by the Goths. In the translation of the Bible into Gothic by Ulfilas, the term *thiudans* signifies the former, the sacred king of the nation; *reiks* (pronounced somewhere between "rix" and "reex"), although certainly kin to the Latin *rex* etymologically, denotes "commander," "governor," or "military official," in other words, a person of rank in whom one-man authority is invested, but one in whom sacred personal connotations are minimal.[5]

The *thiudans* had his origin in tribal religion. By placating the gods better than others could do, he assured military victory and prosperity through the very fact that he lived and was adhered to. The *thiudans* was probably a chief priest in some tribes, but he invariably had certain priestly functions. His great function was, of course, doing well for his people through personifying the tribe in a manner pleasing to the god or gods which the tribe worshipped, but there were various concrete acts that a king of the *thiudans* type performed to make use of his *Heil* on the tribe's behalf, and these resembled ordinary priestly functions. Tacitus reports, for example, that Germanic kings of his own time interpreted the neighing of white horses, the most sacred auguries among the Germans, and that they ruled not so much by force of command as by the fact that their words had highly persuasive force at tribal assemblies, where they were always the first to speak.[6]

The *thiudans,* if analogies from the study of later primitive tribes are admitted into evidence, had his origin in the magnification of a father-type or father-image. He was variously the oldest, the most evidently capable, or simply the most conspicuously fortunate adult of the extended family unit, the clan or tribe. Once the societal unit was sufficiently extended to include a number of branches, or houses, within a tribe, the *thiudans* role was associated with a particular house.

The king of the *reiks* type, too, had an easier time asserting his position if he came from a royal house; however: "The criterion for his election, which was carried out by his retainers, was not his origins, but a decisive victory, an outstanding success in settling newly won territories, in sum, a glorious heroic effort which proved his kingly qualities."[7] Tacitus evidently thought of Germanic kings as of the *thiudans* type when he wrote that kings were chosen among the Germans *ex nobilitate* (i.e., because of the reputed excellence of attributes in their families), while military leaders were chosen *ex virtute* (i.e., because of their valor or merit as individuals).[8] At the same time, he seems to have been aware that the Germans were apt to recognize one of their military leaders as fulfilling the same functions as a king, at least on occasion.[9]

In the period which English and American historians have until recently termed "the barbarian invasions" and German historians, "the migrations of peoples," the kings of the *thiudans* type were rapidly losing out to those of the *reiks* type. A *thiudans* fitted a stable, well-ordered society in which laws and conventions could be taken for granted and in which there were few crises without precedent. Under those circumstances, a king qualified to rule chiefly by the reputation of his bloodline for good fortune would suffice. But when hordes of human beings were on the move in the last centuries before the breakup of the Roman Empire in the West, and the threat of starvation accompanied the grim alternatives of invade and conquer or be invaded and be conquered, good bloodlines were obviously not sufficient for real tribal leadership, and the times called for a *reiks*.

As increases in tribal size and more ambitious attempts to control larger territories made individual ability more of the essence than royal blood, the *thiudans* became less of a reality and more of a memory. Still, the first Germanic warrior kings whose stories are known were aware of the advantages in taking on attributes of a *thiudans*. In their demonstrably new royal houses there was a craving to claim rulership with a mystique which would set their houses apart from others since time immemorial. No *reiks* cared to think of being succeeded by a different *reiks* on the basis of heroic or other distinctions. While the acquisition of *thiudans'* attributes never assured the survival of a king in a period of great stress and setbacks, the *reiks* obviously needed an opportunity to relax between displays of virtue without losing his position; consequently, he and his adherents emphasized that his kingship was based not only on valor but — stealing from the *thiudans'* tradition — on the noblest blood as well. The newly royal stock wanted to demonstrate that it possessed royal fortune and that the *Heil* implanted in its house could be passed on in a smooth succession. By and large the people and their priests seem to have obliged enough in this respect, by according the warrior-king an ancient ancestry. After all, claims to rule the tribe on two different bases would have produced intolerably unstable competitions for power.

THE ROMAN MODEL

The monarchical heritage which the barbarians took from the Romans contributed to their conception of kingship in several ways. The Roman emperor presented the most striking model of monarchy which their rulers could imitate. Roman theorists and panegyrists contributed historical data and reasoning to make monarchy the one form of government conducive to bringing about human happiness on earth in the perception of most medieval people.

The Roman road to imperial monarchy had actually been anything but a straight one. According to ancient Roman sources, Rome had been ruled by kings from the time of its founding in 753 B.C. to 509 B.C. While the dates in question have lost their serious authority, there is no doubt that a period of kingship preceded the Roman Republic. Unlike the Germanic tribes, however, the Romans described by their earliest historians showed great aversion to kingship or monarchy as a dominant principle of government. Titus Livy, prominent Roman historian in the time of Augustus Caesar, equated the abolition of the Roman monarchy and the institution of annually elected consuls in the place of kings with the achievement of Roman liberty. For Romans the excesses of the Tarquins, the last ruling house, had tainted the name of "king" among the Romans once and for all. In Livy's expansive *Roman History,* as in other accounts, revulsion over the rape of the noble matron, Lucretia, by Sextus Tarquin, son of King Tarquin the Proud, had sparked a revolution. Resentment had been festering over the king's use of free Roman commoners, and veterans at that, as a labor force for erecting public buildings and digging sewers. The queen, too, had been an object of popular hatred: she was thought guilty of murder and sacrilege in the death of her father. But while the revolutionary leader, Lucius Junius Brutus, became "the Liberator" in Roman tradition because of his role in casting off the rule of the Tarquins after they had proven themselves unworthy to be kings, it seemed perfectly logical to Livy five hundred or so years later that the sequence of events should have ended the whole period of monarchical government on a note of animosity towards kingship in general rather than with the search for better kings.[10]

At the instigation of Brutus, the whole Roman people were supposed to have sworn an oath "that they would tolerate no man as king nor any who threatened her liberty to be in Rome."[11] Fictional as such an oath probably was, it reflected the sentiment of a later day accurately enough. The Roman Republic managed to hold kingship in ill repute over nearly five hundred years, for during the last five pre-Christian centuries, the Romans continued to associate kingship with selfish arbitary rule and arrogance. Their prejudice against kingship was reinforced by contacts with peoples to the east: "oriental despotism" had already been portrayed by early Greek writers as demeaning for the best of the human species and, at least in pre-Hellenistic times, as very un-Greek and worthy only of slavish, effeminate, Asiatic barbarians. By the time the Romans came under Greek influence, the Greeks themselves had long since submitted to the Macedonian kingship and the rule of Alexander's successors, but the Romans easily absorbed the idea that oriental despotism was as manifestly un-Roman as it had earlier been un-Greek. This in itself helped to keep them estranged even from milder forms of kingship.

The Roman aversion to kingship made it a deadly fault to reveal evidence of kingly ambition. While the sweeping land reform proposed by Tiberius Gracchus as tribune of the people in 133 B.C. no doubt gave wealthy landowners of the senatorial class ample justification for wanting to get rid of him, he was really destroyed by the ease with which the ingrained Roman suspicion of kingly pretense could be evoked. According to all accounts, his leadership promised to be effective, but he made himself vulnerable to charges of arbitrary behavior and a desire to concentrate too much power in his own hands. In the particular account of his death passed on by Plutarch, Tiberius made the mistake during a mob scene of lifting his hand to his head, as a sign to his friends that he sensed an armed attack on himself. His adversaries quickly spread the rumor that he was motioning for a crown to be brought to him. Their ruse was successful, and the defenders of Tiberius among the people were thrown into such confusion that Tiberius was soon killed.[12]

The role of the king as placator of the gods, on the other hand, lasted — in much attenuated form — into the Roman Republic in the person of the king-sacrificer:

> Because certain public religious ceremonies had been performed by the kings in person, a King Sacrificer was created to keep people from wanting kings back on that account. This office, however, was put under the pontifex, to keep the honorific part of the name from threatening liberty in any way. . . .[13]

In other ways, too, the Roman aversion to kingship was not absolute. Romans with some degree of sophistication could see, for example, residues of kingship in such things as the curule chair, official seat of the consuls, adorned with ivory much like a throne. Livy, in fact, had no hesitation in stating that the earliest consuls exercised royal powers in their entirety and retained all of the royal symbols in duplicate, with the exception of the "rods," the symbol of life-and-death authority, which was given to only one consul at a time.[14] The ideology of checks and balances, which intellectual defenders of the Roman Republic were committed to, had its roots in the detestation of the long-term arbitrary power associated with kings. At the same time, the Romans recognized easily enough that in the persons of the consuls they retained a certain element of one-man rule in the republic: the two consuls had a wide scope of decision-making power in their executive positions, particularly since defense preparations and military operations were under their direction. The Hellenistic historian, Polybius, congratulated the Romans on having preserved a necessary component of monarchy in the constitution of their republic, but only as one element offset by the aristocratic power of the Senate and by what was supposed to be the democratic power of the Roman people assembled.[15] In dire emergencies the two consuls could appoint a man to the office of *dictator,* which gave him absolute power for six months, although he was expected to resign when his task had been completed. From the standpoint of ancient political theory, this was even more of a monarchical office than that of consul. When Sulla stretched his dictatorship to three years (82–79 B.C.) and Julius Caesar some thirty-five years later accepted the dictatorship for life, the end of the republic, in which monarchy was a constitutionally limited element, was already in sight.

The familiar story of Julius Caesar's assassination shows how lingering the Roman aversion to kingship was. Whether or not Caesar really hoped to resurrect the Roman kingship for himself is less to the point than the fact that at the late date of 44 B.C., his appearance of desiring to do so was enough to drive the conspirators to do away with him.[16] When the wars following Caesar's assassination were finally over, the Romans accepted the rule of Augustus Caesar with scarcely a murmur, but even so, Augustus was very careful not to avail himself of offensive, kingly accoutrements. Significantly, he not only rejected the offer of the Roman dictatorship but emphatically refused to accept the salutation "Lord" (*dominus*).[17] The title of "King" was simply out of the question.

The evolution of the Roman title of "Emperor" (*imperator*) is particularly interesting in view of all this. Originally, *imperator* had a high but restricted military connotation. A man who had the *imperium* had the command in a given area or for a particular campaign and was thus *imperator*.[18] Augustus actually used a combination of titles from the republic—chiefly proconsul and tribune—for directing civil affairs and "chief priest" (*pontifex maximus*) for heading the state religion. Being proconsul gave him, among other things, the *imperium* within Rome itself and in those provinces where warfare was likely. Even for Julius Caesar, who had been far more willing than Augustus to live dangerously and who had accepted *imperator* as part of his name, the term had signified "only" a military commander of the old type and certainly not a king. Indeed, for Augustus, too, and the first few succeeding emperors, there was something of the mock modesty which much later characterized the plain-sounding words, *Duce, Führer,* and *Dozhd'*—or, most recently, "Chairman." But that did not last long. It was quite clear that the holder of the *imperium* had become a one-man ruler without meaningful checks on his power. If there had been any doubt about this, which there was not really, by the time of Caligula, it was equally clear that kings within the empire were subordinate as clients to the emperor; and a man whom kings served was bound to be like a king only more so. Thus the term "emperor" went from signifying "less-than-king" to "super-king" in fairly short order.

The long reign of Augustus (27 B.C.–14 A.D.) demonstrably lessened the Roman aversion to pure monarchy. His care not to offend republican sensibilities no doubt played a role in the gradual acquiescence of Romans to his rule; at the same time, his unquestioned success in providing peace and prosperity helped to justify his type of rule as a system preferable to the no longer workable institutions of the republic. The immense popularity of Julius Caesar had, of course, already lessened the Roman hostility to monarchy, and in the age of Augustus Caesar, the ancient aversion had become a mere ambivalence.

It was still, to be sure, an ambivalence to be reckoned with. Towards the end of the first century A.D., Domitian's open assumption of the combined title "Lord and God" (*dominus et deus*) and his reckless demonstrations of the type of arbitrary behavior associated in Roman tradition with monarchy at its worst nurtured enough hatred against him to make his assassination rather easy.[19] For all his violent death there was no real turn on the road to consolidating the monarchical system permanently in the Roman Empire, only an increased awareness that the nearly unlimited power of the monarch's position meant that it was a matter of all-consuming importance to have an intelligent and responsible individual as monarch. The period which followed—that of the five "Good Emperors": Nerva, Trajan, Hadrian, Antoninus Pius, and Marcus Aurelius (96–180)—produced no serious challenges to the monarchical principle.

Nerva, chosen emperor by the Senate, returned a share of responsibility in his administration to that body, but his short reign was more important for the example the emperor set in adopting Trajan as his son because of the military and ruling talents he had demonstrated. Trajan, Hadrian, and Antoninus Pius, who all ruled without significantly sharing their authority, as Nerva had begun to do, followed Nerva in adopting likely successors as sons. Previous selection on the basis of merit, combined with the fiction of son following father, provided for nearly a century of good government, which remained without serious domestic challenges. The series of Good Emperors came to a sudden end, however, when Marcus Aurelius chose not to adopt another promising candidate as his son, but rather to allow his own worthless son, Commodus, to succeed him. A century marked by assassinations, overthrows, civil wars, and competing claimants chosen by different Roman armies—the century of the "Soldier Emperors"—followed.

In both the stable times of the Good Emperors and the tumultous times of the Soldier Emperors, the Romans had learned to live with the emperor's title of *dominus,* and the model of oriental monarchy proved to be sufficiently compelling to graft divinity of a sort onto the emperors as well. But while the emperor as *dominus* became a fact of life, his godlike attributes were more elusive. In the Roman state cult, actual miracles were asked only of emperors who were safely dead. The deification of Julius Caesar after his death had worked as a precedent in this respect. After Augustus had also been elevated to the ranks of the gods upon his death, such deification became an accepted possibility on the death of a popular emperor, although never a routine one. Dead god-emperors could be prayed to for favors to the individual or intervention on behalf of the state: their record of miraculous performance in the popular mind seems to have been neither good enough to inspire much enthusiasm nor bad enough to suggest massive disillusionment with such divinities before the victory of Christianity in the empire. Most living emperors, however, were content to have their persons or images venerated in a variable combination of religious and political awe.

At the end of the near-century of upheavals and chaos which had begun with the assassination of Commodus in 192, Diocletian restored stability to the empire and further solidified the hold of the monarchical system at the same time. Diocletian was the ultimate pragmatist. Within a year after his accession in 284, he was putting together a system of elements eclectically chosen to make monarchy work. On the one hand, he emphasized the irrational, charismatic side of kingship which had been finding its way more and more into Roman tradition through imitations of oriental despotism. Under Diocletian, the emperor became more exalted and more removed from the realm of mortals than ever before. On the other hand, his administrative and military reforms were rational to the utmost: he divided and subdivided the empire into more manageable units. For the purpose of determining taxes in kind, he had all areas assessed for their proportional abilities to yield revenue. He then had his administrators project governmental needs with an eye on available resources. Taken together, these two sets of efforts amounted to a novel experiment in imperial budgeting. To combat inflation, he instituted price controls. He made the military both more mobile and more subject to discipline. Soon he offered an ingenious solution to the awesome succession problem. He divided imperial authority four ways. Two senior emperors, called *augusti,* were to rule larger or wealthier regions; two junior emperors, called *caesares* were to rule somewhat lesser areas. The junior emperors were to succeed the senior emperors after fixed terms and appoint their own replacements to the junior positions.

All in all, Diocletian's reforms were successful in restoring a considerable measure of peace and stability to the empire. From the standpoint of the Roman contribution to medieval kingship, Diocletian's reforms had two main effects: they confirmed the tendency to center the Roman model of monarchy around a ruler exalted into the superhuman sphere (something only partly undone by subsequent Christian emperors). At the same time, they satisfied the felt need for rational support of the Roman model of monarchy through wide reaching administrative machinery — something absolutely foreign to Germanic kingship in the early Middle Ages.

In a third, less direct way, Diocletian's system was to affect the Roman imperial model perceived by medieval people. His system of appointing successors, which was copied in the fourth century by Christian emperors, stood in marked contrast with kingship as a hereditary system. Emperors could, of course, appoint their own sons as *caesares* and, on occasion, the results were as miserable when they did so as when Marcus Aurelius selected Commodus as future ruler. Still, the very need for appointment underlined the consideration that heredity alone was not enough. In the German Empire, where eventually the Roman model was taken most seriously in the Middle Ages, the need for some sort of selection process for the ruler, to offset considerations of mere heredity, was accepted from early modern times into the eighteenth century. In this way, the need for election or special appointment of the head of state entered part of the medieval tradition as a transformation of the lingering Roman ambivalence toward the hereditary principle in kingship. Outside of the Germanic Empire, however, the hereditary principle was overwhelmingly strong. When medieval kings elsewhere raised their sons to co-ruler status during their own lifetime, as they sometimes did in England, for example, they had justification for doing so on the basis of Germanic precedent. There was also the natural desire to give their sons experience before having to undertake royal decision-making completely on their own. In such instances, the Roman model at most may have reinforced this inclination of some European kings to give their progeny a head start at becoming effective rulers.

CHARISMA, GOVERNMENT, AND CHRISTIANITY

Royal blood and military command necessarily gave a barbarian king, whether Germanic or not, an exalted position within the tribe. At the same time, the fact of having an exalted monarchical figure as the tribal head did not particularly hamper the personal freedom of an ordinary member of the tribe. This was true for the simplest of all reasons: such a ruler did not have all that much "government" under him. Unlike his imperial Roman counterpart, he was not particularly concerned with taxes or labor service: the whole business of constructing public edifices, maintaining viaducts and paving roads, or staffing a civil service, was still foreign to him. Here, the most extreme example is the most revealing: that of Attila the Hun.

The Huns were of Mongoloid rather than Germanic origin, but with his hordes of nomadic warriors and his person surrounded by signs, wonders, and prophecies, Attila's role resembled that of a Germanic king writ large. When the much later writer of the *Nibelungenlied* made Attila into everything that a German king would want to be in terms of wealth, power, and personal magnetism, he was not far off the mark. The point is this: in magnificence and military might, the historical Attila towered above eastern and western emperors alike for a time; yet, it was possible for Roman citizens to find contentment under him. Among his people they could enjoy meaningful personal freedom. The fifth-century Graeco-Roman historian, Priscus Panites, records a conversation at the court of Attila with a former citizen of the empire who had been captured by the Huns and who had stayed with them very much of his own free will. For him, peacetime life under Attila meant plenty of free time and a minimum of harassment, while Romans were suffering under heavy taxes, uneven enforcement of laws which enabled the rich and powerful to oppress the poor, and the unwillingness of petty tyrants to let the people bear arms enough for their own defense (in what were obviously unsettled times). Priscus remonstrated about the guarantees of Roman law in contrast with the arbitrary rule which the king of the Huns could exercise, but from the standpoint of this voluntary subject of Attila all that was irrelevant. The theoretical advantages of civilized Roman rule did not outweigh the fact that the king of the Huns gave his people meaningful protection and let them enjoy whatever they had with a minimum of interference.[20]

At the onset of the Middle Ages, rulership in the Germanic tribes was generally a male affair, but there had been exceptions where queens headed tribes. Earlier, Tacitus mentioned one Veleda as having had an extensive domain in the area around Cologne; many tribes apart from her own people, the Bructeri, ascribed magic powers to her while she lived.[21] By way of contrast, rule of any sort by women in the Roman imperial system was possible only behind the scenes, with one fleetingly brief exception.[22] There is probably some significance in this contrast which reveals the ancient and medieval mind at work. Germanic kingship was, we may recall, essentially charismatic and religious. Roman emperorship developed more from rationally felt needs for one-man government. The premodern world was willing to attribute charisma to women well before it was willing to attribute sustained rationality to them. The dowager queen, Hatshepsut, became a female pharaoh in ancient Egypt (the ultimate position of charismatic rulership in the ancient world), but there were no female archons in ancient Athens.

To the extent that the two components of medieval kingship discussed thus far can be treated as abstractions, it would be fair to say that the Germanic tradition of kingship tended more to satisfy the prerational, psychological needs of a people, while the Roman model tended more to suggest the rational need for subordination and administration in a governmental system. The temptation to leave the division at this—perhaps with the customary precautions against isolating elements, particularly as abstractions, from the total fabric of medieval civilization—is a considerable one. This is particularly the case since late-ancient and early medieval authors occasionally did so themselves. For example, the poet Claudian at the end of the fifth century referred to the basis of rulership as differing between Roman emperors and even the greatest of non-Roman kings. Kings, Claudian observed, base their claim to rulership on their nobility or blood, while Roman emperors base their claim on *virtus,* or individually proven merit.[23]

Claudian's observation corresponds handsomely with the two-fold division of bases for kingship stressed thus far; however, even by Claudian's time, any reference to concepts such as "nobility" or "merit" in a framework removed from the Christian scheme of things was becoming unreal. Claudian was one of the last pagan writers of significance. Well before he wrote, events were transpiring which were to influence decisively both the medieval perception of kingship and the lasting sources of authority to which medieval protagonists and critics of kingship were to resort.

In the fourth and fifth centuries, the Christian perception of what was valuable and important began to color the total concept of kingship. These tints were sometimes deep and sometimes faint, but they were never to be overlooked throughout the entire Middle Ages. The Christian vehicle of the sermon carried ancient history and ideas down to common levels of understanding to a degree which has only been appreciated within the last forty years or so. Challenged as the power of the Church assuredly was during the Middle Ages, churchmen had a near monopoly in the propagation of ideas. Even the first attempts at a renaissance, notably those associated with Charlemagne and his immediate successors, did not reduce the clerical contribution to medieval perceptions of the world in general and kingship in particular. The reverse was also true. One of the first things reborn in the Carolingian Renaissance was an appreciation of patristic literature and ideas. [24]

The events which constituted Church experience during the patristic period drove emerging Christian theories of kingship back and forth over a wide terrain. Since they were formulated at different points during the course of ecclesiastical vicissitudes in the fourth and fifth centuries, the resulting theories seem to conflict with each other on certain key points. They were cited against each other in medieval disputes involving kingship. Together with their underlying biblical sources, however, they remained the only theories medieval people had to draw on. Innovation was not readily accepted in the Middle Ages, and the patristic perceptions of kingship would be reformulated many times during the centuries following, before men would admit that they were cutting loose from church teachings when dealing with phenomena of the secular world. There is thus no way to avoid a retracing of the interaction of events and ideas which produced the Church's idea of kingship in its formative period for the Middle Ages; nor is there any need to apologize for taking such a route, since it is, all in all, a quite interesting one.

Chapter 2

The Church and Kingship at the Onset of the Middle Ages

CAESAR AND THE TRIBAL KING

The biblical treatment of kingship is anything but uniform, and no theologian ever succeeded in bridging the gulf which separates the attitude toward the ruler in the Old and New Testaments. The Old Testament's David and Solomon, anointed by an agent of God to lead their people, make an entirely different impression upon the reader or hearer than does the New Testament's Caesar, to whom Caeser's due must be rendered. In broad outline, the story of the relation of biblical teaching to the position of the medieval Church on kingship is one which begins with emphasis on New Testament attitudes and — roughly to the extent that kings and their supporters could see the value of invoking the precedent of Old Testament kings — shows a gradual increase in the influence of the Old Testament.

In the New Testament, Caesar is clearly absolute in the temporal sphere. He is foremost among those powers which Christians may resist only at the risk of eternal damnation. His exalted position is, however, not derived from a view of the Roman monarchy as particularly worthy; on the contrary, it is derived from the other-worldly orientation of the New Testament, which is apolitical. It is an understatement to say that Caesar's authority reflects no glory on him in the New Testament. He is absolute because power and wealth are his domain, while Christians should not want to have anything to do with that world of power and wealth. On a different level, it is the devil who is referred to in the New Testament as "the prince of this world."[1] Caesar is never equated with the devil, but the fact that Caesar has ostensible, temporary authority in the sphere of this world, which is the devil's domain, does not speak well for his office either.

Occasionally the early Church found the empire of the pagan Caesars useful. The empire provided relatively easy communication among its lands, which was advantageous in spreading the Gospel. Orderly Roman legal procedures meant that the empire's courts would treat its Christian citizens with dignity when it was not killing them — or even when it was: Saint Paul, according to tradition, was beheaded as a Roman citizen, while the noncitizen Saint Peter was crucified, and upside down at that. But as long as the emperor remained a pagan, and pagans persecuted Christians, no glorification of kingship was possible for the faithful, either in terms of individual Roman rulers or as a principle of government. Apart from this, the "state" appears in the New Testament in large part in its judicial function, and the words of Christ do not allow much to be expected from it:

> Come to terms with your opponent in good time while you are still on the way to court with him, or he may hand you over to the judge and the judge to the officer, and you will be thrown into prison.[2]

While Saint Paul commanded obedience to the state, he condemned Christians for voluntarily taking cases before the "lawcourts of the unjust,"[3] by which he seems to have meant any of the courts known under the empire. Because pagans sat upon the benches did not make the courts "unjust" for him in the sense of prone to violate the written law, but the taint of paganism did make the courts unfit places for Christians to settle disputes.

Before the conversion of Constantine the most Christians really wanted from the state was to be left alone in peace, like other subjects of the emperor who obeyed him in matters of secular law. As decades of persecution wore on into centuries, it seemed clear that imperial authorities had no intention of letting alone those who failed to venerate the emperor's statue or the traditional gods of Rome. Tertullian, who had been a lawyer before he was converted to Christianity and assumed priestly duties in or near Carthage at the end of the second century, looked back with bitter complaints about the injustice of even the relatively conciliatory Emperor Trajan several generations earlier. Trajan enjoyed an excellent reputation for fairness, objectivity, and common sense among pagan Roman contemporaries as well as among modern writers. About 111-113, Trajan had approved what seemed to him a just and expedient way of coping with an insidious Christianity without excessive bloodshed. Christians, he wrote, should not be sought out, but Christians who, without being sought out, came into the custody of the law and after being given ample chance for repentance refused to adore Roman gods were to be executed. For Tertullian this was neither consistent nor honest:

> He says that they should not be sought — as though they were innocent; then prescribes that they should be punished — as though they were guilty! He spares them, yet vents his anger upon them; he pretends to close his eyes, yet directs attention toward them! Judgment, why do you thus ensnare yourself?[4]

Caesar was, of course, not the only monarch with a role in the New Testament, and kingship was never entirely separated either from its religious or its tribal background in the early centuries of Christianity. For Tertullian, to be sure, it seemed natural to refer to Christ as "the Emperor" in order to emphasize Christ's sovereignty over the universe.[5] Christ portrayed as the divine emperor necessarily stood in contrast to the Roman emperor. Tertullian's usage remained rather exceptional, however. Although "emperor" and "empire" were the normal concepts to convey universality of rulership in the West during the first five centuries, early Christian writers in general used "King" in referring to Christ, and "Kingdom" for the divine domain instead. We are inclined perhaps to assume that the original New Testament usage of "king" and "kingdom" must have settled the matter. As a matter of fact, the Greek terms *basileus* and *basileia* were regularly understood and translated as "emperor" and "empire" after the first century A.D., as well as "king" and "kingdom."[6]

A partial explanation for the entrenchment of "king" and "kingdom" in the religious, as well as secular, vocabulary of Christians, can be found in the tendency of early Christian writers and biblical translators to emphasize Christ not only as the ruler of a domain not of this world, but also as an apparent tribal king as well. To make intelligible to his fellow Goths the famous question of Pilate to Christ, "Are you the King of the Jews?" the biblical translator Ulfilas fell back upon the old tribal term, *thiudans*.[7] In any language, Pilate's question to the chief priests, "Shall I crucify your King?" and the response, "We have no king but Caesar" had a distinctly tribal reference, as did the "RI" for the title *Rex Iudaeorum* in the abbreviation, INRI, over the cross. From a modern perspective, this whole matter is at most a side issue demonstrating a misunderstanding of Christ's relationship to the Roman emperor, but in the Middle Ages every biblical portrayal of their relationship was significant. It was not difficult to infuse the position of tribal kings with the Old Testament tradition of kingship. As the Middle Ages progressed, we shall see this particularly in the development of Frankish kingship. The New Testament, however, presented more problems, and the concept of Christ as tribal king was a welcome aid to those looking for New Testament approval of kingship.

The understanding of Christ as *rex* or *thiudans* was no doubt intensified by the desire of most Christian writers (unlike the contentious Tertullian) to avoid using *imperator* in a sense which specifically contrasted with the imperial Roman title. Because of the mark left by the lasting Roman ambivalence toward kingship, the term "King" was, oddly enough, the one high and mighty title which the rulers of Rome did not normally apply to themselves before the Middle Ages. Consequently, it was more nearly "free" for Christians to use for Christ than "emperor" would have been. Then, too, the Near East background of the Judaic-Christian tradition was one in which rulership was generally conceived of in ethnic, religious, and charismatic terms. These were more easily transplanted to other cultures as attributes of familiar tribal kingship, than as attributes of the Roman emperorship, which a unique combination of military, political, and administrative necessities had fashioned in a way quite foreign to the experience of most tribes in western Europe at the onset of the Middle Ages.

All this notwithstanding, it was still Caesar who remained the foremost secular ruler in the eyes of those Christian writers of the early centuries whose works were to have the greatest impact on medieval kingship. It is important to keep in mind the attitude of such a man as Tertullian, who lived under the emperors before Constantine and who wrote while persecution in the Roman monarch's name was still a reality. Later Christian writers who defended the empire were to make something quite different out of the relationship of Christians to Roman rulers. They looked back on the first three centuries from a safe distance in an empire which itself had become Christian. During their first three historical centuries, Christians obeyed the emperor in nonreligious matters; they sometimes prayed for the emperor and for Roman victories; and some of them fought in the Roman armies. With rare exceptions, however, any emotional commitment to the view that Caesar enjoyed an exalted relationship with God was still quite foreign to them.

THE ROMAN MONARCH BEGINS TO DEFEND THE FAITH

The conversion of Constantine to Christianity and his victory over his rival, Maxentius, in October 312, after Constantine had been inspired to have something like a Christian symbol painted on the shields of his soldiers, changed all this in short order.[8] Suddenly, for the faithful, the monarch was no longer the head of forces which might repress them at any moment; instead, he became the guarantor of their equality among Roman subjects. The most important questions dealing with the relation of the monarch to the Church were all raised in the fourth century. Time and again, both supporters of medieval kings and their opponents were to cite fourth-century precedents in Church-state relations, either to confirm the right of kings to deal rather summarily with churchmen or to challenge precisely that right.

The fourth century ultimately stood the older Church-state relationship on its head. At the beginning of the fourth century, Church and state in the Roman Empire were not only separate but hostile. By the end of the fourth century, Church and state were very much fused — and in a manner which could scarcely have been foreseen at the outset. Early in the fourth century, the Church came to rely on Emperor Constantine for the strength of his hand in settling doctrinal questions. Late in the fourth century, the

Church let Emperor Theodosius know in no uncertain terms that it would direct his hand in deciding political questions with doctrinal implications.

The personalities of fourth-century Roman monarchs and churchmen played a major part in this change, as did the course of controversies within the Church itself. Constantine's initial policy towards all religious groups was one of toleration in the strictest sense of the word. Where early modern policies of toleration tended either to be limited in their application or to arise from the relative indifference of their proclaimers, Constantine's policy was at first not limited nor did it, at any time, stem from his religious indifference. This policy is reflected in a constitutional decree for Bithynia, issued to its governor by Constantine's co-emperor Licinius on June 15, 313, who notes that Constantine and he had decided

> . . . that no man whatsoever should be denied the freedom to devote himself either to Christian worship or to any religion he should find to be best for himself, so that the Highest Divinity, worshipped by us with free spirits, will continue to grant us His favor and benevolence.[9]

Constantine certainly never felt that his policy of toleration obligated him to official impartiality; he was too much of what our own age might call a "religious activist" for that. Ultimately his religious zeal led him to take one position, that under his successors was to make a shambles of religious toleration, and another which was to prove an enduring source of conflict. Both were of the utmost importance in providing precedents for later sovereigns in their relationship to the Church over more than the next thousand years. The first simply established the monarch's obligation to help the true faith prevail over error for the public good. The second implied the monarch's right to direct churchmen when questions of dogma were to be decided.

In the months following his victory over Maxentius, Constantine was already taking steps toward the first position, for he immediately went well beyond restoring Church property that had been seized during the persecutions. He granted a handsome sum from the public treasury to Caecilian, bishop of Carthage, for unspecified Church expenses and offered more if it should prove inadequate.[10] He instructed Anulinus, proconsul of Africa, to reward "those men who in due holiness . . . offer their personal services to the ministry of the divine worship" and to see to it that all Catholic clergy be exempted "from all public burdens of any kind whatsoever." His justification for giving them this preferential treatment was simple and to the point: "It is certain that if they will conduct the most devout worship of the divine majesty, the greatest benefit will redound to the state."[11] Later he extended to churchmen a small share in the governance of the Empire: beginning in 318, he let two parties contending at law take their case to a bishop for a final verdict; in 321, he made manumis-

sions before a bishop legally valid. By the end of his reign, the civil authority of the Church had grown to the point that either party in a civil suit
could bring it for verdict to the local bishop from whom there was no
appeal.[12] The overlapping court jurisdiction of secular and church authorities, which was greatly to complicate life for medieval kings and bishops,
had begun.

Constantine's mind had, of course, become gradually closed toward
pagan worship, a process hastened by two wars with Licinius. As Constantine came to see the Highest Divinity mentioned in their joint edict more
and more as the Christian God alone, Licinius took more and more to
seeing the same officially neutral deity as Jupiter. The first conflict was
touched off in 314, when Constantine sought to establish a separate *caesar*
in Italy, and Licinius attempted to corrupt the appointee into betraying
Constantine's interests. This was terminated inconclusively in 315, but
another conflict followed from Constantine's invasion of territory assigned to Licinius in pursuit of marauding Goths in 323. Measures taken
against Christians by Licinius may have prompted Constantine to look for
a fight. Licinius had begun requiring the performance of pagan sacrifices
as a test for office. This, of course, eliminated Christians from his part of
the imperial service; he was also harassing the Church with a series of
annoying prohibitions.

In Constantine's second war against Licinius, we can already discern the
outlines of the holy wars and crusades medieval kings were expected to
wage. During his battles Constantine had his Christian standard, the *labarum,* carried to wherever the fighting was thickest and the men most in
need of inspiration. For his own inspiration he frequently retired to a
prayer tent. His Sunday policy discriminated conspicuously against pagan
soldiers. Christian soldiers were given time off to attend church, while
pagans were required to take part in a parade and then to recite a neutral
but monotheistic prayer to the Highest Divinity.[13] Licinius responded in
kind with appeals for victory to the ancient gods. When Constantine
defeated him decisively with lesser forces, the outcome strengthened the
view to which Constantine was already tending: the Christian God he
worshipped was all-powerful; the pagan gods of Licinius were powerless
against Him. In the struggle God had been helping His own followers in
His own cause.

Constantine did not prohibit pagan worship after his victory; on the
contrary, he confirmed toleration in a new edict. But it reflects Constantine's victory over Licinius in its condescension for the pagans: "Let those
who err gladly enjoy the same peace and tranquility as those who believe,"
and his allusion to "the customs of the temples and the powers of darkness" certainly let the pagans know where their religion stood in his
mind.[14] Then, too, even his proclaimed toleration was not so complete.

He closed a few renowned pagan temples and despoiled many more of their art works and gold, including the gold covering of the cult statues themselves.[15]

Clearly, in the Emperor's exaltation of Christianity and his denigration of paganism, Church and monarchy were slowly joining forces against a common enemy. Although nothing would have been farther from the mind of the pious Constantine than attempting to improve on a key biblical phrase, it is significant of the changed relationship of the Church to this world that Constantine referred to the devil, not as the old "prince of this world," but as an earthly outlaw, "the enemy of this world."[16]

The second great precedent Constantine set for medieval kings was that of taking a considerable part in Church quarrels. For our purposes, it is sufficient to look briefly at his epoch-making role in dealing with two of these, the Donatist and Arian controversies.

The Donatist issue revolved around a pair of related questions: how much resistance should Christians have offered to their recent persecutors? And, did the sacraments lose their effect when they were administered by a lapsed priest, i.e., one who had yielded too easily to the persecutors, particularly in the matter of handing over the Scriptures to imperial agents for destruction? Even before Constantine came to power, these questions had divided Christians in Roman Africa. On one side, those who were to be called Donatists (after one of their subsequent leaders, Donatus of Casae Nigrae) insisted that martyrdom and no cooperation with persecuting officials was the only acceptable course for Christians. On the other side, various shadings of moderates garnered the name "Catholic" for themselves during the course of the dispute. These were willing to make allowances for human frailty under duress and stressed the validity of all sacraments dispensed by a legitimately ordained priest regardless of his personal shortcomings.

Constantine's restoration of the property of the Church in Roman Africa made these issues public matters. It was only during the course of his attempts to undo the effects of his persecuting predecessors that the positions on both sides were actually clarified or, at least, stated with more consistent extremity. At the advice of Ossius (or Hosius) of Cordova, Constantine supported the moderate Caecilian, whose resistance to the persecutors had not been of the fullest before he was ordained as Bishop of Carthage. The Donatists refused to accept Caecilian as bishop; instead, they demanded the church property which the emperor's directive to Anulinus had assigned to him and his supporters. Social cleavage deepened the religious schism: the Donatists in Roman Africa tended to be poor and often of unassimilated stock, such as the Berbers; the Catholic supporters of Caecilian tended to be well off and aristocratic. Violent acts against Church property and persons followed an exchange of recriminations.

Constantine attempted to settle the matter amicably by appointing a commission of three bishops to hear the arguments of both sides. The commission found the Donatists' charges unfounded, but the Donatists appealed the decision to Constantine, who asked a large council of western bishops to convene at Arles to consider the matter thoroughly. He even provided transportation for them to attend. Again the Donatists lost, and again they appealed. Even then, Constantine, although annoyed, hesitated to take action against the Donatists before sending two bishops to Carthage in hopes of negotiating a compromise. This effort failed also, and the Donatists continued what had become resistance to imperial as well as orthodox clerical authority with acts of violence against the Catholics and Church property in Catholic hands.

Frustrated in his attempts to provide conciliation, Constantine intervened heavy handedly in order to keep the peace and the unity he felt necessary for the prosperity of the empire. Even in the first year after his victory over Maxentius, he had shown himself aware of the difference between Catholic and heretic.[17] Now he felt compelled to overcome the difference. To this end, he announced in a letter to Celsus, his vicar in Africa, that he would come to Africa himself to set the clergy straight once and for all on the proper worship of the deity and promised that he would "strike down and scatter" those who did not comply with his directives.[18] Constantine did not, in fact, get to Africa, and the subsequent persecution of the Donatists was an on again, off again sort of thing, applied usually when the Donatist violence provoked military intervention and bloodshed. He ultimately found this course unsuccessful and cancelled the coercive measures against the Donatists.[19] But the fact remained that Constantine had tried to force the obstinate Donatists to unite with the recognized Catholics. Thus a Christian emperor had been provoked into using the arms of the state toward achieving a goal not qualitatively different from that of the persecuting pagan emperors who had sought to impose a semblance of religious unity on the empire. It was the first step toward persecution of religious dissidents in the name of Christian unity, another duty that was to be required of medieval kings on occasion. Constantine had been provoked into action and had used a reluctant and temporary minimum of force, but later rulers did not feel obliged either to wait for any such provocation or to limit coercive measures dictated by the goal of religious conformity.

CAESAR ASSUMES A BISHOP'S ROLE; MONARCHY BECOMES GOD'S OWN
FORM OF GOVERNMENT

In contrast with the Donatist schism, the Arian-Trinitarian rift when it first arose had the look of a purely theological issue which Constantine thought could be quietly laid to rest. Arius, a priest of Alexandria, had begun teaching around 313 that the Trinity could not consist of equal persons. If the terms "God the Father" and "God the Son" are used at all, there must have been a time when there was a God the Father but no God the Son; hence the Son's existence, let alone power and glory, must have come from the Father. To be sure, Arius had a predilection for Greek philosophy and did not put his propositions quite so simply, but when they were reduced to terms comprehensible to less learned minds, this was indeed what they added up to. Orthodox churchmen perceived a real threat in his doctrine, which became popular enough to be worked into verses and sung in the streets by his adherents even after his excommunication in 318.[20] They saw Christ being demoted from full divinity in being made subordinate to the Father.

Since the dispute seemed at first to involve neither recriminations about betraying the faith nor social dissension, Constantine reacted to it only considerably later. In 324, he sent a mild admonishment to Alexander, the orthodox bishop of Alexandria, who had excommunicated Arius, and to Arius himself. In this message to both he stressed that extremely partisan religious attitudes, provoked "by the frivolity of an idle hour," were doing the Christian cause a great disservice. The dispute itself, he felt, was trivial, academic, and unnecessary; such potentially divisive points "we should lock up within our hearts."[21] Ossius carried the dispatch to Alexandria with Constantine's instruction to negotiate a compromise that would bring Arius back into the fold. In Alexandria, Ossius found the situation much worse than anticipated: the Arian controversy raged with such furor that he seems to have given up attempts to mediate it before half beginning.

Constantine then took the momentous step of calling the first ecumenical council, to resolve these troublesome dogmatic questions before they disrupted the peace and unity of Christianity and the empire any further. Thus it was that the Roman monarch—and not a cleric—ordered the Council of Nicaea to assemble for the purpose of agreeing on a uniform creed. Although Constantine made motions of deference to the "three hundred bishops distinguished in life and learning" who attended, the fact was that he not only presided at the council but offered his own formulation—that God the Father and God the Son were of one *essence*— to settle the main disputed point in favor of the Trinitarians and against the Arians. The Arians were in a minority at the council and no doubt would have been defeated anyway. Still, Constantine used the awe, which as Roman emperor he could have been expected to and did inspire, in order to have his phrasing accepted. He then proceeded to enforce religious uniformity on the basis of what the council, called by him, presided over by him, and strongly influenced by him, had decided.

This was a precedent which medieval kings in Europe were never in a position to make full use of, although when modern times were dawning secular princes such as Henry VIII were also to have churchmen of their realms decide questions of dogma much as they chose for reasons much more narrowly secular than Constantine's. For the Middle Ages, Constantine's action did provide a precedent on the basis of which it was possible to dispute the sole authority of the papacy to decide doctrinal questions. It proved to be of considerable use to kings in challenging the whole clerical governance of the Church in favor of more determination by the temporal sovereign in Church affairs, with or without convening a council. In the fourth century, however, orthodox churchmen seem to have felt only gratitude at having the Roman emperor on their side. They were undisturbed by the fact that the principle of later Roman law, *the will of the prince has the force of law,* was quietly being extended to the realm of dogmatics. As for the Germanic kings of the time, they were far from arrogating to themselves the legal claims of Roman emperors in either the secular or the religious sphere.

During the main part of Constantine's career, he remained a pillar of orthodoxy according to Eusebius of Caesarea, his friend and biographer, whose eulogy of him is expansive enough usually to be called the *Vita Constantini.* It is altogether possible that Eusebius modified the words and deeds of Constantine as he recorded them, in order to make Constantine correspond with his own ideal of rulership. Since the Constantine portrayed by Eusebius was that Constantine who served in turn as a model for medieval kings and their biographers, the degree of possible fiction in the Eusebian portrayals of Constantine need not delay us. At any rate, Eusebius records that on one occasion he heard Constantine call himself "a bishop of those outside the Church." This is a vague appellation and, of necessity, a figurative one, but it can be taken to connote vast spiritual authority and responsibility residing in the person of the monarch. Eusebius approvingly notes that "what he did conformed to his words; for he governed all his subjects with a bishop's care and gave them every encouragement he could to lead devout lives."[22] In an oration held at the celebration of Constantine's thirtieth year of rule, Eusebius had already praised Constantine's combined religious-secular energies:

> Our emperor, friend of the Saviour, acting as interpreter to the Word of God, aims at recalling the whole human race to the knowledge of God; proclaiming clearly in the ears of all, and declaring with powerful voice the laws of truth and godliness to all who dwell on the earth. . . .
>
> Having purged his earthly dominion from every stain of impious error, he invites each holy and pious worshipper within his imperial mansions, earnestly desiring to save with all its crew that mighty vessel of which he is the appointed pilot.[23]

Probably carried away by the thought that the reign of Constantine, in which the will of the emperor turned many desires of orthodox churchmen into state measures, would remain a model for subsequent rulers to imitate without essential change, Eusebius gave his unconditional support to monarchy as an institution:

> Lastly, invested as he is with a semblance of heavenly sovereignty, he [the emperor] directs his gaze above, and frames his earthly government according to the pattern of that Divine original, feeling strength in its conformity to the monarchy of God. And this conformity is granted by the universal sovereign to man alone of the creatures of this earth: for He is the author of sovereign power, who decrees that all should be subject to the rule of one.[24]

The tone of all this represented something quite new within the Church. In a single leap, Eusebius went well beyond the passive acceptance of the Roman monarchy characteristic of the New Testament and the qualified endorsement of kingship found in the Old. Monarchy has become the only form of government in harmony with God and nature; by implication, popular rule is discordant in its very essence. Suddenly, it seems that the Church espouses the idea of the divine right of kings enthusiastically and without express limitation. As a matter of fact, the Church did tend to support the rule of a single king as preferable to other forms of government all through the Middle Ages; but the context in which Eusebius of Caesarea expressed the idea, that of a monarch functioning as a secular ruler in a partly episcopal role, was to be severely revised. Eusebius chose not to take note of a few things in Constantine's later career. While for him Constantine was every barleycorn a bishop and deserved his self-elevation to the company of the Apostles as the thirteenth of their band,[25] it was also true that he had his differences with uncompromising Trinitarian spokesmen, such as Bishop Athanasius of Alexandria, who refused any gestures of conciliation with the Arians. Constantine shifted his favor among leading churchmen a number of times, particularly from about 330 onward, always with the intent of promoting spiritual harmony within the empire. Shortly before his death in 337, he was baptized by another Bishop Eusebius — of Nicomedia — who was known to have been a reluctant signatory of the Nicene articles and to have had a long history of at least sympathetic understanding for Arianism.

They Are Not All Like Constantine; Church Leaders Have Grave Second Thoughts

The half century after Constantine's death in 337 witnessed two developments in the relationship between the Roman monarchy and the Church, developments which were gradual, interrupted, and not particularly compatible with each other. The first was the erosion of what remained of Constantine's toleration policy toward the pagans, as most subsequent emperors applied a variety of state measures to hasten the triumph of Christianity within the empire. The second was a drawing back on the part of churchmen from the position of letting the emperor's will prevail as law within the Church.

In a series of acts beginning three years before his death, Constantine provided for the empire to be ruled in five sections by his three surviving sons, Constantine II, Constans, and Constantius II, and two of their cousins. He had given every evidence of planning to make the Roman monarchy hereditary; perhaps he thought that he had already done so. With rare exceptions, men of both the Roman and medieval world tended to see dynastic influence as a legitimate component in the determination of a ruler, even when his office was nominally elective. Dynasties of a sort had actually been more the rule than the exception in the early Roman Empire, although particularly during the second century the procedure of having a reigning emperor adopt his chosen successor as his son blurred the distinction between determination through choice and determination through family, as medieval kings were to blur the distinction in other ways. To help make his "Flavian" dynasty (in itself a bogus designation taken to establish a link through blood with earlier emperors) hereditary, Constantine had associated his sons with high office throughout their lives. The oldest survivor, Constantine II, had been a *caesar* since the age of one.

All the actual and potential rivals of Constantius II, except the later Emperor Julian, met violent deaths over the next eighteen years in a process which Jacob Burckhardt termed "sultanism," the destruction of princes of the blood until there is only one unchallengeable survivor.[26] Before Constantine I had been dead long, a conspiracy of generals and advisors of Constantius II brought about a massacre of three uncles and seven cousins of the late emperor's sons. Constantine II was dissatisfied with the way his murdered cousins' lands had been shared. In 340, he crossed the Julian Alps from Gaul to Italy, which belonged to Constans, in a poorly conducted invasion in which he was killed. His Gallic provinces passed into the hands of Constans, who was murdered in 350 at the command of Magnentius, a military leader of barbarian origin, who usurped the imperial title in the West. This gave Constantius the right and duty to march westward with a large army. When Magnentius committed suicide after being defeated, Constantius emerged as sole ruler.

Constantine II seems not to have occupied himself much with religious policy during his brief reign, but measures for the suppression of paganism were a part of the agenda of both Constans and Constantius. In 341 Constans decreed the following in a directive to his vicar in Italy:

Superstition is to cease. The insanity of the sacrifices is to be eliminated. For achieving this, anyone who shall dare to perform sacrifices contrary to the law of the divine ruler, our Father, and to this command of our Clemency, is to be brought to judgment and his sentence carried out immediately.[27]

A later edict ascribed to Constantius is considerably more sweeping:

It is our pleasure that in all places, and in all cities, the temples shall be immediately shut, and carefully guarded, that none may have the power of offending. It is likewise our pleasure that all our subjects should abstain from sacrifices. If any one should be guilty of such an act, let him feel the sword of vengeance, and, after his execution, let his property be confiscated to the public use. We denounce the same penalties against the governors of the provinces, if they neglect to punish the criminals.[28]

Since both Constans and Constantius had religious enthusiasm of a sort, it is quite possible that these edicts expressed their own ideas for proceeding against paganism, but they also had some support from spokesmen for orthodox Christianity. Firmicus Maternus, a recent Christian convert from Syracuse, addressed his book, *The Falsehood of Profane Religions,* to Constans and Constantius. For Firmicus, there was no sense in tolerating impious pagan forms of worship any longer:

They should be cut short and rooted out, Most Sacred Emperors, while you see that things are put right with the severest clauses of your edicts. . . . God has given you the Empire for the purpose of using us to cure the sores left by this plague of theirs. . . . There is still a bit to be done by your laws to lay the devil flat and to make the death-defiled contagion of a lifeless idolatry go under. . . . God has let you partake of His glory and His will. A gracious command of Christ finally entrusts you with wiping out idolatry and destroying the profane temples. Remove, Most Sacred Emperors, remove without fear the ornaments of the temples. Let the flame and fire at the mint melt down their gods of metal. Take all the offerings made to them for your own use. . . . If you do this, everything will turn out to your fortune. You shall have victories, opulence, peace, plenty, health, and triumphs, to the end that you may govern the world happily under the divine majesty.[29]

Yet Constans did not undertake any such drastic program as this. It will be noted that the pertinent decree of Constans prohibited only sacrificing, leaving other forms of pagan worship alone. While the decree of Constantius is sweeping enough to have satisfied even Firmicus, there is no evidence that in practice he went beyond prohibiting sacrifices generally—if he did that much. In regions where Christians had a substantial majority, the temples were closed down and the pagan priesthood was dissolved, but this seems to have happened as much under local pressures as under imperial guidance. In 384, the pagan man of letters, Symmachus, was to use the conduct of Constantius on the occasion of a visit to Rome later in his reign to illustrate model tolerance in a Christian emperor:

> He took nothing away from the privileges of the vestal virgins; he enabled the Roman nobility to fill the priesthood again. He did not refuse funds for the old Roman ceremonies, and through all the streets of the eternal city in the company of the rejoicing Senate, he viewed the shrines with a look of pleased interest. He would read the name of the god inscribed in the temple pediments, ask about the origins of the temple, commend the work of its founders—in short, although he had different religious beliefs himself, he preserved these, too, for the empire, leaving to each man his own ethical system and to each man his own rite.[30]

At the same time the emperors were moving at an uncertain pace against paganism, they continued to be drawn into church quarrels simply to keep the imperial peace. For example, a quarrel in 342 over who was the rightful Bishop of Constantinople erupted in a riot in that city, in which a general (*magister militum*) of the Roman army was killed and his body dragged through the streets. One account notes there were over three thousand dead before the installation struggle ended.[31] No doubt this sort of thing prompted the emperors to intervene whether they wanted to or not. Sometimes the bitter disputes centered around personalities. More often than not, a quarrel over dogma set off or at least exacerbated the fights. It fell to Constans, whose dominions included Roman Africa, to put down the Donatists whose violence had again gotten out of hand. The most radical of the Donatists, called Circumcellions from their prowling around country houses, had taken to righting social wrongs with their cudgels. They continually threatened moneylenders, slaveholders, substantial property owners, and, of course, enemies of the Donatist clergy. They showed their contempt for the whole existing order by halting the carriages that on North African roads were preceded by running slaves and making the masters run in front while the slaves rode inside.[32] Donatus himself put Constans in his place by replying to his legates, sent with funds to mollify the restless population and indirectly to subsidize the Donatists out of independence: "What does the emperor have to do with the Church?"[33] In a protracted effort the officials and emissaries of Constans brought down the Donatist opposition with four types of measures: alms or largesse, distributed in centers of Donatist influence; persecution in the form of flogging, executing, or exiling the unyielding Donatist leaders; military suppression of and retaliation for Donatist violence; and, finally, the sponsoring of a council at Carthage in 348, which made certain perfunctory compromises with moderate Donatists and allowed them to re-enter the fold without sacrificing their whole self-respect. Gratus, the bishop of Carthage, opened the council by thanking God for having inspired Emperor Constans to undertake this work of union, and again, for the time being, it appeared that the emperor's hand in Church affairs was in the interest of the orthodox and the empire.[34]

The effect of the next chapter of the Arian controversy, however, was quite different for the relation between the Church and the Roman monarchs. With or without enough vague formulations to slip by the Nicene Creed, many varieties of Arianism continually emerged after the death of Constantine I. Generally, Arian sympathizers were stronger in the East, ruled by Constantius, than in the West, ruled by Constans. While the two emperors tended to share the opposing views of their "own" leading bishops, both of them had an interest in settling doctrinal questions on an empire-wide basis. Constans and Constantius agreed to have a council convoked in Sardica (the modern Sofia) in 342 or 343, and delegations of prominent bishops arrived from both East and West in that city ostensibly to reconcile their differences. Instead, however, after conferring separately among themselves, members of the Arian faction refused to meet jointly with the Catholics and left the council. The Catholic bishops then excommunicated them, one and all, and the rift continued to widen.[35]

The extent to which the emperors were forced to take the part of one Church dignitary against another broadened to include affairs bordering on the trivial and even humorous. Once, for example, when some western bishops were visiting Antioch in 345, several servants of Stephen, bishop of Antioch, paid to have a prostitute slipped into the house where they were staying. The plan was to surround the house and, on a given signal, to enter and expose Stephen's western adversaries as vice-ridden lechers. The lady was badly coached, however, and lost her head with the result that wails and lamentations both from her and Bishop Euphrates of Cologne, whom she was sent to compromise, aroused the household. The seizure of some of the accomplices of the plot who had burst into the house to bear false witness put an end to the unlikely scene. The next day the high officer assigned to escort the western bishops went straight to Constantius for redress of this grievance, and Constantius agreed to have an inquiry held, which led to the deposition of Bishop Stephen.[36]

On the other hand, the struggles within the church that put the two emperors at serious odds with each other were anything but trivial. Bishops of Trinitarian orthodoxy in the East sought support from Constans in the West. Arian bishops favored by Constantius carried his influence into western councils. Eventually, when Constans and then Magnentius had been killed, Arian bishops enjoyed something of a triumph, since the absence of another secular authority strong enough to balance that of Constantius meant that their opponents would have to get along without governmental support. While, superficially, Constantius continued the role of his father within the Church, there was a considerable difference in the way the two men acted. In spite of vastly inferior accomplishments, Constantius' personal conceit was much greater than his father's. Where Constantine had intervened in Church quarrels with consistent reluctance, Constantius, although at first forced to intervene, seemed later rather to enjoy disputations and the opportunity to adjudicate them.

It was under Constantius that the first dissension between a pope and a Christian sovereign opened in a manner foreshadowing the same type of strife in the Middle Ages. Although the spiritual sovereignty of the papacy even in the West was still far from being established in the 350s, the bishop of Rome enjoyed a certain primacy deriving partly from the associations of Saint Peter and Saint Paul with the city and partly from the political and historical significance of the old capital itself.

Julius I (r. 337–352) had been "excommunicated" and "deposed" by the Arian faction at the Council of Sardica, which, of course, had no effect on his status at home. Liberius, who succeeded Julius as bishop of Rome at the time Constantius was avenging the death of Constans by marching against Magnentius, was a convinced Trinitarian and refused to acquiesce in the condemnation of the Alexandrian Bishop Athanasius, the most vocal and durable advocate of Catholic orthodoxy against the Arians. Constantius attempted to have Liberius won over with pleas and none too subtle bribery—one of his eunuchs emptied a purse of gold before the altar of Saint Peter's—and when this failed he sent men to Rome to kidnap the pope. Brought to the emperor at Milan, Liberius held firm for a time, but he was sent away to Thrace, where, after two years of cajoling by Bishop Demophilus of Berea, he signed a condemnation of Athanasius and a doctrinal formulation neutral enough on controversial points to be satisfactory to the Arians.[37]

In the meantime, however, Constantius had appointed one Felix as antipope. Popular protest against Felix in Rome was strong enough that Constantius felt compelled to restore Liberius, which he might well have done anyway after his defection from Catholic orthodoxy, and for a time the imperial government recognized the joint rule of Liberius and Felix. Felix was eventually driven into retirement, and Liberius righted himself with the orthodox. This battle was thus lost from the monarchical standpoint, and Constantius was a sufficiently black sheep that no medieval king admitted to following his example. The point, however, is not that Constantius established a precedent which medieval kings were to resort to, as they were to do with those of Constantine I, but rather that a pattern of behavior associated with the Middle Ages could be seen in the relations between high churchmen and a determined monarch within a few decades after Christianity emerged as a recognized religion. The secular ruler, feeling himself to be a true Christian, had seen fit to have hands laid on a bishop, even a pope; he had secured the installation of a competing pope;

and he had been behind the prolonged persuasion exerted on a pope to gain his support of the ruler's own ideas in a Church dispute.

From the standpoint of the Catholic clergy, events had taken a pernicious course. Not long before, they had applauded the Roman monarch for putting down the clearly heretical and subversive Donatists and had looked on approvingly as both Constans and Constantius closed in on a paganism in retreat. But in facing Constantius, whose Arian sympathies came increasingly to the fore after the death of Constans, orthodox churchmen were forced to reconsider the value of the precedent of Constantine's intervention which had given the will of the emperor legal power in deciding so many questions affecting the Church. In 355 a statement admonishing the faithful to accept Arian positions appeared as an imperial edict.[38] Two years later, Constantius arrived at Sirmium, where leaders of the Arian faction were meeting: a declaration of bishops soon was made public there. It specifically removed the of-the-same-essence wording from the relationship of God the Father to God the Son and stated that the Father was greater than the Son, thus making short work of the Council of Nicaea's main accomplishment.[39] In the interest of harmony, the Arian phrasing was toned down a bit at the Council of Ariminum (modern Rimini) in 359, but the crevasse could not be bridged and, obviously, Constantius was standing on the wrong side of it from the orthodox viewpoint.[40]

The inevitable result was that all but the Arians helped by Constantius turned once again to thinking of the monarch as at least a vaguely hostile force and to favoring a totally separate sphere of authority for the Church. Now one could hear the Catholic clergy paraphrasing the question of Donatus: "What has the emperor to do with the Church?" Constantius, for his part, obviously thought that he had a great deal to do with the Church. In condemning Athanasius by decree from Milan as unworthy to be bishop of Alexandria, Constantius had explicitly and arrogantly claimed for himself the right to legislate concerning the faith and the status of clergymen, a role which Constantine had taken upon himself only implicitly and with reluctance. "Whatever I will, let that be a canon," Constantius told a group of orthodox bishops. "The bishops of Syria let me speak thus. Either obey or go into banishment."[41] According to Athanasius, the orthodox bishops left for exile, but before they went

. . . they used great boldness of speech against him, teaching him that the kingdom was not his but God's who had given it to him, whom also they bid him fear, lest He should suddenly take it away from him. And they threatened him with the Day of Judgment, and warned him against infringing Ecclesiastical order and mingling Roman sovereignty with the constitution of the Church, nor to introduce the Arian heresy into the Church of God.[42]

Later, from Spain, Ossius wrote an admonition to Constantius, darkly referring to him as the grandson of the persecutor Maximian (rather than as the son of the pious Constantine) but still beseeching him to mend his ways:

> Fear the Day of Judgment, and keep yourself free of guilt in preparing for it. Do not intrude yourself into ecclesiastical matters, nor give commands to us concerning them; instead, learn from us. God has put the empire into your hands; He has entrusted Church matters to us. Now, just as any man who would steal the empire from you would resist the ordinance of God, you should likewise show fear, lest by forcing your command upon Church matters you commit a great crime.[43]

When Constantius persisted in his course and when, under his protection, Arianism threatened to become the state religion, the voices of the orthodox grew more shrill. Athanasius, in a work written in exile, and Hilary of Poitiers, in a work possibly intended only for the underground orthodox readership of the day, both sought to widen the distance separating the Catholic Church from the monarch by specifically making Constantius into the Anti-Christ.[44] For good measure, Athanasius compared him with Ahab and Belshassar, the most evil kings in the Old Testament,[45] while Hilary linked his persecution in the chain of great persecutions under Nero, Decius, and Maximian.[46]

Although Antichrist, Ahab, and Nero, would seem to be the end of the line as symbols to reflect clerical dissatisfaction with a ruler who claimed power to decide religious questions, Constantius was succeeded by a man who made Church spokesmen grope for still more odious comparisons: Emperor Julian the Apostate. While Constantius was conducting a campaign in the East against the Persians, Julian in the West at first reluctantly and then decisively took the title of *augustus* and set out to wrest control of the empire from Constantius, whose death in 361 following an illness averted a civil war. Julian was the last out-and-out pagan to rule the Roman Empire. Blaming Constantius with considerable justification for the deliberate murder of his family, with much less justification he made Constantius' religion, Christianity, responsible for the miseries of the Roman state and people.

Although Christians soon saw in Julian a persecutor, his reign was marked more by subtle measures than by wholesale violence against them. His decrees kept Christians from public teaching posts, and most other Christians employed by the state were dismissed as well. Christians were forced to pay restitution for pagan temples they had destroyed, and Julian's provincial masters used torture, sanctioned by the Roman legal system, to obtain satisfaction when payments were not made. Several Christians who broke cult statues or offered similar insults to pagan worship were executed. Occasionally, Julian's toleration edicts produced strife among Christians, since they allowed trouble-making heretical exiles to return home, but generally the oppression felt under Julian forced Catholics and Arians into a working alliance. In one famous instance, a bishop known for his Arian sympathies became a common symbol of resistance: under the protection of Constantius, Mark of Arethusa in Syria had earlier been responsible for destroying a pagan temple. Catholic spokesmen soon joined in publicizing his sufferings during Julian's reign for this act, telling in effective, gruesome detail how he had been stripped naked, beaten, and subjected to an array of tortures (his ears were sawed off with fine ropes as a starter) and how eventually he was beaten, poured over with honey and exposed to insects; Julian at length ordered him spared, but his heroic defiance of pagan authority made him a hero to Catholics and Arians alike.[47]

Since the Catholic clergy had already rejected any active role by a Roman monarch in deciding Church questions when they resisted the spiritual encroachments of Constantius, Julian's reign did not introduce any noteworthy changes in their attitude towards this aspect of Church-state relations. Constantius, of course, looked better to them in retrospect after Julian, but this fact had no new implications for their political theory. The thought that it was possible to have not only an Arian but an openly pagan ruler who might oppress the whole Church strengthened their conviction, whether conscious or unconscious, that Christian support of the Roman monarchy should be no more than minimal unless the monarch were a pious Christian ruler. The increasingly political role of the Church in the late fourth century is partly explainable by the consideration — obvious enough to individual Christians dismissed from the imperial service and to congregations forced to pay pagans restitution — that the Church *needed* some sort of political power, if only to protect itself against the whims of bad rulers.

VALENTINIAN TO THEODOSIUS: TOWARD A DELINEATION OF SEPARATE SPHERES

Near the end of June 363, Julian died from battle wounds in a war against the Persians after a brief reign of twenty months. His successor, the orthodox Christian Jovian, died of uncertain causes within eight more months. There followed the dual reign of Valentinian and Valens, which had more than a superficial resemblance to that of Constans and Constantius in that Valentinian in the West moderately supported the Catholic cause, while his brother Valens developed into as much of an Arian as Constantius had been. The parallel should not be overdrawn, since Valentinian, unlike Constans, was the more dominant and resourceful of the two. It was he who had been elected by an assembly of army officers and public officials after Jovian's death and had appointed Valens to rule with him. But, quite like the older pair, the two new emperors were continually brought into disputes affecting the Church and, all in all, confirmed the orthodox clergy's disdain for imperial decisions in Church questions.

Early in his reign, Valentinian was obliged to decide between the supporters of Auxentius, bishop of Milan, an Arian installed under Constantius, and the Catholics led by Hilary of Poitiers, who resorted to a popular uprising in attempting to remove him. Valentinian was then present in Milan, which he maintained as the capital of his empire in the West. When Hilary ignored his edict condemning the disturbance, the emperor had a commission conduct an inquiry. During the proceedings, Valentinian was satisfied by an ambiguous statement of faith made by Auxentius to prove his orthodoxy and let him stay as bishop of Milan.[48] In Rome, Valentinian reluctantly let imperial troops intervene on behalf of Pope Damasus, after the death of Liberius in September 365, to put down an opposition which accused Damasus of popularity among Roman matrons for the wrong reasons and of having once been too willing to accept the antipope Felix under Constantius. This opposition supported one Ursinus in his claim to have been elected bishop of Rome. The dispute produced riots and violent deaths; only Valentinian's rescripts kept Damasus in steady control of his diocese.[49]

In the East the Arian party had lost considerable strength since the time of Constantius and controlled fewer bishoprics. The indifferent Julian had allowed a number of Arian bishops to be replaced by Catholic ones, and they had, of course, remained under the Catholic Jovian. At the urging of his Arian advisors, Valens issued an edict early in his reign deposing these Catholics with the obvious intention of putting Arians in their place. He thus touched off a never-ending feud between followers of the Catholic bishops already installed and their appointed Arian successors.[50] In 370 Valens encountered particularly violent opposition with a decision to support Demophilus, whose persuasive influence had been responsible for the lapse in exile of Pope Liberius years before, for the vacant see of Constantinople. Eighty churchmen from a delegation organized to protest against his installation were put on board a ship, which was ignited at sea and abandoned by its crew.[51] Whether or not Valens was entirely responsible for this and other atrocities, he was made so by the reproaches of the Catholics who saw in him a more malevolent persecutor than Constantius.

While in the West, Valentinian personally favored the Catholic cause, he was inclined to pursue a policy of toleration in the matter of Christians versus pagans and to intervene only as a last resort on behalf of Catholics against heretics. If a bishop of questioned orthodoxy could administer his diocese peacefully, Valentinian generally let him do so. When orthodox bishops of the East who had been deprived of their sees by the Arians supported by Valens sent a message of protest to Pope Liberius in Rome, they also sent a delegation to Valentinian; however, he seems not to have reacted to their approach at all.[52] Valentinian also showed himself indifferent to the whole Arian–Catholic controversy by taking as his second wife, Justina, a woman with strongly Arian sympathies who was to challenge exclusive Catholic control of the Church in the West after his death. At the same time, Valentinian became the first monarch to take under his purview the moral reform of the Christian clergy. In an edict of 370 addressed to Damasus, he placed special strictures on the relations of priests and monks with female parishioners, under pain of civil punishment.[53] Church leaders in the West seem to have accepted regulations of this sort without protest, but, coupled as they were with Valentinian's reluctance to intervene for the purpose of helping Catholics overcome Arianism, such measures increased their desire for more clearly defined areas of authority between Church leaders and even a well-meaning Catholic emperor.

In the East, on the other hand, Valens kept intervening often and discriminatingly in the interest of the Arians. He issued, for example, a decree ordering "certain lazy sectaries" then residing among Egyptian monks to be forced back into discharging their obligations as secular citizens with the justification that they had taken clerical orders only to escape their responsibilities. His soldiers were conducted by Arian priests to locate the "sectaries" and the monks who sheltered them; a large if undetermined number of the orthodox were killed by the military in carrying out the edict.[54] In view of the vastly different degrees of partisanship with which the Catholic Valentinian I and the Arian Valens handled questions of interest to the clergy, it was natural that Catholic praise of Valentinian tended to be tepid, while Catholic laments over excesses committed by Valens were boundless. When Valentinian died suddenly in 375, his devout Catholic son, Gratian, succeeded him as ruler of most of the empire in the West. Three years later, Valens was killed in a war against the Goths. For modern historians the defeat and slaughter of his Roman forces at Adrianople was a landmark in the decline of the empire, but for medieval perceptions of kingship its significance was—as a counterpart to the lesson of Constantine the Great and his victories—that a heretic wearing the purple robe of a ruler could only lose disastrously in battle.

Gratian was hailed as an excellent ruler by the Catholics of his own time and later. He was the first emperor to make a concrete reduction of his personal authority in the interest of the Church, for he rejected the title of *"pontifex maximus,"* which Roman emperors had borne since Augustus Caesar as chief priests of the empire and which the Christian emperors had incongruously retained.[55] The vacant title went, of course, to augment the rank and dignity of the bishop of Rome. There in the old capital, Pope

Damasus was still having trouble maintaining himself against the threats of Ursinus' party. A petition from an assembly of Italian bishops in Rome in 378 addressed to Gratian is remarkable for its delineation of authority between the secular monarch and the bishops. The bishops stated that Valentinian's policy provided for no imperial intervention in purely Church matters. (This was not quite true, since Valentinian had seen to it that Auxentius acquitted himself of charges of Arianism when his position as bishop of Milan was challenged, but, all in all, it was a fair generalization.[56]) This nonintervention was, said the bishops, fitting and just; however, unless the emperor took upon himself the enforcement of decisions reached by the bishops concerning the deposition or support of those whose offices were questioned, threats to the public order would arise. The petitioners cited the precedent of Valentinian in suppressing with police force the opposition to Pope Damasus. They urgently requested Gratian's assistance to insure that sentences of deposition were carried out and to suppress the activities of deposed bishops which tended to stir up strife within the Church.[57] Forty years' experience with sovereign enemies — Constantius II, Julian, and Valens — had wiped out the desire for imperial intervention in doctrinal matters. Let the emperor restrict himself to enforcing Church decisions with implications for the imperial peace when these are reached by the orthodox. But definitely let him do that much!

SAINT AMBROSE: THE CHURCH TAKES ON A DOMINANT ROLE

At the end of February 380, Theodosius, who had been appointed by Gratian to succeed Valens as emperor in the East, had himself baptized before resuming the war with the Goths and thus became the first Catholic emperor to have been fully received into the faith while still in the full vigor of life. Immediately afterwards he made Christianity the state religion, although the wording of his edict aims far more directly at getting rid of heretics than at forcing pagans into the fold:

> We desire that all the peoples governed by the moderation of Our Clemency shall keep within the faith which true religion declares was taught the Romans by Saint Peter the Apostle and preserved from that time to this. . . . And so, let us believe according to the teachings of the Apostles and the Scriptural doctrine in one deity of the Father, and of the Son, and of the Holy Ghost under an equal majesty understood as the Holy Trinity. Art. 1. We command that those adhering to this doctrine enjoy the name of Catholic Christians, while the insane and wild remnant are condemned to sustain the infamous name of heretics in dogma, and their gathering places shall not claim the name of "churches." First condemned by divine judgement, they are to be subsequently punished by measures which we, heeding the heavenly will, shall put into effect.[58]

Within a year, Theodosius forced Arianism underground in his capital, Constantinople. He personally gave Bishop Demophilus the choice between conversion to the Trinitarian faith or the loss of the great cathedral built by Constantine, the Hagia Sophia, and his see. Like the Catholic Liberius before the Arian Constantius, the Arian Demophilus before the Catholic Theodosius chose exile rather than a pretended conversion. Unlike Liberius, however, he neither wavered in exile nor returned. The monarch's troops soon cleared the Arians out of the rest of their churches in the capital. Gregory Nazianzen, the Catholic successor of Demophilus as bishop of Constantinople, expressed regret that the capital looked like a city recently conquered by barbarian troops because of the hordes of imperial soldiers necessary to protect his installation,[59] but he accepted the needed aid from Theodosius gratefully all the same. Although Gregory himself was later ousted by synodal intrigues, the Arian opposition in the East was thoroughly overcome.

In the West, meanwhile, in 382 Gratian withdrew the state funds required to maintain pagan worship and soon removed the Altar of Victory from the hall in which the Roman Senate assembled.[60] In an extreme measure which he promulgated (although certainly did not enforce to the unenforceable letter) he made violations of divine law — even acts of omission resulting from ignorance — equivalent to the capital offense of sacrilege.[61] Gradually, Gratian began neglecting imperial concerns in favor of horsemanship, archery, javelin throwing, and hunting. Too much of these diversions and a bad choice of favorites contributed to a revolt against him, which ended in his death and the usurpation of Maximus in his stead (383–388). Although the laws of Theodosius and Gratian heralded persecution by an orthodox sovereign, the distinction of first killing people for their opposition to the Catholic faith belongs to Maximus, whose subordinates executed gnostic heretics in Spain. The distinction for publicly opposing these murders, in which all forms of due process were dispensed with, belongs to Saint Martin, Bishop of Tours in Gaul — territory held by Maximus — and Saint Ambrose, Bishop of Milan.[62] Since Valentinian II and his mother, Justina, had been designated by Valentinian I to rule in Italy, Saint Ambrose was outside the jurisdiction Maximus claimed for himself at the time; however, it was not difficult to discern the usurper's designs on Italy as well as the rest of the West.

The political role of Saint Ambrose in the late empire was only beginning. Twice he went as an emissary to Maximus from Justina and Valentinian to dissuade him from invading Italy. Before Gratian's death, his position had been made difficult in Milan, still the western capital, by Justina's desire to protect the Arians from suppression. This had brought him into conflict with her. He had refused to heed her request that one church — any church — in Milan or close by be set aside for the Arians' worship; on the other hand, when the Arian clergy favored by Justina and Valentinian II were threatened with mob violence, Ambrose firmly intervened to save them. An edict from the imperial court at Milan had shown Justina's determination: the death penalty could be inflicted on anyone interfering with the free exercise of religion by Arians. Under this grim edict of toleration, Ambrose could in theory have been executed. Instead he was sentenced to go into exile, which he refused to do. He and his followers defended the cathedral and episcopal palace in Milan against imperial troops, who failed to attack the inspired and determined supporters of their bishop.[63] Justina was badly worsted in the contest, her popularity among the Catholic majority in Italy was low and falling, and when the forces of Maximus appeared on the horizon in 387 her position was so untenable that she had to flee to Theodosius in the East with Valentinian and other members of the imperial household, leaving Maximus a free field in Italy. The next year, Theodosius took the field against Maximus, and in the ensuing Italian war Theodosius defeated the forces of Maximus, who was killed soon afterwards.

Two encounters between Theodosius and Saint Ambrose produced the final stage of Church-state fusion begun by Constantine. The few incidents of Ambrose's career cited above already point to his being a man of extremely strong will. He was determined to see the interests of the Church well served, and he had no sympathy for any independent sphere of secular authority which could ignore these interests. In Theodosius, he found a pious Trinitarian Christian, who although a courageous and resourceful ruler in other respects could not bring himself to assert the claims of the state against Ambrose's forceful demands for what amounted, in one instance, to a veto power by the Church on imperial acts affecting the Church and, in another, to the right of the Church to call the emperor to account for abuses of his authority. Stories of both of these encounters were to color medieval perceptions of kingship.

Fateful differences arose in 388 when an official report accused Christians in Callinicum, a small town near the Persian border, of burning a synagogue at the instigation of their bishop. At about the same time, some monks, having been hindered in a procession by a group of gnostics, had burned a chapel belonging to their sect. Theodosius, perhaps recalling the role of Constantine or Valentinian as emperor of all the people, or perhaps simply putting political considerations ahead of religious ones in a ruler's natural desire to discourage violence, decreed punishment for the Christian offenders. The local bishop was to rebuild the synagogue with church funds; the monks who burned the gnostic chapel were to atone for their crime, although it is not known exactly how.

Ambrose's written admonition to the emperor is a horror from a legal or logical viewpoint. But it is significantly portentous for medieval political theory and shows the kind of attitude that kings who stood up for the public order against church interests would have to confront for more than a thousand years. The guilt or innocence of the bishop is irrelevant to Ambrose, because in his eyes the crime was no crime. Far from it, when the synagogue caught fire, "its burning was by God's judgment." Ambrose declares, in fact, that he wishes the emperor had accused him instead of the bishop in faraway Callinicum. "I would declare that I set fire to the synagogue, or anyway that I ordered those people to do it, so that there would be no building in which Christ is denied." Surely the emperor will come to his senses, if he has not already done so: "Although I have not yet read that the edict has been revoked, let us agree that it is revoked." Does the emperor really want to make an apostate out of the bishop, by making him build a *synagogue*? Or does he want to make him a martyr for refusing to do so? Of course not: "There is really no cause for all this commotion, people being punished so severely for the burning of a building, and much less so, since a synagogue has been burned, an abode of unbelief, a house of impiety, a shelter of madness which God Himself has condemned." As for the gnostic chapel, Ambrose asks: "What is it but a temple where heathens gather?" The monks were provoked to burn it, and besides it was only "a shrine of those people in some country village thrown together on the spur of the moment." Plainly it is outside the sphere of imperial protection.[64]

Theodosius did not heed Ambrose's advice immediately, whereupon Ambrose assailed the emperor in church with biblical accounts to support his point. After the sermon, Theodosius made the obvious remark: "You spoke about me."

"I preached what pertains to your own good," said Ambrose.

"About the synagogue having to be rebuilt by the bishop, I did make too harsh a decision," Theodosius admitted, "but that has been changed." Somewhat defensively, he added: "The monks do commit a large number of crimes."

This seemed to take care of the matter of rebuilding the odious edifices but left the question of a modified punishment up in the air. Then Ambrose, relatively diplomatically, conveyed to Theodosius his intention not to offer the sacraments in his presence until he had given his assurance that the whole matter should neither be investigated further nor punished. This was an obvious hint at impending excommunication (no sacraments — no communion) and Theodosius took it. "Go ahead," he said to Ambrose, "on my promise." Ambrose went ahead to the altar, and the matter was indeed dropped.[65]

Yet during the following two years, Theodosius cultivated the friendship of the pagan nobility, and, in the summer of 390, issued a number of edicts which placed restrictions on the clergy. One of these was a measure to keep men from deserting the financial responsibilities of city-council membership by entering the clergy: members of city councils who became clergymen were required first to turn over all their worldly goods to the councils they left behind. This measure may possibly have been welcomed in some quarters of the Church as keeping opportunists out of the clergy.[66] The other acts were distinctly unflattering to the Church, however: widows could not be deaconesses until age sixty, nor could they name the Church as beneficiary in their wills[67]; monks were prohibited from living in cities, and assigned to "abandoned areas and desert wastes" for their habitation.[68] While Theodosius stayed clear of legislating for the Church in doctrinal matters, his setting rules for *clergy as clergy* was still unmistakably secular interference in the religious sphere.

Whether or not Ambrose sought to put the emperor in his place for these encroachments, he ultimately did much more than this, for in the fall of 390 he not only subjected Theodosius to open reproval for a senseless act of vengeance but received a clearly implied admission from him that the Church could make even the highest secular ruler atone for his misdeeds. Unlike the earlier instance of the burning of the synagogue and chapel, in which modern sympathies will probably remain with the emperor in his opposition to the high-handed bishop of Milan, the deed for which Ambrose exacted public penance from Theodosius was so clearly a wanton crime by ancient and modern standards alike that Ambrose emerges at least in part as a figure championing justice against tyrannical outrage. The background for "the Thessalonian massacre" was something like this: Butheric, the garrison commander in Thessalonica, imprisoned a popular chariot racer for acts of sodomy committed on a handsome slave boy belonging to the commander. Local chariot-racing fans demanded the charioteer's release from Butheric but failed to obtain it. The garrison forces seem to have been depleted by the war of Theodosius against Maximus in Italy; at any rate, they provided insufficient protection for their hapless commander and several of his officers. A mob murdered them and dragged their bodies through the streets. On hearing of this, the emperor's rage knew no bounds, and he either commanded or approved (the point is disputed) a wholesale massacre of Thessalonians. Later he changed his mind, but the rescinding order came too late: a multitude of unsuspecting Thessalonians were lured into attending games at a circus, but instead of being treated to a performance they were set upon by soldiers and several thousand of them were murdered.[69]

Again a forceful epistle from the bishop of Milan to the emperor: this time the misdeed of Theodosius was not only incomparably greater, but it had already been committed, and the emperor's exclusion from communion with the faithful became a matter of fact. "I do not dare offer the sacraments," he wrote, "if you intend to be present. Can that which is not allowed after the blood of one innocent man is shed, be allowed when the blood of many has been shed? I think not."[70] Saint Ambrose's intervention was this time of a quite different nature for another reason: although to judge by his name, Butheric came from some Germanic tribe, and Germanic troops leaned strongly towards paganism or Arianism while Thessalonica was looked upon as a Trinitarian Christian city, the dispute obviously went far beyond Christian-pagan dissension. Ambrose was inveighing against Theodosius not for the religious crime of allowing pagans to exact retribution from Christians—Butheric's murder was anything but a religious one—but rather for the secular crime of homicide.

Subsequent historians may have over-dramatized the setting of the emperor's excommunication by having Ambrose turn Theodosius away as the emperor attempted to enter the church in Milan. Perhaps he did, perhaps not.[71] What is important is that Theodosius accepted his sentence of excommunication and Ambrose's requirement that he do public penance, confessing himself to be a sinner and imploring forgiveness for allowing the massacre. This he fulfilled, and on Christmas Day 390 he was readmitted to the sacraments.

Saint Ambrose did not present this encounter as any sort of triumph for himself or the Church at the emperor's expense. Far from having suffered, the prestige of the penitent Theodosius seems to have risen immeasurably in Christian eyes. He was easily the emperor most respected by Saint Augustine and by Orosius, as they wrote of Rome and rulers a generation later, and in contemporary accounts he became the beneficiary of a number of miracles on the battlefield. For example, in telling of how young Valentinian II met his end after Theodosius had reinstated him as emperor in the West, Saint Augustine recalled that:

> Theodosius . . . put down the usurper Eugenius, who had illegally been installed in that Emperor's place, prevailing against his very powerful army more by prayer than by the sword. Some soldiers who were there have told me that all the spears they were throwing were snatched from their hands by a very strong wind, which blew away from Theodosius's side in the enemy's direction, and that it not only gave greater force to whatever they threw against them but even turned back the spears which the enemy soldiers were throwing into their own bodies.[72]

But the long-range effect of this encounter between Theodosius I and Saint Ambrose was to furnish medieval churchmen in the West with an important precedent, showing the supremacy of the Church over secular rulers where their claims to power conflicted. Saint Ambrose was not, of course, technically head of the Church, since he was bishop of Milan, western capital of the Roman Empire, more or less constantly from the time of Diocletian to 404, rather than bishop of Rome. Nor did the bishop of Rome himself have a clear title to supremacy within the Catholic Church even by the end of the fourth century. Still, medieval popes who were to contest the independence of the secular ruler's sphere were quick to seize upon the example of Ambrose's assertion of authority over the emperor. If a bishop of Milan could excommunicate an ancient Roman emperor, then a pope could most assuredly excommunicate him, and he could surely depose him, for deposition was a trivial thing compared to excommunication. Secular rulers were, of course, to challenge or ignore the relevance of the precedent, but it was to remain a weapon in the papal arsenal for centuries to come nonetheless.

AUGUSTINIAN INTERLUDE: ARE EARTHLY KINGDOMS WORTH THE TROUBLE?

During the early fifth century, Saint Augustine of Hippo formulated ideas concerning kingship, as indeed he did concerning many another political and social topic, which were to carry considerable weight in the Middle Ages. Saint Augustine had been a student of Saint Ambrose and evinced all due reverence for his teacher's acts and doctrine; however, when Augustine discussed the place of kings of the earth, he did so in reaction to historic events in which rulership figured quite differently than it had in Ambrose's time. The most obvious difference in the attitudes of the two men is Saint Augustine's relative unconcern about the struggle for authority between the Church and the secular ruler. In the whole formative period of the Church's attitude toward kingship, Eusebius of Caesarea, Augustine, and Pope Gelasius I stand out as the foremost contributors to written political theory. The fact that the Church's view of kingship in the Middle Ages was as supportive or positive (in the modern sense) as it was, is due in considerable part to the fact that both Eusebius, who wrote under the mighty Constantine, and Augustine, who wrote chiefly under the uninspiring successors of Theodosius who governed the West from Ravenna, lived in periods in which the Christian monarch did not challenge the Church's authority in any fashion unwelcome to most orthodox churchmen.[73]

Saint Augustine added to the Church's view of kingship in two ways which can be taken to complement each other or to contrast with each other in an inconsistent way. On one hand, in the tradition of Eusebius, he delineated quite specifically what good a Christian ruler could do in his earthly estate. On the other hand — and here he is more the continuator of Ambrose in spite of the difference — he stressed the ultimate worthlessness of the earthly sphere ruled by kings and implicitly relegated the king to a distinctly subordinate activity. Saint Augustine did not write a specific work on kingship, and, since his political concerns were always incidental to his theological ones, there is no point in holding up the contrast between his two basic stances in confronting kingship. Instead, it is more of the essence to note that his theological responses to history were capable of either exalting or denigrating kingship, "depending on the situation."

On the level closest to Eusebius, Augustine sometimes associated the prosperity of the state with the ruler's Christianity. Many of his remarks on secular rulers are found in his *City of God,* which was begun under the impact of the sack of Rome by Alaric's Arian Visigoths in 410. Since he took some pains in the first books of that great work to answer the pagan charge that the adoption of Christianity had brought about Rome's decline, it followed from his polemics that Rome under its pagan rulers was shown to be worse off than Rome under Christian rulers. Consequently, he let the Christian ruler's religion function on occasion as a shield for the state. It was in this connection that Theodosius had won his miraculous victory, "more by prayer than by the sword," described by Saint Augustine in the passage cited above. The reverse side of this is that pagan and heretical kings are apt to suffer miraculous defeats with the same good results for the Christian empire:

> When Radagais, King of the Goths, was already threatening the Romans' very necks with his huge and savage army encamped near the city, he was beaten in one day with such speed and in such a way that not one single Roman was wounded, let alone killed, while well over a hundred thousand of his soldiers were struck down, and he was captured and soon put to a deserved death. For if such a godless man with such equally godless troops had entered Rome, who would have been spared by him? What shrines of the martyrs would he have respected? In dealing with what person would the fear of God have restrained him? Whose blood would he have wanted to leave unshed and whose chastity unravaged?[74]

For Augustine, the goodness of Christian monarchs can bring not only military victories but also earthly advantage to their subjects in peaceful and prosperous reigns:

> It follows that if the true God is worshipped and served with true rites and good morals, it is a benefit for good men to have long reigns over great territories. This is actually not of so much use to themselves as it is to their subjects, because as far as they themselves are concerned their own true faith and righteousness, which are great gifts from God, are enough to give them the true happiness that lets them live this life well and attain eternal life afterwards. Thus the reign of good men here on earth does not serve their own good so much as it does human concerns.[75]

It is possible to see Augustine's description of the Christian monarch in the tradition of the "Mirrors of Princes," a genre ostensibly didactic but more often than not merely flattering, which had developed in the East at the time of Alexander the Great, was widely used in imperial Rome, and subsequently flourished in both the Byzantine Empire and the medieval West. In the "mirrors," the virtues of the perfect ruler are held up for examination, and the real-life rulers can be rated — or congratulated — according to the degree of correspondence between them and the ideal image. There is no evidence that Augustine thought of directly influencing the rulers of his time, and, certainly, flattering them was altogether foreign to his personality. Nonetheless, the attributes which he brings out in his description of true Christian rulers are precisely those which went into the model of kingship in the western Middle Ages, at the same time that his "mirror" would have given a subdued reflection by eastern standards. His connection of historical rulers with a Christian standard of good rulership is in these terms: if they meet it, they have the satisfaction of having striven well to achieve the true happiness which can be theirs in the life to come. Here Augustine asserts that in contrast with those who equate political and military success in themselves with the happiness of the best rulers, "we" hold certain Christian emperors

> . . . to be happy if they rule justly; if they are not carried away by conceit in the midst of voices praising them extravagantly and by men hailing them with a debasing show of excess humility, but remember that they are men; if they turn their power into a very servant of the Divine Majesty, by using it to spread the worship of God as far as they can; if they fear, love, and worship God; if they are slower with punishments, inflicting them only when pressed by the requirements of governing and defending the state but not for settling scores out of hate for enemies, and are all the more quick with pardons, not in order to let crimes go unpunished but in the hope of rehabilitating the offenders; if they make up for often necessarily harsh decrees with kind acts of mercy and with sweeping generosity; if they restrict their luxury all the more as they can freely afford luxury; if they prefer ruling firmly over low desires within themselves to ruling over any given nation; and if they do all this not out of a passion for vain glory but out of a love for eternal happiness, without failing to offer their own true God the sacrifice of humility, mercy, and prayer for their sins.[76]

Earthly rewards, incidental as they are to the happiness of true Christian rulers, may well be granted to them by God. The career of Theodosius is an obvious case in point, for Augustine; that of Constantine is another:

> On Emperor Constantine . . . God bestowed such an abundance of earthly favors as no man would dare wish for. He permitted him to found a city to share in the imperial rule of Rome, a daughter, so to say, of Rome herself, but without any temples or images of the demons. He reigned for a long time, maintaining the whole Roman world as sole Augustus. He was most victorious in directing and waging wars; he was always successful in putting down usurpers. He was very old when he died of sickness and age, and he left sons to rule after him.[77]

But—and here Augustine parts company silently but resolutely with Eusebius concerning that writer's depiction of Constantine as having earned these rewards by his own faith and deeds—Augustine does not acknowledge that even Constantine merited all these blessings on earth. With his characteristic willingness to explain what motivates God to let things happen, Augustine presents cause and effect in Constantine's case as God's desire to disillusion the pagan world about the chances for victory and prosperity produced by the worship of the pagan gods. Again in contrast with the Eusebian viewpoint, Augustine asserts that God does not even wish rulers to take up Christian worship in the belief that this will bring them earthly rewards.

> On the other hand, to dissuade any emperor from being a Christian in order that he might earn the blessings of Constantine—when everyone ought to be a Christian for the sake of eternal life—God took Jovian away far sooner than he did Julian.[78]

The pious Emperor Gratian, he also notes, was killed by a usurper's sword.

Perhaps because Augustine was forced to spend so much time in the practical matter of ministering to the temporal needs of his North African flock and to do so all the more urgently because of the inability of the Roman Empire to cope effectively with the barbarian invasions and refugee problems, Augustine perceived more clearly than many churchmen of the fourth century that things went much worse for Christians on earth when government posts were not manned by men of conscience and determination. He was the first Church writer to call upon Christians to assume governmental office as a matter of religious duty. He notes that the carrying out of governmental tasks, tied as these are to subjecting men to tribulation, torture, and sometimes death, is a most unpleasant duty for Christians; and yet, he holds that as long as the earthly city endures, Christians must not refuse a contribution of their talents to human society.[79]

The grim and ultimate responsibility for keeping "the peace of Babylon," that is, imposing order on a disorderly world, belongs to the secular ruler. Consequently he is to be obeyed unquestioningly by one and all. It seems that for Augustine the secular ruler should exercise his divinely assigned office without much deference to popular demands because—among other reasons—his competence is usually greater when he reaches decisions alone than when he yields to his subjects' requests. In most cases, he notes, we find that subordinates are best served "by not giving them what would injure them if we did give it to them."[80] Where Ambrose had invoked the parent-child analogy most pointedly to assert the rightful dominance of the Church over the secular ruler, Augustine (without, of course, denying the primacy of Church interests) invokes the parent-child relationship most pointedly in referring to intelligent monarchical rule. Since the monarch's task is difficult enough as it is, no one should presume to call him to account for performing it, as long as he does not command an act contrary to the known will of God. With perfect consistency he notes that the same Christian soldiers who refused to obey Julian in his command to offer sacrifices to the pagan gods obeyed his command with alacrity when he ordered them "to march against this or that nation."[81] In a word, Augustine stresses the rightful absolutism of the ruler. Whatever he decrees in the secular world is lawful. No Christian ever has cause for resisting even the decrees (again, as long as these do not include crimes against the faith) of a tyrant. Tyrants are set over men by Providence, and Providence will in due time remove them. Sometimes tyrants rule as part of God's just punishment of man and sometimes for greater ends known only to God. They can do no real harm to the City of God, that body of the elect who are but pilgrims in this world, who glory in earthly suffering and martyrdom.[82]

Rulers should, of course, go beyond merely keeping the peace of Babylon by using their power "to spread the worship of God as far as they can," and Augustine, although he earlier opposed the persecution of heretics, ultimately developed into one of the most sanguine defenders of coercion by the state for the ultimate good of the coerced.[83] In the final stage of the enduring Donatist controversy in North Africa, it was Augustine who adapted the parable of the great man who had his servants force reluctant people away from the lanes and hedgerows to come in and join him at a banquet he had prepared for others who did not come.[84] Taking the hiders and loiterers from the lanes and hedgerows to represent heretics and schismatics and the master of the house to represent God, he states that his command meant compelling heretics back into the fold. Thus it was that *Compelle intrare!* ("Make them come in!") originated as an admonition to religious persecution, although Augustine himself did not go to the length of medieval theorists who were to allow the death penalty as part of the forced-entry process. To the obvious objection that nothing is further from the spirit of the New Testament than using Caesar's force to gain converts for God, Augustine could reply that obviously times had changed since Saint Paul's day: such a policy would have been impossible then under the pagan emperors, but Nebuchadnezzar's change of heart from persecuting adherents of the true God to decreeing that "whosoever should speak against the God of Shadrach, Meschach, and Abednego should suffer the penalty which their crime deserved," shows that God had made use of the royal power for similar coercive purposes in Old Testament days and thus would have approved of applying it — only as a last resort, to be sure — against heretics in the Christian empire.[85]

The other side of Augustine's presentation of kingship, however, does not merely modify the Eusebian enthusiasm for the Christian monarch from whose good works the state and people prosper, but nearly negates it, if it does not do so entirely. For Augustine, the span of mortal men on earth sometimes seems so short as to render all their doings ultimately trivial: one reason for not arguing with the king about matters of state is that they are not worth arguing about. The Roman monarchy is filled by "a constant going and coming of dying men":[86] since in the context of eternity to eternity death presses upon every man so soon after birth, the brevity of life equalizes what might seem to be the horrendous distinction between the lot of the emperor and that of a slave. Augustine does not equate the earthly city with the Roman Empire or any other historical kingdom. The earthly city is the agglomeration of worldly interests which claim the primary attention, the best efforts, and consequently also the souls of most men. A ruler whose mind is directed toward God and who acts according to his Christian faith can escape the damning citizenship of the earthly city; however, in so far as his earthly concerns demand his attention for their own sakes he is required to function in a sphere alien to true godliness.

This brings us to a cardinal point with Augustine: kingdoms as kingdoms are not only trivial enterprises but thoroughly rotten ones. The Christian monarch's leadership of the Roman Empire has a place in the divine scheme of things, to be sure; it is all to the good that monarchs since Constantine have often used their ruling powers to further and strengthen Christian worship. When rulers and their dominions, however, are viewed merely as rulers and dominions without regard to the service they render the faith they are nothing more than the embodiment of greed and crime. The only thing that distinguishes kingdoms from robber bands is that kingdoms bestow formal legality on themselves. Just as robbers maintain peace and harmony among themselves for the purpose of plunder, royal governments functioning purely as royal governments use threats of violence, take people's property, and kill people, all for reasons of the flesh. If the power of a robbers' band

> . . . increases by having desperate men add their numbers to the point that the resulting plague can control territory, establish bases, seize cities, and subject people to its rule, it takes on in public the name of "kingdom," which is now really granted to it all the more openly — not because its greed is any less but because it now acts with more impunity. It was really an elegant and true reply that a certain captured pirate gave to Alexander the Great: when the king asked him what he thought he was doing by terrorizing the sea, he answered freely and defiantly: "The same thing you think you are doing. But because I do it with a little ship, people call me a robber. You do the same with a big navy, and so people call you an emperor."[87]

It is perhaps an understatement to say that, viewed from this perspective, Saint Augustine's advocacy of absolutism no longer dignifies monarchy. When he admonishes subjects to obey even tyrants unquestioningly, this can be seen in the light of the original New Testament quietism, which boils down to this: Do what the kings of this world tell you, because secular quibbles are so tainted with spiritual death that even arguing about them will taint you as well. Augustine separates the sphere of secular rule from that of religious governance according to the render-unto-Caesar principle: secular rule belongs entirely to the king or emperor; the governance of religion belongs entirely to God. While disputes over claims to authority by Church and state do not concern Saint Augustine nearly so much as they had many fourth-century spokesmen opposing imperial encroachments and were to concern others again in the latter half of the fifth century, Augustine can still be seen to have supported the conception of separate spheres of jurisdiction, with the superior one assigned to the Church. Superficially, Augustine's emphasis on separate spheres for the secular monarch and the Church implies a certain coequality, but the fact that the demands of the earthly city, which require so much of the secular ruler's attention, are minor distractions in comparison with the demands of the City of God means that the theological sphere is necessarily the determining one. The king's authority is subordinate in the sense of being required to take directions from the Church and to give way in the face of Church claims (largely hypothetical for Augustine as he discusses his own times), should the jurisdictional division between the two spheres be unclear.[88] This is also true of the ruler's power to suppress heresy. This is a political-religious act which at first would seem to overlap the two spheres of jurisdiction, but — since it is necessarily the province of the clergy to decide who are and are not heretics — the secular ruler's task amounts to the implementation of decisions reached by the clergy.

Augustine did not actually speak of the Church's sphere as separate from the emperor's in the crucial passages, but referred instead to God's sphere. Nor did he exactly equate the City of God with the institutional Church. But in questions of dividing the ruling spheres, his distinction between (1) the City of God, whose citizens are the heavenly host and the predestined elect and (2) the visible Church, headed by the clergy in this world, with its fair share of chaff mixed in with its wheat, had little practical meaning. The Church as an institution had to speak and act for the City of God — Augustine would certainly not have approved of any other authority in that role — and thus later churchmen could use the term "City of God" as nearly a synonym for the institutional Church.[89] Within thirty years of Saint Augustine's death, Pope Leo I in a letter to the eastern emperor exhorted that ruler to continue furthering the cause of true worship with the secular arm, so

> . . . that the Catholic faith, which alone gives life to and hallows mankind, may abide in one confession, and the dissensions which spring from the variety of earthly opinions may be driven away, most glorious Emperor, from that solid Rock on which the City of God is built.[90]

Here there is a verbal distinction: the Catholic Church is a rock and on it the City of God is built, but obviously, as the custodian of the rock, Leo is speaking as the City of God's defender in this world. Again, this is not so much an abuse of Augustine's theory as its logical extension. Since no one else is appointed to speak for the City of God in this world, sooner or later the leader of the institutional Church was going to give directions to the emperor on behalf of the City of God. The fifth-century emphasis on Saint Peter and the papacy in disputes over authority is a separate matter altogether and is dealt with at length below. Before leaving Augustine, the fact is worth noting that no one even attempted to put together his political and social thought into a single whole until quite recent times. This meant that his description of the ideal Christian ruler could be cited separately in the Middle Ages with its emphasis on what the secular ruler alone could do for the furthering of Christian worship. The idea that the City of God could literally be built — that a great king could refashion his kingdom in accordance with Christian principles to make it a truly blessed kingdom on earth — proved to be one of the great mirages in the development of medieval kingship. The plan for a kingdom of God on earth before the Second Coming is altogether foreign to Augustine, but he deserves the credit or blame for providing the materials and the inspiration for it.

LEO I TO GELASIUS I: THE INFERIOR STATUS OF KINGSHIP IN CHURCH THEORY

To the extent that the fifth-century development of the Church's attitude towards kingship involved an attempt to restrict the power independently exercised by the secular monarch, it continued the direction taken in the late fourth century. Saint Ambrose could still serve as a convenient symbol in the fifth century for the practical challenge offered secular rulers by determined churchmen. In a different way, the bulk of Saint Augustine's discussion of the natures and relative duties of the two spheres of governance could also be taken to support the Church's claim to primacy. That the monarch should give way to Church counsel in political questions affected with a religious interest, that it was the duty of the monarch to see to it that orthodox Christianity prevailed — all this was established doctrine in the fifth century, unchallenged from any quarter in the West. Assertions to the contrary survived in some of the older works of history, but there alone was clearly where they belonged: in the history of a day that was done in the West, as far as the Church was concerned. For example, *The History of the Donatist Schism* from the mid-fourth century could still be read, but its attitude toward secular rulership was clearly antiquated. Back then, in the glow of good Church-imperial relations all around, when Constans sharpened Constantine I's discrimination against heretics into outright persecution, its author, Saint Optatus, had invoked the authority of Saint Paul against the Donatist assertion that the emperor had nothing to do with the Church and drawn the conclusion: "The state is not within the Church, but rather the Church is within the state, that is the [Roman] Empire."[91] Since the emperor's will was the law of the empire, this clearly implied that the emperor stood above the Church in matters of ruling. This had been the attitude of the great historian, Eusebius of Caesarea, too, but it was obsolete all the same. As if to clear up any misunderstanding about the imperial role in religious affairs, deriving from memories of the benign intervention of Constantine I, Constans, or Valentinian I, Saint Ambrose had declared: "The emperor is within the Church, not above it,"[92] and thus it stayed in the western Church for century after century.

The fifth-century novelty was the substitution of the papacy, in place of the relatively undifferentiated authority of the Church at large characteristic of the fourth century, as the chief challenger to monarchical authority in disputed areas. The fifth-century development of the western Church's view of kingship is, in fact, inseparable from the growth of papal monarchy in idea and reality. As before, the reaction of determined personalities to sometimes only incidentally related historic events played a considerable part in the development of the Church's position.

In the East, the imperial administration had suffered some difficult times early in the century under Arcadius, the dissolute and incompetent son of Theodosius I. But Arcadius' son, Theodosius II, had had an able regent to rule for him upon his father's death in 408, and beginning in 414, when he was thirteen, he and his older sister, Pulcheria, ruled jointly over an eastern empire which remained relatively firm and effective in the face of barbarian invasions. In the East, too, the Hellenistic tendency to make the monarch into some sort of image of God on earth had deeper roots and enjoyed wider currency than in the West. At any rate, Theodosius II and subsequent eastern emperors tended to act with more self-assurance than their western counterparts in dealing with the Church. Consequently, fifth-century papal claims to power, which were of great significance in questioning or opposing the independence of medieval kingship, grew out of papal resistance to the attempts of eastern emperors to govern the Church somewhat as they governed the empire. Saint Ambrose remained, of course, an authority for the advocates of papal power in challenging eastern emperors; however, from the mid-fifth century on, popes occasionally found themselves contending not against monarchs of the type of

Theodosius I, whose basic reverence for the Church made him yield to Church authority in gray areas, but against monarchs as confident of exercising quasi-sacerdotal power as Constantine had been and without Constantine's self-imposed restraint.

In 448, Theodosius II deposed Bishop Irenaeus of Tyre. The following year he had the Second Council of Ephesus convene, appointing its president, Bishop Dioscorus of Alexandria, and setting its course with imperial letters. The council deposed Bishop Flavian of Constantinople — who was supported by Pope Leo's message and legates — and a number of eastern prelates, and thus earned Leo's wrath and the appellation Latrocinium Ephesium (Ephesian Highway Robbery) under which it has gone down in a fair portion of Church history. Theodosius may have been merely trying to find a tenable middle ground in settling a series of disputes on the nature of Christ, but to Leo, Theodosius II was not really suppressing the extremists on both sides. In Leo's view, Theodosius was allowing himself to be used by the Monophysite faction, who taught that Christ had only a single, divine nature, for the suppression of orthodoxy. Leo's own position that the human and divine natures were "united without confusion" in Christ was that of Flavian and had been pointedly ignored at Ephesus.[93]

Leo enlisted the support of western Emperor Valentinian III, his wife Eudoxia, and dowager Empress Galla Placidia: soon both papal and western imperial letters entreated Theodosius to reconsider what had been done at Ephesus. Flavian died on his way to exile, but Leo continued to press the matter.[94] The conflict was really resolved when Theodosius II was thrown by a horse and died of the injuries. Pulcheria, who had not been able to act freely before, openly took the part of Leo and the supporters of Flavian, while Marcian, a senator who became emperor when Pulcheria married him less than a month later, did the same. In 451 the Council of Chalcedon was held at Marcian's command under the direction of imperial officials, who accepted considerable assistance from Leo's legates: after several sessions, Leo's definition of the true relationship between the two natures of Christ was accepted as binding, most of those who had suffered from the proceedings at Ephesus and had not yet received restitution were given it, and the prelates and monks who had condemned Flavian were repudiated in one fashion or another. Their leader, Dioscorus, who had added to his outrages at Ephesus by pronouncing excommunication against Pope Leo, was dismissed from the priesthood. On the surface, Leo had prevailed in an important test of strength.

The Council of Chalcedon was not, however, as clearcut a victory for the papacy in its relation to the monarchy of the East as what has been said might indicate. To the extent that Leo's rout of Dioscorus and the enemies of Flavian was a victory over imperial encroachments, these had come from a dead emperor, not a living one. Marcian, the living emperor, had actually proceeded to right some of the wrongs of Ephesus before the Council of Chalcedon met. The contemporary Church historian, Theodoret, who had been one of the victims of the Latrocinium,[95] had complained to Leo bitterly when he was deposed, but it was Emperor Marcian who reinstated him in 451. As Theodoret saw it:

> Our Christ-loving Emperor, after reaping the empire as fruit of his true piety, has offered as first-fruits of his sovereignty to Him that bestowed it, the calm of the storm-tossed churches, the triumph of the invaded faith, the victory of the doctrines of the Gospel. To these he has added the righting of the wrong done to me.[96]

The letter is long, but for all the praise of the emperor and empress, there is no mention of Leo one way or the other. The one session of the Council of Chalcedon which Marcian attended was marked by great pomp and splendor, the council hailed him as "priest-emperor" (sacerdos imperator),[97] and since he had first ordered the council to meet and his officers had presided over it most of the time, he was naturally given credit for its results, particularly in the East. Then, too Leo's legates had not been able to stop the Council of Chalcedon from granting Constantinople a rank equal to that of Rome among the bishoprics.[98]

Nevertheless the whole controversy had moved Leo to insist on and improve the arguments for papal supremacy. The primacy of Rome as a see had already been asserted with some force by Damasus in the previous century against the claims of Constantinople. In 422, Boniface I had linked the idea of sole ruling function (principatus) with Damasus' claim that Rome was the one apostolic see (apostolica sedes).[99] Leo's own innovation — one more of trenchant phrasing than of substance — had been the conception of the Petrine vicarate: according to Leo, the pope functioned *in the stead of Saint Peter,* prince of the Apostles, and was thus his regent on earth.[100] Leo's depiction of the pope as Saint Peter's vicar added strength to the existing papal claim of exercising jurisdictional authority over all other bishops, and consequently it was also of some help in disputing the authority of an emperor who defied the ruling of the Roman pontiff in doctrinal matters and intruded upon the pope's jurisdiction by deposing bishops.

Just as Damasus certainly had not challenged Valentinian I or Gratian for secular authority or any portion thereof, Leo was certainly not challenging the western emperor of his own time for secular authority. There were signs that, had the emperors in the West of his time been more secure in their authority, they might have encroached on his, but the point is that this did not happen.[101] In the West, the papacy faced an entirely different situation. From the emperors in the West, neither the church at large nor the papacy in particular had to fear unwanted influence in the fifth century. In fact, the Church in the West suffered more from the absence of imperial authority to stave off barbarian attacks than it did from imperial encroachments. A repeated sequence of events was the flight of secular Roman officials while the clergy remained in place, with the result that bishops often ended up dealing with the barbarian conquerors as best they could. By the middle of the century, the pope himself was forced into this role. When Attila the Hun invaded northern Italy, leaving whole cities destroyed in his wake, Valentinian III fled from Ravenna to Rome and did no more than send a delegation to meet with the conqueror. Pope Leo headed this delegation, and in Attila's tent he negotiated a ransom for the city of Rome and the rest of Italy. Obviously, by this time in the West the pope had as much political authority as he wanted – and maybe a little more – without disputing it with the feeble court at Ravenna. No secular spokesman thought of Leo as exceeding his authority, for example, when Attila demanded and received from the negotiators the promise of having Princess Honoria, the emperor's sister, delivered to him as a future bride.

Something over three years later, when the murder of Valentinian and then of the Roman noble who succeeded him had left a complete power vacuum at the center, Leo had the unenviable task of trying to talk Geiseric, king of the Vandals, out of destroying Rome without being in a position to offer him anything he wanted that he could not simply take without resistance. Leo's persuasive eloquence was legendary, and he did get Geiseric to agree to restrain arson, murder for its own sake, and the torture of captives, but the Vandals did not actually adhere to many restraints when they sacked Rome for two solid weeks. They took with them all the valuables left from the ransom already paid to Attila which they could locate – everything from the golden candelabra taken by Titus' army out of the temple in Jerusalem four centuries earlier to the bronze-gilded roof of the capitol – and several thousand Roman captives.[102] More political power and responsibility for the Church in the West at that point would have meant only a greater hand in presiding over the disintegration of the Roman Empire in the West, which was certainly no clerical goal.

Popes after Leo's death in 461 continued to have little trouble with the hapless succession of emperors who governed in the West. When Anthemius was about to assume his duties as western emperor in 467, Pope Hilary was informed that he might decree toleration for some dissenters from Roman orthodoxy. Hilary demanded that Anthemius promise not to take such a step, and he yielded.[103] This was the only event which even faintly approached a challenge to papal authority in the West before the collapse of the western empire in 476.

But in the East, particularly in the last quarter of the century, caesaropapism flourished in both theory and practice. The Monophysite faction was sufficiently strong in the decades after Chalcedon to contribute to frequent riots, in which adherents of the decisions reached at Chalcedon were, at the very least, temporarily forced from their churches. Probably with the thought of quelling strife by bringing about a compromise among tractable elements of both the orthodox and the Monophysites, Emperor Zeno in 482 issued the *Henotikon,* or "Decree of Union," significant as the first decree on purely doctrinal matters issued by a secular ruler without the authorization of a Church council.[104] The basic theological point in the *Henotikon*—that one Person of the Trinity became incarnate and that there were not two Sons—was harmonious enough with Roman doctrine, but its failure to mention the doctrine of the two natures of Christ, which the papacy and the Council of Chalcedon had stressed, seemed like a pointed omission to Pope Simplicius. His suspicion of the document's intent grew when Emperor Zeno deposed Calendion, patriarch of Antioch, and backed a rival to John Talaia, the newly elected patriarch of Alexandria who had championed Roman opposition to the Monophysites. Zeno recognized Talaia's rival—a man called Peter the Hoarse, who was a known Monophysite and a special offender in the eyes of Rome for taking part in the *Latrocinium Ephesium*—as patriarch of Alexandria after he agreed to the *Henotikon.* Pope Simplicius protested Talaia's replacement to Zeno. Emperor Zeno and Acacius, the patriarch of Constantinople, failed to heed the pope's pleas; Acacius installed Peter the Hoarse, and Talaia's case took on the hue of suffering in a just cause due to caesaropapal usurpations.

The result was an open controversy, in which Pope Felix II,[105] who followed Simplicius in 483, excommunicated Acacius after milder measures had failed. Acacius was seen as the real author of the *Henotikon* and consequently as the promoter of caesaropapal encroachments on the authority of Rome. It was in response to this culmination of events in the East that Gelasius, first in drafting the letters of Felix II and then as pope in his own right (492–496), clarified the ideas of Ambrose and Leo into a comprehensive position, generally referred to in medieval intellectual history as the "Theory of the Two Swords," although Gelasius does not use the phrase. To speak of the Gelasian "Two Swords," representing the spiritual and secular powers, is, in fact, a bit misleading, to the extent that the metaphor implies a greater degree of separation and a greater likeness in kind than is Gelasius' intent:

> Two elements, August Emperor, go into the means for ruling this world: the sacred authority of the pontiffs and the regal power. In their exercise, the responsibility of priests is the heavier, all the more so because they must render an account before the divine judgment for the kings themselves.[106]

Throughout his discussion of Church-state relations, Gelasius pursues the theme of subordination, not separation, and certainly not equivalence. His theory is ultimately based on the duality of flesh and spirit found in the New Testament, which appears in Saint Augustine's work as the duality between the earthly and the heavenly city. With Gelasius this duality is simply that of secular and spiritual concerns, much as it had been for Saint Ambrose in challenging the legitimacy of Theodosius I's intention to have the synagogue destroyed by Christians rebuilt at their expense. Leo had already fit Saint Ambrose's use of the secular-spiritual duality into the emerging theory of papal monarchy, by emphasizing the sole right of the papacy to final decisions in Church affairs. Gelasius only makes perfectly clear what Leo had already implied, namely, that the emperor is subordinate to the pope when the pope decides that a disputed question is within his jurisdiction. For Gelasius there is no legitimate conflict between the jurisdiction of pope and emperor, for the hierarchy which he postulates recognizes no conflict which is any more than an ignoring of the places assigned above and below. But, since spiritual concerns are so obviously more weighty in their consequences than are secular concerns, when a conflict appears to arise between the two spheres, the emperor, whose rightful province is secular, should give way to the pope, whose rightful domain is spiritual. As a layman, the emperor should not presume to intrude upon the spiritual authority, although, of course, the papacy will leave purely secular matters to his discretion.

Gelasius comes close to presenting this theory as: heads, the emperor obeys the pope; tails, the pope directs the emperor:

> To do their own work properly with heavenly ends in view, emperors are to stand in need of popes, while popes are to make use of imperial arrangements, when it is a matter of conducting worldly affairs.[107]

To defend this thesis, Gelasius uses a variety of arguments, which, although they overlap in his presentation of them, can be reduced to three essential types: historical, legal, and functional. Part of his historical defense rests on the simply untrue assertion that since the time of the great and general conversion to Christianity, emperors had not held the office of pontiff. This act of abstaining from such an office followed what he calls "a marvelous dispensation" of Christ — the last priest and king in one person — which had separated the offices of priest and king forever.[108] Actually, we recall, Emperor Constantine and his successors retained the title of *pontifex maximus* until Gratian finally gave it up. Even in the fifth century, Valentinian III, Marcian, and Anastasius (the last of these reigning during Gelasius' own pontificate) were on occasion styled *pontifex inclytus,* "illustrious priest."[109] A different part of his historical argumentation, however, is convincing enough if one makes allowances for broad approximation in his parallels, for he presents a substantial list of religious leaders who gave strong rebukes to secular rulers. He notes how David yielded to the indictment of the prophet Nathan and Theodosius I to that of Ambrose; then he vividly describes Pope Leo I opposing Theodosius II, Pope Hilary opposing Anthemius, Pope Simplicius opposing both the usurper Basiliscus and Emperor Zeno, and Pope Felix II opposing Zeno. His rhetorical flow seems to carry a point which his history, strictly speaking, does not. Since it was a matter of record that David, Theodosius I, and Anthemius had given way, it might well have seemed a trivial objection that none of the papal censures of eastern emperors cited had had any influence on the conduct of the emperors at which they were aimed.

In a defense based more than anything on Roman legal tradition, Gelasius stresses the difference between the monarch's power (*potestas*) to rule, placed as he is in the world's highest secular rank, and the authority (*auctoritas*) for his ruling, that is, the source which entrusted him with his power.[110] The distinction is almost the same as the modern distinction between executive power and the constitutional authority from which it derives, although we would probably use the term "authority" in both instances. For Gelasius, God is naturally the authority for the monarch's power to rule, but God's delegation of the authority to loosen and to bind puts the pope in God's stead when it is a question of directing those affairs of this world which have a bearing on the salvation of souls. The emperor's responsibility in caring for human transience in this world is necessarily lighter, as befits a man exercising mere power, than the heavier burden retained by the pope, who exercises the ultimate authority. The wise or well-instructed ruler will recognize this relationship to the point that he lets the priesthood advise and direct him as he governs; on the other hand, he will certainly not presume to direct the priesthood or punish its members.

Gelasius' functional defense of his thesis is part and parcel of ancient organic theories of political organization. An exponent of the functional or organic theory of political and social organization often avoided direct arguments about rights in conflict with each other, by the simple expedient of matching up divisions of humanity with parts of the human mind, or body, or both, and then drawing conclusions from these analogies. In the *Republic,* Plato had matched a class of military guardians to the emotional, honor-sensitive part of the soul and concluded that, since emotions should be subordinate to reason, the guardian class should be subordinate to philosophers, whom he equated, in turn, with the rational part of the soul.[111] According to a myth incorporated into the early history of Rome, the Roman plebeians, who had withdrawn from the city in protest over having to work while the patricians did not, were persuaded to return to the city by a penetrating analogy: in the human body, a member which from external appearances could be thought to do no work and exist parasitically (the stomach equals the patrician class) really serves a function necessary to the more obviously working members.[112]

Gelasius proceeds in exactly the same manner as the Roman patrician spokesman, by adapting to his purposes an old Church tradition, which separated the laity from the clergy into "orders" within the one body of Christendom. Gelasius points to "the single structure of the body of Christ," i.e., of Christendom or the Church, "where parts are joined in a single head in a most glorious society of love."[113] For him the Roman pontiff functions as the head or guiding force of this single body, a fact which in itself leaves the emperor the function of caring for that body's needs as determined by the head. The organic theory of Christian society was to enjoy great currency in the Middle Ages. In its most famous and complete twelfth-century presentation, the priesthood was seen to be the soul of the Christian body politic, princes the head, officials and soldiers hands, etc. Obviously, in this analogy, the soul rightfully prevails over the head and the rest of the body; hence the priesthood prevails over the secular government and arguments about authority are nipped in the bud. While Gelasius lets the papacy represent the head (as controlling organ, not as a point of contrast with the soul) of such a body, he does not rigidly stick to this metaphor. Elsewhere he is more inclined to speak of the Church headed by the papacy as administering spiritual medicine to the body of Christendom.[114] But the result is the same. For Gelasius, the function retained by the secular ruler is subordinate by virtue of its analogy with the care of the physical body. Once the analogy is admitted to be a true one, it follows that the ruler in his assigned function should not think of interfering with the more important functions assigned the priesthood under the pope. Medicine for the body is no more medicine for the soul than a hand is the mind, and the secular monarch remains with what is left over in the function of ruling after the pope has decided what he needs for himself.

The Gelasian theory, which relegated kingship to a status distinctly inferior to clerical, particularly papal, authority, held its own in the western Church through the early centuries of the Middle Ages. Historically, as we have seen, its final formulation was the result of efforts to maintain papal authority against the eastern emperor and the patriarch of Constantinople; however, a theory which is developed to oppose one set of rival authorities can obviously be used against another. Thus it was to happen that medieval kings in the West were to be struck by missiles hurled from those lofty theoretical ramparts of papal power which had been constructed to resist the sweeping arrogations of Hellenistic monarchy.

There was, of course, much more to the Church's attitude toward kingship than a merely partisan position in the struggle for authority. Implicit acknowledgment of kingship as divinely sanctioned turns up in ecclesiastical rhetoric during the centuries of controversy reviewed even where it seems out of place. Valentinian I is called *sanctus rex* (holy king) in the work of Hilary of Poitiers which condemns the effects of his interference in affairs of the Church.[115] The Christian king was, after all, not casually but vitally necessary to the Church and its mission. The theories of Eusebius, according to which Christian kings earned victory in battle and ruled long and prosperously over great dominions, were buried but not dead. As catastrophe piled on catastrophe in the western empire during the fifth century, which witnessed the final political-military collapse before Germanic and generally Arian invaders, Eusebius lost his relevance: he could not have provided orthodox churchmen with much of a guide for the times. But new Constantines were to arise almost immediately in the Germanic states which took over from the empire in the West. Another century or two, and new Eusebii would make the old connection between a ruler's faith and his inevitable triumphs.

Chapter 3

Early Medieval Kingship as the Art of Stabilizing and Balancing

NEEDS OF THE DAY

When the Roman Empire in the West became irrevocably defunct in reality, if not yet in theory, and at the same time the mass movements of barbarians from the north and east became less frantic, kingship was more than ever the form of rule most nearly taken for granted in Europe. Looking back at that age with the advantage of hindsight, we can easily discern that kingship was to be a mighty instrument of progress then and for a thousand years to come. At the time, the word "progress" was anything but in vogue. Nonetheless, people were much concerned with having peace, justice, and stability, while kingship appeared to hold the only promise of increasing these elements in the life around them. Law and order was much on the minds of men and women from the early through the later Middle Ages. Succeeding generations in the surviving cities and towns of western Europe worried about the safety of the roads, while even within city walls; arson, rape and murder were still more frequent occurrences than anyone was willing to write off as inevitable. People were still found in the early Middle Ages working the land under conditions which varied from rent-paying in the northern thinly settled parts of Gaul to more onerous sharecropping which shaded off into slavery on the *villae* of the surviving senatorial class.[1] These classes were, of course, guaranteed a security of sorts by their lords of the manor. Even this security, however, was worth precious little when their own lord was at war with another lord; blood feuds and the felt need for ready vengeance made violence hang like a cloud over the early medieval scene a good deal of the time.

The protection which only a strong overlord could give seemed, in short, essential. He had to be strong enough that no one would give *him* trouble for providing law and order. He did not actually have to be called a king, although any sizeable political unit controlled by an overlord was apt to be called a *regnum*, which is usually translated in English as "kingdom." *Regnum* actually signified no more than "ruled territory"; its origin in *regnare* (to rule) is fairly evident. There were any number of rulers, called *duces*, who ruled over *regna* as extensive as some ruled by kings. Such tribes as the Herules, Gepids, and sometimes even the Lombards, found that kings were not entirely necessary to their tribal existence and that dukes would do instead.[2] The history of the early Middle Ages is full of vigorous nonroyal principalities, something which can be used to support opposing points of view: on one hand, the fact that there was such a plurality of them over whole centuries can be taken to show that viable alternatives to kingship remained for the political units not under a royal dynasty[3]; on the other hand, the fact that they were all eventually absorbed into kingdoms or empires — or in one way or another let ducal rule give way to royal or imperial rule — can be taken to show that their viability was more in appearance than in reality.[4]

By settling for the title of *dux*, an independent warlord could avoid certain problems: not quite so much *Heil* would be expected from him, and as a nonroyal ruler he would not pose quite the same tempting target for assassination that a king did; nor would the resentment of lesser lords over his superior airs be kindled so regularly. If he had a powerful king as a neighbor, he knew that he was much better off to remain a duke because the neighboring king would be sure to see in his assumption of royal status a threat to his own position.

Still, it generally took a king with all of the force that charisma and monarchically oriented church doctrine could add to ruling talents, to provide stability in the Middle Ages over large territories. The nonroyal *regna* had a way of becoming royal *regna*, although this did not seem to be a necessary or irreversible trend until Carolingian times. To assume kingship through any of the ancient rites, such as being raised on a shield by warriors, was more dangerous certainly at the outset than resting content with ducal status, but where the attempt was successful it was likely to be worth it.

On the European continent, the centrifugal forces which had broken up the Roman Empire were still to be reckoned with for centuries afterwards, and a successful king was one who could control them, often by playing them off against each other. Among the many ruling systems which filled the vacuum left by the Roman Empire, Frankish kingship came to overshadow that of royal and nonroyal competitors alike until the tenth century. It was the Franks whose kings understood the art of cornering opposition and balancing forces against each other, all the while profiting from anarchy and uncertainty elsewhere. The Franks, too, revealed an early sense of the usefulness of the clergy for providing the intellectual support for their monarchic system: if the Church did not exactly give the Franks a theory of kingship until later, it at least supplied them with a much better memory of their past than most of their contemporaries had and reinforced their collective identity in the process.

Although Roman historians began taking note of the Franks as part of the Germanic threat to the empire from the mid-third century on, distinctive attributes of Frankish kingship escaped their notice until the fifth century. The first Frank to attract attention as exercising what amounted to individual ruling power was Arbogast, a general in the Roman army in the West who had made himself powerful by appointing other Franks to high positions and undermining the authority of Valentinian II, before the demise of that emperor in 392.[5] But Arbogast did not identify particularly strongly with the Franks, having been expelled by them. On the contrary, he successfully attacked some of the Franks, who had defeated the Roman General Bradfords of that time by skillful retreats and forest ambushes in which they decimated the Roman forces with hails of poisoned arrows. Arbogast subdued them out of season, when winter's defoliation had stripped them of their forest cover.[6] He was determined to employ Frankish warriors in the service of the empire, and Frankish kingship did not seem to concern him one way or the other. After the death of Valentinian II, Arbogast made the Gallic rhetorician Eugenius the nominal emperor in the West. In the civil war which eventually followed, the newly conquered Franks fought for the usurper against Theodosius. Thus they were among the victims of the storm, cited by Saint Augustine as divine intervention, which hurled back the arrows of that pious emperor's enemies upon themselves. Then, in best old-Roman fashion, Arbogast committed suicide after Theodosius soundly defeated his armies in Italy.

At that time, the Franks were still divided among several tribes. During the following decades of insurrection, civil war, and barbarian invasion in the western Roman Empire, the Frankish tribes were at least as willing to side with a usurper, such as Constantine or Iovinus, against Emperor Honorius, as they were to support the empire, which most of them did under the imperial general, Stilicho, in 406 against the Visigoths. It would probably have seemed very unlikely to contemporaries that within a century, their kings would be moving fast in the direction of claiming the traditions of Roman monarchy.

Actually, the Franks, like the other barbarian tribes during the period of the later Roman Empire, showed a curious ambivalence towards the Roman monarchy as well as everything else Roman. On one hand, they resented the limitations which Roman governance put upon their movements and the perceptible feelings of superiority which Roman officials were capable of displaying towards non-Romans. On the other hand, the Roman tradition was capable of a high degree of assimilation: it is no surprise that Italian settlers in Gaul considered themselves *Romani*, but it is perhaps remarkable that the non-Italian inhabitants considered themselves as *Romani*, too. Roman citizenship had been extended to all inhabitants of the Roman Empire in 212, and a feeling of belonging to the Roman world remained among them, even when the power of the western empire disappeared along with the imperial title in the West. The very fact that Latin culture provided a unifying influence resulted in the prolongation of the feeling that the empire was still a thing of importance, as somehow or another the universal language, literature, legal concepts, and (for Catholic Christians) religion continued to point back to Rome:

> The new states were established by the kings of a rich variety of ethnic and linguistic groups. Only scarce evidence of documents and semi-official sources, such as inscriptions and legends on coins and medallions, remains. But all of them betray the same fact, namely that these very kings carried Latin titles, issued laws, diplomas, and all kinds of administrative acts in Latin, and used what I would propose to label a "Latin state vocabulary."[7]

The absence of known and reliable alternatives in the instruments of government and law made even the still unassimilated barbarian leaders hesitant to throw themselves against the whole complex of ideas and institutions which made *Romanitas* live on. It made much more sense to attempt to act on behalf of the Roman tradition when dealing with inhabitants of Gaul who considered themselves *Romani*. It is also quite likely that most barbarians were sufficiently impressed by the sophistication and self-assurance of the *Romani*, to want to imitate them consciously or unconsciously. While it is common practice to refer to the "successor states" which replaced the Roman Empire, there are reasons why this term should be used with caution, if at all. The new states run by barbarian kings were often perceived in their contemporary world not as replacements for Roman authority but rather as part of a continuing Roman world system.

The ambivalence of the barbarians towards Rome was strong enough to appear full of out-and-out contradictions. There is, for example, the prologue to the subsequent law code of the Salian Franks, the *Lex Salica*, which attempts to put distance between the Franks and their Roman opponents:

> The illustrious tribe of the Franks, established by God the Creator, brave in war, faithful in peace, wise in their counsels, of noble body, of immaculate purity, of choice physique, courageous, quick and impetuous, converted to the Catholic faith, free of heresy . . . . Such is the nation which, because they were courageous and strong, shook off the hard yoke of the Romans in battle.[8]

It would be hard to imagine a more nationalistic self-image than this or one more consciously hostile to Rome. The Frankish author who wrote this paid no attention to the fact that the Franks received their Catholic faith as the faith which distinguished the *Romani* from most of the Germanic tribes, the latter preferring Arianism, nor to the fact that when the Franks fought massive battles against the empire they lost, while by the time they finally did become militarily dominant in Gaul and western Germany there was no Roman yoke left to throw off. Such a statement as this obviously is not consistent with the fact that the great Frankish King Clovis accepted the Roman title of "Patrician" (*patricius*) from the emperor in the East nor with a great many other things.[9]

Procopius recites the story of "the Arborychi," in context, probably the Armoricans, Gallic inhabitants of the maritime provinces in what became Brittany, who had revolted from the Roman Empire and set up a state of their own. When the Visigoths invaded Gaul and Spain, however, the Arborychi fought as Roman soldiers, *joining forces with the Franks who were previously their enemies and intermarrying with them on the basis of their common loyalty to Rome.* The Arborychi, having thrown in their lot with the Franks,

> . . . handed down to their offspring all the customs of their fathers, which were thus preserved, and this people has held them in sufficient reverence to guard them even up to my time *[some one hundred fifty years later and well after the end of the Empire in the West]*. For even at the present time they are clearly recognized as belonging to the legions to which they were assigned when they served in ancient times, and they always carry their own standards when they enter battle and always follow the customs of their fathers. And they preserve the dress of the Romans in every particular, even as regards their shoes.[10]

The story of the Armoricans, with or without mixing that of the Franks with it, shows resentment against the misgovernment of the later empire, but still a marked preference for things Roman when faced with the possibility of Visigothic domination. Traditional historiography has tended to ignore the similarity between (1) revolts of the fourth century and earlier led by Roman generals, often from the provinces and often of barbarian origin, with the purpose of taking over the emperorship or conquering part of the empire to rule themselves, and (2) the fifth and sixth-century military exertions of warrior chiefs and kings among the barbarians which had analogous aims of bringing chunks of the empire or what had been the western empire under their control. It has recently been shown, however, that no clear line of demarcation in aims can be drawn between the two types of military actions, both of which were often seen more as restoration attempts by their leaders than as attempts to supplant the Roman world order at all.[11] In view of the fact that some writers of history in the High Middle Ages stressed the institutional continuity between the Roman

Empire and the Germanic Empire this begins to make even more sense.[12] It is even possible to fit Arbogast into the picture. Was he not, after all, leading forces dedicated to the ideals of classical Roman civilization and paganism against the forces of the East and Christianity? Regardless of the fact that Arbogast was a Frank, his own puppet emperor, Eugenius, was a Roman rhetorician, while his opponent was the eastern and most Christian emperor, Theodosius. Perhaps, "Regardless of the fact that he was a Frank" is even a prejudicial way of introducing such a statement: there seems to be every reason to believe that many barbarians valued their *Romanitas* as much as the born inhabitants of the eternal city. It is obvious that barbarian kings had nothing against appropriating a bit of the purple and gold of the Roman tradition in their self-appointed tasks of conquest and pacification. It is at least likely that doing so came fairly natural to them.

GOTHIC VARIATIONS ON A THEME

History catches first sight of a kingdom of the Goths in the first century A. D., in the central Vistula region, from which base the Goths spread toward what is now the Ukraine. To stop their destructive raids on the empire in the Balkans and Asia Minor in the third century, the Romans bought them off with the province of Dacia (roughly present-day Rumania and Bessarabia) and financial support. Around the middle of the fourth century, a great Gothic *thiudans* by the name of Hermaneric or Ermaneric turned the unstable situation in eastern Europe to his own and his people's advantage and spread his rule over a large area between the Black and Baltic seas. Hermaneric was to become a legendary figure in Gothic kingship. According to a sixth-century Gothic account he died at the age of a hundred and ten, undefeated in battle but overcome by treachery, after ruling an area from the Black to the Baltic seas and from the mouths of the Danube and Dnieper to the mouth of the Vistula.[13] Whatever the extent of Hermaneric's empire may have been, it really lasted only a few years, and later eastern emperors wisely helped to keep the Goths divided by recognizing several leaders among them at once and employing the mercenary services of their warriors to keep them friendly to their own empire. Like most of the Germanic tribes, the Goths had converted to Arian Christianity, a fact which isolated them from Romans in the empire as much as did their barbarian heritage.

By the time of the invasion of the Huns around 370, two main Gothic nations were discernible: the Visigoths living west of the Dniester River, who wanted Roman imperial protection against the Huns, and the Ostrogoths, east of the Dniester, who became subjects of the Huns. The Visigoths were one of the few Germanic peoples to get along without a king over their whole tribe from the time they formed a recognizably separate grouping. This fact, hypothetically extended back a little in time, makes King Hermaneric necessarily an Ostrogoth, since the Ostrogoths demonstrably did have kings even under the Huns. This might be a poor way of putting it, however, since the Visigoths may have taken on a separate ethnic identity only with the dissolution of an older all-Gothic kingship.[14] Be this as it may, neither major group of Goths was inherently hostile to Rome, and several of their most successful rulers were to hold high Roman imperial posts.

From at least the 360s on, the Visigoths were led by military commanders, who are called "judges" in the Roman sources which take note of them. The Gothic word behind that term is unknown, but several facts concerning Athanaric, the first Visigothic leader of whom something beyond the mere name is known, make it likely that the "judge" was to all intents and purposes a *reiks*. He held power on the basis of his talent rather than his blood heritage, and he could be replaced for failing to ward off military threats to his people.[15] Assumedly the Roman choice of the term "judge" implied some responsibilities of the title holder for overseeing justice among the Visigoths; however, the Roman writers who used it were interested foremost in military matters and were unconcerned about the Visigothic "judge's" relation to tribal law.

Under Hunnic pressure, the Visigoths asked and received permission to cross the Danube for Roman protection; however, Roman officials treated them so badly as refugees that they waged war against the Romans and dealt the Roman legions a startling defeat at the battle near Adrianople in 378 at which Emperor Valens was killed. Frithigern, their leader, was the first Visigoth referred to in a Roman source as a king by name, although the reference is a rather casual one.[16] His command, like that of Athanaric, seems to have been neither permanent nor binding on the Visigoths. After their great victory over the Romans, the Visigothic warriors ignored Frithigern's advice and went on to launch a hopeless attack on the heavily fortified city of Adrianople itself. In 382, Frithigern was still alive but had been replaced by other leaders. During this period of the later fourth century, multiple rulership prevailed among the Visigoths: apart from kings of the *reiks* type, heads of small tribal units based their rule on both "dignity and descent." It is possible that they were called by a name etymologically akin to "king."[17]

Emperor Theodosius I befriended the Visigoths, and he reconciled them sufficiently to have them fight on his side against the forces of Arbogast, the Frankish-Roman general, and his puppet emperor, Eugenius. A large Visigothic contingent was led at the decisive Battle of the Vippaco by a young chief, Alaric, who belonged to the *Balthi*, meaning "the bold ones," the family or clan best known to them for furnishing war leaders. The victory of the combined forces of Theodosius effectively ended the imperial war in Italy and brought the whole empire, East and West, for one final time under a single rule. Alaric felt assured of receiving a high position in the Roman army and considered himself cheated when no such appointment had materialized by the time Theodosius died the next year, in 395. Shortly afterward, Alaric was acclaimed chief over all the Visigoths. Although Latin sources do not call him by the earlier name of "judge," they vary at first between calling him *dux* and *rex* and only later settle on *rex* consistently. It seems reasonable, then, to suppose that Alaric began to lead the Goths as a *reiks*, or as an elected warrior king by one name or the other, but that he developed his position into that of *thiudans*, or permanent tribal king, before his career was over.[18]

Roman military power in the West at the end of the fourth century was effectively wielded by Stilicho, a German who had concocted the post of "Master of Both Services," i.e., of infantry and cavalry, which amounted to being commander-in-chief.[19] Final authority in the West rested with Emperor Honorius, the weak son of Theodosius I, when he chose to use it. Stilicho had defeated the Goths on several occasions, but he did not forget that Alaric had been firmly on his side against Arbogast, and, in general, Stilicho much preferred using the Goths in the service of the empire to fighting them. In 405, Stilicho let Alaric combine his Gothic kingship with his long-sought Roman generalship: Alaric became a *magister militum* and was ordered to occupy Epirus, the region in Greece bordering on the Ionian Sea.

King Alaric was not above using his combined position of tribal leader and Roman general for leverage and blackmail. He made his people more formidable and strengthened his own position among them by supplying them freely with arms from Roman arsenals. In 406-407, Stilicho more than had his hands full with invasions of Vandals, Sueves, and Alans, and usurpations of a series of pretenders to imperial power. Alaric, claiming lack of Roman support for his occupation of Epirus, demanded four thousand pounds of gold in compensation. Stilicho and the Roman Senate agreed to pay, hoping to use Alaric's Visigoths to help put down the most threatening of the usurpers, Constantine in Gaul. Soon Stilicho's power and influence proved to be his undoing, and he was treacherously murdered with the connivance of Emperor Honorius. His murder was taken as a signal for the massacre of barbarians in Roman military service and their families by Roman troops. Huge numbers escaped, however, and marched off to join Alaric, who now found himself warrior-king and general over a greater horde than ever. King Alaric intended first to settle differences by negotiations, but Roman intrigues and Gothic impatience eventually brought him into fierce hostility against the empire, which ended in the Visigothic sack of Rome in 410.

Even then, Visigothic kingship did not place itself in permanent opposition to Rome and the empire. Alaric had gone through the motions of establishing a puppet emperor of Roman stock: he did not attempt to end the empire or to take it over in his own name. On the same topic, the contemporary historian Orosius has recorded an interesting vignette of the outlook of Athaulf, Alaric's brother-in-law, who married the imperial hostage carried off from the Gothic sack of Rome, Emperor Honorius's sister, Galla Placidia. When Alaric died, the Visigoths elected Athaulf king. Orosius, on a trip to Bethlehem, had heard an old soldier who had served under Theodosius and had been on a familiar basis with Athaulf (assumedly from the time the Visigoths supported Theodosius against the Franks and Eugenius) tell Saint Jerome how Athaulf,

> . . . a man of great force of mind, body, and ability, would often swear to the fact that at first he had burned with the desire to wipe out the Roman name and make the Roman Empire into a Gothic one and call it that and let it be in such a way that the man on the street would say that "Romanland" had become "Gothland," and there would have been Athaulf now like Augustus Caesar himself, but that much experience had shown that the Goths were not at all able to make laws because of their unbridled barbarian nature, while it was impossible to write off the matter of a state's laws, without which a state is not a state, and that he finally chose to seek glory for himself in completely restoring the power of the Roman name with Gothic forces, so that posterity would see him as the cause of Rome's restoration, after he had found Rome's transformation beyond his powers. For this reason he was inclined to abstain from war and to strive for peace, particularly when he was influenced and encouraged by his wife, Placidia, a remarkably intelligent woman and quite sound in religious matters, in all his efforts to get results from his good policies.[20]

Athaulf, as Orosius also notes, was murdered by the treachery of one of his own men before he really had a chance to do much, but this contemporary account is perhaps most significant for underlining how Germanic kingship could be perceived by a Roman — Orosius was of Roman-Spanish provincial origin and one of the last enthusiasts and optimists in the West concerning the future of the Roman Empire — as supporting that great international order, the *orbis terrarum Romanus*. Athaulf and Galla Placidia had named their royal son Theodosius. With Athaulf, we have the first clear indication of Visigothic kingship perceived as something to be inherited, and only at this point do we have a Visigothic *thiudans* or *thiudans*-and-*reiks* in one person who has left the elective principle of warrior kingship behind, in favor of the principle of royal stock. Although this Theodosius died as an infant, the choice of his name can be taken as symbolic of his parents' vision of a revitalized Roman Empire with a Gothic king reuniting, pacifying, and defending the West. Nor was this sheer fantasy: Theoderic the Ostrogoth would make a noble stab at achieving exactly this before another century had passed.

Galla Placidia's talents served the empire and its people in a different way after Athaulf's death. No longer queen of the Visigoths, she returned to marry the most prominent Roman military figure in the West, Constantius, in 417. Constantius held the evolving title of "Patrician," which would soon come to signify the highest commander appointed by the emperors.[21] Four years after the marriage of Constantius and Galla Placidia, Emperor Honorius was dead, and Constantius became emperor, although he died a few months later, leaving their healthy, if never very able, son, Valentinian III, as prince and future emperor. Galla did more ruling of the western Empire officially and unofficially in his name in the second quarter of the fifth century than anyone else.[22] She eventually used her influence to get the Goths, along with other Germanic tribes, to oppose the Huns, a policy which proved its worth a year after her death with Attila's invasions and his defeat in the Battle of the Nations on the Catalaunian Fields in 451.

Germanic leaders, whether as kings of tribes or Roman generals, or both, could not be emperors. Roman ethnic self-consciousness was still too strong for this: the rumor that Stilicho was plotting to take the imperial title for himself or his son had, in fact, triggered his assassination. One option still open to German commanders, however, was the setting up of puppet emperors, as the Frank Arbogast and the Visigoth Alaric had attempted to do. A more successful practitioner of the same art, the Suevian officer, Ricimer, freely removed and installed emperors in the West from 456 until his death in 472. Ricimer had gained his prominence by defeating the Vandal fleet in 456 and remained in effective control of most land and sea forces in the West, but he rested content with the title of "Patrician," which underscored his status as an imperial appointee.

When Odoakar disposed of or survived the last claimants to emperorship in the western empire, he was equally careful not to challenge the authority of Zeno, the emperor in Constantinople. Zeno somewhat ambiguously gave him Ricimer's previous title, "Patrician."[23] He also took the title of "King" for himself. With this, a momentous change seems to have taken place. Italy was no longer controlled by a Roman emperor but by a German king. This has seemed to historians a reasonable point at which to close discussion of the western empire, since there were in fact no more western emperors. Odoakar's takeover dealt the empire's influence in Italy a blow from which it never really recovered in spite of Justinian's later restoration efforts. King Odoakar, however, did not choose to emphasize anything new or unusual in his regime. His official stance was that of holding Italy for the emperor in the East. Only later, when his relations with Constantinople became unbearably strained did he hint at challenging the empire by taking an imperial element for his own title. Even then, he preferred to take for himself a proper-name element which had imperial associations, rather than an element clearly designating imperial rank. Coins of the realm began to show his own picture with the inscription: "FL. OD" for "Flavius Odo(v)akar."[24] Flavius was the name borne by Vespasian and his sons when they ruled as first-century emperors. It had been appropriated by later emperors with less distinguished genealogies, and Emperor Constantine himself had made it into a quasi-dynastic title. It had also been assumed by a variety of high Roman officers of barbarian origin during the fourth and fifth centuries.[25] "Flavius" thus hovered somewhere between signifying an official title and claiming the blood of rulers. At any rate, Odoaker evidently felt that it would add something extra or even something necessary for a man ruling Romans as well as Germans.

With or without the Flavian title-additive, the position in Italy of *Odo(v)akar rex*, as he is entitled in a donative document from Syracuse issued in 489,[26] was a remarkable one. Who or what was he king of? He was a Scirian, but he would have had everything to lose and nothing to gain by deriving his authority from any such diminutive tribal source: "King of the Scirians" was out of the question. Odoakar defended the interests of many of the German military settlers in Italy and consequently was a sort of *de facto* king of the Germans. Still, the different German tribes had not chosen him as such, and, besides, even if he had somehow gotten himself elected by all or most of them, Odoakar had sense enough to see that Italians in their own country would not take kindly to being ruled by a *rex Germanorum*. More than anything, he was king of the Roman army in Italy, but that reality certainly could not furnish him with a recognizable title. And so he let well enough alone and called himself simply *rex*, without specifying of whom or what, evidently hoping that his self-designation would be acceptable to most of the barbarians in and around Italy and would not offend any tribal sensibilities since it indicated neither a too presumptuous inclusion of all Germans nor a too parochial limitation to his Scirians. On the other hand he continued to use the title *patricius*, to present himself to the Italians as the high official delegated by the emperor in the East to preside over Italian affairs. This title, in turn, probably went a certain way towards making his kingship credible, if not palatable, to the Romans as long as his power lasted.

It was characteristic of Odoakar's caution that he did not presume to date documents or events by the years of his own rule but continued to use the Roman imperial system for dating as it was continued in the East. This sort of ostensible modesty in relating to Constantinople was equally characteristic of Odoakar's much greater successor in Italy, Theoderic.

The point was not lost on Theoderic, looking at Italy from the outside in

489, that Odoakar was actually king of almost no one in particular, while he had gained the title *patricius* rather much by usurpation and retroactive legitimization. What King Odoakar did, King Theoderic did much better. Odoakar was plagued from the outset by the shakiness of his tribal or national basis of power and his uncertain relationship to the empire. Theoderic, on the other hand, was supported by the imposing numbers and might of the Ostrogoths, and his relations with Constantinople were far more solid.

Theoderic led an Ostrogothic combined invasion and migration into Italy, officially to restore Italy to Emperor Zeno's control. In some ways, Theoderic's outlook and policies could show him as a veritable model of medieval kingship, in spite of certain defects and a rather unsavory personal act at the outset of his governance of Italy: he murdered Odoakar with his own hand on a pretext of requiring blood vengeance not long after his own victories and siege of Ravenna had led to a treaty between them which divided the control of Italy. All in all, Theoderic's background for kingship was far more impressive than Odoakar's. He was acclaimed as the sixteenth king of the Amal dynasty, whose members were supposed to spit fire and to be descendants or, even later, incarnations of Gaut, chief god of the ancient Goths as pagans.[27] We might have thought that this sort of thing could not sit well with his tribe's new Christianity, whether Arian or Catholic, but it evidently did not matter. In a similar way, popular imagination in the British Isles continued to associate kings with descent from Woden long after the date that we should expect to find with the mass conversions there to Christianity.[28] Theoderic's birthdate at the time his father, Thiudimer, led the Ostrogoths in the final defeat of the Huns at the Battle of Nedao[29] reminded those who cared to make the connection of Alexander the Great's birth at the time his father defeated the Illyrians. Even his name was auspicious: "Theoderic" was only what Greeks and Romans made out of *Thiuda-reiks*, thus "nation-king" and "warrior-chief" in one person. The all-around luster of his name and descent was enough to attract a substantial Germanic following, not originally limited to Ostrogoths, who soon took on Ostrogothic identity.

Once having gained the firm upper hand in Italian affairs, Theoderic began the supreme royal tasks of keeping the peace, enforcing the laws, and protecting the realm against external enemies by conquest, peaceful annexations, and alliances. He perceived part of his peace-keeping function to be the elimination of competing sources of power, while keeping those men reasonably content who could not be deprived of access to the means of coercion. Odoakar's partisans were easily overcome, and Theoderic confiscated the lands which they had recently received from Odoakar to give to his own loyal men.[30] He kept Goths in all the military posts of any significance. On the other hand, he appointed Roman citizens to the main civilian offices of his kingdom—provincial governors, the vice-regent in the city of Rome, finance officers and a host of minor officials. He allowed them to administer his government and, continuing an old Roman abuse, to become rich in the process.[31] The two pyramids of power, military and civilian, were thus kept quite separate, and Theoderic, on top of them both, had no difficulty keeping possible rivals from combining forces against him.

Even more important in keeping the peace was impressing on his subjects the certainty of punishment for resorting to force or violence on their own. Unless he could make his Goths law-abiding, he had no chance of establishing a secure state in Italy. Orosius's judgment that without laws "a state is not a state" was, after all, based rather much on fact. In enforcing the laws, Theoderic had to be mindful of the Goths' image of themselves as a people with a proud heritage of maximal freedom, as well as of Italian sensitivity to being given laws by a king of foreign origin who still appeared to be a barbarian to many. An obvious step toward enforcing the laws was setting down the ones in writing about which there was some doubt, while producing other statutes for new contingencies. Theoderic thus issued decrees individually when necessary and even promulgated a collection of them, the *Edictum Theoderici,* but at the same time he stressed that he was not making a new set of laws for the Romans.[32] Instinctively perhaps, Theoderic or his advisers perceived that for a half-way orderly society a written law code was necessary but that there would be less doubt about accepting its articles if they were thought of as stemming from ancient usage. Theoderic saw no need to complicate matters by pushing the idea of Roman citizenship for his people; in fact, the only Goths in Italy who possessed Roman citizenship were Theoderic himself and a small number of his family. The sole significant exception to the Roman-Gothic, civil-military separation of powers noted above was the office of the *saio,* which included duties derived from the Roman civilian institution of *tuitio*: the assigning of a civilian officer by a judge to guard a person who had cause to fear for his personal safety or that of his property.[33] Theoderic had Gothic officers give Roman proprietors this sort of protection, but since Theoderic generally assigned the *saiones* himself, the overall effect of this office under him was to strengthen his royal image as the source of peace and protection under law. Contemporary accounts indicated considerable success in Theoderic's exemplary attempts to rule over a law-abiding country. In the peace of Theoderic's reign, iron and gold mining were furthered, marshes were drained to increase available farmland, and there was an overall increase in the working farm population. With more commodities made available for trade, Theoderic saw to it that land and water routes were open for both domestic and foreign trade, which contributed to Italian prosperity and that of the Gothic occupiers alike. In seasons where crops were short, he attempted to head off inflation with government controlled channels of distribution which kept the prices of grain moderate. In his economic and political enactments, he was able to convey a sense of fairness which had been missing in the reigns of fifth-century western emperors:

> For he was exceedingly careful to observe justice, he protected the land and kept it safe from the barbarians dwelling round about, and attained the highest possible degree of wisdom and manliness. . . . And although in name Theoderic was a usurper, yet in fact he was as truly an emperor as any who have distinguished themselves in this office from the beginning.[34]

The statement that in Theoderic's reign merchants could send quantities of money to other places in his kingdom as securely as if the sums never left the enclosures of the city walls, or the variation on it that a man then could safely leave a purse of gold in a field and return sure of finding it where he had left it, was the sort of thing which symbolized success in the reign of later medieval kings.[35]

Again in the model image of a medieval king, Theoderic attempted to enhance the possibilities for lasting peace in his own realm by pacifying adjoining territories in present-day Austria, Bavaria, large parts of Baden-Württemberg and Switzerland, and part of Yugoslavia. Sometimes he pursued this policy by forcibly reasserting older claims of a hereditary nature, sometimes by offering favorable terms of alliance and protection.[36]

Theoderic and his family also pursued goals of foreign policy by entering into marriages with ruling families of other Germanic tribes. Theoderic himself married Audafleda, sister of Clovis, king of the Franks, about whom considerably more will be said shortly; his sister, Amalafrida, married Thorasamund, king of the Vandals; one of his daughters, Ariagne, married the Burgundian King Sigismund, another the Visigothic King Alaric II; and Amalabirga, a niece, married Hermanafrid, king of the Thuringians; ". . . and thus he achieved peace with all the nations round about."[37] Theoderic's marriage policies went beyond the obvious purpose of helping to keep peace with foreign tribes:

> The efforts of lesser rulers to share part of the *Heil* and magnificence of glorious dynasties by marrying into them played an additional part here; on the other hand, people were conscious that it was a special act of favor when the king of a small realm was accorded the honor of taking the daughter of a famous dynasty for his wife.[38]

The gradation of kinship—sister, daughter, and niece, in that order of importance—showed the degree of favor and recognition. Marriage policies of this type, then, could further international acknowledgment of the superiority of the more famous dynasty and thus help in stabilizing an international order based on dynastic rank and hegemony. These unions did not achieve much in the way of lasting results for Theoderic, except perhaps in the case of the Visigoths in Spain,[39] but such alliances were to become characteristic instruments of foreign policy for medieval kings.

Theoderic had more than a normal portion of ambivalence toward *Romanitas* for a Germanic king. *Romanitas* necessarily exerted a great hold on him in his peculiar position as ruler of Italy at the behest of the Roman emperor in the East. He accepted titles which could be taken to signify ruling on behalf of the eastern emperor until he was acclaimed king a second time at Ravenna. Afterwards, his normal title, *Flavius Theodericus rex,* resembled Odoakar's.[40] As such, it might seem at first glance unnecessarily bare: unlike Odoakar, Theoderic led the tribal constellation which effectively controlled Italy. Still, his motives for keeping his title lean were much like Odoakar's. Theoderic did not want to present himself as "King of the Goths," which would estrange the Roman loyalists by stressing that they were being ruled by the king of a foreign nation, nor could he have expected their sensibilities to accept his title as "King of the Romans." Plain "King" plus the Flavian title-element might be a little vague, but it had imperial associations, and under the circumstances there were distinct advantages in not being too specific.

Theoderic and the eastern emperors with whom he dealt seem to have paid fairly close attention to the origins and shadings of his kingship titles. On one hand, Theoderic had first been chosen king by the Ostrogoths, a fact which Zeno acknowledged well before Theodoric's expedition to Italy. According to Jordanes:

> When the emperor Zeno heard that Theoderic had been appointed king over his own people, he received the news with pleasure and invited him to come and visit him in the city, sending an escort of honor. Receiving Theoderic with all due respect, he placed him among the princes of his palace. After some time, Zeno increased his dignity by adopting him as his own son-at-arms and gave him a triumph in the city at his expense. Theoderic was made Consul Ordinary also, which is well known to be the supreme good and highest honor in the world. Nor was this all, for Zeno set up before the royal palace an equestrian statue to the glory of this great man.[41]

It would seem then that Zeno went all out to recognize Theoderic's royal rank when he first attained it. But then again according to Jordanes:

> It was in the third year after his entrance into Italy . . . that Theoderic, by advice of the Emperor Zeno, laid aside the garb of a private citizen and the dress of his race and assumed a costume with a royal mantle, as he had now become the ruler over both Goths and Romans.[42]

This can only be taken to mean that Theoderic was graduating in the eyes of the eastern emperor to a qualitatively different kind of kingship which made his Ostrogothic tribal title look like that of a private citizen by comparison. The simplest explanation for all this is that the title of rulership over Italy as a territory was emerging. This would also explain the otherwise odd fact that in 493, after Odoakar and Zeno were both dead, the Goths made Theoderic their king without waiting for the command of the new emperor.[43] For all intents and purposes then, Theoderic aspired to make himself king of Italy. Still he left it for subsequent historians and literati to make this explicit in designating his position; he did not do it himself. He did, however, retain the imperial service title of "Patrician" explicitly and the military rank of *magister militum* implicitly.[44]

The education of kings being a prime point of interest for medieval writers on kingship, that of Theoderic is worth looking at in a little detail: having spent some years of his youth in Constantinople as a well-treated royal hostage before returning to his people at age eighteen, Theoderic had received a varied education.[45] He was exposed to the combination of physical, liberal, and general education, along with training in the military arts, which a Greek was supposed to be able to use as preparation for a future position of power. Theoderic seems to have made the most of the first and last of these elements in his royal education. His physical prowess and endurance added greatly to his reputation, and he proved to be a master not only in military strategy and tactics but also in getting across to his own army the importance of training with new weapons and of maintaining military discipline with peacetime drill. It was at his prodding, for example, that the Goths seriously pursued archery, after having probably come to rely too heavily on sword-wielding and cavalry tactics for their victories.[46] His military skill also showed itself in an ability to meet unfamiliar situations. In the speed with which he came up with a navy when it was needed, Theoderic showed more tenacity and ingenuity than any other recorded monarch before Peter the Great. The Goths at that time, like the Russians later, were not exactly famous for being sailors, and yet one fleet gotten together by Theoderic was able to blockade the two harbors of Ravenna in the struggle with Odoakar, and a later one produced in equal haste succeeded in clearing the southern Italian coasts of marauders.[47]

Theoderic showed less than indifference, however, concerning the book-learning part of his own royal education. He evidently found something soft and unmanly in being all too familiar with reading and writing. Whether or not it was pure affectation, he made a show of being illiterate. He "made his mark" on documents by drawing through a stencil plate with letters.[48] He is reported to have expressed his contempt for Roman or Greek style schools of reading and writing for boys with the remark that a boy who had learned to be afraid of the schoolmaster's strap would never face up to a real sword or spear.[49] While he held at least an excess of reading and writing to be effete for the royal male, this did not prevent him from allowing his daughter Amalaswintha to engage in literary pursuits and having his niece presented to King Hermanafrid as "well-versed in letters, knowledgeable of society's ways, a credit not only to her race but to the worthiness of womanhood itself. . . ."[50] Royal women did not have to worry about losing their sword-wielding capacity through preoccupation with letters and fine phrases.[51] While he wanted no part of literary education for himself, it was part of Theoderic's total self-image as king to be something of a patron of letters, as he was of architecture, engineering, and the performing arts. He supported the Roman senatorial intellectual, Cassiodorus, making him head of his chancellory and chief minister. Cassiodorus later produced a history of the Goths, and, although it is lost in its original form, much of what is known about Ostrogothic kingship derives directly or indirectly from his efforts.[52] Theoderic entrusted Boethius, a leading Roman scholar and philosopher, with many offices, including that of Consul in 510, a rank to which he also named Symmachus, the early teacher and father-in-law of Boethius, although, to be sure, as soon as he suspected them of disloyalty he had them killed.

Romanitas with Theoderic was more pervasive than with other barbarian kings of the migration period, but it was also more forced. Theoderic was no doubt happy to be saluted as a new Valentinian or Trajan[53] — the latter being, incidentally, the ultimate compliment to kings throughout the Middle Ages — but he found the appeals of Boethius and Symmachus to Roman liberty annoying and eventually dangerous. As Gibbon pointed out long ago, Theoderic's task in a tradition-conscious society was analogous to Augustus Caesar's:

> "It had been the object of Augustus to conceal the introduction of monarchy, it was the policy of Theoderic to disguise the origin of a barbarian."[54]

The similarity in problems faced, however, is offset by the contrast in the degree of lasting success. Theoderic's synthesis of elements did not survive him for long. His problems were, of course, in many ways greater than those of Augustus: to combine barbarian kingship with *Romanitas* was hard enough, but to establish lasting kingship over Italy and part of Gaul at the head of a small minority of only superficially assimilated barbarians compounded the difficulties.

These difficulties were heightened still more by the religious problems he faced. It was Theoderic's religious position more than anything else which kept him from being considered an ideal king in the Middle Ages, in spite of his success in providing the peace and prosperity which most medieval kings aimed at during his long reign in Italy of thirty-three years. One of the prime tasks of a medieval king was the furthering of the faith, and as an Arian, Theoderic was in an impossible position. He recognized the necessarily suicidal results which would have come from attempting to impose Arian Christianity on Catholic Italy and felt that the best course was one of religious toleration. The problem was that a toleration program with any teeth in it — criminal sanctions against those who interfered with the religious liberties of their opponents — was taken to be persecution. In the short run Theoderic succeeded where Theodosius I had failed: he punished those who destroyed the property of religious opponents, and he never apologized for doing so.[55] To win in this respect, however, was to lose in the long run. Any medieval king who would punish sincere Christians for burning "abodes of unbelief" was plainly incapable of advancing the faith. As a king, he might be tolerated of necessity, but he could never be a model for medieval kingship. Theoderic's enforced toleration policy and his murder of Boethius were perceived as two sides of the same coin.

Then there was the matter of Pope John I: Theoderic sent him to Constantinople, to negotiate a more tolerant imperial religious policy with Emperor Justin.[56] His mission was less than successful, and when he returned to Ravenna Theoderic gave an order for him to be placed under arrest — or worse.[57] Pope John died a few days later, and Theoderic did not long survive him. Upon his death, he was given magnificent entombment by Amalaswintha in a structure which he had built during his lifetime.[58] The tomb of Theoderic stands today in Ravenna as a monument both to the great king of the Goths and to Gothic artistic and engineering creativity. The sarcophagus is empty today, however, standing there before the eye of the tourist for all the world like a giant, whistle-clean bathtub of porphyry. The massive roof, made of a single, hewn slab which must have strained Gothic and Italian ingenuity alike to hoist and place, has a tell-tale crack in it, caused, so the legend goes, when the soul of Theoderic was seized and carried off to a destination variously given as Mount Aetna or the Volcano Island in the Liparis. Medieval accounts were highly specific on this point, and many included what was recorded as an eye-witness statement of a hermit to a sailor who had sought him out while his boat was being repaired off the coast of Sicily:

> "Do you know that King Theoderic is dead?"
> "That cannot be! He was alive when we parted from him and no such news has reached us as of now."
> To this the servant of God replied: "Indeed he is dead, for yesterday at three o'clock in the afternoon he stood out distinctly and wretchedly, with his hands bound in chains, as he was escorted away between Pope John and the patrician Symmachus and hurled into the pot of this nearby volcano."[59]

Some versions, to be sure, allowed Theoderic a little more dignity: one, for example, let him ride his horse through the sky into the volcanic flames, and by the twelfth century the whole incident was subject to some scholarly doubt.[60] But, still, it is reasonably clear that any version of this story widely told of him was never going to make him much of a model for medieval kingship, however many ideal royal attributes his reign might otherwise contain. Charlemagne and Maximilian I recognized one of their predecessors in Theoderic, but they were quite exceptional in this regard.

On his deathbed, Theoderic is recorded as having in effect admonished his Gothic chiefs to maintain his grandson Atalaric as king by the same delicate balance of elements which he had used:

> As though uttering his last will and testament, Theoderic adjured and commanded them to honor their king, to love the Senate and Roman People and to make sure of the peace and good will of the Emperor of the East, as next after God.[61]

Amalaswintha was to act as regent until Atalaric was of age. What happened instead was that Atalaric was played against Amalaswintha by the Gothic nobility. After turbulent years culminating in Atalaric's early death and then the murder of Amalaswintha in 535, the emperor of the East, by then, Justinian the Great, "was aroused as if he had suffered personal injury in the death of his wards."[62]

While there is no indication that the official reaction was Justinian's personal one, the occasion provided him with an excuse for dispatching forces to take over Italy again in the name of the empire. The Ostrogoths were defeated after some sixteen years of intermittent war which began in 537 against Justinian's forces: one of their kings was eventually taken to Constantinople to die with the honorable but quite nonfunctional title "Patrician" and two final elected successors met heroic deaths in battle. But by 553, Ostrogothic kingship was ended. The disappearance of the Ostrogoths as a people soon afterwards offers the most dramatic example of the dependence of a people in the early Middle Ages upon kingship for their tribal identity:

> The Gothic tribal name vanished in Italy after the loss of the kingship to the extent that only research carried out in the most recent times has been able to establish that the Goths did not emigrate but rather were assimilated.[63]

THE MEROVINGIANS MAKE THE MOST OF AN OPENING

The first clear historical reference to Frankish kings indicates nothing concerning their position within the tribe except that tribal loyalty to kings who lost wars against Rome was not a Frankish strong point. According to the poet Claudian, writing about 400, the Franks were contentedly serving the kings put over them by Stilicho some five years earlier; the Franks had not only accepted the Roman exile of their own king, Marcomer, for violating a treaty with the empire, but had even murdered his brother,

Sunno, for his attempts to avenge Marcomer's exile.[64] Marcomer and Sunno were among those already defeated by Arbogast before their loss to Stilicho. The use of the word "kings" for Frankish rulers of even the late fourth century should probably be qualified. Claudian writes *reges* unambiguously enough, but then he was writing a panegyric, a genre not famous for conveying the accuracy of titles. The only other possibly near-contemporary source, Sulpicius Alexander, used slightly different terms for Marcomer and Sunno: *regales,* "men of royalty," and *subregolus,* a new word obviously derived from *regulus* ("petty king") and made a bit lower in rank by the prefix, *sub.*[65] But, *subregolus* to whom? The Roman emperor perhaps, but this is only conjecture. At another place he does mention "kings" of the Alamanni and Franks, but without any helpful elaboration.

For all the good it did them, Marcomer and Sunno probably set themselves off from the rest of their tribe by wearing their hair quite long. This is the sole certain aspect of distinct appearance for the earliest Frankish kings.[66] To trace and authenticate most developments in early Frankish kingship, historians are generally rather dependent for better or worse on the *Ten Books of History* (usually called *History of the Franks*) which Gregory, bishop of Tours, completed in the early 590s. Gregory vouched for the antiquity of the custom of Frankish kings' wearing long hair, and other nearly contemporary sources and findings bear him out. A short-haired king was no king to the Franks, and Frankish kings were to resort to having the heads of potential rivals to their thrones sheared: they would then send them with their unwelcome tonsures to take up monastic life. The impermanent nature of the tonsure, however, meant that royal ambitions might return. According to Gregory, a dowager queen of the Franks once received a messenger with a pair of scissors and a drawn sword: the point was to give her the choice of agreeing to the tonsuring of two young princes or to their death. The queen refused to approve the scissors, and the boys were killed by their royal uncles.[67] In another of his sketches, at least two involuntary clerics of royal extraction were decapitated when word reached the king that they seemed to be thinking of letting their hair grow long again.[68] Hair might grow back; heads would not. Most Frankish kings, however, were able to let the mild custom of tonsuring unwanted male royalty take the place of the *morbus Gothicus,* the grim tradition of their neighbors to the south.

In the second quarter of the fifth century, Frankish power emerged as a sinister force from the Roman standpoint, as a Frankish king named Clodio or Clojo led the Salian Franks on a mission of conquest from Germany to northeastern Gaul, taking the Roman-held cities of Tournai in modern Belgium and Cambrai in modern France.[69] Not much is recorded of Clodio's abilities as a leader except that he was cautious enough to use reconaissance in order to determine that a city was defenseless—as indeed Roman cities of Gaul and Germany often enough were in the later Empire—before attacking.[70] It is fairly certain that he succeeded in etching the outlines of a future Frankish kingdom on the ever-changing western map. Although he was once surprised and driven to flight by the imperial General Aetius, the Franks under him harried Cologne, Trier, and Mainz, to the despair of Roman authorities. A little over half a century more and these cities would be solidly inside the region of Frankish authority extending from the Rhone deep into central France.

It was characteristic of medieval kingship that the accomplishments of a people were seen as the single accomplishments of the king, and, in fact, the combination of courage, proper caution, and intelligence that characterized a good ruler then and now frequently did make the difference between tribal survival and extinction, let alone between fame and obscurity. The Franks were as convinced as the remaining tribes that they fought and prospered best under the leadership of one man, but the Frankish custom of dividing territories among sons—a survival of primitive Germanic custom long after it was dangerous to do this where large territories and potential armies were involved—kept a plurality of royal leaders always at least in the background. This lent a dynamic but impermanent tendency to Frankish kingship. The Frankish kings were kept on their toes by the threat of being toppled by brothers who had shared in their inheritance, but who felt that their shares could be larger. Outwitting a brother or cousin with cunning, a shameless exercise of brutality, or a deftly forged alliance became second nature to the more determined and resourceful among them.

Clodio's successor was the Merovech, or Meroveus, who gave his name to the Merovingian dynasty. While he cultivated ties with the empire, a rival in his family, not to be outdone, allied himself with Attila the Hun and supported his treaty partner in his invasion of the West. This proved to be a formidable aid to his own aggrandizement in the short run, but also to be his ruin after Attila's defeat. Merovech's Franks fought with the Romans and Goths against the Huns and were to profit by taking up some of the slack in the wake of the Huns' invasion. Numerically, however, the Salian Franks were inferior to the Visigoths alone, and for his own part Merovech seems to have been content to consolidate a kingdom of modest size, chiefly in present-day Belgium.

Beginning with Merovech's son, Childeric, we have both artifacts and narratives which bring the Frankish kings into focus as individuals. Childeric's grave in Tournai, dating from 481 or 482, was discovered in 1653. It contained "magnificent wargear, a cloak embroidered with some three hundred gold 'cicadas,' a fine gold bracelet and buckles, a crystal globe and a miniature bull's head in gold, the severed head of his warhorse caparisoned in precious materials, a signet ring bearing his name and showing him wearing his hair over his shoulders, a purse of one hundred gold coins and a box of two hundred ornamental silver coins."[71] The signet ring was probably a royal emblem, particularly since it portrays the king with a spear, which is known to have symbolized Frankish kingship at a later date and must have had a pre-Christian origin going back to Childeric's time and before.[72] The purple color of the cloak gives it similar royal associations. In Gregory's sketch of Childeric, it is impossible to sort out fact from legend, but the story is still useful for our purposes in showing the kind of attributes the Franks attached to their early kings.

The portrait is one of unscrupulousness, tenacity, and success. King Childeric was expelled by the Franks for living a dissolute life and for ravishing their daughters. He sought refuge among the Thuringians, whose king and queen, Bisin and Basina, let him stay with them for eight years. Childeric returned to his people when it was safe for him and resumed his rule—the Franks having accepted a Roman general as their ruler in the meantime—and afterwards Queen Basina left her husband and country for Childeric:

> When he anxiously inquired what had made her journey to him from so far away, she is said to have answered: "I know your capability and that you are most courageous. For this reason I have come to live with you. You can be sure that if I knew of a man beyond the seas who was more capable than you I would surely have wanted to go live with him." At this he rejoiced and took her in marriage. And she conceived, and she bore a son and called his name Clodovech [Clovis]. He became an extraordinary warrior.[73]

In the story, Childeric has obviously broken basic rules of conduct. He first abused his royal authority to an intolerable degree by sexual rapaciousness at home and then gave his host, King Bisin, an ill reward by appearing so capable as to be irresistible to Queen Basina. But much could be forgiven a successful medieval king, it seems, and the tone of Gregory's account by the end is devoid of any reproach. In fact, notice how he works in just a hint of Scripture for the advent of Childeric's progeny with that phrasing: ". . . and she bore a son and called his name. . . ."[74]

The artifacts and treasure from Childeric's grave show that he had prospered as tribal leader and done well for his people by their gods and his.[75] The time was ripe for leadership capable of unifying a large area of land no longer protected adequately by the Romans and of providing its inhabitants with more than a modicum of peace and stability. There was a real opening for a talented king who could overcome the Arian-Catholic division which separated the Gallo-Romans from most recent Germanic settlers, as a first step toward mutual acceptance and eventual assimilation. Young Clovis was to make the most of such an opening.

CLOVIS: MASTER OF THE TOTAL GAME

Clovis was ten years old when Odoakar finally closed the curtain on the western empire's fading performance. At first the Franks did not profit from this act at all. Roman governors or military leaders, sometimes functioning with only local support, sometimes under the auspices of the eastern emperor, exercised some control here and there in Gaul; and Odoakar had left much of Europe beyond the Alps and west of the Rhine to the Visigothic king, Euric. But Roman leaders had difficulty holding the makeshift political units together, while the main base of Visigothic power was in far-off Spain. Although Euric did maintain a tenuous sovereignty over most of Gaul from Gothic settlements in southern France he did so with difficulty. The Franks were to profit greatly by the antagonism created by the Arian Visigoths among Gallo-Romans. The Franks at the time were out and out pagans themselves, but for Clovis it later proved to be of the essence that the Goths in Gaul were in the business of hindering Trinitarian Christian worship, while the Franks were not.

Clovis became king of the Salian Franks upon Childeric's death in 481 or 482, and Euric's death in 484 opened the way for his career of conquest and consolidation.[76] Clovis's military and political accomplishments are easily summarized: he defeated the last Roman governor in Gaul able to maintain vestigial power in spite of the collapse of the imperial structure; he defeated the Visigoths and thus disposed of the most serious non-Frankish opposition in Gaul; he conquered some of the smaller Germanic tribes; and he united the Franks in a new kingdom with its capital at Soissons and then Paris, before he inevitably, as a Frankish ruler, divided this newly united kingdom among his sons.

In telling particularly of Clovis and his successors, the work of Gregory of Tours is useful for showing how a medieval historian could propagate both the Eusebian and Augustinian views of kingship with varying degrees of consciousness and no particular sense of contradiction. Gregory himself made much more use of Orosius than of Augustine in looking for material on early history, and the Eusebian idea, passed on by Orosius, that good Christian kings win their battles and cause their peoples to prosper underlies a good deal of Gregory's reasoning about the careers of Christian monarchs. In Gregory's descriptions of the kings of his own time, however, the pervading pessimism of Augustine makes itself felt: the Earthly City is not to be uplifted. Things change in the world, generally for the worse. The world is in a state of decay, from which no earthly will or labor can redeem it. But — back again to the spirit of Eusebius and Orosius — all is not exactly lost either:

> Would that you, too, o kings, might sweat blood in battles like those in which your ancestors fought, to make the nations, who would be terrified if

you had peace among yourselves, submit to your might! Remember what
Clovis, who started off your victories, did: he killed the hostile kings, defeated the threatening tribes, and subjugated the dominions, to leave you a
whole realm and a strong one.[77]

Yes, if only you royal epigones of the late sixth century would make
yourselves familiar with the methods and outlook of a real king like
Clovis, Gregory seems clearly to be saying, things would go much better
for the Franks. Most of the illustrative stories of Clovis which Gregory
presents do indeed focus on King Clovis's ability. At the same time, some
of them point up the overwhelming primitiveness of Frankish kingship no
more than a century before he wrote and the fact that the mystique which
Gregory himself sees in Frankish kingship had not been enough by itself to
enable an earlier king to have his way. He gives, for example, an interesting account of how Clovis dealt with a challenge to his authority that
stemmed from a tradition-bound and democratic view of the rightful
position of chiefs and warriors. It seems that once, while the Franks were
still heathens, they plundered a church along with the rest of a town, after
which Clovis and his warriors took back the booty, to be divided among
them according to custom. The king was evidently not entitled to a particularly leonine share of it, because when the local bishop came and asked as
a special favor that one particularly beautiful vessel be returned to his
church, Clovis sought to comply, probably with a desire not to antagonize
the most powerful man in the vicinity for an expendable item of loot, but
he did not feel free to give the bishop the vase right away. Instead, he
ordered the booty openly displayed in Soissons and promised that if the
vessel fell to him by lot, he would give it to the bishop. Evidently the vessel
did not fall to him by lot, and Clovis decided suddenly to pull rank on his
fellow tribesmen: " 'I ask you, brave warriors to show me your favor by
letting me have that vase, besides what I have gotten by lot.' "

The warriors, whom Gregory calls "those of a healthier mind" agreed.
Their chorus is really Gregory's own, that of a learned man impressed by
the charisma and consequently the exalted right of kingship: "All things
that we see, o glorious King, are yours, and we ourselves are subject to
your rule. Do whatever you please now. No man can resist your power."

But one "light-headed, envious, and reckless man" was unimpressed by
this display of monarchy in the making and drove his tomahawk into the
vessel with a loud yell[78]: " 'You shall have nothing except what the lot
really gives you.' "

The king took this with outward calm, but the following year, according
to custom, he called for a mass assembly of his warriors in the field on the
first day of March.

" 'No man takes worse care of his weapons than you do,' " said Clovis to the headstrong vase-smasher in the course of his inspection. " 'Your spear, your sword, and your battle-ax are useless.' " Taking the warrior's ax, he threw it on the ground. The man started to bend down to pick it up, but then, raising his own ax, Clovis drove it into the warrior's head.

" 'That is what you did with the vessel in Soissons,' " said the king to the dying man.

For Gregory this was a salutary example: ". . . by this deed, the King implanted a great fear of himself. He waged many wars and won victories."[79]

The conversion of Clovis to Trinitarian Christianity proved historically to be of tremendous influence in making the Franks preeminent in western Europe for centuries to come. Gregory's story of the event underscores at once a variety of notions concerning kingship. On one hand, it sanctions the idea that the faith of the king decides the faith of the people, a principle which was to live on after many transformations into the seventeenth century as *Cuius regio eius religio.* Simultaneously it affirms the Old Testament and early Christian idea that the faith of the king determines how God is going to treat the people. In the Middle Ages it became more nearly axiomatic than ever that a king strong in the right faith meant victory and prosperity, while a religiously deviant king meant disaster. On an entirely different level, Gregory's story attempts to hook Frankish kingship onto the most impressive traditions of Christian Roman monarchy. Clovis is not merely the first Christian "King" of the Franks: he is, because of the significantly analogous turns of events in his conversion, another Constantine.

According to Gregory, Clovis subdued the Thuringians, evidently without his paganism proving to be a hindrance, but was frustrated in his attempts to defeat the Alamanni. Then, in the midst of a great battle which was going badly for the Franks, Clovis cast his eyes upon the Heavens and referring to the excellent reputation of Christ as a deliverer in need, which he knew of through his Christian wife, Chrodechilde, promised allegiance to Christianity if he won his battle.[80] Clovis did not exactly see a sign, such as Constantine's fiery cross, but the Alamanni did turn and flee, which was obviously a close enough parallel to the Battle of the Milvian Bridge for all but the pedantic. The Alamanni then saw that their king was dead and surrendered completely to the Franks.[81] There is a certain parallel in the intermediary function of the Christian woman in the total conversion process: in the Constantine story it was the ruler's mother, Helena, whose piety and example were supposed to have brought masses of people to Christianity after she was converted by her son[82]; in the case of Clovis, queen Chrodechilde took the initiative in converting her husband.[83] Just as hordes of Romans were depicted flocking to the baptismal font upon Constantine's conversion, Clovis's battlefield experience was now followed by a mass conversion of the Franks.

A medieval king did well to imitate a worthy predecessor, and it would be hard for medieval clerics to have thought of a better one than Constantine taken as a whole, but it was all to the good for king and people if the king in question could go just a little beyond his worthy predecessor. The Romans, in the earlier Constantine stories at least, followed their leader into the faith by a more or less logical act of imitation. But while Clovis in Gregory's account is fumbling for words with Bishop Remigius about how to justify his conversion, and even thinking of hesitating lest he alienate his subjects, all the Franks, moved by the Holy Spirit answer in a chorus: "We renounce the mortal gods, o devout King, and are ready to follow the immortal God whom Remigius preaches." Gregory leaves nothing to the imagination, however, and points out explicitly that Clovis went, "a new Constantine" to his baptism, which was performed by Remigius, a bishop "so distinguished in piety that he equalled Saint Sylvester (Constantine's chaplain) in miracles." Remigius was said to have, among other things, raised a man from the dead. Perhaps in reminiscence of the conversion of three thousand Jews, recorded in connection with Constantine's baptism, Gregory writes that "more than three thousand men from his army" followed Clovis into baptism.[84]

In the same ceremony Clovis was both baptized and anointed by Remigius "with holy oil under the sign of Christ." Anointing the newly baptized was common enough in early Christian times, and there is now general agreement that Saint Remigius did not consecrate Clovis as king on that occasion.[85] In this connection, the significant step for kingship was taken later with the Carolingians when the anointment of kings as such began on the basis of Old Testament examples, and it was quite a bit later that legend embellished the story of Saint Remigius, Clovis, and the holy oil, with the assertion that the Holy Ghost in the form of a dove had brought it from Heaven.

Yet Clovis's Christianity did not keep him from aggrandizing his kingship with tooth and nail. Gregory recounts how he gained the region around Cologne from Sigebert, one of the remaining independent Frankish kings: First he dispatched a letter to the king's son, pointing out that the king was getting old and limped. " 'If he were to die, his kingdom would rightfully be entrusted to you with our friendship.' " The prince heeded this advice and had his father murdered; then he offered Clovis whatever he chose to take from his father's hoard of money and valuables. Clovis sent some men to look at the treasure, not to take anything: when the prince was bent over a chest, and had plunged his hands deep into the gold pieces in search of something special to show them, one of these emissaries drove his tomahawk into his skull. When the messengers reported the success of their mission to Clovis, he rode up near the palace and called the rulerless people together. According to Gregory, he not only denied complicity in the murders but offered logical proof of his innocence: " 'For I certainly dare not spill the blood of my relatives, and it would be quite shameful if I were to do so. But,' he went on, 'since things have gone this far, let me make a suggestion and see if you like it: turn to me, so that you may live safely under my protection.' " The people greeted this modest proposal enthusiastically, and Clovis graciously assumed responsibility for their peace and prosperity.

Gregory not only fails to chide Clovis for this act, which obviously violates primitive as well as sophisticated moral codes in so many ways that they can scarcely be counted, but instead sees God even here on the chosen king's side. He does point to God's justice and how fitting it was that the *faithless son* was killed. But as for Clovis: "And so, day for day God cast his enemies before him on the ground and increased his dominion, for the reason that he walked with a righteous heart before Him and did what was pleasing to His eyes."[86]

Clovis continued to dispatch rival rulers, including more of his relatives, with less drama but equal effort. To the last, Gregory's portrait of his model king is unretouched, where moderns would expect the bishop to clean up the acts, or at least the motives, of the first Trinitarian king in France and Germany. Nearly on his deathbed, Gregory has Clovis say of the relatives he had murdered:

"Woe is me that I now remain like a stranger among strangers and have no more relatives who could grant me aid, if misfortune should overtake me." But he said this really not because he was sorry about the deaths of these people but for reasons of cunning, so that perhaps one more would turn up for him to kill.[87]

THE SIXTH-CENTURY FREE-FOR-ALL: THE LOST MODEL, ROYAL EPIGONES, AND THE WILD QUEENS

In contrast with Theoderic's direction of Ostrogothic kingship, which separated his Goths from the Italo-Romans, Clovis's acceptance of Catholicism had greatly reduced tensions between his people and the Gallo-Romans. Institutional segregation of Franks and Romans seemed uncalled for. Both could hold the same offices, and they could intermarry.[88] Eventually, Frankish kingship turned out to be a very successful amalgam of German and Roman elements. Merovingian kings gained something from the Germanic conception of magic power inhering in the royal blood. Their attachment to their Germanic heritage is shown in their choice of names: with two insignificant exceptions, Merovingian kings gave their heirs purely Germanic names.[89] They also kept their own royal blood remarkably pure, in spite of their policy of allowing their subjects to cross ethnic lines in marriage: with only two exceptions, Merovingian kings confined themselves to Germanic wives and even concubines.[90] They also profited from the Germanic idea that the *kingdom* was the most natural political unit, where the Romans tended to think of a multinational empire of cities and principalities with some local autonomy as the most natural form of political organization. On the other hand, Frankish kingship under the Merovingians took on late-Roman aspects, too, enlisting Roman concepts of law, administration, and (after some rough false starts) taxation.

The amalgamation process itself took place almost automatically in the century which followed Clovis's death in 511, and it was just as well that this melting together of elements did not then require conscious planning by Merovingian kings. Far-sightedness in policy was not the strong suit of many Frankish kings of that period. The main thing which Gregory's portraits of royal personages of his own time in the second half of the sixth century indicate is that several generations after Clovis a great deal of agility was still in reality demanded of Frankish kings bent upon surviving, let alone maintaining their kingdoms intact for subsequent divisions among their heirs. Kingship is still the art of playing one potential enemy off against the other, of grabbing weakly defended territory, and of staying alive largely by seeing that persons with the means and motive to commit regicide are themselves done away with first. Its practitioners continue to aim at bringing stability to their political units, and they even experiment a little with new economic measures to give them the more steady income of a type which later kings would use to support a full program of law-giving and peace-keeping. But by and large in Austrasia and Neustria, roughly the east and west portions which emerged from Clovis's (originally four-way) division of his own kingdom among his sons, the rulers are too preoccupied with doing each other in and trying to protect themselves against each other to accomplish much else. The indiscriminate violence practiced against enemies real and imagined — torture, mutilation, murder — weighs occasionally on the consciences of some of the main Frankish kings and queens Gregory describes when the victims are close relatives or churchmen, but only occasionally. Everyone seems to agree that it is unfortunate that kings and brothers do not keep their word for any longer than their immediate interests coincide and that royal rivalries have indeed contributed to making the times uncertain ones.

In Gregory's stories, the career of Fredegund, queen of Neustria and then dowager queen during the roughly two decades in which Gregory was chronicling contemporary events (573–591), shows what an ultimate practitioner of tooth and claw methods could achieve in a sixth-century royal

Frankish household. Rising from lowly origins as a bondmaid, she first became the mistress of the Neustrian king, Chilperic I. Eventually she induced him to murder the lawful queen, a former princess of the Visigoths named Galsvintha, and to make her queen of Neustria instead.[91] Merovingian royalty seems to have gone in for paramours generally more than the Frankish nobility and to have been surprisingly unconcerned about producing offspring from wives or mistresses of low degree. It seems possible that we ". . . may be in the presence of ancient usage of polygamy in a royal family — a family of such rank that its blood could not be ennobled by any match, however advantageous, nor degraded by the blood of slaves."[92] Fredegund's rise to queenship, however, brought complications with it, for Galsvintha's sister, the Visigothic princess Brunhilde, who happened to be married to Chilperic's brother Sigebert, king of Austrasia, did not take the matter lightly. No doubt, Brunhilde thought of vengeance then and afterwards, but Fredegund gave her little opportunity to implement her ideas. Her henchmen murdered Sigebert with poisoned knives during one of the frequent wars between Austrasia and Neustria, causing the rule over Austrasia to devolve to Sigebert's five-year-old son and an ineffectual regency for the time being.[93] At home, she helped inspire murderous wrath in her husband against Merovech, his oldest surviving son from a union antedating Galsvintha's brief queenship, who did not survive much longer; his marriage to the newly widowed Brunhilde had made him a threat to both Chilperic and Fredegund.[94] Following the death of two of her own young children, Fredegund brought about the death of the next Neustrian royal heir, Merovech's only surviving brother, Chlodovech, ostensibly seeing him behind magic arts exercised by the mother of "a girl his eye had lit on," that caused her two children to die.[95] In spite of the fact that Fredegund's wholesale dealing in royal victims gained her considerable enmity all around, she proved resourceful enough even after her husband's death to raise her infant son Chlothar II to rule (although, of course, at first only through her and her hastily cultivated allies) for an all-time record among Merovingian rulers of forty-four years (584–628).

Evidence of Fredegund's Christian faith emerges only sporadically in Gregory's narrative, but it is there nonetheless. He somewhat fancifully attributes a drastic act of hers to her belief in the divinely sent nature of her misfortunes and her resulting remorse: as queen, she seizes the tax registers for recently introduced royal assessments on vineyard-land and slaves and hurls them into the fire, encouraging King Chilperic to do likewise.[96] Later, as queen dowager, she saves the life of the mortally ill Chlothar with the pledge of a large sum of money to the Church of Saint Martin in Tours.[97] By and large, however, she remains impervious to threats of worldly and divine vengeance alike. Gregory describes, for example, how she has a bishop stabbed in his church in Rouen; pretending that she wants to find his assailant, she attempts to comfort him but hears him curse her for her guilt as he dies. Another bishop attends his funeral, and in the ensuing protest a local magnate reproaches Fredegund for her crime; she pretends to conciliate him with a cup of wine in friendship and thus poisons him. Finally, after a third bishop, this time of Bayeux, orders the churches of Rouen closed during an inquiry which, predictably, points to the guilt of the queen dowager, Fredegund sends killers after him, too, although "since he was well guarded by his men, these were able to do him no harm."[98]

Often in perusing Gregory's account of this savage, crafty queen, the reader has a certain feeling of *déjà vu,* for, in spite of the fact that Gregory praises the first Clovis and condemns Fredegund, the latter's temperament all too faithfully reflects that of the kingly archetype. This is true not only concerning the grand strategy of eliminating all possible rivals, but also in terms of small tactics as well. For example, quite in the manner of henchmen acting at Clovis's instructions, she tricks her rebellious daughter Rigunthe into stooping over a chest and burying her arms deep in jewelry, only to slam the lid on Rigunthe's neck and choke the hapless princess, who is rescued only at the last moment by guards responding to the shrieks of one of her maids.[99] Yet, neither large nor small parallels can change the fact that while Clovis's frequent barbarities led to a strengthened Frankish kingdom, those of his later successors did not. Gregory tends to condemn murder except when it can be depicted as fulfilling divine vengeance or serving some other good end: while such an exemption justifies a fair number of royally backed homicides, it does not begin to cover all of them. Still, even murder for the worst of reasons, greed and jealousy, seems rather routine in the real world of kings, as Gregory conceives of it. While kingship is certainly a tarnished concept in his accounts, it seems scarcely to occur to him that this could be otherwise — except that it could be more successful. When he laments the decline of Frankish kingship, his regrets indicate only that he feels that Frankish kings could display less luxury and more steadfast determination in imitating their victorious ancestor Clovis.

GUNTHRAMN: MODEL OF THE GOOD AND CHRISTIAN KING

Yet Gregory does have a contemporary model for kingship, too, in Gunthramn (ca. 525–592), brother of Sigebert and Chilperic, who reigns in a kingdom to the south, consisting chiefly of Burgundy. For him, alone among contemporary kings, Gregory uses the term *rex bonus.*[100]

What does a king do to be a good one in Gregory's own time? Briefly, he fears God and His saints, judges his own subjects justly, and takes no more than his due in wealth and territory from fellow Christian rulers, even when an excellent opportunity for aggrandizement presents itself. That a God-fearing king shows benificence to the poor and the churches is, of course, understood: Gunthramn's excellence here is in the frequency of his donations, the urgency he feels in coming to the aid of churchmen in distress and the contrast with other modern rulers in his refusal to indulge in luxury or display. Gunthramn's consuming awe of holy places is of equal importance with his charity in making him a good king. He cannot be induced to tamper with the right of sanctuary, even when sorely provoked. Once, for example, a man attempts to assassinate him as he goes toward the altar to receive communion. The would-be murderer is seized almost in the act of stabbing King Gunthramn, dragged from the church, and the names of conspirators behind the crime are tortured out of him. Gunthramn himself listens to the assassin's explanation of his sacrilege: the man says that the king's bodyguard and thorough security consciousness *outside* of the church made attempts on his life impossible except *in* church. Subsequently, Gunthramn has many of the named planners and accomplices executed, but limits the punishment of the man sent to kill him to a beating, "for he could not sanction having a man killed who had been taken forcibly out of a church."[101]

King Gunthramn is fairly stern in meting out punishments to keep his own kingdom reasonably well pacified most of the time, but he can still temper royal justice with Christian mercy when he feels that leniency will not endanger the peace of his kingdom. At the request of Gregory, he forgives adherents of an enemy who invaded his kingdom after the men have become suppliants of Saint Martin.[102] In another case, convinced that an old enemy captured by one of his dukes has a hand in a new plot to overthrow him, Gunthramn announces to the man without further ado that his life is to be forfeited; however, he is willing to take the accused at his word when the man explains away the circumstantial evidence against him, and he lets him go.[103] There seems to be no question about the king's power of life and death, unencumbered by institutional restraints: in this instance, Gunthramn conducts something like a trial, sentences the accused to death, and commutes the death sentence, all in a matter of minutes.

Self-imposed restraint in seeking earthly gain rounds out Gunthramn's kingly qualities for Gregory. Once when his brother Chilperic has invaded his lands and occupied Arles, one of Gunthramn's cities, Gunthramn takes Avignon, one of Chilperic's cities, and retakes Arles. He has every reason to keep both, but—and Gregory points out that this was according to his customary goodness—he does not do so, but returns Avignon when peace has been restored.[104] When King Sigebert's death has left Austrasia in the hands of Queen Brunhilde and guardians for their son, Childebert, the regents entrust Gunthramn with administering half of Marseilles for

Childebert. That Gunthramn accepts the responsibility to take care of Childebert's half of Marseilles as well as his own is, of course, not surprising: what distinguishes Gunthramn in the transaction is that he does not absorb the entrusted territory into his own kingdom, but when Childebert comes of age, gives it back to him.[105]

By Gunthramn's time, royal tonsuring as a mild, Frankish alternative to murder had apparently fallen into disuse.[106] Gunthramn senses catastrophe about to descend on the Franks from their frequent killing of present and future kings, either for settling an old score in the interminable feuds among Frankish royalty or simply for personal gain.[107] Apart from the loss of his brothers, greed and envy in his own household had cost him, in Gregory's mind at least, two sons: his wife Marcatrude poisoned his son by a previous union, whereupon divine retribution took from her the son she had borne Gunthramn. Two sons born in a still later marriage also died, so that Gunthramn was left without any sons and had every reason to set a premium on what remained of the younger generation of Frankish royalty in his nephews, Childebert II in Austrasia and Clothar in Neustria. Bearing this in mind he addresses what must seem like a — for a king — modest appeal to the dormant better instincts of the Franks one day in a church in Paris:

> You men and women here, I plead with you to keep your faith with me unbroken and not to kill me, too, as you did my brothers. May I be granted at least three more years to bring up the nephews of mine that I have adopted as sons! This is to keep — and may eternal God not allow that — your downfall from following my death with those small boys, since then there will no longer be any strong shoot from our tree to protect you.[108]

Still, for all Gunthramn's virtues and relative lack of faults in Gregory's history of him and his times he is not so much of an ideal kingship figure for Gregory as Clovis remains. Gunthramn's immense personal piety is, to be sure, credited with working at least one miracle, and his direction of his people is clearly extended to the spiritual sphere in a fashion not attributed to Clovis:

> The King himself, as we have often said, was great in almsgiving and always ready for vigils and fasting. At that time [588] it was told that Marseilles was wasted by bubonic plague and that this disease had spread to a village by the name of Octavus in the territory of Lyons. But the King, like a good bishop mindful of the means whereby the wounds of the populace could be healed, commanded the whole people to congregate at the church and to celebrate the litany with the greatest devotion. He commanded that nothing be consumed but barley bread and clean water along with it and that everyone should be at the vigils without interruption. This was done at that time.[109]

The culmination of the story is, however, not what one might expect. The plague is not lifted immediately for most of the inhabitants of Marseilles. Instead, Gregory goes on to tell of quasi-magical powers inhering in the king's own person:

> After three days, at a time when his alms were flowing with even greater largesse than usual, he showed such anxiety for all his people that he was thought to be not so much a king as a bishop of the Lord, placing all his hope in the Lord's mercy. He threw all the thoughts which rose within him upon Him by whom he felt in the total integrity of his faith they could be given effect. Then it was generally told among the faithful that a certain woman, whose son was suffering from quartan fever and lay fearfully ill in bed, approached the King's back in a crowd and, having secretly torn off some fringes of the royal garment, put them in water and gave them to her son to drink. On the spot the fever receded and the man became well.[110]

While certainly pointing to the divine nature of Christian kingship, such a miracle does not seem to have much to do with the success of the ruling art in Gregory's narratives. Pious and even occasionally thaumaturgic Gunthramn may be, but his overall image is a less fortunate and authoritative one than Clovis's. In contrast with Clovis, Gunthramn often manifests a woeful inability to keep his own armies in hand. When Gunthramn, in the fashion of Constantine, Theodosius, and Clovis, places all his hopes in God for victory, he sometimes does very well, as, for example, in marching to defend his territories against the early predations of his brother. But in other instances, in spite of express commands by Gunthramn, the royal armies allow themselves to be tempted by booty to ravage the countryside and shed blood in the churches themselves. To Gunthramn, or Gregory speaking through him, cause and effect are clear: the excesses of godless modern times will bring ruin to the Franks and their kings:

> How can we win victory in our time, if we care nothing for what our fathers respected? By building churches, putting all their hopes in God, venerating the martyrs, and honoring the priests of God, they won victories and often subjugated hostile peoples with sword and shield thanks to God's aid. We, however, not only fail to fear God, but also ravage His sacred places, murder his servants, and even mock the relics of the saints by plundering and destroying them. Where such sins are committed, victory cannot be won. . . .[111]

CHLOTHAR AND DAGOBERT: PAPYRUS, PARCHMENTS, AND ROYAL JUSTICE

As king in his own right, Fredegund's son, Chlothar II, later turned out better than anyone would have had a right to expect. In a seventh-century historical compilation which has come down to us as the work of Fredegar,[112] his ruler's image appears with decidedly more significant plusses than minuses:

> This Chlothar was quite determined and well-read; fearing God, he made generous gifts to the churches and priests and bestowed alms on the poor. He showed himself to be kind towards all and full of piety. [But] he was excessively devoted to hunting, and at the very end he was too much inclined to follow the suggestions of women and girls, which brought blame upon him among his followers.[113]

Chlothar did, to be sure, have his rough side. When Brunhilde at about age eighty had finally been discovered in one murderous intrigue too many — the last one on behalf of her great-grandson Sigebert — Neustrian forces under Chlothar prevailed over the Austrasians, who had decided in advance to let him win, and Brunhilde was brought to what passed for justice before Chlothar. With a rhetorical flourish worthy of Clovis in Gregory's work, Chlothar charged her with the death of ten Frankish kings including two whom he himself had ordered killed.[114] After three days of diverse tortures, he consigned her "to be tied by her hair, one leg, and one arm to the tail of a very wild horse, and so by the hoofs and the speed she was torn limb from limb."[115]

The Burgundians as well as the Austrasians submitted to Chlothar, who thus succeeded in uniting all the Frankish territories under him. It was really only Chlothar and his son Dagobert after him who maintained a single Frankish monarchy for any significant length of time between Clovis and the Carolingians.[116] Chlothar was still a long way from ruling over a single nation, but an assimilation process had nonetheless been underway for a long time which made his kingdom quite different from the Gaul which had been united under the Romans. The older Gallo-Roman tribal groups, such as the Arverni, Turonici and Andecavi, had taken on a general ethnic identification as *Romani,* although by Chlothar's time this term itself was increasingly reserved for the "senatorial" upper class and some of the clergy. On the Germanic side, only the Burgundians, Alamanni, and those Goths and Saxons who came under Frankish rule maintained much of a separate identity under Chlothar's monarchy.[117]

The combination of the earlier tribal groups into larger ones made it somewhat easier for a king to represent in himself the nations over which he ruled, whether he was responsible for Austrasia, Neustria, Burgundy, or a united Frankish kingdom. While the region or subkingdom might determine the allegiance of Neustrians or Austrasians in fighting each other, they perceived their conflicts to be internal and consequently unnatural: "In those days," an eighth-century source would write of a Neustrian-Austrasian conflict, "at the devil's instigation, Franks again launched invasions against Franks and wrought mutual destruction on each other in the woods of Compiègne."[118]

The idea of a single Frankish nation was not of much practical help to the Merovingian successors of Chlothar and Dagobert, although it was to be of great assistance to the Carolingians in the eighth century. On the other hand, the association of the king with the fair adjudication of disputes and the rule of law, which became firmly established in the period from Gunthramn to Dagobert, did turn out to be of lasting use to the Merovingians, even when real power was slipping from their grasp, although the Carolingians were to make even greater use of this as well. Chlothar made himself available for the dispensation of justice and even showed some initiative in inviting litigants to appear before him. Fredegar notes in this connection, for example:

> In the thirty-third year of his reign, Chlothar summoned to the villa of Bonneuil his majordomo, Warnachar, and all the bishops and notables of Burgundy. There he supported all their just petitions by issuing written judgments.[119]

Chlothar also strengthened the image of the king as lawgiver. The Edict of Paris, which he issued soon after uniting the Frankish dominions under his rule, balanced the concessions to nobles and bishops which he felt obliged to make with affirmations of royal power: the kingdom is to be governed by his own "ordinances, statutes and decrees"; the royal tax on commerce, the *teloneum* is confirmed; and those who defy the royal measures of this edict for keeping the peace and good order of the kingdom are to be promptly sentenced to death as a warning to other would-be offenders.[120] His law codification apparently extended to the Alamanni as a separate people: the *Pactus Alamannorum* stems from a Merovingian chancery of the early seventh century. Between 613 and 623, Chlothar held his court at Marlenheim in Alsace and "was gradually concerning himself with law and order" among the Alamanni.[121]

Whether it was a matter of providing a full code or merely of giving a judgment in an individual case, the king's maintenance of peace and justice was becoming firmly linked with the issuing of written documents. Royal documents served a variety of purposes: most frequently they were issued as charters or *praeceptiones,* types of decrees which in form and content ranged from ordinances to injunctions to grants. The oldest surviving original charter is that of Chlothar from the year 625 for the Monastery of Saint Denis.[122] Since monasteries tended to hold on to their grants more successfully than other recipients of royal documents did to theirs, a large number of donations and privileges accorded to monastic houses have remained intact which is perhaps disproportionate to the original number issued for secular and clerical recipients alike. Whether the documents are huge grants of land, however, or merely directives to officials, they carry a rather set form. The issuer—the king himself in royal documents—identifies himself in the *intitulatio* with the precise designation he wishes to be known by. This is followed by the *inscriptio*, the designation of the persons to whom the documents is addressed, often in the form of a salutation. Then follows the *arenga*, outlining the motivation for issuing the documents in general terms of popular theology or folk wisdom, typically, something about the need to prepare the way to salvation with good deeds on earth or about the need to have things written down since human memory fails after a while, which leads into the *promulgatio* or *publicatio*, in which attention is called to the will of the issuer with a formulation such as: "Let all faithful Christians know that. . . ." or "Let it be known that. . . ." This is followed by the *narratio*, the findings or accepted allegations of fact which underlie the decision, and then the *dispositio*, the royal action itself which the document puts into effect.

The documents are always dated. Religious seriousness is imparted to them by a chrismon, which the Carolingians supplemented and then replaced by a formal invocation of the Divinity at the beginning.[123] Something common to all the Merovingian documents, however, is the note of personal authority: grants and directives are made by the king on the basis of his personal weighing of the interests involved. "One is struck, too, by the growing number of occasions when the king is sought out by parties to an agreement that would be legally valid without his intervention. There is no greater protection to property, secular, or ecclesiastical, than a royal writing."[124] From the standpoint of Americans, who (probably from looking at the development of monarchy in modern Europe) tend to see kings as chief executives, an equally striking thing about all this is the role of the king as a comprehensive, one-man judicial system of the first and final instance, issuing what are clearly judgments in civil cases along with certifying a variety of real-estate titles. Actually, the medieval king functioned as high judge in his realm over civil and criminal cases alike from the moment he expanded his warrior-chief functions into those of domestic peace-keeping. In doing so, he was both reassuming part of the ancient role of the Germanic *thiudans,* who was called upon to settle tribal disputes brought into his presence as well as to placate the gods, and continuing the late-Roman tradition which saw the emperor as the ultimate judge and issuer of documents to settle disputes, although seldom as the judge of the first instance. Consciousness of continuing the Roman imperial tradition appears in Merovingian royal document writing not only in some of the forms taken from Roman imperial rescripts but even in the use of papyrus. Papyrus was a rare, imported material in the seventh-century land of the Franks, but it was felt worth the while to get it for royal charters until both the inroads of common sense and the Mohammedan control of the papyrus trade led to adopting the much more durable parchment sheets, which have figured prominently in high legal or ceremonious documentation ever since.

There is no evidence of much in the way of real elections of kings having taken place among the Franks since before the time of Clovis; however, the *idea* that the king was indeed the choice of the tribe was an enduring one. Something like the show of an election took place whenever a king of part of the total dominions of the Franks annexed the territory of a brother or cousin. Even in the case of a king gaining new territory without real opposition, an election was a useful means to secure legitimization. As we shall see later on in more detail, the general principles of heredity, cooptation, and election were not held in the least to exclude each other as methods of choosing kings in the Middle Ages. The succession of Dagobert illustrates this in rudimentary form. In 623, Chlothar made Dagobert, his son, a king nominally equal to himself in placing him over the Austrasians. Heredity made this appointment much easier, although it certainly did not make it inevitable. Six years later, when Chlothar died, Dagobert wanted to take no chances with his inheritance of his father's realm, which would enable him, like Chlothar, to become sole king of the Franks. He thus mobilized his Austrasian forces and ". . . directed deputations to go to the Burgundians and Neustrians, to insure that they would choose his rule."[125]

Ubiquitous as they were, hereditary considerations worked both forward and backward in the kingship-consciousness of the age: forward in the sense of limiting to a king's blood relatives the list of his possible successors or corulers, backward in the sense of supplying the reigning dynasty with an increasingly more impressive genealogy. We have already seen this process at work in the appropriation of the "Flavian" inheritance by Roman rulers, and then in the search by Ostrogothic kings for deeper and more impressive roots. Fredegar's *Chronicle* documents two separate processes of upgrading first the Frankish people in general and then the Merovingian dynasty in particular. The Franks suddenly appear as descendants of the Trojans and thus as a people with an eminently respectable national heritage,[126] while a *Quinotaurus,* something like a sea-going minotaur, appears as the father of the original Merovech in a new story of his birth two centuries earlier, thus linking the Merovingian dynasty in all events with the supernatural and, possibly for those having a little knowledge of ancient history, with an aura of rulership deriving figuratively and collaterally from the court of the great King Minos of Crete.[127]

Dagobert furnished Fredegar with both a good and bad model of kingship. Unlike the case of Chlothar, this was not so much a mixture of elements in his character as the development of that character over a period of time. Be that as it may, in both the good and bad attributes we

see the emergence of royal stereotypes, which have left Gregory's model of
the warrior-king Clovis far behind. As the model of good kingship, Fredegar's Dagobert shows his godly devotion to law and justice with patience
and stamina. A year before his father's death, Dagobert made a royal tour
of the subkingdom of Burgundy:

> His arrival . . . shook the high clergy and nobles of rank, whether they were
> his own men or not, with a fear that made everyone marvel; however, he
> evoked great joy among the poor seeking justice. When he came to the city of
> Langres, he dispensed such justice among all his subjects, rich and poor alike
> as was no doubt pleasing to God. He could not be influenced by any bribe or
> respect of persons, nor did anything but justice, which the Almighty loves,
> have command there. Arriving at Dijon from there and then staying at Losne
> a few days, he made every effort to give justice by judgments to people
> throughout his whole kingdom. His good will made him so full of determina-
> tion that he caught no sleep and ate no food, his mind intent on seeing that
> everyone who sought his presence should return with justice.[128]

As a model of bad kingship, after he had become sole king of the Franks
and moved his residence to Paris, in Neustria, Fredegar's Dagobert shows
the attributes which were to become increasingly those of a tyrant, as the
Middle Ages progressed: indifference to law, greed, bad treatment of the
Church and wantonness:

> [He] forgot the justice which he had loved earlier and, driven by greed for
> what belonged to the Church and to his men, he turned his keen senses and
> determination to amassing treasure anew from all sources and by all means.
> Inclined then to excessive self-indulgence, he took for himself three queens
> and many concubines. . . . With all this, his heart was turned away from
> what we noted earlier, and his thoughts of God departed from him.[129]

Frankish kingship was, of course, judged only partly by its correspondence to a good or bad image of a ruler's behavior. It was also judged in
terms of achievement. The maintenance of a semblance of domestic law
and order was the chief measure of a king's practical success, but the
results of foreign policy came to weigh heavily in the balance as well.
Negotiations and diplomacy could be used to maintain peace with neighboring tribes, but war was in the seventh century, as it has generally been,
"the continuation of politics by other means." Conducting military campaigns still belonged to the king's duties, but with Dagobert these took on a
new aspect, particularly when they were directed against Avars, who
posed a threat on the eastern frontier. When Dagobert confronted them in
Germany, it was in defending "what amounted to the territorial interest of
a settled people."[130] Protecting permanent settlers from the threat of hos-

tile barbarians was becoming the external equivalent of enforcing the king's peace at home. It was something the people soon came to expect, and the failure of Dagobert's successors to provide it helped to hollow out the authority of Merovingian kingship over the century which followed Dagobert's death.

Chapter 4

Carolingian Kingship: Problems of *Regna* and the *Imperium*

A LONGER GAME, LESS FLEXIBLE RULES

Taken one with another, seventh-century Merovingian kings after the death of Dagobert I in 639 were an altogether sorry lot.[1] While they continued to occupy the nominal seat of secular authority, their loss of actual power seemed to be dissolving the image of Frankish kingship into a pale ghost of its former self. The French term for them, *les rois fainéants* ("the do-nothing kings"), seems increasingly apt as the seventh century wears on. Local lords were quick to exploit royal weakness. When Chlothar II had agreed, as early as 614, to select counts only from the great landholders in their own provinces, he was simply legitimizing the claims of his strongest rivals to wield independent power; probably he was hoping for the best because he had no other choice. With Chlothar and Dagobert gone from the scene, the centrifugal forces gained strength all around.

The thought of becoming a king remained a tremendous attraction to the boldest of the nonroyal magnates, but the Merovingians kept their long hair and crowns for a remarkable period of time after they had lost any evidence of ruling talent. The greatest challenge to them came from their own major-domos, or "mayors of the palace." This position originally signified the director of the royal household with duties as chief overseer of work done on the royal lands and also as chief auditor for the deliveries of goods in kind to the king's court. The first Pippin, who was major-domo to Dagobert I when he became king of Austrasia at an early age, functioned *de facto* as the boy's regent; later, under mature but ineffectual Merovingians, the major-domo could easily expand his court and household responsibilities into the power of decision making where the finances and defense of the kingdom were concerned.

The royal major-domo was, in brief, the Merovingian equivalent of a later Japanese shogun, wielding the power of the realm for a shadowy ruler whose charisma made him indispensable. Like the shogunate, the position of royal major-domo became hereditary in practice, although there was originally no theoretical justification for its being so. Enterprising major-domos naturally thought of increasing their family's power and influence: qualitatively, this did not distinguish them from other magnates, but on a large enough scale this amounted to their thinking, again, like the shoguns, in dynastic terms. Pippin married his daughter to the son of Arnulf, who was later looked back upon as the eponymous ancestor of the Carolingians; early members of that dynasty before Charles Martell are still often called the "Arnulfings." Arnulf had his own unique power configuration. He was bishop of Metz, the Austrasian capital; his personal service to the Austrasian king gave him a lever to substantial influence; and he eventually managed six provinces, nominally for the king, which had previously had separate administrations.[2] With so much power concentrated in the family, Pippin's son Grimoald attempted in 660–662 to direct as major-domo the replacement of the feeble King of Austrasia, Dagobert II, with his own son, who attempted to rule as Childebert III.[3] Grimoald, however, failed miserably in his efforts to secure Austrasian support for his son as king. According to one source, both he and Childebert were betrayed by the Austrasian nobility[4]; at all events it is certain that they fell into the hands of Neustrian enemies and were killed. The Franks evidently had no intention of forsaking the ancient Merovingian blood line for the sake of more talented usurpers.

"Shocked by the stout resistance of their peers and the obviously poor support by the 'people,' who were in awe of their sacred kings, the Carolingians switched over to a policy of a gradual and very cautiously prepared takeover."[5] Is it possible, however, that the Carolingians held to a single strategy for close to a century in pursuit of the elusive goal of kingship? To credit them with this would be to ascribe to them a tenacity of will and continuity of purpose worthy of successive generations of Bismarcks or Lenins. For some scholars, the thought that a dynasty could have seen ahead so far to its possible attainment of kingship and planned accordingly is untenable:

> But the Arnulfings cannot have seen this and cannot have known that the *progenies sancta* of Clovis was doomed to extinction. Nor can they have known that Rome would one day sanction, and in a sense make possible, the transference of royal authority to themselves. All this was unforeseeable. For this reason it is as well to think twice before accepting any account of the *'rois faineants'* in which the Arnulfings struggle ambitiously for the crown through a whole century, and finally achieve it in their moment of triumph.[6]

While it is eminently reasonable to think twice before accepting such a theory, the evidence makes it highly likely: one small step after another over four generations brought the emerging dynasty all previously royal rights short of the crown and title of king. The Carolingians were already tantalizingly close to royal rulership from their major-domo positions. The growing importance of the power to assign land holdings, as feudalism developed, offered them many opportunities to increase their scope as royal administrators on whom there was no effective check.[7] Kingship was really the only meaningful step up from where they stood, and they could not have closed their eyes to the possibility of advancing toward it even if they had wanted to.

The gradual measures the Carolingians took from the 660s on met the two basic requirements for magnates with kingly aspirations. The first requirement was to assume enough functions *de facto* of the medieval king and to exercise these well enough and long enough, in order for it to seem natural for the functions to belong more to them *de jure* than to their decrepit, nominal possessors. This meant defending the realm and advancing the faith with prolonged and substantial success. Grimoald's experience, however, had already shown that something else was necessary. The second requirement was to acquire that certain extra charismatic something which meant that it was all right, tradition-sanctioned, and God-ordained, rather than arrogant, unfaithful, and contemptuous of custom, to wear long hair and a crown. In brief, the twofold task meant doing a complete king's job without the royal title and then acquiring enough of the air of rightful possession of the title, in order to take it over without shocking the sensibilities of anyone powerful enough to do anything about it.

It all went together: winning battles and pacifying the realm showed the divine favor subsumed under the earlier heading, *Heil*; this divine favor, also to be expected from good works in the form of generous benevolence to the Church and its saints, made a dynasty look like the most natural one to perform royal functions. Looking natural in the role of defending the realm and advancing the faith was an aid in itself in overcoming enemies and preserving the peace.

The Merovingian kings had already been shown wanting in *Heil*. Fredegar describes at some length how in spite of Grimoald's earlier quite loyal service to Merovingian King Sigebert, the Austrasians led by the young king against Radulf, duke of the Thuringians, were badly defeated in 639. Sigebert was overcome with grief and humiliation and sat weeping on his horse for those he had lost. To Fredegar this scene was plainly not in the image of what royal *Heil* should provide for.[8] Grimoald's later abortive *coup d'état* ended, of course, with a momentary setback for the Carolingians. Afterwards, however, in Neustria, a major-domo named Ebroin of a different house began making himself obnoxious to the Neustrian nobility by pushing too far the royal claims of his nominal master against them. The nobles there first appealed without results to the Neustrian king to restrain Ebroin, then revolted against him, and finally sought aid from

Austrasia. The second Pippin, son of the elder Pippin's daughter and Arnulf's son, seized the opportunity to revive the family name from temporary eclipse. He led Austrasian forces against Ebroin, who was killed in 680. In waging war against the new Neustrian major-domo, Berchar, Pippin later defeated the Neustrian king, Theuderic III, in 687 at the Battle of Tertry.

Under Pippin's guidance, the parts of the ancient kingdom of the Franks received a semblance of new unity. He, of course, retained power over major economic affairs and defense, letting the Merovingian royalty continue their attenuated functions under his direction. The relation between this Pippin, called variously "Pippin of Heristal," "the middle Pippin," or "Pippin II," and the succession of Merovingian kings he worked with was truly symbiotic at the time. Pippin needed royal documents for such things as adjudicating and assigning large inheritances in land, approving land transfers among monasteries, granting exemption from the tax on commerce, officially confiscating land from faithless vassals, and bestowing comparable favors on faithful ones. Royal charters accomplished these things much more smoothly than his own would have done; all in all, the king was quite useful in settling disputes with a minimum of controversy and resentment. On the other side of the ledger, the Merovingian kings survived as such, thanks to Pippin's ability to manage the defense and finances of the kingdom.

Shortly before his death, Pippin named his six-year-old grandson, Theodoald, as royal major-domo, specifying that the princes of the realm and his wife, Plektrude, should function as his guardians. Obviously he was treating the title as hereditary; the fact that it could be held by a boy and its responsibilities administered by the boy's mother made it resemble a princely rank far more than an office in the normal sense. At the same time, Pippin kept the title of duke (*dux*) for himself, even after establishing his older son, Drogo, as duke in Burgundy. The right to appoint new dukes had traditionally rested with the king, but was evidently being assumed by the Carolingian major-domo. The retention of the ducal title also proved to be of considerable significance, since more than *maior domus* the *dux* title "had the capability of transforming itself into the functional title of a ruler."[9]

A revolt in Neustria and an alliance of discontented Neustrians with Frisians, Saxons, and Aquitainians put an end to the government of Theodoald and his grandmother, but the Carolingians were saved at the last moment when Charles, Pippin's son by a wife of lesser status,[10] escaped from the confinement in which Lady Plektrude had been keeping him, rallied a mighty following, and defeated the Neustrians and their allies in a series of hard-fought battles from 715 to 719. It was significant that before even holding the position of major-domo a new Carolingian could gain support in sufficient numbers to challenge such a formidable alliance on the basis of his family's accustomed leadership role. He contented himself with the old major-domo title under a nominal Merovingian king, along with his ducal title, after he had reunited the Frankish dominions under his control.

The record of Charles's establishment of new religious foundations and of his generosity to the churches in Austrasia attests both to his economic power and to the credit he naturally gained for advancing the faith, while the history of his military exploits in defense and offense shows him to have retained complete control of the Frankish armies. All the while, he kept up the policy which his father had sometimes resorted to of helping himself to Church lands when he needed them, in order to build up a loyal following of armed retainers to keep peace in the kingdom or extend its borders, depending on the alternation of threats and opportunities. In this way, over a period of several generations, the Carolingians came close to founding "a new aristocracy of landowners."[11]

In an age where much religious importance was attached to the possession of relics, it was fitting that the royal family should care for at least some of the most precious of these. Saint Martin having been the closest thing to a patron saint for all of Frankish Gaul, a Merovingian court cult venerating what survived of the famous saint's cloak, which he had charitably split with a beggar, was a predictable development. By 710, however, this *cappa* of Saint Martin had either come into the possession of the Carolingians outright or was at least used by them for having men take the most solemn oaths on it in their own private chapel.[12] Charles, at any rate, appointed special keepers of Saint Martin's cloak.

It was Charles's lot to face the threat of Moslem invasions through Spain into France. With the perspective of history and particularly by way of comparison with the Byzantine reversal of the full-scale land and sea attacks which the Islamic world hurled at Constantinople only a few years earlier, the Frankish victory over the Moorish invaders no longer looks quite as impressive as it once did. There is some doubt now as to whether Charles was even facing the advance guard of any army enjoying the complete support of the Caliphate; the Berbers from North Africa who invaded over the Pyrenees were of questionable Mohammedan orthodoxy. Be this as it may, the Moslems looked quite threatening at the time, and they were rather close to one of the most sacred spots in the Frankish Kingdom, the Monastery of Saint Martin in Tours. Whether it was the result of successful propagandizing by Charles Martell's admirers or the human tendency to simplify complex events into great victories and defeats personalized as the efforts of single men, the image of Charles's victory at the Battle of Tours remained worthy of a forerunner of royalty for twelve hundred years:

> North of Poitiers, where the Clain flows into the Vienne, the Arabian Army was decisively defeated in October 732. Posterity thanked the Major-domo for the smashing blow he dealt for it by adding "The Hammer" to his name: as Charles Martell he lives on in history. But it was more than even such a glorious victory of the Frankish Army. . . . His victory preserved the West from the threat of the Islamic flood and enabled it to preserve the germs of its own individual culture and to let these mature.[13]

This is from a heavy volume on the Middle Ages written for popular consumption in the twentieth century. While historians of the eighth century took no note of the tender shoots of Western culture protected by Charles's victory, they more than made up for this in their tribute to the divinely ordained outcome of the major-domo's triumph. The reports of his subsequent campaigns, too, sound like a conscious attempt on someone's part to lend a charismatic quality to his prowess. When Charles Martell besieged a city held by the Saracens in 737, for example, one writer noted:

> Then as once before Jericho, the armies gave a great shout, the trumpets brayed and the men rushed in to the assault with battering rams, and they took that strong city and burned it with fire, and they took captive their enemies, smiting without mercy and destroying them, and they recovered complete mastery of the city. Victorious, therefore, Charles, the dauntless, mighty warrior, crossed the Rhone with his men. . . .[14]

There was no need to paint a contrast with the *Heil*-less Merovingians: twice in the preceding century, against the Thuringians and at the Battle of Tertry, they had led their armies to resounding defeats; things had gone best for their armies when they simply had stayed out of the way. Just how dependent on Carolingian direction Merovingian kingship had become is shown by a series of events beginning with Charles Martell's act of constituting Chlothar IV king in 718. When Chlothar died the following year, Charles asked Duke Eudo of Aquitaine to return Chilperic II, who had been removed in the course of Charles's wars against the Neustrians, to the nominal kingship. When Chilperic died in 721, Charles then brought out a royal Merovingian consignee to a monastery, to grow long hair again and "rule" as Theuderic IV until 737.[15]

The Church of Saint Martin in Tours shared with the Monastery of Saint Denis, north of Paris, the distinction of being an old and highly venerated religious center, whose favor was of great weight for leaders of the Franks. These centers had also remained as the most important beneficiaries of royal Merovingian patronage down to the eighth century, a connection no doubt patently obvious to the Carolingians. The religious piety of the Carolingians was sincere enough, if their founding of new churches and their bequests for the saying of masses for the salvation of their souls can be taken as evidence, but this did not keep them from showing extra favors to those religious institutions whose leaders would be a great help or hindrance in case some controversy over political authority should arise. Charles Martell enriched the Church of Saint Martin after his victory over the Saracens at Tours. In 741 he went so far as to give a Merovingian royal villa to the Monastery of Saint Denis. This was with one of his own charters, not one of the king's.[16]

When we come to his son, Pippin "the Younger" or "the Short," also called "Pippin III" (as major-domo) or "Pippin I" (as the first Carolingian king), not even a skeptic on the topic of Carolingian aims spanning generations can entertain any doubt that we are looking at a conscious contender for royal status. At first, since Charles Martell left his position and power to be divided between his sons, much like a Frankish king dividing his kingdom, Pippin controlled only Neustria after Charles's death in 741. Charles's older son, Karlomann, was given Austrasia.

While Pippin kept up the network of retainer relationships which his predecessor had begun to weave long ago, the particular focus of his efforts was on cementing a reliable alliance with the Church and gradually perfecting his title to rule in, as we shall see, a literal sense.

It was Karlomann who took the first initiative. Saint Boniface, the great Anglo-Saxon missionary and easily the most influential figure in reforming Christianity among the Germanic tribes, was finding "only undisciplined remnants of Christianity left behind by earlier attempts at conversion."[17] Boniface seemed to need a strong secular hand to carry out both his structuring of the Church and his reformation of Church teachings in the areas controlled by the Franks, to conform with Roman guidelines. Karlomann more than obliged him:

> He summoned Boniface and communicated to him a plan for the reform of the whole Frankish church. Soon afterwards the bishops of the newly founded dioceses (mainly Anglo-Saxons), together with Boniface, met in a synod in which the question of ecclesiastical discipline was discussed. [Karlomann] undertook to enforce the decrees of the synod and incorporated them as capitularies [collections of ordinances] into the laws of the kingdom. A moment of great significance had been reached. Boniface had to suffer the secular ruler to take the initiative in ecclesiastical matters to a degree unprecedented even during the height of Merovingian power.[18]

The formal Carolingian title became more striking and distinctive as it appeared in the promulgation of these capitularies in 742 with the addition of *princeps,* a term which from the time of Augustus Caesar through the close of the Middle Ages could designate the ruler of a political unit, large or small. *Princeps* had a more modest sound than *rex,* a fact which had served the original purposes of Augustus; in the plural it could also be used to designate the high nobility generally.[19] In the singular, all the same, it connoted something like sovereignty, and in this sense it was used by politically independent dukes. "When a non-royal 'ruler' bears the *princeps* title in the eighth century, he is looking for a manifestation of his rulership equal to that of a king."[20] In Karlomann's capitularies of 742, he styled himself "*dux et princeps Francorum.*" The Carolingians had been carrying the *dux* title for a long time now, but never officially the title of *princeps.*

Unofficially, to be sure, there was a certain Carolingian precedent. Pippin II had already picked up the title posthumously in the *Liber Historiae Francorum.*[21] Then two years after Karlomann had made official use of it, Pippin III took it for himself as he promulgated analogous synodal decisions in capitularies with a casual reference to the *priores principes.* In Pippin's formulation, the "*anno secundo Childerici regis,*" which follows, shows plainly enough that while the Merovingian, Childeric III, might be occupying the position of king, his doing so is useful for purposes of dating decrees while Pippin as *princeps* has the function of issuing them. There is another interesting twist in that Pippin addresses the document in rather traditional form to the nobility, but he calls them "*comes et optimates Francorum*" (counts and magnates of the Franks), underscoring the fact that he, the *dux et princeps Francorum,* is no longer in their subordinate league.[22] A few years later, Pippin even tossed a "most glorious" poor Childeric's way, as he dated his judgment of disputed properties in favor of the powerful Monastery of Saint Denis: "*anno VIII regni gloriossisime Childerici regis.*"[23] Pippin, Childeric, and the non-Carolingian magnates seemed to be stabilized in Frankish officialese in their rightful places.

The *intitulatio* was a regular part of late-Roman and medieval documents, in which the issuer of the document gave the title which he wanted to be known by. For the Merovingians in earlier days this had been simply "*rex Francorum.*" It was followed by an address, "*viro inlustri*" or "*viris inlustribus*" ("to the illustrious man or men") whom the document concerned. Legal writing in Merovingian times inclined strongly to the copying of familiar forms — a tendency of legal documentation equally familiar in the twentieth century — and the utilization of abbreviations. The formalized address on the documents was consequently used and copied as "*v. inl.*"

The Carolingians had been among the designated "illustrious men" since at least the days of the hapless first Grimoald.[24] The address form, however, could be turned into a title form easily enough: the *v. inl.* generally came in the first line of the document after the *rex Francorum,* and because the abbreviation omitted the dative endings, there was the latent possibility of construing the phrase as "*vir inluster*" and, consequently, as part of the *intitulatio.* When it appeared advantageous to transfer the gradually acquired and generally recognized "illustriousness" of his family into a formal title element, Pippin was to make use of this possibility.[25] That time was not far off.

In 747, Pippin became the *de facto* ruler of the whole Frankish kingdom when Karlomann voluntarily "put aside the labors of administration in an earthly kingdom,"[26] and entered monastic life in Italy, leaving Neustria to the control of his brother. Then in 751, Pippin sent to Rome to obtain papal advice "about the kings in the realm of the Franks, who possessed no royal power, and whether this was good or not." A pope who was willing to consider such a loaded question was bound to give the answer which Pippin (and probably Saint Boniface) wanted, namely "that it was better for the one who had the power than for the one who remained without royal power to be called 'king.' "[27]

The final step in establishing the Carolingians as the formal rulers of the Franks was taken in November of that year. The record of it is simple and concise: on the basis of the results of consultation with the pope, Pippin became king and his wife, Bertrada, became queen. Following the ancient *ordo* (which in context, seems to signify something between ancient custom and ritual), Pippin was chosen king by all the Franks, he was consecrated by the bishops, and he was accorded homage by his magnates.[28] The consecration took the form of anointment, which has been shown to have been a rite in Spanish-Visigothic usage during the previous century but one which was unknown until then in a Frankish coronation ceremony.[29] The rite conveyed the charismatic Old Testament image of God-appointed kingship, by evoking associations with Saul and David, and at the same time confirmed those pagan conceptions of divine kingship which had already been coated with a thin veneer of Christianity and were to be retained throughout the Middle Ages.

Pippin felt the need to substantiate the legality of his act from as many sides as possible. To still the qualms of any who might feel a need to remain loyal to the Merovingians because of some combination of tradition, Merovingian royal charisma, and solemn oaths, it was pointed out that Childeric, as a man holding the kingly title without performing the attached functions was a man "falsely called King."[30] With the terrible name of "false king" almost ascribed to Childeric, Pippin may have prided himself on his own kindness in only sending him, tonsured, to end his days in a monastery. Dropping now the superfluous *"dux et princeps,"* Pippin was finally free to style himself *"rex."* Filling the traditional *v. inl.* of Merovingian documents with a new signification, which seemed familiar but was to amplify the Carolingian *intitulatio* with a worthy distinction nonetheless, Pippin became officially: *Rex Francorum vir inluster.* Then, in 754, when Pope Stephen II travelled to meet Pippin at his royal palace at Ponthion on the Marne in search of help against Lombard encroachments, Pippin guaranteed him that assistance; in return for this commitment, Pope Stephen gave Pippin the further title of *patricius Romanorum,* which the Exarch of Ravenna had been using as the head official of the East-Roman Empire in the West.

Having all this behind him, Pippin intended to insure that the same measures he had just taken would not be applied against him or his descendents. Part of the ceremony made him, with his wife and queen, the exclusive founders of a royal dynasty. Pippin did not want the concept of the rights of royal blood applied too loosely. He saw to it that Pope Stephen anointed him a second time on the occasion of his visit — assumedly the charisma would either work better or be more obvious if it came from the papal hand itself — and also anointed his sons, another Karlomann and Charles (the future Charlemagne) as his successors. Possibly he was concerned about competition to his line from the offspring of his brother, the elder Karlomann. At any rate, a papal document was to appear which threatened with excommunication those "who should ever dare to presume to choose a king from other loins than his for all eternity."[31]

ALTERNATIVES TO KINGSHIP: THE NONROYAL PRINCIPALITIES

Although kingship proved in the long run to be the most viable system for political stabilization in the Middle Ages, it was required to prove itself generally through the tenth century and was occasionally afterwards in jeopardy. We have seen with the Carolingians and their undermining of the Merovingians before replacing them how dukes or major-domos could personally challenge a dynasty by taking over within the kingship system. From the outside institutional kingship could be challenged equally well or better by those who erected independent bases of power, sometimes with the clear intent of establishing independent kingdoms themselves, sometimes apparently content with lesser aims. Potentially independent bases of power existed in the nonroyal principalities. Attempts to build on their independence affected the development of kingship in two ways: it subtracted ruling responsibilities and authority from kings in areas where royal power showed signs of ineffectiveness, and it forced royal rulers to be creative beyond their predecessors' capacities in order to meet the challenges posed by nonroyal rivals.

Although there were many nonroyal principalities from the early Middle Ages through Carolingian times, developments in two of them, Aquitaine and Bavaria, will suffice to illustrate the dynamic tension which characterized the relationship between them and the adjacent kingdoms.

Aquitaine, the region in the southwestern part of what is today France as far as the Pyrenees, was an example of a generally nonroyal principality with a certain historic independence, or at least separate identity, as a political unit. Several factors made this the case. Aquitaine had a Church history of its own: no less than three archbishoprics rivalled each other for primacy in the region. Toulouse, one of its major cities, had been the seat of the Visigothic kingdom in southern France. In later Merovingian times, the simple need for organizing to resist the threat of Arab invasions no doubt added something to the Aquitainian feeling of cohesiveness, since Aquitaine was obviously the first point of attack for Arabs crossing the Pyrenees from Spain.

Earlier, in the time of Diocletian, the region had been divided into three provinces, but all were obviously thought to belong to the same group for each began with the name "Aquitania." The Roman names, *Aquitania Prima, Secunda et Novempopulana* (literally "First and Second Aquitaine and Aquitaine of the Nine Communities") scarcely reflected any interest in local roots; in fact, the opposite is to be inferred. Still there was a tradition of regional identity going back still centuries earlier, when we find references to one Julius Vindex, "of Aquitainian royal blood" but also a Roman governor, leading an unsuccessful revolt of Averni, Aedui, Viennenses, and Sequani in the last year of Nero's reign.[32]

In 507 Clovis had defeated Visigothic King Alaric II, and the following year he took Toulouse and absorbed Aquitaine into the Frankish kingdom. Later Aquitaine was to be a part of the total Frankish kingdom when it was unified, or the region was divided in some manner among the rulers of Neustria, Austrasia, and Burgundy when these parts of the Frankish Kingdom were under different kings. The latter state of affairs was by far the more normal.

In the 660s, a low point in the ebb and flow of Carolingian fortunes and the normally low Merovingian ebb during the later seventh century, greater political independence was sought for Aquitaine by its chief magnate, a duke. There is some evidence of Aquitaine's tending to become an independent principality in the records of the Council of Bordeaux, which met from 673 to 675. Its decisions were announced "by the mediation of Duke Lupus," who still protected himself with a reference to the reigning *princeps,* Merovingian King Childeric II, as authority for their promulgation.[33]

Using both the confusion which followed Pippin of Heristal's death and the increasing threat of Arab invasions, Aquitanian Duke Eudo did his utmost to gather forces and resources under his own control in the early eighth century. When the Arabs did in fact invade Aquitaine, Eudo defeated them in 721 and forced them to retreat back over the Pyrenees. A few years later, a second Arab invasion succeeded in penetrating as far as Burgundy, in considerable part because Eudo had chosen to reach a diplomatic understanding with the Arabs rather than fight them. For this Charles Martell punished Duke Eudo and the Aquitanians by burning and plundering their lands. When the third Arab expedition, which was to culminate in the Battle of Tours, went through Aquitaine, Duke Eudo, now back on the side of the Franks under Charles Martell, suffered a defeat before Charles's victory in 732.

A sign of Eudo's independent power all the while was the way he could coerce the Church into contributing to his cause. In a series of steps much like those of Charles Martell, Eudo compelled churches and monasteries to lend him the use of land belonging to them. This would be turned over to a vassal in return for an increase of support for Duke Eudo and a small share of the annual income obtained from the fief for the ecclesiastical owners. In theory the fief would be returned to the church or monastery it came from; however, when the fiefs in fact passed to the next generation of the duke's vassals, such a reversion began to seem unlikely, at least for the duration of the Arab threat which had brought on these virtual confiscations for defense purposes to begin with.

Eudo's successors, Hunald and Waifar, resisted reincorporation into the Frankish Kingdom, until Aquitaine was finally subdued by Charlemagne. After the Frankish defeat at the Battle of Roncevalles, which gave rise to the famous *Song of Roland,* Charlemagne took care to organize Aquitaine better against both Basques and Arabs and concentrated on establishing effective resistance to invasion under the counts of Toulouse. These counts were, of course, selected in considerable part on the basis of loyalty to him. Aquitaine as such was still important enough for Charlemagne to give it as a kingdom to his son, Louis (later Louis I or Louis the Pious).

In Bavaria, which in the Middle Ages meant southeastern Germany including parts of what is now Austria, the alternative of ducal rule proved more solidly based and longer lasting than in Aquitaine. Since a good deal of the area had been nearly depopulated by the wars of the fifth century, there was less continuity from ancient times than in Aquitaine. Like Aquitaine, however, Bavaria had a number of active bishoprics: Freising, Regensburg, Passau, and Salzburg were founded or restored by Boniface as important points from which missionary activity radiated and as centers which were to retain considerable autonomy throughout the Middle Ages. The Bavarian Church consequently served as a regionally cohesive force, particularly from the eighth century.

Various historians have attempted to derive the Bavarians from the Boiarii, a branch of the Marcomanni who inhabited Bohemia during the later Roman Empire, or from the Lombards, Vandals, or even Ostrogoths. None of their findings have held up particularly well to exhaustive criticism, and the safest assumption at the moment appears to be that the Bavarians evolved as a new constellation of diverse tribal elements after the great migration period. The Franks acquired control of their territory in the sixth century, and Bavaria endured as a nonroyal principality under the Frankish or Burgundian Agilolfing family from about 555 to 788. The significant thing for our purposes in all this is that by Carolingian times the Bavarians thought of themselves as an independent tribe and consequently attached importance to being ruled in a fashion which respected their distinctiveness.

The Agilolfings were demonstrably rivals of the Carolingians in the eighth century and probably even before. One of their dukes, Theodo, gained virtual independence for his principality about 717, although soon afterwards Bavaria was subdued by Charles Martell.[34] When Hiltrud, Pippin the Short's sister, married Agilolfing Duke Odilo, the Carolingians took the match much amiss, and their feelings turned to greater resentment when the match produced a capable administrator and military leader in the person of Duke Tassilo III, who ruled Bavaria for nearly forty years. Tassilo did homage to Pippin, to be sure, when he came of age in 757, but he allied himself with the Avars, enemies of the Franks, and as a son-in-law of Lombard King Desiderius, his position toward the Carolingians was one of potential hostility. His titles, too, pointed in the same direction. One of Tassilo's ancestors, the Alamannian Duke Godofrid, had begun to sport a *vir inluster dux* in his *intitulatio* about the same time that the idea of doing so occurred to the Carolingians.[35] The *vir inluster dux,* which Tassilo's *intitulatio* shows in 770, and then the superlative *illustrissimus dux* some six years later, proclaimed him as all too much of an equal of the Carolingian kings.[36] By further taking the title of *princeps regni,* in 772, he stressed his independence from the Carolingians beyond any mistaking, while his original title, *dux Bauuariorum,* continued to convey the tribal roots of his rulership.[37] Tassilo's father, Odilo, had already used the quasi-royal plural for himself, another bit of independent ruler plumage which the son adopted as well. In still another approximation of royal majesty, Tassilo had his son, Theodo, anointed by the pope. The Lombard connection showed up in his titles also: there was the superlative of glorious, *gloriosissimus* and the special favorite of Lombard kings, *praecellentissimus* (most excellent). Although Tassilo never quite brought himself to adopt the final term, *rex,* officially for himself, his admirers did not hesitate to refer to him, after an impressive victory over a Slavic tribe, as a new "King Constantine" (*rex Constantinus*).[38] Eventually, the grammar of his *intitulatio* collapsed under the sheer weight of Lombard superlatives in the ablative absolute and Carolingian-style nominatives, as a charter was granted, *"Gloriosissimo atque praecellentissimo Tassilo dux Bauuariorum vir inluster."*[39]

By the 770s, however, Charlemagne was engaged in incorporating anything that looked like an independent and rival principality into his own realm. In 774 he absorbed the Lombard Kingdom and enlarged his own kingly title from *rex Francorum* to *rex Francorum et Langobardorum;* then in 781, he made his son, Pippin, *rex Langobardorum* in the same way that Louis was to be *rex Aquitanorum.* After a lengthy struggle, Tassilo was forced to yield his own duchy to Charlemagne, who treated it as another subrealm, the *regnum Bauuariorum.*

We are certainly not at the end of a story; instead we are forced to step out of a recurring cycle of events which would carry us too far. For the *regnum Bauuaviorum* passed as a significant political entity into the ninth century, when it provided a springboard for an illegitimate but capable Carolingian to depose an East-German king and even to assume the imperial title. While Bavaria spent most of the remaining Middle Ages as a duchy, another, much later emperor, Napoleon I, made its duke a king under him, while Bismarck incorporated the Kingdom of Bavaria — by his time, reconstituted as such for about sixty years — into the German Empire of 1871. The whole long history of nonroyal principalities in their relation to kingdoms reveals the same tense and dynamic play of centrifugal and centripetal forces as the shorter American story of states' rights in relation to the power of the federal government. Consciousness of the latter relationship figured in a decision after World War II, when American occupation authorities leaned toward granting more autonomy to the individual German states (by now, *Länder*) in their relation to the federal republic, and the state (*Land*) of Bavaria, which had existed for most of its twelve hundred years or so as a nonroyal principality, proved to be an excellent choice as a guardian of particularistic rights to offset federal power.

Returning, however, to the fate of nonroyal principalities in the eighth century, we might find it strange at first glance that Charlemagne should choose to reconstitute duchies, whose independence he had effectively taken away, as kingdoms. After all, a kingdom is even more independent than a duchy, and if both may go by the Latin name of *regna,* then a king of a *regnum* still is potentially more independent than a duke with his. The fact was, however, that there was no essential difference to be expected in the political behavior of a duke and a king, if we consider the title in isolation. If a duke had enough resources and tradition behind him to make his duchy able to function independently and felt either tempted or threatened into doing so, he would pursue a starkly independent course. If either a duke or king, on the other hand, were quite subordinate to the emperor, as Louis with his *regnum Aquitanorum* and Gerold, Charlemagne's brother-in-law who received the *regnum Bauuariorum,* most surely were, then this posed no threat of political insubordination in any nonroyal principality which had merely become a subrealm by the emperor's direct designation. As a matter of fact, in making a formerly independent duchy into a subrealm headed by a member of his own family, Charlemagne may have been partly motivated by a desire to keep the

Aquitanians a bit more in line: they would be ruled by a king with a more impressive title and stronger connections than the local duke had possessed. Bavaria, to be sure, was not given a king right away in its status as a Carolingian *regnum* after Tassilo's surrender, but this may have been a matter of available, suitable personnel in Charlemagne's family. The exposed nature of the Bavarian *regnum* may have dictated to him the assigning of it to Gerold, who proved his military prowess in fighting the Avars and, in fact, died in battle against them in 799.[40] In the ninth century, however, Louis the German, the Carolingian King of the East Franks, also held the title of Bavarian King.[41] The relationship of the subrealm to the overall ruler, then, was itself the problematic one: if the subordination relationship held, it was an indifferent matter whether the ruler of the dependent subrealm or *regnum* held a royal or ducal title; if it did not hold, then the royal title was an advantage to the lesser ruler if he could maintain his independence.

Looking at the matter from the standpoint of the nonroyal rulers' policy options in Aquitaine and Bavaria, the question arises: why did the dukes of Aquitaine and Bavaria fail to take the final step and make themselves kings in those periods when the neighboring kingdoms posed less than the normal threat to them?

The answer is that the assumption of kingship by a duke offered advantages — charisma, extra Church sanction, increased prestige and authority — but also could bring future trouble. A new king invited challenges from his own magnates who lost by the new distance put between him and them. He was also bound to appear either somewhat pretentious or bent on expansion, or, at the very least, ambitious to place himself on an equal level with neighboring kings. He thus invited more trouble from the outside. As a duke, such a man could face the possible recovery of strong royal neighbors or their protagonists, as Duke Lupus had done in Aquitaine, without seeming to challenge them or invite their enmity. With the need for gaining Church sanction to become a king, even more time and maneuvering were required for success than the difficult process of accustoming the people to royal airs and quasi-royal titles would have required by itself. All in all, it was a dangerous undertaking.

There was no getting around the fact, however, that for exercising real rulership, there was limited room for initiative left to the nonroyal ruler. The goals of Tassilo III could not be achieved without assumptions of quasi-royal rulership. By that assumption he heated the wrath of his Carolingian neighbors against him. This is not to say that they might not have annexed his duchy eventually anyway but that his act made such a possible sequence of events far more likely. All along, Tassilo had manifested two main overlapping aims: the solidification of his rights as ruler of the Bavarian duchy through the claims of tribal leadership, and recognition of the independence of his ruling rights from higher secular authority.[42] The first goal was probably impossible without achieving the second, and steps to achieve the second were alarm signals for Carolingian intervention to put him down as an upstart who had no business wanting such independence.

While the nonroyal principality offered a constant challenge to kingship as an alternate system in the early Middle Ages, this challenge never amounted to offering a stable alternative, particularly as time wore on, for the nonroyal principalities simply could not maintain the absolute independence of their original status. One by one, like Aquitaine and Bavaria, they were absorbed into the larger royal units, sometimes only nominally, as in the feudal system which linked their rulers to kings as vassals, but more often as subordinate units within the larger realm. The only exceptions were those with rulers who turned their ducal rights into royal or imperial ones, as the dukes of the Normans and those of the Saxons were to do. Even these exceptions were more apparent than real, for what we really have in these instances is the arrival on the historical scene of more talented practitioners of kingship who were able to exploit a power vacuum for their own ends.

THE IMPERIAL CONNECTION

From the moment the Carolingians got in sight of Frankish kingship for themselves, they developed a special relationship with Rome, the popes, and the residues of imperial authority. "Residues of imperial authority" should be understood here in two contexts. The Carolingians dealt with eastern emperors, who claimed the undiminished authority of the old Roman Empire for themselves, on terms of greater equality than did other western rulers. By doing so, they conveyed the impression that the "Roman" authority of the ruler in Constantinople was something less than universal. At the same time, they moved toward appropriating at least some of the residual imperial authority in the West which the popes had been holding in escrow since the end of the fifth century. The papacy had, after all, been operating in a vacuum more often than not as far as centralized military and political power was concerned. Since the time of Clovis, the Catholic kings of the Franks had enjoyed a certain preferential position, especially well defined from the papal standpoint. Some king or nation needed to exercise the coercive power which the pope was incapable of exercising himself, and the Franks with their kings had proven more tractable in this respect than others. In 595, Pope Gregory the Great had written to Childebert II, who was ruling Austrasia with considerable help from his mother, Brunhilde: "Just as royal dignity surpasses all individual men, in the same way the Frankish Kingdom excels all other peoples."[43]

It must have taken some papal imagination to espouse this idea during inauspicious moments when Merovingian family quarrels divided Frankish kingship into warring factions from which Rome could not expect much support. The Carolingians, however, were more credible in the role of fighters on behalf of the Roman Church. Charles Martell's victory over the Saracens at Tours could obviously be depicted as the achievement of a warrior for Rome. The *Annals of the Frankish Kingdom (Annales Regni Francorum)* stress Pippin in exactly the same role. Pippin sought *justice for the Apostle Peter,* when he led his troops to Italy in fulfillment of his pledge to help the pope against the Lombards.[44] Charlemagne simply follows his father and grandfather in this respect. The *Annals* portray his wars in and around Italy in a quite different tone than his interminable wars with the Saxons. The former are emphasized as waged on behalf of Saint Peter; the latter are not, although they included measures of virtually forced Christianization which Charlemagne was later to associate with his imperial rule.[45]

Eighth-century popes developed something much closer to a relation of one-to-one reciprocity with the Carolingians than with other secular rulers. This is evident in Charlemagne's special rendering of thanks in Rome in 786–787 after an impressive series of victories, as it is in the special recognition given to him by Pope Adrian I:

> Then King Charles, mindful foremost that he had peace on all sides through the abundance of God's grace, planned a journey for the purposes of praying at the threshold of the Blessed Apostles, of putting matters in Italy aright, and of negotiating agreements with a delegation sent by the [eastern] Emperor. . . . Then King Charles arrived in Rome on the journey mentioned and was received by the Apostolic Lord Adrian, who showed him great honor, and he stayed several days with the Apostolic Lord.[46]

In Italy, Charlemagne brought about the submission, however transitory, of Benevento, whose independent duke was at odds with Pope Adrian. Soon afterward, Adrian supported Charlemagne against the old enemy of the Carolingians, Duke Tassilo III, about as strongly as the leader of western Christendom could do, among other things, threatening Tassilo and his magnates, according to the *Annals*, with the ban of anathema

> . . . if he were not obedient to King Charles, his sons, and the Frankish people. . . , and if this same duke remained obdurate and offered less than obedience to the words of the Pope referred to here, then King Charles and his army would be absolved from every danger of sin to the extent that whatever happened in that land (Bavaria) in the way of arson, homicide, or other evil deeds would be counted the fault of Tassilo and his followers, while King Charles would remain untouched by any guilt in the matter.[47]

Striking evidence of the special relationship between Rome, Charlemagne, and the Church can be seen in the gifts which the new pope, Leo III, sent to Charlemagne after Adrian's death: the banner of the city of Rome and the keys to Saint Peter's tomb.[48] When Pope Leo subsequently came to Paderborn to request Charlemagne's aid, he was following in the footsteps of Pope Stephen who had personally journeyed to Pippin for help. Leo certainly needed aid: at least two contemporary sources state that he had been blinded and had his tongue cut out.[49] If that is a bit much for the modern mind, since he saw and spoke well enough at a later date, it is certainly true that he had been deposed in Rome on the basis of heavy charges of misconduct made against him. The fact that Leo either agreed or even requested to have Charlemagne sit as judge in a trial to decide his guilt or innocence can be taken to stress either Charlemagne's preeminence among rulers or the pope's great trust in him. Either way, it underlines the special relationship which had been developed by Charlemagne with the papacy. Certainly the pope had no idea of entrusting any local tribunal (or any other ruler) with such judicial authority over him.

The papal invitation to the Carolingians to assume responsibilities in Italy helped in itself to prepare the way for their empire, beginning with Pippin's wars against the Lombards. Territorial responsibilities implied military control, which in turn implied political power. Responsibilities, control, and power in Italy necessarily applied with only minor reservations to Rome itself and helped to make quasi-imperial authority come rather naturally to the Carolingians. The *Annals* speak quite openly of "the glorious Lord King Charles having subjugated Italy itself and put it in order," early in his reign.[50] Much later, an alternate way of counting the years of Charlemagne's reign was to date it from his conquest of Italy.[51]

In holding councils to decide religious questions, the Carolingians also assumed a religious jurisdiction which should have been distinctly reminiscent of the best and worst of old Roman emperors from a papal standpoint. On his own, Pippin in 767 "held a great council attended by Romans and Greeks on questions of the Holy Trinity and the images of saints."[52] The latter issue, the iconoclastic controversy with its roots in the Byzantine world, was of the highest import for international Christendom in the eighth century. In 794, Charlemagne held the Council of Frankfurt in a manner which strikingly resembled Constantine's direction of the Council of Nicaea.[53] There, Charlemagne straightened out true faith from heresy in no uncertain manner as king of the Franks in the condemnation of Adoptionism and the worship of holy images.[54] Later, as emperor, he convoked a council at Aachen to handle the matter of the procession of the Holy Spirit. There was no difference, really, in the way he held the two synods or councils. If anything, the one he held at Frankfurt was the more impressive and authoritative. There was no indication all the while of any papal discontent with all of this; on the contrary, the various popes seem heartily to have approved all along.

Once established, the international scope of the Carolingian empire was impressive. Even the Huns (between the end of the fifth century and the coming of the Magyars this term signified the Avars) turned to Charlemagne to order their affairs.[55] Still more surprising, in view of the fact that the Carolingian empire never controlled the British Isles, was the successful attempt of the king of the Northumbrians to be reinstated by Charlemagne on his throne after he had been driven from his homeland. It seems that the persuasive force of emissaries from Charlemagne and Pope Leo was sufficient to achieve this.[56] These two incidents illustrate the extent to which the Carolingians accumulated authority throughout Europe well before actually assuming the imperial title. Again, Charles Martell and his victory at Tours over the invading Moors can be seen as more than the victory of one tribe over another, even if the religious issue is left out of it. It was later to Charlemagne's court as Frankish ruler that the Saracens sent negotiators when they wanted to deal with the West. By the same token, the Byzantines showed special attention to Charlemagne's court before he became emperor. A brief but remarkable entry in the *Annals* for the year 797 shows the extent of Charlemagne's general European preeminence as king of the Franks:

> Also in his palace at Aachen, he received the Saracen Abdellah, son of King Ibn-Muawijah, who was living an exile's life in Mauretania after having been overthrown by his brother and who now sought his [Charlemagne's] protection. Also an emissary of Nicetas, Governor of Sicily, a man named Theoctistus, came to him there bringing a letter from the [Eastern] Emperor. He gave him a magnificent reception and let him go a few days later.[57]

Charlemagne is best remembered in the English-speaking world as emperor rather than king: Christmas Day, 800, the day when Charlemagne was crowned emperor by the pope, is one of half a dozen memorable dates which students generally pick up in the course of a college education. After all, it can be seen as the starting date for the Holy Roman Empire, which lasted a thousand years, and so must be important.

In view of this, it should be pointed out that governing with Roman imperial authority turned out to be rather a mixed blessing for the Carolingians. Until quite recently it has been maintained that Charlemagne himself not only did not aim at acquiring the imperial title but seriously objected to having it thrust upon him. This is exactly what Einhard, his foremost contemporary biographer, said even in the context of relating Charlemagne's subsequent law giving and reform program to his assumption of the imperial title.[58] One influential twentieth-century analysis of the imperial title ends on the note that as a matter of cold fact it did not add a thing to Charlemagne's official authority exercised already as king of the Franks and of other nations, too.[59] Apart from this, taking the title of emperor was sure to annoy the Byzantines and perhaps stir up trouble on the eastern border of the wide reaches of Charlemagne's European domains.

And yet, the Carolingians did seem to have been aiming at a special relationship with Rome from the moment they assumed the kingship. King Pippin I had conducted careful negotiations with the bishop of Rome before taking over the Frankish kingship from the Merovingians. He became something like the pope's military commander-in-chief in the agreement which left him responsible for protection and conquest of lands in the name of the papacy. Protection of lands in the Middle Ages presupposed at least military control, and the assumption of these protective responsibilities had led to a further *de facto* extension of Frankish control.

From the other direction, there were certain unmistakable signs that popes of the later eighth century saw the Carolingian kings as qualitatively different from other western rulers and accorded them appropriately distinctive honors well before Charlemagne's coronation. Papal reliance on Pippin for protection had meant, of course, a special position for him at the outset. For Charlemagne as king but not yet emperor, the evidence for a special position in papal eyes includes the use by the papacy of dates counted from his year of accession as King of the Franks, references to his rule on papal coinage, pictorial representations of him in place of the eastern emperors, and the use of special prayers in the Church, along with liturgical praises of a type associated with eastern emperors.[60]

Einhard records that to fulfill the wish of Pope Adrian I, Charlemagne made an exception to his otherwise firm refusal to put on foreign clothing. In Rome in 787, he put on a long tunic, the chlamys (a short mantle, which in purple and gold had imperial associations), and shoes of a distinctive, Roman type. A man of Charlemagne's bent of mind did not play dress-up for nothing: to put on Roman costume meant associating his rulership for the moment with the grandeur of the ancient capital. We can be even more sure of this, because he later did the same thing for Pope Leo III, who pleaded with him to put on this costume.[61]

Then there was the matter of the negotiations on December 23, 800, in Saint Peter's Cathedral. At that time, Pope Leo III cleared himself of charges levied against him. If, as according to one contemporary source, the "whole Christian people" — meaning representatives of Franks, Lombards and Romans — decided then and there that Charlemagne should become emperor, it is highly unlikely that Charlemagne did not know of such a plan for two days.[62] The meeting was not even supposed to be a secret one.

All this does not mean, of course, that Charlemagne wanted to be *only* Emperor, as was true of Louis the Pious. His real political foundation was and remained rulership as king, which his [new] title indeed did not renounce. The imperial superstructure was, so to speak, a thing for high festival days, while sober everyday life presented other demands.[63]

The evidence is that he viewed the imperial title as a nice something extra for his exercise of Frankish kingship and that he was fully in agreement with the council's plan:

> King Charles himself refused to deny their petition, but in all humility feeling himself subject to God and the petition of the priests and the whole Christian people he accepted the name of emperor.[64]

All this adds up to a high probability that Charlemagne had been aiming at the imperial title for some time — or at the very least, meeting it as it came toward him. This is further supported by previous references in the correspondence of Alcuin, Abbot of Saint Martin's at Tours and intellectual leader of the Carolingian Renaissance, to the "Christian Empire," an authoritative structure needed for reforming, strengthening, and unifying the Church. Perhaps Alcuin, more dimly, perceived a "Christian Empire" as the means for raising Charlemagne, in theory as well as in fact, above rivals jealous of his power of command in Europe. A work composed by one of Charlemagne's court poets in 799, well before his coronation, calls him *augustus* in a distinctly imperial context.[65]

What seems like a mystery or contradiction in Charlemagne's apparent willingness to assume authority as secular ruler over Roman or western Christendom, while at the same time expressing great reluctance over the way it was given to him in the papal coronation, is easily explained if one separates the two. The ceremony of his accession came logically out of the "petition of the priests and the whole Christian people": they were to acclaim him emperor. Old Roman emperors, it will be recalled, wore diadems or tiaras, but it was their being acclaimed, not any coronation, which made them emperors. The "people," at any rate, had been coached to say: "To Charles, most pious Augustus crowned by God, the great and peace-bringing emperor, long life and victory!" (*Karolo piisimo augusto, a Deo coronato magno et pacifico imperatore, vita et victoria!*[66] — both the term, *augustus,* "senior emperor" in the system deriving from Diocletian and *imperator* were thus used in the formulation.) What Pope Leo did, however, evidently without warning, was to go ahead and crown Charlemagne before the official acclamation. Giving him the crown after the acclamation, which the previous arrangements seem to have called for, would have been a symbolic recognition of the title which the Frankish, Lombard, and Roman peoples with their clergy had bestowed on him.

Pope Leo's upstaging of the acclaimers, however, made the bestowal of the emperorship into his own act.

It was an underhanded maneuver, but safe. Pope Leo could feel reasonably sure that the unsuspecting Charlemagne, just arising from prayer at Saint Peter's altar, would not pull himself together and tell him then and there to wait for the acclamation. If Leo attached importance, as pope, to crowning Charlemagne, he was right. Later popes would take his act as a precedent, asserting that a king could not be made an emperor without it. If, conversely, Charlemagne was annoyed at the pope's performance, he had every reason to be. His own monumental political and military strength kept any quarrel over authority from developing with the papacy, but some of his successors were to have a terrible time trying to govern as emperors with papal opponents telling everyone that emperors were made only by popes, who could take imperial power away as well as give it. If popes had that kind of authority over emperors, then they could logically wield power over mere kings, outranked as kings were by emperors. Later, when Charlemagne designated his son, Louis the Pious, as emperor, he saw to it that the coronation took place with no clergy bestowing the crown. In so doing, "he showed how to his liking things should have been done on 25 December 800."[67]

The imperial connection brought with it an undoubted preeminence of Carolingian rulers and for those later Germanic kings from the tenth century on who acquired it. It also brought a multitude of problems with it, which have left their imprint on nineteenth and twentieth-century history. It is an exercise in futility to try to determine whether the medieval Germanic Empire beginning with Otto the Great's accession to the imperial title in 962 was a continuation of the Carolingian Empire, something new, or a partial revival. The fact is that the same preeminence and the same complications went with the title of ruler in both empires. This is true whether they emphasized their imperial titles more than their royal ones, as was true of the Carolingian Louis the Pious and the Saxon Otto III, or whether they were kings first and emperors second, as was the case with the German Carolingian Charles III and the Hohenstaufen Philip of Swabia.

Chief among the problems was the unusual link with the Church. All medieval kings were expected to cooperate with the Church. This expectation complicated things greatly when popes made a renewed claim to wield secular authority, beginning in the late eleventh century. The Holy Roman emperors were also called on to intervene earlier and more often in Church affairs than other kings, whether by Church reformers who wanted alterations in the Church (Alcuin is something of a prototype here) or by enemies of the papacy who sought the emperor as a counterweight. Closely related with this was the Italian problem. Germanic kings with their imperial titles wasted their resources trying to control the Italian peninsula with their armies, when the need to develop central government at home was most pressing.

The imperial connection added greatly to the problem of even determining where Germany was; that is, literally where it was on the map. It took an ambitious lawyer to try to disentangle the geographical sphere of a Germanic ruler's authority as king of Germany from that which he wielded as Roman emperor. There was, of course, the initial geographical problem that Germany, unlike England, France, and Spain, had very little in the way of natural borders to begin with; but the problem was greatly exacerbated by the fact that the German emperors were to claim authority well outside of the German-speaking lands, while forced to rule inside them with less authority than the later feudal or earlier national monarchs. If German rulers had attempted to differentiate their kingdom from their empire, Germany would have had more of a chance to develop as a nation state along with its western European counterparts. An emphasis on their role as German kings, however, would have gone against the universal claims of emperorship which the Conrads, Henrys, Ottos and Fredericks generally chose to stress from the tenth to the thirteenth centuries.[68]

The strength of territorial lords inside Germany was directly proportional to the weakness of the German king or emperor. The fact that he was kept busy so often elsewhere—in eastern Europe, in the region to be claimed by French kings, but above all in Italy, rebounded to the advantage of these territorial lords and the eventual weakness of the German kingdom. While emperors continued to outrank kings and could even make kings when they felt so inclined, one still has some hesitation about using the term "monarch" for a German ruler at home in speaking of a period when it can be applied without hesitation to French and English kings. The weakness of the imperial position derived partly from its elected nature: the princes who did the electing could demand and get guarantees in advance that their territorial rights would not be interfered with. That factor alone was sometimes enough to weaken the imperial position, as the elective kingship similarly proved disastrous in Poland.

It is true that the male line ran out among German emperors more often than with the kings of those countries which were to develop Germanic kingship into successful feudal and then national monarchy, but it is also true that the elective principle, maintained in Germany largely through the imperial connection, enabled changes of dynasties more often, and with less limitation on which the next ruling house would be, than adherence to the hereditary principle would have provided for.

The ancient Roman tradition that emperors were selected on the basis of promising merit, while kings merely inherited their throne, continued to exert some force. While Charlemagne had become king of the Franks by heredity, he had been personally chosen as Roman Emperor by ostensible representatives of the Franks, Lombards, and the Romans, as well as, of course, the pope. Whether or not the same man held them, kingship remained hereditary, but emperorship remained theoretically elective. Almost every German emperor made an effort to turn the imperial title into a hereditary one, but all efforts to establish the principle before the Hapsburgs (and even after some Hapsburgs) met with no more success than the attempts of an ancient Vespasian or Constantine to make the old title of emperor hereditary. As with some of the ancient Roman emperors, strong Holy Roman emperors could often assure themselves of being succeeded by a son or designated heir. They also stood the same excellent chance of having their wishes ignored. Emperor Henry V clearly designated as his successor the closest likely relative of his dynasty, Frederick of Swabia, whom the electing princes passed over in favor of Lothar III. Emperor Frederick II stirred up so much opposition that many of the electing princes seemed determined to avoid considering any of his progeny at all in choosing a successor. Rather than accept another Hohenstaufen, they fought his descendents for eighteen years and let the title remain vacant for another five.

The ancient Roman prohibition against ruling empresses was also a part of the imperial baggage which the Germanic rulers carried to the end of the Middle Ages and beyond. During the Carolingian period, the prohibition was updated by Pope Leo III's claim that the immediate reason for giving Charlemagne the imperial title was its illegal assumption in the East by Irene, who as a woman could not head an empire, even though she used the Greek male title, *basileus,* rather than *basilissa.* We find repercussions of this renewed prohibition very late in the history of the empire, in fact, in the middle of the Enlightenment itself. In the eighteenth century, after the imperial title had been held constantly by the Hapsburgs for some three hundred years, it still took Emperor Charles VI some twenty-three years of diplomatic negotiations and concessions to gain assent for having his daughter, Maria Theresa, follow him as ruler over most of the Hapsburg dominions; another twenty-three of intermittent warfare passed before she was able to hold them in peace. Even then, there was no thought of her holding the imperial title in her own right: the solution reached in Maria Theresa's case was something like the arrangements entered into by the ancient Roman empresses, Pulcheria and Galla Placidia: beginning in 1745, her husband, Francis I, and then after his death in 1765 their son, Joseph II, became Roman emperors, much as Marcian and Constantius III had in the fifth century because there was no possibility for their imperial wives to rule in their own names. Although popularly called empress, Maria Theresa had been left instead with the titles of queen of

Hungary, queen of Bohemia, and archduchess of Austria, and she could not have been the choice of the electors who had to name an emperor.[69]

In the following chapter, the development of feudal monarchy in Germany can be seen as constantly beset with more problems than the same institution in England and France, and the imperial connection is related to most of these problems. It eclipsed the constitutional significance of the Kingdom of Germany and helped to prevent it from becoming a meaningful political unit in its own right. During Charlemagne's own lifetime, however, the imperial connection added prestige, if not exactly authority, to Frankish kingship, while the problems remained submerged.

PUBLIC RELATIONS AND THE CAROLINGIAN RENAISSANCE

The Carolingian influences which were of decisive importance for medieval kingship for nearly a century (roughly 752–843, with the decades near the turn of the century the most significant)[70] are inseparable from the broader revival now generally called the "Carolingian Renaissance" in the English-speaking world. The characteristic direction of the Carolingian Renaissance as a period of intellectual history was "back to late-ancient times"; in this connection it had a revived emphasis on literary production and education in common with the great Italian Renaissance of the fourteenth and fifteenth centuries but not much else. The political orientation of the Italian Renaissance moved from support of monarchy to one of nostalgic longing for the ancient Roman Republic, while the Carolingian Renaissance favored kingship from beginning to end, but the differences between them went much deeper. Where the later Italian Renaissance was imbued with an intensely humanistic spirit, that of the Carolingian age sought to educate men in writing and speaking to regenerate society on the basis of biblical teachings and those of the Church fathers of the fourth to sixth centuries.

In looking at kingship during the Carolingian Renaissance, one is struck by the fact that the kings and men around them seem conscious of how kingship is perceived. They pay close attention to all manifestations of the institution, from the royal title to the shoes the king puts on when foreign ambassadors are to arrive. They speak with disdain of false imagery; at the same time, they are constantly mindful of a need to cultivate the best image of the ruler as he relates to the Frankish people, to other nations — particularly the rival Byzantines — and to the Church, from the papacy to the parish clergy.

The regeneration of the power of Frankish kingship under the Carolingians brought with it an exaltation of the Franks as people. Even though much of the imagery and phraseology seems to have been suggested from the outside, i.e., from the papacy (Alcuin himself was from near York in

England), Frankish nationalism permeated the Carolingian Renaissance as long as it lasted. Frankish nationalism meant this: an emphasis on the Franks as a nation chosen by God, headed by divinely selected and consecrated kings, and worthy above all other peoples to be the vehicle for a divinely inspired reform of Church and society throughout Europe. Looking at it from the other end, the Carolingian Renaissance can be seen to have lasted only as long as the idea of manifest destiny for the Franks as a people and the divinely assured success of their rulers were both credible.

The Franks were given their first official designation as the people of God (*populus Dei*) in a document of Pippin the Short's brother, Karlomann, in 742.[71] The phrase stuck: its meaning was to become that of a people who had replaced the Hebrews as the chosen people. From here on, the Franks would be the one chosen people as opposed to the many still unregenerate tribes for the duration of the Carolingian age. Latin Bibles suggested this distinction in their general use of a different term for the chosen people (*populus*) in distinction to other peoples (*gentes*).[72] As the Hebrews were custodians of the Word of God in Old Testament times, while God assured them prosperity and victory through their kings, prophets, and judges if they would keep His commandments, so too the Franks, guided by their rulers, were entrusted with a true understanding of the Word of God and were to cultivate and spread Christian worship with every assurance of success.

Since the emphasis in all of this was religious, there was not as much need to emphasize cultural uniqueness on the part of the Franks, apart from their orthodoxy in religion and their valor in war. Unlike modern varieties of nationalism, there was almost no emphasis on the Frankish language. The reason was simple. Latin was the language of the available Scriptures, of the writings of the Church fathers in original or in translation, and of all the written law that mattered. Only to Charlemagne himself, among the leaders of the Carolingian Renaissance, did it seem to occur that the Franks as the *populus Christianus* should cultivate their own language. He showed an interest in preserving old songs in Frankish, appropriately enough, "those in which the deeds and wars of the kings of long ago are sung about," and even began work on a Frankish grammar.[73] Einhard relates these activities to Charlemagne's assumption of imperial responsibilities beyond his royal ones. If there was a connection, Charlemagne must have been thinking of the Franks as having taken a new position of leadership among the tribes of Europe which the empire encompassed. This would have justified such an emphasis on their cultural identity as an interest in their grammar and war songs implies. Whatever his motivation for these efforts may have been, no one else seemed interested enough to continue them.

Since the king was universally acknowledged to be the head of his people, it followed that what exalted the Frankish people exalted Frankish kingship. The medieval king continued to represent his people in the literal sense of embodying their identity, and politically this led in several directions. On one hand, royal concern for the people became an important part of the ideology of the Carolingian Renaissance. Carolingian laws are full of measures to protect *miserabiles personae,* those without means of defending their rights, particularly widows and orphans. The Carolingian court system was also to give a certain status to free men of the counties who were chosen to agree on local judicial sentences.[74] The overall emphasis of Carolingian ideology, however, was no more democratic than that which underlay Hebrew kingship. Between 765 and 769, the Carolingians adopted the formulation, probably new for kings in the West, of *Dei gratia* ("by the grace of God") as an element in their official title not long after they had introduced anointing with sacred oil to the rite of royal consecration.[75] An anointed king who ruled by the grace of God could reasonably expect to count on the support of his people. After all, if God's grace gave this particular king to the Franks as the chosen people of God, it would be a sacrilege for the people not to support him. Look what happened to the Hebrews when they rejected the king whom God chose to send them! The more directly a king's selection, and consequently his rank and dignity, came from God, the less the people had to do with it. The people were emphasized as the object of royal concern throughout the Carolingian Renaissance but never as the rightful source of royal power.

The responsibility of the Frankish Kingdom and later of Charlemagne's empire for advancing the faith could mean simple conquest and the imposition of Christianity on a non-Christian people. This was essentially the Carolingian policy toward the Saxons and some of the Slavic peoples to the East. It could also mean attempts to liberate Spain from Moslem domination. Frankish kings, however, generally preferred to use peaceful instruments of diplomacy in their foreign relations. In their constant sending and receiving of ambassadors and delegations to and from foreign rulers, the Carolingians kept themselves informed about problems and opportunities presenting themselves abroad and at the same time impressed on those same foreign rulers the strength and scope of the Frankish monarchy. Proper attention was always given to presenting an impressive royal or imperial image on such solemn occasions as a reception for foreign dignitaries. Charlemagne would wear a bejeweled sword; he would put on clothes woven through with gold and shoes studded with more precious stones. These also provided some of the rare occasions when he would wear his gold crown, resplendent with still more jewels.[76] Gift-giving on both sides reflected the opulence of the giver and the esteem accorded the recipient. Alfonso II, Christian king of Asturias and Gallicia in Spain, shared some of his finest booty with Charlemagne:

> After plundering Olispona [Lisbon] on the far side of Spain he sent cuirasses, mules and captured Moors to Charles as a token of his victory.[77]

For all the Christian-Moslem conflicts on the Iberian peninsula and Charlemagne's own border problems with Spain, Carolingian rulers maintained fairly cordial diplomatic relations with various Mohammedan rulers there and elsewhere, particularly with the caliphs of Baghdad. From one of these, Haroun-ar-Rachid, who was first perceived at the Frankish court as the "King of the Persians" and then as "King of the Saracens," Charlemagne received one of his most prized possessions. This was an elephant named Abul Abaz that lived at his court for eight years. The animal's death in 810 was noted in somewhat more detail than that of the emperor's oldest daughter a few weeks earlier by the court official recording the Annals of the Frankish Kingdom.[78]

The reputation of the Carolingian Empire among its neighbors was responsible for the apparent ease with which Charlemagne and the pope could cooperate in restoring Eardwulf, the deposed king of the Northumbrians mentioned above. Rival claimants for the throne of Denmark turned to the Carolingians on several occasions, and Louis the Pious combined great patience and restraint with diplomatic effort over some fourteen years to carry through his support of one of them to a successful conclusion.[79] Delegations from a long list of Slavic tribes[80] and from unnamed "heathen peoples, all who lived round about,"[81] flocked to the Carolingian court to give and receive gifts and to bring their problems to the attention of the emperor. The Carolingians publicized the guarantees they gave that emissaries on route would not suffer harm and the stiff penalties in store for those attempting to rob or kill them.[82]

Relations with the Byzantine Empire were a delicate matter for the Carolingians, who wanted to keep peace with the eastern emperors but at the same time wanted their due when dealing with them. Several Frankish-Greek dynastic marriages were the object of diplomatic contacts in the later eighth century, but no Carolingian-Byzantine marriages were successfully negotiated. The failure to reach an agreement on one in particular toward the end of the 780s placed an extra strain on Frankish royal relations with Constantinople.[83] Charlemagne's conduct of the Council of Frankfurt in 794 was an assertion of the high status of both the Franks and their ruler in the international Church which could not help but be felt as a threatening gesture towards Eastern authority. To no one's surprise, eastern monarchs regarded Charlemagne's acceptance of the imperial title which they had considered solely their own as a final act of usurpation.

Fortunately for Charlemagne, the Byzantines were vulnerable both to intrigue and to attack at their outposts in Sicily and Venice. In 804, forces friendly to the Franks and hostile to Constantinople took over Venice.

Although the Byzantines soon won it back, Charlemagne's son, King Pippin of Italy, kept the Byzantine fleet busy with threats against Venice and towns on the Dalmatian coast.[84] Charlemagne was also helped by a turnover in Byzantine rulers in the early ninth century sufficient to let the Frankish affront to their claims of sole Roman emperorship fade into the background. Eventually, he was able to trade a firm offer of peace for full recognition of his imperial title: Byzantine ambassadors obliged him at Aachen by chanting before him the Greek liturgical praise to the emperor.[85] Charlemagne was thus officially recognized as emperor by his only potentially serious rival in the Christian world.

Charlemagne's extensive building program reflected both his devotion to the Church and his creative energy; at the same time it enhanced his own ruler's image. Contemporaries were much impressed by the great bridge across the Rhine at Mainz, although it burned the year before his death, and even more by the Basilica of the Holy Mother of God at Aachen.[86] From ancient Egyptian through Roman times, it held true that a ruler conveyed something of his power and authority by the number, quality, and size of the structures he erected. Medieval kings continued to give their reigns monuments in this way, beginning with Theoderic the Ostrogoth, who sought to rebuild and preserve ancient walls, aqueducts, and public buildings for contemporary Romans and posterity. This clearly reflected his image of himself as the restorer of Roman greatness and counteracted the image of barbarian and destroyer which he disliked. It was entirely in keeping with the religious emphasis of the Carolingian Renaissance that in its architecture kings and emperors manifested their greatness by erecting church buildings.

Superficially the Carolingian rulers were in a very strong position in their relations with the Church. The papacy needed their support and exalted them above other rulers of the earth in order to get it. The most reform-minded of the high clergy in the Frankish realm saw Frankish kingship as the great instrumentality by which clerical behavior could be made to conform to moderately ascetic Christian ideals and by which the Church would consequently be strengthened. The Church further needed the support of Frankish kings for internal defense of Church lands and property, for the protection of frontier missions to the north and east, and even for making sure that people paid their tithes.[87] On a local level, most parish priests appear to have accepted the role of popular educators assigned to them, to the extent of what can be known about their reactions.[88] At least in the directives on the frequency and emphases of their preaching there is none of the frustrated repetition of orders of the type which admonished the courts to take their administration of justice seriously. If it is objected that this is an unfair comparison, then it should be stressed that priests in a preaching and teaching role commensurate with the dignity of their office fit in well with Carolingian reform programs; counts in their (by then) traditional role as strong territorial lords did not. When it came to instituting reforms in monastic houses with measures like enforcing celibacy there was considerable indifference to royal policy, but even fairly strict monastic reform measures did not evoke the public expression of opposing ideas or any organized resistance. All in all, Carolingian kingship enjoyed international backing from the papacy, support from at least the most influential bishops and abbots at home, and general cooperation on the part of parish clergy.

All this nonetheless amounted to a superficial relationship of strength for two reasons. For one, it was at the price of furthering a clerical monopoly in the public expression of ideas beyond those pertaining to functions of government in the narrowest sense. Leaders of the Carolingian Renaissance thought of kingship as an instrument in the service of faith. To be an instrument, then as now, is to be subordinate when power relationships are clarified, as they were, in fact, to be when the Carolingian Empire approached disintegration in the course of the ninth century. For another, any talk of secular rulership's strength in relation to the Church just went counter to the whole spirit of the Carolingian Renaissance. There was no room in the political thought of that age for developing either the concept of Church and state defending their respective spheres against encroachment by the other in pursuit of a balance of separate powers or the concept of one power's effective domination of the other.[89] Ideas of this sort were expressed only anonymously and were nipped in the bud before they could contribute to serious public controversy.[90] The byword instead was "peace and concord" between secular government and the Church in a way which played down any conscious diversity of interests, let alone any opposition of powers.[91] It made no more sense to the main luminaries of the Carolingian Renaissance to speak even of Charlemagne as strong in his relation to the Frankish Church than it did to speak of a human head — to which the medieval king was quite frequently compared — as strong in relation to the body joined to it or to the spirit which inhabited it.

But as long as the theory could be maintained that a complete unity of interests prevailed, the Church stepped in mightily to advance the ideology of a regenerated Christian society under divinely chosen kingship. In a largely illiterate population, the chief vehicle for popular enlightenment was the sermon.

> Sermon and parochial organization complemented each other rather effectively. In the agricultural sections public and social order was represented by the parish priest, not by the count, not by royal officers. . . .[92]

Because the king and his leading clergy reached the people most effectively through the parish priests, they were necessarily committed to a comprehensive program of educating and supporting priests who were qualified to drive home theological and moral points in a vernacular which their parishioners would understand. It was quite logical for the Carolingians as secular rulers to stress propaganda for humility, love of one's neighbor, charity, modesty in behavior and in demands, and respect for authority— all of which, if accepted and acted on would make the task of governing much easier and much more productive of results. Since Charlemagne and his successors, however, did not limit themselves to thinking solely as secular rulers, they valued the propagation of the true faith and the Christian virtues of chastity, Sabbath observance, and temperance just as much. Behavioral strictures with a theological basis found their way more easily than ever into the laws promulgated by Carolingian rulers.

While the papacy did much to enhance the image of the Carolingian kings in public relations, eighth and ninth-century popes also worked from time to time on propagating the idea of papal authority through the Petrine theory. The papacy naturally attached great importance to its rights in Italy, where spiritual authority and secular power seemed as closely linked as elsewhere. We recall that in 754, King Pippin promised for the record to let Pope Stephen and his successors hold the lands which he would take from the Lombard king. He made good on this promise,[93] which became known as the "Donation of Pippin." Then, in 774, Charlemagne not only confirmed the papal right to hold these lands under his protection but placed a permanent deed of ownership to all lands and cities which his father had conquered with papal approval for the Roman Church in Italy on the altar of Saint Peter's Cathedral.[94] These were obviously steps in the right direction from the papal standpoint. Almost casually, Pope Adrian I "reminded" Charlemagne a few years later: "And do not forget the donation made to the Holy See by the pious Emperor Constantine in the days of Pope Sylvester. . . ."[95]

The "Donation of Constantine," easily the most breathtaking forgery of the entire Middle Ages, "documented" how Constantine I, in return for Pope Sylvester's having cured him of leprosy, ceded all secular power in the western empire to the pope. Actually composed around the middle of the eighth century by someone within or close to the papal curia,[96] it purports to date from the time of Constantine's departure for the East to found his new capital in Byzantium. In this "Donation," Constantine first made the pope supreme over all possible rivals:

> To the extent that earthly imperial power is ours, we have decreed that his holy Roman Church shall be honored with veneration, and that the most sacred seat of the blessed Peter shall be gloriously exalted more than our empire and earthly throne, since we are giving the power, worthiness of glory, forces and imperial honor to it.[97]

That done, imperial property "in Judea, Greece, Asia, Thrace, Africa, Italy, as well as the various islands" is transferred to the papacy in mild contradiction to the underlying idea in the document that the emperor is transferring the geographical locus of his own secular power from the West to the East.[98] Ultimately, the pope receives not only imperial status but every bit of the imperial regalia:

> Wherefore we do give by this present our imperial Lateran Palace, which is to be preferred above all the palaces of the whole world, then the diadem, that is the crown on our head, and at the same time the tiara and also the shoulderband, that is, the strap that usually goes around our imperial neck; and indeed, also the purple mantle and scarlet tunic, and all the imperial raiment; and also the rank of a commander of the imperial cavalry, conferring also even the imperial scepters, and at the same time all the standards, banners, and the different ornaments, and everything that goes with our exalted imperial position and processions, and the glory of our imperial power, to the Blessed Sylvester, Supreme Pontiff and universal Pope of the city of Rome, and to all his successors as pontiffs, who are to sit in the seat of the Blessed Peter even unto the end of the world.[99]

Since we recall that two popes particularly asked Charlemagne to put on the imperial costume and that Leo III made a point of giving him the imperial crown, the "Donation of Constantine" seems to make little sense in the context of the times. Instead, the popes appear to be making monstrous claims of imperial power for themselves precisely at the time they are building up the special scope of Carolingian kingship. The confusion is made all the greater by the modern finding that the document originated in southern France or northern Italy, at any event in territory conquered by the Franks. The oldest surviving manuscript is preserved at the Monastery of Saint Denis, a sacred place to Frankish kings, who were its patrons.

The "Donation of Constantine" can have been intended only as a tool in a public controversy over what secular authority the papacy had. The closest thing to a logical explanation for its appearance at the time of Carolingian-papal cooperation is this: popes in the third quarter of the eighth century were much concerned about their rights in Italy, particularly those which Frankish kings were not in a position to protect for them. The document was fabricated to support the papal stand in a likely controversy with the Byzantine Empire, probably over Venice, Ravenna, and the Adriatic coast in general. This would explain why the "Donation" does not give to the popes lands which at that time were under Frankish control (except, of course, for those in Italy), again in spite of the motive imputed to Emperor Constantine of renouncing his own imperial rights in the West, in order to reassert them in the East. Popes during the actual Carolingian period had no occasion to make real use of the document as things turned out, but it remained a bombshell which would later help to explode the myth of complete harmony in imperial or royal cooperation with the Church, which public relations in the Carolingian Renaissance had so carefully fostered.

THE KING AS LAWGIVER AND DEFENDER OF THE FAITH

In looking at kingship in any of its medieval centuries, we find kings confronted with the main tasks of providing justice, defending the realm, and advancing the faith. In his approach to these rulers' obligations, Charlemagne came to be a model, along with Constantine, for medieval Europeans who discussed kings and kingship.

Charlemagne's concern with restoring and codifying older law, with introducing necessary amendments, standardizations, and plain changes to meet new situations, and with assuring fair judicial procedures and sure execution of sentences throughout his realm appears in all his biographies. The biography of Charlemagne most often used by medieval people and moderns alike for a concise, factual and, at the same time, human depiction of his total personality as king and emperor is that of Einhard, a monk who had known him well. Einhard's work, the *Life of Charles the Great (Vita Karoli Magni),* already used as the basis for some of this chapter, enjoys a great reputation for credibility both because of its contemporaneity and because of its restraint in depicting Charlemagne, whom legend soon afterwards portrayed as a larger than lifesize and a quite perfect model of kingship.

Einhard wrote his work using the classical biographies of Suetonius as a stylistic sourcebook. He adopted a striking number of phrases from that writer's *Lives of the Caesars,* particularly his biography of Augustus Caesar, for his own *Life of Charles the Great,* and he follows Suetonius in a more general way by seldom introducing material that evokes admiration for his subject without qualifying it. Einhard seems always conscious of a ruler's devotion to law and justice as the constant criterion for his greatness. He presents Charlemagne as a great lawgiver and judge for his people. At the same time, his classical model's moderation leads him to bring out quite candidly the limitations of Charlemagne's reform efforts. According to him, upon becoming emperor, Charlemagne

> . . . noticed how much was lacking in the laws of his people, for the Franks have two legal systems, which are divergent in many instances. He then contemplated adding what was missing, unifying what was discrepant, and correcting what was wrong or unsuitable, but of these things he did nothing further than to add a few sections — and these were incomplete — to the laws. He did, however, order the laws of all nations which he conquered and whose laws were unrecorded to be written down.[100]

In the basically truthful restraint of this summary there is also some of the caution with which a medieval writer depicts legal innovations by a ruler whom he admires. Einhard's reader gets the impression that even in his long-range goals, Charlemagne sought only to revitalize and standardize older codes. Charlemagne himself was less hesitant in this respect. It was a sign of the immense power he wielded and the respect he confidently enjoyed that he did not resort to circumlocutions in his legal innovations. No doubt he stayed mindful of his broader mission of reforming the lives of his people by amending and correcting rules for governing them, but he did not trouble himself to justify his abrogation of traditional laws for this purpose. Laws as such came from him, on the basis of advice and consent of some of the nobles and high clergy of the realm, to be sure, but they were still enacted and promulgated by him. If custom contradicted these laws, it could mean only that the king's new written law was at a variance with an older idea of law on the same subject, which would now have to give way:

> It is Our pleasure to establish that where there is a law it shall take precedence over custom and that no custom shall be superimposed upon law.[101]

This is from one of Charlemagne's capitularies. The capitulary, issued by the king, was the typical Carolingian instrument for coping with sets of legal problems as they arose. In content they varied from statements of basic constitutional philosophy, such as that just cited, to administrative directives to royal officials. The capitularies increasingly focused on the elimination of certain offenses, which Charlemagne had taken upon himself to wipe out: "highway robbery, homicide, encroachments on churches and on *miserabiles personae,* perjury, incest, and certain cases of revenge or *faida.*"[102] It was still too early in the day to think of abolishing "the rule of personality of the law," that is, the old idea that people were to be judged according to whether they were Franks, Goths, Alamanni, or Burgundians, each subject to the written law of the whole realm, but Charlemagne confronted the major problems which abuse of legal "personality" could give rise to. Parties in a dispute had to declare in advance which system of national law bound them, to keep those who might have a choice of nationality claims from selecting the law code with the most favorable provisions to themselves in the case to be tried; at the same time he stressed the need for presiding officials in his courts to know tribal legal distinctions and to verify their applicability.[103] Where differences in tribal law seemed to encourage abuses, he attempted to eliminate them, particularly after becoming emperor. For example, Bavarian tribal law permitted the appropriation of goods which could not be proven to belong to anyone with less formality than Frankish tribal law, which meant that a Bavarian could claim goods lost or stolen from someone easier than a Frank, until Charlemagne's *Capitulare Bawaricum* introduced Frankish safeguards on any property with temporarily unidentified ownership.[104] He also introduced a provision with empire-wide scope which prevented double jeopardy and at the same time prevented anyone from seeking to reopen a case which his court system had decided at the highest instance provided for a category of litigation.[105]

Charlemagne was well aware that while he alone was responsible for the overseeing of justice, such a task was considerably more than he could handle efficiently by himself. Consequently he devoted great attention not only to court proceedings which he could preside over but also to delegating appropriate judicial authority. His counts, of course, were supposed to function as judges. The familiar term, "county court" has, in fact, its origin in the Merovingian and Carolingian courts held by the counts for "counties," in the sense simply of lands under their jurisdiction. To make their judgments less arbitrary, he introduced some time in the 770s permanent bodies of assistant judges, called *scabini*. At least seven *scabini,* who were supposed to know the law and were empowered to make findings of law, were required to be present at each legal proceeding.[106] Eventually, these assistant judges replaced the nonpermanent jurors or assessors called *rachinburgii,* who assisted counts in reaching decisions in the more purely Germanic areas east of the Rhine.[107]

Both to keep the counts in line and himself informed, Charlemagne regularly sent out royal legates, the *missi dominici,* who were also empowered to appoint the assistant judges and remove them for dishonesty or incompetence.[108] While he decreased the general litigation before his own palace court by improving the quality of justice in the county courts, he increased the competence of his personal court to deal with special types of cases. Partly he wished to reserve to himself personal authority to deal with those crimes which he felt to be the most despicable; partly, too, he felt it necessary to maintain a line of judicial authority above local secular or ecclesiastical courts. It was not exactly that he wanted to make his own court an appeals court, although some of his measures tend in that direction; rather it was that he wanted to use the weight of his own judicial authority against those who refused to accept duly authorized decisions at a lower level, such as free men who refused military service demanded of them in the emperor's name or monks who refused to accept certain rulings from their bishops and abbots.[109] His idea was not so much to review local justice, which was becoming more uniform and dependable through the work of his royal legates, the assistant judges, and reform-minded ecclesiastics, but to back it up.

Kings like Gunthramn, Chlothar II, and Dagobert I had been aware of the importance of their own rendering of justice, but it was Charlemagne who took the greatest strides before the twelfth century to introduce a total system of royal justice. Throughout the rest of the Middle Ages, the justice of the king's court and of those administered under fairly close royal control was to contrast favorably with that meted out by the local nobility in the absence of checks from a king or emperor. Royal justice was to become a strong link in the later chain which bound interests of the medieval monarch together with those of the rising middle class.

Charlemagne made sure that the *missi dominici,* if they happened to be magnates themselves, were used outside the areas where their control of land gave them independent power.[110] Thus he could expect that they would not be distracted from serving the ends of the king's law enforcement. The *missi dominici* also had responsibility for making the counts and the assistant judges familiar with new royal capitularies. These officials would then sign a copy of the new law, which the *missi* would then take back to the king or hold for future reference. Ignorance of the law on the part of officials was not to be an excuse for injustice in Charlemagne's territories.[111]

All in all, Charlemagne counted heavily on having his wishes carried out with the least hesitation by those outside the feudal power structure who owed their positions solely to his appointments. This may also have influenced his educational program of training boys who were not from noble families at the palace school.[112] Although most of those educated in this fashion were destined for the clergy, Charlemagne used the clergy for quite secular ends as well as religious ones; he used bishops repeatedly as *missi dominici.*[113] Still, this sort of thing went against the spirit of the times. Feudal nobles did not take kindly to being corrected or even advised by low-born officials of the king.[114] This aspect of Charlemagne's government, like a number of others, depended on the strength of his personality to make it work.

The medieval king's task of advancing the faith figures prominently in Charlemagne's legislation. The *Dei gratia* element in the Carolingian royal title had already underscored this commitment. The title of emperor, linked as it was to that of a supernational Christian empire, heightened it further, with Charlemagne basing his whole rule on the concept of peace and concord between secular and religious authority, as indicated above. Instead of attempting any separation of the spheres, his idea was to insure harmony by suffusing his government with the Christian spirit, as he perceived it, and harnessing the efforts of churchmen and royal officials alike in the service of the same ideal.

The highpoint of Charlemagne's efforts to promulgate a legal basis for a total, combined religious-secular ordering of affairs of the realm came in 802 when he summoned the leading nobility and clergy to meet with him in Aachen and issued a series of capitularies to the *missi dominici.* The importance of the new legislation can be seen in the type of *missi dominici* used to carry it to the counties. Instead of using, as he generally did, vassals who had few resources of their own and whose loyalty to the emperor was assured through their immediate dependence on him for this service, Charlemagne in 802 employed the highest ranks of nobility, including dukes and counts, along with high ecclesiastics.[115] Evidently he was more concerned on this occasion with having men of rank and dignity use their weight to have the capitularies accepted than he was with any accrual of additional and dangerous power to already strong nobles through a royal position given them.

The capitularies of 802 stress imperial power, particularly in the sense of the direct loyalty of every subject to the emperor. It requires that each subject shall give or affirm such loyalty and confirm the emperor's right to summon an army of his free subjects as well as his complete authority to issue commands.[116] The swearing of loyalty was intended to give a religious emphasis to service to the ruler, and the same capitularies also stress the emperor's responsibility before God for his subjects' proper faith and attitudes. Feudalism, as will be discussed in the next chapter, was less than a century old in any half formal sense, but already the king and emperor can be seen trying to free himself from limitations on his power imposed by the feudal demands which often split the loyalty of people between lords to whom they owed service. Charlemagne's notion that the real chain of command went from subject to king or emperor and from there to God, with others as necessary intermediaries but only that, was offset by his willingness to let the clergy guide him and by his organic view of Christian society as a whole. Kings with fewer self-imposed restraints, however, would one day let this notion develop into the absolutism of early modern times.

Charlemagne never faced the issue of what was right or fitting when high churchmen disagreed with him — of what might happen if the pope commanded that one thing be done and he as king or emperor felt that something else was required. He never had to face it, a fact which reflects the strength of his reign but also its partial inadequacy as a model for later kingship.[117] Charlemagne simply did the best he could for Church and secular government alike and received the thanks of his contemporaries for his devoutness and his thorough interest in advancing the cause of the faith along with his own power. Church reform certainly figures prominently in the capitularies of 802. Clergy were encouraged to lead "a common life," that is, accept the life of monasteries and nunneries, while the autonomy of monastic houses was reduced in favor of the authority of bishops (who in practice were named by Charlemagne himself). Charlemagne also wanted to regularize other aspects of the Church hierarchy within the empire by expanding the jurisdiction of "metropolitans," or archbishops, to the point that together they could effectively administer and control the activities of the bishops in whole provinces.[118] Ecclesiastics were also to be required to have a knowledge of the law which they would need in their capacity as secular administrators as well as of canon law.[119] In an assembly of the secular clergy convoked by Charlemagne, canon law was officially accepted as binding within the empire.[120] Consciously or unconsciously, he seemed to be balancing Leo III's coronation maneuver. If it could be asserted that the emperor's authority came from his papal crowning, it was equally or more true that ecclesiastical law had become the law of Christians in Charlemagne's empire on the basis of synods held under the emperor. This sort of argumentation was foreign to Charlemagne's own reign, but subsequent protagonists of strong royal power in dealing with the Church used him along with Constantine as a model for the type of kingship they wanted.

Later medieval kings were to expand the concept of the "king's peace" into ultimate royal responsibility and authority for all the significant judicial activity in their realms. They began with a perception of crimes against the king's peace — crimes against people on the highways, violence against persons in the king's presence, and the like. Charlemagne moved in this direction in taking such special crimes under the royal purview. His own measures at different times to make highway robbery, violence against pilgrims or against emissaries enroute to the court, encroachments against the royal desmesne, and refusal of military service to the emperor into crimes for which the emperor decreed special punishments, were the sort of steps which later led in England and France to establishing or expanding the concept of the king's peace. For Charlemagne, however, the religious focus of the Carolingian Renaissance gave all this a somewhat different twist. He took under his personal purview not only such things as affected the peace of the realm or royal power as a whole, but also those crimes which, as leader of a Christian people with his own direct responsibility to God, he felt a personal responsibility to prevent. These ranged in seriousness from crimes such as incest and clerical offenses against chastity to the relative misdemeanor for clergymen of keeping hunting dogs and birds.[121] An often-cited passage from Einhard refers to Charlemagne's enjoyment in having Saint Augustine's *City of God* read to him. If much of his legal program did not really help to develop the concept of the king's peace, precisely because it attempted to cast too wide a net, we can perhaps find one of the causes for this in the way Charlemagne looked back to the models of Constantine and, even more, of Theodosius, which Augustine held up.[123] In Saint Augustine's depiction of what it is like to have a truly Christian emperor head a state, the rationale emerges for the sort of program which Charlemagne attempted. If an abbot kept falcons and this kept him from devoting his attention to the salvation of souls entrusted to his care, then it was just as much the king's job to do something about that state of affairs as it was his task to keep travellers on the highway from being robbed of their silver and gold.

Charlemagne's campaigns against the Mohammedans in Spain to defend and advance the faith were to inspire later generations of Christian warriors and ultimately the crusaders themselves with an ideal. As a matter of fact, however, they were not really very successful. The same can be said about Charlemagne's efforts, as lawgiver in the role of the Christian king and emperor, to reform morals along with repairing law codes. What was worthwhile in his law codes was later taken up, when a narrower concept of the king's peace and royal protection served the development of feudal monarchy better. It is an open question, however, whether Charlemagne's greatest contribution to medieval kingship was in this sphere at all. Perhaps, instead it was in furthering the mystique of kingship upon a religious basis.

ROYAL MYSTIQUE: OLD TESTAMENT IMAGERY AND POPULAR NOSTALGIA

In the ideology of the Carolingian Renaissance, the Old Testament rite of anointment with oil had bestowed sacred rulership upon Pippin the Short and his successors. One official, metaphor-wrenching statement made this into a simple, known fact: "It is quite evident that Divine Providence anointed Us onto the throne of the kingdom."[124] Scholars during the whole Carolingian era enhanced the charisma of kingship with Biblical allusions. Comparisons of the Frankish armies with those of the Hebrews before Jericho and the adoption of the term "people of God" for the Franks in the 740s were only the beginning. Alcuin gave Charlemagne "not only the name, but also the dignity of the biblical king David,"[125] and others amplified Hebrew associations for their Frankish kings without restraint. Angilbert, or perhaps another ecclesiastic and poet at Charlemagne's court, could compare his master to King David and, going unconsciously beyond the Hebrew tradition back into that of the pagan Near East, to the sun itself:

> King Charles is letting the luster of his name shine brightly to the stars. As the sun sheds light with his rays, David illuminates the lands with his great and devout majesty.[126]

Old Testament phraseology in general and the name of David in particular were applied to Charlemagne's youngest son, Louis the Pious, who became sole ruler of the Franks when the emperor's other sons died before his own death in 814. Thegan, who wrote the first biography of Louis, went to some trouble to show how younger and youngest sons in the Old Testament, such as Adam's Abel and Isaac's Jacob, were often preferred by God above their brothers.[127] When Louis showed Pope Stephen IV all due honor near Rheims by prostrating himself three times before him, the pope responded: "Praised be our Lord God, who has given our eyes a second King David to see."[128] As things turned out, it was more in his troubles than in his accomplishments that Louis the Pious resembled King David. Thegan chose not to stress this point, but it was picked up and even interpreted in Louis's favor by another contemporary biographer, generally called "The Astronomer," who saw Louis "imitating the example of the blessed David, who was badly mistreated and wounded by his son, but who was still struck by great grief at his death.[129]

The sacred nature of kingship and the sacred nature of the priesthood were held to be akin but different in both the Merovingian and Carolingian periods. Sacerdotal appellations for Merovingian kings were rare, even in the purely literary sources. Of all the kings discussed by Gregory and Fredegar, only Gunthramn appeared a time or two to combine priestly with royal functions.[130] The few explicit references to a Merovingian priest and king in one person have more the look of rhetorical flourishes than politically significant designations. Fortunatus, for example, once honored Childebert II as a Melchisidek.[131] Taken literally, this would have meant that Childebert was being given the royal-sacerdotal title which Gelasius I had found quite inappropriate for the Christian era; however, there is no indication that this was anything more than a figure of speech in the context of the times. In the Carolingian era, the attribution of being at once priest and king begins to sound more serious. Pope Stephan III, at a time when he needed the aid of Charlemagne and Karlomann, referred to them in biblical phraseology as coming from an entire "holy, royal, and sacerdotal race."[132] The Lombard historian, Paulus Diaconus, called Charlemagne *rex et sacerdos*,[133] and yet, for all Charlemagne's functions as governor in Church affairs as well as secular ones, the rhetoric of his own court gave no more than a figurative force to the idea of a priest-king in the ruler's person. In Alcuin's words: "He is a king in his power, a priest in his sermon."[134] Charlemagne did not hesitate to enter into theological decision making, as he did, for example, in presiding at the Council of Frankfurt in 794, which dealt with the matter of image-worship as allegedly practiced in the East; but even when he took a hand in formulating doctrine, he clearly recognized a division of authority with the papacy in which each partner had plenty to do without infringing on the rights and duties of the other. In fact, it was largely for overstepping the bounds of secular rulership and laying claim to divine attributes that his own *Libri Carolini* condemned Byzantine rulers.[135]

This distinction was also clear in the Old Testament model which the Carolingians used. While King David was the Lord's anointed and even wrote Psalms, he was not a priest and assumed no ritual function. It is true that "The Astronomer" said of Louis the Pious: ". . . he was more of a priest than a king,"[136] but even here the reference is to the ruler's use of secular authority to reform the life styles of the clergy and his allocation of money to Church projects, together with his protection of Church interests in his realm. The same source compared Louis at one point to Job of the Old Testament and indicates that God rewarded him for his faith and perseverance by striking down enemies whom he could not conquer by force of arms[137]; but this, too, is something quite different from casting him in a sacerdotal role.

Ninth-century commentators on kingship tended to write as if they had before them lists of good and bad royal attributes taken from the Old Testament. With little disagreement, they exhort kings to further justice by preserving the law and obeying it themselves; to protect widows, orphans, and other helpless persons; and to stand in fear of God, who gives and takes away royal power.

In a rather typical treatment of kingship for the later Carolingian period, Cathwulf, who refers to the ruler as God's regent or vicar in the limited context of having responsibility on earth for the enforcement of God's laws and the advancement of the Church, counts off the characteristics a true king should have:

> Eight pillars support the rule of a just king: the first is truth in the exercise of kingship; the second, patient forebearing in conducting all his affairs; the third, generosity in rewarding service; the fourth, a convincing way with words; the fifth, correction and restraint of criminals; the sixth, elevation and public praise of good men; the seventh, lightness of taxes levied on his people; the eighth, equal justice to rich and poor.[138]

In a similar vein, Jonas of Orleans drives home the point that the king must provide his people with peace and justice, defend the faith, and keep himself from getting carried away by the glory of his office:

> It is the particular function of the king to govern God's people, to rule with equity and justice, and to try hard to ensure peace and harmony. First of all, he should be the defender of the churches and the clergy. . . . With arms and through the Church of Christ he should assure the protection of widows, orphans, other poor persons, and each and all that lack the means to defend themselves. . . . He is to know that it is God's doing and not man's which has committed these responsibilities to him. . . . It follows that those, too, who have power under the king . . . must recognize Christ's people as equal to themselves by nature . . . and will administer justly, not injuring them with arbitrary measures, nor requiring tribute of them, nor oppressing them for the sake of their own glory, for such things are not part of justice, but rather of tyranny and the unjust exercise of power.[139]

Hebrew kingship as such stands out in the history of the ancient Near East as having been conditional, if not constitutional, monarchy. Hebrew kings, unlike their Egyptian or Assyrian counterparts, were distinctly under the law. They were subject to considerable control by the priests and even more by the prophets, who could rebuke them and, in rare instances, call for their removal as a consequence of shameless behavior and violations of God's laws. Contrary to a widespread present-day belief, the Old Testament does not give the divine right of kings an unqualified endorsement. Jehovah's sanction of kingship is, in fact, a backhanded one at the outset: the Children of Israel had earlier had no need for kings, but since they stupidly wanted them in imitation of foreign peoples they would get them, and they would be sorry.[140] On the other hand, since God loved the Children of Israel, He would not allow their kings to get completely out of hand either. Kings were anointed of God, all right, but the special relationship between God and the Hebrew people meant that their kings had special responsibilities for their subjects' well-being. If they ruled unjustly they betrayed their trust, and their unction would not protect them. Saint Augustine's idea that without justice royal government is nothing but robbery on a grand scale fits in perfectly with the Old Testament conception of kingship and was frequently cited by writers in the later Carolingian age.[141]

The validity of the Old Testament model for Carolingian kingship is further reflected in the fact that Pippin and Charlemagne, who were themselves ideal rulers in the eyes of their contemporaries and later generations, allowed their exercise of power to be confined by the same set of boundaries as their Hebrew counterparts: acknowledgment of the supremacy of God's law over them as over other mortals; a policy of heeding the wishes of the papacy and the institutional Church, which had taken the place of the Old Testament priesthood, in formulating their programs; and the assumption of a paternalistic role toward their subjects.

In an age which set great store by names as invoking the essence of the thing pronounced, there was great stress on the name of "king" as containing justice in itself.[142] The connection between the names of "king" and "justice" was crystal clear to those who, like Jonas of Orleans saw *rex* derived from doing *recte* (rightly, righteously, or justly).[143] Saint Isidore, easily the most authoritative source of etymologies in the Carolingian age, derived *rex* from *regendum* (ruling), as had Saint Augustine, on the basis of a long tradition before him, but he gave a positive twist to his source's derivation by adding:

> Whoever fails to right things does not rule. A king who acts rightly will thus keep the name of king; falling into abuses, he will lose it.[144]

The fate of Old Testament kings — the just who prospered and the unjust who were cast down — remained as an inspiration for rulers to exercise royal courage and mercy and as a warning against royal arrogance and capriciousness in the later Carolingian age. Exactly how tyrants were to be cast down, that is, who had the authority to rise against them and when, was left rather vague, but then the more sophisticated and refined theories of kingship in the twelfth century never tackled that problem effectively either.

For all its conditional aspects, the Old Testament model did not allow for meaningful limitation of kingship rights through secular institutional checks. The people remained as the objects of great royal concern in the ideal image of Carolingian as of Old Testament kingship, but the model did not give the people any share by right in the lawgiving process or in imposing restraints on royal action. In practice, the scope of Church activity and the self-imposed commitment to further the faith and cooperate with the Church were the strongest forces limiting kingship under the first three Carolingian rulers.[145] By the late ninth century, Carolingian kingship became so weakened by the growing difficulties of keeping the peace at home, coping with powerful feudal lords who reasserted their independence, and repelling foreign invaders, that institutional limitations on royal power did not seem very important. What borders were set to Carolingian kingship thus arose from voluntary restraints in the earlier period and from factual helplessness in the later one.

Although the power of the Carolingians was waning in the later ninth century, the name of King David and imagery from the Old Testament were associated with their house until the end. One work from the Carolingian twilight period is of particular interest for its display of popular longing for an effective ruler and its larger-than-life-size depiction of the greatest Carolingian as a model of kingship. The combination provides an immensely effective mirror of princes; in fact, it is probably the most convincing as well as the most readable work of that genre before the twelfth century. This is the *Deeds of Charles (Gesta Karoli),* written by the monk Notker the Stutterer about seventy years after Charlemagne's death for his descendant, Charles III.[146]

King David is so much on Notker's mind that he appears in both likely and unlikely places in the *Deeds of Charles.* Notker tells the story of how Charlemagne's father, Pippin, once heard his own short size disparaged among seditious members of the nobility. Showing his figurative kinship with the Old Testament giant-killer, he decapitated with a single stroke of his sword both a lion and a bull which the lion had thrown to the ground:

> "Does it perhaps seem possible to you now," he asked, "that I am your master? Haven't you heard what little David did with that giant Goliath. . . ?" Then they fell to the ground, as if struck by a thunderbolt, saying: "Who but a madman could stand in the way as Your Highness rules over mortals?"[147]

In describing the magnificence of Charlemagne and the imperial family, attended by Frankish magnates from far and wide, Notker, like Angilbert long before, brings together the sun and King David. The scene, incidentally, is one in which emissaries from the Byzantine Empire, where Charlemagne's own representatives had been treated with neglect, are put in their places. Charlemagne, standing by a window and adorned with gems, "was sending forth rays as the sun at sunrise." The splendor of the emperor and his assemblage was such "that if David had been present he would have had every reason to burst into song. . . ."[148]

After Charlemagne's death, Notker notes, the fierce Normans were still cowed "in the same manner in which neighboring peoples, subdued by David's firm hand, continued to pay tribute to his peace-loving son, Solomon. . . ."[149] As the biblical parallel suggested, the Normans continued to defer to Louis the Pious just as long as the spell lasted. Having made Louis the Pious into the Frankish counterpart of King Solomon, Notker begins to extend the parallel from Hebrew dynastic history further. Upon the death of Louis, the kingdom is threatened by invaders whom Notker compares to the dissidents who rose against King Rehoboam, Solomon's son, saying, " 'What share do we have in David; what have we inherited in the son of Jesse?' "[150] At this point in time, however, Notker terminates the drawing of parallels between Frankish and Old Testament kings, and none too soon, for three verses later in the Book of Kings, which he is citing, Israel deserts the House of David permanently. Writing in the days of the hapless Charles the Fat, whose incompetence and uninspiring personality would soon cost him the crown, Notker may have been reminded in spite of himself that the parallel between the dynasties did extend further and that division and strife was the undoing of the Carolingians as it was of the Hebrew rulers.[151]

Notker does not trouble his narrative with any analysis of sacred aspects of Frankish kingship, but the personal relationship between God and Charlemagne looms very large in his work. Charlemagne serves God willingly and draws on God's help in running the empire. The king's intimate relation with God in some ways gives him a more special status than would an official priestly role in itself. When Charlemagne names a man to succeed a deceased bishop, for example, and the new appointee celebrates with feasting and drinking to the point that he is among the missing next time when the clergy at court chant responses, the emperor removes the previously favored "proud man who showed neither fear nor honor either for God or His special friend."[152] Alcuin had reasoned that since God had established the imperial office for His purposes, He would grant power and wisdom to the man He had chosen to fill it.[153] There is a certain overlapping of this idea with the old Germanic notion of a king's *Heil,* or charisma, according to which the personal superiority of the king and his good standing with the gods reinforced each other in making him suited for his role. In both instances God or the gods let the king see and understand things which remained hidden to his subjects.

As king, Notker's Charlemagne shows uncanny powers of perception: on seeing some Norman ships off the coast one morning, he alone can tell from their speed and the way they are rigged that they belong to enemies and pirates, while all the other Franks with him go far afield with their guesses.[154] On the other hand, his Norman enemies seem to know that Charlemagne is no ordinary leader and flee in the belief ". . . that all their arms would be dulled on him or would smash apart in the tiniest pieces."[155] The power of Charlemagne's glances and words borders on the supernatural: Notker tells how a "lightning bolt" from the emperor's angry eyes struck an offending bishop senseless to the floor.[156] On another occasion, it is Charlemagne, "the wisest of men," and not a bishop, who interprets a sign in the form of a cattle epidemic sent by God ". . . either as a test of Israel, of the sort found in the Scriptures, or as punishment for our sins," and calls off a military expedition.[157]

Considerable Carolingian legislation, we recall, had gone into attempts at reforming the morals of the clergy. In Notker's work, Charlemagne watches over the conduct of bishops and priests as "Justice's strictest investigator." On one occasion, he sends officials to test a priest rumored to be guilty of fornication: they surprise him early one morning and require him to celebrate a mass without a chance for previous confession and absolution. A terrible fever overcomes the priest, and he dies forthwith.[158] Notker does not say exactly that Charlemagne has subjected the priest to a version of trial by ordeal thought up by himself and enforced by God, but this is certainly the general impression which the story makes.

But while Notker lets Charlemagne assume something of a higher bishop's role to correct the clergy,[159] he tells another story to illustrate the gross impropriety of a bishop's wish to appropriate a little royal splendor for himself. While Charlemagne is off fighting the Avars, a bishop whom he has left at court to protect Queen Hildegard gradually becomes so bold that he asks her if he might hold the king's scepter on a festive state occasion. Hildegard minimizes the seriousness of the incident, but Charlemagne upon his return sternly and publicly puts the erring bishop in his place without naming him:

> Bishops are supposed to have contempt for this world and awake a desire in others for Heavenly things by their example. Now, however, they have been corrupted beyond other mortals to the extent that one of them, not content with the most choice episcopate in Germany, which he holds, has desired to take up Our scepter, the golden one which We carry as the sign of rulership. . . .[160]

It seems that, for Notker, the king's occasional role as a bishop over bishops implies no obligation of even small, symbolic reciprocity.

In Notker's portrait of the ideal king, Charlemagne's uncanny perceptions and inspired decisions shade off into plainer forms of mental and physical superiority. Charlemagne can see, for example, that a very unlikely looking informant whom others want to ignore is worth hearing, and thus he discovers a plot on his life.[161] He has a keen sense of what is appropriate royal splendor and what, on the other hand, is stupid extravagance. He is "the best at sports among the most athletic Franks,"[162] which in itself would not be a sign of special grace, were it not for the fact that it fits in too well with the way Charlemagne's grandson, Louis II (Louis the German), is described as breaking swords with his bare hands and with Pippin's sword wielding in imitation of David — depictions which let Carolingian feats of strength go beyond ordinary mortal limits.[163]

True to the Old Testament model of kingship, Notker's Charlemagne is merciful when no harm is likely to result but ferocious and even genocidal when dealing with a serious threat to the peace of his realm. He is able to forgive sleeping sentries, when he is sure that they have learned their lesson,[164] but he shows no mercy to invaders, evidently Slavs in his mind, who have devastated the northeastern parts of his dominion. Notker described Charlemagne personally measuring captive children of the invading tribes with a sword and sending off those who were taller than its length to be executed. There is no factual basis for such an incident, nor even a record of any Slavic attacks during the period he indicates. Instead, Notker seems to have incorporated this sort of atrocity from earlier Franks' stories of their rulers, to illustrate that element of necessary severity in kingship.[165] In general, medieval writers who dealt with kingship had no compunctions about consigning captives of dangerous tribes in mass to the fate of the Hazorites, the Anakim, and other enemies of the Israelites in the Old Testament.[166] As we will see, even the eminently civilized and sophisticated John of Salisbury, writing at the height of the Renaissance of the Twelfth Century, could confirm the wisdom of backing up royal pacification efforts by annihilating Welsh children.

Notker's borrowing of incidents from other biographies to round out the *Deeds of Charles* is symptomatic of the greater need he felt to depict an ideal king than to keep events in the stories they belonged to. A problem with the whole Carolingian conception of kingship, however, was that it took a larger-than-life-size king to fill simultaneously the roles of dispensing justice, administering the demesne, defending the realm, advancing the faith, building great edifices, and looking after the enlightenment of his people — generally with a minimum of assistance. Notker has Charlemagne personally administering his demesne with careful attention to its productivity and personally overseeing construction projects. In fact, in all the great royal undertakings, it is only the educational one in which Notker recognizes the apt and successful efforts of the king's helpers. Even in the schoolroom, however, Notker paints a remarkable portrait of Charlemagne on a visit, arranging the good pupils of modest background on his right hand and the lazy pupils of noble background on his left in a conscious imitation of Christ with the saved on his right hand and the damned on his left at the Day of Judgment. The emperor then personally praises and condemns each group for the quality of its letters and poems in truly apocalyptic terms.[167]

All in all, it seems that in too many places it is only the great king's presence which yields action on the spot; in his absence, the wheels of the Carolingian Empire are likely to stop turning. Notker mentions the administrative officials and persons to whom Charlemagne delegates authority, particularly in his building program,[168] but he shows no particular interest in the *missi dominici* or other institutional mainstays of Carolingian kingship from the later eighth and ninth centuries. They evidently made so little impression on him in his own day that it did not occur to him that Charlemagne's use of them could have had much to do with making his government function as it was supposed to.

Notker's lack of interest in royal officialdom necessarily further magnifies the king, who in the *Deeds of Charles* is thrown back more than ever on his own resources and God's help. In a direct and special way, God helps Charlemagne by keeping his subordinates in line when his back is turned: "Thus God's court kept watch for the most religious Charles, when other imperial business distracted his attention somewhat."[169] This remark follows the story of an abbot entrusted by Charlemagne with responsibility for construction work at Aachen, who extorts money and valuables from some artisans and overworks the others brutally—again the Old Testament parallel—"like the Egyptians once did with God's people." The greedy abbot is then killed by a flaming beam when a fire breaks out in the midst of his ill-gotten gains and he attempts to salvage them. Then there is the Emperor's head steward, Liutfrid, a man guilty of embezzling public money which was to have been used for feeding and clothing construction workers who had been brought from far and wide for the imperial building program. Liutfrid was suddenly found dead after a giant resembling Polyphemus led a camel through the dream of a poor laundryman, revealing that he was on his way to Liutfrid's place to seize and carry him to hell.[170] In a similar fashion, the monk Tancho of Notker's own Saint Gall was quite literally struck dead when he embezzled the silver Charlemagne had entrusted to him for forging a great church bell: God caused him to pull the clapper out of it onto his own head.[171] A consistent theory underlies Notker's observations in all these instances: that royal performance in the service of God and justice is rewarded with divine aid in keeping embezzlers, thieving contractors, and other antisocial elements from getting out of hand. The more a man is a true king, the more God will help him out as he fulfills his duties. This is, of course, no help to royal mediocrities who would like God's assistance to offset their own weaknesses, but it is not supposed to be. Notker seems to sense that the reciprocity of cause and effect in a king's successful furthering of God's law and justice, followed first by God's support of such a king and then by the king's achievements meriting further divine aid, is a difficult cycle to break into. All the while it was becoming abundantly clear that Charlemagne's successors had not been able to develop governmental foundations that would support the peace and stability of the realm. Lacking personal superiority, they forfeited any chance of enjoying enough of God's trust to compensate for their lack of commanding talent.

Ostensibly, Notker offers hope: quite unlike Gregory of Tours with his invocation of Clovis, Notker does not hold up his model Christian ruler in order to disparage the state of the kingdom as the result of ineffective epigones' failures. On the contrary, he asserts his admiration for Frankish kingship as the worthy successor to Roman imperial rule and emphasizes the family connection between Charlemagne and Charles III in a fairly reassuring manner. Notker's writing includes professions of optimism which jar with the actual observations it contains on matters of political and military fact. He hesitates to point out too baldly to Charles III that he is losing his empire to the Normans and to chaos, but he lets the increasingly destructive presence of the Normans hover over the *Deeds of Charles* in allusions to their raids on seaports and the destruction of monasteries. It seems that Charlemagne himself had a premonition that while he could cope with "those zeroes and nothings" (the Normans who fled before him), their victories over his successors and subjects would follow his death.[172] It is difficult to imagine a conclusion to Notker's work which would bring together his expressed faith in the Carolingians and his noting of facts which add up to a drastic decline in their fortunes and effectiveness since Charlemagne's day. Symbolically enough, the concluding part of Notker's work on Charlemagne as the ideal of Frankish kingship was lost before the surviving copies were made. His fame in the Middle Ages rested not so much on his being its author as on his accomplishments in writing choral sequences, the most famous of which was probably that epitome of medieval Christian asceticism: "In the midst of life we are in death" (*"Media vita in morte sumus"*).[173]

Notker began his *Deeds of Charles* in 884. Three years later Charles III, for whom it was written, was deposed in favor of Arnulf of Carinthia, under whom Carolingian rule in Germany took a brief step toward recovery before disappearing altogether in the tumultuous reign of his son, Louis the Child. The mystique of kingship was of little help to the Carolingians in their decline. It seems clear in retrospect that the Merovingian royal charisma, which had protected the feeble rulers of that dynasty so long, had been entrusted by the Carolingians to the Frankish Church with the idea that the Church would bestow it on rulers of their new dynasty, as needed, by the grace of God and anointment. The institutional Church, however, which the early Carolingians had greatly aided and from which they obtained enthusiastic support, did not strain itself to help the last Carolingians. At the same time, the Frankish royal charisma never became quite the property of the Carolingians in the way in which it had belonged to the Merovingians. The image of Carolingian rulership, stemming from the time of the great major-domos, was one based on military and political talent and was never quite superseded by one based on their royal blood. Before 752, each successful Carolingian had gained his fame and power rather much like a latter-day *reiks,* and, in the last analysis, a bit too much of the *reiks*-principle stuck to the kingship of the Carolingians for their own good. In the absence of military successes, they no longer lived up to their image, and the Church and the peoples they ruled simply looked elsewhere for rulers.

Chapter 5

Kingship, the Feudal System, and the Embryonic Nation State

THE KING AND THE FEUDAL PYRAMID

Easily the most significant event in the development of kingship from the eighth through the twelfth century was the regularization of the king's position at the top of the feudal pyramid. Political and economic power under the feudal system, which reached its fullest development during these four centuries, depended on the control of land use and tenure. Such control had a legal and ideological basis in the feudal contract, but it took ingenuity and great exertion on the part of medieval kings to turn the whole feudal system of sworn loyalties and mutual obligations to the advantage of the monarchy in the future nation state where it was emerging.

It is important in tracing the main outline of events relating kingship and feudalism to keep the often blurred distinction between feudalism and manorialism as clear as possible. Manorialism, the system whereby a lord traded protection for the services and produce of workers on his estate is a discernibly older institution in European history than feudalism. Manorialism can be seen evolving from the late-Roman *latifundium,* a large ranch or plantation maintained by slave labor. Etymologically the term *serf* evolved from the Latin *servus,* the slave working the estates, which were generally called *villae* in the transitional period from Ancient Times to the Middle Ages, although the one man, one soul value system of Christianity spared the medieval serfs some of the worst indignities of outright slavery. Kings were manorial lords in their own right on their own lands called the demesne. The story that Charlemagne counted the eggs from his royal farms casts him in the role of manorial lord, offering some of his serfs protection in return for the meat and dairy products they produced on his demesne.[1] The demesne as a manorial entity was a significant royal source of power only when it was huge and could supply support for knights in abundance.

Where manorialism rested on lord-serf relations and the running of individual estates, feudalism was based upon the apportioning of estates. When medieval kings could operate the levers of land apportioning — their constant aim in the feudal period — they controlled a powerful mechanism indeed in a society based on agricultural holdings.

The origins of land apportionment among the Germanic tribes reach back far before the relatively late institution of feudalism. Tacitus notes in the first century, A.D., that when the Germans took over new land they divided it up "according to rank or position."[2] Somewhat later, the warrior kings of the migration period were in a position to oversee the apportioning of land after victories. To be sure, the story of Clovis and the vase at Soissons illustrates plainly enough that there was no guarantee that even a king could have his own way in dividing up any sort of spoils of war. Still, all in all, the more resourceful medieval kings got their way eventually by creating repositories of land conquered by the tribe. This became the source of the royal demesne and, at the same time, the backing for a good deal of the fisc, or royal treasury. For medieval kings themselves, however, the extent of their land repository was the royal fisc. When around 584 Chilperich I exclaimed in desperation, "How poor our fisc is left!" he meant, in context, that he and his predecessors had apportioned away so much land that there was very little left to furnish the royal Merovingians with the means of governing.[3]

The Carolingians made very extensive and systematic use of land apportioning in order to solidify their own power. In doing so, their chief innovation was to combine the institutions of *vassalage,* the personal element in nascent feudalism, with *benefice,* the property element in it. Through most of the Merovingian period the two had been fairly separate. Under the Merovingian kings it happened that men unable to support themselves would take an oath pledging their lifetime service to a lord rich and powerful enough to provide for them. They received a guarantee of food and clothing from the lord, and in pledging their service to him as vassals, they traded in a good deal of their self-respect in the bargain.[4] The actual term *vassal* derived via the Latin *vassus* from the Celtic *gwas;* it meant "boy" and had the same derogatory association in adult relationships which American blacks object to. No man would be another man's "boy" in this sense if he could help it in Merovingian Gaul.

There was also, however, among the Germanic tribes an institution of equally great antiquity, the *comitatus,* which can be translated roughly as "military followership" or "armed retainership." Tacitus describes how the most distinguished warrior chiefs — assumedly he is speaking again of the *reiks* type of king if kingship is involved at all — would gain a following of young men.[5] By way of contrast with the vassalage of the sixth to early eighth century, based on a public acknowledgement of need and implicitly reluctant dependency, there was, according to Tacitus in his own century,

. . . no embarrassment in being seen among these retainers. . . . They depend on their chief's generosity for their war-horse and their lance, stained
with blood and aimed at victory. . . . They actually think that it seems lazy
or cowardly to acquire by sweat [of labor] what they could get by blood.[6]

Something of this spirit survived in the relationship between the Merovingian kings and their retainers called *antrustiones*.[7] These resembled
vassals in their dependence, to be sure, but they were perceived more as
military followers of the king than as mere economic hangers-on who
could not support themselves.

The most basic property element in the development of feudalism was
the benefice. This term originated as a point of contrast with the usual
tenement of late-Roman times in the sense of land assigned to a tenant on a
share-cropping basis. Where the terms of an ordinary tenement were often
hard for the tenant to meet, the benefice was put at the disposal of a tenant
to show favor to the grantee. "The *beneficium* or benefice may thus be
defined as a tenement held on easy terms or even gratuitously, and which
the tenant owes to the generosity of the grantor."[8] In Merovingian times,
the benefice was normally bestowed on abbeys and monasteries, although
a layman could receive one, too. There was still no firm idea, however, of a
necessary exchange of values, something to be given for something received in the bestowing of benefices. The benefice continued to reflect the
liberality of the king — naturally enough perhaps, since the main recipients
were churches.

The Carolingians changed all this by putting vassalage and benefice
together with an added twist as they bestowed benefices on laymen. Their
idea was that significant personal service was due from the grantee in
exchange for the property allotted to him. Although isolated examples of
such a combination can be cited from the earlier Merovingian period, it
was the middle Pippin and Charles Martel who put the two together on a
large scale in the early eighth century, first as an emergency measure to
cope with internal threats of war, and later as one to repel Mohammedan
invasions and win external conflicts. They took lands which had been
church benefices and assigned them to men whose loyalty and fighting
ability could be counted on, with the firm understanding that their holding
of these lands made them vassals who owed services. This was a handy
means of organizing a class of dependable, obedient retainers for the
service of the state. The success of the Carolingian major-domos in restoring the unity and order of the Frankish Kingdom while repelling the Moors
stemmed in considerable part from exactly this policy. Cavalry may have
gained substantially in importance when Charles Martel adopted the
stirrup — if, in fact, he did — for the Frankish army and thus multiplied its
effectiveness.[9] Increased reliance on cavalry meant a greater need for men

with estates broad enough to support horse raising and the training of more riders. The Church lost, of course, in the process, while the new landholders did well for themselves and supported the Carolingian major-domos.

The strengthened personal position of the Carolingian major-domos through this combination of vassalage and benefice aided them in making their final jump to royal status. Predictably, the first Carolingian kings continued to make real and sustained use of the successful invention of their dynasty. Under them, vassals of the king (*vassi dominici*) served as their legal and administrative officers, as well as sometimes their military commanders. They received their grants of land for their own lifetime, on condition of the faithful performance of service. All the while, the hope of acquiring new benefices was a constant incentive to serve the king well.

The fact that the Carolingian kings consciously relied so much on the *vassi dominici* brought about other significant changes: for one thing, the *antrustiones* disappeared as a discernible group; the designation became meaningless and was dropped by the Carolingians since all the *vassi dominici* were the king's immediate followers. For another, the social stigma entirely disappeared from vassalage. The *vassi dominici* were no one's "boys"; they were the king's *men*. The language of the time showed this; *homo* (man) replaced any conscious synonyms for "boy" in the new feudal relations.[10] The origin of *vassus* was conveniently forgotten, and being one of the "king's men" became a clear designation of honor.[11]

It soon turned out that the new combination of elements could work in two directions, against royal power as well as for it. Service or expected service continued to be rewarded with estates from the king, which in itself increased and strengthened obligations toward the monarchy. On the other hand, the fact that the benefices were earned and protected by contractual arrangements made royal power look rather conditional. Men contracted with the king as they did with other lords for services; kings, like other lords, could default on their contracts when they failed to give the protection they pledged to give or violated the stated terms in any other way. When they defaulted, they lost their rightful claim to the loyal service of the grantees. In the long run, Western civilization benefited by the notion that royal power was conditional and dependent on any number of contracts, written or unwritten. In the earlier Middle Ages, however, when the most widely felt political need was that of a government stable and powerful enough to provide a minimum of law and order at home while defending the realm against Saracens, Vikings, and Magyars on the borders and coasts, this long-term benefit did not loom very large on the social horizon. Instead, the old question remained: How can men be kept obedient to the law? Or, looking at feudal relations as mainstays of the public order: How can a king keep the support of men who received their rewards of benefices long ago? The later Carolingians were never able to come up with a satisfactory answer to this question. The law, of course, provided for the punishment of vassals who broke their faith, but this did not happen in the more typical and problematic instance of a vassal who yielded to minor temptations or who took his earlier rewards rather too much for granted at a later date and served the king half-heartedly.

Eventually, for purposes of plain peace keeping, the Carolingians felt forced to make major concessions to territorial lords and thus to strengthen their most obvious competitors for power. Territorial lords, of course, had vassals of their own, and when royal power was weak, it was much easier for a king to try to make a territorial lord responsible for breaches of the peace in the area he controlled than to use the uncertain force of the royal government directly. Professor Ganshof has furnished some pointed illustrations of this phenomenon:

> In the Capitulary of Servais of 853, Charles the Bald ordered the *missi* to take action against the brigands who infested the kingdom, and commanded that no man should offer asylum to them and that all should lend their aid to the royal officials. If anyone disobeyed this injunction, "his lord, if he have one, shall be responsible for bringing him before the king. . . ." In other words, in order to secure that a guilty person shall be handed over, the king has to apply to the lord. Thirty years later, matters have got much worse. Carloman laid down at Compiègne in 883 that if a vassal takes to brigandage, his lord must hand him over to the king so that he may suffer the punishment that the law prescribes, and that if the lord does not succeed in delivering him up he must pay the fine on his behalf. . . .
>
> The fact that the lord has now to be made responsible for the vassal's conduct shows with peculiar clearness that the immediate authority which the state should expect to exercise over a free man who had become a vassal had been reduced to next to nothing.[12]

This was the story all over again of Merovingian kings conceding too much law enforcement power to the counts. Two further factors exacerbated the weaknesses of later Carolingian kingship: decreasing land resources for apportioning purposes and the constant strength of the hereditary tradition. Bestowing land as a major means for gaining support presupposed considerable new land to bestow. The measure resorted to by the Carolingian major-domos of compelling churches to let secular lords use their land "by order of the king" (*verbo regis*) was no real solution, as the first Carolingian kings recognized, since strengthening the Church belonged to their own acknowledged tasks. Pippin the Short had carved benefices galore out of lands conquered or confiscated from rebels in Aquitaine and Lombardy, while Charlemagne had done the same thing in other parts of Italy and in Bavaria. After Charlemagne, however, there was not very much newly conquered land available for granting as benefices.

In theory, the feudal system required that benefices be granted anew on the death of the grantee. Heredity, however, exerted as great an influence on this aspect of medieval life as on many others. Medieval people took what their parents had possessed to be their own with even more assurance and less hesitation than people in other periods of history. In time, heirs came to take it rather much for granted that they would be entrusted with the estates of their deceased father or close relative, and if the fief had already been bestowed on several generations of the same family, this expectation became all the more natural.

Carolingian efforts never succeeded in putting kings at the top of the feudal pyramid in a way that enabled them to keep the centrifugal forces of the realm in check in the long run. Their ingenious combination of vassalage and benefice, however, did produce a useful instrument in the hands of later kings. It was also true that even the strengthening of the territorial lords was not a complete loss for medieval kingship. Territorial lords might pose a threat to the peace of the kingdom, particularly during the reigns of weak or incompetent kings, but they, too, had a vested interest in the peace and defense of the realm. It took some doing to make the territorial lords into the mainstays of feudal monarchy, but precisely those kings who were able to do this laid the firmest foundations for nation states in their realms.

There was no clean break between the increasingly feudal nature of Carolingian kingship and the early feudal relations of those monarchies which brought feudal kingship to its height. This was true even in France, where feudal monarchy was to develop most successfully. It has been shown that during the three quarters of a century following the takeover of continual royal power by the Capetians, ". . . the nature of the royal power, its instruments, and its spheres of authority, even its political exterior, did not differ from those of the later Carolingians."[13]

The art of ruling as king in the feudal period, however, became increasingly that of making the most out of overlordship or, as it was eventually to be called, "suzerainty." Where a king could indeed make himself effectively the lord over the lords of the realm, feudal monarchy prospered, as in England and France; where such efforts failed, feudal monarchy either gave way to other governmental forms, as in Germany, or maintained itself in generally little better than figurehead form over the quasi-anarchy of control by local nobles, as in Poland.

Kings in the feudal period acquired vassals in the same manner that other lords acquired them: a man would become a vassal by contracting to render homage or service to a lord. This was symbolized by the "mixing of hands" (*immixtio manum*), in which the man showing homage would put his hands in those of his future lord. A supporting oath of fealty or fidelity was then sworn to on relics of a saint or on Holy Writ. Fealty was sometimes negatively put; oaths survive in which the vassal promised no more than to abstain faithfully from doing his lord any injury, but attempts were made from the first to breathe into the contract a spirit of positive obligation to promote the lord's interests. A convenient phrase for the vassal's obligations was *auxilium et consilium,* signifying originally aid in the form of military service and availability for consultation.

In return for his vassal's service and fealty, a king, again like any other lord, would grant him protection and maintenance. The latter concept occasionally signified support in the lord's household but more often meant being granted a benefice for use during the lifetime of both contracting parties. Beginning in the tenth century, the term "fief" began to replace "benefice," particularly for land grants to lay vassals, but the meaning remained the same as that of the Carolingian benefice.[14] At the time of contracting, the agreement was generally sealed with a kiss of some sort; afterwards the relationship was often symbolized in the rendering of some small but obvious service, such as the vassal's holding the stirrup of his lord. Sometimes real, functional services to be rendered at regular intervals were spelled out in the contracts; sometimes these, too, were of a symbolic nature. Such services characterized the feudal contract as long as feudalism flourished. For example, in the late twelfth century, the English King Henry II granted a manor and a fully equipped mill to a lesser vassal in return for the service ". . . of keeping a white hound with red ears and delivering it to the king at the end of the year and receiving another puppy to rear." In a similar spirit, Edward III later granted a manor for the annual service of having his chessmen counted and returned to their proper places when he finished his games on Christmas Day.

The right to a vassal's consultation, however, was always considerably more than a formality, particularly for kings. This right enabled kings to develop working councils and prompted the development of royal courts. Since the idea developed at almost the same time that the king had an obligation to avail himself of his vassal's advice before making important decisions, the practice also contained the seed of a late-flowering but highly significant plant: the requirement that a king obtain *consent* before acting. From the first, the institution of *consilium* enabled kings to share the responsibility for necessary but unpopular decisions. Finally, it was a means for forcing a vassal to appear in instances when he would rather have stayed away, i.e., it developed into the right of summons with regard to vassals.

Even when the concept of "suzerainty" was fully developed, it implied no more than being a lord's lord. When the king functioned as suzerain, he gained in authority as the person to whom vassals of his own vassals could appeal for redress of grievances. This was useful from time to time in putting pressure on the great territorial lords, but it did not in itself guarantee the service and loyalty of vassals who owed homage to two or more lords, even if one were the king. William the Conqueror coped with this problem directly for England in 1086, when he

> . . . travelled about so as to come to Salisbury at Lammas, and there his councillors came to him, and all the people occupying land who were of any account over all England whosoever's vassals they might be; and they all submitted to him, and swore oaths of allegiance to him that they would be faithful to him against all other men.[17]

The Oath of Salisbury was unique for its time. All that remained for Henry I early in the following century to do in this connection was to formulate its content into written law. From his time on, every feudal contract between lord and vassal included a reservation of primary loyalty to the king.[18] Outside of England, the problem was attacked by instituting "ligeancy," a practice allowing a vassal to have a plurality of lords but only one to whom he owed fealty (his "liege lord") in cases of conflict among them.[19] French kings were able to become liege lords of vassals holding fiefs from more than one lord; rulers of Germany made a late and ultimately unsuccessful start to attain this right for themselves.

While overlordship was a real enough relationship, the times had to be right for it to be exercised. An impressive case in point is the suzerain relationship of the kings of France to the dukes of Normandy. It all started before the Normans lived in France at all but regularly descended from their Norse homeland in order to plunder French coastal towns. The Carolingian French king, whom contemporaries called "Charles the Most Patient" and subsequent historiography has termed less kindly, "Charles the Simple," became convinced that if the Normans held the coast under feudal contract they could not raid it any more. There was a certain grandiose logic to the scheme from the beginning: if the Norman Duke Rollo were given that great coastal region of France as a fief then he would be going against his own interests to wreak havoc on it. At the same time, King Charles would be spared the impossible task of defending it.

A small, very welcome victory by the French in 911, in reversing Norman advances at Chartres for the time being, allowed Charles to negotiate from something other than his usual position of helplessness against the Normans. According to Dudo of Saint Quentin, Charles' emissary asked Rollo to accept Christianity and told him of the king's willingness to let him marry Gisela, a princess "of legitimate birth on both sides, slender of build, set apart, as we have heard, by a striking beauty, a virgin entirely intact, able to give prudent advice in the administration of affairs, gifted in speaking generally and very nice to talk with. . . ."[20] Along with Normandy, this was a pretty good bargain, and Duke Rollo came to meet with King Charles at Saint Clair on the Epte and accept the terms. Rollo is said to have ". . . put his hands into the King's hands, something which neither his father, nor his grandfather, nor his great-grandfather had ever done." Evidently he thought that this was going far enough, and when it came to a symbolic act of outright humility, Rollo drew the line. Some of Charles' advisers held it to be essential that he kiss the king's foot; after all, it was a very rich, big chunk of territory that Rollo was getting:

> The bishops said to Rollo who was unwilling to kiss the king's foot, "Whoever receives such a gift should salute the king's foot with a kiss." Rollo replied, "I will never bend my knee to anyone's knee, nor will I ever kiss anyone's foot." But when the French kept pleading with him, he was persuaded to order the King's foot kissed by one of his warriors. The warrior immediately jerked the King's foot up high, threw him on his back, and put his kiss on the foot while he was standing up and the King was flat on his back.[22]

Still, this contract was a valid one, and by mutual agreement King Charles was lord and Duke Rollo was his vassal. Sixteen years later, the same King Charles was probably not looking forward to the ceremony whereby the same gigantic fief was to be bestowed on the next Norman chief, William Longsword, but by that time the Normans had quieted down a bit, and the event unfolded in crisp, proper, and eminently civilized fashion. "[William] committed himself in service into the King's hands, pledged his fealty, and confirmed it with an oath."[23] The Norman dukes continued to swear fealty to the French kings and, of course, created vassals of their own, who then had the king of France for their lord's lord or suzerain. This was not changed when the Norman Duke William took England in 1066, to start making his real marks on history as William the Conqueror, while some of William's descendants, even as kings of England, were dukes of Normandy holding that great fief as vassals of the king of France.

Nearly a century and a half later, King Philip Augustus of France was in a position to exploit his suzerain relation with a contemporary duke of the Normans who, even as king of England, bore little resemblance to the formidable foe whom poor Charles the Most Patient could do nothing about. The holder of the Norman fief was, in fact, the hapless, impulsive King John of England, who conveniently provided the French king with an excellent opportunity to make use of his suzerainty. With the intention of strengthening his weakened position in Normandy, King John did not hesitate to do one of his vassals in France, Hugh the Brown, count of La Marche, a grievous wrong. He suddenly married Hugh's fiancee, Isabel, daughter of the count of Angouleme, after reaching an agreement with her father. Hugh and his family waited the better part of a year for at least some compensation from their feudal lord, King John. When nothing happened, they appealed to John's lord, King Philip Augustus of France, to do something. Philip made full use of the position which his title as suzerain gave him.[24] King John was soon fighting with Hugh's family and taking their territories in retaliation for attacks by them on him. From a feudal standpoint, this compounded his guilt. Philip Augustus summoned John as his vassal to appear before him, and naturally enough John did not appear. Then Philip Augustus, with the advice and consent of his barons who had obeyed his summons to appear used his suzerain power to condemn John to the loss of his fiefs in France, including, of course, Normandy.[25] King John continued to compound his feudal felonies by doing away with Prince Arthur, his nephew, who was also King Philip's vassal and serving Philip's cause against him. In reaction to all this, many of John's Norman barons turned against him. Over the next twelve years, King John lost Normandy together with other significant territories in France to the French crown. It was no accident that shortly thereafter the defeated and discredited English monarch was forced by his barons to make his own contribution to English constitutional development by signing the Magna Carta.

From the standpoint of long-term strengthening of royal power, an alliance with the middle class was to prove extremely effective. In the continuing search for means of stabilizing and balancing volatile political and social elements during the period of feudal monarchy, however, such an option was not always either evident or available. In Germany, notably, it proved impossible for the monarchy to cultivate enough ties with the merchant and artisan class to offset the power of the territorial lords effectively. Elsewhere, too, particularly in the early period of feudal monarchy, the great lords were often able to hold on to the power which the monarchy wanted, and the king's most difficult task was that of mobilizing their interests on behalf of his own policies. In attempting to increase their own power and weaken that of an adversary, kings occasionally recruited each others' vassals for service against their lords. King John did this with vassals of Philip Augustus, the counts of Boulogne and Flanders. From the other side, Philip won most of John's Norman vassals away from him. John's son, Henry III, later supported French barons in revolt against the regency of Blanche of Castile during the minority of Louis IX.

At home, too, it was possible for the feudal monarch to use the vassals of a great or middling great lord against him for the purpose of centralizing more power in the king, but this was dangerous business and apt to alienate the support of the feudal nobility as a whole. Often a less overt policy of letting the territorial lords vent their jealousy toward each other or against too successful feudal newcomers would benefit the monarchy equally well in the long run. An example of this phenomenon is provided by the policy of the French king, Philip Augustus, and his son, Louis VIII, in acquiring large and wealthy land areas to the south of their kingdom. During the period of King Philip's controversy with John of England, he was faced with having to do something about the Albigensian heresy in a broad area around Toulouse. There his vassal, Raymond VI, count of Toulouse, had allowed the heretics to flourish in his domain in southern France.[27] Matters had been brought to a head when a papal legate was killed by an inhabitant of the Toulouse area, and Pope Innocent III called on Philip to lead a crusade of northern Frenchmen against Count Raymond in order to restore the Catholic faith as the exclusive one in his region. Instead of leading an expedition against one of his own vassals directly, however, Philip had encouraged a baron named Simon de Montfort to undertake the project.

De Montfort, one of the most capable generals of the Middle Ages, recruited a considerable army (although its fighters were bound to him very loosely and for individually short periods of time), led what became known as the Albigensian Crusade to the south and crushed the opposition with a series of military victories and civilian massacres. In 1216, King Philip recognized him as count of Toulouse as well as feudal lord of other significant territories near the border of Aragon. The great lords of France, however, were cool towards the Montfort success, while most of the nobility of the conquered area remained hostile. The French king gave Simon and, after Simon's death, his son Amaury rather vacillating support against strong indigenous revolts against them, and by early 1226 Amaury de Montfort had no choice but to cede his claims to his father's territorial conquests back to Philip's son, Louis VIII, as crown lands.

The last stage of the Albigensian Crusade illustrates another point of interest: the importance of direct royal involvement in waging campaigns in the feudal period. By 1223, Pope Honorius III, worried about the resurgence of heresy to the south of the French kingdom, had become convinced that only a crusade led by the king of France himself could compel the new, locally supported Count of Toulouse Raymond VII to suppress it. After some hesitation, Louis VIII accepted the idea and decided to treat the crusade partly as an effort to recover crown lands. This enabled him to require full military service from all his vassals, and the effect was overwhelming. There was only one significant confrontation in the ensuing campaign, Louis's three-month siege of Avignon, but its success terrified all but the most resolute of the defenders of towns which might have offered resistance in support of Raymond VII's independent course. It was thus the king's crusade which "established French rule permanently in the south."[28] To be sure, the king died the same year, Raymond VII was eventually given royal recognition of a much diluted title of count, and the last Albigensians were not wiped out for several generations more, but all that is beside the point. The warrior-chief role of the king was undergoing transformation in the feudal period, and in a different guise its importance was increasing. In England, kings made the most of their ancient right to call on all free men for the defense of the realm, a tradition which has remained a factor in English history all the way through the Middle Ages into the day of modern constitutional monarchy, when men are called up for military service by the crown. Even in those countries, however, where the royal right to summon direct military support applied largely to the king's vassals, the cumulative effect when they in turn summoned their own men was to put a formidable army in the field.

In practice, a king in the feudal period either had to lead his armies himself, or personally see to it that they were well commanded. It is no accident that many of the most successful feudal monarchs, regardless of the century or country, were experts in contemporary military tactics and strategy: Louis VI in France, Otto I and Frederick Barbarossa in Germany, and William I and Henry II in England. The relative speed and completeness of their victories, of course, remained conditioned by the size and reliability of armed forces at their disposal.

There was never any doubt from the first that the vassal pledged some military service in the feudal contract to his lord, whether a king or not. The obligation of "aid" (*auxilium*) or any synonyms or paraphrases for it implied that much, but outside of England monarchs in the feudal period were often troubled by the question of how much aid, or, more concretely, how many knights' service, their vassals owed them.

In England, the primary vassal relationship of all fiefholders to the king, which resulted from the conquest, made it easier for English kings to fix precise and extensive military obligations on all of them. To obviate the lack of military obligation between a suzerain and his vassals' vassals, English kings built on the conception of William the Conqueror that *fiefs owe knights*. Every fief bestowed had a given value translatable into the number of knights it could support, and it is with this number that the vassal was expected to appear, no matter how far the fief might be subgranted to vassals down the line.[29] Fiefs were then tied in the following century to the furnishing of equipment; Henry II required that suits of armor, helmets, shields, and lances were to be owned and ready for use in numbers proportionate to the fiefs of a landholder.[30] The special, technical use of the term *honor* in England, which spelled out the very substantial military obligations due from the chief barons of the realm, the king's tenants-in-chief, added to the systematization of service to the monarchy.[31] The results of such a systematic approach to military service can be seen in the kind of feudal contract which English kings were able to get from the same vassals who escaped with services to other lords which were formulated more vaguely and fulfilled with considerably less effort and expense. In the early twelfth century, the Count of Flanders received a vassal's protection from the king of France by furnishing only twenty knights. For the same relationship with the king of England, however, he had to pledge service with a thousand knights in Normandy or England and five hundred in Maine.[32]

The need for royal armies to outweigh those of the kings' nearest possible competitors put strains on royal revenue from the beginning to the end of the period of feudal monarchy. It was evident from at least the eleventh century on that the simple procedure of granting benefices as maintenance in return for services, as the Carolingians had done, was not sufficient for meeting this end. The fact was that royal lands in abundance had to be kept for yielding revenue; it remained the overall desire of medieval kings to increase their territorial base in order to have more revenue-producing lands than before. This in itself placed limits on how much land could be granted from the royal demesne, if the feudal monarchy were to be strengthened. In Germany, Frederick Barbarossa sealed the fate of the monarchy's fiscal independence when political developments running in an opposite direction from those in France required him not to rejoin permanently to the royal demesne any of those lands which had been granted as fiefs to the nobility.[33]

Where they were indeed kept intact or increased, the royal demesnes continued to yield substantial dues. One of William the Conqueror's most lasting financial advantages for the crown was the construal of "the forest" — vast preserves of woods not assigned as fiefs — as belonging entirely to the king. Frankish kings had enjoyed certain forest rights which kings on the continent continued to claim,[34] but English kings exploited royal ownership of the forest with a vengeance. Not only the game but the greenery was protected by royal decree, and heavy fines for violations, which went to the royal treasury, were levied with the acquiescence of the barons. In dealing with royal forest rights, the *Dialogue of the Exchequer* from the reign of Henry II flirted with the idea — generally abhorrent to medieval political theorists, as will be seen in the next chapter — that at least in the forest the king was above the law:

> It is true that regulation of the forests, including fines and corporal punishment or the absolving of offenders, is set apart from the rendering of other justice in the kingdom and is subject to the king's will alone. . . . [The forest] stands then under its own laws, which are said not to be based on the Common Law of the kingdom but on the will of the prince, and so it can be said that what is done according to such a law of his is just according to the Law of the Forest, not just in any absolute sense.[35]

Henry II made it quite clear that the trees and game in the forest were his and his alone in an article of his "Assize of the Forest," requiring that his foresters be able to account even for the king's trees destroyed. Another article extends the king's protection to keep "his own wild animals" from being hunted at night outside the forest "wherever they generally go and have peace." Violators faced "a year's imprisonment, with fines and restitution money to be set at the king's will."[36]

One gets the impression of a modern Frenchman who has heard just about enough about the English heritage of common law and constitutional rights, in Petit-Dutaillis' summary of English Forest Laws:

> The forest is, at the same time, an expression of the king's pleasure and a financial instrument. It provides the king not only with tyrannical pleasures but also with arbitrary revenue. It is not subject to the custom of the kingdom but is the refuge of despotic power.[37]

William I and his half-brothers owned directly nearly half the land of England after the Norman conquest, and what was not carefully granted as fiefs remained crown land.[38] Forest lands yielded revenue also from the sale of lumber, and if lumber was not legally a royal monopoly in England the vastness of the royal forest made it certainly a profitable crown enterprise.

Property and income taxes occurred to medieval kings with the passage of time as means for raising revenue, but these often proved difficult to collect on the domains of the more powerful lords. Louis IX (Saint Louis) did collect taxes of this sort regularly. Most feudal monarchs in France found that splitting the tax revenues with the territorial lords was the most effective means of obtaining the cooperation necessary for royal tax collections in the long run.[39] While English kings had an easier time of tax collection in the feudal period than their continental counterparts, not even in England would any combination of direct or indirect taxes in the usual sense, together with income from the royal demesne, take care of royal expenses, in which personal and governmental costs were seldom differentiated closely. Medieval kings were also required to work at gaining revenue through their positions as feudal lords.

The older concept of *auxilium* as military aid to be given by a vassal to his lord was expanded to include financial aid when the lord had special need of it. All vassals in the feudal system eventually had certain monetary obligations towards their lords. When an old vassal died and a new one took over the fief, the lord could require a payment for the new investiture, a payment known as the "relief" of the manor, which in general practice came to equal the value of a year's income derived from the fief.[40] Lump sums from vassals became customary, too, and were eventually fixed in law. These were, typically, substantial monetary gifts when the lord's eldest son was knighted, when his eldest daughter married the first time, when the lord went on a crusade, and when the lord was captured and in need of ransom. The last of these, when the king was the captured lord, amounted to a huge sum. Richard I's vassals raised "a king's ransom" indeed (since all free subjects were called on to contribute in England) and retrieved him from his captor, Emperor Henry VI. From the standpoint of the latter, the incident shows something about royal revenue raising as well; capturing a king and holding him for ransom was a lucrative venture when successful. While Richard's poor subjects had to pay a quarter of their movable goods to get him back,[41] this money provided Henry VI and his vassals with magnificent funding for their projects. With his part of the money, Austrian Duke Leopold was able to enlarge Vienna to about four times its previous size and establish the town of Wiener Neustadt, which was to grow and serve the Hapsburgs in the fifteenth century as something of an imperial capital. This sort of thing had its limitations, however, since the Church frowned on one Christian king taking another captive, particularly when the royal hostage was a crusader against the Saracens, as King Richard had been. If kings felt compelled to sign treaties with tribute or subsidy provisions, in something like the modern spirit of "reparations," the king could levy a special "aid" on his vassals, as Louis IX in 1259 "for the King of England's peace."[42]

Kings eventually let vassals account for military service with a monetary payment (scutage or "shield-money"). In a way, this was contradictory to the very nature of the feudal contract, in which the lord promised maintenance in return for service; in fact, some of the old contracts had provided for "money fiefs," which were essentially annuities paid by lords to vassals in return for present or expected service.[43] But while monetary payments from vassals to lords contradicted the logic of feudalism in theory, and, as things turned out, helped to put an end to feudalism in both theory and practice, they represented an extremely fortunate turn of events for kings at the time. The income derived from vassals' service, when commuted into cash, would support many more infantrymen than knights, and warfare was becoming increasingly a matter of at least a substantial infantry component as the Middle Ages progressed. The Normans had already proven the effectiveness of combined infantry and cavalry efforts by the early twelfth century. Acceptance of the importance of having foot soldiers in large numbers was an uneven development at the royal courts of Europe, but the trend was irreversible and so were its results. Just as Charles Martell's increased reliance on cavalry had made kings dependent on the nobility at the onset of feudalism, the later reliance on infantry weakened the feudal nobility's hold on the king.

DIVINE RIGHT AND THE RIGHT OF RESISTANCE

As the High Middle Ages approached, European kings and their supporters had a wealth of sources to draw on when they wanted to go beyond the idea of royal power emanating directly from God. Nearly everyone agreed that somehow or another royal power, like everything good in itself, came from God. Disputes were likely only over the matter of the *direct* receipt of power from the divine hand and over the question of accountability, which boiled down to this: to whom *besides God,* if indeed anyone, did the king have to answer for what he did with his power?

To stress the corresponding directness of God's grant of power to the king and the absence of any intermediate power to whom the king was responsible, royalists availed themselves of two themes in particular which had been spiraling around each other since antiquity and which would adorn the Baroque pillar of royal absolutism at a later day. The first theme was that of God's rule of the universe as a monarch, which could be taken to show that monarchy was the most preferred form of government in the divine eye. The second was that of the sacred character of kingship bestowed by God, which could be taken to rule out any contradiction by subordinates.

Both themes could be easily documented from Eusebius:

> [S]urely monarchy far transcends every other constitution and form of government: for that democratic equality of power, which is its opposite, may rather be described as anarchy and disorder. Hence there is one God, and not two, or three, or more: for to assert a plurality of gods is plainly to deny the being of God at all. There is "one King"; and his Word and royal Law is one: a Law not expressed in syllables and words, not written on tablets and therefore subject to the ravages of time; but the living and self-subsisting Word, who Himself is God, and who administers His Father's kingdom on behalf of all who are under him and subject to his power.[44]

There was also the lasting model of sacred rulership in the Byzantine Empire, where the ruler, unlike the western Emperor Gratian in the fourth century, had never laid down the title of "chief priest." Great care should be taken in referring to anything Byzantine as a paradigm for the western world, since a complex love-hate relationship colored the characteristic western view of the East with its ancient and sophisticated civilization, but the centuries-old model of the Eastern priest-emperor was there for purposes of argument when Western polemicists chose to use it.[45]

The rather improvised nature of monarchical theory between the end of the Roman Empire in the West and the rise of the Carolingians, coupled with the fact that political theorizing in the earlier Middle Ages was generally done by churchmen anxious to retain at least some secular authority for the Church, had muted the divine-right themes until the eighth century. Although they resounded again during the Carolingian period, they had no dissonant effect because of the seriousness with which the early Carolingian rulers took the need for peace and concord between Church and state, which meant not pressing any theory of royal authority in a form which would detract from the authority of the Church.

In the declining decades of the Carolingian era, the unitary conception of Church and state suffered as the increasingly ineffective Carolingian rulers heard their supporters and critics argue about whether and to what degree a king might have to yield to some earthly authority. For example, when Lothar II wanted a divorce from Queen Tetberg, Hincmar of Rheims noted critically:

> Certain wise individuals have now taken to pointing out that this ruler (*princeps*) is a king and subject to neither laws nor judges but only to God, Who established him in the kingdom which his own father left him; and if for this or any other reason he should wish to do so he will resort to a decree or a synod, while if he is negatively inclined he will dismiss these freely and at his pleasure. They then reason that he is not to be excommunicated by his own bishops, whatever he may have done, nor to be judged by other bishops, since he ought to be subject only to the ruling power of God, by Whom alone he could be established, and what he does and how things are in his kingdom are so through the divine will, as the Scripture states.[46]

A problem remained, of course, with the second of the main absolutist themes noted: God bestowed sacred kingship necessarily through His representatives on earth, namely the clergy. But, of course: "The Lord giveth, the Lord taketh away. . . ." Why could this not apply to kingship, too, especially since churchmen could be found on occasion ready and willing to do the Lord's taking away for Him? Defenders of unbounded royal power attempted to cope with this problem on several levels: on one, they pointed out that clearly sacramental acts were meant to be permanent. Entering the priesthood or marrying a wife were steps taken and sanctified before God and not to be reversed. The anointing of a king could be seen as a sign of God's own sanction which not even the clergy could revoke. If clergymen insisted on attempting such a revocation, then they were guilty of wicked innovations and were certainly not the representatives of God they purported to be.[47]

On another level, a man who was consecrated king through anointment and coronation rites could be seen as transformed into a qualitatively different species of mortal. Medieval kings could bring about miracles in a way that other laymen could not. We recall that even before the advent of royal consecration rites King Gunthramn in the sixth century had enjoyed such divine favor that broth made from his garment could cure fever. It is true that in general the influence of Christianity worked during the early

Middle Ages against the ancient conception of sacred royalty: immediately after the great migration period was over, "their [kings'] political power was stronger than ever, but they ceased to pass for divine personages at least officially."[48] This fact, however, may be a bit beside the point. No one portrayed medieval Christian kings then or later as divine personages wielding any miraculous power of their own. It was instead the belief that they could tap holy power more readily than others through prayer and the invocation of the divine name which distinguished them.[49] This was certainly the case with Charlemagne. In a popular twelfth-century German account of the blinding and cure of Pope Leo III, it is a rather firm prayer by that king of the Franks which brings about the needed miracle of the pope's restored sight:

> Charles fell before Saint Peter's resting place and made a fervent plea to Christ, saying: "Lord God in Heaven, how could I be any good to you as king, when you let such shame befall me? Sinner that I may be, I do make every attempt to judge the people in a manner worthy of you. The Romans swore allegiance to a pope, and you granted him a portion of your power that he might release the people from their sins and also bind them. What more can I do? I recall to you your sublime martyrdom and your divine resurrection that you may give the evil people of Rome something to recognize your hidden power by: then they will know for certain that you are a true God. Grant me this, Holy Christ!"
>
> Charles, the noble King, fell to the ground a second time and said: "Hail, noble Saint Peter! You are really a divine stalwart of God, a watchman of Christendom. Think now, my lord, what I am going through! You are a summoner of the Kingdom of Heaven. Just look at your Pope! I left him sound of body in your care. Blinded was how I found him, and if you do not heal the blind man today I shall destroy your Cathedral and ruin the buildings and grounds donated to you, and then I shall leave him for you, blind as he is, and go back again to Ripuaria."
>
> Quickly the noble Pope Leo made himself ready and said his confession. As he spoke the last word, he saw a heavenly light with both his eyes. Great are the hidden powers of God.[50]

In the story, the king's prayer is answered with the prompt restoration of Pope Leo's sight. It is the power of prayer and not the independent power of the monarch which the anonymous author wishes to stress.[51] At the same time, the distinction is scarcely significant in terms of the power drawn upon or invoked by the king. It is evident that the king has seen fit to deal with divine beings on a level of familiarity and near equality which would have made a lesser being guilty of several kinds of sacrilege at once. Grotesque as the scene appears, it reflects nothing more than an extension of the extraordinary belief in the efficacy of prayer offered by an emperor like Theodosius I[52] or a king like Otto I,[53] both of whom served God well according to medieval historians and could count on His aid in moments of great need.

The power of healing scrofula, attributed to kings of France from the early eleventh century on and to kings of England beginning about a century later, both narrowed and strengthened the thaumaturgic power of kingship.[54] Church spokesmen tended to further belief in it rather at the expense of more general wonder-inducing royal powers. At the same time, having the king heal afflicted persons with his touch put miraculous efficacy more directly—in fact, literally—in the king's hands. As popular acceptance of the royal power to cure this disease grew, scrofula came to be called "the king's evil," since only kings could heal it directly:

> Come to England to the present King of the English, and take with you any Christian at all who has the king's evil, regardless of how long or how seriously and disfiguringly he has had it. After saying a prayer, laying his hand [on the suffering person], and giving a benediction, he will cure that person in the name of Jesus Christ.[55]

Defenders of royal power could point to the obvious impropriety of seeking to depose or even correct a ruler by the grace of God with thaumaturgic power in his fingers. Faith in this sort of thing lasted through the rest of the Middle Ages into the age of royal absolutism. The Stuarts, true to their divine right conception of monarchy, made quite a point of healing the king's evil by their touch. For the record, their Puritan opponents flatly denied any curative powers inhering in royalty. And yet, after the Puritans went on to behead King Charles I, it was noted that handkerchiefs which had soaked up some royal blood at his execution had acquired value for their healing power; even officers of the Puritan army were accused of keeping such relics and—worse—of believing in their efficacy.[56]

When it was a question of positioning the ruler as the "vicar of Christ," the "friend of God," the "image of Christ," or the like, we find fewer restraints observed in the empire than elsewhere,[57] but the Anglo-Normans could also countenance extreme statements of royal priestly powers:

> By divine authority and also through the teachings of the Holy Fathers, kings are ordained in God's Church and are consecrated at the holy altar by the sacred unction and benediction that they may have the power of ruling the Christian people, the people of the Lord, the chosen group, the holy race, the people of God's acquisition, that is the Church of God.[58]

The anonymous writer goes on to ascribe not only the power of ruling the total Christian community but also explicitly sacerdotal functions to the king. In doing so, he actually went beyond any caesaropapal claims made for Byzantine rulers.[59]

On a still more basic level, sacred objects imparted a splendor to the royal or imperial personage. The crown, sceptre, and throne were seen as far more than the mere symbols of an exalted position which they suggest to the modern mind. Instead, they radiated the authority of a divinely chosen ruler from something within them. To diminish such authority would be to show contempt for the supernatural source of those divine emanations. Sometimes an object in the ruler's possession had an original sacred efficacy of its own. The Holy Lance, for example, which was believed to contain a nail of the True Cross, aided the Burgundian Rudolf II and passed to the German emperors with Henry the Fowler. It was credited with a substantial role in Otto I's decisive victory over the Hungarians in 955 at Lechfeld.[60] As a rule, however, sacred objects of authority had origins associated with a particular ruling title. It did not require any abstract theorizing to drive home the point that the king or emperor in possession of these objects stood above the common run of humanity in his direct relation to things divine. With the growth of the territorial conception of monarchy — of kings as ruling countries with the people in them, as opposed to the earlier conception of kings ruling peoples in whatever lands they happened to be — the splendor of the sacred objects began to cover the territorial integrity of a kingdom. The possession of the royal insignia came to equal the right to rule the territories embodied by the sacred objects.[61] Again, to the extent that possession of the characteristic regalia manifested a king's rightful rulership, they lessened any need for a king's accountability to any other visible authority in his country.

The ability of kings to impart miraculous power to otherwise nonsacred objects was, by and large, limited to the few dead medieval kings who had become saints. For example, an old hat of Louis IX was found good for making water recede from flooding basements in the name of the Father, the Son, and the Holy Ghost, while his saintly bones worked no less than sixty-four other publicly certified miracles on which his canonization was based.[62] In England, however, a ritual developed whereby living kings with no particular claims to future sainthood could have rings with great curative value produced from consecrated coins. Sorcerers, it seems, had a similar art at their disposal, but only kings of England could impart such power to these metal objects in an aboveboard fashion. As part of an elaborate Good Friday ceremony, the king would crawl in utmost humility on his stomach toward the Cross on the altar, where he would place silver coins of the higher values. Then he would "buy them back" with equivalent sums placed on the altar. After taking the first coins from the altar, he would have them made into rings. At first these were held to cure their wearers of ailments in general, but by the fifteenth century their curative power was concentrated upon muscle spasms. Above all, the king's "cramp rings" were thought to cure epilepsy.[63] Thus, the "sacred disease" of ancient Greece, whose divine origins and curability through "incantations and purifications" Hippocrates once attempted to refute, regained something of its sacred character as the object of English kings' thaumaturgic efforts.[64] In a small way, the cramp rings helped to set kings off from common mortals as men entrusted by God with special rights besides those symbolized in their crowns and sceptres.

Finally, New Testament teachings epitomized by the words of Saint Paul could be thrown into the mix of nascent royal absolutism. It was bad business, of course, to pursue them too far, lest European kings be put on a level with pagan and potentially persecuting Roman emperors, but if one stopped at the right place the implications of such passages as Romans 13: 1–4 were quite serviceable for the cause:

> Let every person be subject to the governing authorities. For there is no authority except from God, and those that exist have been instituted by God. Therefore he who resists the authorities resists what God has appointed, and those who resist will incur judgment. For rulers are not a terror to good conduct, but to bad. Would you have no fear of him who is in authority? Then do what is good and you will receive his approval, for he is God's servant for your good. But if you do wrong, be afraid, for he does not bear the sword in vain; he is the servant of God to execute his wrath on the wrong-doer.

Such scriptural support also provided a defense of expanding royal prerogative against those churchmen striving to control or depose rulers, whose behavior presented a striking contrast with the patient forbearance of the early secular leaders of the Church; although for kings and their supporters to condemn others for lack of humility was often enough to throw stones from glass houses.

Overall in the Middle Ages, what the Church seemed to be looking for politically was a set of kings to whom enough God-given power could be ascribed in order for them to protect everyone's rights effectively, but who also had common sense and humility enough not to let themselves get carried away by the exalted power they wielded — kings who could hold their peoples in awe like the monarch Eusebius alluded to, but at the same time monarchs who were mindful of the insignificance of worldly aims in contrast with the task of promoting salvation, like the Christian emperor described by Saint Augustine. The practical political question, however, for the Church in the Middle Ages was not so much what the model of kingship should be, but rather what, if anything, should be done about the acts of less-than-model kings. Put perhaps a little more crudely but accurately: how far did a responsible churchman let an erring king go his own way, before stepping into the role of Saint Ambrose and applying sanctions against him?

Some, although certainly not all, extreme assertions of the divine right of kings were clearly reactions against growing papal claims for absolute authority within the Church and the new use of the old Ambrosian or Gelasian veto over political acts affected with a religious interest, particularly the claims advanced by the stern and reform-minded Pope Gregory VII in the later eleventh century.[65] On the other hand, the more extreme claims for royal authority produced extreme antiroyal reactions themselves.

Sometime between 1083 and 1085, a German monk named Manegold of Lautenbach, reacting against imperial objections to Gregory's assumption of new prerogatives, produced a full-blown theory of popular sovereignty and social contract all in one. According to Manegold, a people places a king in his ruling position, ". . . to provide defense from the tyrannical and malicious acts of others." If he should turn tyrannical or malicious himself, the people should dismiss him like a man who is hired to herd and protect pigs but who proceeds to lose, slaughter, and steal them.[66]

Manegold's pamphlet is a model of clarity and consistency, but as a democratic theorist the man was way ahead of his time. By and large in the feudal period, churchmen shrank from any conscious demeaning of kingship in relation to the popular will. It is likely that the medieval papacy's summary rejection of democratic accountability within the Church restrained clerical talk in general about the political primacy of the people. Still, within limits, the notion found its supporters that the power churchmen as God's representatives had bestowed on kings in good faith could be withdrawn when that faith was disappointed. In its mildest form, this idea justified resistance to a monarch when nonroyal secular authority had already withdrawn support from the king or emperor. "How long should we hesitate, colleagues?" asked the archbishop of Mainz when Emperor Henry IV was losing power in 1105:

> Is it not within our duties to consecrate a king and to invest him with his office after consecration? Should that which can be imparted after the decision of the princes [the high nobility of the Empire in their electoral capacity] *not* be able to be withdrawn again also by their authority? Why don't we divest the man whom we invested when he deserved it, now that he is unworthy of his office?[67]

Such a stance was generally more real in Germany, where the election of rulers by an established body gave status to the electors as holding legitimate authority altogether independent of the monarch, than elsewhere in Europe. It also made considerable sense to those Italians who were none too happy with the dominant role of the German king as Roman emperor and who respected the established authorities of their own city-states, often to the point of resisting the emperor. Not only anti-imperial Guelfs in Italy but even Saint Thomas Aquinas as a moderate thirteenth-century monarchist presented the idea of legitimate resistance to wayward monarchy by using nonroyal public authority.

It was much less easy to make a case for public authority resisting the king in England before the development of Parliament or in France during the Middle Ages as a whole. Absolutist ideas were countered there, too, by the Church, the nobility, and eventually by the middle class, but on a different basis than in Germany or Italy. In western Europe, fundamental opposition to the unlimited expansion of royal rights arose partly from the strong medieval sense of law as binding the king along with his subjects. The ancient Germanic idea persisted that most basic laws had nearly always existed and that any new laws needed the consent of those they affected. The corollaries were that the good king sought to rediscover and restore laws which had prevailed "in the days of our ancestors" or "since time immemorial" and that he should seek approval for his legal innovations. These Germanic principles turned out, oddly enough, to exert far greater influence in France than in Germany itself and were eventually to have their most lasting influence in Britain.

Under the Norman kings, the English legal system had been centralized and produced systematic law books well ahead of any legal systems on the Continent, where the demand for comprehensive law books came late enough to be strongly influenced by the revival of Roman law. In spite of the fact that the Norman kings pursued law codification largely to increase their own power, a result of their successful standardization of the English common law was that both the direct absolutist tendencies of revived Roman law and the Roman conception of the final word in law coming by right from the government (which indirectly aided monarchical absolutism) came to be seen as foreign and sinister to many Englishmen in the Middle Ages and to still more of them during the great constitutional struggle of the seventeenth century. The basic Christian idea of equality of souls may have exerted some influence in checking absolutism; however, it would be hard to prove that it did. On those rare occasions in the Middle Ages when the equality of man was urged in any political or social sense, the enemy was generally the overbearing aristocracy rather than the monarchy. On the other hand, the medieval sense of community demonstrably did work against absolutism. It was a commonplace of medieval political thought that the function of the king was to protect every person in his station. When kings swore to maintain the ancient "orders" or "dignities" of all their subjects as well as the safety of their persons they stated in effect that they were not going to preempt whatever decision-making rights people in different social stations had previously enjoyed.[68] Popular memory was retentive in medieval society, when important facts had to be known by heart and transmitted to succeeding generations in the absence of the written word, and it figured prominently in this connection.[69] Royal claims impinging on remembered customary rights evoked mistrust and resentment — as the English forest laws, curfew bells, and similar innovations did from the days of the legendary Robin Hood to those of the Enlightenment radical, Thomas Paine.[70]

BISHOPS BETWEEN KINGS AND POPES

Medieval kings and popes depended on each other in a way that assured at least occasional friction. The insufficiency and often the complete lack of a papal army, or, for that matter, of any effective measures of political-military coercion outside of Italy, meant papal dependence on secular rulers to provide the minimum of peace and security necessary for the Church to function. Economically, too, the Church was dependent on tithes or donations of one sort or another, which presupposed that crops were peacefully harvested and that labor in general was profitably applied. The Church, like any other proprietor, had a strong interest in keeping its holdings safe from the depredations of lowly outlaws and feudal aristocrats alike who scorned the protection afforded monasteries and cathedrals by their patron saints. Again, in view of the alternatives, strong monarchical government appeared best suited to taking on all these responsibilities. On the other hand, strong kings were apt to show rude independence on occasion, as they protected the Church according to their own concepts of how to do so.

Medieval kings took it for granted that promoting salvation by furthering the faith was a main part of the royal mission. On a slightly different level, the idea of God's protecting His own continued to mean that a king would have a much better chance of achieving victory and prosperity in his reign if he kept on the good side of God's visible representatives, the clergy. Most medieval kings were religious enough to be full of awe before the Church. Like other medieval Christians, kings thought of the monasteries in particular as multiplying the "treasury of merits," that store of salvation-bringing credits amassed in heaven through the good deeds, prayers, and pious lives of their monks. Sinful Christians from the royal to the lowly would have to draw one day from that great depository, to keep from going to hell or to lessen their time in purgatory. A Christian ruler might help himself to Church lands and money if he felt really hard pressed, but by and large he preferred the role of benefactor. If he took away with one hand today, he tried to give tomorrow with another, in the way that Pippin the Short had once felt obliged to compensate for his own confiscations of Church lands by making the payment of tithes obligatory. From still another standpoint, it was natural for kings to strengthen the power of bishops, in order to cut down on the strength of territorial lords. Clerical celibacy, while often ignored in the early Middle Ages, was adhered to frequently enough to keep bishoprics from becoming hereditary most of the time. There was consequently nothing at all odd about the fact that medieval kings generally backed reform movements within the Church, particularly those which kept Church offices from being sold and the clergy from behaving like independent territorial lords.

In retrospect, it may seem obvious that a strong, effective, and reformed Church would desire to shake itself free of royal control. From the Carolingian period to the mid-eleventh century, however, the actual power at the disposal of the papacy and the religious orders was still too slight to make such a sequence of events seem at all likely.

Germanic kings and emperors worthy of the name stayed in the business of Church reform, and bishops in the German Kingdom were to feel the pull between Church and secular monarchy more intensely and more often than others. The development of the imperial connection itself meant closer ties to the papacy and consequently more occasion for friction than was the case with the nascent national monarchies. As Charlemagne had judged the case of Pope Leo III, restored him to his papal rights and received the imperial crown from him, Pope John XII was to crown Otto I in 962 and thus make a German king officially an emperor — only to find that Otto would eventually judge him much more severely than Charlemagne had Pope Leo.

Otto consciously patterned his own rulership to a great extent on Charlemagne's, but as a matter of fact he took more liberties with the authority over the Church assumed as he deposed and restored more popes than any western emperor since Constantius II. When men loyal to Otto intercepted letters written by Pope John to incite foreign opposition to the emperor, bishops and other clergymen equally loyal to him swore to a list of colorfully compounded allegations against the pope. They heightened the charge that Pope John had consorted with loose women by the accusation that he had kept his own father's mistress; they made the charge of gambling in a manner unbecoming a clergyman extremely felonious with the marvelous specification that Pope John had implored "the aid of Jupiter, Venus, and the other demons" while shooting dice.[71] When John ignored the emperor's summons to appear, a clerical assembly responsive to Otto called upon the emperor to depose him and appoint a good man of his own choosing in his place, which Otto lost no time in doing. At some point in the confusion of events, an imperial document appeared which stated that no pope would be consecrated without taking an oath before the emperor,[72] but in spite of it, the Romans soon rebelled against Otto's man. The emperor promptly besieged Rome to insure that Leo VIII, his loyal and reasonably reform minded appointee, would be restored as pope. Again, however, after Leo's death in 965 and the installation of Otto's appointee, John XIII, subsequent resistance forced the emperor to besiege Rome once again and restore his man, who had been imprisoned and then banished.

In enforcing his self-decreed right to give or withhold approval in the selection of popes, Otto I established a strange but powerful precedent for later Holy Roman emperors. In the following centuries expeditions to Italy to order secular affairs, establish or restore the candidate favored by the emperor and set things aright in the Church were often threatened, although less frequently carried out. Under the Hapsburgs, who generally pursued a policy of thorough cooperation with the papacy, such a threat was less constantly in the air, but it did not disappear altogether until the Counter Reformation. As late as 1527, the Hapsburg Emperor Charles V became outraged at the foreign intrigues of Pope Clement VII; soon imperial mercenary troops marched on Rome and ended by sacking the city.

Otto's immediate successors shored up the imperial right to name popes or at least strongly influence papal elections, and Germanic emperors in the following century made some use of that power in the service of Church reform. A later chronicler could note almost casually the control exercised by Henry III at the Council of Sutri:

> In the year 1046, King Henry led an expedition to Italy and was received by the Romans without strife. He deposed three popes who had not been installed in the proper manner and raised Suideger, the second Bishop of Bamberg, to the papacy. On Christmas Day, he and his wife Agnes were then raised by the imperial consecration. . . .[73]

Far from representing a cynical desire to impose his own will on the Church, Henry III's deposing of the three claimants to the papal throne reflected a devout ruler's desire to rid Church leadership of corruption and incompetence. His own appointee, Leo IX, presided jointly with the emperor at a reform council in Mainz in 1049 which condemned simony and clerical marriage. Leo, with the emperor's approval, then went on to organize the College of Cardinals from a largely ceremonial body into a functional and permanent council. Henry showed no regret as Leo and the cardinals made imperial interference in Church governance seem unnecessary, and a few years after the deaths of Leo and the emperor the College of Cardinals pursued the spirit of reform to its logical conclusion by electing Nicholas II their candidate to the papacy, without consulting the boy, Henry IV, who became king of Germany in 1056.

When the fervent and energetic Church reformer, Hildebrand, was elected pope in 1073, he faced the old problems of bishoprics bought and sold, of bishops invested with several bishoprics at once and indifferent to spiritual concerns in any of them, and of clergymen not only taking wives but now occasionally grooming sons to succeed them in lucrative posts. As Gregory VII, he backed the cause of those who reasoned with some justification that the lack of discipline among his bishops derived from the fact that they were named by secular rulers who remained as their feudal lords after investing them with benefices and that this made them immune to papal reform efforts. Consequently he took it upon himself to strike at the root of what he perceived to be the real evil: excessive power in the hands of kings and emperors and not enough in his own.

Shortly after his accession in a work entitled very frankly "Dictate of the Pope" (*Dictatus Papae*), he took the secular bull by the horns and, building evidently on the "Donation of Constantine," asserted, among other things, an exclusive right of his own to bear the imperial insignia, a right to nullify the obligations of subjects' fealty to "wicked men" (in the context of the times the right to release the vassals of kings and emperors who opposed him from their duties to their lord), an exclusive right to depose and reinstate bishops, and a right to go well beyond even the radical measure of excommunicating rulers by deposing emperors from their worldly station.[74] Since the hand of the secular ruler was much stronger in Church affairs in the empire than elsewhere in Europe, it followed in the nature of things that these papal claims struck first and foremost at what Henry IV and his supporters in Germany considered their traditional prerogatives.

Henry IV took up the challenge, and soon Germany was the scene of a complex tug of war. The German bishops generally supported the king who had invested them with their offices. Much of the feudal nobility took advantage of Henry's rift with the papacy to oppose him and assert their independence all the more strongly. In fact, an open alliance developed among the duke of Saxony, who was in revolt against the king, other princes of the empire, and Pope Gregory, who heightened the conflict further by explicitly prohibiting the investing of bishops by laymen at the Lenten Synod of 1075.

Henry had appeared willing to make concessions when hard pressed, but he was really in no mood for compromise. He had become unhappy in retrospect about the election of popes by the College of Cardinals without his being consulted in accordance with Otto I's stipulations, and Gregory's own actions naturally confirmed his hostility. He proceeded to appoint more bishops, even for Fermo and Spoleto in Italy. There were as yet no territories clearly defined and acknowledged as papal states, but Gregory VII had been moving toward international suzerainty for the papacy and regarded Italy in particular as his domain. In response to the pope's predictable protest and threat of deposing him, Henry IV convoked a council of his German bishops at Worms in 1076. The bishops willingly convicted Gregory of usurpation of authority and criminal interference in affairs of the empire, and they demanded his abdication. Their decision, contained in a letter from "Henry, king not through usurpation but through the holy

ordination of God, to Hildebrand, at present not pope but false monk,"
spells out the essentials of the divine-right theory of kingship clearly
enough. Gregory is accused of daring "to rise up against the royal power
conferred on us by God," and of having violated the ancient and accepted
Church teaching that, as king, "I am not to be deposed for any crime
unless, which God forbid, I should have strayed from the faith, [but] am
subject to the judgment of God alone."[75]

Gregory held rather negative opinions concerning the divine right of
kings:

> Who does not know that kings and princes derive their origin from men
> ignorant of God who raised themselves above their fellows by pride, plun-
> der, treachery, murder — in short by every kind of crime — at the instigation
> of the Devil, the prince of this world, men blind with greed and intolerable in
> their audacity. . . ? Does anyone doubt that the priests of Christ are to be
> considered as fathers and masters of kings and princes. . . ?[76]

In this connection, Gregory cites Gelasius for authority, but his own view
is substantially different from that of Gelasius, who did not stress evil in
the origin and nature of kingship but only its natural subordination to the
guidance of the Church in areas of possible conflict.

This utter condemnation of secular rulership is actually contained in a
letter to a bishop some five years after the Council of Worms. As an
immediate response to its actions Gregory simply made good on his threat
to excommunicate Henry and declare his subjects absolved from their
feudal obligations to him. He also renewed his alliance with the high
German nobility. The princes of the empire convoked an assembly at
Tribur on their own and invited Gregory to come to Germany, where a
council planned by them would try King Henry for usurpation of powers
and criminal interference in affairs of the Church. The pope set out for
Germany.

At this point, most of the German bishops gave the king's cause up for
lost. Henry headed for Italy to intercept the pope, who was on his way to
Augsburg, with an offer of repentance and a plea for mercy. He met him in
January 1077 at Canossa near Modena and easily outdid any previous
monarch — including Theodosius I, whose record had stood unchallenged
for nearly seven centuries — in self-abasing and public penance. Some accounts describe him as barefoot in the snow, others as lying there prostrate
waiting to kiss the pope's feet, but all agree that his show of repentance
lasted at least three full days until the pope finally received and forgave
him.[77] Unlike the public penance of Theodosius, however, Henry IV's
submission was no more lasting than the press of dire necessity. When he
was again back in Germany and the pope safely on the way home, Henry
cultivated an alliance with the towns of the empire to offset the continued

opposition of the nobles. The high nobility elected an antiking, Rudolf of Swabia, but the strength of the royal alliance with the towns swung the German bishops back to Henry's side, and soon Henry was confident enough of his position to begin investing bishops again.

There is no good reason to believe that Gregory VII was taken in by the king's display at Canossa; on the other hand, it would have been most difficult for the pope to refuse forgiveness to him under the circumstances. When Henry had lapsed again into his old ways, Gregory excommunicated him again, but the German and some Italian bishops met and once more deposed Gregory, electing the king's choice as antipope. In the same year, 1080, Henry defeated Rudolf, who was killed in the decisive battle, and invaded Italy. After a long siege, Rome yielded to his forces, and the pope fled, only to die in exile.

Henry installed his antipope as Clement III in Gregory's place and finally had himself crowned emperor in 1084, but his apparent victory was as short-lived as Gregory's at Canossa. For another twenty years civil war racked Germany, with Henry desperately trying to keep the bishops, towns, and some of the nobility on his side, while most of the princes and a succession of embittered popes struggled against him. Eventually, opposition leaders induced his own sons, Conrad and the future Henry V, to defect to their side.

Upon Henry IV's death in 1106, Henry V succeeded without much difficulty to his father's position. Having fought his father and even treacherously entrapped and imprisoned him, Henry V now began to inherit his old problems and to imitate his policy. To insure himself the support of loyal bishops he too practiced lay investiture, and in 1110 he too led a military expedition to Rome; however, both he and the pope, by then Paschal II, had had about enough of the interminable conflict and were inclined to compromise differences. Paschal II made a bold offer: if the German ruler would give up lay investiture, the papacy would let the bishops do without their "regalian rights," that is, the secular authority and assured income which they had as temporal lords holding land and privileges from the king or emperor. A treaty was drawn up in 1111 to put this into effect, and it included further concessions by the Church to the German monarchy. All nonpapal estates received by the Church from earlier emperors since Charlemagne were to be returned to the imperial demesne, and Henry V would be crowned emperor without further ado. The basic problem with this solution was, however, that while it was fine for the future positions of emperors and popes, it completely withdrew from the bishops the income and power as large fief-holders which they were used to. The bishops raised such a storm that the compromise was scrapped, and the negotiations ended with Henry V taking Paschal II a prisoner and extorting a new treaty from him which conceded lay investiture to the emperor, which the pope promptly repudiated as soon as he was free.

After more than another decade of conflict and the death of Paschal II and the next pope, a compromise was finally reached in 1122 between Henry V and Calixtus II in the Concordat of Worms. The German king or emperor would allow bishops in Germany to be elected in his presence; while he would refrain from attempting to appoint them himself, he retained some power to help decide disputed elections. The agreement stressed the difference between a bishop's regalian rights derived from the king — his secular power and his manorial grants — and his rights of spiritual office derived from the Church. The king would bestow the regalian rights on the episcopal candidate first, and then the archbishop with jurisdiction would consecrate him in his official Church position.

There is still no agreement about which side gained the better bargain at Worms concerning the German settlement. On one hand, the Church ended lay investiture of bishops as bishops; on the other hand, the very presence of the king at elections was of great influence, and the possibility of withholding the regalian rights to land and income could influence the choice of a candidate as well. In Italy and Burgundy, where the Concordat provided that investiture with regalian rights would follow a bishop's investiture with his spiritual office automatically, the royal loss and the corresponding papal gain could not be disputed.

The compromise reached in the Concordat of Worms lasted for quite a while, but even after half a century of struggle among the parties, the conflicting interests of the king, the pope, the bishops, the towns, and the nobility, continued to divide Germany. In the last half of the twelfth century, the capable Emperor Frederick Barbarossa succeeded in once more consolidating the power of feudal monarchy in the German Empire, but in the thirteenth century the old conflicts flared up again with more disruptive force than ever. Although under Otto I the German Empire had been the most successful example of feudal monarchy in Europe, it fell well behind its rivals in spite of their later starts as the Middle Ages continued.

If medieval kings could not appoint bishops outright, they naturally wanted at least to exercise some control over them. The next important round of the struggle between a monarch attempting to keep churchmen somewhere within the feudal pyramid and a pope concerned with keeping the Church hierarchy free from secular control and responsive to Rome took place in England.

The first three Norman kings of England had pursued a policy of letting papal decrees and papal legates enter the realm only with royal consent. They also tried to keep English laymen and clergy alike from journeying to

Rome without royal permission. Gregory VII had predictably complained about this:

> No king, not even a pagan king, has presumed to act against the apostolic see in the way that William [the Conqueror] has acted; no one has been so irreverent and insolent as to prevent bishops and archbishops from going to the threshold of the apostles.[78]

But in spite of differences over William's policy of isolating England religiously and over a claim that William himself owed fealty to the papacy, relations between them were not generally hostile. With all his disdain for earthly kingship, Gregory had once given William what (for Gregory) amounted to a clean bill of health:

> Although in certain matters the king of the English does not comport himself as devoutly as might be wished, nevertheless he has neither destroyed nor sold the Churches of God; he has taken pains to govern his subjects in peace and justice; he has refused his assent to anything detrimental to the Apostolic See, even when solicited by certain enemies of the cross of Christ; he has compelled priests on oath to put away their wives and the laity to forward the tithes they were withholding from us. In all these respects he has shown himself more worthy of approbation and honour than other kings.[79]

William was thus ranked as a Church reformer in his own right, and the papacy willingly allowed him considerable discretion in Church-state affairs. William II and Henry I maintained much of the same independence in dealing with the Church, but the weak reign of Stephen of Blois saw a growth of papal influence and the formation of a definite propapal faction within the English Church.

When Henry II became king of England in 1154, he wanted to restore the royal independence of an earlier day in relation to the Church. The earlier issues of internal reform of the Church were no longer so much in the forefront as was the question of a king's right to exercise judicial authority over the clergy. The contemporary pope, Alexander III, was no fanatic on the independence of churchmen from secular control, but neither did he want to see the results of international consolidation efforts during the past century of reform in the Church hierarchy be whittled away. The main bishop caught between king and pope was, of course, the famous Thomas Becket, archbishop of Canterbury. In issuing the Constitutions of Clarendon in 1164, Henry insisted that the king was merely recording for himself a recognition "of a certain part of the customs, liberties and rights of his ancestors," but although older claims were in fact confirmed, the resulting package was heavily weighted with innovations. The article which was to unleash the most controversy as things turned out went like this:

3. Clergymen who are charged and accused of anything shall come, on being summoned by a Justice of the King, into his court, in order to answer there for whatever it may seem to the king's court they should answer for there and in the ecclesiastical court for whatever it may seem they should answer for there. Accordingly, the King's Justice shall send into the court of Holy Church to see what the basis is for having a case tried there. And if the clergyman is convicted, or if he confesses, the Church should not give him further protection.[80]

Other articles which seemed calculated to undo the new papal influence in England reserved to the king the right to let "archbishops, bishops, and parsons of the kingdom" leave the kingdom, placed restrictions on the use of excommunication, made the benefice-holding clergy accountable as secular lords to the king for justice in their territories as well as liable for the *consilium* part of vassal service, and gave the king substantial influence over the investiture of high clergy whose bishoprics or abbeys had come from crown land.

Becket momentarily agreed to the Constitutions of Clarendon, but he later reversed his stand. With regard to the crucial Article 3, Becket insisted that a clergyman should be tried only by his fellow clergymen for a crime; if he were found sufficiently guilty, he should be stripped of his clerical status and made subject to the king's justice for any further offenses. Becket's stand was unacceptable to the king, who felt that his own administration was being undermined by clerical independence:

... for it was intimated by the judges to the king, who was diligently occupied in the concerns of the state, and who had ordered all malefactors to be indiscriminately banished, that many crimes against public order, such as thefts, rapines, and murders, were repeatedly committed by the clergy, to whom the correction of lay jurisdiction could not be extended. Finally, it was declared, in his presence, that during his reign more than a hundred murders had been committed by the clergy in England alone.[81]

When Becket proved intractable, King Henry had charges brought against him which had very little to do with the basic issues that divided them—charges which were obviously intended to intimidate him and others of the propapal faction. Thomas came close to being convicted of treason and fled to France in November 1164, but he had only begun to fight against what he held to be royal usurpations.

Pope Alexander sympathized with Becket, but he vacillated in his support of him, urging him to "act with gravity and deliberation by every means at your disposal, with a view to recovering the favour and good will of the illustrious king of the English, so far as is consistent with the liberty of the Church and the dignity of your office."[82] Alexander was then having difficulties with Emperor Frederick Barbarossa, so that he had every reason to avoid making a complete enemy out of the English king. It was consequently an oddity of this particular segment of the royal-papal struggle that from 1165 to 1170 we find not so much a bishop caught between pope and king, but a pope caught between king and bishop. Thomas was easily the more forceful of the two men, and his stature was certainly greater in the popular imagination than Alexander's. A contemporary chronicler told how Thomas's radiant presence turned water into wine for Alexander, well before the archbishop's martyrdom enabled him to work miracles from the grave.[83]

Becket ignored even the pope's call for moderation. From exile he declared his patience exhausted with the king: "Enough and even more than enough, have we put up with our lord, the king of England. . . ." He went on to declare the Constitutions of Clarendon repealed: "[W]e have rendered of no effect, and have made null and void the authority of that writing, as also the writing itself, together with all the corruptions that are therein contained and more especially the following: . . ." after which the offensive sections are cited one by one. In the same imperious document, issued to "his suffragan bishops" in his own name, Thomas excommunicated several English bishops, particularly those who had profited by his exile, for various crimes. As for King Henry:

> As yet, indeed, we have delayed pronouncing this sentence [of excommunication] against the person of our lord the king, in the hope that perchance, by the inspiration of the Divine grace, he may recover his senses; still, we shall very shortly pronounce it, unless he shall make haste so to do. . . .[84]

Outraged as he was at the time, the king mellowed toward his old friend after a few more years, and by 1169 a reconciliation had been negotiated whereby Thomas would return to take up his duties as archbishop of Canterbury again. King Henry greatly complicated things, however, by having his son, Henry, crowned as his successor before Thomas's arrival back in England, which meant that precisely those high clergymen who had taken the king's part in the controversy and had exploited Thomas's absence for their own benefit would officiate at the awesome coronation ceremony. Thomas was incensed at this, and Pope Alexander turned the king's bad timing into a major confrontation by dropping his moderate stance in order to back Thomas with papal letters of excommunication against Thomas's rivals. Back in England, Thomas rather triumphantly entered Canterbury and announced the excommunication of the erring bishops.

It is well documented that four knights who acted as if they were fulfilling the king's wish then murdered Thomas in his cathedral on December 29, 1170. Whether Henry actually intimated a desire to have Thomas done away with cannot be confirmed so easily, but it seems likely. He is recorded by a reliable source as having acknowledged that the murderers could have hatched their plan after "some words of his too incautiously uttered, when, hearing of the suspension of the prelates, he spake unadvisedly."[85] Certainly, the king's penitent act of stripping down and accepting a whipping from the Canterbury monks implies a considerable sense of responsibility for the murder, for unlike the German Henry IV at Canossa, he was not under any strong external compulsion to do penance.

The king's penance assuaged the indignation of the papacy, as well as the English adherents of the new martyr. Henry yielded most of the way on his demands to make the clergy accountable for secular crimes in his own court system. In fact, the only claim which English kingship salvaged for a while from the Constitutions of Clarendon as these affected control of the Church by the crown was the old right of adjudicating controversies arising from Church appointments, which Thomas had not raised any particular objection to. All in all, Henry's concessions brought about good relations with the papacy, as Pope Alexander made up for lost time by sending over four hundred papal decretals to bring the English Church into the mainstream of international Catholicism.

Henry II's son, Richard the Lion-Hearted, had his share of quarrels over royal appointment and taxation rights,[86] but his role as a leading crusader against the Mohammedans made him enough of a hero in the eyes of the Church to offset this most of the time. King John, on the other hand, had no such redeeming attribute, and bishops during his reign were caught in the papal-royal struggle more tightly than ever.

The prerogative which English kings retained of adjudicating disputed episcopal elections was similar to that granted to the German emperors in the Concordat of Worms. When the Archdiocese of Canterbury became vacant in 1205, King John used his influence to get monks of Christ's Church in Canterbury, who had the right canonically to elect a successor, to elect his candidate after they had already decided on another man. This soon led to a conflict: the real problem was that the election was disputed only because King John had made it that way, and Pope Innocent III would not accept the king's interference as legitimate. Innocent suggested still another candidate, Stephen Langton, and the Canterbury monks obediently elected him. John, however, balked at confirming the pope's appointee, partly because Langton, an English cardinal, had not been in England for some twenty-five years and seemed likely to adhere to papal policy in any conflicts John might have with the Church.[87]

The sides hardened. John took the substantial revenue from holdings of the Canterbury archdiocese and forced many of the Canterbury monks to move elsewhere. Innocent responded with a threat to put England under the interdict, that is, to prohibit all public worship there. John still refused to accept Stephen Langton as archbishop. Innocent then made good on his threat of the interdict, from which only the Cistercian order was excepted. John remained undaunted: when the clergy stopped saying mass and administering the sacraments, he declared them in default of services owed and seized more Church property. Innocent eventually excommunicated the king himself, but not before King John had taken enough additional money from the English Church to reduce his own war levies on his barons.[88]

In short-range terms, the king was doing well for himself economically, but he soon found that his quarrel with the papacy, which had turned into a general struggle with the Church as he removed and exiled clergymen who opposed him, added greatly to his overseas problems. He was, after all, faced with massive discontent in Normandy. The Welsh and the Scots were giving him trouble, and his vassals were beginning to claim that they could not serve an excommunicated king. Reappraising the situation, he agreed to confirm Langton as archbishop of Canterbury, to restore exiled clergymen to their positions, and to make restitution for property and income taken from the Church.

Then, in a step as grandly conceived as Charles the Most Patient's bestowal of the future Normandy on the Normans, he gave all England and Ireland to Innocent III, who let him have them back again as fiefs. This, of course, made John the pope's vassal, and it gave the pope the obligation to protect him from harm.[89] Harm was approaching rapidly with John's loss of Normandy and the revolt of the English barons, but partly thanks to this feudal maneuver at the crucial point, John did have a powerful ally in the pope, who attached importance to gaining fiefs for the papacy and who could hardly abandon him to his enemies. It was his old enemy and former papal protege, Stephen Langton, who drew up the Magna Carta for the barons who forced John to sign it at Runnymede; however, John now enjoyed papal protection. Pope Innocent promptly denounced the Magna Carta as shameful and illegal and freed John from any obligation to abide by it.

Taxation rights remained another source of potential friction between medieval kings and the papacy. Kings were bound to be made a bit unhappy from time to time by the outflow of money from their realms in the form of Peter's Pence and other payments to Rome. It was the asserted right of kings to tax Church property and incomes, however, which opened that part of the papal-royal conflict which turned the tide in favor of secular monarchy and against the papacy.

Pope Boniface VIII confronted the problem squarely in 1296 in his bull, *Clericis Laicos*.[90] In it, he prohibited rulers from taxing the clergy and clergymen from paying taxes imposed by kings without papal consent; violators were to be excommunicated. Although Boniface sounded the same strident tones as Gregory VII in asserting papal demands against royal claims, he was in a far weaker position. The whole ascetic value system of Christianity, in the form which had justified the massive papal reform efforts beginning in the eleventh century, was eroding, as developments in the coming fourteenth century were to make clear. This value system had come under attack from the worldly orientation of groups as diverse as the troubadours, burghers, and scholarly humanists. Further, in the 1290s the crusading ideology had caused reaction against Rome. It was no accident that the power of the papacy had soared when Europe was aflame with zeal to heed the papal summons and recover the Holy Land. But then in 1244 Jerusalem fell to the Turks, who were to hold it until World War I. Efforts to regain it met only with further losses, and in 1291 the Moslems took Acre, the last significant crusader outpost in the East. It was not a good season for popes to be making fresh demands on kings.[91]

King Philip IV of France responded to Boniface's taxation orders by prohibiting the taking of any money at all from France to Italy. King Edward I of England went him one better by declaring the clergy outlaws in his realm. At this, Boniface retreated a step and qualified his position: kings could collect taxes from the clergy after all, if they determined that a state of emergency existed which made it necessary for them to do so. This resolved that aspect of the controversy for a time, but the conflict between the French king and the pope was only beginning.

As things turned out, the papal-royal struggle culminated in France at an advantageous period for French kingship. At the time of the original Investiture Controversy, the French kings were too weak to pose much of a threat to papal reforms. They held appointment rights to less than a third of the bishoprics and abbeys of their country, in contrast with the German rulers who then dominated high ecclesiastical appointments. Further, the fact that a greater number of French church appointments then fell under the control of the nobility ruled out any possibility of the papacy gaining aristocratic support against the king in any all-out attack on lay investiture in France. This would have made more enemies than friends of the papacy among the French nobility. All in all, before the last part of the thirteenth century, French kings either had passively accepted papal rebukes for allowing simony and loose living among their clergy, or they had actively implemented the reform programs with the aid of their own high clergy. In the eleventh century, Philip I had done penance imposed on him by Gregory VII after pursuing a sordidly corrupt policy of, in effect, handing out bishoprics to the highest bidder. He also paid little attention to Church strictures in his marriage and family affairs and was excommunicated twice, but although he never made good on promises to improve himself and reform the Church in France, he did not ostentatiously defy the papacy either. In the decades after his death, Abbot Suger of Saint Denis ably served both Louis VI and Louis VII in a position of what amounted to prime minister, while furthering a policy of Church reform at the same time. Relations among popes, kings, and bishops remained generally good in France during the twelfth century, a period when they were sometimes strained severely in England and Germany. Louis VII had a rather ascetic outlook which made him fall into the role of a friend of the reforming papacy far more naturally than was true of any of the Plantagenet kings of England or the Hohenstaufen emperors of Germany. The same could not be said for Philip Augustus in the early thirteenth century; however, he was able to stand by and profit from Pope Innocent's embroilments with King John and consequently had little reason to challenge papal authority. His son, Louis VIII, profited somewhat similarly during his brief reign from papal hostility to his competitors for power in southern France. Afterward in the thirteenth century, Louis IX led the effort in France to strengthen the Church and revive the flagging crusading spirit; again there was far more reason for cooperation than challenge in relations between the French monarchy and the papacy.

That was recent but decidedly past history in the time of Philip IV, who after more or less winning the argument over taxation, challenged Boniface VIII on the same issue which Henry II of England had taken up at the time of Alexander III: the right to try clergy in royal courts. When the king instigated proceedings against the bishop of Pamiers on charges of treason, simony, blasphemy, and heresy, the pope threatened to declare him a heretic if he persisted in doing so. Philip answered that threat by defiantly heightening his claim to rightful control of significant Church financial affairs within his realm:

> Let Your Great Fatuousness know that in temporal affairs we are subject to none. Filling vacant Church offices and assigning benefices with their proceeds are for us to do by royal right, and the grants we have already made or shall make are to be considered valid. We shall defend their holders against everyone.[92]

Boniface responded in 1302 with the bull, *Unam Sanctam,* essentially a restatement of the Ambrosian-Gelasian position as heightened by Gregory VII:

> In this Church and in her power are two swords, the spiritual and the temporal. . . . Both are in the power of the Church, the spiritual sword and the material. But the latter is to be used for the Church, the former by her; the former by the priest, the latter by kings and captains but at the will and by the permission of the priest. The one sword then, should be under the other, and temporal authority subject to spiritual. . . . If, therefore, the earthly power err, it shall be judged by the spiritual power, and if a lesser power err, it shall be judged by a greater. But if the supreme power err, it can only be judged by

God. Furthermore we declare, state, define and pronounce that it is altogether necessary to salvation for every human creature to be subject to the
Roman pontiff.[93]

Thus both king and pope claimed an absolute right to be accountable to
none but God in the area of political-spiritual authority which they left
themselves free to delineate. Each declared himself an irresistible force
quite able to impel as movable objects all other human beings in the realm.
Either king or pope had to surrender a part of his claims.

King Philip can be seen making the step from feudal monarch to national monarch in his act of calling representatives of the clergy, nobility
and townspeople to the first meeting of the Estates-General to give him
backing. This was in contrast with the development of the English Parliament which had its origins in the English king's need for money and his
desire to legitimize what would have to be unpopular decisions. The armed
forces at Philip's disposal also corresponded more nearly to those of a
national than a feudal king. He correctly calculated that he could move
militarily against the pope if need be without serious interference.

Philip planned to hold a general council of the Church in France, to
kidnap the pope for the purpose of bringing him there to be tried, found
guilty on charges made to order, and deposed, and then to assure that a
successor with an outlook more compatible with the interests of the
French monarchy would be chosen. He came reasonably close to carrying
out this wild scheme; when Boniface was in his home town of Anagni,
Philip's followers, aided by an antipapal Italian faction, invaded the papal
palace there and took him prisoner. In the confusion which followed, the
pope was momentarily freed and escorted back to Rome, but he died
there. Philip's influence on the College of Cardinals was sufficiently
strong that they elected a Frenchman who, as Clement V, moved the seat
of the papacy from the Vatican to Avignon and took care to appoint
enough like-minded Frenchmen to the College of Cardinals to keep a
succession of fourteenth-century French popes in office there.

The authority of the Avignon papacy was duly challenged during the
following decades by the emperor with an antipope, and in time it led to
the anomaly of the Great Schism, when two popes, and then for a short
time, three, divided the allegiance of European Christians among them.
As far as the development of medieval kingship is concerned, however, the
point is that the papal-royal struggle was decided in favor of royal power
in France in the early fourteenth century. The esteem and authority of the
Church was significantly reduced by the scandal of the Great Schism, and
although the rift was healed and a single pope reinstated in Rome, thereafter the Church scarcely placed serious checks on the ascendancy of

national monarchy until after the Reformation in the sixteenth century.

ROYAL JUSTICE AND PROTECTION

Where feudal monarchy achieved success, much of it was due to the quality of justice which kings alone, or persons directly responsible to them, could dispense. "Quality" should be understood here in the simplest possible sense: people came to expect that royal justice would really be more fair and impartial than they could have gotten from the decisions of lords of the manors to whom they might take their cases.

Royal courts acquired an early reputation for impartiality, and historians tend to agree that on the whole it was well deserved. Any medieval king, who would be judged himself on the basis of how well he kept the peace and defended the realm, had substantial motivation to keep his people satisfied and loyal. Settling their disputes fairly was a means of insuring both, while, of course, promoting his own status, power, and wealth at the same time. There were medieval kings of the type of Philip I of France, who were too short sighted to pay much attention to this series of facts, or who were indifferent to how contemporaries or posterity would judge them. Under them royal consolidation of control of justice moved slowly or not at all. But even rather materialistic and greedy kings had a reason to enhance the concept of royal justice.[94] Justice was quite lucrative for those who dispensed it. Fines and forfeitures went to the authority in whose name sentences were imposed. The wider and lower the king's legal jurisdiction spread, the greater the royal income from those sources became. In this connection, a king's vested interest in impartial justice stemmed from the desirability of having, so to speak, more satisfied customers and consequently more people seeking royal justice. This was, of course, much more true of the western monarchies than of the empire, where feudal lords were strong enough to prevent the king or emperor from reaching even the middle class with his dispensations of justice.

Apart from its quality in the sense of inherent impartiality, royal justice was better than that available from local lords because of the personnel which a royal court could maintain. When it was a question of using men educated in the written law, kings were at a distinct advantage. The experts were often clergy trained in the law, and these were to be found far more often in the service of kings than in that of the lesser nobility. With the continued interest in legal codification, supplemented by a revived and sustained interest in Roman law from the eleventh century on, the worth of this advantage increased.

Developments in England showed this trend in action. There, as elsewhere, the concept of "the king's peace" originally had a fairly narrow focus, in guaranteeing such things as protection from highway robbery and ambush or the safety of royal officers and of persons in the king's presence from harm. At the most, it provided that on special occasions and at certain places violence would be answered with royal retaliation. In the later eleventh and twelfth centuries, the concept was often expanded to supersede the peace-keeping functions of the feudal barons. Any crime of violence was construed as breaking "the king's peace." At first this was a fiction in that only a designated and limited number of violent crimes could be shown to come under this heading, but it came to be accepted as fact. The concept of "felony" originally signified a breach of fealty within the limited context of the feudal contract. This, too, was broadened to cover major crimes of violence quite apart from those which could be linked to betraying a feudal lord in the earlier understanding of the term. The idea developed that commission of any, at least major, crime could be a felony in the sense of breaking the implicit feudal contract which all free men had with the king. "Alone, these fictions and powers might have failed; they succeeded because the king sold a better brand of justice than competing courts could offer."[95]

This sort of thing was, of course, easier in England than elsewhere. The Norman Conquest gave its leader, William I, the opportunity to reshuffle fiefs in such a way that no older territorial lords in England gave the monarchy much trouble. While the Norman barons were later to challenge the growing power of the king, they did not do so effectively until after the idea of the king as the guarantor of public order throughout the realm had taken firm hold.

Elsewhere the task facing feudal monarchs was made more difficult by the deep roots of local power which territorial lords had used to ensconce themselves during preceding periods of weak monarchy. In France, kings fell into the role of judge in deciding disputes between their own vassals easily enough, but it was a far more difficult task to make them behave with regard to the public order. Several of the early Capetian kings had made efforts in this direction, although more as dukes of France — the Duchy of France stretched from Normandy to Flanders — than as kings. It was really only Louis VI in the early twelfth century who was willing to wage the necessary constant war with his nominal vassals in the interest of general peace.

Louis VI would often summon a baronial vassal to appear before him to answer charges made by people whose goods he had seized or by the relatives of persons murdered, injured, or held prisoner. When the baron failed to answer the summons, his default on the vassal's obligation would be noted, his fiefs would be forfeited, and Louis would march against him. The royal campaigns were long and hard, but Louis had the advantage of being able to pursue his rivals for power at times of his own choosing and could thus pick them off one by one.

Doubts were occasionally raised in the feudal period concerning the extent to which law emanated from the king, and certainly royal abuses of the law-making power engendered opposition among the feudal nobility. Since kings and their courts had much leeway in defining wrongdoing, any noble opposition to expanding royal power had a way of appearing in royal documents as tinged with crime well before it went over into rebellion, if in fact it was headed in that direction at all, which was not necessarily the case. This fact no doubt dampened on occasion the enthusiasm for royal justice felt by aristocrats who saw their own power dwindling before it, but it was not enough to offset the popular support, particularly in England and France. Even when the king's law-*making* power was questioned by either the nobility or the Church, there was no doubt whatsoever that the king as the source of justice and protection in the realm was the highest judge in the kingdom. The view of the king as the ultimate judge is amply illustrated by those feudal monarchs who made the most of the role, Henry II in twelfth-century England, and Louis IX in thirteenth-century France.

Through the twelfth century, royal dispensation of justice was both aided and impeded by the peripatetic nature of the royal court. We recall the examples of Chlothar II and Dagobert I, each handing down judgments in the course of a great itinerary. The advantage in this system was that royal justice remained a constant threat to wrongdoers; the king could descend on them without much warning, particularly if local complaints grew loud enough. The hope that indeed the king would hear a plea and grant justice on the spot, if only word would reach his ear, also served to make the prestige of kingship more immediately felt throughout the realm:

> The king [Henry II] was equally accessible to scholars and to the meanest of his subjects, and if he knew how to delay affairs that he did not wish to settle, he could not be accused of being difficult to approach. As soon as he left his residence, he might be assailed by a crowd of noisy suitors, shouting their pleas and complaints, and dragging the king along with them; yet he would hear each man out, and bear no anger for the almost physical violence offered to his person, although if too hard pressed, he would withdraw again to more peaceful places.[97]

The reverse side of this was the often erratic, hit-or-miss nature of royal justice. There was certainly an immense quantity of luck in who happened to have his suit heard by the king. Also, any on-the-spot response to those pressing a suit would have its arbitrary side. Smoothing the way to royal justice with gifts was a practice which obviously made access or a successful outcome easier for the rich to obtain than the poor, in spite of the ideal of treating subjects equally before the law. Henry II had a reputation for fairness, while his son John had a reputation for prejudiced responses, but even the former saw nothing wrong with accepting a gift in advance of hearing a case. "Men who wished to obtain a speedy hearing of their lawsuits knew that a good falcon was the gift most acceptable to the king."[98] A trained falcon was actually worth a small fortune and plainly miles beyond the reach of "the meanest of his subjects" who might be lucky enough to have his case heard by the king in passing. There was, perhaps, a distinction between a gift to get the king to hear a case expeditiously and one to get him to decide in the suitor's favor, but again, there can hardly be much doubt that this made the course of royal justice more erratic in either case. Like Dagobert I, Henry II was given to dispensing justice with such fervor as to sacrifice food and sleep; however, when he chose to do so was a rather chance matter:

> Once, when a knight from Lincolnshire came to him with seven commandments which the king was to obey, and which had been dictated by a voice from heaven, Henry sat up all night dealing with cases of justice which he had delayed too long, but at daybreak thought better of it and dismissed the remaining suitors.[99]

Louis IX is recorded as having been greatly struck by the words of a Greyfriar preacher, who claimed to have read "both the Bible and the books which speak of infidel princes" and to have found that never had "any Kingdom . . . been lost or . . . changed its ruler except through some offence against justice," concluding with the admonition to King Louis: " 'Let him take care to give his people true and prompt justice, that Our Lord may allow him to hold his Kingdom in peace all the days of his life.' "[100]

While Louis gained more lasting credit for his gradual and painstaking reform of the royal judiciary system, he was known to his contemporaries for his instantaneous rendering of sound judgments. He is cited as having laid down without a moment's hesitation a royal policy concerning excommunicated persons in a manner which protected royal prerogative while satisfying the high clergy of the realm, after a bishop at the head of a delegation had asked for his intervention.[101] By way of contrast with Henry II of England, he seemed to radiate calm and serenity whenever he made himself available to people seeking justice:

> Often in the summer he went after Mass to the wood of Vincennes and sat down with his back against an oak tree, and made us sit all around him. Everyone who had an affair to settle could come and speak to him without interference of any usher or other official. The King would speak himself and ask "Is there any one here who has a case to settle?" All of those who had

would stand up and he would say, "Quiet, all of you, and your cases shall be dealt with in turn."[102]

It seems that everyone's turn came and that justice was more than adequately rendered on the spot. By this time, however, Louis IX was generally relying on expert assistance for legal cases, a step also taken by Henry II of England in the previous century, in spite of his confident pronouncement of lone judgements on occasion. Medieval kings interested in expanding the scope of royal justice could not help but feel a need for officials to assist in making their judicial processes more regular and effective. The king, after all, could only be at one place at a time to hear cases, and whether a king's special avocation was wenching, stag hunting, or prayer and meditation, hearing cases all day every day would leave no time for it. For coping with anything less drastic than signs of rebellion in a baron or serious problems of Church-state relations, the royal presence was not really necessary anyway.

And so it happened that the second half of the twelfth century saw a revival of official overseers of public peace and justice responsible to the ruler alone, those officials who appeared in on-again, off-again fashion from Diocletian's *agentes in rebus* in the third century through Theoderic's *saiones* in the fifth, to the Carolingian *missi dominici* in the eighth. Since the downfall of the Carolingians, officers of this sort had been used in the principalities of Aquitaine and Normandy. Those established by the French kings, first, at least conspicuously, by Philip Augustus, were called *baillis* (Latin *baillivus,* Anglicized as "baillifs") in the north of France, although they went by the manorial designation of "seneschals" in the south.[103] Their immediate task was to counteract the "provosts," to whom royal authority for governing and managing demesne lands had been extended. These officials had come to treat their offices and lands as practically their own by hereditary right and, in their arbitrary spirit of independence, were often hated and feared by townspeople, peasants, and clergy alike. The *baillis,* by way of contrast, had neither local roots nor power of their own in the areas to which they were sent to conduct hearings and render justice in the king's name. The problem remained, of course, of how to allow people to seek royal justice without flouting feudal ideas of local jurisdiction to the point that the barons would be aroused to opposition. Consequently, Philip Augustus and Louis VIII proceeded firmly but also cautiously and slowly in using the *baillis* to expand royal jurisdiction where the nobility was concerned.

Although the legal rights of a suzerain over the vassals of his own vassals were originally as nonexistent in law as his military claims, feudal custom came to allow vassals whose own lords refused to hear their suits to take these to their suzerain. Louis IX interpreted this to mean that if a vassal felt that his lord's decision was unjust, he could take his case to his suzerain. In context, this meant endowing French kingship with appellate jurisdiction in all cases involving feudal lords lower than the king.[104] This was a very useful instrument in suppressing private warfare, a main source of disruption during the whole feudal period. Vassals who were too weak to defend their claims could be counted on to ask for a royal hearing of their case rather than resist with force of arms. In the thirteenth and fourteenth centuries, French kings then had laws enacted against many of the practices of feudal warfare, which made it an increasingly sure thing that claims and appeals would be brought for the purpose of involving the king and the royal *baillis:*

> St. Louis hedged private war about with complicated rules that took most of the fun out of it. Before attacking your neighbor you had to give him notice, and you had to ask his relatives whether or not they wanted to be included in the war. If your enemy asked for a truce, you had to grant it. You could not slaughter your foe's peasants or burn their crops. Royal officials stood ready to enforce these rules.[105]

The constant stream of litigation and the impossibility of following the king around on his journeys throughout the kingdom led to the establishment of permanent royal courts, which acted in the king's name. In France the court which acted on the king's behalf, but which was separate from the king's council as an institution in spite of the fact that councillors were members, was called the "Parlement of Paris." The term "parlement" had signified "discussion," and in thirteenth-century France it signified a hearing in which there was considerable give and take with men pressing a suit. When, one day in 1253, the prior of Saint-Martin-des-Champs appeared before "the councillors of the King of France holding Parlement," he was in effect appearing before the highest tribunal in the country apart from one in which the king himself rendered justice.[106] The Parlement of Paris was to continue in this role down to the eve of the French Revolution, when its judges refused to support King Louis XVI on a crucial tax issue, to the undoing of the whole *ancien regime.* (While the term has the same source, the English Parliament had, as will be noted later, a different origin as an institution, as well as a different function and fate.)

In England, royal government had more of a judicial system to start with than elsewhere. While the strength of local tradition taxed the imagination of English kings, most of the rulers from William the Conqueror through Henry II proved quite equal to the task of using it to strengthen royal government. Experience in governing Normandy served them in this connection as did certain earlier English judicial practices which they adopted and adapted without difficulty. They inherited from their Anglo-Saxon predecessors the tradition that in the courts which dispensed justice on a shire or county level according to local custom there were three presiding officials. One of these, the sheriff, was a personal representative of the king, and another, the earl or ealdorman, was an official at least nominated by the king.[107] William I and William II had strengthened the office of sheriff considerably by generally appointing barons to it who could enforce local-court decisions. The strength of the sheriff-barons made them sometimes undesirably independent, much as was true of the provosts in France. Henry I sent officers called "justices," who were to be the English predecessors of the French *baillis,* through the counties to hear pleas under royal jurisdiction and also to check up on the dispensing of justice under the sheriffs.[108] Henry II made the itinerant justices regular officials with fixed circuits, who heard cases related to that expandable concept, "the king's peace." It is quite possible that Philip Augustus consciously copied the institution of the *baillis* from Henry II's itinerant justices because of the latter's success with them.[109]

The Norman kings found it expedient to share formal judicial responsibilities on the highest level with a council. Anglo-Saxon kings of England before them had consulted rather informally a collection of secular magnates, members of the royal family, high churchmen, and some of the few functionaries of the royal household, called the *Witenagemot,* which translates roughly as "the Council of Wise Men." William the Conqueror replaced most of the secular personages in the sense that he took so much land from most of the Anglo-Saxon landholders that they were no longer magnates; his own family and his principal office holders were, of course, new to the realm. Still, the Anglo-Saxons looked upon the Norman king's great council as the successor to the *Witenagemot,* nor did the Normans object, although they used the term *curia regis* for it. While the court was useful in giving extra force to royal legislation by consenting to it, the Norman kings were strong enough to do things like regulate lower courts and the coinage without consulting much of anyone when they chose. Members of the court also advised the king as he tried important cases, usually those involving treason or some breach of the feudal contract. Occasionally the *curia regis* altered the king's intention in the early Norman period, but only on rare occasions did it challenge him. The only significant instances of *curia regis* opposition to the king stemmed from the barons' being torn in their loyalties between the king and the Church.[110] ". . . [T]he autocratic Norman kings had their will 95 percent of the time but used the court as a sounding board for public opinion."[111] In so doing they both got their way and conveyed the impression that royal laws and judgments had the backing of the most important men of the kingdom and through them of the people governed. As the twelfth century progressed, this body was more usually called the "King's Great Council" (*magna curia regis* or *magnum concilium*), but until the reign of King John it generally served the purpose of giving the king the advice he wanted and legitimizing his decisions.

The minimal core of officials desired by English kings for minor legal enactments and the dispatch of routine litigation became known as the King's Small Council. There was no formal differentiation between those who met with it and with the Great Council, nor between their duties. Kings simply used the Small Council, supplemented by some local barons and bishops when they were travelling about, because the Great Council was too unwieldy to convoke for all but the most important occasions. The king chose most of the Small Council's participants on the basis of their competence and loyalty. The different position of the two councils, while difficult to define precisely, can be seen in the way Henry II used them during the trial of Thomas Becket. Becket was tried before the Great Council, since Henry wanted to share responsibility for what was likely to be an unpopular decision with as broad a group of magnates of the realm as possible; however, while the trial was going on, he sought the advice of the Small Council on possible courses of action.[112] In civil business, too, while the king's authority still sufficed for issuing charters, his councillors served him by drawing these up and witnessing them. For ordinary charters, the king drew principally from his Small Council; however, at least some men who met with the Great Council without attending Small Council sessions witnessed the most important charters.

English kings were required to spend a great deal of their time in Normandy from the time William I conquered England as Norman duke to the early thirteenth century when King John disposed of the royal need for being in Normandy by losing it. While they were out of the country, they were required to delegate authority in England. It is significant in underlining the king's desire to be associated with the rendering of justice that the person most often entrusted with vice-royal powers in the king's absence was the member of the Small Council who officially specialized in legal matters, the king's justiciar (*justiciarius*).[113] The origins of the office were very gradual, and it died a lingering death in the thirteenth century. It combined some attributes of a modern American attorney general and chief justice all in one, with some of the administrative responsibilities of a European prime minister, although any modern parallel in constitutional government is misleading because the justiciar's responsibility was only to the king.

In Germany this sort of thing was lacking. The administrative apparatus of a German emperor was negligible. Nevertheless, not only the notion of the ruler as the ultimate judge but also his itinerant pattern of governance persisted in Germany well after the English and French monarchies had settled down to make capitals of London and Paris. In Germany the *Reichstag* evolved precisely from the institution of the travelling monarch dispensing justice. In Middle High German, the emperor was frequently referred to, in a telling example of personification, as "the empire" (Middle High German *rîche*, modern German *Reich*). *Rîchtac*, later *Reichstag*, meant literally empire day in the sense of "the day when the empire (that is, the emperor) is in town dispensing justice." A *Reichstag* was, of course, not limited to a day; it could go on for weeks. The institution lasted in almost that form to the sixteenth century, when, in a famous example, Martin Luther was summoned to appear before a *Reichstag* being held by the emperor, who was still rather itinerant, in Worms.

The sporadic efforts made to change the administration of justice in Germany were unsuccessful. Perhaps the most concentrated effort was made by Frederick II, the Hohenstaufen emperor who had grown up in Sicily, where royal government did have a fully developed administrative apparatus. To expedite and regularize justice through the central monarchy, he even proposed instituting an official something like the English judiciar in his imperial "Decree on the Maintenance of Peace in the Land" (*Landfriedengesetz*) in 1235.[114] This high judicial official was to be appointed by the emperor on an annual basis, to oversee the prosecution of justice within the empire. The power of the German territorial lords, however, was too great by his time for even the emperor's personal rendering of justice to strengthen the monarchy, let alone that dispatched by his representative.

Kings in the feudal period found punishments for crimes drastic and brutal, and they usually left them that way. Their contribution towards progress in this regard was chiefly in having retribution applied more systematically and in such a way that guilty men had less chance of escaping and again endangering the peace of the realm. Medieval kings did, to be sure, introduce different types of punishment. Louis IX, who as a saint, was opposed to "filthy oaths," designed a special iron, round with a small spike, for branding the noses and lips of blasphemers, which he may actually have demonstrated once on a citizen of Paris.[115] William the Conqueror had gone so far as generally to abolish capital punishment in his own administration of justice. His idea was to replace it by blinding, castration, cutting off hands or feet, and other forms of mutilation, so that what was left of the punished party would serve as an example to other likely wrongdoers. The *Anglo-Saxon Chronicle*, while deploring the Norman tyranny, grudgingly compliments William on the success of his criminal-justice policy:

[With] other things we must not forget the good order he kept in the land, so that a man of any substance could travel unmolested throughout the country with his bosom full of gold. No man dared to slay another, no matter what evil the other might have done to him. If a may lay with a woman against her will, he was forthwith condemned to forfeit those members with which he had disported himself.[116]

William, in the parlance of our own time, "wasn't afraid to experiment." It seems, however, that being forced to see or be around those who had received this sort of royal justice was too much for the sensibilities of medieval Englishmen, and Henry I finally restored capital punishment, to everyone's relief.[117] Mutilation, while no longer either the most stressed deterrent in the arsenal of royal justice or carried out so thoroughly, nonetheless remained a punishment for some crimes in England as elsewhere.

Since even a criminal matter could be brought to the attention of one of the king's justices only on the basis of a personal complaint, the fact remained that crimes against those who had no friends or relatives of a mind to complain went unpunished. To rectify this, and to bring more business before royal jurisdiction, Henry II introduced the "presentment jury," the forerunner of the modern grand jury. Twelve men from each division of a hundred in the country and four from each township were summoned to appear before the king's justices and declare on oath the names of those they believed to be guilty of crimes.[118] On the first occasion introduced by his decree, the Assize of Clarendon in 1166, the recollection of the presentment jurors was supposed to go back to 1154, the time of the king's coronation; afterwards, the sessions were limited to indictments for recent crimes.

The Angevin kings also furthered the petty criminal jury at a later date, but Henry II himself rested content with the ordeal by cold water. A person indicted by the presentment jury would be tied up and thrown into water. If the water accepted him and he sank, he would be fished out as innocent. If he floated, he was judged guilty. The king decreed in the Assize of Clarendon that a man failing the ordeal should lose a foot and leave the realm, with his goods reverting to the royal treasury. Evidently this was thought too mild a punishment for probable criminals; in the Assize of Northampton guilty parties were additionally condemned to the loss of their right hand,[119] while even in the earlier Assize of Clarendon, Henry stipulated that men "of bad reputation" should be banished in spite of successfully passing the trial by ordeal.

Under medieval kings the advance towards rational adjudication of civil disputes was more rapid than towards that of criminal ones. Henry II provided that questions of rightful occupation of land and inheritance could be brought before the royal chancery, where a writ would be issued directing the sheriff of a county to summon twelve men to testify on the subject of who had possessed what and when. These "possessory assizes" were significant in deciding questions of right by inquiry and testimony rather than with trial by battle or ordeal, which endured into the late thirteenth century in criminal cases.

KINGS AS PATRONS OF THE MERCHANT CLASS

While a medieval king needed the support of loyal fighting men which feudalism offered, and while his administrative apparatus was so thin that he could not govern effectively in peacetime without the support of the feudal hierarchy, it was also true that the greatest threat to medieval kingship from the ninth through the thirteenth century remained the independence of feudal lords whose control of land was so wide that they had their own political bases of power. To be able to deal with such men, it was necessary for the king to cultivate alliances with groups who suffered from the threat of an excess of power in the hands of territorial lords in the same way that he did. Groups in such a position were the lesser nobility, churchmen, and the productive and commercial elements of the towns whose most visible representatives were the merchants.

Royal attempts to strengthen the monarchy by giving advantages to lower lords in the feudal pyramid had a long record of producing unintended results. The development of "immunity" is only one of the more illustrative encapsulations of this phenomenon. Originally, the institution of immunity united the interests of lesser lords and the kings against territorial lords, beginning with the counts of the Merovingian period. It worked like this: when a king would make a landholder an immunist, this meant that his land holdings could not be entered by counts, other nobles, or even royal officials except by invitation. Kings retained the right to enter such estates personally, but they seldom exercised this right. The immunist was left with the responsibility for collecting taxes and pursuing criminals on his estate. In the short run, this helped Frankish kings to offset the power of the counts as territorial lords, particularly where control of church lands was concerned. Immunity, however, was not confined to land held by abbeys and monasteries. Lay immunists were created, of course, but only among men whose loyalty to the crown was considered at the time to be unwavering. There was nothing in the long run to keep a layman, as immunist, from using his practical freedom from royal inspection and coercion to increase his own wealth and power. He was less subject to royal control than before and could end up compounding the problems of a king by competing with the nobility for independent political power.[120] Much of the story of provosts in France and even of sheriffs in England merely varied the same theme. Strong royal support for a lesser lord simply meant that he would eventually be in a position to throw his weight around like a more powerful lord, which put the king back where he had started.

Churchmen were necessary royal allies in running a medieval state, as has been shown above, but as nonfighters exempt from most taxes they had obvious limitations when kings were looking for military strength and economic support for the monarchy.

The shift to a money economy as the feudal period continued would have given kings a strong reason to attempt to link the interests of the merchant class to their own even if they had no other grounds for doing so, since it was from the merchant class that ready cash was most likely to be forthcoming with the fewest complaints. The attitude of the merchants themselves, however, provided feudal monarchs with equally strong motivation to support their common interests from another standpoint.

Although law and order seems to have loomed large on the mental horizons of nearly all medieval people, this was particularly true of the merchant class. Merchants had to worry more than others about roads being safe from bandits. They had to worry about territorial lords exercising arbitrary power, in stringing chains across roads and rivers and collecting tribute under the name of taxes from transporters; and they really had to worry about receiving fair treatment in judicial proceedings. Buying and selling, particularly over long distances, was not quite a savory way of making a living in the minds of many medieval magnates. The way the merchants seemed to make large profits from small investments with little sweat of the brow looked something like usury, and merchants consequently looked too much like fair game too much of the time. This suited them not at all. They reasoned, naturally enough, that the stronger their kings were, the more the local barons would be held in check. Their notion of cause and effect here was much the same as that of American blacks in the twentieth century, who have generally favored strong federal government to offset abuses of local authority; it was also that of Jews in nineteenth-century Germany, who favored a strong, united central government which seemed sure to protect them against blatant and arbitrary local discrimination.

All in all, the merchant class had more reason to pay income and property taxes more cheerfully and more fully than did other groups on whom the feudal monarchies attempted to impose them. It made more sense to pay the king's predictable taxes than to continue to yield to the irregular exactions of the local nobility.

Kings in the feudal period furthered their alliance with the merchant class by increasing the political freedoms of towns in which their interests were dominant.[121] In France, Louis VII had begun to do this, but Philip Augustus pursued such a policy with real determination, granting charters of franchises to selected towns, and approving a considerable amount of self-government for the municipal corporations, or "communes."[122]

When talented commoners in the towns could acquire some education, medieval kings were often to find in them useful officials whose loyalty to the crown could be depended on. Enjoying no feudal benefits or heredi-tary authority, they owed their positions entirely to royal appointments. The previous absence of any such pool of educated labor had been a recurring problem for medieval kingship since the seventh century, when the supply of secular officials dried up, leaving kings almost completely dependent on the clergy for officials who had the necessary reading and writing ability.

It was the French bourgeoisie who furnished King Philip Augustus and his successors with the *baillis*, administrators who remained dependent on the king in every way. They received set salaries from the king, they were removable at his will, and they were transferred among regions to prevent them from sinking roots deep enough to give them aspirations as future territorial lords. The French kings did not replace the provosts and vis-counts, who earlier had been allowed to acquire local power through quasi-independent control of land, but they aimed at making them in-creasingly accountable to the crown in the manner of *baillis*. In an impor-tant decree to "Our *baillis*, viscounts, provosts, mayors, and all other officers, in whatever matter it may be and whatever office they may hold," Saint Louis seems consciously to have lumped all his officials together with the intent of making them relate to him in a civil-service rather than a feudal way. He specifies that they are not to receive money, "indirect benefits, nor any other thing, except fruit, or bread or wine, or some other present up to the value of ten *sous*," from anyone for what they do in the king's service. The royal salaries are obviously meant to be sufficient. There is also to be no extending of money, goods, or services upwards by "Our provosts, Our viscounts, Our mayors, Our foresters, and Our other officers" to "their superiors"; in other words, there are to be no separate feudal, hierarchical arrangements to offset the chain of command within the royal administration. The *baillis* themselves are prohibited from pur-chasing or indirectly acquiring "any lands that may be in their own baili-wick, or that of another, so long as they remain in Our service . . . without Our express permission."[123]

In France as elsewhere the clergy remained prominently represented among the king's officials, but, even so, bourgeoisie and clergy were not groups with mutually exclusive attitudes towards kingship. Reading and writing—those skills indispensable to royal administration—were attri-butes of the clergy long before they became the property of other classes. Clergymen who were at the same time lawyers of middle-class background diligently supported the centralizing efforts of French kings in the feudal period.[124] From the twelfth century, it might be well to distinguish such men in France and elsewhere as members of a special group. Still calling themselves *clerici*, they remained clergymen largely in the sense that they had been educated under Church auspices in the universities, which were then springing up in Europe. Once in the service of the king, they formed in practice a class between laymen and churchmen in the sense that they were not practicing priests and monks.

English kings lagged behind their French counterparts in utilization of middle-class talent. This was partly due to the position of the first Norman kings as conquerors: William I and William II used the great barons who had assisted in the conquest of England and their sons for royal officials. Henry I turned to the lesser nobility for his sheriffs and constables, and even Henry II generally took men from the lower feudal ranks for his service rather than from the middle class in spite of his emphasis on developing responsiveness to the king alone in his judicial officialdom.[125] Possibly Saxon preeminence in the merchant interests and lingering Norman-Saxon tensions prompted him to do this. Of greater weight, however, in this regard was probably the simple fact that in the reign of Henry I and in the later one of Henry II the English monarchy seemed securely enough atop a stable and quite satisfactory feudal pyramid to make any search for balancing elements from the middle class unnecessary. Then, too, while trade and town life were developing in England, nowhere except London did townsmen or the merchant interests wield real political power through the first half of the thirteenth century, although they were to make up for lost time in this respect later.

In Germany town life and a feeling of common interests among the middle classes were fairly highly developed in many localities. The German towns, we recall, had been significant enough to enable Henry IV to maintain himself against much of his own nobility at the time of the Investiture Controversy. The town of Worms and its merchant-class citizens had distinguished themselves early in the conflict, and Henry had acknowledged their devotion to his cause in a charter releasing them from payment of tolls at six stations. This document from 1074 is worth citing at some length as a monument of royal solidarity with merchant-class citizens. Notice that the king refers to his commoners of Worms as displaying precisely the *fealty* which his actual feudal vassals lacked. They are consequently to receive *benefices*, not of the older feudal, land-grant type, but those which merchants can use in their given station in life:

> In the name of the holy and indivisible Trinity. Henry by God's grace king.
> It is fitting for the royal power and piety to respond to the service of all men with appropriate benefices, so that those who show themselves more prompt in devoted service may rejoice to be judged more eminent and more worthy too of remuneration for service. We have judged the inhabitants of the city of Worms worthy of not the least but the greatest special reward . . . since we have learned that they were loyal to us with especially great fidelity in the worst turmoil of the kingdom . . . We say it is extraordinary because they alone were loyal to us, rushing as if to death against the

general will, while all the princes of the realm were raging against us, having abandoned the ties of fealty . . . Worms alone facilitated our arrival with support of arms by the general approval of all her citizens. Therefore let those who were the advance guard in devotion to service be the first to receive the rewards of service. Let those who excelled all in preserving the bond of fealty be an example to everyone of the response due for service. Let the inhabitants of all cities rejoice in the hope of royal munificence, which the citizens of Worms have obtained as a result of this event. May all learn to keep faith with the king by imitating those who proved their good will in the service of the king . . .[126]

Such "hope of royal munificence" for services rendered may have figured in the adherence of many towns in the Rhineland to the king's cause after Canossa. In his conflict with Rudolf of Swabia, the towns throughout Germany were generally on his side. In his invasion of Italy, he secured even the support of northern Italian cities by making lavish commercial concessions to their merchant interests.[127]

In the twelfth century, however, the successors of Henry IV let such ties with the towns and the middle class slide in favor of cooperation with the nobility. Even Emperor Frederick Barbarossa, for all his ambition to centralize power in the German monarchy, came to accept the higher nobility as the potentially strongest force in German political struggles. Consequently, he also declined to renew the same sort of alliance with the towns and the merchant interests which Henry IV had initiated. For Barbarossa the situation was complicated by the fact that some of the strongest merchant interests in his empire were located precisely in those Italian city-states, such as Milan, who resented his policy of imperial consolidation the most; it would have been hard indeed for him to work on the development of direct monarchical power through their support.

An abortive attempt to cultivate an alliance with the German towns against the nobility was made by one Henry who is not usually numbered among the kings of Germany, although he reigned there from 1230 to 1235. His father, Emperor Frederick II, had earlier procured Henry's election as king of Germany, intending that he rule his German territories for him while Frederick himself governed Italy and took care of pressing problems relating to the papacy and the crusades. Henry's policy, however, of building on merchant-class support in the towns, much in the manner of contemporary French kings, led to a severe antiroyal reaction by the German territorial lords. Eventually, Emperor Frederick II came in on their side, fought his son, and kept him prisoner until the latter's death.[128] In spite of this treatment, the German towns continued to flourish, but the territorial lords had secured their victory and were successfully to head off any effective alliance between townspeople and the monarchy until the close of the Middle Ages.

What developed in Germany under feudal kingship instead of the French *baillis* or the English king's "justices" was the unique institution of the *ministeriales*. These were men taken actually from below the status of freemen, but nonetheless entrusted with some administrative duties for the monarchy. They were certainly quite dependent on the ruler, and their lowly origin kept the feudal nobility from worrying about them to the point of creating overt trouble. On the other hand, the fact that men of the knightly class and above balked at having to take orders from unfree men, whether they were designated the king's or emperor's own men or not, lessened their effectiveness as royal officials. When the emperor's *ministeriales* actually executed a noble, the count of Burghausen, in 1104, the feudal lords were ready to take this as a cause for renewed revolt against the monarchy.[129]

German rulers were, of course, not indifferent to what the merchant class had to offer, and they were all in favor of mutually beneficial arrangements which did not put them between the towns and the nobility in a power struggle. In Germany, as elsewhere in Europe, cooperation between the monarch and the merchant class can be seen in the abundance of fairs put on under royal charters. Fairs in the Middle Ages featured great exhibitions of products from near and far. By American standards they were gigantic "markets" rather than "fairs," their activity centering around retail and wholesale transactions. Royal protection of fairs was a great help to the merchants. It helped insure the safe transportation of products to the grounds and, since the royal charter often also included a grant to administer justice on the spot, it did something to alleviate violence and thievery. Merchants sought royal or imperial charters partly to free themselves from exactions or the use of force by the nobility when they took their goods to their fairs. A typical charter issued by Frederick Barbarossa for fairs at Aachen and Duisburg, for example, stipulates:

> Merchants shall have the right to ascend or go down the Rhine under our protection for their persons and goods, and on other waters of our empire. If anyone presumes to use force against them or to injure them, he will be deprived of our favor forever.[130]

At the same time, the local nobility or territorial lords could profit legitimately from a share of those tolls which were authorized by such a charter. They also gained indirectly from the prosperity and enjoyment which such fairs would bring the inhabitants of their lands. Consequently, responsible members of the nobility were happy to sponsor them, and royal fair charters were sometimes issued to them. (The one cited immediately above, for example, was issued to Count Philip of Flanders.)

Finally, there was the contribution to central military power made by all the non-noble classes as the feudal period began to draw to a close. In their original conception of non-noble *equivalents* for knightly service, English kings were ahead of their continental counterparts. In 1181, Henry II decreed that a given level of income from rent (sixteen marks a year) obligated a man to maintain for the king's service the military equipment of a knight.[131] Then, when infantry became more important and sudden increases in the size of armies became an overall trend, the merchant class became an indirect military mainstay of all European monarchies. This was not through direct furnishing of much in the way of manpower, since it was chiefly former peasants and mercenaries of one sort or another who found their way into the rank and file of the new armies; however, tax revenues from the merchant class furnished soldiers' pay. This economic aid was what kings and their military advisors in the later feudal period were looking for when war clouds were on the horizon.

KINGSHIP AND EARLY NATIONAL IDENTITY

The term "national identity" signifies a perception by members of a group that they are related to each other through common bonds of heritage and culture strong enough to set that group off in significant ways from others. A people's sense of national identity necessarily precedes the nation state and remains a primary requisite for its continued success. In the Middle Ages, the group memberships by which people characterized themselves were often primarily religious, occupational or social (the *orders* of society), or of a clan or tribal nature smaller than anything we would recognize as national. Still, writers even in the early Middle Ages revealed a certain conviction that people were often what they were by virtue of an extended tribal membership.[132] Certainly, Jordanes thought of the Goths and Gregory of Tours of the Franks as having enough important common attributes — heroism, fortitude, intelligence, a glorious history — to make Franks or Goths distinct from other tribes by their very birth. It is no more out of order to call such extended tribal groups "nations," even when speaking of the early Middle Ages, than it is to repeat such historically unchallenged appellations as "the Iroquois nation" or "the Cherokee nation" for groups which appear to have had a similar sense of identity.

A medieval man was capable of feeling that his *natio* — his birth and all the characteristics that being born of a given stock in a given estate brought with it — was a matter of being a knight, farmer, or even baker, but he was also capable of perceiving his *natio* as that of a Frenchman, Dane, Saxon, or Bavarian. Not all the medieval *nationes* of this type developed into national kingdoms, let alone nation states, but that is beside the point. To the extent that a man perceived the tribal part of his identity as embodied by his king, it is almost tautologically true that he felt a sense of shared identity with that very king. We may recall the role of the *thiudans* as the personifier of the tribe, particularly in its dealings with the gods, a figure from the dawn of history constructed partly from anthropological evidence but at least sketchily alluded to in the period of the great migrations. There is evidence of this office having lasted in Welsh and Irish tradition in relatively unchanged form well past the year 1000.[133] Such events as the Alamanni going to pieces on the death of their king, or the Ostrogoths failing to maintain their identity as a people after the dissolution of their kingship testify to the continuance of the primitive principle of tribal embodiment in royal rulers into the early Middle Ages. The personification of the Franks in their king in the work of Notker Balbulus and the personification of the Germans in their kings and emperors in the anonymous *Book of Emperors* attest to the survival of this principle, at least on the level of popular consciousness, afterwards.

The fact is that every successful medieval king was at least something of a *thiudans,* although on the Continent the word and its cognates as royal designations died out with the Goths.[134] Kings who enjoyed the unswerving loyalty of a tribal following continued to do so partly because members of the tribe felt their unity to be at least associated with, and sometimes actually derived from, their king. Problems arose, of course, as political units grew larger. The parallel Strasburg Oaths of 842, taken by the followers of Charles the Bald and Louis the German to confirm an alliance against their brother, Lothar, in what would develop many centuries later into the French and German national languages, mark a step along the way to national consciousness in terms of larger units. The abandonment of the terms "Neustria" and "Austrasia" in favor of "Francia," a development which proceeded gradually from Charlemagne's own reign to the early tenth century, marks another. The first Norman kings of England necessarily treated the Anglo-Saxons a good deal of the time as a conquered people: yet, in time, their successors subsumed an amalgamation of tribal identities, and later Englishmen would think of themselves as Englishmen partly by virtue of having a kingship worthy of the free, courageous, active, and right-thinking people which, like any nation, they perceived themselves to be. Superficially, the development of the territorial conception of kingship meant less individual attachment to the king as the personal leader of the nation and more to the impersonal concept of the realm, but only superficially, since the personal control of the monarch over the realm was growing at least as fast as the importance of the territorial notion of the realm itself. Even after this development from personal to territorial kingship was fairly complete, Shakespeare's audience could still understand "France" as the person of the king of France in no different a fashion than "Kent" signified its earl.[135]

The early medieval class differentiation into estates had undermined the primitive sense of national identity in the king in two ways. It had not only made personal identity more dependent on belonging to a particular order of society at the expense of identity with the nation, but the pyramidal fashion in which it developed also placed blocks of intermediaries between the ordinary run of people and the king as the personification of the nation. Perhaps instinctively, perhaps through design, the most successful medieval kings attacked both aspects of the problem. One common bit of policy which we have seen running through all the preceding sections of this chapter represented royal attempts to turn the higher orders of society, aristocratic and ecclesiastic, into instruments of royal administration and communication with the population at large. Equally important were the links which kings established — or reestablished if we think of the older structure of the tribe — with all free men of the realm, whether in the context of taxation, soldiery, or the administration of justice. In the founding of new towns or the rechartering of old ones, royal protection was the best apparent guarantee for a reasonable degree of freedom and independence. In France, many communes outside the royal demesne requested the king to confirm their charters. In effect, they traded immediate dependence on feudal lords for later dependence upon kings.[136] Settlers in frontier regions, such as those recently taken from the Slavs in eastern parts of the empire or those reconquered from the Moors in Spain and tenuously held, were granted liberal terms of governance by rulers who were glad to have buffer zones occupied by their own kind of people until the areas could be fully absorbed.

The interaction of kingship and the Church, whether direct or indirect, friendly or hostile, could not help but further the development of early national identity. From a direct and positive standpoint, the Church had been working through tribal or national kings since the days of the first concentrated missionary efforts. Later it was rather obvious that when the papacy wanted to push reform or otherwise influence events in the European churches, the voluntary cooperation of the secular rulers was a great asset. The fact that money from royal treasuries was necessary for building churches and monasteries, for granting them land, and for supporting them in their undertakings kept the institutional development of the Church tied to national frameworks. From time to time, the papacy accorded different rights and privileges to churches on a national basis. Medieval historians showed an early and strong tendency to relate Church events to national developments: the Venerable Bede's *History of the English Church and People* is only the most obvious case in point. While until the time of Henry VIII, no king in the West succeeded in making himself the head of the Church in his country, other medieval kings accumulated long experience in supporting and sometimes directing church affairs in their dominions. The point is that the very fact of kings' having responsibilities for the Church in their lands led — insofar as inhabitants of their countries identified with their own churches — to still another increase in national identity perceived through the guidance and person of the king.

It was also true that if kings increased their standing through helping the churches which their subjects felt to be their own, they were sometimes equally successful in gaining national support during their conflicts with the Church. The papacy in particular represented an accumulation of international authority. National kings who challenged it credibly on behalf of the interests of the realm could reckon with considerable support at home. King John himself was never more popular than during his lengthy battle with the papacy.[137] This was due partly to realization that conflicts such as his concerned the sensitive issue of taxation. Englishmen, like other peoples north of the Alps, harbored resentments over the outflow of money from their own country into Italy for disbursement. A century after John, King Edward I heightened his own popularity with the Statute of Carlisle, which prohibited the payment of taxes threatening to draw off wealth from England into the papal treasury.[138]

Philip IV mustered considerable national support in his conflict with Boniface VIII. He was careful to couch his hostility to the papacy in terms of liberating the French or Gallican Church from the pope's unsavory influence. This gave an entirely new twist to the idea that a king was obliged to unsheathe the sword of state against heretics and unbelievers. Heretics and unbelievers had become the papal minions who threatened the cherished position of the French Church. The French king was to be seen as "the temporal deputy in his kingdom of King Jesus Christ" and the "agent of His victories" over enemies.[139] Philip shared his glory with his countrymen by professing confidence that France was Christ's specially favored kingdom:

> Jesus Christ the Highest, finding a stable basis in this very kingdom for the holy faith and Christian worship and considering the deepest devotion accorded to Himself, His ministers, and His servants here more than in other parts of the world, realized that He is loved, feared, and honored in it before the rest and thus ordained that it should be honored before other kingdoms and principalities with certain particular and outstanding signs of primacy.[140]

This was the sort of faith that might not move mountains but could very well move the papacy to Avignon in France, where Church leadership could benefit by the wholesome influence of a king and people so deserving.

The growing acceptance of the divine right of kings, as well as the constant, if lesser, phenomenon of belief in their thaumaturgic power, tended to reinforce national identities when people compared kings of different countries. Not all kings could be equally Christ's deputy ruling the most Christian kingdom; foreign kings' claim to rule by divine right tended to seem at least a fraction less valid than the home king's claim. Nationalism or something very close to it entered into popular perceptions of the relative degree of thaumaturgic power wielded by kings. Guillaume de St. Pathus reports how an Englishman mocked French devotion to Saint Louis "and said that King Henry of England was a better man than the blessed Saint Louis," only to be struck by paralysis in one leg; he was not cured until he was transported to Saint Louis's tomb and offered that French saint and king a candle as long as his leg.[141] Englishmen at home were not above alluding on occasion to the way the English king could cure scrofula and others could not, although, in general, the scrofula-curing attribute was the one most willingly conceded to French and English kings alike.[142] Valdemar I of Denmark was portrayed as giving health to children and abundance to grain through his touch as he travelled through Germany—thaumaturgic achievements implicitly beyond the powers of German rulers themselves in the eyes of the Danish writer.[143]

In this connection the struggle between the papacy and the secular ruler had a different effect in Germany than in the western European countries in spite of a comparable sort of national popularity which figures such as Henry IV and Frederick II enjoyed from time to time in Germany. One rather comprehensive reason for the decisive difference in the outcome was the fact that the national monarchy in Germany was submerged in the concept of the Holy Roman Empire. When the empire suffered losses in territory, prestige, and power, these were necessarily born by the emperors in their capacity as German kings. The empire suffered substantial losses of this nature during the thirteenth century, when the last of the Hohenstaufens were hunted down. Imperial governance passed to Rudolf of Hapsburg, who could not find the time, in spite of strenuous exertions elsewhere, to cope with political problems in Italy, where centrifugal force proved to be the greatest from the standpoint of the empire's German rulers.[144] The beneficiaries of the undermining of the empire simply could not include kings of the *regnum Teutonicum* or German Kingdom as such. Those profiting the most from its losses were instead the rulers of the principalities at the next territorial level, such as the dukes of Saxony and Bavaria. They developed a new independence of a type which the consolidation of national monarchies in western Europe ruled out: to the extent that they succeeded in doing so, emperors and German kings had to reckon without a useful sense of national identity in their subjects. In western Europe on the other hand, the sapping of the international authority of the empire in the thirteenth century and the eclipse of the international authority of the papacy with the Babylonian Captivity favored the development not only of national identity but of nationalism through the simple process of removing two of its chief obstacles.

Somewhat more indirectly, transformations in the feudal system aided the growth of national consciousness. That such a consciousness was to help undermine and then destroy feudalism is incidental here. It was more as feudal lords than in any other role that European kings amassed the ever-larger land holdings which were to become the nation states under their personal control. In the most obvious example of this, the Capetian kings gradually extended the royal demesne from modest holdings in north-central France to include an area approaching the modern borders of the French nation state. Their suzerainty over the Norman-held territories was tenuous at times, as we have seen, but it gave them their basis for later sovereignty there, nonetheless.

The Normans themselves used elements of feudal control to solidify royal power wherever they established governments. In Sicily they imposed a feudal pyramid on the island with the king more firmly in control from the first than those kings who had to make concessions in gathering territorial holdings together. Their relative lack of success there and in southern Italy, which was joined to Sicily in the same kingdom, was due in considerable part to their inability to create a common national identity among themselves and the inhabitants they found when they arrived. They failed in Sicily in the manner of Theoderic, who had imposed his Gothic rule on Italo-Romans in a way which ruled out assimilation, although in the early thirteenth century Emperor Frederick II, whose father had acquired Sicily by marriage, used Norman feudal precedents to good advantage. Frederick himself was much aware of the need to propagandize for a common national identity among the Arabs, Greeks, Latins, Jews, and Normans who populated Sicily. He even went to the extent of making it difficult for Sicilians to marry "foreigners" because:

> When the men of Sicily ally themselves with the daughters of foreigners, the purity of the race becomes besmirched, while evil and sensual weakness increases, the purity of the people is contaminated by the speech and by the habits of others, and the seed of the stranger defiles the hearth of our faithful subjects.[145]

From the standpoint of allowing a common national identity to develop, the same Norman tribe succeeded in England in the manner of Clovis and the other Merovingian kings who allowed Franks and Gallo-Romans to overcome their differences. It was in England that the Norman William I restructured the feudal pyramid in such a fashion that, in spite of limitations put upon the crown by the barons at Runnymede in 1215, and by later parliaments, the power of the monarchy was not so shaken. The Lancastrian kings were able to restore it in part, and the Tudor kings in its entirety, before going on to greater things.

In fact, the Magna Carta and royal concessions to the parliaments should be seen in a different light than that of weakening English kingship, particularly in comparison with kingship on the Continent. England was almost unique in having a monarchy so strong that there was any greatly felt need to limit it during the thirteenth century. Only Denmark had a similar experience at that time through anything like analogous causes.[146] All the while, however, it was true in England, as elsewhere, that even when the feudal nobles gained temporary victories in disputing power with the king, the results of their struggle helped both to refine the royal art of government further and to assure the regular participation of lords or magnates in it, thus renewing kingship with the old stamp of feudal, as well as the new stamp of national, legitimacy. It was precisely this integration of late-feudal interests with national identity that was to serve subsequent kings in particularly good stead when they made further moves in the direction of absolutism.

VARIATIONS ON FEUDAL MONARCHY: FRANCE

The transition from personal and tribal to territorial kingship proceeded gradually and smoothly most of the time in medieval France. When Hugh Capet became king in 987, he assumed the old title, *rex Francorum,* which Merovingians and Carolingians had used earlier and which the Capetian dynasty kept from that time on.[147] In doing so, they were capitalizing on the legitimacy of the ruling tradition which they were picking up from their predecessors; at the same time, they benefited by an expanded understanding of that title, an understanding no longer limited to the Franks as a tribe, wherever they might be, but to the realm of France.

This shift toward a territorial conception of kingship represented both a revival and an innovation. After all, the Romans had certainly thought of Gaul as a place, and the Franks remained at least dimly conscious all along that they had roots in a heartland stretching across central France north of the Loire and extending to the Rhein. In the early tenth century, we find a reference in a document from the chancellery of Charles the Most Patient to *Gallia,* signifying in context the western part of this heartland of the Franks which seemed not to be covered any longer by the designations of Austrasia, Neustria, or Burgundy. On the eastern side, a main portion of the area where the Frankish population was concentrated in the early Middle Ages had been given to Lothar I at the Treaty of Verdun in 843 as Lorraine. When tenth-century writers referred to Lorraine as *pars Franciae* (part of France), they were clearly implying that in some way France was a unit. Sure enough, when Charles the Most Patient became ruler of Lorraine the result was that *Gallia* plus Lorraine became *Francia* in his documents.[148] Although Lorraine was soon lost again, Charles is thus perhaps the first king to reach consciously for the territorial reality of France as a kingdom:

> Whether as "King of the Franks" or "King of the French," the title, *Rex Francorum,* continued to fill up that little area with reality, all the while giving a very favorable impression to the outside, since the honorable Carolingian tradition in the long run secured a recognition of equality for it when the Carolingian Empire was renewed in the East.[149]

One of the advantages of the territorial concept for French feudal kingship was the way it could be used to carry the loyalties of vassals from one king to another. The king appeared more and more as the guardian of the realm and less and less as its owner, in spite of the factual increase in French royal landowning from the tenth through the thirteenth centuries. Vassals were perceived to have sworn their loyalty to the kingdom and to relate to the king most of all in their obligation to maintain it against loss. Thus when a king died, royal vassals were not absolved of their oaths of service and fidelity; instead, the loyalty they owed the kingdom was transferred to the new king.

As was true of the kingdoms themselves, Churches within them were thought of increasingly in territorial terms as the Middle Ages continued. This was the case with the Gallican Church, which French kings came to view as an integral part of their realm. During the feudal period they were all the more able to make the Gallican Church a national one since they were spared really poor relations with the international Church until they were strong enough to win out in a contest rather easily. In the eleventh century French kings had been able to invest only a fraction of the bishops and abbots within their kingdom. There were so many members of the higher nobility exercising lay investiture that a papal attack on it in France would have cost the pope at the same time the support of the king and the secular magnates. By way of contrast, German kings and emperors deposed popes often enough in the Middle Ages, but certainly none of them succeeded in any such power play as transporting the papacy to Germany. After the conflict between Boniface VIII and Philip IV ended with moving the papacy to Avignon, the fourteenth-century Avignon popes were to be sufficiently obedient to the French kings to cause the papacy to forfeit some of its international prestige. By the time the papacy was finally restored to Rome, the Gallican Church had been strengthened with more royal support and, of course, paid the price of more royal influence in its affairs.

While the last Carolingians perceived France as a territorial unit, they were certainly unable to rule it as such. Throughout most of the tenth century, the Capetian family wielded real power as counts of Paris and as dukes of France, often under nominal Carolingian kings, in something like the way that Carolingian major-domos had exercised power during nominal Merovingian rule. One major result of this was that when Hugh

Capet became king, he and his successors had to develop feudal monarchy from a royal demesne that had dwindled in size to less than the province of the Ile-de-France.

The smallness of the royal demesne at the outset of the Capetian dynasty had two significant consequences in turn. One was that the early Capetian kings had to enlarge their power base by using their holdings as dukes of France, chiefly in what had been Neustria. The other was the necessary abandonment of the Merovingian-Carolingian practice of splitting the kingdom among sons. The increasing tendency during the first half of the tenth century to perceive the French kingdom in terms of a prenational but still distinctly territorial unit had probably rendered this practice impossible anyway. In fixing the succession, the Capetians moved toward royal primogeniture, the practice of leaving the kingdom to the oldest son, but they did so step by step. When the Carolingian line had first grown feeble, the French nobility had fallen back on the ancient custom of electing their kings. Having thus been elected himself, Hugh Capet had no intention of letting French kingship slip away from his family in a future election. To head off such a possibility, Hugh resorted to a different ancient practice and crowned his son, Robert, as associate ruler and his successor. This step of designation established a precedent for French kingship, and every king of France afterwards until the thirteenth century succeeded to the throne as a *rex designatus.*[150]

The problem remained of providing for younger sons of the king in the face of the previous tradition, which would have given them an expectation of some substantial part of the kingdom. When the Capetians extended their royal land holdings, they did not split the realm into subkingdoms; instead, at first unwillingly but later by design, they provided them with substantial fiefs for maintenance. In 1034, Henry I of France gave Burgundy to his brother, Robert, in settlement of a war which broke out following their father's death. In the following century, Louis VI provided for his younger son, Robert, with the county of Dreux before his own death and thus established a pattern which was to last for centuries. The institution which developed was that of "royal *apanages,*" large land grants made to brothers of the future king with agreements required of them that the *apanages* would revert back to the French crown when their lines of direct heirs ran out. Eventually, specific, written assurances were considered not altogether necessary, as reversion to the crown became "the custom of France."[151]

In 1223, Louis VIII succeeded to the throne without having formally been a *rex designatus;* from that point on, the principle of primogeniture can be taken to have won out in France, although Louis VIII himself took the precaution of having the most powerful barons and bishops of the kingdom promise to serve his son, the future Louis IX. The system of royal *apanages* was continued, however, and by and large they furthered the interests of the king and kingdom; they were large enough to provide for comfortable maintenance but, at least after the extension of royal control in the twelfth century, not large enough in proportion to furnish bases for active resistance. Not all royal sons received *apanages*. Only certain family members who because of near-seniority or outstanding talent would have been likely candidates for partial kingship in former days obtained them. When a prince with an *apanage* became king himself, as happened during a series of short reigns and early deaths of kings of France in the fourteenth century, his lands reverted to the royal demesne.[152] The recipients of *apanages* were carefully chosen and "cheerfully served the king more or less as provincial viceroys."[153] There was nothing quite like this in the other feudal monarchies. Arguments could arise over reversions of *apanages* to the crown and did, but, all in all, first through designating future kings and later through developing the *apanage* system, French kingship remained free of serious or prolonged succession struggles even through most of the Hundred Years' War.

The degree of near sovereignty wielded by local lords in medieval France was considerably greater than in England, although not so great as in the empire. The Capetian kings could not have set themselves against the feudal structure of their kingdom if they had wanted to, and they did not try. "As long as their vassals, direct or mesne, performed their feudal duties and services, the kings were well content."[154] The French kings did develop a large and complex bureaucracy in comparison with that of the other feudal monarchies, which certainly did end by working against the independent power of the feudal nobility. The centering of governmental operations in the capital city was also more pronounced in France than in other western medieval kingdoms. The Parlement of Paris, which functioned as a sort of supreme court of the realm, greatly served the interests of French kingship by adjudicating a large volume of business in the king's name. The Parlement also proved quite useful to the monarchy — particularly during periods of boy kings and regencies — in taking charge of disputes among nobles or suits against the crown. Early *apanage* controversies exemplified only one type of dispute which the Parlement generally decided in favor of the king's rights.[155]

The real test of the work done by the feudal kings of France and their supporters came when French defeats during the Hundred Years' War set the scope of royal holdings and actual power back to the days of the early Capetians. Both national identity and royal traditions, however, had been firmly established by that time; it was not nearly so difficult nor so long a process to reestablish the dominance of kingship in France the second time.

ENGLAND

In England, feudal monarchy developed with as great success as in France, although partly for different reasons. The most important of these reasons was the uprooting of English society when the Normans conquered the Anglo-Saxon kingdom and the ability shown by William the Conqueror in making use of the materials he found.

The loose organization of the early Anglo-Saxon kingdom is somewhat deceptive. Alfred the Great and other kings of the Wessex dynasty had put together many useful elements of government which were to serve William's purposes well. Anglo-Saxon kingship furnished him not only with a functioning system of local judiciary, which he easily adopted with a few centralizing modifications, but also with a tradition of administrative-military action which had developed to meet the Norse threat. The collection of *Danegeld,* the tribute required by the Danes, was an example of concerted action on a larger, more nearly national scale than could be found in continental Europe in the eleventh century. The assemblage of all free men for combat against invaders from the north on those frequent occasions when the *Danegeld* did not have its desired effect was another. In a similar way, William was also able to capitalize on the Anglo-Saxon experience in acting against enemies native to the British Isles, particularly the Welsh and Scots. The whole Anglo-Saxon custom of calling subjects to arms to face formidable enemies became under William the primary duty of all free Englishmen to serve the king when needed and render him their primary loyalty even during peacetime. The royal Norman idea that the king's subjects "who were of any account"[156] owed him service for whatever land they held, since it all came from him, might have been sufficient for this purpose by itself, but certainly the native tradition made it easier to apply.

William's application of some useful native elements of political tradition and his rejection of others were possible only in the state of malleability which characterized England after William's main opponents had exhausted each other and he had led his Normans to victory against the survivors in 1066. This allowed him to impose his eclectic and strong kingship on England so firmly that in spite of later internal strife, rebellion, and restrictions on the monarchy, the power of kings would continue to consolidate the realm for the rest of the Middle Ages.

The only contemporary parallels to the initial freedom he enjoyed were found in the Kingdom of Sicily and in the crusader kingdoms. Western settlers who conquered territories in the Near East codified feudalism in a model pyramid, leaving ample power to the king at the top, and they eliminated, at least on parchment, the ambiguities and inconsistencies which feudal kingship in most of western Europe was forced to live with.

Like William the Conqueror, they did not have to accept any patchwork of inheritance in laws and customs which could work at cross purposes and prevent a stable, hierarchical establishment. On the other hand, the few useful native elements of governance which they were willing and able to adopt did not add much durability to their feudal realms in the hostile Mohammedan environment, and the crusader kingdoms fell in the course of the twelfth and thirteenth centuries.

The Anglo-Norman monarchy suffered severe losses, it is true, in Normandy itself during the thirteenth century and was to lose its territory in France altogether before the close of the Middle Ages. These losses, however, were more than compensated for by consolidation at home. It was probably all to the good for English kingship that the demands placed on its military and financial resources were not those of a supernational empire. There were demands enough as it was. Continued threats were posed by the Welsh, Irish, and Scotch; however, these proved incapable of overtaxing the resources of English kingship in the way that the Italian involvement overtaxed the resources of the German rulers.

The limitations put on English kingship through the Magna Carta and subsequent constitutional documents did not hold back the growth of royal authority and prerogative in the long run, in spite of the fact that all the important restrictions continued to apply. Although the Magna Carta was declared null and void by Pope Innocent III in defense of his vassal, King John, subsequent English kings directly or indirectly recognized its articles as binding. Aimed as it was against abuses of royal power, it not only left the king's exercise of initiative intact, but, by defining the king's obligations clearly, sanctioned his position.

The Magna Carta is more than anything else a feudal document; nevertheless, its articles are not limited to the protection of the rights of the nobility only. Its Article I guarantees the general freedom of the English Church and the specific freedom of elections within it, before going on to specify that the remaining liberties to be enumerated are "for all free men of our kingdom . . . to have and to hold in perpetuity for themselves and for their heirs from us and from our heirs."[157] Possibly the most remarkable sections of the Magna Carta as a feudal document — in view of the traditional hostility between merchants and aristocracy throughout Europe — are those guaranteeing rights to townsmen and merchants. Article XIII confirms all chartered and traditional liberties to London and all other cities and towns, while Article XLI spells out the right of merchants to travel around and stay for purposes of buying and selling without being subject to any arbitrary taxes but only "to the ancient and right customs."[158]

The desire of Archbishop Stephen Langton to align a broad front against the king explains a small part of this unusual ecumenicity in the bestowal of rights by a baronial group, but the uniqueness of medieval English class structure explains a larger part. Even here, in the context of cutting down the king's independent powers, we see English upper classes developing quite propitiously for the ends of monarchy. William the Conqueror had kept the nobles from holding large, compact fiefs of a type which made figures like the duke of Aquitaine or the margrave of Flanders so formidable on the Continent.[159] Deprived of sovereign rights and great expanses of territory on which to base their independence, the English aristocracy began fading off into the gentry several generations after the Norman conquest in a fashion which left the nobility less of a distinct class than elsewhere in Europe. The result of this for medieval kingship in England is significant: since the nobility furnished the most organized and strongest resisting force to medieval kings anywhere, the blurring of upper-class lines made the nobility less of an independent entity and consequently less of a force to be reckoned with for challenging royal jurisdiction. While it is true that English kings were slower than their French counterparts to enlist middle-class talent in their administrations and that outside of London there was little early cultivation of the alliance between the towns and the king which solidified royal rule on the Continent, this proved to be no great hindrance to English kings in their centralizing efforts. The English middle class still responded to royal leadership. Middle-class opposition to vestiges of the manorial economy and middle-class enthusiasm for expansion of the concept of the king's peace, as it extended to more crimes and led to a more regular execution of justice, put that class in the royal camp as long as these issues remained live ones.

In spite of difficulties under the early Plantagenets and some later problems in the English relationship to the Avignon papacy, English Church-state relations were mutually satisfactory and supported the development of kingship through most of the Middle Ages. English kings came out of their disputes with the papacy over judicial and taxation rights well enough. They banked successfully on popular support when national independence from a Church under Italian or French control was an issue, and they were amenable to change and compromise when it was not (as during the later Conciliar period, discussed in the next chapter). The early Norman kings had been able to retain as much control of the Church as served their purposes. They had brought with them from Normandy the Frankish tradition of a strong secular hand in the administration of ecclesiastical affairs: a considerable part of their success in England is attributable to their forceful application of administrative skill in dealing with the clergy there. It is also true that one of the useful elements which Anglo-Saxon society offered them in the eleventh century was the institutional veneration of the royal person.

Throughout the Anglo-Saxon period, English kings were portrayed in a more "peculiar and sacral relationship with the divine" than most of their counterparts on the Continent.[160] English kings played a leading role in the conversion of their people, and this was a difficult and demanding task since paganism remained alive and entrenched in the British Isles well after it had declined to insignificance in Gaul. The early Christian king in England had been entitled *Christus Domini,* a phrase probably going in the sacral direction somewhat beyond "the Lord's anointed" in its signification.[161] English kings were honored as *pastores,*[162] which could be construed as "shepherds entrusted with keeping God's people," but in a plainly analogous sense to the way "pastor" still denotes a clergyman.

> It is very rightly the duty of a Christian king to be in the place of a father to a Christian nation, and in watch and ward as Christ's vice-regent, so as he is accounted. . . . Lo! through what shall peace and support come to God's servants and to God's poor save through Christ and through a Christian king?[163]

The ancient pagan notion of a king's marriage to his land may have survived in England into Christian times in allegorical form. Bede describes a seventh-century bishop named Paulinus accompanying the Christian princess Ethelburga of Kent to Northumbria, to marry the still pagan King Edwin:

> But he was further determined to bring the nation to which he was sent to the knowledge of the Christian truth, and to fulfill the Apostle's saying, "to espouse her to one husband, that he might present her as a chaste virgin to Christ."[164]

In due course Edwin was converted and thus brought Northumbria as a bride to Christ.[165] To Bede it seemed fitting to stress "the parallel of the country led as a bride to Christ and the princess as a bride to Edwin."[166] It is impossible to tell at what level this sort of thing survived in the English mind, but the notion of a king as husband of the land was a sufficiently familiar one to have survived the Middle Ages and emerge as an image in Jacobite poetry of the seventeenth and eighteenth centuries.[167]

Christian kings in England appear to have been held responsible not only for victories and defeats, as evidence of their *Heil* or lack of it, but also at least occasionally for good and bad seasons in the manner of Scandinavian royalty.[168] There was also, and here the Scandinavian parallel is quite clear, a "well-established class of royal martyrs," of which King Edmund, killed by the pagan Danes in 870, was only the most famous example.[169]

In the tenth century, Alfred the Great had worked out a theology of kingship which was remarkably like that applied to successful Carolingians in infusing kingship with divine trust, but it also stressed the king's freedom of choice in the exercise of temporal power more than the Carolingian models do.[170] In law codes as well as literary sources, the English king's vice-regency for God appears. Ethelred the Redeless, for example, presented himself as "Christ's deputy among Christian people,"[171] not long before the conquest of Canute the Dane, who had no difficulty retaining this bit of royal tradition. Poets saluted Canute as guarding his land in just the way that God guarded the Kingdom of Heaven, and the king mixed thoroughly his own authority with God's in his decrees, as he referred to "the law of God and my royal authority or secular law" and to the "faith which you owe to God and to me."[172] The early Norman kings toned down the exalted expressions of their divinely sanctioned office, but they incorporated the Anglo-Saxon religious awe for kings and the notion of the king as God's representative into their own ruling tradition, thus laying the groundwork for the concept of divine right as it later developed in England.

Primogeniture did not become the firm principle for determining the succession of English kings until the fourteenth century with the accession of Richard II (r. 1377–1399).[173] At the same time, the strength of the English monarchy was such that the lack of primogeniture as a fixed rule did not lead to as many difficulties in England as it did elsewhere. In general, medieval kingship encountered three types of difficulty occasioned by the absence of primogeniture throughout Europe: uncertainty as to the succession of one member of the royal family as opposed to others and strife among their partisans; the danger of weakening the monarchy through splitting up the realm among sons; and the similarly weakening effects of bargaining and concession-making when doubts about the succession led to a royal election by magnates of the realm, which was, of course, the normal course of events in the regularly elective monarchies.

Except for the confused period of Stephen of Blois (r. 1135–1154), English kingship rarely suffered from struggles over the succession before the establishment of royal primogeniture. Nor, from the other side, did its acknowledgement as a principle head off strife when serious doubts arose about royal competence. Richard II was the first king to accede to the throne in a manner clearly traceable to general acceptance of primogeniture. He became king as a boy of ten after the death of his grandfather, since his father, Edward the Black Prince, had died before him, but he was deposed by a rebellion of Henry of Lancaster, who defeated him and established a new dynasty in 1399. The lack of a predetermined choice let King John with all his faults accede to the throne in 1199 over young Arthur of Brittany, who would have become king if primogeniture had been observed, simply because John was in a much more powerful position on the death of Richard I. John remains an isolated disaster among those Norman and Plantagenet kings who would not have acceded to the throne under primogeniture before the later fourteenth century. We might perhaps see a residue of the ancient Germanic custom of dividing the realm in such decisions as that of Henry II to leave his son, Geoffrey, the Duchy of Brittany; however, the resemblance to the *apanage* policies of contemporary French kings is considerably greater. England itself was not divided. As for concessions, we find Henry I winning the support of magnates of the realm with a charter of liberties, in order to be confirmed as king against the claims of his older brother, Robert, who was returning from the First Crusade at the time of the previous king's death, but the concessions he made were neither unreasonable nor weakening. Several of the more important ones, for example, the restriction of royal feudal rights over the Church, limitations on the amount of relief due the king upon the death of a vassal, and a reduction of arbitrary royal authority in exercising wardship and in controlling marriages of the women in vassals' families, made their way into the Magna Carta.[174] After a time, the matter of concessions took the form of a king's assuring upon his accession his adherence to principles of the earlier charters and traditional English liberties, a practice which the subsequent adoption of primogeniture as the rule of succession did not affect. No matter how English kings succeeded to the throne, they found it the best course to take coronation oaths with such assurances contained in them. These did not have the effect of turning an excess of power back to the aristocracy or leaving the crown too weak to provide for the effective administration of the realm. Instead, in implicitly acknowledging the rightness of former demands for guarantees against arbitrary rule, they functioned in the same way as the Magna Carta itself by presenting the idea that English kingship in its existing form was the choice of everyone who mattered from past and present generations.

GERMANY

The German experience with feudal kingship has been used frequently thus far to illustrate unsuccessful efforts at achieving national monarchy, in contrast with the more productive efforts of English and French kings. Regarded in itself, as well, the story of kingship in Germany from the Ottonian period is basically one of decline. After some auspicious but false starts in the tenth century, rulers of Germany failed to find the necessary means for coping with a feudal order of society, in order to turn it into the basis for national monarchy. German kings were forced to mortgage potential national power, to keep up with the impossible task of maintaining their international empire.

In their essence and almost by definition, the universal claims of the empire were at a variance with the ideas on which future nation states were to be built. Periodically, German kings resorted to two ways of dealing with this problem, neither one particularly effective. One method was an attempt to establish a hegemonic position for the German people within the empire, something like the early Carolingians had been able to do for the Franks. Such efforts inevitably came to nothing. This was due partly to rejection of German hegemony by the Italians and other European peoples on whom it was imposed. It was also due partly to internal German disillusionment with the eternal ventures into Italy and other foreign expeditions, in the interests of imperial unity, that necessitated extra military and financial efforts which produced only sparse results. There was a certain unintended symbolism in the fact that the vassals and some of the subvassals of a German king had the special obligation of accompanying him to Rome, the center of their chimerical non-nation.[175]

Another way of coping with the problem, although probably not a conscious one, was to treat it as if it did not exist and to let imperial achievements pass for national ones. Appearances permitted this, particularly during the twelfth and early thirteenth centuries, when the German king and emperor seemed to be pursuing successful national missions. The most obvious of these was the movement now referred to, more often in English-language histories than German ones, as the *Drang nach Osten,* during which the subduing of the Slavs by the German knights and settlers, sometimes under imperial leadership, redounded to the credit of the German nation. Accounts like those of Henry of Livonia, for example, freely mix German national feelings with expressions of religious rapture in telling how the Livonian Brothers of the Sword carved new domains out of the Baltic regions held by pagan Slavs.[176] Diminishing returns set in here rather soon, however, for it took a great deal of conquest on the eastern frontier to have much of an inspiring effect on the Germans who had not left home. Often, too, neither German kingship nor imperial auspices were credited with either victories or conversions in the new settlements. Instead, the dukes who led the Bavarians, Swabians, Franconians, and Saxons would be recognized in their own right for leading the campaigns and protecting the settlers; the same was true of the heads of the larger religious orders.

The elective nature of the emperorship, inherited as it was from ancient Rome via the Carolingians, kept the German rulers from using primogeniture to centralize the power of either the German Kingdom or the empire. The elective practice also had the effect of weakening kingship because of the possibility it left open for the territorial princes as electors to extort weakening concessions before they agreed to the election of a king or emperor. Often the past ruler's son was their choice, but bargaining and trading in imperial elections with the goal of securing a ruler who appeared unlikely to strengthen the central government of the empire could also characterize electoral behavior. This was exemplified in the choice of

Conrad III in 1138, before the lay and ecclesiastical princes were organized into the Electoral College. It was also exemplified at the end of the Middle Ages in the choice of Charles V in 1519, more than a century and a half after the College had been regularized.[177] The electors were badly fooled about the apparent harmlessness of Charles V, but they did their best to restrict the scope of his power by demanding that his representatives sign "election capitulations" in thirty-four articles before electing him. Even when no open trading was in evidence, the gravitation of electors toward a weak ruler was more natural than toward a stronger one who could be expected to diminish the authority of rulers of principalities. The extraction of concessions had worked well in shaping English kingship, but only because the English monarchy was strong enough to begin with. German rulers had never succeeded in holding on securely to the demesne lands acquired by their predecessors from other dynasties. Partly because of the frequent changes in dynasty, this factor took a certain toll.

To be sure, German rulers could still use feudal practices and sanctions sometimes to strengthen their positions, in spite of the power of the magnates. If they had not been able to, the empire simply would not have survived. Royal vassals had helped to prevent the early German monarchy from being eliminated by the powerful lords who had acquired ducal titles for Saxony, Franconia, Swabia, and Bavaria in the early tenth century.[178] Later, Otto I gained the support of the dukes by recognizing the legitimacy of their titles and by making them his vassals, too.[179] As both tribal duke of the Saxons and king of Germany, Henry I then attempted with some success to curtail the independent power of the other dukes. His son, Otto I, gained their support by recognizing the legitimacy of their titles, while they in turn became his vassals. During the eleventh and twelfth centuries, the autonomy of the German tribal duchies suffered some setbacks. The tribal dukes were faced with the hostility of the lower nobility and were unable to maneuver well through the storms of the Investiture Controversy. They tended to side with the pope against their liege lord, the king, and consequently forfeited the trust of much of the remaining feudal world in Germany. Frederick Barbarossa, the most successful German king and emperor during the feudal period, was able to invoke the aid of his vassals against Duke Henry the Lion of Bavaria, who had defaulted on his feudal obligations in a particularly flagrant way by refusing to give Frederick the service he owed him against the Lombard League. The fact remained that the strength of the nobility, even divided as it was into classes with opposing interests, could not be challenged effectively over the long run by a monarchy which had developed no effective alternatives to reliance on aristocratic support.

German kingship was never strong enough to initiate and maintain the flow of land control to the crown, as the Capetians did in France, let alone impose an order with the crown as the apex of landholding, as William the Conqueror had done in England. The principle conceded to by Frederick Barbarossa that lands once granted by the crown had to be granted again immediately upon the termination of the feudal grant which covered them remained in force throughout the Middle Ages. This limited the ability of the German monarchy to acquire enough control of land to make feudalism work for it. The occasional willingness of German rulers to alienate crown lands as hereditary in the families of their recipients[180] and the difficulty in transferring demesne lands from one dynasty to another mentioned earlier also limited the control of land by the German monarchy. All these factors meant that German rulers did not have the secure land base under them which was necessary to make suzerainty an effective instrument, let alone to turn suzerainty into sovereignty.

The strength of the German feudal lords was such that royal courts or circuit judges never penetrated their domains with a popular form of justice to enhance kingship. Nor, even apart from the lack of an effective application of royal justice down to lower levels, did German kingship ever succeed in building up an administrative apparatus to serve as the basis for a modern state's officialdom. The sole exception in the empire was found outside of Germany in the Kingdom of the Two Sicilies under Emperor Frederick II,[181] but when he tried to extend its administrative system no further than to Lombardy he failed. Then, too, reliance on the originally unfree class of the *ministeriales* for royal administrators evoked the hostility of the aristocracy much of the time without enlisting comparable support from the German middle class. It is true that the *ministeriales* worked out quite well as officials in some of the newly acquired imperial territories; in Austria, where so many of the old noble families died out, the *ministeriales* were free to replace them without opposition. All in all, however, they could not furnish the German rulers with the support of an officialdom as effective as that which served the kings of France and England.

The papal-imperial struggle, which had long German chapters in all of the centuries from the tenth to the fourteenth, sapped considerable energy from German kingship. Germany remained the one country where the struggle between kings and popes did not serve to strengthen either national identity or the power of kingship in the national period. Much of the German nobility was as ready to side with the papacy as with the German king or emperor. German rulers countered by strengthening the power of bishops, which proved to be of rather little help in the long run. It was true that bishoprics were not hereditary, which solved some of the problems of land alienation from the crown, but the loyalty of the bishops was not entirely assured, e.g., the bishop of Mainz was as ready as the next lord to depose Henry IV and a good deal more eloquent about it. Even when bishops did not behave in a particularly independent or troublesome fashion, the favoritism shown them frequently alienated some of the nobility further. The German nobility remained sufficiently powerful that kings and emperors had to throw in their lot with them most of the time, to the neglect of the royal or imperial alliance with the merchant class, an alliance which Henry IV had carefully cultivated in the eleventh century but which remained a rather sporadic affair for the rest of medieval German history.

All this does not detract from the fact that from the tenth century on the empire east of the Rhine made it possible for a German state to arise which gave some semblance of unity to ethnic groups and regions which might have otherwise gone their own way entirely. It is even unlikely that Germans would have come to think of themselves as one people at all, if it had not been for the unifying experience of the empire in the Middle Ages. At the same time, the centrifugal forces in Germany which promoted the German equivalent of "states' rights" exerted great pressure on the imperial structure of government to which the German kingdom was committed. When the later Hohenstaufens overtaxed its resources, particularly in imperial conflicts centered outside Germany, the German Kingdom was prevented from developing into a nation state.

ARAGON

We recall that the Visigothic kings in Spain had been so insecure in the power they wielded over a turbulent nobility from the second quarter of the sixth century that *morbus Gothicus* (the Gothic disease) became an early jocular medieval name for regicide. Their kingdom was erased by the Islamic invasions of the early eighth century, but warrior bands of Visigoths, Basques, and other Christian inhabitants held out in the Pyrenees and the Cantabrian mountains. They raided the Muslim state in Spain soon after it was established, and eventually such guerilla bands formed the nucleus of the kingdoms of Leon, Navarre, Aragon, and Castile.[182] Other feudal monarchies emerged on the Iberian peninsula as the Mohammedans were pushed further southward in the great crusading movement known simply as "the Reconquest," but among them, those of Aragon and Castile are perhaps worth examining in more detail as monarchies which ultimately combined to form the basis for the Spanish nation state.

At the outset, the king of Aragon had neither the authority of tradition behind him nor the physical resources at his disposal to establish anything like control of the reconquered areas. He received a share of the lands taken from the Muslims; the rest went without any particular recognition of the king's rights in them to the warrior lords who had accompanied him on successful expeditions.[183]

Any efforts at royal centralization were further hindered by marked differences among the territories under the king of Aragon: a royal marriage joined Catalonia to Aragon in 1137, and the successful invasion of James I, or James the Conqueror, added Valencia in 1238. Each part of the realm kept its own institutions and distinctiveness, particularly with regard to feudalism. A loose feudal structure had developed in Catalonia and southern Aragon, while James was strong enough to parcel out most of the land acquired from his conquest of Valencia as fiefs.[184] In Aragon north of the Ebro River, however, feudalism made few inroads on the rough equality of kings with the barons, who protected their independence by keeping land as their own property rather than fiefs from the king. The Aragonese part in the Reconquest had been played early: in the High Middle Ages, Aragon did not feel that threat of Moslem counterattack in recently taken territory which caused the Catalonians to concentrate so much on building walled towns. The more rural and sedentary quality of life in Aragon thus let something closer to a regular feudal system develop in most sections,[185] although it was not until James I in the thirteenth century (quite late, by way of contrast with England and France) that a king of Aragon could be seen at the top of the familiar feudal pyramid.

Aragonese kingship continually met a united spirit of resistance among the classes, again in contrast with Castile, which gave form and substance to the opposition to kings from James I to Peter IV (r. 1319–1387) who attempted to centralize power in the direction of absolutism.[186] The nobility was firmly convinced that it maintained the traditional liberties of the land by preventing royal powers and prerogatives from developing along Castilian lines. As a result, kings of Aragon were in even less of a position than their counterparts elsewhere to levy taxes without first consulting with the nobility and granting concessions to them.

The special strength of the nobility in Aragon is shown in the organization and membership of the Aragonese Cortes, the counterpart of Parliament in England—the development of which it may actually have influenced[189]—or the Estates-General in France. In it the secular nobility constituted half the orders, rather than one out of three on the more usual European pattern, and its orders were easily the most powerful ones. The first branch (*brazo*) or estate was that of the upper nobility. It was made up of the heads of thirty-nine leading families, who, very much in contrast with their English counterparts, accepted only the most minimal sort of feudal obligations, if any, to the king. Eleven of them owed the king no service at all and ruled their dominions with the independence of kings themselves. The other twenty-eight noblemen admitted to owing the king three days of military service a year, which assuredly ruled out any guarantee of their support in an extended military campaign. For what it was worth to the crown, the child of either a mother or father from a family owing service to the king inherited both the noble status and the obligations which went with it. This was in a statute recording ancient rights and privileges (*fuero*), but kings of Aragon were often unable to enforce even this meager claim of being able to extend the service owed to them.[188]

In attempting to assess the relative strengths of theories of divine right and the right of resistance in Spain, there is perhaps a natural tendency to begin with the familiar and most Catholic kings of Spain in the sixteenth century and project their image backward in history toward a conclusion that kingship and the Church must have strengthened each other in the period of feudal monarchy in Spain more than elsewhere in Europe. This, however, was not generally the case in Spain; in Aragon it was not the case at all. While the common hatred of the Mohammedans during the early Reconquest period may have made support of the Church in Aragon all the more natural, the dominance of the nobility was so heavy then as to leave the clergy almost inarticulate until the fourteenth century. The Church in turn did not tie in its own lot particularly closely with early Aragonese kings, preferring instead to support the nobility much of the time. It is true that leading clerics often administered the chancellery and served the kings as advisors, but they caught the royal ear more as the holders of vast estates than as clerics.[189]

During the high Middle Ages, Aragonese and Catalonians cited theories of kingship both in favor of a Church-sanctioned right of resistance and opposed to it:

> The kings and their supporters could counter the nobles point for point. If John of Salisbury favored tyrannicide, the kings would counter with St. Thomas Aquinas, who reminded all that Saint Peter taught reverence "not only to good and moderate rulers, but also to the harsh."[190]

Kings of Aragon by and large did not push claims to rule by divine right until their increased strength and their hostility toward several of the Avignon popes during the Great Schism of the later fourteenth century led them to do so. Toward the end of the preceding century, Pope Martin IV, an obedient puppet of the French king, excommunicated King Peter III of Aragon for invading Sicily, but the decision obviously had so much to do with politics and so little with religion that Peter safely ignored it.[191]

While individual theorists might advocate absolute authority of the kings, this plainly ran contrary to the tradition of the Aragonese limited monarchy. In Aragon, the nobility retained more rights and the king fewer than in any other feudal monarchy. It was Aragonese nobles rather than kings who decided who would lead military forces and who would serve under which leaders. Aragonese kings did not even have control over the coinage: the Cortes determined not only the number of coins minted and their values, but even their designs.[192] The consent of the Cortes was absolutely necessary for the acceptance of new legislation in Aragon. It was scarcely necessary there to underline a right of resistance among nobles who felt that kingship was limited and conditional to begin with.

Enough versions of a recorded oath of precisely such conditional loyalty to the king survived after the unification of Spain, to make its final words an enduring battle-cry for Aragonese independence. A typical one goes like this:

> We, who are worth as much as you, make you our King and Lord provided that you guard for us our *fueros* and liberties, and if not, not.[193]

While it now seems fairly certain that such an "oath" in this form is only a sixteenth-century approximation of earlier Aragonese sentiment concerning the monarchy, there is no doubt but what it reflects that sentiment accurately.[194]

The Church took part in solemnizing royal coronations, although rather late — in fact, beginning only in 1204. As elsewhere in Europe, the Church supported primogeniture in Aragon to guard against divisions of the realm and to insure royal succession with the least chance of strife, but the Aragonese Church shared with secular dignitaries more of the solemnities as the heir apparent determined by primogeniture was readied for the throne than was customary in the other feudal monarchies. At age fourteen, the heir apparent had to swear an oath in Saragossa to preserve the ancient liberties of Aragon, an oath taken before the people and the *Justicia* or justice of Aragon. Upon the old king's death, an almost entirely civil ceremony gave the heir apparent his interim jurisdictional powers with an oath taken before the *Justicia,* one deputy from each of the four estates of the realm, and three jurors of Saragossa. Finally, in an inaugural ceremony, the king would swear to preserve the *fueros,* and the estates would swear to obey the king. It was most of all the presence of the *Justicia* in the Cathedral of Saragossa for the purpose of receiving the king's oath that made an heir apparent's assumption of royal power valid.[195]

It was an Aragonese peculiarity that the *Justicia,* in contrast with the English justiciar, whom he resembled in being the chief judicial officer of the land, served as much as a counterweight to royal power as he did as an instrument of the king's justice. The *Justicia* served as a mediator between the king and the nobility, when the nobles wished to appeal royal decisions. There are indications that the office originated in the early twelfth century; however, the *Justicia* became powerful only in the thirteenth and fourteenth centuries as a result of a compromise. Aragonese kings had been learning the efficacy of written law, particularly after James II joined Sicily, with its highly structured administration, to the Aragonese-Catalonian Empire. On the other hand, the Aragonese nobility was made uneasy by Roman and canon law, in fact by any written law. "Once the laws became codified, the nobility could no longer settle juridical problems either by force or by private discussion."[196] The nobles were also apprehensive about the way James I and Peter III had employed outsiders to enforce the royal will. Consequently they gave up some of their more extreme claims to judicial independence and placed considerable power in an official who was to understand the fine points of written law which they did not and who would have power to check arbitrary royal decisions. The kings of Aragon accepted the office willingly enough, in order to gain the compliance of the nobility in the new rule of written law.[197]

The *Justicia* fit well into the political environment of Aragon, where the early possibilities for centralizing and expanding monarchical power through royal justice and protection were limited by the relatively weak executive power vested in the king, in contrast with the uniquely strong legislative power in the hands of the nobility. The *Justicia* was responsible for the protection of prisoners on trial or awaiting judgments, and he could reverse those judgments which he found contrary to law. His duties included that of interfering to prevent all sorts of abuses of power, but mostly those which could be expected to come from an overly strong or arbitrary monarchy: the torture of any free man except for counterfeiting; the levying of any tax without the consent of the Cortes; arraigning, trying, or condemning any Aragonese by a foreign judge or at a location outside the realm; compulsion exercised to obtain hospitality in the course of travels; changing the value of the coinage without the consent provided for by law; entrusting any castle in Aragon to a foreigner; and secret trials or imprisonments.[198]

In medieval Aragon, the royal alliance with the middle class was slow and uneven in developing. In Aragon proper, the nobility was strong enough to hinder its advancement for a long time. It took root first in Catalonia, where the merchant class by the end of the thirteenth century was on the way to achieving a dominant economic position. In Aragon, kings tried the normal method used by their contemporaries to the north of winning over townspeople by granting them charters of rights. They varied their schemes with ingenuity: one twelfth-century king attempted to work nominally within the feudal system by the process of declaring the town of Alcañiz a fief of a religious order, thus putting himself in a suzerain position to the townspeople when he granted them local autonomy. No amount of imagination, however, could enable him or his successors to overcome several basic problems until the fourteenth century. In rural Aragon, alodial ownership — that is, the holding of lands as property outright rather than as fiefs — was widespread. This type of ownership was entrenched enough in Aragonese tradition to affect the towns, too, where the nobles often held the centers as alodial property.[199] When kings attempted to repopulate the often dangerous and unattractive reconquered areas, they were able to recruit settlers only by including independence from much royal control among their privileges. Throughout Aragon townsmen as a class were well aware of royal weaknesses and somewhat like their counterparts in central Europe did not generally respond with more than minimal support in return for royal privileges and immunities.

In the late thirteenth century, Aragonese kings began to have better luck pursuing alliances with Catalonian merchants and financiers on two bases of mutual benefit: the common interest of kings and the commercial classes in the spread of Roman law, and the willingness of kings in financial need to borrow money at substantial rates of interest. The merchants, of course, preferred a nonfeudal legal system based on written codes, while Aragonese kings, apart from profiting by the chance to extend royal justice and protection under written law, also relished the thought that the Roman-law principle of monarchical will might one day become reality in Aragon: "What pleases the prince has the force of law (*Quod principi placuit.* . . ." See ch. 2).[200]

Under James I and Peter III, money borrowed from Catalan merchants strengthened the monarchy against the nobility. A significant part of the funds went to employ mercenary troops which lessened royal dependence on feudal military service. Sometimes merchant communities even recruited troops for the kings. In 1283, for example, the Catalonian Jewish community furnished Peter III with troops to meet an impending invasion from France.[201] There was an added advantage to the crown in borrowing from the merchants: when royal real estate had to be put up as collateral for loans, the merchants generally did not occupy the lands, whereas nobles who lent kings money expected to do just that. In time, Catalonian businessmen grew aware of the advantages accruing to them from Aragonese royal power, not only to oppose the feudal nobility, but also to break the commercial monopoly of Italian cities. Kings of Aragon proved willing to strengthen the hands of their merchant subjects by fair means and foul. In the venture of licensing piracy they preceded Queen Elizabeth of England by nearly three hundred years. The oddity of their policy was in the way in which it figured in their alliance with the merchants. Merchants were effectively permitted to employ privateers against the ships of foreign city-states and countries. In 1299 and 1301, James II even went so far as to put royal ships under the control of merchant interests for rent and as much as fifty percent of the loot taken by them in pirate raiding.[202]

While the merchant community generally preferred to support royal interests against feudal ones, it attempted to check royal abuses in the economic sphere. It was the merchants who put a stop to royal coin-debasing and counterfeiting by refusing to accept light-weight new coins or imitations of Arab and Castilian coins, which the crown was attempting to pass off in the thirteenth century. It seems to have been merchant influence in considerable part which took the power to control the coinage out of exclusively royal hands and — in a rare display of solidarity with the nobility — entrusted final power to regulate it to the Cortes and the *Justicia*.[203] More enlightened kings of Aragon, however, had no desire to tamper with the coinage. Such embarrassments as this were more than offset by merchant support of the monarchy both as a class and individually. Kings of Aragon made Jews royal officials at least partly because of their double dependence on the crown for any position they might hold. They eventually recognized a pool of available talent in their commercial class which could be used to fill royal offices and, from still another standpoint, make the crown less dependent upon the nobility and the high clergy with its aristocratic mentality.

CASTILE

Castilian kingship had beginnings as modest as those of Aragon, in furnishing leadership to Basques and the amalgam of Hispano-Romans and Visigoths as their slow recovery of parts of northern Spain from Saracen conquerors began. In comparison with their counterparts in Aragon, who made similar attempts to turn their loose control of warrior bands into an effective monarchy, medieval Castilian kings encountered less organized feudal opposition; however, by mid-fifteenth century their attempts to consolidate power had not proven successful. At most, their sporadic efforts developed instruments of governing which rulers from the time of Queen Isabella were to put to good use.

Castilian law evolved from the constantly amended Visigothic codes of Euric's successors. The main code of the High Middle Ages, the *Fuero Juzgo,* still incorporated much of the material which survives in the *Lex Visigothorum.*[204] In the fifth century, the Visigoths had brought to Spain the ancient Germanic notion that kings were responsible to the warriors who elected them. This lived on in Castile, even when the monarchy became hereditary, in the idea that a king could legislate only with the consent of the Cortes. It survived even longer in the defiance shown by the highest nobility to royal attempts at centralization.[205] At the close of the Middle Ages, one of the more extreme statements justifying tyrannicide appeared in a work by the Jesuit writer, Juan de Mariana, *On the King and the King's Education (De rege et regis institutione).* In its advocacy of killing heretic kings, it sent chills down the spines of Elizabethan Englishmen and other Protestants, who cited it with much indignation. While it did not interest them at all that Mariana was also a first-rate national historian, the fact that he was one and was quite familiar with the Visigothic practice of doing away with undesired kings led him to join his contemporaries during Spain's golden age in turning the threat of regicide into something of a Spanish constitutional principle on historical grounds after a thousand years.[206]

Their proud heritage of independence led the Castilian nobles to offer formidable opposition to royal authority from time to time, but local conditions, particularly the constantly shifting borders during the Reconquest period, an era which lasted longer for Castile than for Aragon, worked against the establishment of much of a feudal system, in spite of the fact that feudal practices had early origins in Spain.[207] Sharp social and political distinctions divided the Castilian aristocracy, while the links among its members as lords and vassals were fewer and weaker than in Aragon. At the top, the *rico hombre,* or grandee, felt that his title and authority in his own domain were not only derived from origins independent of the monarchy, but also quite beyond the power of a king to bestow on other nobles. The second rank, that of *hidalgo*, came to denote earned nobility; Castilian kings regularly awarded it as a title and even sold it. Its holders were often at odds with the grandees, while the class of *caballeros,* or knights, did not perceive its interests to be particularly close to those of the noble groups above it.[208]

Partly because of divisions among the nobility and partly because representation from the towns was a strong element in the Castilian Cortes from its inception, unlike the Cortes of Aragon, it was never an effective instrument for restraining the monarchy on behalf of feudal interests.[209] Castilian kings had the services of loyal counsellors at their disposal, and from the mid-thirteenth through the later fourteenth centuries they turned an informal advisory body into a formidable political instrument, the *Consejo Real,* or Royal Council, which aided the royal administration, particularly in the field of finance.[210] To be sure, the Royal Council often exercised authority for child rulers and at times established its right in law to wield what amounted to a veto power in the crown's civil, military, and diplomatic affairs. Among other things, the council sometimes prevented the king from naming bishops to vacant benefices, from granting pensions beyond a certain limit, and from alienating the royal demesne without its consent.[211] Later, however, the council's powers would be undermined by the simple fact that members were selected by the kings themselves. In 1385, King John I appointed twelve men to form his Royal Council, four from each estate: clergy, nobles, and commons. Although he called it a *Cortes*, it plainly did not rest on the principle of election which had characterized earlier bodies of that name, particularly in Aragon.[212] Some recollected Visigothic traditions of limited monarchy survived to uphold the idea that kings of Castile should legislate only with the concurrence of the Cortes[213]; however, they were not sufficient to keep the crown from legislating on its own behalf. It is true that John II and Henry IV ruled Castile quite ineffectively during most of the fifteenth century (1406–1474), but Henry's sister and successor, Isabella, was able to strengthen monarchial power decisively through the ancient art of balancing interests of the

estates of the realm against each other. The Castilian Cortes was sufficiently divided in its branches that it proved possible for a strong monarch
simply to dispense with the functions of a dissident estate in legislating,
and, in effect, to treat the whole body as merely an advisory one.

Although medieval Castilians did not distinguish themselves through
support of the papacy, the crusading fervor of the Reconquest flamed
higher and longer in Castile, strengthening the position of the clergy beyond what was the case in Aragon. Castilian tradition told of how Saint
James, whose tomb in Compostella was a site much venerated by pilgrims,
appeared in the air on a milk-white steed, bearing a white banner with a red
cross, to inspire Christian soldiers against Moslem invaders.[214] The Castilian Church took both responsibility and credit for victories against the
Saracen infidels, and Castilian priests often led armies in battle to bring
these victories about. When towns were reconquered from the Arabs,
religious orders normally received a generous portion of the territory and
spoils. High ecclesiastics often wielded more secular authority than the
nobility. For example, the abbess of Huelgas had jurisdiction over fourteen medium-sized towns and fifty villages. The archbishop of Toledo,
who combined the offices of primate of Spain and grand chancellor of
Castile, was from a Castilian perspective, the highest ranking ecclesiastical figure worldwide after the pope. He came closer than any other magnate in Castile to making feudal obligations work for him systematically,
in that he could count on more vassals answering his summons than could
any other high crown vassal in the kingdom. He maintained secular jurisdiction over fifteen large towns in Castile as well as a multitude of smaller
places.[215]

The church in Castile backed a form of royal primogeniture which
transferred the succession through the direct line, male and female. Castilian laws and commentaries stressed the divine origin of kingship at the
same time they enumerated rights and prerogatives of the crown.[216] Still,
memories of the early elective kingship survived vividly enough into the
fifteenth century to prevent theories of divine right from having much
impact on behalf of royal absolutism. A Cortes in which the estates of the
realm were represented was supposed to approve the title of an heir apparent before the old ruler's death. Upon his succession the new ruler had to
swear an oath to uphold the liberties of the kingdom; only then would the
estates in turn vow to uphold their end of the contract.[217] This did not
always work in practice, to be sure, and kings acceded to their offices on
several occasions well before their approval by the Cortes,[218] but the
ancient elective rights of the Cortes were periodically evoked to keep royal
independence from becoming an acknowledged part of Castilian tradition.

Neither sacerdotal nor thaumaturgic kingship existed in medieval Castile, which produced no counterparts to Saint Louis or the Anglo-Saxon and Scandinavian saint-kings. The fervor of Spanish religiosity in general did not permit the king to assume religious powers simply by virtue of his royal office. The only exceptions, possibly resulting from French influence and without lasting historical significance, came up in the Kingdom of Navarre, where Sancho II and Carlos Viane were believed to have cured scrofula by their royal touch.[219] In Castile, Alfonso X explicitly condemned the notion that kings could cure scrofula as

> . . . not worth one rotten fig. . . .
> For you say I have that power,
> And you speak nonsense.[220]

Even the outstandingly pious and successful Ferdinand II, who permanently united Castile and Leon, persecuted the Albigensians obediently at the direction of the Church, and waged several victorious wars on the Mohammedan frontier, had to wait for the seventeenth century for his canonization.

While Rome gave to members of the clergy the unifying stress on education which set them apart from and above the rest of the population, the clergy made use of both education and special position to show strong independence from Rome when Rome accepted ecclesiastical rights and prerogatives later from kings in Spain. Papal prerogatives themselves were slow to gain recognition in Castile, where until the twelfth century kings maintained judicial rights over the clergy and an only slightly veiled form of lay investiture in their right to confirm clerical elections or declare them void.[221] By the thirteenth century, the papacy had made its claims felt both concerning the independence of the clergy from royal court jurisdiction and the freedom of ecclesiastics to conduct elections without royal interference. Alfonso X, or Alfonso the Learned, who followed Ferdinand II and ruled Castile from 1252 to 1284, stressed written law in order to give a sounder basis to royal rights, but in borrowing from both Roman law and canon law he conceded to the pope, in effect, the right to grant benefices. This, in turn, meant many benefices in the hands of foreign-born ecclesiastics. The instinctive reaction of Castilian clerics to their own losses in benefices was to seek indirect compensation from the crown for themselves in the form of immunity from taxation.[222]

Differences between popes and Castilian kings over investiture and taxation rights opened a chapter in the story of similar conflicts all over Europe. It was complicated by the strength of the religious military brotherhoods in Castile, particularly the Order of Calatrava and the Order of Santiago (Saint James). Having been continually engaged in the Reconquest since the twelfth century, they demanded the privileges of both the clergy and the aristocracy for themselves. The papal-royal struggle in

Castile, which reached its height during the Babylonian Captivity and the Great Schism, differed from that in other European countries in two main ways. One of its distinctive features was its tripartite division of sides. The Castilian clergy generally supported its own cause without allying with either the royal or papal factions. The other was the hesitance of Castilian kings to press the conflict as a national or imperial cause in the way that other rulers from Henry IV in Germany to Philip IV in France had done. It simply remained unresolved until the time of Queen Isabella.

Kings of Castile would seem to have had greater opportunities than those of Aragon to capitalize on the appeal of royal justice and protection. Townsmen who stood to benefit from it were more numerous in Castile than Aragon, while the aristocratic elements in the Castilian Kingdom, who could be counted on to oppose or subvert it, were more divided among themselves. And yet the shortcomings of its court system proved to be one of the major weaknesses of the Castilian monarchy. The townsmen were often jealous of their right to run their own courts, while the nobles and higher clergy succeeded in turning to their own advantage many of the royal efforts to expand a central judiciary system, in spite of conflicts within their own ranks.

Local judicial authority in Castile had two main origins. One was in the high degree of autonomy granted to the many fortified towns which at one time or another were exposed to Arab attacks and whose citizens had broad responsibilities for their military defense and government. The other was in the need for granting privileges of self-government and the corresponding independence from royal control to the inhabitants of frontier regions, as part of an inducement to get more people to settle there and hold the land. On the basis of royal charters, citizens often elected judges through their councils, and local judges so chosen administered civil and criminal law, although from at least the thirteenth century on their decisions were subject to appeals to the royal tribunal. Castilian kings sought to protect the minor judges in their localities through sending out inspectors called *pesquisidores* with the mission of reporting abuses. These early inspectors also helped to introduce a practice, new to Castile, of preferring charges in the king's name against well-known breakers of the law, without waiting for a local plaintiff to bring charges. The purpose was to bring to trial powerful men of the nobility, who would be normally able to intimidate potential accusers among the townsmen. This was certainly a step in the direction of expanding the concept of the king's peace; however, townsmen remained at least mildly suspicious of the royal inspectors. In the fourteenth century, Alfonso XI sent out judges appointed by himself, the first *corregidores,* to aid local judges in enforcing the written law and the king's peace. Some of the *corregidores,* however, soon used their positions to attain power in the fields of finance and general administration, as well as taking over the more important work of the locally elected judiciary. The result was that municipalities objected mightily to having such officials assigned to them without their consent.[223] The powers of the office remained intact, but its holders did little to popularize the judicial system of Castilian kings until considerably later.

Early kings of Castile had handed down decisions in the company of magnates informally selected for their ability to give advice on legal questions. Until the thirteenth century, no clear line of demarcation separated such a group from the Royal Council, whose membership was equally irregular. Then in 1274, Alfonso X created a separate and supreme tribunal with the purpose of having some judges always present at the royal household to hear cases. The king retained his position as the highest judge in the kingdom: he intended at first to preside over the administration of justice in the tribunal for three days a week, although the pressures of other business eventually cut down his personal participation to Fridays. The supreme tribunal was rather elaborately put together to assure that there would be judges from different parts of the kingdom; it was also divided into a group of twenty-three judges particularly familiar with the *fueros* to hear appeals.[224] Since it could function in the king's absence, it had a certain standing and authority of its own; however, Alfonso's successors did not make effective use of it until the mid-fourteenth century.

The overall judicial situation in Castile was complicated by the fact that royal appointments to judgeships in the outlying regions were sometimes made in a way which allowed their recipients to turn them into hereditary offices and to combine them with military power. The result was a conflict of authority and jurisdiction, which royal centralization efforts were only partly able to overcome before the reign of Isabella. The nobility continued to exercise judicial rights in their own domains or to pass them on to councils of their own choosing.[225] Even for the supreme tribunal Castilian kings tended to select judges from nominations made in the Royal Council, where nobles were more likely than others to exert influence.[226] The *ricos hombres* posed perhaps the greatest problem, in that they never pretended to accept royal jurisdiction even in times of conflict: instead, they reserved to themselves the right to renounce allegiance to the king if they chose to do so.[227] From still another standpoint, the nobility stood in the way of royal efforts at judicial standardization by dominating the military-religious brotherhoods, which demanded clerical immunities from royal courts.

The materials for balancing forces against each other to the advantage of the crown may have been available to Castilian kings, but taken one with another they were not equal to the task. The personal element was, of course, significant in itself. With a few exceptions, such as Ferdinand II and Alfonso X, Castilian kings were neither a creative nor a talented lot. The exasperation of contemporaries and immediately succeeding generations lives on in the epithets attached to many of them, including "Henry the Ailing," "Alfonso the Bewitched," "Peter the Cruel," "Alfonso the Slobberer," and "Henry the Impotent."[228] Feudal monarchy never reached the stage in Castile where the feudal lords felt obliged to render even lip-service to the monarch as suzerain, let alone sovereign. Still, it developed such institutions as the supreme tribunal and the *corregidores* for more capable hands to use, and all the while it remained true that the opposition to Castilian kingship was terribly disorganized and at odds with itself, in spite of victories by default.

SCANDINAVIA

Kingship of a sort which has distinct parallels to that of England, France, and Germany shows up in medieval Scandinavian history from the first. In attempts to reconstruct it, the general paucity of documents and the virtual absence of chronicles or annals for Scandinavia, particularly Sweden, in the early medieval period throw the historian back upon two devices: extracting a maximum of factual material from basically legendary sources and speculating backwards in history on the basis of considerably later documentary evidence.

With that caveat, we can claim to find early Scandinavian history revealing the figure of the chieftain or small king in the combined role of priest, military leader, and administrator of justice. Even when these functions later emerge as more differentiated, the sacral nature of Scandinavian kingship, above all the role of the king as placator of the gods and guarantor not only of victory but of good harvests, remains more pronounced than in European kingdoms farther south.

Because of the strong role in government played by tribal assemblies, called *Things* in Sweden and Norway and *Tings* in Denmark, they modified the development of kingship in Scandinavia more than comparable bodies elsewhere. In the "prenational time," i.e., before the consolidation of provinces or smaller territories into Norway, Sweden, and Denmark, kings were "permitted to rule only during good behavior. . . ."[229] The Uppland *Thing* continued, well after the historical period had begun, to require the early kings of Sweden to submit to its authority.[230] For European kings to promise upon their accession to respect prevailing law and custom was nothing special, but for them to be held responsible to a political body in any way was almost unique to Scandinavia in the early period. The closest points of comparison are provided by the Cortes and Justicia in restraining the monarchy of Aragon and by the Witenagemot's influence on the Anglo-Saxon kings of England. Similarity with the latter is probably not accidental, for there had been considerable institutional borrowing back and forth between England and Scandinavia in the tenth and eleventh centuries before the Conquest.[231]

While the Viking Age lasted, successful Scandinavian kings, functioning as chiefs over warriors who fought without being greatly divided by rank, did not have to worry about aristocratic opposition. Following defeats, however, royal chieftains were likely to be deposed. When more settled times followed the Viking Age, the richer and more powerful men who were to form the nobility generally resisted royal attempts at centralization.

Feudalism in the northern lands never developed very fully. No chain of vassals and subvassals ever held all the land from the king even in theory: manors could be privately owned and frequently were. On the other hand, when a king such as Harold Fairhair, who became the first king of all Norwegians in the late ninth century,[232] did begin making grants of land to his nobles, these tended to remain valid for one lifetime only,[233] so that what feudal tenure there was did not erode under the hereditary principle to anything like the extent characteristic of France and Germany.[234] For both better and worse, the northern nobility was never arranged into anything like the model feudal pyramid. Scandinavian, particularly Norwegian, kings could frequently count on loyal military service from their vassals, but the groups beneath the king's vassals had to be dealt with directly without the aid of the institution of suzerainty. Only as the feudal period neared a close was the nobility structured into royal governance: in the 1270s the Norwegian King Magnus VI (the Law-Mender) made a regular institution out of the Council of the Realm and thus gave secular and ecclesiastical aristocrats a formal advisory role in royal administration. Toward the end of the thirteenth century, the Swedish King Magnus I (Barnlock) attempted to enlist aristocratic power by making an assembly of nobles and high ecclesiastics, which had previously been entitled to meet independently, into an instrument of the crown as the royal council.[235] From the standpoint of strengthening royal power, these measures had little immediate effect. In Denmark, an analogous experiment at the end of the thirteenth century ended with independent power vested in a council which kept the monarchy limited by the nobility and clergy from the late fourteenth century through the end of the Middle Ages.[236] At most, they provided precedents for later kings to juggle the composition of bodies speaking for the nobility until the age of absolutism approached.

In general, the notion of a king's divine right to rule was much weaker in medieval Scandinavian minds than the idea of resisting an unsuitable or tyrannical king. Northern kings backed the Church and the work of conversion, while the Church supported Scandinavian kingship against its enemies; however, the relationship was often an equivocal one. Conversion to Christianity began later in Scandinavia than it did farther south and proceeded more slowly. Early Scandinavian royal converts to Christianity, like their Anglo-Saxon counterparts, were apt to alienate their pagan subjects to the point of losing their thrones and sometimes their lives. In the early eleventh century, two Swedish kings, Olaf Sköttkonung and Inge, had to flee in the wake of a pagan reaction when, as kings, they refused to perform the heathen rites which went with their office.[237] It was, of course, not only Christian kings in the north who met disastrous ends for malfunctioning in their role as placator of divine power, although adherence to Christianity obviously heightened the related risks. According to one account, the Norwegian king and unconverted pagan, Harold Greycloak, paid for a series of bad seasons and harvests in the 960s with his life.[238] According to Snorre Sturlason's version of the *Ynglinga Saga,* at least two kings had met the same sort of fate in pagan Sweden. In one instance, the people attempted to overcome famine by sacrificing oxen; when that failed they offered men the next year. Then

> . . . for the third harvest many Swedes came to Upsala at the time when the sacrifice should be held. The chiefs then took counsel, and held to a man that Domaldi their king must be the cause of the bad seasons and also that they should have to sacrifice him in order to have a good season, that they should bear their weapons against him and kill him and dye the altars with his blood. And so they did. . . . Domaldi's son was called Domar, and he next held the kingdom. He ruled for a long time, and there were good seasons and peace in his days.[239]

Later, Olaf the Tree-Feller met a comparable end, when hungry Swedes burned his house with him inside.[240]

Church spokesmen in Scandinavia did not generally either preach the sacredness of kingship with particular fervor or stress the principle of legitimate hereditary succession as necessary for kingship. Although kings of Norway until 1162 claimed direct descent from Harold Fairhair through the male line, the Church agreed to switch the following year to a claimant through the female line, Magnus Erlingsson, who subsequently gave the Church considerable leeway in the determination of the succession.[241] In Sweden, the Church went right along with the elective principle until the end of the Middle Ages, when Gustavus I established the Vasa dynasty in hereditary kingship early in the Reformation period. Church-state relations were perhaps closest in Denmark of the three countries, both in terms of mutual support and of friction. Danish kings belonged to the Estrith dynasty for nearly three centuries (1047–1332), but hereditary succession through the eldest son had not been established as a matter of principle. In the early twelfth century, the Danish King Niels provided the Church with tithes and the immunity of clerics from royal court jurisdiction; at the same time, he received Church support for royal acquisition of court fines, shipwrecks, and treasure troves.

Medieval Scandinavia saw the loyalty of bishops stretched between kings and popes as part of the European-wide tension between the forces of Church and state. In the eleventh century, Harold III (Haardraade or Hard-Ruler) attempted to keep Church appointments under royal control, maintaining that "There is no archbishop in Norway but me."[242] In the late twelfth century, King Sverri insisted on keeping the established Norwegian practice of having bishops elected by the clergy and people in the presence of the king rather than appointed by the pope or a Norwegian archbishop. Like Harold III, he frankly claimed the power of archbishop for himself,[243] but he was practical enough to realize the need for tolerating a clerical archbishop so long as he would agree to accept the king's restrictions on the money he could collect, on the jurisdiction of ecclesiastical courts, and on the retinue he could maintain. The last demand ignited Norway's bloodiest medieval conflict, the Crosier War, between supporters of the king and those of Archbishop Eirik Ivarsson, whose education in Paris had made him a fervent protagonist of Church independence and papal supremacy. Sverri won the war, but stable Church-state relations were restored only when his son, Haakon III, made concessions enough to meet the papal party halfway.[244]

Pope Innocent III intervened in a royal power struggle in Sweden on behalf of King Sverker the Younger, who had exempted the clergy from the jurisdiction of secular courts and Church property from royal taxes, against his rival, Erik. Neither papal support nor military assistance from the Danish king was enough to keep Sverker from defeat and death; however, Erik proceeded immediately after his victory to conciliate the papacy. His successors confirmed and extended the privileges of the clergy with the result that the papal faction had few complaints to lodge against the policies of Sweden's kings until the middle of the fourteenth century, when the unpaid loans of the Papal Curia to Magnus II added fuel to another kind of papal-royal conflict leading to the excommunication of Magnus in 1358.[245]

In Denmark there was a distinct analogue to the Becket controversy and one which occurred close to it in time. Archbishop Eskil, an outspoken advocate of Church independence, supported Alexander III against the antipope named by Emperor Frederick Barbarossa, who was the liege lord of the Danish king, Valdemar I (the Great). Valdemar and bishops loyal to him supported the emperor and his protege, and Eskil had to flee to exile in France. Good relations were temporarily restored when Eskil agreed to canonize Canute Lavard, Valdemar's murdered father, in 1170. The king made some concessions on Church freedom from royal control, and Eskil anointed Valdemar's young son as future king, a step which seemed to sanction hereditary kingship in Denmark.[246]

Thirteenth-century Denmark, however, saw an even more heated power struggle of the same sort, with most Danish bishops siding with the king, Erik Klipping, against Archbishop Jacob Erlandsen. All Denmark ended up under a papal interdict, as England had in the reign of King John. In a turn of events paralleling King John's misfortunes in another way, the Danish nobility took advantage of royal problems with the Church to press for a chartered confirmation of aristocratic rights. It was out of this struggle that the Council of the Realm of Denmark established significant legislative rights and a share of governing responsibility with the king for some three hundred years beginning in 1319.[247]

In Norway, where kingship had become stronger on the basis of its own resources than in other Scandinavian countries during the High Middle Ages, kings tended to use the Church less for ideological reinforcement until the reign of Haakon Haakonsson in the thirteenth century. While the temporarily successful unification of Iceland with Norway is usually seen as Haakon's major achievement, he took care to advance the interests of the Church at the same time. Although he had already been ruling since 1217, a papal envoy performed special coronation rites for him in 1247 which were new to Norway, and, that being the season of massive papal discontent with Emperor Frederick II, Haakon was mentioned as a likely Roman emperor.[248] The period of close cooperation between the Norwegian Church and monarchy between that time and Haakon's death in 1263 proved to be exceptional and did not set a pattern for Haakon's successors.

Justice in medieval Scandinavia remained for a long time under the power of the *Things,* which meant that a need for royal justice and protection was generally less strongly felt in the North than elsewhere in Europe. Life was cheap enough in ancient Scandinavia when Viking bands readily dispatched victims with war axes and swords, but as a stark point of contrast with wartime behavior and a readiness to offer human sacrifices, the law of the time was applied rather gently. If later Icelandic practices can be extended back in time on the mainland, the acceptance of the law had a large voluntary element in it: persons were bound to accept justice from kings or the tribal assemblies largely by virtue of having placed themselves under their protection.[249] Punishment was largely confined to payments imposed as the price of a man killed, fines of different sorts, and outlawry. Torture, mutilation, or death sentences were rare, while imprisonment was almost unknown. The law itself was largely memorized and spoken by a "lawman" or "speaker of the law," from whose function the office of speaker in modern parliamentary systems circuitously derives.[250] The emphasis of law among the early Norsemen, as among other Teutonic peoples, was the adjudication of disputes to prevent blood feuds from arising. The readiest means to assure this was a system of compensation for crimes so that the injured party or his survivors could be bought out of a desire for revenge. There were crimes, however, even in pagan days, which could not be paid for, those which were felt to affect society at large, such as manslaughter in sacred places, arson, inland piracy, and sorcery. Combating these offenses became the narrow basis on which the king's judicial responsibility rested at the outset in Scandinavian countries. As elsewhere in Europe, the concept of the king's peace was expanded as the area increased in which kings purported to defend the interests of society at large, and the king's role as the ultimate judge in his realm expanded proportionately. By the mid-thirteenth century, the judicial role of the king could be perceived as his primary one, as the following prayer written by a Norwegian cleric for kings to recite would indicate:

> [G]ive me the right understanding, self-control, and sense of justice, elo-
> quence, purpose and good intentions, so that I may be able to judge and
> determine the causes of rich and poor in such a way that Thou wilt be
> pleased, while they rejoice that justice is done among them.[251]

The power of kings, particularly when supported by clerics in their service who had received some education in jurisprudence, grew at the expense of both the assemblies and the lawmen, as written law gradually replaced oral tradition. Canon law sometimes clashed with the oral law of the people, particularly in matters of land assignments and bequests, and when it did, clergy in the royal service were prone to favor the former. In Sweden, a bishop served as royal chancellor through most of the Middle Ages,[252] while lesser clerics served in royal record-keeping and administration as in the rest of Scandinavia. The concept of the king's peace made slower headway in Sweden and Denmark than in Norway, but even in the former countries it made the common sentence of outlawry far more effective by making it apply to the whole realm equally. A banished person was no longer able merely to take refuge in an adjoining province.

As an administrative service heavily staffed by clergy, the growing primacy of written law, and kingship itself all tended to further and strengthen each other, Scandinavian kings got into the business of making law outright. In Denmark, the royal-clerical administration of justice was greatly furthered by the organization of the new towns which sprang up on the coast in the twelfth century: judgments in the town court system were based on written law and showed a "tendency to become summary and radical" in contrast with the earlier system of justice under the clans and the *Things*. In 1241, King Valdemar II (the Victorious) standardized the administration of justice by having a royal committee draw up a set of laws, the Jutland Code. This was then passed by the *Landsting* of Viborg, which enjoyed a certain primacy among the assemblies, and was promulgated by the king for the whole country.[253] Throughout Scandinavia, it became common practice for a king to present new, amended, or standardized law for confirmation by an assembly. Thus the kings made law into a more stable and predictable instrument of government, while at the same time depriving the assemblies of their initiative and yet alienating them from the king as little as possible. This turn of events was less obvious in Norway, where in theory the *Things* retained power to introduce as well as pass legislation. Even there, however, kings could introduce law proposals or bills, which were usually passed, to standardize or unify the law. Most Norwegian kings paid attention to cultivating good relations with the four major legislative *Things*. From the twelfth century, many of the delegates to the *Things* were appointed by the king's own officials. Finally, in the later thirteenth century with the approval of the *Things*, King Magnus VI or Magnus the Law-Mender standardized the laws governing town life in the direction of providing greater security for productive town inhabitants. With the same eye towards advancing the economy of the country in long-range terms, he introduced a measure to require that a fourth of all arable land should lie fallow at any one time.[254] In such instances the assemblies passed the actual laws but followed royal initiatives.

Although Scandinavian traders carried on considerable commerce by sea, the general sparseness of population in this region tended to hinder the growth of a large urban business and commercial class. This was the case in Norway, in spite of the efforts of such far-sighted kings as Magnus VI, somewhat less so in Sweden, and markedly less so in Denmark. In Sweden, a large proportion of the trading was carried on by Germans who settled with royal encouragement and protection, to further the country's urban development. Many of the first Swedish town councils were dominated by German settlers, which meant that they were even more responsive to the kings than their Danish counterparts.[255]

Scandinavian kings occasionally appealed to the interests of free farmers against the nobility. For example, Magnus Barnlock earned his sobriquet by protecting this class from powerful lords who had fallen into the habit of travelling around with their retinues and forcing farmers to feed them and their horses without payment. Magnus prohibited this practice and helped to make it workable by seeing to it that a man was appointed in each village to buy travellers' provisions from farmers and sell them under royal protection.[256] But, in general, throughout medieval Scandinavian history we find very little of the alliance between kings and native middle classes which helped to solidify monarchy in France and England. Royal taxes in Scandinavia do not appear in the context of a king's accepting middle-class support to become less dependent on the nobility. In Sweden, royal taxes which were applied to rural areas in the thirteenth century fell particularly on peasants in the royal demesne, while those working the estates of other lords or renting land from them were generally exempt from the king's taxes.[257] At the same time, Swedish kings kept pursuing their earlier policy of encouraging German traders to establish settlements. These prospered; one of them flourished under the walls of a fortress built for protection against pirates and furnished a good part of the nucleus for the future city of Stockholm.[258] The same sort of thing was happening in Norway: one convincing theory of the eclipse of later medieval Norway blames the failure of the Norwegian kings to promote native commerce and establish more new towns as a basic economic policy, rather than relying upon commercial development in foreign hands. The policy actually pursued by Norwegian kings can be tied in with their chronic financial embarrassment in the period which began medieval Norway's decline. The acute Norwegian royal dependence on foreign loans undermined the independence of the monarchy.[259] The overall result of this lack of a royal alliance with a middle class was that Scandinavian kings, somewhat like the emperors in Germany, were thrown for support more and more on the nobility that demanded a high price in influence and independence for its cooperation.

Just what degree of independent power a truly enterprising and successful Scandinavian nobleman could wield under a king is demonstrated by the development of the office of royal justiciar in Sweden. At roughly the same time that Henry II and Richard I in England were turning the office of justiciar into a mainstay of royal government, Birger Brosa, the first great Swedish justiciar, was acquiring such influence under King Canute Eriksson that his career soon had more in common with a Merovingian major-domo's than an English justiciar's. He assumed leadership of the army in wartime, acquired and assigned landholdings to loyal followers, concluded treaties with foreign powers, and soon maneuevered his family into the position of furnishing candidates for the throne itself.[260]

Scandinavian kingship furthered national identity along familiar lines both with and without assistance from the Church, which favored a stronger, centralizing monarchy as long as its own interests were not threatened. Thaumaturgic kingship in the form of good kings assuring good seasons had deep roots in Scandinavia, as the fate of the kings mentioned above who were found inadequate in this respect would indicate. Just how deep those roots went, however, is demonstrated by the attachment of the people to the body of Harold Fairhair's father, Halvdan the Black:

> Of all the kings he had been the most fortunate . . . in having good seasons, and all loved him so highly that, when they learned that he was dead and his body was being taken to Ringerik (where they would give him a grave), the great men of Raumarik and Vestfold and Hedemark went there and they all demanded his body for themselves to lay it in a howe in their own district, for they expected good seasons if they had the body. Finally it was agreed that

they should divide the body into four parts, and the head was laid in a howe
at Stein in Ringerik, whilst each of the others took home his part and laid it in
a howe. . . .[261]

While Halvdan was no saint, royal martyrs at the hands of antiroyal forces
or foreign pagans became both saints and objects of national pride. In
early medieval Norway, Olaf II enjoyed the support of a nationally
minded Church in his conflict with the old nobility, who held out for
paganism. When he was killed by peasants commanded by a nobleman,
miracles were attributed to him, and he was regarded as the patron saint of
Norway a century before his canonization in 1164.[262] The day of his death
became the earliest Norwegian national holiday.

Although he was never canonized by the Church, the Swedish king Erik
IX acquired enough posthumous fame to become patron saint of Sweden
after he led a Christian crusade against the pagan Finns and — in a sequence of events which may or may not have been historically related —
was murdered by a Danish prince.[263] In Denmark, Canute IV supported
the Church but otherwise ruled in anything but a saintly manner, as he
pressed royal forest and water rights to an extreme, rigorously imposed the
duty of supporting and supplying his entourages through the realm, and
collected fines in the administration of royal justice and the enforcement
of royal prerogatives with particular harshness. When his attempts to
impose fines on a large group of farmers who had failed to make themselves available for a raid against England provoked a rebellion, he was
forced to flee and was killed in a church at Odense in 1085. His brother
negotiated his canonization, trading royal support of Church independence in return for Church stress on the sacrilege of rebelling against the
king as the Lord's deputy and recognition of Canute as saint and martyr.[264] A few years had to pass before much national pride could be evoked
by the memory of Canute IV, but royal and Church cooperation and
propaganda succeeded eventually in making him a national hero as well as
patron saint of Denmark.

From a different standpoint, Scandinavian kings furthered national
identity, although less successfully, by putting national interests, both
secular and ecclesiastical, against those of the papacy or international
Church. In Denmark, Valdemar I had rallied considerable, but quite temporary, national support in his stance of opposing Pope Alexander III and
Archbishop Eskil. Royal descendants of Saint Erik in Sweden took a
pronational stance in their struggles with a traditionally propapal family
to win out a few times in obtaining Sweden's elective kingship.[265]

In general, royal and ecclesiastically supported efforts in Scandinavia
moved in the direction of national delineations into the kingdoms of
Sweden, Denmark, and Norway, although Scandinavian kings were

happy to unite two or even all three of the kingdoms in a personal union when opportunity presented itself. The nobility generally stood for the ancient traditions of provincial self-government. In native works of history written by clergy loyal to the kings, national consciousness stands out from the first. Foremost among these is the work of Saxo Grammaticus, secretary to Valdemar I's foster brother, Absalon, whom the king had made a bishop and then, in his conflict with Eskil, archbishop of Denmark. Saxo gave a new luster and permanence to the legends of early Danish kings, bringing his work down to the day of Valdemar himself. It was first in Saxo's descriptions that we find faith in Valdemar's healing children and increasing the abundance of harvests as he walked along.[266] Since the king continued to embody the people in Denmark as elsewhere, this sort of thing served the exaltation of Danish kingship and the heightening of Danish national consciousness simultaneously. Reflecting either a conscious or unconscious perception of a people's identity in their kings, Saxo's work which features Danish kingship is entitled *Deeds of the Danes (Gesta Danorum)*.

It is one of the least debated facts in the reconstruction of ancient Scandinavian history that kings and chieftains were elected and could be deposed by warriors. In Snorre Sturlason's account of the Swedish Olaf Sköttkonung, a lawman reminds the king that such a great decision as that of war or peace is not his alone to make:

> Now we *bönder* [free men] wish thee to make peace with [Olaf the Fat], King of Norway, and wed thy daughter Ingegerd to him. . . . But if thou wilt not have it as we say, then we shall go against thee and slay thee, and endure no more unrest and lawlessness of thee. Thus have our forefathers done before. At the Mula Thing, they pitched down into a well five kings who had been too haughty as thou art now to us. . . .[267]

An early Norwegian law stipulates matter of factly:

> No man shall attack another in his home, neither the king nor any other man. If the king does this, the arrow shall be sent forth through all the shires; and [men shall] go upon him and slay him, if they are able to seize him; and if he escapes he shall never be allowed to return to the land.[268]

Through the early period of national differentiation, kings in Denmark and Sweden were still usually elected, while those of Norway, after Harold Fairhair, gained their throne most often through hereditary right. These distinctions are anything but absolute, however, since in Norway nobles and clergy could juggle the line of succession somewhat, as noted above. In Denmark and Sweden, kings attempted with varying degrees of success to position their sons as future rulers in the manner of the first Capetian kings of France. King Valdemar's son, anointed as coregent, had succeeded to the Danish throne in 1182 as Canute VI, but this sequence of events did not set any lasting precedent. In the later thirteenth century, King Erik Klipping of Denmark attempted to have his son crowned during his own lifetime, but the uncertainty of his step was underlined by his need to protect himself with German troops at the time. Fear of "a hereditary monarchy upheld by foreign forces" sparked a revolt among the nobility which turned out to be only the first in a series of conflicts leading to the confirmation of elective monarchy during the fourteenth century.²⁶⁹ In fact, a prohibition against the king of Denmark's seeking to name his son as successor remained in the law of the land until 1536. Aristocratic resistance to the hereditary principle in kingship was less drastic in Sweden, where, for example, Magnus I had his son, Birger, accepted as his successor in 1284; but in principle elective kingship lasted almost as long in Sweden as it did in Denmark.²⁷⁰

All in all, Scandinavian kingship in the High Middle Ages was characterized by the greater restrictions placed upon it, by the failure of divine-right theories to gather much momentum, and by the lack of much middle-class support. It consequently comes as no surprise that its relative strength from time to time depended on the military and administrative talents of outstanding individuals in the royal office, who were aided somewhat by the popularity of royal justice and protection and also by a nascent consciousness of national identity. The importance of national identity as a factor in relation to kingship is seen dramatically in the case of Norway. With the assumption of the Norwegian crown by the rulers of Denmark in the fourteenth century, the country suffered not only the economic decline noted earlier but entered a period of "495 years in the shade."²⁷¹ It was only the restoration of separate Norwegian kingship in 1814 which reestablished the nation with a place in the Norwegian perception of world history.²⁷²

The ancient sacral role of the king lasted in Scandinavia through the Middle Ages well into the seventeenth century. It was transformed, of course, with the advent of Christianity, but it remained more consistently a focal point of popular attention than was true in the case of European monarchies elsewhere. Its endurance remained a rather doubtful blessing for Scandinavian kingship, however, where such concrete matters as warding off revolts or strengthening the king's authority in Church affairs were concerned. In theory, the way it associated the king with the fruitfulness of seasons and the constancy of the forces of nature should have helped to strengthen his office. What actually seems to have happened in historical times, however, is that good seasons were enjoyed with no more than perfunctory thanks to Scandinavian kings; it was a more than offsetting deficit for the same kings to be held responsible for droughts, excessively long winters, and famines.

Chapter 6

Theories of Kingship in the High Middle Ages

From the twelfth century, kingship became the object of much concentrated study in its own right. In looking at the transition from antiquity to the first medieval centuries, it was reasonable to speak of the main theorizing about secular rulers as "the Church's view of kingship," for churchmen then did the only serious writing on broad political and social topics. They dealt with kingship—the art of ruling well—only as an instrument for enabling the Church to do its work or, on occasion, as a threat which could undermine the efforts of the Church and encroach upon its sphere of authority. In the High Middle Ages, churchmen were keenly aware of the old problems of Church and state. From one standpoint, the confrontation between Gregory VII and Henry IV at Canossa was over the same issue that had brought about the confrontation between Theodosius and Saint Ambrose centuries earlier. Bishop Otto of Freising in his *History of the Two Cities,* the High Middle Ages' counterpart to Saint Augustine's *City of God,* saw an ominous parallel between the excommunication of Theodosius and that of Henry IV. For him it signaled the approaching end of the earthly city altogether.[1]

Yet in the development of Western political institutions, superficial similarities between the two events were misleading. Saint Ambrose, after all, had faced an empire in the West which had less than a century of life left in it. In the High Middle Ages, on the other hand, in spite of Church rebukes and occasional victories of the clerical party over the royal one in cases of conflict, secular monarchy was a rising phenomenon, not a declining one. Individual kings and emperors could be overcome, but kingship was an art of the present and future all the same. As a result, and often in spite of grave reservations, clerical writers were forced to focus more and more on kingship as a separate institution and to construct theories concerning its nature and proper exercise, instead of merely looking at kingship when it suited them or seemed to threaten them. Only at this point does it make sense to speak of "theories of kingship" as such, rather than "the Church's view of kingship."

By the end of the thirteenth century, a new element was added. Churchmen no longer monopolized the world of ideas. Secular writers, such as Dante, were more apt to look at the Church in its relation to kingship rather than kingship in its relation to the Church. They were also more apt to discuss restraints upon rulers in terms of other secular institutions than their early medieval predecessors had been, although there was certainly no agreement about the legitimacy or wisdom of such restraints. Then, too, there were clerics, such as Marsiglio of Padua, who looked at the Church's efforts to bend kingship to the demands of the ecclesiastical hierarchy as wrong.

In discussing kingship within the framework of political theory from the mid-twelfth to the later fifteenth century, this chapter will focus on a broad trend: the evolution of the framework in which kingship was seen. The first was an organic view of Christian society with an unchallenged acknowledgment of the primacy of Church interests, a view which differed from that held by Saint Augustine or Gelasius I chiefly in the tremendous importance it attached to kingship. The eventual treatment of kingship as an institution was one in which the institution could be analyzed in terms of its own merits and shortcomings.

JOHN OF SALISBURY: TWO REAL SWORDS AND THE ORGANIC THEORY OF KINGSHIP

The revival of learning, now sometimes called the "Renaissance of the Twelfth Century," necessarily had its impact on political theory. Where the Carolingian Renaissance had sought to rejuvenate Christian society with learning in the spirit of the Bible and the Fathers of the Church, the Renaissance of the Twelfth Century was less narrowly focused. Its leaders were interested in ancient learning in general, and it remained an inescapable fact that most ancient social and political learning was overwhelmingly secular in the values it defended. Medieval Christian writers, who took clerical authority and the stress the Church had always placed on the salvation of souls for granted, could integrate classical learning into their world view, but it was an uphill labor. In the long run, it was a losing proposition.

John of Salisbury's work, *Policraticus,* completed in 1159, if perhaps not quite "the first attempt to produce a coherent system which should aspire to the character of a philosophy of politics"[2] in the Middle Ages, was at the very least a monumental effort to use the new learning on behalf of the traditional organic view of Christian society. At the time he wrote, Henry II of England was consolidating royal power in what was slowly becoming the English nation state with a considerable degree of success.

There are passages in the *Policraticus* in which John cautions the monarch to recognize the just bounds of his royal power, but within these limits John is all in favor of strong monarchical rule. The tone of John's work is confidently didactic when he deals with kingship, rather than polemical. It is as if his delineation of the good ruler and his functions, put together from the most appropriate ancient, pagan, and Scriptural sources, together with later history and personal observations, is so self-evidently a correct one that it needs only to be stated properly to be accepted. He simply proceeds to outline an ideal of kingship by describing the relation of the true king to the whole of Christian society. He then validates his conception of the monarchical ideal by showing what happens when a historical king lives up to it or fails to do so. John thus uses a "mirror of princes," although his mirror for kings is clearly a segment of the larger one reflecting the whole Christian community. Along the way, he also employs a mirror of reverse images, to demonstrate the prototype of the bad ruler, the tyrant.

In spite of many a lengthy excursus, it is always clear enough what John considers to be the main functions of the king. The king is the man divinely ordained to exercise power on earth in order to keep the peace and to render justice to his subjects. With the advice of the clergy, whose task of saving souls the true king recognizes as superior to his own, the king is further obliged to use his secular power to strengthen the faith. But it is a bit misleading to talk about the king's functions in the *Policraticus* as if they were at all finite, for John's king is more than the ruler of his people: he also embodies the whole of his people to the point that his fate is theirs. Consequently, the fact of his living an exemplary Christian life serves not only to inspire imitation but actually determines what sort of divine rewards or punishments shall be visited on the people, as he himself is rewarded or punished. If the king is deficient in fulfilling his role, the people must generally bear with him in deference to the divine source of his power; however, there are cases in which the king's default is so great that he no longer is a true king but a tyrant, the vicar not of God but of darkness. When the tyrant comes into view in the *Policraticus,* the question arises as to whether to put up with him or to remove him; tyranny is not a form of kingship but its perversion.

John claims to have adopted his organic conception of the state, or the "commonwealth," from Plutarch[3]:

> First of all, the prince should examine himself thoroughly and give careful attention to the whole body of the commonwealth, in whose behalf he prospers. For the commonwealth is a certain body, as Plutarch liked to put it, brought to life by the grace of divine favor, moved to action as the greatest demands of justice require, and controlled by the moderating faculty of reason. Those things which institute and cultivate religion in us and which

are instrumental for the worship of God (I do not follow Plutarch here by saying "of the gods") take the place of the soul in the commonwealth. Thus those who have charge of religious worship ought to receive that great respect and devotion rightly due the soul. Who, indeed, would doubt that the ministers of holiness are God's own representatives? Further, just as the soul has ruling authority over the whole body, those whom Plutarch calls governors of religion have charge of the whole body. Augustus Caesar was subject to the sacred power wielded by the priests until—to avoid being subject to anyone at all—he made himself a pontiff of Vesta, and a little later he was raised to the company of the gods, while still living. In the commonwealth the prince has the place of the head, subject to God alone and to those who act as his representatives on earth, seeing that in the human body the head receives its vital force from the soul and is governed by it,[4]

This is, of course, not the real Plutarch speaking. "Plutarch's" *Instruction of Trajan,* which John cites, seems to have been an educated medieval man's idea of what a great political biographer and moralist like Plutarch might well have said about the state and the sort of thing that Trajan (the twelfth century's prototype of good ancient rulership) might well have been guided by. Calling those entrusted with religious worship the instrument for controlling the body politic, as the soul controls the body, reflects a Christian rather than a pagan Roman view of the proper position of the priesthood.[5] Such an equation does, however, perfectly illustrate the idea of a secular sphere under the authority of a spiritual one, which developed in the century between Saint Ambrose and Pope Gelasius I. Again the thought of any legitimate conflict between the two spheres is suppressed at the start: a conflict between the soul and the head is a disease and nothing more.

We are reminded that the Carolingians, too, had stressed an organic view of the *populus Christianus.* During the Carolingian Renaissance, special circumstances had permitted Pippin the Short and Charlemagne to function with clerical approval as heads of the body politic; however, the Frankish clergy at the time did not emphasize their own equivalence to the soul controlling the king as head. The Carolingians had been content to stress fusion of secular and ecclesiastical power and had never faced the problem of conflicts within overlapping spheres of jurisdiction. Through reviewing the history of the intervening centuries, however, John of Salisbury evidently gained the insight that any real discussion of kingship had to deal with this problem concretely.

In spite of his head-soul analogy and an explicit statement that the king is inferior to the priests in their authority,[6] John speaks of the two swords of Christian rulership in a way which implies a greater degree of real equality than Gelasius' pronouncement on spiritual and royal power had permitted. John's presentation of sacred and secular rulership, as rightfully enjoying together all coercive power within a kingdom to the exclusion of all other claimants, brings out what the two forces have in common by virtue of this shared legitimacy:

> Two swords are enough for Christian rulership; all others belong to those who approach as enemies with swords and cudgels, in a desire to capture Christ and wipe out his name.[7]

While John emphasizes the ruler's subordination to the clergy in matters of religion, the secular framework within which he generally elaborates on the art of ruling well keeps this subordination relationship very much in the background for long stretches at a time. An immediate contrast between John and fourth- or fifth-century churchmen who dealt with kingship is evident in the attention which John devotes to the skills which a king must acquire to rule well. Here Eusebius had gone no further than admiration for the learning, acuity, and diligence of his patron, Constantine the Great. A monarch's ruling skills were quite beyond the interests of Augustine and Gelasius. *Policraticus* is aptly translated "The Statesman's Book." It is to a considerable degree a kind of handbook of skills and learning necessary for a king, if he would reflect a good image in the mirror of ideal Christian rulership. Pious inspiration and good will may set the king on the right path, but it is the exercise of self-discipline and the acquisition of a considerable body of knowledge which enable him to function as a king should. For example, the king must learn to read things himself, no mean or lightly assumed skill for secular men in the Middle Ages, for he must know at first hand what God enjoins upon him. John approvingly recalls a letter of Emperor Conrad III, in which that German ruler urged Louis VII of France to have his children given an education in the liberal arts, including the German ruler's "tastefully added comment that an illiterate king is like an ass who wears a crown."[8] In the ruler's education, John assigns a special place to controlling and properly deploying armed forces. Again, the king must understand military science himself, for the defense of the realm and its internal peace are his own responsibilities: this, in fact, becomes for John "the field in which the wisdom and justice of the ruler shine out the most."[9]

Most of the things John's good king must learn sooner or later contribute to the art of living up to the law and being able to enforce it. In executing justice, there are two sets of recurring problems which the king must learn to deal with: he must spurn the temptations of pleasures and the pleas of favorites; he must also learn to be wary of the extremes of severity and leniency.

John's admonitions to the king to be chaste and avoid avarice are about what one would expect any Christian moralist to advise any layman with broad opportunities to make free with his subjects' women and money.

There is also a certain predictable quality to his warnings against parasites and flatterers, who will attempt to corrupt the king's justice. Of more interest perhaps is the great care which John enjoins upon the king in the matter of choosing counselors; here he implicitly underscores the loneliness of the medieval king in his ruling task and the fact that he could take no functioning of any organ of government for granted. John's king must personally see to it that his military commanders know the arts of war and discipline their soldiers properly. He must inform himself to make sure that judges in his realm do not turn the administration of justice into a lucrative business.[10] Only judiciously selected counselors can help him weigh evidence and reach decisions in public matters: they are the king's heart, and weakness in them will make him rule badly in spite of himself.[11] John is not overly optimistic about the prospect of finding perfect counselors. While he never settles for anything less than the ideal in depicting the true ruler, he goes rapidly from the ideal counselor to the counselor that the prince can actually hope to find:

> I really do not think that the ruler can expect to find a man for counselor who has never done wrong, but only one who has no inclination to wrongdoing, who hates sin, who takes pleasure in what is right and fervently wants to see it done—what you might call "a man of good will." Still even this requirement should not be made of a man down to his toenails; instead, the man should be chosen who is "as good as possible," as people often say, one who seems quite upright not in any absolute sense but in relation to others.[12]

On the question of leniency versus severity, John ostensibly seeks the middle ground of firmness tempered by mercy. Particularly in dealing with individuals, it would seem that royal kindness is a great virtue. A king is foolish whose harshness makes him hated. It does no harm for the sovereign to cultivate a manner of speaking that implies good will toward his subjects. Doing permissible favors for difficult men will frequently turn them into supporters of the king.[13] The chapter in which he deals at length with the rightful place of beneficence and reconciliation in royal power contains several ancient citations on the healing art of the ruler, much to the point in view of John's organic view of the body politic, for when a king destroys his own subjects he destroys part of his own body. For John, anything like the Biblical injunction to pluck out one's offending right eye is a resort for the last extremity only. On this subject, John purports to expound on the wisdom of his beloved Trajan:

> He was given to calling a man insane who would prefer to gouge out his inflamed eyes rather than cure them. He would say that a man's nails should be cut if they were too sharp, not pulled out. If lute players or those with other stringed instruments take great pains in removing the fault of a string that is out of tune, to get it into tune with the rest, and if they achieve the

sweetest harmony from the discordant members, not by breaking any strings but by tightening them or loosening them as proportion requires, then how much more, indeed, should a ruler modulate sometimes with the harshness of justice and sometimes with the mildness of clemency, so that he will make his subjects of a single mind at home with each other, so to speak, and make a great and complete harmony out of discordant members by works of charity and by care of them with an eye towards peace.[14]

Elsewhere in the same vein John emphasizes that a king's desire to do justice should not lead him to abridge the ancient liberties of his kingdom, lest he become justly hated as an oppressor. He should always show restraint and good sense enough to listen to honest criticism, freely expressed.[15] At the same time, restricting local autonomy, as opposed to taking away freedoms from individuals, can be all to the good. John is a sufficiently astute observer of his own world to see clearly that, given the normally volatile state of political relations in the Middle Ages, a concentration of power in royal hands tended to be beneficial, while a diffusion of power in the hands of local lords was an invitation to perpetual strife. Again, in discussing Trajan, his constant model of a good ruler, John notes that he bestowed economic benefits on the cities and provinces of the empire and increased the riches of deserving individuals as well. At the same time, however, Trajan extended the boundaries of imperial control and kept his authority everywhere intact.[16] Firm monarchical rule and the general enjoyment of freedom in prosperity are, for John, simply two sides of the same coin.

When it is a question of the king's repressing organized threats to the peace of the realm, John's recommendations for mercy fade into the background. He recounts with evident approval how Edward the Confessor sent an able commander, Duke Harold, to deal with the marauding Welsh from around Mount Snowdon. Through apt methods of warfare the Welsh were beaten in a campaign lasting two years, and the whole male Welsh population that the Duke could find was killed off down to the little boys. King Edward received the heads of the chiefs as a token of some sort, and afterwards "this Duke's valorous achievement so finished the Britons [Welsh] that almost the entire tribe seemed to disappear, as by the indulgence of that same King their women were married by Englishmen."[17] For good measure, royal officials were to have the right hands cut off of whatever Welshmen survived and ventured beyond a set point with weapons. Strictly speaking, John uses the story to illustrate good generalship rather than royal policy, but the point is crystal clear that when pacification is an issue, a king's cause should be served with the utmost severity.

Whatever task confronts the king, he must obey the laws of God and those of his kingdom. While effective employment of his armed forces remains the supreme test of royal wisdom and justice, obedience to the law is the standard for determining who is a king and who is a tyrant. Obviously nothing could be of greater importance, for kings are to be served unquestioningly, while tyrants may be killed with impunity. But what obedience to the law means in this sort of discussion of the lonely medieval king, who decrees what secular law is in his own right, is something else again. Beyond stressing that all Christians, and the king among them, are bound by the laws of God or laws which answer an eternal purpose, [18] John does not take up the question of clearly defined checks upon the king. It is enough that the true king considers himself bound by the laws, assumedly those of his predecessors with the additions and modifications he has made himself.

John's conception of the ruler's relationship to his subjects is nearly as paternalistic as Saint Augustine's: subjects are wards of the king, worthy of his indulgence to be sure but not entitled to pass in any way upon what measures the king decides are good for them. John is aware of the Old Testament's limitation on the royal power — the matter of binding kings in chains and nobles with links of iron — but it is characteristic of him that he cites it as a subterfuge employed by unscrupulous elements in order to justify their misdeeds. [19] This abuse has its counterpart in the wanton invocation of the render-unto-Caesar principle by unjust men with some sort of claim to royal protection, as they speak wildly of lese majesty. Real lese majesty is one of the most heinous crimes a subject can commit in John's book, but charging others with it can also be the last refuge of scoundrels. [20]

John sees the king's role in strengthening the faith primarily in terms of his setting a good example of Christian morality in his own life, while refraining from taxing the Church either with demands for money or with appointments of his favorites to Church positions. In his negative assessments, he may be alluding critically to Henry II's high taxes levied on the clergy prior to his expedition against Toulouse[21]; he certainly criticizes Henry II openly and bitterly for naming the wrong men to ecclesiastical posts:

> Ask our very fortunate King of the English and still quite unconquered Duke of the Normans and of Aquitaine what he really thinks of the men he thrusts into these offices, and it is my opinion that he will say that there is no evil afflicting the clergy that these men are not the cause of. [22]

John does not chafe, however, at the thought of a secular monarch's setting rules for the conduct of candidates for clerical office, if these are laid down in good faith. In another example of his taking the "Two Swords" of Christian rulership more to heart than Gelasius himself had done, John thoroughly approves of Justinian's decrees concerning selection of the clergy according to their proven moral excellence.[23] These statutes had been the consequence of that Byzantine ruler's view of "two ministrations" under imperial purview, which was in itself rank caesaropapism of a type foreign to the Western tradition. John supports the Justinian ordinances, however, with the remark that since the ancient doctors of the Church set too high a standard for the clergy of his time to maintain, these rules set by a secular monarch should be followed as a minimal norm.

As a loyal churchman, John is, of course, concerned that what belongs to "that exalted City on High which is our Mother"[24] should not be encroached upon by the king or any other man. Still, his denunciations of simony as a current danger gravely threatening the Church do not make a consistent target of the king. His horror over corruption inside the Church on occasion offsets his statement that the maladies besetting the clergy are all traceable to royal appointments of self-seeking prelates, as he dwells on adversities which cannot be laid at the king's door by any stretch of the imagination. These include the challenges to the Church establishment from wandering friars whose conspicuous poverty and holier-than-thou attitude John finds a great affront to Church unity.[25] He sees a host of worldly ambitions which corrupt the Church hierarchy outside as well as inside England. Although John defends the spiritual overlordship of the papacy, he sees the whole environment of the papal court as inescapably corrupting.[26]

For John, the way a king lives his life determines the fate of his people, quite apart from the decrees he hands down to them. The king as the head of the body politic represents the whole people, as well as rules them, much as in portraiture where the head can represent the whole person. The king and the people share the same fate, according to John, for "the people are shaped by what the prince deserves, while his government is shaped by what his people deserve."[27] John is convinced that a king can earn a prosperous reign and even a lasting succession. He refers to the divine *promise* made to pious and deserving rulers, and, obviously, what is promised to good rulers in the way of a prosperous reign also belongs to their peoples to enjoy.[28]

In a mystical way as well, the king holds within himself the well-being of his whole people, for the people are identified with their king to the point that their very continuance as a people can depend on him. John sees in the symbolic raising of a king, taking as his example Saul's being lifted onto the shoulders of his people, a sign of the king's assuming responsibility for the people's well-being. Why should this be done, he asks,

> . . . unless the man who is to be set over others should be one whose spirit

and countenance show that he is able to embrace the breadth of the whole people in the arms of his good works, so to speak, and to protect them by being more learned, more holy, more careful, and more distinguished by every other excellent quality.[29]

All this is symbolic of the natural feelings which should prevail between king and people and hence of the king's value as a source of inspiration to his people. It is not an indication that the king as a matter of fact excels his subjects in any extravagant way. John's conviction that such a bond is natural and proper does not prevent him at one point from subjecting it to some analysis. John was familiar with the phenomenon, often observed in ancient times and later, that when a king was killed in battle that battle was lost for his army. Their king's death could turn a powerful fighting force into an abject and disarrayed mass of fleeing warriors. John further recognized that this sequence of events did not necessarily have anything to do with how effective or deserving a king was. It was instead the fact of losing the tribe's collective existence in the living institution which gave the members a coherently united being. As an illustration of the point, he takes a case from classical antiquity. The Illyricans and Thracians defeated the Macedonians, whose old king was dead, but afterward the Macedonians brought their infant king close to the line of battle. From his nearness and the fear of his loss they caught the will to win. In spite of their enemies' better training, the Macedonians defeated them and showed "that in the former conflict the Macedonians had been lacking a king, not fighting qualities."[30] He notes that they had placed the royal cradle near the front "as if they had been defeated" earlier for want of a king. While he leaves open the question of whether "superstition or loyalty" was the causal factor, the incident confirms for him that only a king can inspire this sort of determination in a people.

The identification of the king with the people heightens the problem of tyranny in the *Policraticus*. A tyrannical sovereign is sometimes taken by John to be simply a plague inflicted by Providence for the punishment of the people or for some unknown end. Having a king and his people share the same fate can also mean that evil in a monarch taints the very being of the people and leads to their undoing.[31] What, then — if anything — should a man do who sees his people not only oppressed but tainted by tyranny in the land?

John's answer is difficult to present concisely, for the simple reason that his work is strewn with contradictory statements on the subject of bearing with tyrants or doing away with them,[32] as has been amply shown. Yet it would seem fair to give precedence to those statements which John makes with particular fervor as being those which he feels most deeply to be true and to those which he supports with an abundance of detail as being those which he has most carefully thought out. That John firmly believes that a people need not put up with tyranny seems amply borne out by the tone of this passage:

> In whatever way this [tyranny] arises, it is clearly an attack upon divine grace, and in a way it is a battle challenge hurled against God. The prince fights for the laws and the people's liberty; the tyrant thinks no act worth his while that does not make a hollow mockery of the laws and condemn the people to slavery. The prince is a certain image of divinity, and the tyrant is the image of the proud defiance and depravity of Lucifer, our Old Enemy, since he imitates him by trying to place his throne in the north and by assuming attributes of the Most High God with His goodness left out.[33]

If God is thus challenged by a man who imitates the devil, then it would follow that God's people should take up the fight, and indeed:

> The prince, image of the Deity, is to be loved, revered, and obeyed; the tyrant, image of depravity, should instead be killed in most instances.[34]

A little later, John seems to explain why this is true "in most instances" (*plerumque*) rather than always: killing a tyrant is a praiseworthy act, providing that the perpetrator is not bound by fealty to the tyrant, does not avail himself of such an insidious means of dispatching him as poison, and avoids everything else in the process which might cause him a "loss of religion and honor."[35] Here his specific modifications underscore the general imperative for tyrannicide. At the same time, John sets great store by the legend of Saint Mercurius, who rose from his grave to kill the tyrant, Julian the Apostate, at the express bidding of the Virgin Mary. He also describes how the long dead English king, Edmund the Martyr, executes the divine judgment against tyrants with the sword and with disease.[36] These stories do nothing to offset John's idea that tyrants should be killed, but they do imply that Christians may do well to wait until they feel divinely admonished to rid the land of a tyrant and that the hand of God, rather than human planning, should be the moving force in tyrannicide.

THE BOOK OF EMPERORS: KINGSHIP IDEALS FOR POPULAR CONSUMPTION

In our own day, the term "theory" is the subject of considerable definitional controversy in political science, but two aspects of John of Salisbury's writing will indeed certify him as having a theory of kingship even for the purists who insist upon the construction of universal models as the essence of political theory. John does indeed engage in analysis by abstracting the elements of good and bad kingship out of a wealth of examples, to construct universal models. At the same time, his cause and effect demonstrations prove at least to his own satisfaction the validity of his models.

At very nearly the same time John was writing the *Policraticus* in England, an anonymous cleric of Regensburg was composing a German vernacular work for the most popular audience he could reach. In doing so, he presented a similar theory of kingship but in a quite different format. The result of his efforts, now generally and somewhat misleadingly called the *Kaiserchronik,* is first and foremost a book about good and bad ruling types rather than historical subjects as such. Its older name, *The Book of Emperors and Kings (Der Kaiser und der Könige Buch)* describes it better, and, since it deals with hardly any kings who were not imperial rulers, *The Book of Emperors* describes it best.[37] To be sure, the author refers once at the outset to his work as *"Crônicâ"* and insists on the truth of his verse stories of old Roman, Byzantine, and German emperors, but in neither form nor content is most of his book a chronicle or any other form of historiography recognizable to moderns. It is instead the portrayal of model rulers. By focusing upon one or more important attributes — persecuting, Christian, faithful, apostate, just, negligent — he lets the attribute determine the biographical sketch. Where an attribute is firmly linked with a ruler by history or legend, the writer feels free to incorporate all sorts of instructive material to illustrate this attribute as part of this emperor's story, even when it means borrowing from the real or legendary life of a quite different ruler.[38]

The epic Middle High German form of *The Book of Emperors,* and the author's explicit statement that people who waste their time and endanger their souls listening to the falsehoods of singers of fiction would do better to listen to his "good song," indicate quite different expectations of an audience than John of Salisbury could have had with his learned Latin treatise. *The Book of Emperors* is written to be read or chanted to literate and less than literate alike, assumedly in installments, for its 17,283 lines comprise the longest work of any type in German before 1200. This makes the parallel ideas in the *Policraticus* and *The Book of Emperors* all the more striking with regard to the nature of true kingship and what can be expected from those whose lives reflect the ideal model.

For the German author, quite like John, a king needs considerable education in the sense of acquiring both the requisite character traits and knowledge. Luxury and idleness are, of course, constant dangers, and young rulers-to-be must be taught self-reliance through overcoming severe hardships. This, at any rate, is the ideal. Faustinian, a benign, just, and altogether legendary emperor inserted in *The Book of Emperors* between Caligula and Claudius, approves of a thoroughly Spartan course of training for his two older sons:

"Proper discipline and fear in a boy are all to the good: the man who lets tenderness keep him from instilling these into a boy most often raises a faint-hearted man, one who will never observe any standard in doing things or leaving them alone when he has reached the age of understanding and is supposed to take over himself what is left to him. . . . My boys are to be forced to let freezing, hunger, trouble, and heavy labors help them put their youth behind them. What they learn will do honor to the Empire, so that they will live afterwards well content and justly famous."[39]

Nor can book-learning be neglected either. Faustinian predicts that from studying under wise teachers in a far-off land his sons "will be equipped early with a knowledge of excellence that will bring great honor to us, too."

After the apparent loss of his two older sons, sent abroad to study, and of their mother, who afterwards went seeking them, Faustinian leaves his throne to wander after them. Addressed to the Roman nobility, his parting words concerning the education of his remaining heir resound with the limp platitudes driven on by the brute conviction of their rightness which have made pedagogical theory justly famous:

"I entrust the boy Clement, my youngest son, to you. Have him taught the books, and bring him up so that he is a credit to yourselves. As long as he is a child, do not let him go around with nothing to do. Idleness and laziness leave only bad effects with age. Acquired wisdom enhances manliness, while self indulgence spoils it. Learning as a young man the proper bounds of speaking well and keeping silent when he should will help him do well for himself. Observing proper limits and keeping faith must go hand in hand: wherever these get separated, bad things are sure to follow. The one who is to sit surrounded by Senators at Rome, deciding the right course of action as he upholds justice in his wide domains, will need a full measure of knowledge."[40]

Later, all his sons—for none are really lost, but have been instructed meanwhile in the true faith by Saint Peter—make the best possible use of their skill in logical and theological disputation, acquired variously by studying Epicurus, Plato, Aristotle, and, of course, Scripture. They convert their own philosophically minded father, Emperor Faustinian, to Christianity.

The final note of the story does, to be sure, let the uses of royal learning take an unusual turn in *The Book of Emperors,* particularly since Faustinian becomes so imbued with religion as to become a monk and abdicate his secular office. The norm is, of course, for kings to keep putting their acquired wisdom to use as kings.

More typically, the author is content to let his examples of excellence in rulers speak for themselves: good kings will follow good models. Once, for special emphasis, he directs the attention of kings to the career of Trajan. For him, as for John of Salisbury, Trajan is the ultimate model of good rulership. In *The Book of Emperors,* as in the *Policraticus,* Trajan's justice and Saint Gregory's intercession even gain salvation for the emperor in spite of his paganism:

> Let all the kings of the world now heed the example of the noble Emperor Trajan—how he gained such mercy from God for having persevered in righteous judgements while he lived in this world. They will be sure of the same mercy, if they keep Our Lord in their administration of justice.[41]

The king's primary function remains throughout that of insuring justice by a speedy and impartial application of the law. Trajan, as prototype of the good ruler

> . . . handed down just judgments to the lord and to the serving man. His justice cost poor people no money at all. No man could gain such wealth or power as to be of avail against him. As for those miswrought and criminal rogues who richly deserved maiming and hanging, neither silver nor red gold was of any help to them: death was always awaiting them. No one dared offer him any sort of payment, and no one dared support guilty men. His was a kingly life.[42]

As an example of the just ruler in action, the author recounts how, on one occasion, Trajan called his army together and prepared for a campaign against the Normans. "He already had one foot in the stirrup," when a widow came up to him and demanded justice against the murderer of her son. She remonstrated with the emperor about his leaving, perhaps never to return, without doing his most important duty. Trajan, knowing her words to be true "dismounted from his horse and, alighting upon the ground, said with tears in his eyes: 'My lady, I shall not depart from here without fulfilling your wish for judgment.' " The accused had taken upon himself the avenging of his brother's murder, when, of course, he should have sought justice under the law from the ruler. Trajan heard the case, had the man executed, presented his head to the widow, received her blessing, and went on to win a great victory over the Normans.[43]

This was what kingship was all about, and our author foresaw no pedant in the banquet hall who would interrupt his reading with the observation that Trajan ruled hundreds of years before the stirrup was invented or the Normans threatened the peace of Europe.

Before Trajan, other righteous pagan rulers, notably Augustus and Titus, distinguish themselves in *The Book of Emperors* in much the same way. The Law of the Empire has, for the author, a divine as well as a human origin, which naturally makes it all the more binding on the ruler. Where a more sophisticated work would later trace the source of the human (positive) law to various gradations of natural or divine law, *The*

Book of Emperors puts the relationship in terms much easier to grasp. In it, the Law of the Empire was already a standard of justice in the time of Titus, who upon his accession to the throne "called for the Law of the Empire to be brought forth" in the same way that other figures in *The Book of Emperors* call for Scripture or some other solid authority to be brought out for settling some controversy. Titus "would never hand down justice except as the Law commanded him."[44]

This same Law of the Empire was then later perfected by the workings of the Holy Spirit at the time of Constantine and Sylvester. During the whole week following Constantine's conversion, these two men, emperor and pope, prayed, meditated, and set down inspired articles together. These began with the prohibition of pagan worship and progressed through the institution of cardinals, bishops, and priests. Finally, on Saturday,

> . . . they brought the Law of the Empire to fulfillment: the King prescribed for his court—and it is still written down this way—what dukes and counts and all those under them should be and the way that all those bearing the name "knight" should live their lives.[45]

Then in the time of Charlemagne, after "the Law of the Empire had fallen into sad neglect," which is as close as the author comes to conceding the fall of the Roman Empire in the West, an angel recited its articles to the emperor, including some regulations not mentioned before on tithes and gifts of property to the Church and a quite detailed statement on what clothes and arms were strictly prohibited for peasants. This sort of legislative process gives new arrangements ancient birth and consequently puts them beyond challenge. The College of Cardinals, actually instituted in 1059, is thus moved back to the fourth century for its origin, while recent decrees to keep peasants from looking and acting like knights are put back at least a few hundred years. All these things emanate from God and are entrusted to future kings to uphold.

In telling of Charlemagne's son, Louis, the author does not make use of a single historical or recognizably near historical fact. The general reputation of Louis, who has come down even into modern history as "Louis the Pious," provided him with a solid basis to build on nonetheless. Since his Louis is a devout and good emperor, he not only obeys the Law of the Empire himself, but sees to it that the nobility of his realm have their children instructed in it. Louis himself uses his proper ban against rebels and, after sentencing them according to the Law of the Empire with the approval of bishops and lay nobles, has them executed. His justice and vigilance lead to a clean sweep of criminal elements: highway robbers are hanged, murderers broken upon the wheel, arsonists beheaded, thieves blinded, and breakers of the peace deprived of a hand, leading the author to exclaim "Hai! What a Peace of God that was!" As a result:

> Peace then flourished in the Empire. The King ruled as mightily as his father had before him. The leaseholds remained whole, untouched by robbery and fire, and the son who took over after his father would find what he inherited to be as pleasing a sight as it had been before.[46]

The fact that the real Louis the Pious could not keep his own sons from waging war against him, much less provide a lasting and general peace for his whole realm, fades into irrelevance here because we are in the ethereal realm of pure theory. It is, of course, more than a little dogmatic to insist that a model of kingship does indeed work well in the absence of support-ing facts, but then there was nothing wrong with being guided by proper dogma in the twelfth century. What could be more reasonable or more consonant with the faith than these propositions? A king renowned for piety is a king committed to the law. Fully committed to the law, he brings about a just and lasting peace with God's help. Under the threefold influ-ence of a pious king, law, and peace, his subjects experience a moral regeneration:

> In King Louis's time, no one could doubt that the least crime, once commit-ted, would be swiftly punished. Thus everyone watched what he did more carefully beforehand. Fidelity and respect flourished then between vassal and lord, as did pleasure, moderation in behavior, great joy and abundance. No man was discontent with what he had inherited but manfully did the best with what his father had left him.[47]

In enforcing the law, the king's medieval role was very often simply that of judge. Many times in *The Book of Emperors,* the ruler's title is given as "Judge" rather than as "King" or "Emperor." For him to be a good judge, the certainty of his punitive sentences must remain a frightening threat to would-be lawbreakers; at the same time, he must avoid stirring up more strife through unnecessarily harsh judgments. He must keep death sen-tences among subjects potentially useful to the kingdom down to a mini-mum. In short, like John of Salisbury's model of restraint in Trajan, he must be committed to correct erring subjects rather than destroy them. *The Book of Emperors* assigns this attribute particularly to Titus and Theodosius. In the hope of reconciling his enemies, Titus first exhausts all hope of using liberality and appeals to their better natures, before their second conspiracy to kill him forces him to have them executed.[48] In his much later reign, Theodosius refuses to heed the advice of the clergy to slaughter heretics, at least until persuasion shall have proved to no avail. Alluding to his office as protector and judge, he calls upon the Holy Spirit to keep him from taking any man's life prematurely and summons the accused Arians to appear before him. "We hear the books tell us," Theodosius remarks with an appeal to ancient custom, "that our forefathers would call a synod, so that arguments could be pursued to a conclusion. We must treat all men alike with enduring patience and kindness. After all, God Himself showed forbearance, so let us harvest souls for God by winning them over in His love."[49]

A king, however, can meet the need for striking fear into foreign adversaries or those from provinces of doubtful loyalty without any such compunctions. *The Book of Emperors*, by adapting an anecdote from Byzantine history, lets Otto I take memorable vengeance on the Milanese for brigandage and "forcing acts of heathendom on the people" after a successful siege of their city:

> The King's wise counselors advised him to take hostages from the city. Accordingly, he ordered twelve of sufficiently noble birth to be selected there, bound with ropes, and led into the open field to avenge the King's anger. He ordered the eyes gouged out of eleven of them, but the twelfth left with one eye so that he could show the others back to their quarters. This filled the inhabitants of the city with anxiety.[50]

There are no more institutional checks, in the modern sense, upon what kings can do in *The Book of Emperors* than in the *Policraticus,* only the same pervasive emphasis on the monarch's need to obey the law and let himself be advised well. In the example of Theodosius and the Arians noted above, the emperor is quite free to reject the bishops' advice and make a contrary decision. More typically, however, Otto I in the subsequent example heeds his counselors. The vital role of the counselor is brought out at considerable length in the story of Adelgêr, a quasi-royal chieftain of the Bavarians, whose life and dominions are saved by the sagacious advice of a tried and true counselor. A good king's important decisions are frequently set down in *The Book of Emperors* as reached "with the general consent of the leading nobility," which has the sound of a constitutionally relevant formulation, to underline the fact that the good king is both nonarbitrary and well advised. Interestingly enough, every time a queen offers advice to her husband in *The Book of Emperors* he ends up taking it, although the author feels some ambivalence about this: In the story of Justinian, the emperor's wife is his only source of good counsel. In the Faustinian story, the queen's advice launches the royal family on a fateful course which ultimately saves their souls but leaves the empire in the bad hands of Emperor Claudius.[51] Unmitigated disaster occurs from the same source in the case of King Tarquin, who is inserted in *The Book of Emperors* after Nero in one of the author's many affronts to chronology. In an altogether new twist to the Lucretia story, it is the queen's nagging expressions of hurt pride and her demand that the king even the score which lead to the famous rape of Lucretia and the expulsion of Tarquin.[52]

Although a perhaps surprising number of pagan rulers are praised in *The Book of Emperors*, the author's ideal of kingship is not complete without the ruler's advancement of the faith. He may do this by showing exemplary piety as does Philip, according to late-ancient tradition the first Christian emperor, by fervent prayer and by manifesting love and faith in the face of death.[53] Theodosius is a prototype of this sort of virtue, too. He implores the aid of God and seeks prayerful solitude before the Cross every day. Liberality towards the Church and aid to the poor in a way which does credit to Church teachings are similar means at the king's disposal for furthering the faith. Philip's Christian almsgiving is noted briefly, but the model attribute of monarchical benevolence is most developed in the portrayals of Constantine and Charlemagne. The former not only heeds Saint Sylvester's instructions by giving silver, gold, and fine clothing, but is known for having "adorned holy baptism" by providing a fund from which the newly baptized received a large cash bonus.[54] Charlemagne aids the Church as a matter of course with such acts as founding the Diocese of Bremen; he shows special thankfulness in building his cathedral at Aachen in a way which commemorates the great victories in Spain which the author's imagination ascribes to him.[55]

Defending the faith against the challenges of heathendom and heresy belong to the king's best tasks. Heretics and Jews, in fact any who offer opposition to Christianity by argument, are dealt with by counter-argument, prayer, and divine signs. To this end, great synods are held under the auspices of the monarch. But physical attacks on Christendom by pagans are something quite different for the author. The medieval age of hysteria in confronting heretical movements was still in the future when he wrote, but the period of crusades against the Moslems was enjoying a vigorous youth. Any number of interpretations have sought to explain the sudden breaking off of *The Book of Emperors*, right where it recounts preparations for the Second Crusade. According to one, the author laid down his stylus right then and there in 1147 under the spell of enthusiasm and went along to the Holy Land with Emperor Conrad III.[56] The bulk of the evidence (such as it is) indicates that at least most of the work was really written in the following decade. Regardless of this, the work is very much suffused with the crusading spirit. To this end, the author introduces strong crusader motivation into very early rulers of the empire. Emperor Tiberius (of all people) reacts in a story told of him much like the ideal Christian king of the Middle Ages upon hearing of Moslem outrages. On being cured of leprosy in a variation of the story which normally belonged to Constantine in the Middle Ages, Tiberius is overcome by just and devout wrath at the fact that the Jews have slain the great Physician, whose image on Saint Veronica's cloth has just healed him. To seek vengeance against the obvious foes of God, he sends his generals Vespasian and Titus to destroy Jerusalem. Thus he fulfills a prophecy of Christ concerning the levelling of the city, which is inserted in full to underline the point, and not one but three pagan emperors of the first century, Tiberius, Vespasian and Titus, are made into really rather conscious avengers of the faith.[57]

While bloody vengeance against enemies of God is normally a good thing with which to adorn a mediocre reign or ornament an already excellent one in *The Book of Emperors*, a king's obligation to show Christian mercy is not completely lost sight of in the work. This is shown by the Byzantine Emperor Heraclius, who fits handily into the crusading tradition anyway by virtue of his having reconquered territories from Khosrau II of Persia, while restoring what was held to be the True Cross to Jerusalem. In *The Book of Emperors*, Heraclius spares a son of Khosrau and becomes his godfather. As the author puts it, "this turned out well for him," for young Khosrau goes on to become Saint Cyril.[58] Things turn out well in *The Book of Emperors* for Heraclius, too. Where regular history lets Egypt, Syria, and Palestine fall into the hands of Moslem invaders during Heraclius' last years, *The Book of Emperors* more fittingly spares him this indignity. The Heraclius story has a further point for medieval rulers in their role as furtherers of the faith: divine assistance is given to those who do battle for the Lord, but they must be careful not to become overly proud as the result of their victories. Having captured the Cross from the Persians, Heraclius leads his army "full of high spirits and pride" back to Jerusalem. There is even some jostling for a preferred position in riding through the famous gate to the city.

> There is no doubt about what happened then: the Angel of the Lord appeared to them above the shining gate. The King was sore afraid at this and hurriedly dismounted. . . . He asked the Angel: "My Lord, since I was commanded from Heaven to undertake this expedition and won back the Holy Cross, what have I done to incur God's disfavor?"
>
> Then the Holy Angel spoke: "Do you hear, still, of how God Himself rode a donkey through this gate, to show His gentle humility?" And still sore afraid, the King took off his shoes, put on a coarse woolen garment, and implored Our Lord fervently for mercy. Clasping the Cross to himself, he went through the gate, glad of heart. He carried it into Jerusalem and into the Temple.[59]

In the taking of Jerusalem during the First Crusade, some fifty years before *The Book of Emperors* was written, the victorious Godfrey of Bouillon manifested such humility that, although he was chosen king and exercised royal functions, he refused to assume the title of "King of Jerusalem" because of the all too obvious contrast of worldly monarchy with Christ's kingly role in that place. The Franks were quite familiar with the story of Heraclius, and it is quite probable that legends similar to those which funneled into *The Book of Emperors* had a direct bearing on Godfrey's behavior. The historical Godfrey then became a prototype of monarchical excellence in his own right in later narrations of the First Crusade which hovered on the border between legend and history. When Godfrey finally appears in *The Book of Emperors,* everything from the battle scenery to the emotions and inspiring words of the leader's exhortations are familiar to the reader, since the crusader monarch is one of the earliest and most reinforced types in *The Book of Emperors.*

In discussing the relation of the monarch's authority to the institutional Church, *The Book of Emperors* nearly ignores the problem of bad royal appointments to clerical office, which had so distressed John of Salisbury. But while the author's loyalty to the Roman Church is as unswerving as to the "Roman Empire," he does manage to share John's disdain for latter-day Rome and the Romans. Actually, nothing much can be implied from John's contempt for Rome and the Romans as far as proper monarchical behavior is concerned. He leaves the whole problem of the Pope's being a "servant" to the Roman "tyrants," while guiding Christendom with all its kings, largely unresolved.

It is quite different in *The Book of Emperors*, however, where the German author is able to see the Holy Roman emperor fulfilling part of his duty by occasionally straightening out the erring Romans himself. Henry III, for example, in marching over the Alps, holding a synod, and deciding among three popes by deposing them all and putting in his own man, is described as doing God's will purely and simply.[60] In the author's Charlemagne story already mentioned, when the Romans assault the pope and blind him, the emperor responds with a siege of Rome, the bloody subjection of the Roman nobility, and a startling scene of imperial remonstrance with Christ and Saint Peter in the latter's cathedral, which is aimed at bringing the Romans back to fear of the true God and accomplishes its end. All this appears to result from the emperor's duties as guardian of Rome and papacy.[61]

Such acts, however, are strictly emergency measures to cope with a ship out of control. Normally, in a healthy division of labor, the monarch is content to keep the secular world on course and take his spiritual guidance rather much as it comes from angels, saints, popes, and bishops. The constant ideal is that of an organic whole of secular-spiritual functions, much like John's literal comparison of the commonwealth with the human body.

It is much to the point for the author that the secular and spiritual spheres do not have anything like opposing interests. The strength of the

Christian dominion seems, on the contrary, sometimes to lie in the lack of differentiation between the two spheres as is true of the Law of the Empire with its mixed spiritual-secular origins. Depicting these two spheres in opposition to each other is as foreign to his mental world as contrasting the interests of the members of the Trinity. For the purpose of stressing the unity of Christian interests, the author suppresses the whole sticky story of Canossa when telling about Henry IV in otherwise considerable detail, since there could be no retelling of Canossa without allusions to competing authorities and the conflicting interests of papacy and empire.

In *The Book of Emperors*, the king's embodiment of his people and the corresponding identity that the people are supposed to sense in their king are more freely brought out because of the author's essential lack of restraint. His exaggerations in letting kings do nearly every major undertaking themselves, so that their personal histories become all of history that is worth remembering, are, from one standpoint, perhaps no more than naive foreshadowings of a familiar type of historical narration. Historiography of this type portrays great events as emanations from great men (generals winning battles under their own name, whether or not their leadership was decisive; presidents and prime ministers personally credited with periods of economic prosperity in which their roles as planners and directors may have been peripheral factors at most). In this connection, we recall lines from the late-medieval "Agincourt Carol":

> Then went our King with all his host
> Through France for all the Frenshe boast
> He spared no dread of least or most
> Till he came to Agincourt coast. . . .

> Then forsooth that knight comely
> In Agincourt field he fought manly.
> Through grace of God most mighty
> He had both the field and the victory:
> *Deo gracias Anglia*
> *Redde pro victoria!*[62]

Henry V did display directive genius and valor at Agincourt, and the songwriter's exaggeration is perhaps nothing more than normal poetic license when he gives the *whole* credit for the English victory to the king and the grace of God which he enjoyed. On the other hand, medieval legend and popular historiography of a few centuries earlier were capable of going well beyond even the broadest limit, in making acts ordered by the king or simply performed during his reign into deeds he literally performed himself.

The ancient and medieval idea of letting champions do personal combat in order to decide the outcome of a conflict provided an intelligent way of saving hordes of men and horses from unnecessary slaughter. It was possible only because of the feeling that the champions sufficiently represented their whole peoples to make their duels roughly equivalent to large scale battles.[63] From a theoretical standpoint, the king as the man who subsumed the being and experience of his people was naturally an ideal champion for single combat, although it seems that the king's choice of a champion was recognized as almost equally good. Kings fought single combats far more frequently in literature than in history, and, as a matter of fact, in neither context did their duels necessarily substitute for full-scale battles. Sometimes kings were described as making a point of seeking each other out in battle with the knowledge that killing a royal opponent would probably be enough to ensure victory; sometimes royal combats were portrayed at the end of an inconclusive encounter between armies. Nonetheless, in the more legendary accounts, the focus of attention was on the physical combat of rulers as decisive for the outcome.[64] This aspect of rulership is introduced very early in *The Book of Emperors* by having Julius Caesar do single combat in conquering the German tribes. Although a great deal of fighting goes on among the armies, it is clear that Julius's own sword-wielding is responsible for the victories.

> [Julius Caesar] turned towards the Swabians and showed them no mercy. Swabia was then the domain of a very daring duke named Brennus, who rode against him with his army. The book tells us that Brennus fought three hours with Julius in battle in the open. They slashed wounds in all directions and bloodied many a shield rim. The Swabians defended the land well until Julius kindly offered to negotiate with them, and they yielded their land to his suzerainty.[65]

Caesar was at this point, of course, not yet ruler. But his very act of personally overcoming German chieftains and making their peoples subject to him is obviously the main thing which qualifies him to start monarchy in the Roman Empire in the author's mind. (Romulus is mentioned but not as king; Tarquin is very much a king in the book, but he is made to rule later, just after Claudius.)

We obtain perhaps the best look at what the author of *The Book of Emperors* had in mind when he showed his rulers doing the noteworthy deeds of their reigns themselves by regarding the work of an equally anonymous drawer of pictures who lived during the author's lifetime. In the artwork which accompanied Otto of Freising's *History of the Two Cities* when it was presented to Frederick Barbarossa in 1157, the literary presentations of the king as the great and ubiquitous doer of the important deeds of his reign have an unmistakable pictorial counterpart. A typical illustration shows the abdication of emperors Diocletian and Maximian and the cessation of persecutions under them. Each emperor is standing in front of a pile of severed heads and bodies; from his left hand a sword is falling, and with his right hand he is removing his crown. The hands of a headless martyr, whom Maximian has just decapitated with his own hands, reach up to take his crown from him.[66] The rich symbolism of medieval art was well adapted to turning the figurative into the literal, and such personification of events was done for purposes of serious illustration in a manner which, in modern terms, falls somewhere between surrealism and political cartooning.

God's rewarding or punishing a whole people in accordance with what the king deserves, one of the most enduring themes in medieval discussions of rulers, is, of course, taken entirely for granted in *The Book of Emperors*. It is most obvious in the case of military victories and defeats, but it also emerges in the responses of nature: that the earth yields abundant harvests in the reign of Louis the Pious rounds out his portrait as one of ideal Christian kingship.

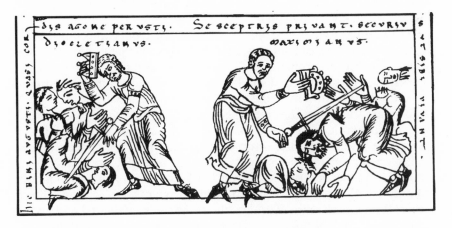

Emperors Diocletian and Maximian suffer a great change of heart and resign their symbols of power and glory to the Christian martyrs they recently persecuted.

One of a collection of mid-twelfth century drawings done to illustrate Bishop Otto of Freising's *History of the Two Cities.* The pictures are bound in the *Codex Jenensis Bose,* q. 6; reproduction kindly furnished by Prof. Dr. L. Bohmüller, Direktor, Universitätsbibliothek Jena, DDR.

Although he heightened the personal element in it, the author had adapted the story of Julius Caesar from the older *Annolied,* an epic which begins as a world history but rapidly turns into a life of Bishop Anno of Cologne.[67] The writers of both works in telling about Caesar dwell fancifully on the origin of the plural "you" as a respectful form of address. For them, it originated in the need to address the ruler as a man who is more than one man. According to the *Annolied,* the custom of saying a plural "you" for one man, instead of the singular "thou," was invented in order to honor Julius Caesar because "he had united in one person all the powers held formerly by many."[68] This telling phrase is taken over in *The Book of Emperors.* There it has been seen not as referring to Caesar's obvious political takeover, which ended the Roman Republic with its plurality of governing institutions, but rather to Caesar's uniting all people of the empire by taking over the authority which had belonged to their individual rulers.[69] Actually, it probably refers to both factors: the brief indications of early rule in Rome by a senate or assembly disappear in *The Book of Emperors* with Julius Caesar; at the same time, different peoples of the empire are indeed subjected to the rule of one man. Hence the ruler is rightfully addressed as the many in the one. Far from showing this as any degradation of the conquered peoples, being joined to the empire through the personal nexus of the great ruler *raises* their status. The Germans are described in the source work as having honored Caesar with this appellation but, in turn, Caesar is said to be honoring them by having this name usage propagated among them.

   The Book of Emperors disposes of the problem of tyrants much in the same way that John of Salisbury does: by indicating that tyrants are killed and that this is according to God's will. The *when* and *by whom* is not something to set down hard and fast rules about. Sometimes the author's tyrants take their own lives under greater or lesser compulsion, as Nero or Maximian; sometimes they are killed by an indignant citizen as the result of a personal injury. His Tarquin the Proud, Claudius, and Justinian all die as the whole or partial result of vengeance for rape or seduction of ladies among their subjects, but the author does not praise the tyrant killers. Examples of tyrannicide, very much as with John, are for potential tyrants to look at and heed — not something to give their Christian subjects ideas. With a great sense of drama, the author tells a variation of the same story which John of Salisbury related concerning the death of Julian the Apostate. Saint Mercurius is roused from his grave by the Virgin Mary, who calls on him to take vengeance upon God's enemy. Saint Mercurius grabs his shield and spear, mounts his horse, and, invisible to all but the terrified Julian, runs the tyrant through the stomach at full gallop. The ending is, as with John, a clear warning to would-be tyrants: Saint Mercurius' spear, it seems, was found outside his grave the next day, and the blood running down it linked him unmistakably with the tyrant's death.[70] But this is clearly not an exhortation for ordinary Christians to slay tyrants, unless something should happen to them on the order of being awakened from their graves by the Virgin Mary. For a king's subjects, the message is evidently that God will choose an instrument for tyrannicide Himself in the rare instances when He wills it.

THOMAS AQUINAS: THE SCHOLASTIC MONARCHIST AND GREEK SECOND THOUGHTS ABOUT KINGSHIP

The introduction of Aristotle's *Politics* into Western political thought marked a turning point in political theory. From one standpoint, the impact of the *Politics* was a part of the strengthening and eventual victory of scholasticism in the thirteenth century over the more casual forms of inquiry and analysis which had characterized the "Renaissance of the Twelfth Century." The impact on kingship, however, was more simple and direct than this alone would indicate. While generally scholasticism won out by offering systematization of thought and definitive answers to long-disputed questions, when it came to kingship the *Politics* raised more questions than it answered. It furnished information and doctrine which conspicuously refused to be synthesized into any system.

Nowhere were the new problems for kingship more in evidence than in the works of Saint Thomas Aquinas, the greatest synthesizer within the scholastic movement. A striking difference between the approach of Thomas and that of John of Salisbury or the author of *The Book of Emperors* toward kingship is Thomas's distinct awareness of alternative forms of government and hence of a serious need to justify kingship against competing forms. Most twelfth-century writers had been conscious enough of aristocracy and democracy as theoretical forms of government, but monarchy was so obviously superior in their eyes that these needed only a perfunctory treatment before being dismissed.

In his most concentratedly political work, *De Regimine Principum (On Princely Government)* or *De Regno (On Kingship)*, Thomas makes a commitment to monarchy quite in line with the older tradition. The fact that he was writing this for the king of Cyprus in 1266 may have led him to take this position: "It seems that the island was then in a complete state of anarchy and that a reinforcement of the royal authority appeared indispensable." In this work,[71] at any rate, Thomas assumes that a political body is something like a human body; consequently there must be a single force to guide and control all the members. Among the three forms of government, monarchy, aristocracy, and democracy, monarchy works best as long as it is not corrupt, because of the unity of command and interest which it assures. Nature furnishes the analogy of monarchy, for the bees have one king.[72] More to the point, God rules the universe as a monarch, not as an aristocrat or democrat, and it is up to human beings to imitate God as much as they can.

In other works by Saint Thomas, particularly the *Summa Theologica*, the suction of Aristotle's *Politics* exerts more force. The commitment to monarchy is still there, based in part on Aristotle's *Metaphysics*, but it is offset by an unequivocal statement that mixed government is best, i.e., one which selects elements from monarchy, aristocracy, and democracy, both for the reason that each pure form has something to contribute in the way of ruling and for the reason that the elite and the common people will accept a government all the more readily if they can have their way some of the time.

Thomas follows Aristotle closely in noting that the purpose of politics is to lead men into living well. Given the dominance of kingship within the best political system for Thomas, this becomes, easily enough, the king's office (responsibility and duty), to lead men into living well.

"The duties of a king commit him to strive for the common good," says Thomas, and by "strive for the common good" the bulk of his examples show him to mean keeping a just peace under the law in the familiar pattern of the ideal medieval king.[73] Thomas gives a trenchant definition of law in general as "a certain, rational order for the good of a group which is promulgated by the one entrusted with the care of that community."[74] He deals at some length with the logical difficulty inherent in having a king as lawgiver who nonetheless is bound to respect the law as if it were over him and he could not change it. Of considerable help here is Thomas's hierarchy of law types, ranging from the immutable to the variable. In this sequence there are: *eternal law* (divine guidance of created things),[75] *natural law* (man's perception of or "sharing in" the eternal law by virtue of the right reason in his nature),[76] and *positive law* (laws of a type generally encountered among different peoples, the *ius gentium,* as well as the body of laws for special contingencies and the particular legal determinations which differ among peoples, the *ius civile*).[77] But even the most particular of human laws must serve the common good as perceived by the lawgiver, whose right reason by its very nature strives to copy, or at least not to violate, God's eternal law. Thus the king's natural exercise of reason in the cause of the common good will cause his legal enactments to be just: "All laws, so far as they claim a share of right reason, are derived from the eternal law."[78]

Thomas nominally accepts the two most nearly absolutist principles of Roman law: "What pleases the ruler has the force of law" and "The ruler is absolved from the laws." He renders them harmless by reasoning that the true ruler will be pleased to enact only what his right reason finds consonant with the natural law. Being absolved from the laws or being above them becomes, for Thomas, merely a reference to the lack of a law-enforcing power above the king himself. Again, since a true king is voluntarily subject to natural law, this presents no problem. A king who ignores his right reason and enacts unjust laws which further his selfish interests is — once more a familiar note — not a king but a tyrant, and what he decrees has only a shadowy claim to being considered law at all.[79]

For Saint Thomas, in addition to his enforcement of laws punishing wrongdoers, the king is responsible for his subjects' economic well-being, for he must see to it that within his kingdom there is "a supply of material goods sufficient to let the people live well."[80] Medieval kings had already paid quite a bit of attention to regulating guilds, licensing trade fairs, standardizing weights and measures, controlling the coinage, and many other aspects of economic life, but writers before the new availability of Aristotle's *Politics* in the thirteenth century tended not to make economic promotion a particularly conscious part of political responsibility, as it had certainly been for ancient Greek political writers. John of Salisbury tended to assume that if a king suppressed criminality and official avarice, economic prosperity would come of itself. *The Book of Emperors* did not go much beyond associating the rule of a pious king with good crops and the subjects' acceptance of their economic duties as a part of their rank in society.

Yet even Saint Thomas does not go into much detail concerning how a king should further the economy of his country. Most of Thomas's discussion of the economic side of rulership concerns equitable taxation. A king has the right to collect taxes for the defense of the realm against outside aggression, internal disturbances, or for any other purpose which is clearly in the public interest. Limits on justifiable taxation are set by what is necessary for the common good. Thomas acknowledges that there is sometimes justification in having regular taxes paid to the royal treasury. These taxes can be only approximately equal to anticipated requirements, but he advises against a ruler's making innovations in this area. If a certain tax is fairly apportioned and has been paid as long as people can remember, well and good; if it has not been, the king should think long and hard before demanding it, for its novelty will engender resentment.[81]

Avoidance of novelty is, in fact, a general rule in good lawgiving for Thomas. The very changing of law carries with it a proportionate threat to the public welfare, because custom is of great importance for the observance of law. Hence it is that human law should never be changed unless the change is so much in the public interest that it compensates for the harm done. Much has been made of the differences between Germanic and Roman legal tradition in the Middle Ages. Germanic traditions insisted that law be discovered or revived from ancient usage rather than made. The Roman tradition was one of having a written code changed by the introduction of new articles by successive rulers. Both systems, however, stressed continuity of tradition. For most medieval writers, a law's antiquity was a probable sign that it was a good and just one (rather than an indication it needed overhauling), regardless of whether it stemmed from a memory of what Charlemagne had done or from the *Corpus Iuris Civilis*.

The need for innovative legislation is minimized for Thomas's sovereign for a different reason as well. Eternal law obviously admits of no novelty.

If a king is guided by natural law, which is the human "share" of eternal law, then those of his decrees which smack of novelty will at most reflect changes in the times, sharpenings of his own perception, and (rarely) emergencies for which there is no precedent. For Thomas, the right to decree law implies also the right to make dispensations from it with or without precedents, but while no one can legally prevent the king from doing this, a good king will make sparing use of this prerogative.

Thomas repeats this admonition that a ruler is permitted to do something but should not in a variety of contexts. In answer to an enquiry from the duchess of Brabant who enjoyed the rights of a virtually independent monarch, Thomas notes that she is indeed legally entitled to sell secular offices, if she is convinced that the purchasers are worthy men; however, even then she should not do this. A ruler should seek out officials strictly according to their abilities. When a ruler is paid for an office, this obviously hinders an impartial selection of the best man for the job.[82] Such a view certainly places a great burden on a monarch's self-restraint and understanding of the common good. Thomas's good king is to derive this self-restraint partly from a normal desire for glory and honor, but more from a personal study of those parts of Scripture pertaining to law or ruling and from a desire to attain "the highest degree of blessedness in heaven," which, it seems, God reserves for good kings.[83] Reflecting both medieval tradition and Aristotle's *Politics*, Thomas ascribes to the non-tyrannical ruler a propensity for arriving at the common good after careful consideration and a willingness to subordinate his own interests to those of the whole community, simply because to do so is inherent in the nature of true rulership, which justifies itself only when the whole body politic prospers from it.

There are certain oddities in Thomas's applications of Aristotle's ideas on kingship which derive from Aristotle's assumption that the normal political unit which people will want to discuss is a city-state. This was simply not true in medieval Europe, where independent city-states were rare outside of Italy. Even in Italy the city-states were not kingdoms, nor was the Kingdom of the Two Sicilies a city-state. Thomas speaks in a disconcerting way of going out to found a new city or kingdom, as if this were a matter of rationally weighing alternatives, to insure the viability of the future unit:

> . . . it is necessary that the founder of a city or a kingdom first of all pick out a suitable location, one which will be good for the health of the inhabitants, sufficiently fertile in its soil to produce food, naturally attractive to the eye, and naturally secure against enemy threats. . . . Next it will be necessary for the founder of a city or kingdom to divide the selected site in such a way as to provide for all the needs of a city or a kingdom. Suppose a kingdom is to be founded: then someone will have to decide what place is suitable for estab-

lishing towns, what place for country estates, what place for fortifications; then, where centers of learning should be established, where military training should be conducted, where public business should be transacted, and such other things that a kingdom requires for its complete functioning.[84]

The obvious pattern here is that of ancient Greek colonialism with inhabitants from one city-state setting up a new city-state with the support of the old one from which they came. Here Thomas is writing for the king of Cyprus. Possibly this advice is given partly in view of the creative opportunities still available in the relatively new crusader states. But as general principles, such abstract considerations had very little to do with establishing medieval European kingdoms, which were usually "founded" when the leader of an extant political unit assumed the title of "King" or took it from a king whose realm he had succeeded in conquering. Thomas's assumption, noted above, that a king is in charge of assuring economic sufficiencies for his realm also stems from Greek city-state experience, which Aristotle, but not Thomas, was entitled to take for granted as the natural model for a political unit.

While Greek political commentators discussed mixed government with a monarchical element, the form as an ideal one was more closely associated in antiquity with the Roman Republic, in which the consuls with their annually elected executive office added monarchy, the Senate aristocracy, and the popular Assembly democracy to the mixture. Roman historians whose works were directly or indirectly known in the Middle Ages saw the mixed government of the Roman Republic as a form very much in contrast with the government of the Roman kings, which had preceded it. Medieval writers, Thomas among them, were also aware that the mixed government of the Roman Republic differed from the imperial government of the Roman emperors and that the demise of the former represented a loss of Rome's ancient liberties.[85]

The task of putting all this together was exceptionally difficult. Aristotle, Thomas's greatest authority in political theory, defended what he called "polity," a mixed government without monarchy, as the best form of government on the basis of both justice and relative durability. Familiar Roman history contrasted mixed government having an executive with limited powers favorably with royal or imperial government. All this notwithstanding, kingship remained for Thomas the safest and most viable form of government in the world he knew.

As if to meet the challenge between his authority and his experience, Thomas's remarkable talent for bonding discrepant parts into a coherent whole comes to the fore. It was at least a small part of the scholastic's business to define the best possible form which the object he was discussing could have. Ultimately, however, Thomas comes up with too many best forms of government to convince the reader that he has found any one of them with certainty. Part of the time his reasoning runs like this: a mixed government with only an institutionally limited monarch is indeed the best political form (*optima ordinatio principum*).[86] In it there is one head to make decisions coordinating the good of all, an elite of virtue and intellect who contribute their efforts to the governing process, and a whole people from whom rulers may be drawn according to merit and from whose consent law is derived. This is the sought-for combination of monarchy, aristocracy, and democracy, which by its very nature absorbs all private interests for the public welfare.[87] This form, however, seems to be so ideal that it tends to be unstable, as the history of the Roman Republic and of the Hebrew rule by judges proves clearly. Human frailty simply will not let it function before dissension from below in the population and corruption from above in the leadership destroy it.[88] The best form of government (*optimum regimen populi*) would then really be monarchy, because monarchy will answer the human need to be governed firmly and is not subject to the inherent instability of a governmental form which requires extensive cooperation and devotion to the public interest by many people at once. Thomas notes it is fairly easy for this logically ideal monarchy to become corrupt because of the temptation presented to a man enjoying such broad power.[89] A corrupt monarchy — and this he says even in his most pro-monarchical work, *De Regimine Principum* — is the worst of all governmental forms.[90]

Elsewhere, he reasons altogether differently and states an absolute preference for monarchy, rather than merely settling for monarchy because mixed government is too ideal for this mutable world. Natural order is best maintained by a natural unity, and what could be more of a natural unity than the rule of one man? Obviously then, "the best government (*optima gubernatio*) is that which is conducted by one man."[91]

Thomas consistently advocates limited monarchy as the best possible form of government only to the extent that for him the true king must obey the law, restrain his demands on his subjects, and accept the guidance of divine teaching and human counsel in striving for the common good. Under the influence of Aristotle's *Politics* and the history of Rome, he can see the advantages of using a balance of institutions to reduce the need to rely on such a great amount of self-restraint and innate reasonableness in a lone king, but for him such institutions still have too much the look of human contrivance and instability to elicit his unreserved commitment to them.

Another major difficulty in transplanting Aristotelian ideas to the Middle Ages was the fact that while for the ancient Greeks the good life had a large spiritual element in it, this was not related all that closely to the prevailing religion. Aristotle discusses the goal of political activity as providing those men who are capable of enjoying it leisure filled with learning and contemplation. Without much ado, Saint Thomas substitutes salvation in Christian terms for Aristotle's philosophical leisure as the primary goal of political science. The king is to lead people in living the good life by protecting them and enabling them to prosper in this world in such a way that their chances of being saved in the next world are made as great as possible.[92]

To this end, the king must acknowledge that in religious matters the Church is to be free from secular interference of any kind. The Church requires the king's protection against internal violence and infidel aggressors; this is within the king's normal and assumed function of peacekeeping and raises no new issue. The king must not undertake the conversion of infidels by force, because forced conversion, Thomas states in another context, is not in keeping with the necessarily voluntary acceptance of the faith.[93] This sounds like a strange assertion after a century and a half of the crusades, but, strictly speaking, the crusades were considered a Christian response to Mohammedan attacks. The Moslems were fought as enemies to be repelled, not as potential converts. On the other hand, the king or whatever official is responsible must take every step he can to keep the faithful in the faith. In a telling, if unconsciously appropriate, illustration of John of Salisbury's statement that the prince receives the duty from the Church of performing the offices of the sword which are unfit for clerical hands to touch, Thomas outlines what the secular government must do in the case of habitual backsliders into heresy. The final step is for clerics to bring the lapsed member of the faithful back into the faith. He is then given over to the secular authorities for execution so that his soul can be saved before he slips back again.[94]

While Thomas does not dwell on an organic analogy, as does John, in accepting the comparison of the body politic and the individual human being, he confirms the old equation of the clergy or the spiritual powers with the soul and of the temporal powers with the body.[95] The clergy are to respect the king's calling by God to his office, and his accountability to God alone, as far as his control of secular activities is concerned. Unlike Gelasius in the fifth century, he does not attempt to separate royal power from authority vested in the clergy. He notes that the clergy are to be obeyed in matters affecting salvation, while the temporal powers are to be obeyed in matters of civil welfare, without emphasizing the primacy of the spiritual powers in the case of disputed jurisdiction. Where, according to the Gelasian formula, royal power was subject to spiritual or papal authority, Thomas's depiction of the king as directly receiving his office from God, however much he may be justifiably called on by the Church to execute a heretic or two, means that he controls human affairs through his own power and authority entrusted to him directly by God.[96]

A title of "King" according to Thomas is "antonomastic," that is, a name properly belonging to a whole species of things which becomes applied to a single individual, as a metonym. Again, we have the notion of the king as the one who subsumes the being of the many.[97] For Thomas this idea is born out of purely rational considerations already mentioned as justifying monarchy. Society is organized with the goal of promoting peace among its members. Peace implies a unity of will. The people are more easily given a unity of goal and will by one man than by a plurality: hence they impart the necessary portion of their will to the king for governing them. His will and abilities are theirs, since the king, to the extent that he is a true king, applies these to the common good. The king consequently takes upon himself "the public person."[98] Even the law is *in* the king, since law can be applied only as a dictate of practical reason, the reasoning of a human being, and consequently of the king as the personification of the public.[99] That a whole people suffers as the result of the king's misdeeds follows as a matter of course. Apart from the effects of bad royal government as such, when the sins of kings incur God's displeasure, the people are justly punished. For the Hebrews to have been led into captivity as a consequence of the wickedness of their kings makes perfect sense: the Hebrews asked God to give them kings, their kings personified them, and the acts of their kings were judged as the acts of the whole people.[100]

In the important matter of deposing a tyrannical king, Thomas comes closer than in other contexts to unreserved support of an institutional check on royal power. Perceiving the dangers inherent in having individuals take the murder of a tyrant upon themselves, even when they feel themselves inspired to execute a just sentence of God, Thomas notes that it is much better to let decisions for the murder or deposition of a tyrant be made "by public authority."[101] In elective monarchies, Thomas notes, the community who elected a man as king may, with justice, remove him as a tyrant. Thomas cannot supply an example of what this public authority would be in the traditional, hereditary monarchies of the Europe of his time. He can only draw on the analogy of the Roman Senate, which deposed and murdered the tyrannical Emperor Domitian, with the obvious weakness that there were no comparable bodies in the royal governments of his time. In his only other example, he refers to the deposition of Tarquin by simply, "the Romans."[102] Since this act was instigated by the Roman nobility, Thomas's approval of it would seem to sanction feudal revolts against a tyrannical king. To see Thomas as giving the nobility the right to decide when tyranny was intolerable and to revolt accordingly against their king would perhaps be going too far in attempting to get at Thomas's meaning. Or would it? Thomas's failure to follow the point through to its logical conclusion may stem simply from his belief that such an action is a measure of the utmost extremity to be resorted to only on the rarest of occasions. To institutionalize it plainly might invite sedition, but there is no harm in having it there in the dim background as a remote threat which might deter potentially extreme abusers of royal authority. Instead, Thomas advises oppressed subjects to rely on prayer and God's eternal willingness to redress grievances for help, the same "Appeal to Heaven" made famous much later by John Locke's *Second Treatise of Civil Government* and the American colonists' Pine Tree flag.

DANTE: THE IDEAL OF UNIVERSAL PEACE THROUGH SECULAR ABSOLUTE MONARCHY

Dante and Marsiglio of Padua introduce a new element into theories of medieval kingship when they advocate freeing the temporal ruler from obedience to the Church in political matters affected with a religious interest. Dante, whose early fourteenth-century work *De Monarchia* is much briefer than Marsiglio's and more stark in its innovative thrust concerning kingship, begins with some propositions which might have qualified as self-evident but which he backs with the authority of Aristotle for good measure. It is the guiding principle of civilization that human beings must have the chance to grow in intelligence.[103] Human beings can mentally develop well only under conditions of peace. This peace must be not only domestic but must exist between the previously powerful, contending political units. Therefore there must be some sovereign power strong enough to keep the existing units, in all likelihood the Italian city states with their perpetual feuding were foremost in his mind here, at peace with each other.[104]

At first it sounds as if Dante were hinting at something like a medieval United Nations, and indeed the *De Monarchia* has been translated as *On World Government,* wording which emphasizes precisely the world peace-keeping function of Dante's ideal sovereign as a visionary contribution of the great poet.[105] However, Dante's solution is not very United Nations-like: his ideal ruler is an absolute emperor ruling over the existing structure of kings and republics. Far from seeing absolute power as absolutely corrupting, Dante demonstrates to his own satisfaction that absolute power is the only type of sovereignty which can be guaranteed against corruption. Strife and abuse of power, he notes, come from greed or even a normal desire for gain. The absolute emperor, on the other hand, since his dominion extends from ocean to ocean already has everything he could want and will have no reason to start wars or abuse his power. With an offhand rejection of the whole medieval ideological framework which had made the king's obedience to law a prerequisite for his ruling well, Dante thus justifies a ruler's will as having the rightful force of law without qualification.[106] Obviously then for him, although he does not make this explicit, at the top level the rule of law is only a formality: if the emperor's

will has the unconditional force of law, no previously established limitations of the law can be binding upon him.

There is a certain disarming simplicity in Dante's theory of kingship: to
the extent that a king approaches absolute rule in his dominion, his personal wants are satisfied without recourse to violence. Since the king, who
has everything to gain from peaceful conditions within his own dominion,
is in his very being the logical guarantor of peace and justice, the king is the
"servant of all" inhabitants of his kingdom, because his interests in preserving peace and justice are inextricably linked with theirs.[107] Any need
for checks on the monarch vanishes into thin air.

Dante says all this of kings in general, and in this fashion he equates
them with representatives in a republic. Kings are obviously better in his
eyes than representatives in a republic because within one man there is less
cause for a conflict of interests than among many representatives; however, as far as ordinary kings are concerned he does not press the point.
Ordinary kings, he notes, taking the kings of Aragon and Castile as examples, have dominions bounded by each other.[108] Thus they have a built-in
reason for wanting to increase their power at the expense of another
sovereignty. The element of royal mystique seems scarcely to interest
Dante as it applies to most of the kings of Europe. The element of uniting
the peoples emotionally to their ruler is of overwhelming importance for
him, but this for him must be in terms of uniting them to one monarch over
all other rulers.

What monarch is so awesome that he shall draw upon the loyalties of all
peoples with or without lesser kings? It can only be the Roman ruler. In
practical terms of the thirteenth and fourteenth century this can only have
meant the Holy Roman emperor, i.e., the German king who, after an
imperial coronation, could claim to be Augustus and Caesar in medieval
Europe. Dante's arguments for his natural supremacy as world sovereign
had, understandably, relatively little to do with the actual contemporary
position of the Germanic emperor relative to the states of Europe. Instead
Dante is content to demonstrate the logical and natural supremacy of
ancient Rome over the world and the legitimacy of Augustus Caesar's
sovereignty, letting the justification for seeing the Germanic emperor as a
latter-day Augustus Caesar rather shift for itself.

Rome, Dante states, won out over other nations in a fair test of strength
decided by God's judgment; therefore, the Roman victory over competing
nations was divinely sanctioned.[109] Did not Christ choose to be born at the
moment when Augustus Caesar instituted his census? And can one imagine Christ responding to an unjust edict? Of course not. Christ's birth in
the reign of the man who solidified the institution of the Roman emperor
for all succeeding time showed divine approval for this institution.[110]
This, of course, was the viewpoint of Orosius. Dante's paragraph driving

home the divine sanction of the Roman monarchy through Christ's birth under Augustus Caesar has the look of being written with Orosius' book in front of the author.[111] There was a great difference, to be sure: Orosius had seen the reign of Augustus Caesar and the birth of Christ in it as the divine negation of previous Roman history, which for him was pagan and hence dark. Dante, on the other hand, saw the same events coinciding to show an improvement in the Roman Republic, which for him had an illustrious history and which had already won the trial by ordeal in establishing supremacy over the non-Roman world. Both men dwelt on the long peace under Augustus and on that sovereign's reputation for justice on a worldwide scale with the same eventual end. As Orosius had ended up by justifying the preeminence of the old Roman Empire as it reeled under the blows of barbarian invasions during the reign of Honorius in the West, Dante ended up justifying the preeminence of its theoretical successor, the German Empire under Henry VII. It is striking, however, that while both Orosius and Dante were free with the name of the illustrious Augustus Caesar, they were sparing with the names of their much less illustrious contemporary emperors. It remained a fatal weakness for Dante's theory of world monarchy that his proofs were derived so much from Aristotelian logic and ancient Roman history and had so little to do with the real-life monarch to which his theory leads.

Implicitly, to be sure, Dante does cope with the problem that Henry VII does not look more like the ideal world ruler that Dante would like him to be. Dante explains at great length the reasons why his once-ideal Roman world ruler is not the powerful awe-inspiring personal institution that God and history intended him to be. The villain of the piece is the papacy, which in its play for temporal power since Constantine, has been sapping the strength of this sole institution capable of assuring world peace. Dante does not call the Donation of Constantine a forgery, but he notes that it was illegal for Constantine to offer it and irreligious for Sylvester to accept it.[112] Thus, obviously, it was null and void. The Church never had any claims for temporal power, least of all at the expense of the Roman ruler. Since temporal power in papal hands amounted to a usurpation, Dante finds it quite in order for the "Roman" monarch forcibly to put things aright and establish his own absolute sovereignty. This, of course, in terms of contemporary current events, was an invitation to Henry VII to invade Italy and destroy the power of the papacy (which anyway had been shifted to Avignon).

Apart from the weakness inherent in transferring ancient concepts to the medieval world, while shying away from the modifications necessary to keep them relevant, Dante's idealization of monarchy suffered from the fact that it was transparently Ghibelline partisan propaganda. It was certainly not transferrable to kingship as a whole, and how much sense it made was ultimately dependent on how strong Ghibelline feeling was running. Henry VII in his invasion of Italy rallied considerable Italian support to his cause, but he was far from being acclaimed universally as the natural world ruler Dante had demonstrated him to be. The Lombards gave him the iron crown of their ancient rulers, and he seemed assured of military success against King Robert of Naples who opposed him. Suddenly in 1313 he died of a fever, however, and his forces were compelled to withdraw.[113]

MARSIGLIO OF PADUA: HALF-HEARTED CONSTITUTIONAL MONARCHIST

On first glance, Marsiglio of Padua, whose lengthy *Defensor Pacis* was completed in 1324, three years after Dante's death, seems to have taken up the cause of independent secular rulership where Dante left off. Marsiglio's presentation overcomes two obvious fantasies in the *De Monarchia:* Dante's pseudo-logical demonstration of the incorruptibility of the absolute emperor and his emphatic claim of rightful world rulership for the monarch. Discourse One of the *Defensor Pacis* includes a patient, detailed defense of the elective form of kingship. In it Marsiglio predictably assigns the king the function of defending the peace by enforcing the law; however, in contrast with Dante, Marsiglio is careful not to let it be implied that the king's will has the absolute force of law or even that he is to rule chiefly by his own discretion. He stresses that ultimate sovereignty resides not in the king but in the people as lawgivers and electors or in — a flexible phrase — "the weightier part" of the people. Although Marsiglio uses the singular, personal *legislator* as his term for the sovereign power, he clearly means a legislative authority in the modern sense of a representative lawgiving body.[114] The king is to function under the law, which he is not at liberty to change himself. In discussing kingship in isolation, Marsiglio's spokesmanship for the Conciliar movement, which sought to place Church authority in the hands of a representative body, appears related to his political theory.

Marsiglio then has in mind precisely what the English-speaking world has long called "constitutional monarchy" as his ideal of kingship. This is true even if we retain in the modern connotation of the term the assumption that the "monarch" does not embody within himself the most important political institution of his kingdom, as the contemporary rulers of the Scandinavian countries and Great Britain exemplify in those monarchies which are so constitutional that the monarch is far from being a one-person ruling institution. For Marsiglio, as for Dante, the purpose of the state is to provide peace and consequently to quell strife for the ultimate improvement of civilization or simply so that all its inhabitants can live well. But while Dante would have the monarch take the state's coercive means in hand as one man, Marsiglio, sees the king as the agent of the legislature and subject to censure and correction by that body.[115]

It perhaps seems a bit odd that Dante, as one protagonist of the Holy Roman emperor, could write as if his were a model of absolutism while Marsiglio, as a partisan of the next Holy Roman emperor, could write on behalf of a constitutional model, something all the more remarkable since Marsiglio and Dante wrote under quite analogous circumstances which included an impending imperial invasion of Italy that both writers looked upon with favor.[116] But since there was a welter of discordant models for kingship in the Holy Roman Empire, either view was quite plausible and evidently welcome enough to contemporary Ghibellines. Dante was looking for his inspiration at those ancient Roman emperors who were most certainly the prime medieval models for righteous absolute monarchs: Augustus Caesar, who appeared as more of an absolute ruler from the start to medieval writers than to moderns, and the indisputably absolute Christian Emperor Constantine. Marsiglio, on the other hand, focused upon the elective nature of monarchy in the Holy Roman Empire and drew from it a theory of executive responsibility on the part of the monarch to his electors, which was considerably more than most real-life Holy Roman emperors would have been willing to concede, at least after they had been duly elected.

In his analysis of kingship, Marsiglio, like Dante, sees no great need to say much about contemporary Germanic emperors. He is specific enough in appealing early in his work to Emperor Ludwig for support of his ideas,[117] and he also names specific contemporary kings when they turn up in his second Discourse as the victims of clerical encroachments, but that is a different matter and only incidentally related to his theory of kingship. In treating kingship as such, Marsiglio prefers to draw his descriptions and arguments from ancient political theory, particularly Aristotle's *Politics*.[118]

This fact is responsible for both impressiveness and weakness in what emerges. Marsiglio covers his subject on many fronts with a considerable display of knowledge and insight, much of which, however, had been so carefully tailored to the world visible from a Greek city-state of the fourth century B.C. as to scarcely fit in with the medieval phenomena Marsiglio is supposedly discussing as real and potential. Marsiglio's division of regimes is taken entirely from Aristotle, beginning with the familiar sixfold division of governments into a genus of three good or "well-tempered" forms, monarchy, aristocracy, and polity with their corrupt counterparts, tyranny, oligarchy, and democracy, comprising a corresponding "vicious" or "diseased" genus.[119] Monarchy, which Marsiglio regularly calls "kingly monarchy" (*regalis monarchia*), redundant to the modern ear but a useful distinction for him since, of course, *monarchia* signified any kind of sole rule, is dissected according to the way kings get to be kings and the way they exercise authority into further Aristotelian subdivisions. These are introduced as: military kingship, oriental despotism, elective tyranny, and then elective kingship with hereditary succession. According to Aristotle, this had been a typical system of the heroic age long past. One would never guess from Marsiglio's recapitulation that this subspecies was the normal form of monarchy for the Europe in which he lived. The list concludes with a rather nebulous catchall for miscellaneous monarchies, particularly primitive ones in Aristotle's mind, where formal safeguards on the king's power might be lacking but where evidently for some reason of tradition or religion, the king would not command with the reckless selfishness which Aristotle and Marsiglio more than sixteen hundred years apart could attribute without hesitation to oriental despots.[120]

All this Aristotelian subdifferentiation was less important for Marsiglio, however, than a criterion for separating all well-tempered from diseased species which Marsiglio attributes with more confidence than accuracy to Aristotle: the voluntary attachment of subjects to their governments. After slipping in the statement, definitely not taken from Aristotle, that kingly monarchy is "a species of good government and perhaps more nearly perfect than the others,"[121] Marsiglio finds it a quite adequate summary of kingship types to say that each monarchy participates in true kingship to the extent that it is governance over voluntary subjects under laws made in the subjects' own interest.

It follows that nonelected kings rule over less willing subjects by laws less conducive to the common benefit than elected ones; hence, given kingship, elective kingship is superior to hereditary kingship. *Given kingship,* that is, and this is the catch in supporting elective monarchy on the authority of Aristotle's *Politics,* a work in which kingship comes off second best, as noted in the discussion of Saint Thomas above. Aristotle's own conclusion, we recall, was that a *polity* (in modern terms, an aristocratic government with democratic checks) generally was the best possible form of government. It is, of course, difficult to reconcile Aristotle, author of the *Politics* and staunch advocate of polity, with the same Aristotle who was hired by King Philip of Macedon as a teacher for his son, the future King Alexander the Great. After all, King Philip did his share to break up the city-state form of polity espoused by Aristotle, while King Alexander seemed intent on eliminating the independence of the city-states altogether in favor of a vast empire. Probably it is best not to attempt a reconciliation of the ideas held by Aristotle as author of the *Politics* and as royal tutor. More than likely Alexander listened with at least half an ear to Aristotle as the world's most renowned teacher of the liberal arts when he felt like it but ignored him and the *Politics* altogether when he saw a serious chance to fasten his monarchy upon the known world with his military skill and whatever philosophical or religious justifications came in handy. Aristotle is supposed to have written a separate work, since lost, on kingship for the thirteen-year-old Alexander. Perhaps he did and took a more favorable stand on monarchy in it, although this is mere conjecture. There is, at any rate, no record of the historical Aristotle ever having pressed the point to Philip or Alexander that monarchy on a broad scale was less ideal for Greece than the politics of independent city-states. Aristotle was well known in the Middle Ages as the teacher of the most renowned king of antiquity. This relationship alone would have given Marsiglio reason to take him as an approving authority in presenting kingship to his audience.

In discussing the choice of a ruler, it is not at all surprising that Marsiglio recommends looking for the man with the most prudence and moral virtue, especially one with a sense of justice. For Marsiglio, the ruler's chief task, difficult enough in itself, is that of carrying out the will of the legislative body by executing the laws according to due process; however, his candidate for kingship is to be especially endowed with *equity*, meaning for him a keen sense of proportion in balancing the deficient letter of the law, in order to fulfill its spirit fairly in individual instances.[122] The arbitrary element which Marsiglio sees a king legitimately exercising is considerable for an author so convinced of the sacredness of law. In rare instances his king should violate the law completely. His justifying example is the Catalinian conspiracy. His model of good executive action is the Consul Cicero's decision to put the conspirators to death in violation of the due process of law, because the security of the Roman Republic would have been too gravely threatened by civil war if all the time-consuming niceties had been observed.[123] The dilemma of government heads faced with political decisions involving a choice between what is legal and what is felt to be absolutely necessary for the well-being of the state has been the despair of political theorists for millenia. Did the Saguntine rulers who decided to adhere to their treaty of alliance with Rome and risk having their people annihilated by the invading Carthaginians do the right thing?[124] Is the United States president justified in making American participation in a war inevitable through maneuverings unknown to Congress, which legally has the war-making power, when he believes his acts to be necessary for national survival? For Marsiglio, however, such questions are not tortuous at all. The king will have to violate the laws on occasion in the interest of the state. The very fact that he must do so is simply the weightiest evidence for the choice of a really prudent king to exercise this kind of authority.[125]

Marsiglio holds consistently to the idea that primary authority and responsibility for governing should be in the legislature, but he never deals straightforwardly with the question of whether such a government might get along better with a different kind of executive than a king. Instead, he proceeds by attacking the weaknesses of hereditary monarchy that are corrected in an elective monarchy. This kind of contrast naturally makes elective monarchy appear much better on the authority of Aristotle than would be the case if elective monarchy were contrasted with Aristotle's preferred aristocratic-democratic synthesis. In best scholastic fashion, Marsiglio sets down the philosophical and practical arguments for hereditary monarchy, as Aquinas did when attacking error, and then disposes of them one by one. Since the Holy Roman Empire was by far the most significant elective medieval monarchy, and Marsiglio was one of its few defenders to dwell especially on its elective aspect, the case he makes in eleven major points is worth looking at in some detail:

1. Hereditary monarchy allegedly insures that a king will take excellent care of a kingdom in thinking of his heirs. Yet this is false, for an elected king will be chosen precisely because of his just and intelligent nature, which means that he will keep the kingdom in good order as a matter of course. His knowledge that only his successful stewardship in the highest political office will incline men to choose his descendants to rule after him is a further safeguard on his actions foreign to hereditary monarchy. [126]

2. It is alleged that hereditary rulers will wear the crown with less despotic arrogance, while elected monarchs in their new glory will manifest the excessive pride of the newly rich. Yet this is false, for the glory of high office cannot corrupt a noble nature any more than do riches properly acquired. (Marsiglio shares the medieval distaste for wealthy upstarts enough to agree that they are "ignorant and morally vicious" and use their recent wealth to give vent to hateful urges; while election is a justified way for a man to become newly royal, there is evidently no justifiable way for the newly rich to have become so.) The elected king will direct his power to its proper end as the proper disposer of riches will use them "for good ends and for meeting the needs of this world." [127]

3. It is alleged that hereditary monarchy induces obedience in subjects because they come to take the ruling family's royal office as a matter of course. Yet this is false. Not only does great new achievement produce awe and willing acceptance of rulers but if subjects ever have the habit of obedience they have it primarily to their governments and laws but only indirectly to their rulers' persons. [128]

4. An illustrious family is alleged to deserve the kingship by nature, in order that their eminent characteristics may benefit their subjects without interruption. Aristotle said this, too, yet it is false. (Here Marsiglio refutes a statement from Aristotle's *Politics* with one from Aristotle's *Rhetoric*. [129]) Greatness inheres in families for certain periods and then disappears in them. Never forget that you can always have the family's next in line after the old king, if you find him good enough to succeed the old king

under the elective principle. Sooner or later, all dynasties run out or a vacancy in the kingship comes up for one reason or another that cannot be filled by an heir: then election must be resorted to and will be.[130]

5. A variation of the same argument alleges that eminent parents transmit excellence both through hereditary traits and the upbringing they provide. Yet, granting that this is more frequently true than not, electing a man who has already shown that he has the traits needed for kingship is a far better guarantee for obtaining a worthy monarch than family background.[131]

6. It is alleged that there are insuperable problems with the electors of a ruler: apart from the scarcity of sufficiently wise and just men, the electoral college choosing the Roman emperor has shown dissension and quarreling incompatible with reasonable choice of a candidate. Electors are subject to bribery and corruption, and they may make a bad selection of rulers out of malice or selfish considerations. This is only too true, but it is still misleading. There were fewer prudent men to conduct elections that produced hereditary monarchies at their beginnings, but the real question is whether divisiveness and corruption inhere in the electoral system. They do not, in spite of some seemingly contradictory experience with electors of the empire. Dissension among the electors (and here is Marsiglio at his scholastic worst) is extraneous to the principle of election, which aims to achieve the public benefit. The real dissension is caused by certain men (i.e., protagonists of clerical political power, particularly papal claims, whose influence must be radically curtailed in the interest of a viable government) who are hostile to the law-making body. The legislature, if permitted, as it should be, to elect a ruler, would not thwart its own will by electing an inadequate executive for the government.[132]

7. It is alleged that it is important for citizens and officials, particularly those serving the state in an advisory capacity, to know the character of a ruler well in advance, and this is easiest when the succession is hereditary. Yet this is false. Having foreknowledge of a coming ruler's character deficiencies is worth far less than being able to reject a faulty heir of the old king and to elect an altogether better man.[133]

8. It is alleged that hereditary monarchy advantageously settles the whole matter of succession once and for all and thus puts a limit to men's excessive ambition. Yet this is false, for ambition to achieve the highest office on the basis of ability is a legitimate aspiration, and suppressing justifiable ambition will give subjects grounds for sedition.[134]

9. It is alleged that an elected king will be hampered by his vulnerability in proceeding against great men, for he must think of their retaliation against his family when his heirs no longer rule. Yet this is false, for the elected ruler will be chosen in large part because of his commitment to justice, which he will forcefully execute against great men. Since it is the

force of the law rather than the whim of the ruler which will punish great offenders, they will have no reason to exact personal vengeance against the elected king's family; if they should unreasonably think of seeking such vengeance, they must fear the next elected king's avenging justice.[135]

10. It is alleged that hereditary monarchy is that form of royal government encountered in most times and places and hence is the most natural. Yet this is false. Even if it is granted that hereditary monarchy has been the most frequent form of kingship throughout history—which might be challenged—hereditary and elective monarchy are two different species of government.[136] In describing different species, the frequency of one of them does not make it any more natural than another one.[137]

11. It is alleged that the unity in hereditary monarchy is fittingly analogous to the single rule of the Ruler of the universe. Yet this is false. It is anything but sure that the rule of the universe can be reflected in the rule of any succession of men. Even if the analogy were recognized, the hereditary aspect of monarchy has nothing to do with the similarity sought for: father and son will tend to be less nearly identical in ruling attributes than a succession in which the king is chosen for having the same traits of excellence as his predecessor and for imitating the perfection of the one Ruler of all creatures.[138]

After presenting elective monarchy as generally having the advantages of hereditary monarchy without its disadvantages, Marsiglio goes on to contrast elective monarchy with the system of vaguely dual Church-state sovereignty which let the Church be accorded primacy in political matters vested with a religious interest. For Marsiglio, as for Dante, sovereignty must be vested in one secular government, which alone may exercise coercive authority. He acknowledges, for the time being, a legitimate difference of opinion as to whether there should be one world ruler or a plurality of something like nation states.[139] Much later he dismisses universal monarchy of Dante's type as unrealistic.[140] Given a plurality of states, these must have sovereignty within themselves: there is no room for a tug of war between secular and clerical authorities. In his discussion of kingship, Marsiglio briefly anticipates what is to be the topic of his whole Discourse Two: the damage done by clerical usurpation of secular prerogatives. His viewpoint, at home within the tradition of ancient and early modern Christian thought, but quite radical within the late medieval tradition, is this: the sole purpose of the Church is the salvation of souls, which can be achieved only through voluntary means. Wealth is irrelevant in the saving of souls, as is "coercive jurisdiction" (coactiva jurisdiccio, usually synonymous in his usage for "political authority"); in fact, both are damaging.[141] "Render unto Caesar" for Marsiglio means to give up the claim to coercive rights in this world; this obviates the question of borderline disputes.[142] It follows that when Marsiglio takes his elective monarchy, in which the legislative body is vested with ultimate sovereignty, and contrasts it with the current system in which Church and state compete for sovereignty, he finds the latter such a living disaster that this time elective monarchy comes off much the better without much argumentative effort on his part.

Marsiglio's insistence upon checks on the ruler is only fitting and obvious if we are to see in him an early advocate of constitutional monarchy. He alludes to the inevitability of human shortcomings in even the elected monarch and speaks of his correction as a necessary responsibility of the legislative body.[143] To be sure, he cautions the citizenry or their legislature to use common sense. Small, rarely committed offenses on the part of the monarch should be benignly glossed over lest his image be tarnished unnecessarily. Still, appropriate punishment must be meted out in the form of a sentence when the offenses are neither small nor infrequent.[144] Although missing from its logical climactic place in Marsiglio's discussion of correcting a king, a brief remark earlier in his work makes it explicit that the lawmakers must depose an unworthy king.[145]

Since so much of Marsiglio's argument turns on the successful election of an outstanding man as king, we would be quite justified in asking for the practical mechanisms whereby his king is chosen. His appeal to Holy Roman Emperor Ludwig and his stout defense of the empire against the papacy would indicate that he supports the electors of the empire as the legitimate persons to choose the monarch and ultimately sees them as the lawmaking body he constantly alludes to as supreme. But this indication leads nowhere. Marsiglio's ability to match his ideal state with the Holy Roman Empire begins and ends with the bare fact of the emperor's election. Not much Marsiglian voluntarism underlay the electoral college of the princes of the empire (three archbishops, three dukes, and the king of Bohemia) who were neither elected by their subjects nor responsible to them.[146] Marsiglio's insistence upon speaking of the ruler as if he were the chief magistrate in a well-functioning Greek city-state of antiquity is altogether divorced from the real possibilities of European kingship in the fourteenth century. At times, Marsiglio's analysis of kingship is saved from near absurdity by the fact that he does not focus clearly on the distinction between what the ruler is and what he should be if all the details of election and executive responsibility were somehow worked out to make the king or emperor the choice and instrument of the "whole body of citizens" or "the weightier part of the citizens."

We can garner a hint, but only that, of Marsiglio's notion of how a ruler should be chosen by looking at the way he would have his general council chosen. He is certainly straightforwardly committed to establishing Conciliar authority for the Church, and he shows clearly enough to his own satisfaction how the whole community of the faithful should be represented step by step in the selection of a general council to decide religious questions:

> To this end let all countries or significant communities elect faithful men according to the rules given by their human legislator, whether one or many, and according to the quantity and quality of their people, choosing clergy first and then laymen for their demonstrated qualities of leading an upright life and experience in matters of holy law, who in applying their judgments shall represent all the faithful, for in this way the authority discussed earlier is transferred to them by the whole units. . . .[147]

Of course, the analogy cannot be pushed very far, for the selection of the general council presupposes the existence of legislatures, while the legislatures cannot presuppose the existence of another body to perform the selection of their members. All we have then is the thought that if the sovereign legislative body which is also to pick the ruler is constituted in terms of territorial and corporate representation, it will then legitimately be the whole people for governmental purposes.

Other weaknesses in Marsiglio's treatment of kingship stem from the fact that when he presents the institution with its functions in his ideal state his mind seems to wander as he describes an imaginary royal institution that is royal for no really good reason. Next to Aristotle, his chief political authority is Cicero, one of the ancient world's most eloquent opponents of monarchy. His examples of the king in action have nothing to do with any recognizable aspects of royalty, and it is evident enough that a republican executive called "archon" or "consul" would fit into his scheme much better than a king. Unlike recent constitutional monarchists, he has no patience with the magic of monarchy.

But if this is so, why did Marsiglio entitle his book *Defensor Pacis,* which certainly meant "the King" to his contemporaries as well as moderns?[148] Why his salutation to Emperor Ludwig IV? Above all, why his readiness to take kingship for granted as "a species of good government, and perhaps more nearly perfect than the others"? Something in the immediate circumstances of his writing and the little which is known of his career can help to explain this anomaly. Marsiglio shared the views of condemned heretics, and his virulent attacks on the clergy in general and the Avignon popes in particular for their usurpations of political authority and wealth make it clear why he was soon to be a condemned heretic himself.[149] In his polemics against the established Church he would not compromise. In Ludwig IV he saw the elected leader of what purported to be the Roman Empire, a powerful man with a following whose cause also opposed clerical political authority. Marsiglio and the supporters of the emperor hated the same enemies with enough passion to make them ideological allies for the time being. A condemned heretic could not be choosy about his friends, particularly if, like Marsiglio, he was looking for righteous action in his cause rather than martyrdom. Marsiglio, considering the circumstances, would have been most indiscreet to press a republican cause and an antipapal one at the same time. There were medieval people who did that sort of thing with a certain glittering success. Unfortunately, they were apt to end by being burned at the stake like Arnold of Brescia in 1155, or murdered by a mob like Cola di Rienzi in 1354 without wresting authority from either pope or emperor for long. Marsiglio instead seems to have muted his republican sentiments precisely by describing his ideal executive as a king, in order to serve something like a united front against the papacy. His solution has the look of a mental compromise: he kept his ideal political system a republican one, but he let a monarch — in the form of a figure suggestive of the Holy Roman emperor by the bare fact of his being elected — stand as the executive as its head. It is possible that he had to swallow hard over thus implicitly treating the electors of the Holy Roman Empire as embodying the will of their subjects in a way he knew that they did not. It is equally possible that he had that strange sensitivity, fairly common to polemical writers, which automatically brings conflicts which separate "our side" from "their side" into sharp focus, while blurring over issues which would divide "our side" against itself if they were ever focused on. The result was the same: unwilling or unable to challenge monarchy outright, Marsiglio painted an ideal king as a constitutional monarch. It is strange that such a momentous concept could have been arrived at by a man whose heart was so obviously not in it.

SIR JOHN FORTESCUE: TRADITIONAL KINGSHIP AND THE COMING "NEW MONARCHY"

In urging that Church authority be placed in the hands of a general council, Marsiglio and other critics of the Avignon papacy shaped the movement called "Conciliarism," which gathered particular momentum when the Great Schism in 1378 divided the loyalty of European Christians between two popes for more than thirty years. The authority of a great council first proved to be ineffective at Pisa in 1409 when the choice of the council became merely a third claimant to the papacy. Then, in 1417, in partial fulfillment of a thoroughly Conciliarist program, the Council of Constance successfully deposed all three claimants and elected Martin V as pope. Once in sole power, however, Martin V attempted to counteract the movement to which he owed his election but which now threatened to limit his power, for the Conciliarists demanded continual authority for their general council.

In large part due to the successful maneuvering of Martin V and his successor, Eugene IV, the Conciliar movement as such lost its strength in the second quarter of the fifteenth century. Some of the ideas it furthered continued to command a following. In particular, there remained the Conciliarists' emphasis on the need for grounding a powerful and independent kingship on law, and policies for the purpose of uniting king and people of a realm in a community of interests. This made as much sense as ever, especially as the century headed in uncertain fashion toward the era of the early nation-state. Often enough, those who resented the Conciliarist protest against papal power felt the same way as their opponents about a need for revitalizing kingship. Even the protagonists of papal authority ultimately contributed to the same theoretical trend. If they remained stubborn and unyielding, their justifications for papal monarchy could be easily appropriated by any defender of secular kingship who chose to make a few substitutions in their terminology or references ("king" for "pope," "realm" for "Christendom," "public good" for "salvation," etc.). Actually, however, the most influential advocates of papal power, men such as Juan de Torquemada and Antonio de Roselli, sought concordats or working agreements with imperial or royal rulers to heal the whole Conciliar breach. The most obvious suggestions they had to offer for reaching these agreements included cessions of bits of papal authority to the emperor or king.[150]

Monarchical theorists ultimately gained either through adaptation of their opponents' arguments or through compromises put forward by men who hoped for an end to the tense opposition between the papacy and secular monarchies. "The concordat policy and the advocacy of monarchical sovereignty thus pointed in the same direction: together they formed the foundation for the royal and princely absolutism which was to be built up in the following century."[151] This is a little overstated, for, as we shall see, an opponent of absolutism could contribute significantly to the foundation of the "New Monarchy," from which absolutism was to develop, without fully realizing the implications of some of his ideas, but it is still largely true.

A vicious cycle characterized the inherent instability of fifteenth century kingdoms. Warfare engendered by the ambitions of powerful nobles frequently eroded royal power to the detriment of peace in the realms. The erosion of the king's peace led to popular discontent and additional uprisings, which encouraged ambitious magnates to make further grabs for wealth and power at the expense of each other and of the king. Predictably, these practical needs and dangers molded the political theories of the age. After the Conciliar controversy had been settled, there were few distinguished contributors to political theory in the fifteenth century, but what political theoreticians there were consequently set about refining models for effective kingship. The threat most of them perceived most clearly was an overly strong nobility, and an alliance between the king and

Commons against that danger came to them with varying degrees of clarity as the basis for insuring domestic tranquility.

In England, the long, disastrous reign of Henry VI and the interminable War of the Roses made the search for a strengthened monarchy more consistently pressing than elsewhere. In the works of Sir John Fortescue, particularly his *Governance of England,* written probably between 1471 and 1475, the whys and hows of kingship are given a thorough reexamination. Fortescue was a prominent jurist and chief justice of the king's bench from 1442 until he was forced to become an exile after the Yorkists deposed the Lancastrian Henry VI. His Latin works, *The Nature of Natural Law (De Natura Legis Naturae)* and *Praises of the Laws of England (De Laudibus Legum Angliae)* brought up the question of absolute as opposed to limited monarchy in the light of history and the English common law, but his *Governance of England* is noteworthy from another standpoint. It is essentially the first constitutional treatise in the English language.[152] While his frame of reference in the *Governance* is peculiarly English, he presents his conclusions as having application everywhere, and his theoretical concerns are quite broad. The thrust of this work is two-fold: (1) confirming, along the lines of Aristotle and Aquinas as he understood them, that true kingship cannot be absolute but must function within a constitutional framework, and (2) proving that monarchy must be independently rich and powerful in the face of all competitors, if it is to be expected to keep the peace and enforce the laws. It seems not to have troubled him that a monarchy strong enough to be independent of the nobility (again, the chief visible source of opposition) might prove to be too strong and independent to be restrained within a constitutional framework. Like many another political theorist before and since, he was inclined to place undue weight on the willingness of men in authority to recognize the long-term interests of groups on which their institutions depended for support.

England had officially sided with the pope in the later Conciliar controversy, and Fortescue shared no part of the resentments against papal claims which smoldered in England from the days of the Lollards to Henry VIII's break with the Roman Church. The fact that Fortescue could support the primacy of the spiritual powers over the temporal and still preach the need for a much stronger monarchy with fervor is a good indication of how general the sentiment for increasing monarchical authority was in the England of his time (as well as elsewhere). In the *Governance of England,* he does not particularly worry about the king's role in advancing the faith. The king he describes has enough to do in the secular sphere with defending the realm against internal and external enemies. Discussion of the king's governance is confined to problems of this world alone. To follow the reasoning of his earlier *Nature of Natural Law*, the pope has the authority to rebuke and punish a king who fails to rule his subjects justly, but since in the *Governance* the primary matter at hand is strengthening the king's power, the question of who can rightfully exercise power over him is not of the moment.

Sir John attempts to base his chief distinction between good and faulty kingship on the work of Saint Thomas Aquinas. Citing Thomas for authority, he states that there is one form of kingship, "*dominium politicum et regale*" (royal and political dominion), exercised under laws approved by the people and financed by taxes which they assent to. There is another, plain "*dominium regale*," (royal dominion), in which the king makes the laws to suit himself.[153] Fortescue has been accused of citing Thomas badly,[154] but the result is a vast improvement on Thomas's largely verbal synthesis of none-too-compatible parts. Unlike Thomas, he does not let Aristotle's discussion of political concepts within a Greek city-state frame of reference get in his way when he discusses the contemporary institution of hereditary monarchy. He uses Aristotle's idea of "polity" and "political" to indicate the consultation of diverse interests, to modify the concept of pure kingship in the way a monarch rules. Fortescue is, to be sure, impeded from time to time in his reasoning by bursts of nationalism, making the English monarchy the model of *dominium politicum et regale* and the French monarchy the model of *dominium regale* to the point of turning differences of degree into absolute points of distinction.

Fortescue is medieval enough to accept the king's embodiment of the people in nearly a literal sense. At the same time, he emphasizes clearly that the significance of this embodiment is what amounts to the ancient and modern concept of government by consent. In speaking of the origins of the English monarchy under Brute,[155] he contrasts the arbitrary rule of one man — understandable enough in those dark days when mankind was still too ferocious to be governed in any other fashion — with "the fellowshippe that came in to this land with Brute, willyunge to be vnite and made a body pollitike callid a reawme, hauynge an hed to gouerne it," for in the case of Brute, the king was freely chosen by the people to be their head.

> And thai and he vpon this incorperacion, institucion, and onynge of hem self into a reaume, ordenyd the same reaume to be ruled and justified by suche lawes as thai all wolde assent vnto; wich lawe therefore is callid *polliticum,* and bi cause it is ministrid by a kynge, it is called *regale.*[156]

After establishing that a king of a civilized nation must not subject his people to arbitrary rule, Sir John focuses his discussion on how to keep the king strong enough to enforce the law and defend the realm. The need for maintaining the peace against crime within and aggression from without, as well as the appropriateness of monarchy for doing so, are for him too nearly self-evident to need belaboring.

Soon several principles emerge, none of them new, but in their emphasis on economics different in their cumulative impact from those of the writers discussed above. The king must see to his economic strength as the basis for his political effectiveness, but his economic resources cannot be taken out of the hides of the commoners. The economic interests of the king and his people are the same, but powerful intermediaries between the two must be guarded against.

For a king to be effective, he must be impressively rich. To put down uprisings properly, he must be able to "ride in his owne person myghtely accompanyed,"[157] and his own wealth must be more than sufficient for putting greater armies in the field than any likely combination of the higher nobility can do. "The harme that comyth off a kynges poverte" is a great evil indeed, for without ready money a king simply cannot guarantee speedy justice or the security of his realm.[158] He must have regular sources of income granted to him, to cover both anticipated expenses and unforeseen contingencies. Fortescue is too much of an English traditionalist to argue that the king should ever resort to unaccustomed taxation measures.[159] There is no need, for as far as he is concerned there are resources aplenty for the king's government. The problem should be solved by continuing the established taxes, such as poundage and tonnage for keeping up the navy, while reaffirming what is for him a natural order of priorities: in fiscal matters, the crown must come first, the interests of private subjects a bit later.[160] Sometimes, mere discretion will dictate reasonable policy: when it is necessary for the king to reward outstanding men for their services, this should be done with money as a single diminution of royal wealth rather than with gifts of land, which represent a perpetual loss of revenue.[161] Sometimes, it is necessary to accept the lesser of evils: maintaining the king in his high estate is more important than doing absolute economic justice in terms of rewards to private subjects.[162]

Fortescue also advises the monarch to circumvent the question of new taxation by increasing his revenue-producing landholdings. Whether it is a question of taking the produce value of demesne lands directly or of leasing them, this means of enriching himself will cause the least possible popular discontent. He should not hesitate to make the fullest use of traditional means to see that his manors grow in size and number: estates forfeited through treason should revert to the crown. The king's wealth, when properly looked after, will enable him to be in a much better position than other men for timely manorial purchases. The king should even make full use of his right to approve and veto marriages among the high nobility to assure that escheats and likely inheritances do not fall some other way, when they might well fall to the crown.[163] At the same time, the king will be undermining the chance for possible rivals among the nobility to amass the landholdings and resulting wealth which will make them dangerous.

At most, of course, the king can provide himself with only a fraction of the needed revenue by these means, and Fortescue stresses that the overall economic strength of the king is in the productive forces of his kingdom. For him it is clear that the Commons produce wealth by their very nature; therefore, when the Commons are strong, the king may easily have ample funds at his disposal. He finds, perhaps predictably from his partisan standpoint, that the history of England proves that the freedom of the Commons to prosper has meant that they could be moderately taxed for the strengthening of royal government to no one's injury. This has further meant that their loyalty to the realm has been solidified. English commoners have been able and willing to supply themselves with archers' equipment and serve as bowmen for the common defense, and this has kept the king's peace.[164] French history proves the same point in reverse: the Commons of France have been exploited by exorbitant taxes, such as the *gabelle,* which he described as a 300 percent to 400 percent tax on salt, and the *quatrime,* or tax of the fourth pipe, on wine. They have been subject to irregular exactions and deprived of their economic security to the point that they have been generally unwilling and even unable to furnish the king with the resources he would need to keep a decent peace.[166] His conclusions are a bit muddied by his observation that actually fewer robberies are committed in France than in England, but this he dismisses as due only to the innate cowardice of the French and the heroic nature of the English people.[167]

Beyond this, the king must not rest content with the economic nonexploitation of his subjects but must actively further their prosperity. It is too early in the day for Sir John to have come up with a detailed set of steps for achieving the goals of mercantilism, but he has a clear, if general, idea of what could be done in this direction. The embryo of mercantilist striving for a favorable national balance of trade is clearly discernible in his work as the search for

> . . . how the goyng owt off the money may be restrayned [and] how bullyon mey be brought in to the lande . . . and also how the prises off the marchaudise grown in this lande mey be holde vp and encressed, and the prises off merchandyses brought in to this lande abatid.

He does not expect any king yet to have the knowledge at his own disposal for bringing this about, but still he feels that these are projects for "wich right wyse men mowe sone fynde the meanes."[168]

Having once stressed the origins of good monarchy in the consent of the governed at a time when people had attained a level of civilization which made absolute monarchy unreasonable, Fortescue does not follow through with a discussion of institutional machinery to keep the king's acts in line with the people's wishes. Nor does he place quite such a heavy burden on the king's sense of self-restraint as John of Salisbury, *The Book of Emperors,* and Saint Thomas all did. In Fortescue's model of kingship, the ruler simply does not require an excess of self-restraint, only normal perceptiveness, to realize the singleness of the interests of himself and his Commons. At the same time, this eliminates the need for placing ultimate authority in a representative body, such as that advocated by Marsiglio.

Fortescue's hesitancy in this connection may seem a bit strange for a critic of absolute monarchy in the land of Magna Carta, but he has his reasons. In his eyes, the problem of keeping king and Commons strong together in the face of challenges from pretenders to the throne and other all too powerful members of the nobility is so overriding that he is distrustful of encouraging reliance on divisions of authority in the process of governing. All this notwithstanding, Sir John does lay great stress on the king's need for a Great Council to help him steer his policy in the direction of the common interest. Unlike Marsiglio's Great Council for governing the Church, however, John's Great Council is to remain an advisory body. The king must be well advised, and this is a matter for expertise. If his people are to be content to maintain the king in his wealthy estate, their interests must be consulted, and, of course, there is no forgetting the earlier point that a king ruling a rational and moral people must do so through the taxes and laws which they approve.

The Great Council which Fortescue proposes must be quite unlike the royal councils familiar to him with their token and hesitant commoners, assemblages which merely had raised the existing divisions of power along feudal lines to threatening levels.[169] These had been so dominated by the great lords, spiritual and temporal, that they spent an undue amount of time on their own divisive concerns and were hardly in a position to deal objectively with conflicts of interest between the king and "thair cosyns, there seruantes, tenantes, or such other as thai owed ffauor vnto."[170] For a council really to assist the king in dispensing justice and setting policy for the realm, its members must owe their positions to the king and be bound by oath and interest to him alone.

In Fortescue's plan for the Great Council, he suggests that twenty-four men be chosen for the mental and moral traits which make them the best men in the kingdom for advising their sovereign and fashioning long-term policy. Twelve are to be laymen and twelve are to be clergy, but evidently not lords spiritual and temporal. Their interests shall not be deflected from the king's service, for they are to be rewarded only by the king himself for their work. This, Fortescue notes, has been the practice for recruiting justices of the king's bench, and it has worked out well.[171] In preferring the members simply to be "chosen" in a manner analogous to the king's justices, he indicates unmistakably that they are to be selected by royal appointment. The *people* in his model are to be consulted and their interests united with the king's in the council at most in this way: the reputation which the twenty-four men enjoy among the people for fairness and intelligence will be the criterion for their selection. It is, of course, impossible even in such a theoretical model, to offer any guarantee that when a king choses council members with the thought in mind that they must be dependent on him for their positions, he would pick the first choice of the subjects themselves. For Fortescue, it is so necessary to guarantee the council's absolute dependence on the king that he is willing to sacrifice something of its representative character. On the other hand, the connection between representation and election never became so self-evident to medieval political theorists that we have any right to find him making this sacrifice consciously.

The matter of popular representation is worrisome in discussing Fortescue's theory of kingship only because of his insistence that the people do indeed assent to the laws. If there were some other institution for transmitting popular assent to governance, the king's choosing his council members and his final authority over them would present no problem at all. How about a Parliament in which the Commons as such are represented?

For Fortescue, the Great Council had some of the responsibilities which later constitutional theorists would reserve to a Parliament or a ministry over which Parliament exercised a certain control. Since the thirteenth century, representatives had sometimes been elected from the Commons in the shires and boroughs of England to deliberate, particularly on tax matters, along with the clergy and nobles in what can be seen as the forerunners of Parliament or even as Parliaments themselves.[172] Fortescue does not write off the function of parliamentary assemblies in the *Governance*, although he mentions them only twice: once, in passing, when he notes that the Three Estates of France, when assembled are like "the Courte of the parlement in Ingelonde,"[173] and once, in elaboration on the beneficial results of thorough deliberations by the Great Council

> . . . wher through the parlementes shall mowe do more gode in a moneth to the mendynge off the lawe, then thai shall mowe do in a yere, yff the amendynge theroff be not debatyd, and be such covnsell ryped to thair handes.[174]

Taken at face value, this would imply a clear veto power of Parliament over legislation as well as taxes, as these are proposed by the king and council, rather much along the lines of the future constitutionalism of England and Western Europe; however, it would appear from the minuscule attention which Parliament, as opposed to the council, receives in *The Governance of England* that Fortescue thinks of the function of parliamentary assemblages as generally that of making only moderate changes at most in proposals emanating from the king in council. Thus Parliament in the sense of a gathering of the estates is a logical necessity for Fortescue to preserve the form of limited government, but the serious weight of governance is shared between the king and his council.

Perhaps in order not to break too radically with what had become tradition, Sir John suggests that at the same time the council is chosen the king should appoint four lords spiritual and four lords temporal annually to counsel him also, but he clearly does not think of them as constituting a separate body. This king is to choose a chief officer, something like a prime minister, from the original twenty-four, not from the eight great lords.[175] In case the expense of the whole arrangement appears to be too great, the number should be reduced in such a way as to retain the same proportion: sixteen laymen and clerics chosen on the basis of merit, two lords temporal and two lords spiritual, so that the nobility remains over-shadowed as a matter of principle.[176] Even the original council seems to be a separate body for Fortescue largely as a matter of physical necessity: advice and discussion from varied standpoints are feasible only in a group setting. He does not think of the council as constituted in a separate body to act as a check on what the king does, but only to make sure that the king has what any reasonable king would want: impartial advice on which to base decisions for the good of his whole kingdom.[177]

In Sir John Fortescue's work we find the culmination of the trend toward presenting a theory of kingship in terms of the merits of the institution as such. The theory of kingship which Fortescue articulated also provides a bridge to modern ideas of constitutional monarchy, although in a peculiar way. On one hand, his ideas that the best form of government originates in consent, that the king continues to function under the laws which his people have assented to, and that important deliberation should be entrusted to a regularly constituted council, point toward the modern goal of constitutionalism pure and simple. On the other hand, his most constantly stressed overall goal remains that of strengthening kingship in power and wealth in order to subdue the king's possible rivals, once and for all. In this context, he would make the ruler more nearly the sole source of political power in all the kingdom and less bound by *de facto* restrictions than before. Historically, the realization of the latter goal turned out to be a very necessary step on the way to constitutional monarchy, and it would be more correct to speak of men of Fortescue's persuasion as providing a bridge to theories of constitutional monarchy in two separate spans. Before monarchy as a European institution could become truly constitutional, it had to develop sufficiently absolutist tendencies to dispose of feudal competition. Only later, after experiencing abuses of absolute monarchy and after absorbing the fact that a medieval balance of estates was neither possible nor desirable, could political theorists stop equivocating about the need for institutions to insure that kingship would indeed be the embodiment of the people's will and interest which medieval political theorists from John of Salisbury through Sir John Fortescue had made it out to be.

Chapter 7

Towards the "New Monarchies" at the Close of the Middle Ages

The last half of the fifteenth century saw a final turn of the familiar spiral whereby medieval kings rose to new levels of power and popularity after another round of feudal anarchy, uncertainty, and disorder. With Henry VII in England, Louis XI in France, and Ferdinand and Isabella in the newly united Kingdom of Spain, medieval kingship was vested in a group now generally known as the "New Monarchs," who were determined to make the king's peace a reality and to limit severely the power of the feudal nobility. As a group, the New Monarchs displayed a high degree of realism and practicality in coping with the problems of government. This in itself was, of course, nothing new for medieval kingship: such kings as Clovis with his tomahawk, Louis VI with his forceful use of suzerainty, and Henry II of England with his itinerant justices had been pragmatists and realists relative to the needs of their time and the means for ruling at their disposal. What distinguished the later fifteenth-century group from their successful predecessors was their ability to manipulate forces for the construction and strengthening of early nation-states. They were no longer bound so much to maintain themselves on top of the old feudal pyramid as they were bound to make themselves independent of it.

> The history of France from the time when Hugues Capet assumed the Crown till the reign of Louis XIV can be summarized in few words. It is a record of the destruction of political feudalism by the monarchy. . . . The royal armies overthrew the feudal territories; the royal law-courts filched jurisdiction from the feudal judges; the royal tax-gatherers thrust themselves between the noble and his vassals.[1]

This turns out to be a horrendous exaggeration for France, as well as for other European countries, if we review the ways that medieval kings until the twelfth century or even later depended on feudal cooperation to govern effectively. But feudalism began to outlive its usefulness to medieval kingship sometime during the thirteenth century, at least in the realms of western Europe, and the above description is a fairly accurate one of what was happening in those countries as the Middle Ages neared their close.

When the dust of the conflict had finally settled, the successful New Monarchs headed governments as sovereigns rather than suzerains. Armies were under royal control. Regular taxes supported the king's domestic projects and foreign expansion, and kings felt far less inhibited than before in making laws. Kings in control of the new nation-states were to increase their popular support, and at least a mild form of nationalism was in the offing. Merchants and traders would back their kings more than ever, and explorers sent abroad by kings would usher in a new age of discovery. Some of these happenings had analogues in the Holy Roman Empire, some did not. Maximilian I, a contemporary of the New Monarchs, and his grandson, Charles V, who followed him, had much the same sort of support and reigned over a much greater expanse of territory than their English or French counterparts. The notion of a universal or multinational empire, however, remained just as incompatible with the concept of a national kingdom as before. Since it continued to govern many of the actions of these emperors, the result for central and eastern Europe was perhaps obvious: late medieval emperors, at least as emperors, never headed nation-states of the type the New Monarchs were shaping.

THE END OF CHIVALRY AND THE ATTENUATION OF FEUDALISM

Rebellions led by nobles rocked the peace of European kingdoms repeatedly during the fourteenth and fifteenth centuries, and yet both feudalism, which had given the nobles their sociopolitical status, and chivalry, the set of ideals which nobles professed to live up to, had been eroding for centuries. When the New Monarchs eventually deprived the nobles of their capacity for waging private war, what was left of chivalry evaporated into airy and apolitical influences on a code of gentlemanly conduct. Although forms of manorialism and the dominance of territorial lords lasted through the rest of the Middle Ages in eastern Europe, the hereditary nobility in most of western Europe had to be content with bearing titles of feudal origin which had neither the political independence nor the responsibilities of early medieval dukes, earls, and counts to reinforce them.

The decline of chivalry and feudalism affected late medieval kingship in two ways. The aristocracy changed its relationship to the crown when the independent fighting noble of the earlier Middle Ages sought refinement and a chance at sumptuous living on his way to becoming a serviceable courtier in the king's service. The type of warfare which kings had to fear from enemies and wage on their own behalf changed even more drastically. Chivalry originally meant cavalry, specifically the heavy cavalry of armored knights, and it retained this meaning throughout the Middle Ages. Cavalry, however, was losing its decisive importance in the fifteenth century. Consequently, the king's dependence on the class which furnished mounted warriors was lessening.

In one of their many roles, medieval kings considered themselves the noblest of knights. In isolated instances they exhibited the personal heroism which chivalry demanded even in its centuries of decline. Sir John Froissart tells the story, for example, of King John of Bohemia, who had lost his sight some six years earlier, at the Battle of Crecy:

> The king said to them: "Gentlemen, you are all my people, my friends and brethren at arms this day; therefore, as I am blind, I request of you to lead me so far into the engagement that I may strike one blow with my sword." The knights replied that they would directly lead him forward; and in order that they might not lose him in the crowd, they fastened all the reins of their horses together, and put the king at their head, that he might gratify his wish and advance towards the enemy. [After the battle it was found that] the king . . . had rode in among the enemy and made good use of his sword; for he and his companions had fought most gallantly. They had advanced so far that they were all slain; and on the morrow they were found on the ground, with their horses all tied together.[2]

Most kings of the later Middle Ages, however, supported the chivalric ideal with considerably less personal participation than this. More typically, King Martin of Aragon had novels with chivalric themes copied for his royal library.[3] Still, even very late medieval kings, such as Henry VIII and Francis I, continued to sponsor knightly tournaments and to take part in them. The same Francis did not accept the challenge of Emperor Charles V to an actual duel when the emperor felt the French king had broken his solemn promise (the Oath of Madrid), but even the tournaments required chivalric-minded kings to risk real danger.[4] In 1559, Henry II of France participated in his last tournament so heartily that he was fatally wounded in it.

The whole image of the knight, however, had been undergoing substantial change from, say, the time of William the Conqueror. The early ideal of feudal chivalry had been based on prowess in the simple sense of an individual's "ability to beat the other man in battle"; on intense personal loyalty to a liege lord; and on largesse, the attribute of generous giving to the point of recklessness.[5] It was fiercely independent and embodied a scale of values which took fighting style seriously enough that it could get in the way of winning a war.

By the fifteenth century, the physical ability of a knight to best his opponent in battle had lost much of its earlier significance due to the development of more advanced weaponry and even more to the development of strategy and tactics which required the deployment of fighting men as masses. As a class, equestrian aristocrats did not go in much for the type of mental work which the application of new weapons or tactical planning involved. Chivalric pageantry lost its relationship to the demands of contemporary warfare, for which it was supposed to provide training. Although an occasionally fatal wound was still possible in them, royal tournaments got rather far removed from their original function of practice melees to maintain mounted warrior toughness. Around the beginning of the fifteenth century, the rules governing tournaments sometimes had to include the proviso "that in the combats on horseback neither contestant should be tied to his saddle." The esthetic side of the performance, aimed at gaining the attention of admiring ladies, certainly had little to do with what was likely to happen in late-medieval massed battles.[6]

Generosity in giving survived as an attribute of chivalry into the late Middle Ages, and it was one generally claimed by kings before the "New Monarchies." The records kept for Edward the Black Prince, for example, show that he would bestow such expensive gifts as a gold mug, a silver cup, or a pony on whatever lords and ladies caught his fancy on his travels.[7] Now if nobles were to keep up the practice of extravagant giving, well and good, but it was a poor policy for royalty who had to worry about depleting the strength of the crown. It was precisely this sort of thing which we found Fortescue concerned with in the previous chapter. The endless strife of the fourteenth century, which feudal lords in western Europe had made the most of, had left them on the whole powerful but objectionable in the eyes of their non-noble or lower-ranking noble subjects. The fifteenth century witnessed a remarkable economic upswing in Europe. With it came an assertiveness on the part of those who had themselves contributed to the new productivity: the farmers and the middle-class inhabitants of the towns. The New Monarchs knew how to distinguish between a need for a certain display for underscoring royal power or for promoting royal prestige and mere wastefulness. Several of them got a name for being miserly, but they knew what they were doing, as consciously or unconsciously they adopted the financial outlook of their allies in the merchant or business class, who valued thrift well above display.

At the same time, the later Middle Ages also saw a general rise in the standard of sumptuousness for maintaining noble status. This ultimately served the interests of kingship extremely well from another standpoint. If nobles spent their time and money trying to live more lavishly than each other, they were less likely than before to stir up trouble. Promoting that turn of events led to occasional apparent contradictions in royal policy. In the spirit of thrift, which their non-noble subjects admired, the French

Charles VII and Louis XI prohibited many tournaments with the justification that they were so wasteful. "Yet both these kings with malicious inconsistency, encouraged certain tournaments for this very reason, hoping that some of their rivals among the great feudal lords would strain their resources in the effort to surpass all others in lavish display and entertainments."[8]

As another chivalric ideal, the personal loyalty of vassals to lords lost its significance for kingship in the later Middle Ages. With the ascendency of the territorial concept of kingship, when loyalty to the realm rather than to the king as a person grew in importance, particularly when the demands of loyalty were placed on all free classes and rendered directly to the king, the worth of the feudal contract in relation to kingship took a marked drop. A demonstrated lack of loyalty to the crown was treasonous, whether committed by a noble or a commoner. Rebellions headed by nobles continued to be an unfortunate commonplace in the fifteenth and sixteenth centuries, but no one could successfully defend them any longer on the basis of a feudal lord's rightful independence. This had been true in England since the days of William the Conqueror, but by the fifteenth century it was generally the case all over Europe except for Castile and Poland. With loyalty to the ruling monarch as everyone's obligation, feudal loyalty ceased to be anything special.

Religious chivalry, as distinct from feudal chivalry, had earlier imparted to knights the ideal of service to God, going on a crusade, or both. The crusading spirit, however, did not generally linger on much after the failure of the thirteenth-century crusades. Except on the frontiers of Christian Spain, where warfare inspired by religious chivalry lasted into the fifteenth century, and in the empire, where the later wars against the Turks furthered the ideal of militant opposition to Islam,[9] religious chivalry lost most of its practical significance. It is supposed to have served the purpose of sanctioning the king's peace, as a force for maintaining the laws of God and man. To the extent that breakers of the king's peace could be identified with enemies of Christian law, the same sort of fervor could be elicited against them as had been turned against pagans and Mohammedans. Kings and their supporters could infuse national missions with religious zeal; however, national missions infused with religious zeal no longer had much to do with chivalry as such. Chivalry was inherently non-national, being both class-based in confronting non-knightly elements in the nation and international in its ideals at the same time.

As far as keeping the king's peace was concerned, late medieval knights were not particularly reliable. The restraints in the chivalric code on the power of armed men lost their effectiveness in the last decades of the Hundred Years' War and other conflicts such as the English War of the Roses, when atrocities under commanders of noble birth multiplied. The

Burgundians were noteworthy for their lip service to the chivalric ideal but equally for their later medieval atrocities after taking hostile towns. To avenge the murder of a herald, a Burgundian commander had all the men of the town of Nesles who appeared to be combatants hanged and a hand cut off of all the noncombatants, including women and children. The capture of another city was followed by the mass drowning of some eight hundred inhabitants. Knights and squires who formed marauding bands in the fifteenth century often distinguished themselves more by their cruelty than by their adherence to any given code at all.[10] They were obviously not going to be of much help in applying the concept of the king's peace as this became the basis for royal law enforcement on a national scale.

Chivalry, of course, could not survive in anything like its earlier medieval forms without its base in feudalism, and feudalism itself underwent drastic transformations after the thirteenth century in relation to kingship as well as in other ways. While in the High Middle Ages the general trend in western Europe was for expansion of the royal demesne to the point that all land was held from the crown, developments in the way land was held in feudal tenure forced kings to base their power less and less on their position as feudal lords, a shift which worked out to their advantage in the long run.

As one significant factor in this connection, the hereditary principle not only made inroads but triumphed as a matter of practice. Even in England, where royal control of landholding had originally been the best defined, it became ". . . accepted that all lands held under feudal tenure passed by hereditary right."[11] This ruled out the use of fiefs to reward or punish men who might be more loyal or serviceable to the king than heirs of the previous lords, unless convincing legal reasons could be found for taking them from the latter. In France, the Capetian kings had tended to grant the most significant royal offices — those of constable, chamberlain, chancellor, royal seneschal, and others — for life. These high appointments came to be looked upon as the rightful preserve of the small group of families who held them before. In this way, too, the hereditary principle was becoming ingrained in a manner incompatible with royal independence. This danger caused the later Capetians often to fill these offices with weak appointees and to let the kingdom get along for an extraordinarily long time without a royal seneschal. Before they did so, the royal seneschal had amassed power in being head of the king's household, controlling royal finances, commanding the army, and sharing judicial powers[12] — in a way probably all too reminiscent of the Carolingian major domos for kings with any sensitivity to practical considerations and any recollection of French history.

As the right of lords, including kings all over Europe, to transfer fiefs or fees to different vassals diminished, the very notion of a lord's continued control of the land became blurred in the face of competition from the increasingly clear concept of private property. The great English jurist, Bracton, put the greatly reduced rights of lordship like this:

> The lord has nothing in the fee except the services due to him, and thus the fee is the property of the tenant, but subject to services to the lord.[13]

The sense of this statement in the context of the later Middle Ages is that the "tenant" is still to render services as a sort of labor equivalent of rent but the rendering of such services does not detract from the fact that holding the land as a "tenant" is equivalent in all other ways to owning the land. Landlords with a sense of what was coming would take pains to assure themselves that they had quasi-ownership rights to the lands they held. The whole notion of the feudal contract could not withstand the impact of the idea that landholding was a matter of ownership and business.

Something of a business mentality also came to influence the process of subinfeudation: the granting of fees down the line to new holders. The grantors passed on their own service obligations to their new tenants — often more obligations in proportion than the land was worth relative to their own fees — while their own lords suffered from the fact that the services in question were now being performed for them less directly. Although any other feudal lord benefited in his role of vassal as well as lost in his role of lord when this happened on several levels at once, the same could not hold true of kings, who had the role of lords but not of vassals within their own countries. There was a general tendency for the feudal dues or incidents, those "encumbrances that went with the land" and were supposed to furnish a source of income for the lord, to get lost in the subinfeudation process, although generally the services themselves were accounted for in some diluted form.[14] In England, with the statute, *Quia Emptores,* the crown attempted a compromise to slow down the process of deterioration. Those who held land as tenants under the feudal system were recognized as having the right to sell it in such a way that the purchaser would render exactly the same services and dues to the lord as the former tenant. The same statute, however, ruled out subinfeudation. In other words, the matter of who could alienate land was being put on a cash basis rather than even nominally in terms of the feudal contract. Since the king's own tenants, the tenants-in-chief of the realm, were not originally affected by the terms of the statute, the result was to eliminate intermediaries between the king's chief landholders and those actually holding the land, while preventing the crown from losing services and revenue through the sale of lands by the tenants-in-chief.[15]

In 1327, however, the tenants-in-chief obtained the right to alienate lands in any way they wished through purchasing a "license" from the crown for such sales.[16] In the short run, the crown lost money since the value of the licenses to sell was small in relation to the diminution of feudal dues which resulted from the sale of these lands. In practice, the obligations which the purchasers were supposed to fulfill were more difficult to oversee than when they were held by the tenants-in-chief. In the long run, however, this whole process turned out quite well for English kings, in getting the control of land more into the market and away from feudal principles of land tenure, for the eventual shift to landholding based on purchase and rent accelerated the shift toward a money economy in general. The money economy made it possible for kings to support themselves and finance their projects through direct taxes on their subjects and indirect taxes on goods which their subjects bought — all in all a more profitable and politically significant business than royal landholding itself.[17] This does not mean that late-medieval kings were unconcerned about increasing the size of the demesne whenever an opportunity arose, but rather that they sought to avoid lord-vassal relations in their new acquisitions. When English victories in the Hundred Years' War put more land in France under English control, for example, Edward III made it plain in 1360 that he wanted it annexed to the crown only and not treated as a feudal holding.[18] At the same time, English kings — who had learned from the way French kings could exploit suzerain rights over their vassals — assiduously avoided putting themselves in vassal relationships to other monarchs from that time on.

In Germany the emperors were unable to make inroads on the strength of feudal tenure from the crown. This continued the growth of territorial rulership already discernible and meant in effect that a successful German king had to start with being the powerful territorial ruler that a Hapsburg was.

Outside of Germany the very identity of the nobles as nobles was at stake within the complex framework of kingship and declining feudalism. If they were not dukes and barons by virtue of holding land on feudal tenure, what was it that gave substance to their titles? Knighthood itself was separated out of the feudal system with the wholesale creation of knights by kings during the Hundred Years' War. By the end of the fifteenth century, French King Charles VIII would think so lightly of a knight's dignity as to bestow the honor casually on strangers in Italy as he passed through.[19] In time, rental incomes and monopolistic privileges would support some of what had been the feudal nobility in England as elsewhere. That trend in itself, however, broke down some of the real, economic distinctions between the nobility as a class and aspiring members of the merchant class, since, when land became saleable, it was possible for successful businessmen to purchase manors and draw revenues from them in the same way. Special status had to be sought somewhere else by the nobles. From the fifteenth century, the most promising avenue of advancement for them was the king's service, although here again they were not free from bourgeois competition.

Feudalism enjoyed a sort of revival in the fourteenth and early fifteenth centuries in England and France, in considerable part because of upheavals wrought by the Hundred Years' War. Feudal lords seemed stronger than ever in their private fortifications with fighting forces under their own virtually independent commands. Their strength was superficial by this time, however, and the resurgence in question is often called "bastard feudalism." The fact was that there was no longer any lasting justification for such independent enclaves of authority within the state. All the overlapping concerns of the non-noble classes and most of the lower nobility — security of life and limb, the administration of justice, protection of property, payments to authorities only in some comprehensible relationship to benefits received — were best cared for without the independent action of the nobility, who were in their final stage of power largely through royal default at the time.

Concerning personal competence to deal with problems at hand, fourteenth-century kings, taking one with another, were as sorry a lot as had been seen since the seventh century. Time, however, was on the royal side, and the New Monarchs of the mid- and late-fifteenth centuries would profit from the foregoing developments. The partial erasure of the economic distinction between the nobility and the upper middle class, which began with the commercialization of landholding, made the nobility more like other subjects and consequently easier to deal with. At the same time, having the best routes for aristocratic distinction lead to the royal palace prepared the day, still well in the future, when the feudal lord with his great castle and private army would be turned into a serviceable courtier.

Nothing happened, as things turned out, to the practice of dividing society into the three estates of clergy, nobility, and commons during the later Middle Ages. In fact, it has been shown that this habit became more ingrained than ever during the fifteenth century itself.[20] Perhaps the blurring and questioning of class lines between the second and third estates made medieval people more conscious of them, since before the divisions were simply given facts of life. Whatever its cause, this fact posed no problem at all for later medieval kingship since it continued to provide the means for the fine art of stabilizing and balancing forces within the kingdom. On the Continent the nobility retained many of its ancient privileges of tax exemption. This fact engendered acute resentment in the middle class and at least through the seventeenth century enabled astute monarchs to further their own absolutist cause by letting bourgeois and noble interests check each other.

ROYAL FORCES BECOME NATIONAL ARMIES

Both the masses of men and the new technology required for later medieval warfare worked against feudal conceptions of the military and in the direction of national armies under royal control. Nobles could still gather formidable marauding bands, particularly during periods of ineffective royal government, but they could not supply the tens of thousands of troops which eventually became necessary to turn the tide in a major war. Except in Aragon, it was rare for the nobility anywhere in Europe to own towns or chunks of them as alodial property. It was equally rare for most of the ranks of the nobility to maintain effective feudal control over large towns. Kings and, on the Continent, the great territorial lords with quasi-royal domains could call upon townsmen for military service as they could for taxes.

The development of the crossbow from the tenth through the twelfth centuries into the most lethal weapon of battle was extremely important in reducing the previous significance of the whole knightly class and its feudal lords in warfare. The new weapon had greater accuracy than earlier bows; it could be drawn and held cocked without difficulty, and, above all, it could pierce a knight's armor.[21] Armed with it, infantrymen could finally begin to hold their own against cavalry opponents, and their value in royal forces naturally increased. Philip Augustus with his accustomed foresight had encouraged French townsmen to practice with the crossbow; part of the result was to make them and their descendants available for service in an effective national militia. In the later thirteenth century, both Philip III of France and Edward I of England made payment of soldiers a general practice in order to carry through plans for prolonged campaigns. Edward linked soldiers' pay specifically to fixed, obligatory terms of service in an attempt to expand his infantry contingents and to help overcome the problem presented by the short spans of time for which men rendered military service under the feudal system. Philip IV took the same concrete steps for the same reasons in France.[22]

Such policies were then pursued by kings of both France and England; however, the change in what it took to win major battles seems to have been understood more slowly in France than in England. The Battle of Courtrai in 1302, when infantry composed of Flemish middle-class citizens defeated the French cavalry, should have marked a major turning point in French military history, but it did not. An outmoded conception of the importance of mounted shock combat cost the French three disastrous defeats in the Hundred Years' War.[23] The Battle of Crecy in 1346 took a tremendous toll in French cavalry against lesser English forces under Edward III and the Black Prince. On that occasion the English may have made the first use of the mobile cannon in European warfare — the point is disputed — but it was the improved longbow[24] in the hands of their infantrymen which proved to be the decisive weapon:

> For the bowmen let fly among them at large, and did not lose a single shaft, for every arrow told on horse or man, piercing head, or arm, or leg among the riders and sending the horses mad. For some stood stock still, and others rushed sideways, and most of all began backing in spite of their masters, and some were rearing and tossing their heads at the arrows, and others when they felt the bit threw themselves down. So the knights in the first French battle [wave] fell, slain or sorely stricken, almost without seeing the men who slew them.[25]

In 1356, the heavily armored cavalry of the French nobility took another historic defeat largely from English longbowmen at the Battle of Poitiers, when the French King John II — who had become aware of the greater flexibility of nonmounted fighters in close combat — attempted to use his feudal cavalry by having the knights dismount once they approached the fray. His knights, however, were too weighted down and too fatigued after lumbering up on foot to their opponents some half a mile away for the king's plan to stand any real chance of success. Dismounting at some distance was a necessary part of the tactic, for getting off the horses and into a new formation was a very cumbersome operation in itself. The knights would have been greatly endangered if they had attempted it too close to the actual fighting.[26] Nearly sixty years later, at the Battle of Agincourt, the mounted French knights allowed themselves to be goaded into a furious, undisciplined charge and into a hail of English arrows. King Henry V had positioned his archers carefully on the wings. They not only killed many French knights while they were still mounted but also closed in on them successfully with axes and swords after the knights had been forced to dismount by the slipping and sliding of their horses on the muddy field and by the barrier of pointed stakes placed in their path by the English infantry.[27] Charles V, who ruled France from 1356 to 1380, was consciously antifeudal and antichivalric in his outlook. His emphasis on infantry, together with his suppression of independent feudal armies, helped to regain much of the territory lost to the English and to earn for himself the name of "Charles the Wise." His son, Charles VI, however, again let the nobility have their way in warfare, and the predictable disasters followed.[28] Most of the immediate predecessors of the New Monarchy in France had thus proven to be slow learners.

The English class structure, in which the boundaries between the lower nobility and the middle class were less rigid than on the Continent, made de-emphasis of noble cavalry and upgrading of non-noble infantry considerably easier than in France. The direct loyalty to the crown which English kings had been cultivating for centuries in their free subjects was another factor making it easy for them to draw on the willing service of all classes in wartime. It was not until later, when the Kingdom of France seemed close to dismemberment, that French patriotic sentiment could be effectively mustered against the invaders. Late as this was, it seemed to Joan of Arc a matter of course that devotion to the French cause would have to be evoked around the French king. Certainly without consciously thinking in those terms, she felt instinctively that a successful French king would have to enjoy the direct loyalty of his subjects if he were to be a match for his English opponent.

Before the fifteenth century was over, French kings had learned to make full use of the large population resources at their disposal and the copious royal revenues in order to provide themselves with standing armies of their own subjects and foreign mercenaries. Louis XI, for example, enlisted twenty thousand French foot soldiers and hired large numbers of Swiss mercenaries at the same time.[29]

The old provisions for feudal military service were practically gone in France by the end of the century, except for rare cases of *harri bannus* or *arrière-ban,* the right of the king to call on all free men, nobles and commoners alike, for the emergency defense of the realm. Even during the preceding century, however, the few French kings who issued the *arrière-ban* were generally willing to settle for cash payments in lieu of service from nobles, so that they could hire still more foot soldiers than before. Philip IV, for example, had received a huge sum in 1304 through the *arrière-ban,* and his successors preferred to view it as simply another type of military subsidy, like scutage, from then on.[30]

There were many reasons for kings to prefer payment from aristocrats to having their cavalry service. The effectiveness of medieval cavalry had declined not only relative to that of infantry, but in absolute terms as well. To help protect themselves against arrows shot from the improved crossbows and new longbows, medieval knights had replaced the old suits of chain mail with much heavier suits of plated armor, which made galloping and maneuvering more difficult. Since so heavily armored a knight was considerably less able than his predecessor to fight on foot if his horse should be shot from under him, or even to dismount deliberately and fight on foot according to a plan, as the Battle of Poitiers had shown, he became more than ever intent on protecting his horse. Suits of the new heavy armor were consequently put on horses, too, which made the horse and rider combination carry something like one hundred forty pounds, dead weight, of iron. This restricted cavalry mobility still more. Kings were powerless to do what might seem obvious: order the knights to wear lighter armor. Enough of the feudal concept of military service survived where cavalry was concerned to leave the choice of armor and most equipment up to the vassal.[31] Feudal contracts occasionally called for minimal equipment standards to be met; limiting the maximum was simply unheard of. The nobles perceived their individual safety as best preserved by heavy armored plating and let it go at that.

From the mid-fourteenth to the mid-fifteenth centuries, the development of artillery also worked against older concepts of feudal warfare. At the Battle of Castillon, the French showed that cannons could strengthen an entrenched line to make it withstand a cavalry onslaught. Then, too, artillery greatly reduced advantages to the defender that had been offered by walls and castles during the high point of the feudal era. From 1450 to 1455, the French "blasted the English out of their castles in Normandy and Guienne," to bring the Hundred Years' War to a conclusion favorable to themselves.[32] When the Turks breached the walls of Constantinople, the world's most strongly fortified city, in 1453, they showed easily enough that strong artillery could put the advantage with the attackers in siege warfare.[33]

By one means or another, late medieval kings had to come up with masses of troops and the most recently developed equipment, particularly when cannons rapidly made catapults obsolete, in order to carry on successful warfare with foreign enemies. The feudal nobility could not be counted on to supply either. In fact, the traditional independence of feudal lords once they were at the head of armies they had raised often made their behavior fit in badly with waging war on behalf of the kingdom. Even if nothing else had done so, the "maturing realization that war and the profession of arms must be set within the framework of national life and interests" would alone have dealt chivalry a fatal blow.[34] The same could certainly be said of at least the military aspect of feudalism. Compromises with the system seemed to work only in the short run: with his indenture system Edward I had originally entrusted much of the recruitment for the new paid, royal forces to the nobles who could command them. By the time of Henry VI, however, the practice of letting commanders recruit large troop contingents had deteriorated into "livery and maintenance." This was a nonsystem from the royal standpoint under which commanders paid and outfitted soldiers at their own expense with few limitations upon them effectively enforced by the crown. "Livery and maintenance" and its continental equivalents were, in turn, one of the bases for "bastard feudalism" while it lasted.[35]

Where the nobility was able to keep its military independence — as in Castile, where as members of the top noble class each *rico hombre* jealously clung to the right to display the banner and cauldron which symbolized his right to raise and maintain an army at his own expense[36] — the royal dominance of military forces was naturally impeded. But wherever kings effectively used their free subjects by the tens of thousands and became free of heavy reliance on feudal cavalry, national armies could be seen developing under their authority.

ROYAL TAXES OUTWEIGH FEUDAL DUES

While medieval kings greatly welcomed scutage and other feudal dues in lieu of service, such revenues could not be counted on regularly, since they could be collected only for war or other special needs. Consequently they could not furnish the basis for modern taxation. Instead, kings were able to transform certain "aids" into modern taxes, while the "aids" which remained in their original feudal form were to lose their significance. The word itself lingered on through many changes in meaning. By 1500 in France, "aid" signified not only a simple tax but an indirect one at that.[37]

At the same time, there were certain medieval assessments — particularly those of manorial rather than feudal origin in the strict sense of the word — which resembled modern taxes at least in their compulsory nature from the beginning. The *taille,* or tallage, began as a levy which a lord could fix on his subordinates whenever he needed it. Although it was necessarily paid in kind by peasants to their lord, kings from at least the early twelfth century intended most of it to be monetary when it was paid to them. Unlike scutage, it could not be classified among the feudal dues or monetary commutations of dues. Although some of the English kings called it an "aid," it did not really belong under that heading either, since aids were to be given only with the consent of those who were asked for them.[38] Further, the tallage, while it was supposed to be levied to meet a need, was not limited as to the kind of need it could be required for. When levied by kings it did not have to be linked to any special occasion or to consent, since it came simply from royal prerogative as an extension of manorial rights in the royal demesne. In England Henry II had his itinerant justices set tallage, and his successors continued this practice. In their capacity as royal assessors, they generally set lump sums for towns and manors which represented a compromise between what the king needed and what the traffic would bear: if the governing body of a town could not deliver the assessment, its citizens would be taxed per capita.[39] The particularly unpopular nature of the tallage as a tax levied without consent led English kings to drop it in the fourteenth century, but in France the *taille* increased in importance as a source of royal income. In fact, as a tax on land which ended by being generally passed on to the peasants, the *taille* remained significant in French royal financing until the Revolution.

The carucage or plowland tax of Norman England resembled a modern real estate tax, the distinction being that at the outset it was levied on land granted as a fief. It derived from the Anglo-Saxon *Danegeld,* money for the Danes which Ethelred the Redeless began to collect around 980 to buy off the invader. This had been the first direct monetary tax which a king in England had levied for the use of secular government.[40] With the passage of feudalism, the tax was increasingly applied to landlords' and farmers' own property, as the term "fief" or "fee" was divorced from the fact of English land granting. It was relatively easy for English kings to remove the carucage from a feudal context since it was already a tax of national scope, levied without regard to the landlord's or owner's status.

The tax on what the Middle Ages called "moveables," i.e., most property other than real estate, was also modern-looking in its resemblance to a personal property or excise tax. It was sometimes combined with a tax on "revenues" in the sense of incomes from landholding in any form. In the twelfth and thirteenth centuries it could yield on occasion more money to the royal treasury than the scutage or any other form of feudal dues commutation.[41] It was, however, not easy for kings to apply. Except for financing a crusade[42] and in instances of *harri bannus,* it could be levied only within the context of feudal "aid." The ransom of King Richard I, noted above, was an obvious example of its use to supply such "aid." When the Magna Carta recognized feudal aids to the king as being payable on three occasions — when the king needed to be ransomed, when his eldest son was knighted, and when his oldest daughter was married the first time[43] — it was probably the barons' underlying assumption that a tax on moveables would bear the heaviest weight.

The trick for medieval kings was to keep the "aid" coming in such a way that it could be spent for regular governmental expenses, not merely the emergencies which its feudal origins specified. Innovating taxes was a most unpopular undertaking in the Middle Ages. It is no surprise that the change of special aids into regular taxes took place without any royal emphasis on what was happening. In retrospect, two breakthroughs, one in thirteenth-century England, the other in fourteenth-century France, appear particularly significant.

The first came quietly in 1207, when King John of England asked his barons for a "gracious aid" of one-thirteenth of the value of their moveables and revenues. John justified his request by pointing to the need to renew the war against the French, but as an event of uncertain future date. The realm itself was not in any immediate danger. "Gracious aid" was originally supposed to be assistance voluntarily offered by the givers, although, of course, the actual degree of free will involved varied from case to case.[44] The barons undoubtedly agreed to give King John their aid in this instance, but there is no easy answer as to why they did so. While the king was still powerful and popular in that early year of his quarrel with the Church, this does not explain why the opposition expressed itself so badly and failed to come up with an adequate ground for refusal. One fact to be considered is that the English barons, like their counterparts on the Continent, were in the habit of asking for "gracious aid" from their tenants, who were in no position to protest, when they needed money and could find no regular excuse within the feudal or manorial systems for demanding it. It may well be that the barons felt difficulty in taking the position that what was all right for them to collect from their tenants was not all right for the king to collect from them. At any rate, King John's agents were soon collecting this "gracious aid," while what opposition there was sputtered on ineffectively. The barons had given their approval. Later, when the king's right to exact taxes was limited by the requirement that he must always obtain consent from them, nothing changed the fact that they had set an important precedent in divorcing "aid" from feudal custom by agreeing to its collection without a tradition-sanctioned special occasion.[45]

The second major breakthrough occurred in France during the early part of the Hundred Years' War in two war-related events: the establishment of the royal salt tax in 1341 and the acceptance of regular levies in the place of special war "aids," following French military disasters in 1356. Thirteenth-century French kings had already advanced sales taxes further as sources of revenue than English kings had done. In fact, the *gabelle,* eventually the best known of medieval commodity taxes, began as a sales tax on a variety of products.[46]

In 1341, Philip VI established the *gabelle* as a tax on salt, simultaneously asserting royal monopoly rights to sell the commodity. Since salt deposits existed on the royal demesne, Philip was exercising a manorial right, according to which a lord could prohibit the importation or use of competitors' products of a commodity produced on his land.[47] In forcing merchants who obtained salt outside the demesne to sell it to his royal warehouses, he was, to be sure, stretching this manorial right to cover the whole kingdom most imaginatively. The reception of this measure was consequently a stormy one, but the monopoly right and the high indirect tax which it enabled remained in force, after a brief interruption, to furnish, like the *taille,* a substantial source of royal revenue until the French Revolution.

After the victory of Edward, the Black Prince, over the French at the Battle of Poitiers in 1356 and the capture of John II, the French had to raise money for the king's ransom. This was, of course, demanded by the feudal tradition itself, but the point is that at this particular time the humiliation of France worked against those forces which would have opposed increased and previously unsanctioned taxes. "Assemblies became discredited, the kingdom rallied to the monarchy as the only hope for restoring order, and the king's ransom necessitated taxes which were not subject to negotiation. . . . Although it was not apparent at the time, the age of the war subsidy was over, and the history of French taxation entered a new period on 19 September 1356."[48] The inability of John's vassals to raise the ransom made the situation more pressing. John remained a well-treated prisoner for four years in Bordeaux and London, until the English agreed to let him go back to France and encourage the ransom-raising himself. From 1360 to 1363, John worked hard on that hapless fund drive, but he was forced to give it up. True to his word, he returned to captivity in England, where he died a few months later. In the whole incident, while the particular need to ransom the king was answered in a traditional way with an unsuccessful attempt to supply a feudal aid, the general need for revenue to avoid the military defeats and national humiliation which the fate of King John symbolized meant less argument about the crown's right to tax subjects on a regular basis.

While the most significant shift between the twelfth and fourteenth centuries in royal taxation was from dues or commutations of service based on land granted in fiefs, to taxes on land and other property, with supplements from indirect taxes on commodities, the shift in what "consent" connoted was of almost equal importance. Medieval lawgiving, including the issuing of taxation edicts, never escaped the traditional stricture of consent. This had both Germanic origins and a Roman law formulation: What affects everyone should be approved by everyone (*Quod omnes tangit, ab omnibus approbetur*[49]). Kings as powerful as Charlemagne and William the Conqueror had once gotten the desired consent without much ado, but less secure and forceful rulers had always had to bargain for it. In taxation matters, the need for consent was complicated by the fact that approval of a feudal contract with all of the dues and aids it included was an agreement by individuals. Thus, taxes arising out of the feudal contract did not in and of themselves carry with them the idea of group consent, that is, the idea that the lords of the realm as a whole, or middle-class citizens as a whole had consented for a present occasion or the future.

This led medieval kings to obtain consent through representation. The empowering of representative groups to vote taxes on behalf of the estates and regions which sent them is usually seen as limiting the royal power. It is certainly true that its end result was to put the power of the purse, the most significant restraint on central government, whether royal or other, into the hands of parliaments and assemblies. In the Middle Ages, however, the fact that representatives could bind the group they spoke for greatly aided kings in their attempts to gain consent.[50] Individual consent of the feudal type could be dispensed with and became an anachronism. In England representation was virtually forced on the last holdouts in the royal demesne near the end of the thirteenth century when Edward I directed them to choose men and give them power enough to make binding commitments for them.[51] The limited nature of monarchy in medieval Aragon, Castile, and Portugal had already led to kings' obtaining consent through representative bodies at an early date, not only for taxes but often for questions of war and peace as well. During the fourteenth century, the principle that what affects everyone should be approved by everyone appeared in the constitutional writings of royalty and clergy alike on the Iberian peninsula without overt contradiction.[52]

Revenue derived from the churches made up a fair portion of royal income. Generally, ecclesiastical leaders recognized the wisdom of giving something to the king for the needs of the state, but preferred to couch this as a free gift. It was a fairly sure thing that if no gifts were forthcoming, royal taxes would indeed be assessed on Church property or revenue by kings who were unconcerned about euphemisms. William II made demands of a type indistinguishable from *tallage* on the churches to help finance his Norman campaigns.[53] In France even the pious Louis VII did not hesitate to take gold and silver vessels, candelabra or censers from French abbeys to meet a tax assessment (*tributum imperatum*).[54] The Church never accepted the royal right to tax it as a matter of principle, and there are many instances in the Middle Ages when the clergy resisted payment of royal taxes. One source of the conflict between King John of England and the clergy of the realm was over the carucage he demanded from them.

All the same, the great and rather conspicuous wealth of monasteries and abbeys was such that permanent resistance to all forms of royal taxation would have been bad policy on the part of the higher clergy. They probably calculated the "free gift" to the king consciously or unconsciously on the basis of a compromise between what the king's analogous assessments on secular holdings were and the minimal sum which it seemed desirable to pay him. In certain instances, the papacy would extend to kings the right to tax the clergy for a limited period of time and for a specific purpose. In the fourteenth century, for example, Pope John XXII granted Charles IV of France a tax on churches amounting to 10 percent of their revenues for a two-year period.[55] The ostensible purpose was a crusade to the Holy Lands, but as a matter of fact the era of the crusades was over and the money ended up in defraying the costs of warfare against the English.

Fines continued to be a substantial royal source of revenue into the period of the New Monarchies. Although the term sometimes had its modern signification, as with King John's fines taken from those who did not cooperate with him during the period of the Interdict, this was not always the case. In some contexts, a "fine" could signify coming to terms with a lump sum payment in order to meet some other exaction which would otherwise be drawn out over a period of years or to avoid the effects of a decision by the king or his officials. For example, non-noble tenants in England sometimes made cash settlements to avoid classification as knights with the heavier military service or monetary equivalents which this would entail. When they did so, they were said to be "fining."[56] Later, a fine could signify money paid as an equivalent of military service, and consequently it overlapped the concept of scutage.

Moneylenders were obvious sources of revenue for medieval kings because they were generally thought to be rich, while their occupation was looked on as parasitic and evil. They were subject to irregular assessments and often forced to make loans to royal governments, which were not necessarily repaid in full. The Jews fared particularly badly in the assessments placed upon them. They were subjected to exorbitant tallages in England through the thirteenth century, although unlike their Christian counterparts they were not in a position to negotiate them. They were under the special protection of the king, which meant that they had no other protectors when a king chose to be unreasonable with them. Roger of Wendover reports that King John seized Jews of both sexes without much official jurisdiction in order to extort money from them and that in one case he put a high individual tallage on a Jew of Bristol, with instructions that he was to have a molar pulled every day until he paid it, which he did after a week and the loss of seven teeth.[57] Assessments on Jews were often couched in criminal terms, which made them look more like fines in the modern sense than taxes. For example, Philip V of France subjected the Jews in 1321 to an exorbitant fine for having engaged lepers and their children to poison wells, wines, and crops.[58] It is doubtful whether the relatively defenseless Jews would have escaped with any amount of monetary assessment if the king had really been convinced that they were guilty of mass murder. After all, he could have had them killed for such a crime and taken all their property. His measure has instead the look about it of a need for money coming first, the availability of it from the Jews coming second, and a need to justify taking it from them coming third.[59] The accompanying propaganda probably took its toll later. It appears that in the Black Death of 1347–1350 masses of people really did think that the Jews had poisoned the wells—something that the earlier charge against them would have made more credible—and went on to kill them accordingly. Still, medieval Jews on the whole supported kingship. In worrying about oppression, it must have seemed to the Jews who had to contend with Philip that with the king for their protector they didn't need any enemies; however, the rural nobles were far rougher on the Jews and less predictable in the forced loan department than kings generally were; besides, there were many more of them. Royal power definitely looked better than aristocratic power to Jews until there were other choices.

THE MIDDLE CLASS BECOMES THE KING'S MOST VALUABLE ALLY

The drive of European kings to secure middle-class support, which had been at least sporadically in evidence since the rise of the towns to economic prominence in the eleventh century, became a matter of compelling urgency in the fourteenth and fifteenth centuries as the need for royal revenues increased. The feudal lords provided the monarchies with no more of the old aids and dues than before. Townspeople continued their earlier support of their kings in most cases; however, when they began to perceive the importance of their consent to royal legislation, they showed a corresponding will to use their consent to influence royal policy.

While kings continued to use middle-class money to man and equip their increasingly large armies, townspeople did not particularly want to give royal military policy their blanket endorsement. In France, in 1318–1319, Philip V attempted to use central representative assemblies to agree to taxes in advance of military campaigns. He found representatives from the towns willing to promise financial support in case of war, while the nobility was reluctant to make any such commitment ahead of time. In the following two decades, however, Charles IV and Philip VI were forced to restrain their tax demands in view of the aversion of townspeople to war in distant places. Wholehearted in supporting the king's efforts to maintain internal peace, they wanted fighting with foreign enemies kept to the unavoidable minimum. In 1338, Philip VI accepted a definition by representatives of southern French towns of the type of war which alone justified royal tax levies: a war to repel foreign invasions.[60] Although humiliations inflicted on them by the English were to modify their stand eventually, French townspeople at that time did not wish to encourage the king to wage war for any such abstraction as the expansion of the realm.

Something of the same attitude prevailed in the towns when it was a question of royal attempts to further commerce. It was in the common interest of the king and the middle class to remove the barriers, physical and feudal, which obstructed internal trade. In England, we find Edward I ordering the removal of those fish-weirs, dams, and mills which might have fit in with the manorial economy but which hindered water traffic. Nearly a century later, merchants and other English townspeople were complaining to Edward III about the lack of enforcement of the statutes which had been intended to get rid of manorial obstacles to water traffic and to counter the attempts of barons to require tolls from all barges passing their estates.[61] Still, for all their desire to be helped by royal restraints on feudal privileges, English townspeople were still reluctant to support royal projects at any distance which would cost them money. Down to the seventeenth century, in fact, Englishmen living inland resisted taxes for support of the king's navy, taxes intended, among other things, to help protect English commerce from the depredations of pirates through increasing available naval forces, on the grounds that it was the time-honored business of the coastal towns and counties to provide the king with ships when he needed them.[62]

In France, the same sort of common opposition to the internal tariffs and commercial barriers which stemmed from manorial usage remained a constant factor in politics until the eve of the French Revolution, but, as in England, townspeople held back with their support of projects which would benefit overall national commerce. Philip V, for example, set forth an economic program in 1321: suppression of the unpopular currency issued by the nobility, revaluation of the royal coinage, and the standardization of weights and measures. This was precisely the sort of thing that French townspeople had been asking for. After hesitations and an apology, their representatives withheld their commitment of even enough financial support to carry out the king's measures. In the same way, Philip VI's project of restoring the harbor at Aigues Mortes was resisted by French communities distant from it.[63]

There is a danger in using the term "townspeople" as if the interests of all those living inside town or city walls were homogeneous. Although they were united by a certain common antagonism to the feudal nobility, poor town laborers and rich town merchants certainly felt quite differently about many political and economic questions. The history of later medieval wage disputes, strikes, and price regulations shows this clearly enough. When internal, economic conflicts first developed in the towns, French kings showed a tendency to side with the poorer or laboring elements, who favored assessments on property as the least evil form of raising the king's revenue, as opposed to the wealthy bourgeoisie, who preferred sales and other indirect taxes. The reasons for such a policy are not clear. It is possible that royal agents were thinking then simply in terms of high taxes and fines to be gained from merchants and town landlords. At any rate, this state of affairs did not last long. By the early fourteenth century, royal officials would often strike a bargain with the merchant-class leaders who dominated town governments to let the town settle for a lump sum tax which would then be raised by whatever local taxes the municipal leaders chose to levy. When disputes over the apportionment of local taxes arose in the second half of the fourteenth century, the king's judges and other officials tended to side with the municipal representatives of the propertied classes.[64]

An unsavory aspect of the royal–middle-class alliance was the outright persecution of commercial groups who had little or no local support. The

Jews were the most obvious case in point, although not the only one. While medieval kings had been extracting forced loans from them all along and had extorted large payments under the name of taxes, kings in the earlier Middle Ages had at least considered them useful and necessary. In those earlier days, when nearly all secular Christian commoners lived from farming, and the few Christians with money to spare did not want to risk the sin of usury by lending it, it was useful to have some Jews around to borrow from. Being in debt or craving more money for enhancing the royal position was an almost normal state of affairs for medieval kings. Consequently, they would issue Jews special letters of royal protection, sometimes as individuals, sometimes as groups within municipalities.[65] After the eleventh century, however, European town life and an increasingly cash economy put more funds into Christian hands. First in Italy and then in cities to the north, Christians overcame their reluctance to lend money themselves.[66] By the thirteenth century, the *Summa Theologica* finally pointed out the obvious: interest did not have to be exorbitant. Money lent for reasonable interest was simply letting somebody use your property for hire, like common rent — not usury.[67] Saint Thomas's lenient view of loans and interest articulated an increasingly popular sentiment, but instead of removing the stigma from Jewish moneylending, the change in attitude led to the result that Christian Europeans saw moneylending as too good an occupation to waste on the infidel Jews. In England, Edward I expelled them altogether, and it remained illegal for Jews to live there for some three and a half centuries afterward.[68]

The crusading order of the Knights Templar shared with the Jews the distinction of providing medieval Europeans with banking institutions in the High Middle Ages. In the thirteenth century, their London temple was the king's bank and the forerunner of the Bank of England. Henry III borrowed enough money from the Templars in 1235 to purchase the island of Oleron. French kings availed themselves of Templar loans for such large sums as royal dowries required. Saint Louis even borrowed some of his own ransom money from them. In spite of this demonstrated utility, a few years after King Edward's expulsion of the English Jews, Philip IV wiped out the Knights Templar in France, taking their revenues and thus both enriching himself and pleasing his middle-class allies who wanted the banking business for themselves. The Avignon Pope, Clement V, obedient in every way to the French King, then proceeded to dissolve the Templar order entirely.[69]

It is true that the Jews often demanded excessive interest rates of around 20 percent, and it is true that some of the charges of intrigue and corruption made against the Templars may well have had some substance to them, but the timing of such sweeping royal actions against both groups suggests that with the increasing acceptability of banking as a legitimate, lay Christian occupation, the Jews and the Templars were suddenly found to have outlived their usefulness.

A similar sequence of developments occurred in Spain somewhat later. There, until near the end of the following century, Ferdinand and Isabella tolerated the Jews in the tradition of previous rulers of Aragon and Castile, but only until the most pressing royal problems had been solved. When the Spanish Kingdom was united, the Moors militarily defeated, and an adequate royal income for all contingencies assured from the Christian merchants and sheep ranchers who shared in the new era of prosperity which enhanced Spain's "Golden Century," Ferdinand and Isabella required the Jews either to convert to Christianity or to depart from Spain and not to return upon pain of death and confiscation of property.[70] Ten years later, the king and queen forced their Mohammedan subjects who had stayed after the defeat of the Moors to accept baptism.[71] Some of the most successful artisans and sheep raisers were Mohammedans. While many of them at least outwardly accepted the royal order that they convert to Christianity, they could no longer be counted on to support Spanish kingship. The loss of productive elements in the Jews and Moslems who left Spain or were put to death by the Inquisition cost the Spanish monarchy a considerable amount of tax revenue, as well as human resources, nor was the loyalty of the forced converts who stayed beyond question. On the other hand, the persecuting measures were bound to solidify Spanish royal and Christian commercial interests and consequently cultivate support from the Spanish merchant class for the crown.

After the French defeat at Poitiers, the Estates-General in France pushed the middle-class desire for influence on royal policy to an extreme degree. With John II in captivity, its members tried to have the old councillors of the king punished for their mistakes and replaced by their own representatives. The regent, the future Charles V, agreed to their demands after a bourgeois-induced revolution in the city of Paris. The leader of the middle-class faction, however, involved himself in intrigue beyond his means and supported a rival claimant to the throne. He and his followers also gave their support to a peasant revolt which ended in massacres and arson in the countryside. These events necessarily discredited French middle-class leadership. When order was restored, the monarchy was stronger than before and the bourgeoisie as a group politically weaker, although as dependent as ever on the monarchy for protection from the nobility. When Charles V took over in this own right as king, he did not hold a grudge against the bourgeoisie, whose impetuous leadership had caused the monarchy so much recent trouble. Instead, he retained able middle-class councillors who gave him sound economic and military advice. In the Hundred Years' War, which was entering its fifth decade at the time of his death in 1380, he kept the French forces united and succeeded in driving the English back to some of the coastal towns.

His successor, Charles VI, was too unstable and generally incompetent to make use of middle-class support. Consequently, the merchant class tended to support a faction led by Burgundians, who favored peace with the English and a resumption of trade. The English reciprocated by supporting the Burgundians against the French king. Charles VII was slow in gaining middle-class support, but it came to him after the success of Joan of Arc in rallying French national feeling on the dubious king's behalf. In 1435, he made peace with the Burgundians, and financial aid from merchant-class leaders was soon at his disposal. It was, in fact, income from the merchant class which enabled him to undertake the major military reform which is credited with driving the English out of all of France except Calais. Although the weight of the *taille* fell on his non-noble subjects, they had every reason to support him with their money. The defense of the realm was a good readily perceptible to most Frenchmen by the second third of the fifteenth century. The standing army that the king acquired with the taxes of his subjects held the promise of assuring internal peace as well as defending the kingdom from the English. Military power under the king posed no threat to the vital interests of the French Third Estate; military power in the hands of the unpredictable nobility most certainly did. The royal service gave regular employment to some twelve thousand cavalry in the *gens d'ordonnance,* which the merchant class could easily see as preferable to twelve thousand potential robber knights, threatening merchants and farmers, either singly or in bands. Charles seems to have been bent on making the most of bourgeois enthusiasm for the royal cause: he backed the organization of townsmen into archer infantry units and, with greater success, offered royal administrative posts to men from the middle class. Both the king and the townsmen had a common interest in keeping high- and medium-level offices out of the control of the nobility. Charles's protomercantile measures of subsidizing nascent industry and older commercial enterprises in his realm made his alliance with the middle class at the expense of the nobility a firm and open one.

Louis XI was perhaps the best suited of the later medieval kings of France for cultivating middle-class support because his tastes and lifestyle resembled those of the middle class in several distinctive ways. He was indifferent to pomp and display, frugal with governmental and consequently with taxpayers' money, and wary of foreign military involvements. Faced with an aggressive neighbor in Burgundian Duke Charles the Bold, who was intent on territorial expansion, he both employed Swiss mercenaries and supported the Swiss confederation against him. The combination of Swiss arms and French royal subsidies defeated Duke Charles. He was killed in battle, and the Duchy of Burgundy passed under the control of the French crown.

In England, also after some vacillation, the middle class came to the support of Edward II to the extent of forcing the barons to relinquish their control over royal appointments and the war-making power. The cause of the middle class was helped by the political alienation of the knights from the great lords. The knights joined with representatives of middle class English citizens in presenting petitions to the king for changes in the laws. Under Edward III, these two groups conferred together regularly. During the Hundred Years' War they gradually gained substantial influence on royal policy by exercising their right to grant or withhold royal requests for funding. In the short run, this limited the power of the monarchy under Edward III, who shared power with the Commons rather indifferently. In the longer run, extending into the later fifteenth and the whole of the sixteenth century, however, it was the power of the feudal lords which was most limited by the political alliance of knights and representatives of the towns. English defeats near the end of the Hundred Years' War and the chaos of the War of the Roses let power fall into the hands of the great lords for a final time, but the new coalition of knights and middle-class leaders needed only a capable monarch to work with. This need was amply supplied by the Tudor dynasty after 1485.

When the future Henry VII defeated his opponents at the Battle of Bosworth Field in 1485 and began the great work of reconciling those interests which had been divided by the War of the Roses, he dealt with a Commons which was more united and organized politically than the Lords. As has recently been pointed out, it was still too early to speak of either a House of Commons or a House of Lords in the sense of permanently established institutions. The Commons, however, had a sense of being represented by spokesmen who were authorized to give assent or withhold it; whereas certain Lords assembled simply upon individual invitation of the king.[72] The barons had been forced to take more partisan stands in the conflict between the houses of Lancaster and York than middle class persons had been. The independence and irresponsibility of the nobility also had led to an antiaristocratic reaction which benefited the king and Commons. Henry VII appointed his share of middle class advisors and other officials. His good working relationship with representatives of the Commons can be seen in the relative ease with which he obtained their consent to taxes, as he went about suppressing "livery and maintenance" by the great lords. The townspeople of London supplied Henry not only with needed tax revenue but also with loans when he needed them.[73]

Henry VII also relied heavily on the justices of the peace, who, in fact, took on much of the importance which the itinerant justices had once had under Henry II. The office of justice of the peace evolved out of that of "keeper of the peace," a sheriff's assistant in the late thirteenth and early fourteenth centuries.[74] Edward III had attempted without much success to rely on justices of the peace to enforce his Statute of Laborers, enacted to keep wages and prices as they had been prior to the depopulation of the Black Plague. During the fifteenth century, the qualification that an appointee must have an income of twenty pounds a year, which was the equivalent of a knight's fee in older usage, meant that they came from "the aristocratic gentry, the rural middle class,"[75] that is, from backgrounds wealthy enough to have more than an average interest in maintaining the king's peace, but still not from the great lords of the realm who might threaten stability and the public order by their own power.

The cooperation of Henry VII and the Commons in raising the office of justice of the peace to a new level of importance can be seen in the passage of one or more enactments dealing with the work of these officials by every Parliament of his reign.[76] Justices of the peace eventually set proceedings in motion against powerful men for unlawfully maintaining private followings under arms and against sheriffs for extortion. As was so often the case in the whole history of medieval kingship, royal appointees were intended to offset the power of local magnates.

While many developments in the royal–middle class alliance ran roughly parallel in France and England, class distinctions in France remained far more rigid than in England and resulted in sharper antagonisms during the later Middle Ages. In the battles of the Hundred Years' War, the English generally showed a remarkable capacity for making their cavalry, archers, and spearmen coordinate their actions with each other. English victories against larger forces in France, attributable to the fact that cavalry and infantry supported each other without hesitation, can be traced in turn to the absence of bitter hostility between the knights as a class and the commoners fighting with them. Here the French experience was quite different until late in the war. French knights had nothing but contempt for either the mercenaries who had been hired or the townsmen who had been recruited by the crown. At the Battle of Crecy, Philip VI became so impatient with the hired Genoese crossbowmen who were fighting on his side but who had not held up well under English longbow fire that he shouted: "Kill me those scoundrels, for they stop our road. . . ."[77] The French knights seem to have taken him at his word and trampled the mercenaries underfoot in a wild effort to get at the enemy to do chivalrous battle. The English archers easily wrought havoc among them as they charged. Nearly sixty years later, Charles VI's field commander, Charles d'Albret, constable of France, actually refused to take along six thousand crossbowmen of the municipal militia in Paris who had volunteered for the action which became the Battle of Agincourt. Even then, the French nobles were still asking what they needed "these shopkeepers" for.[78]

From one standpoint, the New Monarchy was to have an easier time developing toward royal absolutism in France than in England. The depth of class antagonisms made it easier to balance the interests of the French nobility and commoners against each other. Even after the Middle Ages, Louis XIV made use of mutual noble-bourgeois hostility to further the cause of royal absolutism in a way which his English counterparts, Charles II and James II, simply could not do. In the long run, it was not worth it for kingship in France. The fact that French class antagonisms could be overcome only in moments of national crisis — and not completely even then — while a spirit of nationalism normally kept the same differences in the background in England, stood French kings in poor stead in competing with their rivals across the Channel. Whether they could have done anything about it, or whether deep class antagonisms were simply some of the given materials they had to work with, is, of course, another question.

REVIVED ROMAN LAW FAVORS ROYAL ABSOLUTISM

The revival of Roman law was another factor which helped medieval kings assert not only their judicial superiority but also their lawmaking authority over their dominions as feudal kingdoms began to become nation-states. On the face of it, an assertion that Roman law furnished the legal basis for absolutism contradicts much of what our educational system imparts to us concerning the Romans as freedom-loving people who revered their republic and its laws, who hated monarchy, and who accepted emperors and eventually rule by imperial decree only when Roman civilization began its decline. And indeed we know that the antiroyal bias of Roman political theory lingered on surprisingly late in the empire. Such things, however, were not central to the perceptions of those medieval people who thought about the Romans and their law system. Roman law in the Middle Ages was first and foremost the great codes, Theodosian and Justinian, stemming from the later empire, and with them, Ulpian's principle that the will of the prince has the force of law.

Because the Roman law which was known and which mattered in the Middle Ages derived from the period in Roman history when the absolutism of the emperors was not seriously questioned, it helped medieval kings justify their centralization of power in their own realms with ancient, imperial conceptions of governance. Teachers of Roman law in the Middle Ages presented the emperor or prince (*princeps*) as the originator and interpreter of law. Some of them — Vacarius, for example, an early Bolognese jurist brought to England by Archbishop Theobald to teach at

Oxford — went so far as to make the prince the only rightful originator and interpreter of law, leaving no room for the lawmaking work of medieval estates in any form.[79]

Vacarius and his school stressed lawgiving as the natural outcome of the sovereign's will. To the extent that holders of lesser office or representatives might seem to lay down law, they did so only from necessity, that is, because the exact determinations of the sovereign could not be known and applied everywhere and immediately. Some clearly absolutist conclusions follow from these premises. The sovereign is either not bound by law or he is bound by the law no more than his voluntary hesitation to amend or interpret it makes him accept it as binding. A judge's interpretation of law is valid merely in the case of litigants before him and, even then, only insofar as they cannot cite a remedy deriving from the sovereign's known and written laws against that judge's decision. The modification of all legal rules themselves is reserved to the legislator, who, in turn, is the same prince whose will is the operative force in the legislative and judicial systems alike.[80]

Nothing could have been more natural than for ambitious medieval kings to favor this sort of doctrine, substituting, of course, "king" for "emperor" as the *princeps* of Roman law. By 1300, kings of France were called emperors in their own kingdoms largely because they had adopted the role of emperor within the Roman legal system.[81] Lawyers of middle-class background in the king's service often advanced from minor departments of the royal administration to significant careers through their discovery of quasi-imperial rights inhering in the king as sovereign. In their historical research, they were free to use a double standard, subjecting feudal titles and claims to some suspicion and great scrutiny, while validating royal rights on the basis of what was really less solid evidence.[82] "Emperor" as a title retained, of course, the signification of ruling over more than one tribe or nation. As such, being an emperor would have been meaningless in aiding national kings to pursue their first order of political business, gaining supremacy over the top ranks of the nobility who could challenge their right to sovereignty, were it not for the Roman-law connotations of the title.

Although it was generally not a matter of primary importance to most late-medieval kings most of the time, the concept of themselves as emperors in their own kingdoms could be used to defend their national sovereignty against the position of the contemporary emperor in Germany. Whenever they came to view Roman law as favoring the subordination of their kingdoms to his Empire, they were apt to have its teaching overseen in order to prevent this interpretation. Fawtier notes that for this reason caution and reserve toward Roman law periodically characterized French attitudes toward it and led French kings to intervene, at least occasionally, in university curricula. Philip IV, for example, felt it worthwhile to take a direct hand in organizing the teaching of Roman law in Orleans.[83]

In Germany itself, the emperors obviously had less work to do in adapting the ancient Roman concept of rulership to their part of the medieval world. Consequently they favored Roman law more actively than their counterparts in western Europe and with none of their hesitations. Their task was made far more difficult in the later Middle Ages, however, by the fact that the empire they ruled did not resemble particularly strongly either the ancient Roman Empire from which Roman law derived or the national kingdoms where Roman law was successfully being applied by kings in their attempts to centralize power. On the other hand, they were aided by the lack of a national tradition of German law which would have competed with Roman law in the way that the English common law, the French body of customary law, or even the *fueros* of Aragon and Castile presented strong traditional alternatives to it. Local custom in the individual parts of Germany was strong enough to pass for law, but even such major codes as those of the Saxons and Swabians did not draw adherents outside the borders of their duchies. The tribal basis of non-Roman law in Germany was simply too small to attract much of a national following, and — in contrast with what happened in western Europe — the upper classes were willing by the later fifteenth century to see the emperor establish a central court based entirely on Roman law.[84] Territorial lords in Germany who strove for as much judicial autonomy as possible, such as the rulers of Bavaria and Saxony, were successfully imitating the law of the empire in their own legal codes all during the late Middle Ages. Thus, even the emperor's German competitors for authority furthered the Romanization of law. A lasting result of imperial efforts in Germany was nothing other than the establishment of Roman law as the prevailing system from early modern times to the present. The English legal system is sometimes considered to be one of largely Germanic law, but Germanic law never yielded a legal system for modern Germany in anyone's estimation.

There were certain ways in which Roman law limited medieval kingship as well as strengthened it. For one thing, the essence of Roman law was codification in written form. The more seriously written law was taken, the less scope was left to the monarch's will and discretion. In fact, the very emphasis on having the laws in writing, with a consequent permanence of a sort, worked against any broad theoretical extension of the principle that the monarch's will had the force of law. If a king were to make free use of his will in improvising law, he would be undermining the whole basis on which Roman law tended to be promoted among his subjects in preference to traditional or customary law, namely, the attributes of being available in books for people to refer to and of providing security and certainty of results. Those who sought harmony between the two principles in the later Middle Ages generally took the written codification and stability of Roman law to be its primary characteristic and regarded the will of the prince as having the normal function of giving law its proper authority and intervening with innovations in emergency situations only. If a prince let his legal system appear to have the primary characteristic of being ruled by his own will, then he was dangerously close to being an arbitrary ruler. [85] An arbitrary ruler, in turn, was a tyrant in the political notions prevailing in the fifteenth century, just as it had been in those of the twelfth and earlier centuries. No late-medieval king wanted to be thought of under the heading of tyrant if he could help it, for the doctrine that tyrants could, at the least, be deposed lasted throughout the entire Middle Ages. Consequently, even rulers tending toward absolutism in practice welcomed the theoretical harmony of the essentially opposing principles of the king's will as the effective law and the permanence of written law.

Another theoretically limiting aspect of Roman law upon medieval kingship was its claim to be founded on consent. After all, the old Roman emperors, unlike openly hereditary kings, were supposed to have been chosen on the basis of merit. Consequently the legislation which came from them had in theory the prior approval of those who had elected them. We have seen roughly how this worked in some contexts with Marsiglio of Padua: the Roman people consented to what the emperors did because they empowered them to rule over them. [86] In a different way, the principle encountered above, *Quod omnes tangit, ab omnibus approbetur,* clearly implied the necessity of consent at least to major matters of law. And yet, the more adroit kings of later medieval Europe were able to turn this principle to their own advantage by using it to replace individual consent with corporate consent through representatives. Roman law helped them out in this maneuver. While corporate representation was basically foreign to the world of lords and vassals, what amounted to business law under the Roman codes as they were applied in medieval Italy allowed proctors (*procuratores*) to act for organizations in a legally binding way. [87] To the extent that medieval kings were able to overwhelm or dominate representative assemblies, the Roman legal principle of consent helped them to legitimize what they wanted to do. On the other hand, whenever the principle was raised against royal measures that consent was needed, it was more often traceable to custom or tradition than to any Roman-law principle at all.

England presents a rather special case in the way that its kings did and did not use Roman law. It is obvious that the English experience was exceptional: people in the English-speaking countries are generally conscious of living under a system of laws derived from Germanic or Anglo-Saxon law rather than from the Roman law which established itself on the

Continent. Certainly the strength of the native common law and the fact that Roman law always appeared more foreign and suspect in England than elsewhere kept medieval kings from espousing the latter too openly. Nonetheless, the Roman legal tradition did serve the centralizing efforts of English kingship in the Middle Ages, although in more subtle fashion than elsewhere. Henry II had certainly proceeded on the king-as-lawmaker principle. It was obvious from the way he went about having the Constitutions of Clarendon approved that he took the principle of consent about as seriously as a later Roman emperor. The men he summoned to give their consent to his legislation, which contained both old and new articles, were obviously expected to consent to it. At the same time, without being deterred by labels applicable to competing systems, Henry II also stressed the supremacy of written law, whatever its origin, against custom. It was the common law that became acknowledged to be superior to local custom under him, but it was the fact of its *having been written down and being made applicable to the whole kingdom* that determined its superiority.[88] In other words, he was using the English common law in this context, not as a point of contrast with Roman law, but as something which was essentially the same. The English magnates could effectively keep Roman law codes from having precedence over the English common law, when it was a question of the content of many laws. Under their pressure Henry III even forbade the teaching of Roman law in London.[89] Still, the study of Roman law continued at the principal universities, and the precedence accorded to the king's written law — which was as essential to the spirit of Roman law as it was originally foreign to Germanic tradition — has lasted even in those countries with supposed Anglo-Saxon legal systems to this day.[90] When disputes arose concerning the common law, Roman law could be used in England to clarify its terms,[91] and its influence was felt in still more indirect ways as well. Even in the case of the most distinguished medieval English jurist:

> [I]t can hardly be denied that Bracton used Roman terms, Roman maxims, and Roman doctrines to construct upon native foundations a reasonable system of law out of comparatively meager authorities. Roman law supplied him with the intellectual outlook and technical language.[92]

By circuitous routes then, English kings and their supporters were able to infuse the common law with enough Roman legal attitudes and terminology to support their centralizing efforts. The disasters experienced by the first two Stuart kings of England, who seemed to support their programs and prerogatives with Roman law against the common law, proved that their medieval predecessors exercised wise caution in acting as if the basis for their measures were still the native common law.

In relations with the Church, Roman law worked quite well for medieval kings. Frederick Barbarossa, one of the first monarchs to make use of the revived interest in it, had employed Italian jurists to counter the claims of the canon lawyers when he sought to solidify his control over Italian cities of the empire.[93] Other medieval rulers made use of the fact that Roman law normally promoted a secular scale of values. In England, again certainly without any public emphasis on the Roman origins of the king as lawmaker in defense of the interests of the state, Edward I prohibited his subjects with his Statute of Mortmain from making large donations without his consent to the Church for the salvation of their souls. In the same way, in *Circumspecte Agatis* he limited the jurisdiction of Church courts to ecclesiastical matters, leaving all remaining litigation under control of the royal courts.[94]

Roman law, being obviously prefeudal in its origins, took no particular account of an independent nobility. While the patron-client relationship in Roman law had certain characteristics similar to the feudal contract, these did not go beyond interpersonal obligations. The wealthiest patron or the one with the most clients under the Roman system had enjoyed no legal exemptions from the sovereign's control. Consequently, royal officials trained in Roman law had no reason to respect the claims of the feudal nobility to ancient rights and privileges at the expense of royal power. In fact, the whole matter of justifying claims through appeal to tradition or custom was quite foreign to Roman law. Since the two main obstacles to royal centralization of authority were the strength of the feudal nobility and appeals to native custom or tradition, Roman law was of equal help in royal efforts to overcome either or both of these hindrances.

Roman law presupposed the very kind of state which rulers of the early national kingdoms were trying to construct. But while sovereign power in a state was taken for granted during the Roman Empire, this was certainly not the case in the medieval world, where local, feudal, and Church tradition stood in opposition to a uniform, sovereign, and secular exercise of power. Medieval teachers of Roman law, who advocated precisely this uniform, sovereign, and secular power which kings were trying to acquire, did not fail to put it into a general philosophical framework. Previous theories of divine right were helpful here, of course, but many of the advocates of Roman law were also Neo-Platonists. This might seem surprising in view of the Platonic ambivalence toward man-made law of any kind, but it makes perfect sense in the light of the Platonic doctrine of the naturalness of the state.[95] The idea that the state could give an individual his identity was a rather commonplace notion in the ancient world, although it was one stressed by the Platonic schools with particular force. The ancient idea — common to Platonism and Aristotelianism alike — that the state was a unit of organization uniquely fitted by nature to help man fulfill his potentialities and aspirations had lain dormant in the early Middle Ages. Governance was then associated entirely with persons in authority, and the Two-Cities concept relegated the state to a status, at best, of sharing the authority that mattered. The two notions — that the state imparted the most essential part of a person's identity and that the state was the most natural unit of human organization — did not converge until the period of modern nationalism. The foreshadowing of such a convergence and the beginnings of strong feelings of nationalism can also be seen furthering the interests of kingship toward the end of the Middle Ages.

KINGSHIP AND OUTRIGHT NATIONALISM

The fact that two notably international movements, the Renaissance and the Enlightenment, come between the High Middle Ages and the French Revolution has led to a tendency to begin the history of nationalism with the French Revolution or the obviously nationalistic reactions to it.[96] If, however, we use most of the current criteria for nationalism, patriotic attachment to the territory of a nation, to the national language, to the combination of faith and ideals which people feel as characteristic of their nation, and to the feeling of having fought and struggled together as a nation,[97] we find them all in the Middle Ages, particularly the later centuries. Even propaganda intended to instill and cultivate nationalism and censorship with the aim of keeping the concept intact are in evidence and closely linked with the development of kingship.

Although the Roman law which medieval lawyers used for strengthening the power of the state had been designed for an empire transcending nations, it aided kings in heightening national identity into various degrees of nationalism. There is a simple reason for this. The state presupposed by Roman law was a completely sovereign one to which citizens owed final loyalty; since the countries which kings headed were the only large and viable states in Europe, later medieval kingship stood to profit by the state's subsumption of other political loyalties.

We can safely claim to have found nationalism when we see national identity heightened to the point that it becomes more important — even if only temporarily — to substantial numbers of the people of a country than their religious or class identities. We can also be sure of having found nationalism when we see national identity combined with a religious fervor in a cause which large numbers of people in a country are willing to struggle for. These things, in turn, presuppose that "countries" are something like national units. Many of the significant political units in later medieval Europe were still not national units, but some of them certainly were: England, France, Portugal, Denmark, and Poland with no reservations; Bohemia with some; Norway, Sweden, and Spain at the very end.

By and large, the movement toward national monarchies had progressed over the route of assimilating smaller units, counties, duchies, or
simply large estates, into the king's realm through all the means mentioned
thus far in chapters 5 and 7. At the same time, it necessitated the rejection
of any sort of universal or transnational monarchy. It has been pointed
out that the "seam" between universal and national monarchical emphasis
is most evident in the later example of Spain. Emperor Charles V (King
Charles I of Spain) perceived Spain as part of his international empire, the
greatest and most international domain under the control of a European
ruler since the reign of Charlemagne. Upon his abdication, however, his
son, Philip II, pursued policies as king of Spain which seem to reveal
behind them a sense of the primacy of Spain as a national entity.[98] Even in
this instance the change is anything but an absolute one, since Philip was
clearly motivated in many of his decisions on war and peace by his pursuit
of transnational religious unity, the restoration and triumph of the Catholic faith far beyond Spain's borders as well as inside them, and consequently of an international ideal.

Elsewhere the "seam" is harder to find, particularly since the terrain of
universal monarchy was one where theorists were apt to wander far from
the real world around them. Supporters of French kings periodically saw
them as rightful heirs to the universal empire of Charlemagne and the
Romans before him:

> When Providence founded one hundred kingdoms the best was fair France,
> and the first king whom God sent there was crowned by the hands of His
> angels. Since the time of Charlemagne all nations have sprung up from
> France — Bavaria, Germany, Burgundy, Lorraine, Tuscany, Poitou, Gas-
> cony, to the borders of Spain. But the King who wears the gold crown of
> France upon his brow must be a warrior, and be able to lead an army of one
> hundred thousand men, even to the ports of Spain.[99]

A work dedicated to the wife of Louis IV put it this way:

> The kingdom of the Romans is in great part destroyed, but as long as the
> kings of France survive, who ought to rule the Roman Empire, then its
> dignity will not perish entirely, but will live in them.[100]

Philip IV suggested that the empire simply be transferred to the king of
France,[101] and the French royal propagandist, Pierre Dubois, noted that

> . . . it would be expedient for the whole world to be subject to the realm of
> the French, provided always that the King be begotten, born, brought up and
> instructed according to wont, in that realm.[102]

To be sure, French kings in the later Middle Ages generally found it more
to the point to stress their independence from the papacy and the empire.
Still the familiar story of Napoleon I shows that the ideal of a universal

monarchy radiating from France survived even the end of the Middle Ages by several centuries. The modern notion, too, of one nation in the role of international peacekeeper and enforcer of justice, e.g., the British mandate to police the seas,[103] has more than a hint of the universal monarchical ideal in it.

Emotional attachment to the realm as a national entity was in evidence in medieval literature well before the closing centuries. "Fair France" obviously exemplified a territorial conception, and at least from the tenth century loyalty to a *patria* was a recognized virtue, although most pointedly in cases of treason, where malefactors were condemned for not having it. Later medieval kings were able to build on such loyalty in two ways. Quantitatively, they extended the number of their subjects who were to feel it. In the *Song of Roland,* patriotic sentiments for fair France are essentially those of the knightly class. The fighting Archbishop Turpin shares them, but even he sounds like a knight when he expresses them. In the later Middle Ages, on the other hand, kings could sometimes hope to find similar feelings of overriding loyalty to the realm among the middle classes and yeoman farmers.[104] At the same time, European kings sought to make concrete use of the extended patriotic commitment to gain support for controversial royal policies, particularly in peacetime when innovations were most apt to be questioned. By the time of the Hundred Years' War, there was no longer much doubt that loyalty to the king was loyalty to the land.[105] Later medieval kings, however, wanted all their free subjects not only to serve as needed in the royal forces during wartime but also to pay their taxes regularly and more or less of their own free volition even without war.

Roman law helped a bit in making "public duty" to the state and "evident necessity" felt by its leaders justifications for requiring active support by the citizens for "the common profit." A recent study of this development in later medieval France groups the types of necessities which were apt to set off a barrage of propaganda to put citizens on the king's side in fulfillment of their ostensible duties to him. "[C]onflicts involving taxation, coinage manipulation, civil or foreign wars, social reform, or religious controversy, were almost invariably accompanied" by a torrent of royal persuasive words. Edicts regulating commerce, grain prices, and the wages of laborers were sometimes issued in propagandistic phrasing which somehow underscored the king's sovereignty in proclaiming them and the need for subjects to accept them for the national good.[106]

A patriotic attachment to the native language, a sure criterion of nationalism, emerged in several European countries as the Middle Ages wore on. There were basically two reasons for this: the relative standardization of vernacular languages by the fourteenth and fifteenth centuries and the increased consciousness of their worth for vernacular literature and for commonplace writing. The vernacular gradually won out over the Latin tradition in letters. Both factors, particularly the latter, are probably traceable to the increased preponderance of the middle classes in all the varied applications of letters, from record keeping to the composition of epics. The clergy had lost its virtual monopoly of letters which had characterized the early Middle Ages and had greatly furthered Latin as the international European language. By the end of the Council of Constance, which was the first Church council to treat clerical delegates as representing nations in the modern sense, the principle had emerged that nations were recognizable as such by the language spoken by their members.[107]

With wide variations in timing, royal propaganda made early use of the vernacular. In Germany, the international claims of the empire did not keep its twelfth and thirteenth century supporters from voicing its praises in the national language.[108] French kings patronized vernacular writers, who in turn exalted their kings and kingdom with eloquence, fervor, and imagination:

> The chief of all crowns is that of France, and the first king of France was crowned by angels singing: " 'Thou shalt be,' saith God, 'My representative on earth, where thou shalt cause Law and Justice to triumph.' "[109]

Many French royal communications of the fourteenth and fifteenth centuries seem to have been drawn up with the intent of engraving patriotic vernacular phrases such as *la chose publique* and *le profit commun* on popular consciousness.[110]

The Plantagenet kings of England should logically have been hesitant to link English with their military and political causes. It was, after all, through the conquest of their ancestors that French became the language of the king and those nobles who were powerful in their own right, while Anglo-Saxon remained the language of the common people and those natives in higher ranks who accepted their dependence on the Normans. Many, possibly most, Englishmen of any standing were bilingual or even trilingual if they had knowledge of Latin, at least through the time of Henry II.[111] Even so, the Normans had made language a divisive force, separating the conquerors from the conquered. A century later, however, the Plantagenet King Edward I was actually stressing the English language as a unifying force, even though in his day it was still a lumpy and uneven amalgam of Norman French and Anglo-Saxon. Edward had a reputation for being able to speak both pure French and the English of his day (assumedly the Midlands dialect) with equal oratorical skill. In summoning the clergy to his "Model Parliament" of 1295 he played upon a strong English attachment to the language of his realm, whatever it was. "The King of France," Edward noted, "if he should have the power — and may God keep it from him — to back up his detestable plan, conceived in depravity, seeks to wipe the English language off the earth altogether."[112] His queen, Eleanor, who had grown up at the court of her half-brother, Alfonso the Learned of Castile, did her bit for interest in the vernacular by patronizing the translation of Latin works into it with personal grants.[113] Writing under the last of the Plantagenets, Richard II, Geoffrey Chaucer himself could refer in all seriousness to "the king, that is lorde of this language."[114]

It would be stretching a point to insist that medieval kings could see the outcome clearly, but probably the more perceptive among them could sense that usage of the national language was something of a measure of their central authority in the realm at large. By the end of the Middle Ages, French King Henry IV made the connection between the use of the national vernacular and the extent of royal power an explicit one in addressing representatives of recently annexed provinces:

> As you speak the French language by nature, it is reasonable that you should be the subjects of a King of France. I quite agree that the Spanish language should belong to the Spaniard and the German to the German. But the whole region of the French language must be mine.[115]

National identity was further heightened toward nationalism through histories magnifying the deeds of earlier kings and a host of additions to royal legends. The turn which this movement took in later medieval France is particularly interesting in showing a renewed importance attached to Clovis, who had been superseded by Charlemagne in the interim, as the ultimate model of kingship. Lilies had actually been a French royal emblem since the time of Philip II, but by the middle of the fourteenth century legend told how they appeared miraculously on Clovis's shield just before his great victory over the Alamanni at the Battle of Tolbiac. In combining two elements of the much earlier Constantine story (vision of the sacred sign and painting of an emblem on shields before a decisive victory), French tradition seemed once again to be identifying Clovis with the first Christian Emperor in exactly the way Gregory of Tours had begun to do in the later sixth century.

Philip I had made the oriflamme, which was supposed to have been on the banner of Saint Denis, into a royal symbol in the eleventh century. French legend subsequently derived it from a flaming lance in Charlemagne's hand, but by the fifteenth century it was Clovis who had held it. At the same time, Clovis was credited, very much retroactively, with curing the king's evil by his touch.[116] Part of the reason for emphasizing Clovis may have been simply his position as the first great king of the Franks, but it seems significant that in the fourteenth and fifteenth centuries Charlemagne's legends were merely left intact or given slight embellishments, while new work was done to upgrade the image of Clovis. A factor may well be that Clovis established and maintained a kingdom which was easy to identify with the late-medieval Kingdom of France, while Charlemagne founded a Europe-wide empire, something of proportionately less interest from a national standpoint, particularly since the Germans derived the late-medieval empire from his same achievement.

The most effective forms of medieval nationalism were those which harnessed religious energies to the royal cause. It was no accident that the most obviously devout of their ancestors figured very prominently in the genealogical references of later medieval kings. The pious Edward the Confessor was a favorite forefather of his English successors, and the public attachment of French kings to the memory of Saint Louis grew with the passage of time. Charles V declared the memory of Saint Louis to be engraven on his heart as

> . . . the flower, the ornament, the light and the mirror, not only to our royal race, but to all Frenchmen; his memory shall be blessed until the end of time . . . ; his life shall be our eduation.[117]

In stressing the pride which not only the royal line but all *Frenchmen* should have in recalling Saint Louis, Charles V touched on an aspect of medieval kingship which has been part of each chapter of this book: the devout king shares his blessed standing with his people. A line of most-Christian kings means that a people has a distinctive religious past to live up to. They are a people who can expect to enjoy divine favor in a national mission, for "the greater excellence of our kingdom is revealed in that our king is worthier than any other king."[118]

When medieval kings tried to instill a common religious feeling among their subjects of a type which set them off from other nationalities but allowed them to be the custodians of the one true faith all the more, their efforts led naturally enough to demanding more ostensible freedom for the national Church, necessarily at the expense of the Roman hierarchy. This was, of course, the same sort of stress which had sometimes forced bishops to choose between kings and popes in the High Middle Ages, but by the fifteenth century whole nationalities had to take sides. In fact, the strongest stirrings of national feeling at the close of the Middle Ages were so imbued with religious fervor that it is hard to tell whether nationalism or a sense of religious mission was the greater driving force within them.

Although sooner or later national consciousness had to redound to the favor of kings, thus undermining the universal Church and feudal lords alike, the growing feeling of belonging to a country and a whole people did not favor kingship everywhere or immediately. In the earliest fifteenth-century example of national religious fervor, it failed to do so utterly, but largely because the monarch in question, King Wenceslaus IV of Bohemia, could not or would not make sustained use of such a force. Dissatisfaction with the worldliness of the Renaissance Church in general and with the papacy in particular gave the Czech reformer, John Hus, ample cause to stir up considerable rebellion among Bohemians and Moravians. Hus was anything but an original thinker; he has long been recognized as having taken up the reform ideas of Wycliffe without significant theoretical additions, but that is beside the point here. Like Wycliffe, he can be called a nationalist without hesitation. He also foreshadowed Luther in convincing large numbers of his own countrymen that they had a national mission to restore the purity of the true faith. The Church Hus preached against was Italian with a French coloration from Avignon. To Hus, his own people had no share in producing the Renaissance abuses in the Church, and he let the Bohemians and Moravians feel that in leading a moral crusade to reform it they would be bringing to fruition their uncorrupted Christian heritage (which just happened to be a national one).

Considering the force which religious conviction and a strong sense of national identity would unleash among the Germans, Spanish, Dutch, and Swedes, with the ultimate result of raising the authority of their secular rulers during the following two centuries, it is perhaps belaboring a point to explain that the Hussite Rebellion was caused by the fusion of the same two elements in Bohemia and Moravia at the turn of the fourteenth to the fifteenth century. Certainly the religious-national fervor which fired the Czechs during the Hussite Rebellion and then during the opening part of the Thirty Years War much later was of a type equivalent to that of these other European peoples.[119] Wenceslaus, however, was manifestly not of the same enterprising stripe as Frederick the Wise, Philip II, William of Orange, or Gustavus Adolphus.[120] He was ethnocentric enough to expel the Germans from the University of Prague in 1409, and he gave Hus encouragement at first. When Pope John XXIII placed Prague under the interdict, Wenceslaus ordered his subjects to ignore it. After a disagreement between the two over the sale of indulgences, however, Wenceslaus began weakening in his support of Hus. At the crucial moment he abandoned him and his supporters altogether, with the result that the religious and nationalistic fervor of the Czechs did not do much for Bohemian kingship for a while. Instead, Wenceslaus's successor earned the wrath of the Hussites, who continued to stress the unity of religious truth and national mission:

> Therefore we appeal to you out of love and compassion that you have mercy on yourselves and your kindred nation and work together with us so that God's law and all the salutary truths which may be proved from Holy Scripture be freed and safeguarded against the oppression planned by the King and his accomplices. He wishes to despoil us of our salvation, foist upon us his heretical creed as proclaimed . . . [at the Council of] Constance and lead us to damnation. Should you, despite it all, wish to take his side, we should

be forced to believe that you also favor the extinction of the Bohemian nation and to treat you, with God's help, on a par with the Lord's and our nation's public enemies.[121]

Compare events in France only a little later. Joan of Arc appeared on the historical scene in 1428, only thirteen years after Hus was burned at the stake in Constance. The dauphin she persuaded to be crowned as Charles VII did not seem to be much more of an attractive or resourceful figure than Wenceslaus had been, but, sober and willing, he turned the force of the religious-nationalistic fervor which Joan inspired in the French people to the crown's advantage; and it is probably in the unlikely person of Charles VII that New, or Renaissance, Monarchy really first took shape.

Although Charles VII as dauphin was heir to one of the oldest monarchies in Europe, he seems at first not to have thought of France, his future kingdom, as a living organism whose boundaries were predetermined by ties of language and the common history of its inhabitants. His effective holdings had been reduced to a pathetically small area around Bourges. While he no doubt wished from the first to add to his kingdom, which had received the mocking appellation "Kingdom of Bourges"[122] it was clear that he, or at least his closest advisers, did not consider the territory he held too sacred to be whittled down a bit in order to secure peace through negotiation with the restive English, who were occupying parts of western France, or with the Burgundians to the east, who came close to establishing a separate kingdom of their own and one which would have included great chunks of French territory.

In the face of an immediate attack by the English, Charles summoned the Estates-General, which granted him money for the defense of the realm. His trusted advisers embezzled considerable sums, but guns, powder, and provisions for the royal army were purchased nonetheless. By deeding away small tracts of land and a few castles, Charles was able to keep the soldiers in pay and food; however, it was the inspiration which Joan of Arc offered to the royal cause that kept the royal income flowing. Until her arrival, neither the nobility nor the clergy were forthcoming with the sums Charles requested, and even the money from non-noble sources voted by the Estates was collected only in part.

Joan made it clear from the outset that foreign alliances were not to play any major part in the victory for the French king and kingdom which she foretold. With reference to the Treaty of Chinon, which Charles had concluded to secure aid from the Scots, she had declared:

> Nobody in the world, not Kings nor Dukes nor the King of Scotland's daughter, nor anybody else can win back the Kingdom of France, but only I. Yet would I rather sit and spin with my mother, for this is . . . work for

which I was not made. It must be done, however, and I must go to the King, taking up the burden: for such is the will of the Lord.[123]

Joan perceived her mission of driving the English from France to be inseparable from that of restoring true kingship there. In a letter to the king of England and his deputies in France, which was later presented at her trial, she made this quite explicit:

> Surrender to *The Maid* sent hither by God, the King of Heaven, the keys of all the good towns you have taken and laid waste in France. She comes in God's name to establish the Blood Royal, ready to make peace if you agree to abandon France and repay what you have taken. . . . I am sent here in God's name, the King of Heaven, to drive you body for body out of all France. If your men obey, I will show them mercy. Do not think otherwise; you will not withhold the kingdom of France from God, the King of Kings, Blessed Mary's Son. The King Charles, the true inheritor, will possess it, for God wills it.[124]

Things stood better for Charles than he knew. Even before the royal forces led by Joan resoundingly defeated the English as they beseiged Orleans, the French cause was aided by volunteers and partisans in the English bastion of Normandy. It is difficult to estimate the size of this early resistance, which was led by local nobles and members of the bourgeoisie reacting against the confiscations and demands of the English, but the fervor of the movement and the significance of its — at least indirect — aid to Charles is amply documented by the importance the English attached to counteracting it. Several thousand partisans and those who sporadically aided them with food and shelter were tortured and killed. For emphasis, the English buried women alive at the foot of the gallows for merely feeding them. The English offered informers against them six livres, but the partisans punished collaborators with death; and generally the population supported and sheltered the nationalist-minded guerillas.[125]

Joan's rout of the English at Orleans was followed, in large part at her urging, by Charles's coronation at Rheims. Through two simple ceremonies in one, the Dauphin became both the choice of the French people and the anointed of the Lord. First, Charles solemnly swore to fulfill his kingly office by maintaining peace, by strengthening the Church, and by governing in justice and mercy. One of his dukes gave him the arms of a knight, and two of the ecclesiastical peers raised the chair on which he sat. Thus he was presented to his subjects, the crowd in the cathedral symbolizing the people at large and the Twelve Great Peers of France symbolizing the clergy and nobility.[126] The crown was held suspended above his head, as if consent must be forthcoming before he was crowned.

Then the archbishop of Rheims anointed Charles with the sacred oil which, according to additions in the Clovis legend, the Holy Ghost in the form of a dove had brought Saint Remigius in 496 for the anointment of that first French king. A silver reliquary in the form of a dove housed the vial; the oil in it was supposed to stay at the same level, no matter how many French kings should be anointed from it.

For Joan, the ceremony was a great fulfillment. "Gentle king," she told Charles, "now is God's will done, who wished you to come to Rheims and receive solemn sacring to show thereby that you are the true king and the one to whom the kingdom belongs."[127] His coronation seems indeed to have brought over still uncertain spirits to the royal cause. A number of towns sent Charles the keys to their gates; others sent announcements that their gates would be open to the king's army. Charles did not make the most of his opportunity to seize Paris and perhaps unite his kingdom in short order. In fact, his undue caution and only devious pursuit of his goal showed that the mysteries of his coronation were slow to remove his natural timidity. His failure to venture the slightest aid to Joan after her capture was a most unkingly reward in view of his debt to her for having virtually handed him his kingdom.

There were any number of reasons for Charles to abandon Joan to her fate as having served her purpose. She had known his early weakness through and through, including the significant detail that he had once offered a contingency prayer to God for his own refuge in Spain or Scotland.[128] Then, too, God could be seen as having withdrawn His favor from her. For several months, Charles busied himself in negotiations with the duke of Burgundy, who, as the feudal lord of Joan's jailer, alone possibly could have procured her release. But these negotiations concerned a peaceful working relationship between France and Burgundy, and Charles did not raise the question of Joan at all.[129]

Years later, long after Joan had been turned over to the English and burned as a witch and heretic, Charles was systematically at work to strengthen the royal position and, indeed, with considerable success. Confident of his ability to raise an army within France, he had the six thousand Scottish archers assured him by the Treaty of Chinon reduced to two thousand before the treaty was fulfilled with the arrival of Princess Margaret to wed his son, the future Louis XI.[130] To pursue his war against the English, he called the Estates-General, and in 1439 that body authorized the king to pay for his army with a tax on land belonging to non-nobles, the *taille*. This was a fateful step, for having been granted this form of tallage by the Estates-General for the express purpose of pursuing the war, Charles continued to collect it as the Hundred Years' War entered its final phase. He did not consult the Estates any further about it. It was at this point, too, that Charles introduced a sales tax, renewed the ancient *aides,* and added a tax on salt, the *gabelle.* Those estates assembling in the provinces never surrendered the power of the purse as had the Estates-General; nonetheless, they continued to vote the king's taxes and thus helped to finance the royal army and courts.

At the same time, what was left of the Conciliar movement in France continued to work for the benefit of the national monarchy within the framework of the Council of Basel, which had convened in 1431 to continue the work of the Council of Constance and kept meeting in various European cities after Eugene IV officially dissolved it the same year. In 1438, the French clergy declared the supremacy of councils over the papacy and the administrative independence of the Gallican Church from the Holy See in the Pragmatic Sanction of Bourges. No more annates were to be paid to Rome, and the pope was admonished not to interfere in the appointment of French bishops and abbots. This increased the clerical capacity for donations to the royal treasury and indirectly affirmed the royal prerogative to nominate bishops. Although the Conciliar movement nominally came to an end when Eugene's successor, Nicholas V, successfully dissolved the Council of Basel in 1449 with an amnesty for its participants,[131] the kings of France were to profit by the exertions of the Gallican Church for independence from Rome. Charles VII was discreet enough in his nominations for bishoprics to keep the cooperation between Church and monarch smooth. He had made the most of national-religious sentiment in his time of greatest need, but his instinct in this give-and-take with the papacy was to quit while he was ahead.

As the Middle Ages wore on, theocratic justifications for the divine right of kings which had been in circulation since Carolingian days were revived and expanded to fit the national mold. In the High Middle Ages, themes of divine right and the preeminence of the nation sometimes complemented each other, as in the citations from French court singers given above, but the application of divine right in terms of what was being claimed under the heading of ruling gradually changed along with institutional developments. With the enlarged royal administration and the concept of sovereignty in the increasingly impersonal state of the later Middle Ages, much more was at stake in such claims than in the previous centuries of tiny administrative apparatuses and personal rule through often unwieldy feudal structures.

The theocratic conception of kingship emphasized the king as patriarch in the image of God, a stress which royal supporters gave it more and more as the age of absolutism approached. In the reconstructed image of the divinely chosen royal father, we find the same combination of paternal role and religious functions which characterized the oldest of all Indo-Germanic kingly types, the *thiudans*. The *thiudans* was, we recall, an exalted figure and at the same time one with whom tribal members were supposed to feel a sort of intimacy as he embodied their tribe and hence themselves in dealing with the gods. The progressive monarchs of the later Middle Ages, no doubt unconsciously, presented precisely this superficially incompatible pair of attributes, exaltedness and intimacy.

Exaltedness followed naturally enough from the king's rule through divine right; it was also easy for a successful king to convey this with pageantry and court ceremony, as well as with the pompous phrasing of royal decrees. The concept of royal unassailability supported the king's exalted position in still another way, as he projected himself as a man who could not be replaced. Royal blood and exactly the right place in the royal line established legitimacy and irreplaceability. Where in the earlier Middle Ages, the king could legitimately be any one of a number of royal family members, legitimacy in the later Middle Ages became an exclusive concept: there could be no substitute for the one sanctioned ruler. The notion of royal expertise was quietly cultivated to the same end. While a king obviously could not be an expert in every field of government, he presented himself as commanding legions of wise and experienced men. This stress also dealt an oblique blow to competing interests: feudal lords by way of contrast did not have such men at their disposal in appreciable numbers — men educated in Roman law and knowledgeable of the nation's history, who would guard the people's interests in legal disputes.

Unlike exaltedness, intimacy was hard for a king to get across in the ancient nation state, which is where propaganda comes in. Propaganda is certainly a hallmark of modern nationalism, and some of the later medieval kings understood its uses quite well, although the term itself was not coined until the sixteenth century. The essence of propaganda is persuasive communication with masses of people, and the large numbers alone made intimacy a tricky item for medieval kings to present convincingly. Then, as now, a high and mighty personage could convey intimacy with his people only under the headings of *caring* and *concern*. The ruler cares for his people as individuals and in their collective identity as his nation. He is concerned about national well-being on a full-time basis. He needs his people as they need him, and at certain moments he wants them to understand exactly what he is doing and why. Something like mass communication was necessary to achieve this end. Given the technological limitations of the time, later medieval kings reached their real and putative subjects rather well. Edward III had his decrees conspicuously nailed to church doors in the French kingdom he claimed[132]; the duke of Bedford's government went to the extent of displaying "the true genealogy of Henry VI, king of France and England, accompanied by explanatory verses,"[133] in the Cathedral of Notre Dame, to try to convince the French of his rightful claims. In fact, wherever they could do so officials or military men saw to it that royal messages were prominently posted or publicly read in towns. In a less verbal way, public feasts and processionals sponsored by kings, as well as celebrations of national victories, displayed the royal concern for sharing and receiving common national feelings with their subjects.

The reverse side of this was censorship. Antiroyal propaganda could often be suppressed as treasonous, and even papal bulls could be tampered with for popular audiences. It had been a sign of new times in France when Philip IV not only exploited his quarrel with the papacy to improve his own standing but played fast and loose with the letter and spirit of its basic documents. The reproachful letter of Boniface VIII to him was shortened, its hostile points were editorially heightened, and it was released for publication with the spurious last line: "We count as heretics all those who believe otherwise." Philip's ostensible answer, *"Sciat vestra maxima fatuitas,"* was a conscious parody of his own chancellery's adulterated version of the papal letter, complete with a terminal clause: "We count as fools and madmen those who believe otherwise."[134] There is some doubt about whether Philip's reply was actually sent to Boniface in anything like its published form; it was, at all events, intended more for popular consumption than for the pope.[135]

A century and a half later Louis XI was more subtle in his approach but felt equally up to the task of censoring papal communications in the national interest before they reached his subjects. In 1470, he instructed his council to hold up the publication of a papal bull until the members determined whether it contained damaging material:

> If it contains anything specific which would be derogatory or would prejudice our position in any way, or if it contains any points which would make modification or interpretation highly desirable and necessary, take note of what needs work on it and we will have it improved.[136]

If the pope failed to consider royal concerns in a great nation, then it was evidently up to the king to correct the oversight.

Chapter 8

Summary and Conclusion

How did kingship come to dominate the medieval world to the point that major events in the history of the European Middle Ages seem so often to have been decided by what kings and queens were or were not?

The answer is largely that from the early through the later Middle Ages kings appear as living institutions with absolutely necessary functions: they were to keep the peace and render justice to their subjects, while defending the realm against foreign invaders. Then, too, in an age which stressed salvation as the highest value, they were key figures in defending and strengthening the faith.

Why, however, did it have to be kings who met these needs? Certainly most of the classical Greek world and the Roman Republic got along well enough without them, while a host of modern democracies have kept peace, rendered justice, and defended borders with only figurehead kings or none at all. Here much of the answer lies in the class structure of the Middle Ages and the lack of realistic alternatives to kingship under prevailing conditions.

The feudal nobility wielded substantial power in the Middle Ages, but it offered no permanent solutions of its own to enduring political problems. It exercised a considerable check on royal authority, but, all in all, the dukes, counts, and barons of the Middle Ages were too class-based in their interests to show much foresight or adaptability in advancing the cause of peace and stability on a realm-wide scale, except, of course, to the extent that they supported a central monarchy. With their roots in a system based on fighting and one which made the offering of protection a semiprivate matter, a multiplicity of nobles could hardly be expected to serve as the mainstays for a stable social order in areas as large as medieval kingdoms.

Checks on royal power from popular assemblies were real enough in the very early Middle Ages, and even later in Scandinavia and other places where: (1) a rough equality prevailed among warriors, (2) warriors were the bulk of the free men of a tribe, and (3) most of the men of the tribe were free. With increasing class differentiation and the isolation imposed upon population strata in the context of the manorial economy, popular assemblies lost power or faded away altogether. In the later Middle Ages, to be sure, the forerunners of modern representative assemblies made their appearance, but not as institutions which limited royal power. Instead, they came upon the scene most often as groups convoked by kings to affirm royal measures, particularly in taxation. Nearly all medieval kings claimed to make at least their major decisions by consent, and in the later Middle Ages the consent of representatives of the commons was becoming a material and psychological aid in the ruling process.

The feudal nobility retained enough power to keep kings from becoming absolute rulers — a role in which they were often supported consciously or unconsciously by leaders of the Church — but the feudal nobility could exercise independent ruling power without kings only in a way which threatened the peace and stability of the realm. The common people during this time were too weak or disorganized to think of determining anything like the fate of realms themselves. The inherent instability of unleavened feudal domination led the majority of individual nobles to accept the kingship principle. Among the commons, the middle class was able to develop into a politically significant factor, but only in a symbiotic relationship with kings. No alternative seemed possible to either group.

The medieval Church exercised both a restraining and supporting influence on medieval kingship. When we review the actual relationship between the Church and kingship over the course of the medieval centuries, we find material to lay to rest two enduring, if contradictory, myths. The first, a peculiarly American one, holds that the divine right of kings, as found in the Old Testament and propagated by the Church, was a bulwark of unlimited royal power in western Europe in the Middle Ages. By now we have seen that the power of kings was not absolute either in the Old Testament or in medieval portrayals of Old Testament figures. As a matter of fact, in the first medieval centuries, the New Testament's "Caesar," rather than Old Testament kingship, was the focus of Church teaching concerning rulers. It is true that Church leaders came close to acknowledging something like absolute divine right in the highly exceptional case of Emperor Constantine I during the early fourth century, but that view of rulers was held only by an insignificant minority in the Western Church after that emperor's death. Saint Ambrose spoke much more lastingly for the Church toward the end of the fourth century, when he dwelt in public upon the figure of King David for the benefit of the Christian Emperor Theodosius I — not to demonstrate the glory of kings but rather to prove that kings could be rebuked and corrected by those who spoke for the Lord.

Three hundred years later, in the Carolingian Renaissance, King David finally came into his own as an illustrious model for Christian rulership, but those who subsequently stressed the power of kings as independent of restraint because of God's choice in their selection did so—generally unsuccessfully—in defiance of Church authority. The middle Ages were over before any theory of the absolute divine right of kings had the sanction of (as it turned out) divided factions of what had been the medieval Church.

If the Church did not grant absolute power to kings under the heading of divine right, it certainly did not go to the other extreme either. The story of medieval kingship refutes the other myth alluded to, that quaint but persistent notion not so much advocated as taken for a starting point for "dialogue" in our own day, that Christian political theory is inherently democratic. At the time of Constantine I, the influential Bishop Eusebius of Caesarea predictably enough found that monarchy was God's own form of government. While Church spokesmen afterwards were generally less sanguine on the topic, the vast majority who dealt with political matters either supported kingship as preferable to other forms of government or did not consider alternative governmental types at all. Not even Saint Augustine (whose distaste for "the earthly city" led him to equate the rule of kings or emperors with robbery on a grand scale) suggested that Christian principles might call for the people to limit monarchy, any more than Thomas à Becket did much later when he directly challenged royal authority. There were a (very) few advocates of democratic limitations on royal power within the medieval Church. These were lesser figures of the caliber of Manegold of Lautenbach, whose impassioned defense of the embattled papacy led him to strike out in new and unheard-of directions to undermine the papacy's royal opponents. His democratic conclusions are clear. They are based on the analogy of the king as a hired hand with whose work the people must be satisfied if they are to retain him in their employment, but there is no indication that his line of reasoning was influential, even in his own time. The papacy could scarcely encourage democratic theory. Firmly rooted in the monarchical principle itself, the papacy could not encourage democratic values with credible consistency even in conflicts with kings.

What Church spokesman did consistently demand of kings in the Middle Ages was that they respect Church interests. Almost all the salient points in medieval religious-political theory emerged during the course of fourth-century conflicts over the power of the state in questions affected by a religious interest. Depending on who was in power and how he used (or could be expected to use) that power of the state for or against Church interests, Church leaders called for a great variety of policies which covered the spectrum. They were capable of calling now for massive interference by the state in religious affairs and a bit later for the complete separation of religious and secular spheres. By the fifth century, Church doctrine settled on the theory that the secular sphere should be independent except where matters of the faith overlapped affairs of state. In such case, secular rulers should take the guidance of Church leaders. The logic, given the medieval emphasis on faith, was inexorable: saving souls was more important than the concerns of "this world"; therefore, those having charge of saving souls rightfully exercised both the prerogative of making positive demands and veto rights when they dealt with those in charge of the affairs of this world. When jurisdictions seemed to overlap, precedence was to be given to the claims of those whose work and insight could save souls for the heavenly kingdom rather than those who dealt with the distinctly inferior matters of taxation in Caesar's coin and bringing common criminals to the gallows.

There is an intriguing parallel between the claims of the medieval Church to direct kings in the world of ideas when the faith was involved (which was most of the time) and the claims of present-day Communist parties in power to direct the government when Marxist-Leninist doctrine and the interests of the working class are involved (which is most of the time). The most conspicuous contrast emerges, however, in medieval kings' frequent and successful independence of action. Unlike governmental leaders in Communist countries, medieval kings often found important factions willing to support them in their defiance of the sanctioned source of ideological directives. Their periodic gains in recruiting bishops and rallying national sentiments against the papacy did much to dissolve the organic union of Church and state which stood at the center of medieval ideology. By way of contrast, the Dubček and Djilas figures of the later twentieth century have made little lasting headway with their ideals of political action outside party control, and the union of party and state, which stands at the center of current Communist ideology, remains intact.

Medieval kings were able to use nascent national identity to strengthen their ruling positions. In their efforts they were aided by the fact that, at least on occasions, they could be the nation as well as lead it. While the Roman Empire transmitted the rationale for one-man decision making in government to the Middle Ages, the charismatic side of medieval kingship, which allowed the king to subsume tribal identity in his own person, had Germanic origins. The early Germanic *thiudans* personified the tribe in a very real way. His tribe saw in him the best man to please the gods of war and nature because of his *Heil,* that certain something about him the ancient deities liked. His tribe entrusted him with their very identity: the divine liking for him meant a greater probability of victory or survival in the face of calamity than tribesmen could hope for merely on their merits. Then, too, the gods could be expected to favor someone with praiseworthy characteristics: courage, strength, determination and the like. The immersion of tribal identity in such a man resulted in assurance that these virtues permeated the total tribal personality. In his possession of *Heil,* the *thiudans* swayed fate on the tribe's behalf, and as the living embodiment of the tribe in a single royal personage, he gave his people an enduring unity, which was, of course, transmitted by blood through a royal house or dynasty.

The royal role of personifier did not disappear when tribes became Christian, much larger, or both. The divine favor seen as Charlemagne's possession reflected upon the Frankish people he embodied, just as his wisdom and dignity somehow became theirs. Nor did the king as tribal personifier fade away with the emerging nation-state. We have noted that in *King Lear,* the king of France is called simply "France." More to the point, perhaps, in *King Henry V,* Shakespeare takes for granted that his audience will recognize that an insult by the French dauphin to the English king is an insult to the English people sufficient for war. This function of national embodiment has followed charismatic leaders right up into the later twentieth century: the leader assumes the identity of his people and suffuses it with his own power to move mountains; he lets his people glory in the defeat of his adversaries who in a familiar but still mysterious process have somehow become their common enemies.

Kingship was certainly no final answer to problems of instability in the Middle Ages. It proved to be such a tantalizing prize in the sixth and seventh centuries that the murder *of* kings by those who desired to become kings and the preventive murder *by* kings of those who might aspire to topple their thrones was a source of despair even among the Franks, who had made the most of the opportunities presented by kingship after the fall of the Roman Empire. The power concentrated in medieval kingship not only posed the problem of offering such a tempting prize as sometimes to threaten the peace of the realm but also made a corrupt or incompetent king into a tribal (and later national) calamity. Still, there was enough awareness even in the early Middle Ages of the fact that kingship was supposed to be filling the vital function of insuring peace and stability to instigate action when kings failed in this respect. Less-talented kings could rely on subordinates for aid and advice in the ruling arts they lacked, but if kings were bad or inept enough, they were likely to be replaced either by rivals or by the subordinates they counted on. Dynastic changes generally reflected the pervasive feelings of contemporaries that ruling talent had run out in the old line. The Middle Ages saw many variations on the theme of worldly-wise Carolingians replacing feeble Merovingians and being forced to yield in turn to Capetians when their last Louis became "Louis the Sluggard" in the eyes of his subjects.

The most rational and straightforward side of the appeal of medieval kingship remained its potential for keeping order better than any possible competing political structure or system. The rudimentary desire for protection against robbery, assault, rape, murder, and the host of violent acts with which earlier medieval history is replete sustained widespread support for a ruler strong and independent enough to control potential lawbreakers. On all sides, medieval kingship developed precisely the strength and independence which seemed to further the peace and stability of the realm. Royal leverage for this purpose appeared early in a wide variety of forms: the royal right to issue documents guaranteeing possession of land; the inspired combination of benefice and vassalage to make "king's men" of the nobles; the concept of "suzerainty," with the king often as the ultimate lord's lord; the expansion of the royal demesne; the growing concept of "the king's peace"; and a thoroughgoing alliance with the merchant class — to review only the most significant elements. New possibilities for the strength and independence of kingship kept emerging as enterprising kings turned to their own advantage such diverse elements as the taxation opportunities offered by a money economy, the increased importance of royal infantry and the decreased importance of noble cavalry, the revival of Roman law, and the aspirations of townspeople for more royal guarantees of their liberties.

All the while, medieval kings were helping to bring the nation-state into being. The concept of a "state" beyond that of the ruler's personal authority had been quite dim in the early Middle Ages. Charlemagne's sense of reality led him to recognize the fact that his royal person could not be everywhere at once, and he set up a network of officials to help insure royal justice in outlying parts of the realm. Even he, however, had great difficulty in making a lasting institution out of his *missi dominici*. In the same century in which Charlemagne died, Notker Balbulus wrote of him simply as if he were almost every place he needed to be to oversee affairs of the realm, and God took care of royal justice when his back was turned in the remaining cases. The state was still ages away. By the twelfth and thirteenth centuries, however, the great expansion of royal guarantees of justice, the increasing military responsibilities of the crown, and the complexity of royal taxation measures all required substantial groups of officials and a continuity of administration. Increasingly, too, kings found at least nominally representative bodies convenient to bestow legitimacy on controversial royal measures. At first it seemed that most officeholders in the embryonic state were so clearly the creatures of the king that their weight would have to strengthen kingship as a matter of course.

With the onset of modern times, to be sure, this turned out not to be such a matter of course. Judges were to rebel at the mention of the plain fact that most European judgeships originated in posts created by kings for the purposes and convenience of royal administration. Parliaments forgot easily enough that their institutions stemmed from royal initiatives to obtain ready consent to new taxes; their members now thought of limiting royal authority as well as confirming it. The biggest defection was to come from the middle classes. Where in the Middle Ages the merchants and other townspeople could be counted on to support royal authority, their descendants in the post-Reformation period were apt to be among the foremost critics of royal powers, now seen as usurpations. In destroying the power of the feudal nobility by such direct means as outlawing private armies or by such indirect means as domesticating and coaxing them into becoming courtiers, kings unwittingly destroyed the bond which held the middle class to them. The nobility had threatened kings and the middle class in different ways. They opposed royal attempts to centralize political authority at the expense of their own time-honored right to dominate much of the local scene. They opposed the new influence of commoners who justified their right to sway political decisions by the productive contributions they made to the nation. After kings had freed the middle classes from the threat of a strong and independent nobility, it did not take middle-class leaders many generations to question why they should support royal power against a past enemy who no longer threatened them.

Medieval kingship led through its inexorable success to the Age of Absolutism, when kings freed themselves of most secular and religious restraints. Medieval kingship had flourished for a thousand years by combining the rationale for one-man decision making with the charismatic nature of the tribal personifier in a fashion preferable to any imaginable alternatives. The Age of Absolutism was relatively short, for preferable alternatives were soon imagined, and it ended with the unravelling of the earlier strands of monarchy and kingship. The Absolutist notion that the king can do no wrong became the modern European idea that if kings are to stay they had best not do anything controversial. One-man decision making and charismatic rulership have certainly persisted as elements of world civilization, but by the twentieth century serious rulers of men — even the Fascists, who in their pretentious combination of charisma and authority were to caricature medieval kingship in many ways — had become as chary of reaching for crowns as ancient Romans.

NOTES

ABBREVIATIONS

CCSL – Corpus Christianorum, Series Latina
CSEL – Corpus Scriptorum Ecclesiasticorum Latinorum
LCL – Loeb Classical Library
MIÖG – Mitteilungen des Instituts für österreichische Geschichtsforschung
MGH – Monumenta Germaniae Historica
NPNF – Nicene and Post-Nicene Fathers
PG – Patrologia Graeca (Migne)
PL – Patrologia Latina (Migne)
SPCK – Society for the Promotion of Christian Knowledge
SRM – Scriptores Rerum Merovingicarum
WBG – Wissenschaftliche Buchgesellschaft, Darmstadt

CHAPTER 1 NOTES

1. Letter to Roger Sherman, July 18, 1789. *Works,* ed. Charles F. Adams (Freeport, N.Y.: Books for Libraries Press repr., 1969), Vol. VI, p. 430.
2. *Kultur und Religionen der Germanen,* ed. Otto Höfler; 6. unveränderte Auflage (Darmstadt: Wissenschaftliche Buchgesellschaft, 1961), Vol. I, p. 143.
3. Ibid., Vol. I, p. 135.
4. William A. Chaney, *The Cult of Kingship in Anglo-Saxon England* (Berkeley and Los Angeles: University of California Press, 1970), pp. 33–35.
5. Herwig Wolfram, "The Shaping of the Early Medieval Kingdom," *Viator,* Vol. I (1970), pp. 3–5.
6. According to Tacitus, Germanic kings shared in the horse-neighing augury with priests, but when kings or chiefs addressed the tribal assembly, the priests had only the function of assuring silence and order. *Germania,* chs. x–xi; LCL, *Dialogus, Agricola, Germania,* pp. 276–80.
7. Wolfram, op. cit., p. 4.
8. Tacitus, op. cit., ch. vii; p. 274.
9. This comes out in his description of the "king or chief" addressing the assembly noted above: "Mox rex vel princeps, prout aetas cuique, prout nobilitas,

prout decus bellorum, prout facundia est, audiuntur, auctoritate suadendi magis quam iubendi potestate." Ibid.

10. Titus Livy, *Ab urbe condita,* I, lix — II, i; LCL, Vol. I, pp. 208–18.

11. ". . . neminem regnare passuros nec esse Romae unde periculum foret." Ibid., II, ii, 5; LCL, Vol. I, p. 222.

12. Plutarch's *Lives of Illustrious Men,* "Tiberius Gracchus," trans. John Dryden (Chicago: Belford, Clarke and Co., n.d.), Vol. III, pp. 119–20.

13. Livy, op. cit., II, ii, 1–2; LCL, Vol. I, pp. 220–22. The term used, "Rex sacrificulus" or "sacrificolus," may have been understood as a diminutive based on "sacrificus" (sacrificing), which would be an obvious dilution of the kingly name as, roughly, "King for the Minor Sacrifices"; on the other hand, it may have been formed simply by analogy with "sacricola" (sacrificing priest or priestess) without any diminutive connotation.

14. Ibid., II, i, 7–9; LCL, Vol. I, p. 222.

15. Polybius, *The Histories,* VI, xi-xviii; ed. E. Badian (New York: Washington Square Press, n.d.), pp. 222–29. The passages in question probably date from the later 140s B.C.

16. Caesar's accumulation of quasi-royal honors was sufficient even for Suetonius, historian and secretary to Emperor Hadrian in the second century A.D. and a man who took the rule of the emperors to be simply the given system to find that the conspirators had acted justly, all in all: "Praegravant tamen cetera facta dictaque eius, ut et abusus dominatione et iure caesus existimetur. Non enim honores modo nimios recepit: continuum consultatum, perpetuam dictaturam praefecturamque morum, insuper praenomen Imperatoris, cognomen Patris patriae, statuam inter reges, suggestum in orchestra; sed et ampliora etiam humano fastigio decerni sibi passus est: sedem auream in curia et pro tribunali, tensam et ferculum circensi pompa, templa, aras, simulacra inter deos, pulvinar, flaminem, lupercos, appellationem mensis e suo nomine. . . ." *De vita caesarum,* I, "Divus Iulius," lxxvi, 1; LCL, Vol. I, p. 98.

17. Ibid., II, "Divus Augustus," lii-liii; LCL, Vol. I, p. 206.

18. In the development of the title, there were numerous shadings of meaning, depending on such considerations as whether the term was applied to a victorious commander or whether it was used as a "praenomen" or "cognomen." According to Theodor Mommsen, the "praenomen imperatoris" signified the holder of perpetual command. *Römisches Staatsrecht,* Vol. II, Part 2, 3rd ed. (Leipzig: Hirzel, 1887), pp. 767–74. This view is challenged by Donald McFayden, *The History of the Title* Imperator *Under the Roman Empire* (Chicago: University of Chicago Press, 1920), esp. ch. V, "The Connotation of the Praenomen Imperatoris Under Augustus," pp. 44–52, and Mason Hammond, *The Augustan Principate in Theory and Practice during the Julio-Claudian Period,* enlarged ed. (New York: Russell and Russell, 1968), esp. ch. V, "The Uses of the Title *Imperator,*" pp. 48–53. Both of these more recent authors find the signification of the title considerably more limited through the time of Augustus.

19. Suetonius, op. cit., VIII, "Domitianus," xiii-xiv; LCL, Vol. II, pp. 366-68.

20. Priscus gives the story of his embassy to the Huns in his *Historia Byzantina* or *Historia Gothica,* part 8 of what survives. Karl Müller, ed., *Fragmenta Historicorum Graecorum* (Paris: Didot, 1851), Vol. IV, pp. 77-95. J. B. Bury gives a free English translation of the whole account in *History of the Later Roman Empire* (London and New York: Macmillan, 1923), Vol. I, pp. 279-88.

21. Tacitus, *Historiae,* IV, lxi and lxv; LCL, Vol. II, pp. 118 and 126. *Germania,* loc. cit., ch. viii, p. 276.

22. Pulcheria, sister of Theodosius II, ruled the eastern empire in her own right for four weeks (July 28-August 25, 450) following her brother's death. Significantly, however, she considered it necessary to counter the prejudice against a ruling empress by then marrying Marcian, a senator, who was officially given the imperial title, although Pulcheria continued to exercise the very considerable influence on state policies she had while Theodosius was alive. While the Byzantines later seem to have come to terms with the possibility of a woman ruling in her own right in the person of Empress Irene (r. 790 and 797-802), the western recollection of the Roman model furnished a basis for keeping women from ruling the Germanic or Holy Roman Empire down to the eighteenth century.

23. In this connection, Claudian presents the Parthian kingship for contrast with the Roman emperorship. *Panegyricus de quarto consulatu Honorii Augusti* (398 A.D.), 11. 214-23; LCL, Vol. I, p. 286.

24. Walter Ullmann, *The Carolingian Renaissance and the Idea of Kingship* (London: Methuen, 1969), pp. 5-15.

CHAPTER 2 NOTES

1. John, 12,31; 14,30 and 16,11.

2. Matthew, 5,25; cf. 5,40.

3. I Cor., 6,1.

4. Tertullian, *Apologeticum,* ii, 7-8; CCSL, Vol. I, pp. 88-89.

5. Herwig Wolfram, *Intitulatio I. Lateinische Königs- und Fürstentitel bis zum Ende des 8. Jahrhunderts.* MIÖG, Ergänzungsband XXI, 1967, p. 35.

6. Ibid., p. 36.

7. Ibid., p. 39.

8. There is no agreement either in the ancient sources or in modern interpretations about the precise timing of Constantine's conversion, the nature of his inspiration for the shield painting, or the connection between the two. With reference to the Church's view of the Roman monarchy, it is enough to observe that Christians took Constantine's army to have triumphed under a Christian sign and that Constantine, at least in retrospect, was thoroughly

convinced of this as well. Still, as the first symbol of a Christian emperor, the emblem has a significance of its own. The earliest source, Lactantius' *De mortibus persecutorum,* written before 318, states that the night before the great battle Constantine had a dream admonishing him to mark "the heavenly sign of God" on the shield of his soliders. Then: "Facit ut iussus est, et transuersa X littera, summo capite circumflexo, Christum in scutis notat. Quo signo armatus exercitus capit ferrum." Ch. xliv, 5–6; CSEL, Vol. XXVII, Part 2, p. 223. Following Lactantius and evidently assuming that the X was not only turned (which is clear from the passage) but had its legs moved to the point of forming four right angles (which is not clear from the passage) Ramsey MacMullen presents the emblem as ☥ . *Constantine* (New York: Dial Press, 1969), p. 72. Eusebius of Caesarea, on the other hand, in his *Life of Constantine,* written in 337 or 338, introduces the story of a vision seen by Constantine at an undetermined time before the battle. Book I, chs. xxvi–xxix; NPNF (2), Vol. I, pp. 487–90. A.H.M. Jones takes this as evidence that Constantine saw a variety of "halo phenomenon," namely "a cross of light with the sun in its center" well before the battle, which is about the way Eusebius describes the sign, and concludes that the symbol used on the shields was ☧ , the chi and rho as a monogram of Christ devised by Constantine. *Constantine and the Conversion of Europe* (London: English Universities Press, 1948), pp. 94–97. The missing link necessary for Jones's interpretation but not for MacMullen's is the Labarum, a device carried into battle by Constantine's troops: this was a tall pole with a cross bar, from which hung the portraits of Constantine and two of his sons. On the pole, high over the cross bar, was the ☧ , surrounded by a wreath of gold and gems. According to Eusebius, Constantine had constructed the Labarum on the basis of his vision, and, of course, if the ☧ appeared as a result of the vision on the Labarum it would have undoubtedly been the emblem on the shields. The problem is that the Labarum is not documented as having been carried into battle until much later than Constantine's victory over Maxentius. The sons depicted on the Labarum which Eusebius saw were not even born in 312. Hence no evidence derived from the Labarum for what was painted on the shields is admissible. MacMullen's argument for ☥ would seem to be supported by the ambiguity of the sign, for it is much like the pagan sign for the sun deriving from the Egyptian ☥ , and it is hence quite consonant with Constantine's early official references to the "Highest Divinity," which his pagan subjects were still quite free to see as the Unconquered Sun, however much the emperor himself moved toward Christian monotheism.

9. Complete text in Lactantius, op. cit., ch. xlviii, 2–12; CSEL, Vol. XXVII, 2, pp. 228–29. Since this document is essentially a summary of the agreements reached by Constantine and Licinius in January or February 313 in Milan, it is usually called the "Edict of Milan."

10. Eusebius of Caesarea gives the text of the letter in his *History of the Church,* Book X, ch. vi; NPNF (2), Vol. I, pp. 382–83.

11. Text in ibid., X, vii; p. 383.

12. While the Church increased its authority during the fourth century in great part at the expense of imperial authority, events never flowed straight in that direction even within relatively short periods of time. Constantine himself had second thoughts about releasing the clergy from the onerous duty of membership in city councils when it seemed to him that too many men were taking holy orders to get rid of hereditary councilors' responsibilities, and he later excluded those to whom this office would legally fall from the future clergy. His law dating from the 320s, *Codex Theodosianus,* XVI, ii, 3, confirms this prohibition while ruling out a retroactive application of it. After Constantine's death, the unworkable rule that a single party could take any civil case before a bishop was abandoned.

13. Eusebius of Caesarea, *Life of Constantine,* loc. cit., chs. xviii-xx, pp. 544-45.

14. Ibid., II, chs. lvi and lviii, pp. 513-14.

15. There is some reason to dismiss most of the temple-closing as something other than a manifestation of Constantine's growing intolerance of paganism. Since ritual prostitution occurred in some of the temples of Venus, shutting a couple of these can be seen as a police measure in the interest of public morality. When Constantine had gold melted down from the images, his motivation may have been largely financial, since some pagan emperors had also done this. Jones, op. cit., p. 211, and Hermann Dörries, *Constantine and Religious Liberty* (New Haven: Yale University Press, 1960), p. 45. Still, the coincidence of these two types of measures is significant, and no one has thought of a good nonreligious reason for Constantine's closing of the temple of Aesculapius at Aegae in Cilicia. Eusebius, after all, praises Constantine for the suppression of pagan worship, and while he no doubt exaggerates in doing so, it would seem — particularly in view of the wording of the new toleration edict of 324 after the defeat of Licinius — unlikely that his attribution to Constantine of a desire to humiliate paganism through official measures is completely made up.

16. A reference by Constantine in his letter to Arius and Alexander to the enemy of this "world" or "habitable globe" ($o\hat{\iota}\kappa o\upsilon\mu\acute{\epsilon}\nu\eta$) was previously taken to refer to Licinius. Hermann Dörries has shown, however, that a subsequent reference to the second victory over the enemy of the Church at Nicaea — clearly the devil — implies that Constantine had meant by his phrase "enemy of this world" in discussing his earlier victory "not so much Licinius as the power of Evil standing behind him." *Das Selbstzeugnis Kaiser Konstantins* (Göttingen: Vandenhoeck & Ruprecht, 1954), p. 56, n. 1.

17. "Haereticorum factione comperimus ecclesiae catholicae clericos ita vexari, ut nominationibus seu susceptionibus aliquibus, quas publicus mos exposcit, contra indulta sibi privilegia praegraventur." *Codex Theodosianus,* XVI, ii, 1, dated 313.

18. "Epistola Constantini ad Celsum," PL, Vol. VIII, cols, 489-92.

19. "Epistola Constantini de basilica catholicis erepta" (to the Numidian bishops); CSEL, Vol. XXVI, Appendix, pp. 214-15. Another letter from Constantine states simply that heavenly justice will punish the injuries done

to the Catholics by the Donatists; consequently, the Catholics should tolerate them. "Epistola Constantini universis episcopis per Africam et plebi ecclesiae catholicae;" Ibid., App. IX, p. 213. Also in PL, Vol. VIII, cols. 531-32.

20. MacMullen, op. cit., p. 167.

21. Text in Eusebius, *Life of Constantine,* loc. cit., II, lxix, pp. 516-17. Also, with some background material, in Socrates Scholasticus, *Church History from A.D. 305-439,* Book I, ch. vii; NPNF (2), Vol. II, pp. 6-7.

22. Eusebius, *Life of Constantine,* loc. cit., IV, xxix, p. 548; minor alterations in translation (cf. PL, Vol. VIII, col. 75).

23. Eusebius, *Oration on the Tricennalia of Constantine,* ii, 1-5; English text from NPNF (2), Vol. I, p. 583, given with alterations by J. Stevenson, *A New Eusebius: Documents Illustrative of the History of the Church to A.D. 337* (London: SPCK, 1957), pp. 391-92.

24. Ibid., iii. 5-7; NPNF, I, 584; Stevenson, pp. 392-93.

25. Eusebius, *Life of Constantine,* loc. cit., IV, lx; I, p. 555. Constantine had provided for his own funeral arrangements: he lay in state with his own coffin in the middle of twelve other coffins symbolizing the Twelve Apostles. Dörries sees this as Constantine's entreaty for the favor of the Apostles. "Constantine's hope was that crumbs for him would keep falling from that rich banquet table that he had prepared for the Apostles and that the land all around would receive moisture from the flowing spring water." *Das Selbstzeugnis Kaiser Konstantins,* loc. cit., p. 422. A larger number of interpretations, however, some using evidence from August Heisenberg's *Grabeskirche und Apostelkirche, zwei Basiliken Konstantins* (Leipzig: J. C. Hinrichs, 1908), present the scene more or less as an attempt by the ruler to link himself upon dying with the Apostles, not necessarily on a completely equal basis but as belonging to them nonetheless. Compare, for example, the simple statement of Andreas Alfoldi: "He was buried in his new capital as the thirteenth Apostle." *The Conversion of Constantine and Pagan Rome,* transl. Harold Mattingly (Oxford: Clarendon Press, 1948), p. 33. Medieval Germanic emperors were to derive some feeling of special association with the Apostles from the Constantine stories and legends. Their occasional title, Servus Apostolorum, was in the same category with the papal title, Servus Servorum Dei. It was also not uncommon for medieval rulers to assume that they would continue to do a little bit of ruling with God and the Apostles in heaven. Herwig Wolfram, *Splendor Imperii: die Epiphanie von Tugend und Heil* in *Herrschaft und Reich.* MIÖG, Ergänzungsband XX, 3, (1963), p. 120.

26. *The Age of Constantine the Great* (1852), transl. Moses Hadas (New York: Pantheon Books, 1949), pp. 260, 277, and 284-91.

27. "Cesset superstitio, sacrificiorum aboleatur insania. Nam quicumque contra legem divi principis parentis nostri et hanc nostrae mansuetudinis iussionem ausus fuerit sacrificia celebrare, competens in eum vindicta et praesente sententia exeratur." *Codex Theodosianus,* XVI, x, 1.

28. "Placuit omnibus locis atque urbibus universis claudi protinus templa, et accessu vetitis omnibus licentiam deliquendi perditis abnegari. Volumus

etiam cunctos a sacrificiis abstinere. Quod si quis aliquid forte huiusmodi perpetraverit, gladio sternatur: facultates etiam peremptis fisco decernimus vindicari: et similiter adfligi rectores provinciarum si facinora vindicare neglexerint." Ibid., XVI, x., 4.

29. Iulius Firmicus Maternus, *De errore profanorum religionum,* chs. xvi, 4; xx, 7; xxviii, 6; and xxix, 4. CSEL, Vol. II, pp. 100, 109, 125, and 130.

30. *Relatio III.* Q. Aurelius Symmachus, *Opera quae supersunt,* ed. Otto Seeck, MGH, *Auct. Antiquiss.,* Vol. VI, Part 1, pp. 280–83; passage cited, p. 281.

31. Socrates Scholasticus, op. cit., II, xv-xvi, pp. 42–43.

32. ". . . etiam itinera poterant esse tutissima, quod domini de vehiculis suis excussi ante mancipia sua dominorum locis sedentia, serviliter cucurrent. Illorum iudicio et imperio inter dominos et servos conditio mutabatur." Optatus, *De schismate Donatistarum,* III, iv; CSEL, Vol. XXVI, p. 82.

33. " 'Quid est imperatori cum ecclesia'?" cited in ibid., III, iii, p. 73.

34. "Gratias Deo omnipotenti et Christo Iesu, qui dedit malis schismatibus finem, et respexit Ecclesiam suam, ut in eius gremium erigeret universa membra dispersa: qui imperavit religiosissimo Constanti imperatori, ut votum gereret unitatis. . . ." PL, Vol. VIII, col. 774.

35. Hilary of Poitiers, *ex Opere Historica Fragmentum II,* viii. PL, Vol. X, cols. 632–35 and Theodoret, *Ecclesiastical History,* III, vi; NPNF (2), Vol. III, pp. 67–72.

36. Athanasius, *Historia Arianorum,* ch. iii, § 20; NPNF (2), Vol. IV, pp. 276–77, and Theodoret, loc. cit., pp. 72–73.

37. Athanasius, *Historia Arianorum,* loc. cit., ch. v, §§ 35–41, pp. 282–84, and *Apologia contra Arianos,* ch. vi, 89; NPNF (2), Vol. IV, pp. 146–47. It is significant that even at this early date and even in the judgement of a pagan historian, Constantius was seeking Liberius' confirmation as that of a "higher power" in his move to have Athanasius outlawed: "Id enim ille Athanasio semper infestus, licet sciret impletum, tamen auctoritate quoque potiore aeternae urbis episcopi firmari desiderio nitebatur ardenti; quo non impetrato, Liberius aegre populi metu, qui eius amore flagrabat, cum magna difficultate noctis medio potuit asportari." Ammianus Marcellinus, *Rerum gestarum libri qui supersunt,* Book XV, ch. vii, 10; LCL, Vol. I, p. 164. The lapse in exile of Liberius is documented from his own letters by Hilary of Poitiers, *ex Opere Historica Fragmentum VI,* v-xi; PL, Vol. X, cols. 689–95. The story is also given by Sozomen, *Church History from A.D. 323 to 425;* Book IV, ch. xi; NPNF (2), Vol. II, pp. 306–7, and Theodoret, *Ecclesiastical History,* loc. cit., II, xiii-xiv; pp. 77–79.

38. Sulpicius Severus, *Chronicon,* II, xxxix; CSEL, Vol. I, p. 92.

39. The term "Catholic" was, of course, used by the Arians as a synonym for "orthodox" to describe their own doctine: "Et hoc catholicam esse, nemo ignorat, duas personas esse Patris et Filii, majorem Patrem, Filium subjectum cum omnibus his quae ipsi Pater subiecit." Text cited by Hilary of Poitiers, *De synodis,* ch. xi; in PL, Vol. X, col. 489.

40. Full text in Athanasius, *De synodis,* ch. xxxiii. NPNF (2), Vol. IV, p. 461.

Constantius had, of course, a vital interest in settling the dispute with only a partial victory for Arianism, in order to attain passable unity within the Church and empire. With this in mind, he cautioned the bishops at Ariminum: "His ita se habentibus, de fide atque unitate tractari debere cognoscat sinceritas vestra, et operam dare, ut ecclesiasticis rebus ordo competens praebeatur. Discurret namque cunctorum prosperitas ubique populorum, et concordia fida servabitur cum penitus amputatis nec huiusmodi questionibus cunctis sectando commoverit." Text of the imperial letter in Hilary, Ex op. *hist. Fragmentum* VII, i-ii, PL, Vol. X, cols. 695–96. In this spirit, too, the Arian bishops proposed to drop the terms concerning "substance" and "of-one-essence" as "nomina . . . , quae in divinis Scripturis non inveniuntur scripta." Their plea is modestly expressed: "Subveni, pie imperator, Dei summi cultoribus: subveni eis, qui per Christum Dei filium Deum patrem omnipotentem orant: subveni eis, qui judicio tuo offerunt aures, qui nesciunt colere nisi Deum patrem per Dominum nostrum Iesum Christum gloriae eius filium." Hilary gives their statement in "Epistolae missae ad Constantium Imperatorem a perfidis episcopis," Ibid., *Fragm. IX,* i-iii, PL, Vol. X, cols. 703–4.

41. Cited by Athanasius, *Historia Arianorum,* loc. cit., ch. iv, 33, p. 281.
42. Ibid., ch. iv, 34, pp. 281–82.
43. "Cordubensis Episcopi Epistola ad Constantium Augustum," PL, Vol. VIII, cols. 1328–32 (1329).
44. Athanasius, *Historia Arianorum,* loc. cit., 71–74; pp. 296–98. The *Historia Arianorum* was written between 358 and 360, Hilary's *Contra Constantium Imperatorem* in 360; passage noted, ch. xi; PL, Vol. X, col. 589.
45. *Historia Arianorum,* ch. vi, 45; loc. cit., pp. 286–87. Herod is also invoked for comparison with Constantius, and Darius is considered but rejected for the purpose as too warmhearted a king under analogous circumstances. Ibid.
46. *Contra Const.,* chs. vii-viii; PL, Vol. X, cols. 583–85.
47. Sozomen, *Church History,* loc. cit., V, x, pp. 333–34 and Gregory Nazianzen, "First Invective against Julian," 88–91 in *Julian the Emperor,* transl. and ed., C. W. King (London: George Bell and Sons, 1888), pp. 55–59.
48. Hilarius, *Contra Auxentium,* vii-viii and xiii-xiv; PL, Vol. X, cols. 613–15 and 617–18. Hilary was unable to convince the imperial authorities that when Auxentius said he believed "Christum ante omnia tempora natum Deum verum filium" he was really letting the "true" refer only to "son" rather than "God."
49. Ammianus Marcellinus, *op. cit.,* XXVII, iii, 11–15; LCL, Vol. III, pp. 18–20.
50. Socrates Scholasticus, *Church History,* loc. cit., IV, ii, pp. 96–97. Sozomen, op. cit., VI, vii-xii, pp. 350–53.
51. Socrates Scholasticus, op. cit., IV, xvi, p. 104. Sozomen, op. cit., VI, xiv, p. 354.
52. Ibid., VI, x-xi, p. 352.
53. Specifically he prohibited religious celibates from visiting the houses of widows and girls and made it illegal for clergymen to be named beneficiaries

in the wills of women whose confessions they heard or to receive any gifts of money from them. The wording is altogether insulting in places: "Ecclesiastici aut ex ecclesiasticis, vel qui continentium se volunt nomine nuncupari, viduarum ac pupillarum domos non adeant, sed publicis exterminentur iudiciis, si posthac eos affines earum vel propinqui putaverint deferendos. Censemus etiam, ut memorati nihil de eius mulieris, cui se privatim sub praetextu religionis adiunxerint, liberalitate quacunque vel extremo iudicio possint adipisci, et omne in tantum inefficax sit, quod alicui horum ab his fuerit derelictum, ut nec per subiectam personam valeant aliquid vel donatione vel testamento percipere." *Codex Theodosianus,* XVI, ii, 20. As Edward Gibbon notes with obvious approval, while Valentinian "remembered that he was the disciple of the church, he never forgot that he was the sovereign of the clergy." *Decline and Fall of the Roman Empire,* ed. J. B. Bury (London: Methuen, 1901) Vol. II, p. 23.

54. Socrates, op. cit., IV, xxii and xxiv, pp. 106 and 109. Sozomen, op. cit., VI, xx, pp. 357–58. The decree is in *Codex Theodosianus,* XII, i, 63 (dated 365).

55. Zosimus, *Historia nova,* IV, xxxvi, transl. James J. Buchanan and Harold T. Davis (San Antonio: Trinity University Press, 1967), p. 169.

56. On Valentinian's interference, see Hilary of Poitiers, *Contra Auxentium,* ch. vii; PL, Vol. X, cols. 613–14. That Valentinian tended to avoid interference in what he considered purely Church affairs whenever possible is supported by Sozomen, who cites Valentinian as replying to Bishop Hypatian of Heraclea, concerning the latter's request for permission to assemble a council to confirm something like consubstantiation against the Arians: " 'I am but one of the laity and have therefore no right to interfere in these transactions; let the priests to whom such matters appertain assemble where they please.' " Op. cit., VI, vii, p. 350.

57. "Epistola Romani Concilii sub Damaso habiti ad Gratianum et Valentinianum Imperatores," PL, Vol. XIII, cols. 575–83.

58. "Cunctos populos, quos clementiae nostrae regit temperamentum, in tali volumus religione versari, quam divinum Petrum apostolum tradidisse Romanis religio usque ad nunc ab ipso insinuata declarat, quamque pontificem Damasum sequi claret et Petrum Alexandriae episcopum, virum apostolicae sanctitatis; hoc est ut secundum apostolicam disciplinam evangelicamque doctrinam patris et filii et spiritus sancti unam deitatem sub parili maiestate et sub pia trinitate credamus. §1. Hanc legem sequentes Christianorum catholicorum nomen iubemus amplecti, reliquos vero dementes vesanosque iudicantes haeretici dogmatis infamiam sustinere, nec conciliabula eorum ecclesiarum nomen accipere, divina primum vindicta, post etiam motus nostri, quem ex coelesti arbitrio sumpserimus, ultione plectendos." *Codex Theodosianus,* XVI, ii, 2.

59. *Poemata,* II, i: "De vita sua," 1. 1335, PG, Vol. XXXVII, col. 1121.

60. Constantius had removed this famous altar before; Julian assumedly had restored it. Gratian's act in removing it again became the focal point of pagan denunciations two years later, which linked Rome's political and military

decline with official renunciation of the protection of the traditional Roman gods. Herbert Bloch, "The Pagan Revival in the West at the End of the Fourth Century," in *The Conflict between Paganism and Christianity in the Fourth Century,* ed. A. Momigliano (Oxford: Clarendon, 1963), pp. 193–218, reviews the extensive literature on the final pagan resistance.

61. "Qui divinae legis sanctitatem aut nesciendo confundunt aut neglegendo violant et offendunt, sacrilegium committunt." *Codex Iustinianus,* IX, xxix, 1; ed. Paul Krueger, as Vol. II of *Corpus Iuris Civilis* (Berlin: Weidmann, 1915), p. 385.

62. Sulpicius Severus, *Chronicon,* II; CSEL, Vol. I, p. 103, and *Dialogus* II, xi; CSEL, Vol. I, pp. 208–10. Saint Ambrose, *Epist.* XXIV, §12, PL, Vol. XVI, col. 1039.

63. Sozomen places the death-penalty edict after the confrontation with Ambrose at the cathedral. *Church History,* loc. cit., VII, xiii, p. 384. This seems unlikely to begin with, and is made even more so by Sozomen's general chronological confusion in moving the whole sequence of events back to 383, before the death of Gratian, while they make sense only in the context of Justina's subsequent regency.

64. Epistola XL, to Theodosius, December 388, viii-ix and xiv, PL, Vol. XVI, cols. 1104–6.

65. Epistola XLI, to Marcellina, Ambrose's sister, December 388, xxvii-xxviii, PL, Vol. XVI, col. 1120.

66. Evidently Constantine's sweeping decree which prohibited all curiales from entering the clergy (see above, note 12) had proved unenforceable, and Theodosius was attempting to separate the completely sincere aspirants to the clergy among them from those seeking to have the best of both worlds: ". . . si qui de curialibus ad ecclesiam confugissent, omni scirent patrimonio curiae esse cedendum." *Codex Theodosianus,* XII, i, 123, 1.

67. "Nulla nisi emensis sexaginta annis, cui votiva domi proles sit, secundum praeceptum apostoli ad diaconissarum consortium transferatur. . . . Ac si quando diem obierit, nullam ecclesiam, nullum clericum, nullum pauperem scribat heredes." Ibid., XVI, ii, 27. (dated June 21, 390).

68. "Quicunque sub professione monachi reperiuntur, deserta loca et vastas solicitudines sequi habitare iubeantur." Ibid., XVI, iii, 1 (dated Sept. 3, 390).

69. This is basically Gibbon's reconstruction, op. cit., ch. xxvii, from what he acknowledges to be a mixed bag of ancient sources, n. 58. They agree only on the essential points that the Thessalonians had given the emperor sore provocation in the murder of the garrison commander and that Theodosius was in some way responsible for the massacre.

70. Epistola LI, xiii, to Theodosius, written about September 8, 390; PL, Vol. XVI, col. 1163.

71. Accounts of this assumed confrontation seem to rest ultimately on the words of Paulinus, Ambrose's secretary, in his *Vita Sancti Ambrosii,* where he relates that when the bishop heard of the massacre, ". . . copiam imperatori ingrediendi ecclesiam denegavit: nec prius dignum iudicavit coetu Ecclesiae

vel sacramentum communione, quam publicam ageret poenitentiam." Ch. xxiv; PL, Vol. XIV, cols. 37–38. In this context, "denegavit" could refer to Saint Ambrose's statement to Theodosius in the letter cited above. In that letter, Ambrose goes on to tell Theodosius that he dreamed of seeing him come to the church and of then being unable to offer the sacraments (". . . ipsa nocte qua proficisci parabam, venisse quidem visus es ad Ecclesiam; sed mihi sacrificium offere non licuit. . . ."). A recent biography of Saint Ambrose dismisses the widely accepted account of the face-to-face confrontation at the church as altogether legendary: "Byzantine historians have described what Saint Ambrose had written in his letter to the emperor about his dream as if it actually occurred." Angelo Paredi, *Saint Ambrose; His Life and Times,* transl. M. Joseph Costelloe (South Bend, Ind.: University of Notre Dame Press, 1964), p. 390. This seems quite possible but not conclusive.

72. *De civitate Dei,* V, xxvi; LCL, Vol. II, p. 268. Augustine takes due note of the public penance of Theodosius following the Thessalonian massacre, but it is overshadowed by his account of the pious emperor's virtues and victories. Orosius heightens the drama in the miraculous triumphs of Theodosius against overwhelming odds and deletes the incident of the massacre and penance altogether. *Historiarum adversus paganos libri septem,* Book VII, xxxv–xxxvi; CSEL, Vol. V, pp. 525–32. Rufinus in his Latin continuation of Eusebius' *History of the Church* also suppresses the massacre and confrontation between the bishop and the emperor. He gives much the same account of Theodosius' miraculous victory over Eugenius as that of Augustine above. *Hist. Eccl.,* Book II, ch. xxxiii; PL, Vol XXI, col. 540.

73. Early in the fifth century, Gothic invasions of Italy became serious. The western emperor, Honorius, son of Theodosius I, decided in 402 to move the imperial residence from Milan in northern Italy to Ravenna, which could be more easily defended. By 404 Ravenna was generally looked on as the capital of the Roman Empire in the West.

74. *De civitate Dei,* V, ch. xxiii; LCL, Vol. II, pp. 256–58.

75. Ibid., IV, ch. iii; LCL, Vol. II, pp. 12–14.

76. Ibid., V, ch. xxiv; LCL, Vol. II, p. 262.

77. Ibid., V, xxv; LCL, Vol. II, p. 264. Augustine's enthusiasm for Constantine as a ruler is noticeably restrained, particularly in contrast with the panegyric tone of Eusebius. His treatment of Theodosius is considerably fuller and more sympathetic. Ibid., ch. xxvi; LCL, Vol. II, pp. 266–72.

78. Ibid., V, ch. xxv; LCL, Vol. II, p. 264.

79. Ibid., XIX, vi; LCL, Vol. VI, pp. 142–46.

80. ". . . nam pleraque non dando prosumus et noceremus, si dedissemus." *Epist.* CIV, ch. ii, 7; CSEL, Vol. XXXIV (2), p. 587; NPNF, 1st ser., Vol. I, p. 429. Cited by Herbert A. Deane, *The Political Thought of Saint Augustine* (New York: Columbia University Press, 1963), pp. 153, and 310, n. 125.

81. *Enarrationes in Psalmos,* CXXIV, 7; CCSL, Vol. XL, pp. 1841–42; NPNF, lst ser., Vol. VIII, pp. 602–3; cited in ibid., pp. 149 and 308, n. 112. Cf. Ambrose, "Sermo contra Auxentium de basilicis tradendis," PL, Vol. XVI,

col. 1018: "Quid enim honorificentius quam ut imperator Ecclesiae filius dicatur?"

82. There is a certain terminological problem here, in that the Latin "tyrannus" signified "usurper" as well as "tyrant." Augustine's context, however, makes it clear that even a benevolent "tyrannus" in the sense of "usurper" is not to be obeyed against a "tyrant" (in the English sense) who has become the constituted power in a kingdom. *De bono coniugali,* XIV, xvi; CSEL, Vol. XLI, p. 209; NPNF, Vol. III, 406; cited by Deane, op. cit., pp. 144 and 306, n. 94.

83. The whole story of this development is told in Deane's chapter, *"Church, State, and Heresy,"* in op. cit., pp. 172–220.

84. Luke 14, 15–24.

85. Augustine's use of the Nebuchadnezzar story from Daniel 3, 1–36, is an example of the early Christian art and science of finding "prefigurations" of later history, easily convertible into imperatives, in the Old Testament. The change in Nebuchadnezzar is taken here to prefigure the change in the institution of the Roman emperor from an instrument to persecute Christians into an instrument of coercion to be used by Christians. Epist. XCIII, iii, 9; CSEL, Vol. XXXIV, 2, pp. 453–54.

86. ". . . decedentibus succedentibus mortalibus . . . protendatur." *De Civ. Dei,* IV, v; LCL, Vol. II, p. 20.

87. Ibid., IV, iv; LCL, Vol. II, p. 16. The anecdote was probably taken from Cicero's *De re publica,* III, xiv, a work which Augustine elsewhere cites by name.

88. See passages cited by Deane, op. cit., pp. 146–49. Deane refers to "a foreshadowing of the later Gelasian doctrine of the Two Swords" in Augustine's assigning of temporal affairs, as concerns of the body, to one power, and matters touching upon salvation, as concerns of the soul, to another. As will be shown below, Gelasius tightened up existing theory without much innovation of his own. His presentation of the two elements in the ruling process, spiritual and temporal, differs from Augustine's in explicitly subordinating the emperor's sphere to the Church, which both Ambrose and Augustine had done at least implicitly, and by emphasizing papal supremacy in the Church's sphere, which Pope Leo had done in the meantime.

89. This is in spite of his occasional use of the appositional phrase, "hoc est ecclesia," after *civitas Dei.* That this is not the church seen on earth with its elect and damned nominal members alike is made quite clear: "There are those who are connected with the City of God, as long as she is a pilgrim in this world, by the bond of the sacraments, but who will not be with her to share the rewards of the blessed in eternity." *De civ. Dei,* I, xxxv; LCL, Vol. I, p. 136.

90. Letter 162, i, to Emperor Leo, written in 458; NPNF (2), Vol. XII, p. 104. Pope Leo's Letter 156, also to Emperor Leo, written in 457, contains the statement, ". . . the universal Church has become a rock (petra), through the building up of that original Rock," ii. In ibid., p. 100.

91. "Non enim respublica in ecclesia, sed ecclesia in republica est, id est in imperio." *De schismate Donatistarum,* III, iii; CSEL, Vol. XXVI, p. 74.

92. "Imperator enim intra Ecclesiam, non supra Ecclesiam est." "Sermo contra Auxentium de basilicis tradendis," ch. xxxvi; PL, Vol. XVI, col. 1018.

93. Leo I, Letters 27 and 28 to Flavian; NPNF (2), Vol. XII, pp. 38–43. The latter, which was to remain a cardinal document of Roman orthodoxy in combating heresies concerning the nature of Christ, is often called the "Tome of Leo."

94. Leo's own letters of protest and entreaty to Theodosius II and Pulcheria are his nos. 43–45 and 59–70. The texts of the western imperial letters, including one from Eudoxia, Valentinian's wife, are in the collection of Leo's letters as nos. 55–58, while Theodosius' answers to them are nos. 62–64. The most important texts are in ibid., pp. 52–58 and 63–64.

95. Theodoret, Letter 123; NPNF (2), Vol. III, pp. 293–95.

96. Letter 138; ibid., pp. 307–9; passage cited, p. 307.

97. Walter Ullmann, *The Growth of Papal Government in the Middle Ages,* 2nd ed. (London: Methuen and Co., 1962), p. 10, n. 1.

98. The Council of Chalcedon officially requested Leo's assent to having Constantinople rank second to Rome. But since the degree of independence requested "to provide for the good government" of the cities of the East was sufficient to make the authority of Constantinople responsible for directing nearly half the Church, the request was substantially one for equal standing with Rome. Letter from the council is in collection of Leo's letters as no. 98; loc. cit., pp. 72–73.

99. PL, Vol. XX, col. 778, cited by Ullmann, op. cit., p. 7.

100. "Cum ergo cohortationes nostras auribus vestrae sanctitatis adhibemus, ipsum sanctrum Petrum vobis cuius vice fungimur, loqui credite. . . ." Sermo III, ix; PL, Vol. LIV, col. 147.

101. Valentinian III and his mother, Galla Placidia, who really ruled the West until her death in 450, were generally obliging enough to Leo, who simply availed himself of an imperial decree when he thought it necessary. For example, in order to have the Manichaean sect suppressed, he obtained an edict from Valentinian. Text in Leo's Epist. VIII; PL, Vol. LIV, cols. 622–23; not in NPNF collection. The following year he countered the attempt of Hilary of Arles to extend the primacy of his diocese over southern Gaul with another imperial rescript. It is significant, however, that Valentinian hedged on acknowledging the *principatus* of the Roman See. Ullmann, op. cit., pp. 9–10.

102. Prosper of Aquitaine, *Chronicon;* PL, Vol. LI, cols, 603–6. Idatius, *Chronicon,* Vol. LI, cols. 877–80.

103. "Sanctae memoriae quoque papa Hilarus Anthemium imperatorem, quum Philotheus Macedonianus eius familiaritate suffultus diversarum conciliabula nova sectarum in Urbem vallet inducere, apud beatum Petrum apostolum palam, ne id fieret, clara voce constrinxit in tantum, ut non ea facienda cum interpositione sacramenti idem promitteret imperator." Gelasius I, Epistola XXVI, xi; *Epistolae Romanorum Pontificum . . . a S. Hilaro usque ad*

Pelagium II, ed. A. Thiel (Brunsbergae: Peter, 1868), p. 408. (Collection cited hereinafter as "Thiel.")

104. It was, to be sure, ostensibly based on the decrees of other councils. Text given by Liberatus, *Breviarum causae Nestorianorum et Eutychianorum,* ch. xvii; PL, Vol. LXVIII, cols. 1023–24.

105. He is Felix II or III, depending on whether or not the Felix who replaced Liberius for a time and subsequently shared the title of Bishop of Rome with him is counted.

106. Epist. XII, ii; in Thiel, pp. 350–51.

107. ". . . ut et Christiani imperatores pro aeterna vita pontificibus indigerent, et pontifices pro temporalium cursu rerum imperialibus dispositionibus uterentur." *Tractatus* IV, xi; Thiel, p. 568.

108. "Fuerint haec ante adventum Christi, ut quidam figuraliter, adhuc tamen in carnalibus actionibus constituti, pariter reges exsisterent et pariter sacerdotes, quod sanctum Melchisedech fuisse sacra prodit historia. Quod in suis quoque diabolus imitatus est, utpote qui semper quae divino cultui convenirent sibimet tyrannico spiritu vindicare contendit, ut pagani imperatores iidem et maximi pontifices dicerentur. Sed quum ad verum ventum est eundem regem atque pontificem, ultra sibi nec imperator pontificis nomen imposuit, nec pontifex regale fastigium vindicavit: . . . quoniam Christus memor fragilitas humanae, quod suorum saluti congrueret, dispensatione magnifica temperavit, sic actionibus propriis dignitatibusque distinctis officia potestates utriusque discrevit, suos volens medicinali humilitate salvari, non humana superbia rursus intercipi. . . ." Ibid., pp. 567–68.

109. Ullmann, op. cit., p. 24, no. 1.

110. Epistola XII, ii; Thiel, op. cit., p. 351.

111. *The Republic,* IV, 434d–445a; VI, 484a–487a, and 497a–502c.

112. Titus Livy, *Ab urbe condita,* II, xxxii; LCL, Vol. I, p. 324.

113. ". . . una monstraretur compago corporis Christi, quae ad unum caput gloriossima dilectionis societate concurret. . . ." Epistola XIV; PL, Vol. LIX, col. 89.

114. "Sed adhuc apostolicam sedem, sibi medicinalia suggerentem, superbam vocare arrogantemque contendunt." Epist. VIII, ibid., col. 46. The fact that dissident men may oppose the administration of papal medicine to the body of Christendom simply heightens the analogy: "Sic phrenetici solent medicantes quosque vel ut hostes putare vel caedere." Epist. IV, ibid., col. 30. Notice also the medical allusion in the quotation from *Tractatus* IV, xi, note 108 above.

115. *Contra Auxentium,* ch. vii; PL, Vol. X, col. 613.

CHAPTER 3 NOTES

1. In the later Roman Empire and the early Middle Ages, an agricultural worker was commonly called a *colonus*: he was often tied to the land but had certain

attributes of a free man: availability for army service, the right to marry a free citizen, and other family and inheritance rights. In practice, however, it was sometimes hard to distinguish his lot from a slave's: a law of Constantine permitted the chaining up of a *colonus* suspected of wanting to run away, and in the early fifth century, large numbers of *coloni* became ineligible for military service. Legal and factual gradations are discussed in detail by A. H. M. Jones, *The Later Roman Empire, 284–602* (Norman: University of Oklahoma Press, 1964) Vol. II, pp. 793–808.

2. J. M. Wallace-Hadrill, *The Long-Haired Kings and Other Studies in Frankish Kingship* (London: Methuen and Co., 1962), p. 155.

3. J. M. Wallace-Hadrill, *Early Germanic Kingship in England and on the Continent* (Oxford: Clarendon Press, 1971), pp. 7–8.

4. Reinhard Wenskus notes that none of the tribal groups who can be shown to have been without kings in Roman times lasted through the period of the great migrations without at least an interruption of their traditional tribal existence. *Stammesbildung und Verfassung* (Köln: Böhlau, 1961), p. 66. Herwig Wolfram suggests an intermediate position: that the later achievements of the nonroyal principalities — such as the founding of the monastery of Cluny by William the Pious, duke of Aquitaine, or the development of Flanders into the cradle of modern industry and commerce — remain considerable and "unjustly overlooked by a king-centered historiography," but that it was left for the *regna* ruled by kings alone to progress for better or worse to the "centralized and unifying Leviathan — the modern state." "The Shaping of the Early Medieval Principality," *Viator,* Vol. II (1971), pp. 50–51.

5. Suicide was officially claimed at the time. Earlier modern historians, such as Theodore Godefroy and Gibbon, were sure of Arbogast's guilt, but contemporary judgment does not rule out either suicide or murder. Erich Zöllner, *Geschichte der Franken bis zur Mitte des sechsten Jahrhunderts* (München: Beck, 1970), p. 23.

6. Gregory of Tours, *Historiarum Libri Decem,* Book II, ch. ix; WBG, Vol. I, pp. 82–86.

7. Herwig Wolfram, "The Shaping of the Early Medieval Kingdom," *Viator,* Vol. I (1970), p. 1.

8. Cited by Heinrich Fichtenau, *The Carolingian Imperium,* transl. Peter Munz (Oxford: Basil Blackwell, 1957), p. 1.

9. Gregory of Tours has the eastern emperor, Anastasius, make Clovis a consul. Op. cit., II, xxxviii; Vol. I, p. 134. The evidence is, however, that the office was that of *patricius,* the higher one in the context of the times, as well as that of consul. Wolfram, ". . . Early Medieval Kingdom," loc. cit., p. 13. On the *patricius* title, see note 21.

10. Procopius, *History of the Wars,* Book V, ch. xii, 17–19; transl. H. B. Dewing, LCL, Vol. III, p. 123. The validity of this often-cited passage has seemed at least partly questionable to some historians from Gibbon to Ferdinand Lot. It is defended, however, by Bernard S. Bachrach, "Procopius and the Chronology of Clovis's Reign," *Viator,* Vol. I (1970), pp. 22–26. Manfred

Silber notes that Procopius was on the scene in Italy himself and in a position to have seen the Frankish-Armorican army. *The Gallic Royalty of the Merovingians in Its Relationship to the Orbis Terrarum Romanus During the 5th and 6th Centuries A.D.* (Bern and Frankfurt: Herbert Lang & Cie AG, 1971), pp. 68–69.

11. This is one of the main theses advanced by Silber (ibid.), for which he gives evidence throughout his whole book.

12. It is more or less customary in the English-speaking world to see the Germanic Empire of the Middle Ages as an attempt to revive the tradition of the Roman Empire, an attempt which logically presupposes recognition of the fact that the old Roman Empire was defunct before being revived. This, however, was not the medieval way of looking at it. In the twelfth century, the scholarly Otto of Freising was fully aware that Rome fell to the barbarians under Odoakar in 476 (*Chronica sive historia de duabus civitatibus,* Book IV, chs, xxx-xxxi; WGB, pp. 364–66), but this fact fades into insignificance beside his finding that since the time of Theodosius I there has been only one secular state worth writing about: "Unde in sequentibus libellis non solum Romanozum augustis, sed et alis nobilium regnorum regibus Christianis factis, cum in omnem terram et in fines orbis terrae exieret sonus verbi Dei . . . ceptam hystoriam prosequamur." Ibid., V, Prol.; p. 374. Even the Christian states were not worth regarding in isolation from the Heavenly City, although they did form a dominant unity from the end of the fourth century on: "regnis nobilioribus a nostris possessis"; the states outside their orbit were to have a corresponding nonidentity and nonhistory: "illis iam non solum ad Deum, sed et ad seculum ignobilibus, vix aliqua ab eis gesta stilo digna vel posteris commendanda inveniuntur." Ibid., Henry IV can appear "in regnum succedentes" as the ninety-first ruler since Augustus Caesar (ibid., VI, xxxiv; p. 488), as if the fall of Rome and the Byzantine control of the empire before Charlemagne were of no particular weight in identifying successive rulers of the one state. *The Book of Emperors,* an analogous twelfth-century work dealing with the Roman and Germanic empires, but written for popular consumption rather than for scholars, stresses a break in continuity only between the Greek (Byzantine) Empire and the Carolingian one (ll.14,277–14,281). It lets control of the *rîche* pass earlier from Roman to Greek control with considerable ill feeling between Greeks and Romans but no hint of a fall of Rome (11.13,650–13,671; 13,821–13,834). *Kaiserchronik,* ed. E. Schröder; MGH, 1892, photogr. repr. (Zürich: Weidmann, 1969), pp. 328–29, 331, and 339.

13. Jordanes, *The Gothic History,* transl. and ed., Charles C. Mierow, 1915 (repr. New York: Barnes and Noble, 1960), 116, p. 84, and 129–30, p. 87. J. B. Bury, *The Invasion of Europe by the Barbarians,* 1928 (repr. New York: Russell and Russell, 1963), p. 44. The Roman historian, Ammianus Marcellinus, describes Hermaneric as a "bellicosimus rex," who resisted the Huns with great fortitude but committed suicide when the Gothic cause appeared

hopeless against them. *Rerum gestarum libri qui supersunt,* Book XXXI, ch. iii; LCL, Vol. III, p. 396.

14. Dietrich Claude, *Adel, Kirche und Königtum im Westgotenreich,* series *Vorträge und Forschungen,* ed. Konstanzer Arbeitskreis für mittelalterliche Geschichte, Sonderband VIII, (Sigmaringen: Jan Thorbecke Verlag, 1971), p. 11. On the other hand, the same author gives a basically positive review of the philological evidence that the Ostrogoths and Visigoths called themselves by separate names as early as the reign of Emperor Claudius (268–70): *Geschichte der Westgoten* (Stuttgart: W. Kohlhammer, 1970), p. 7.

15. Ibid., p. 15. The topic is pursued at length in Herwig Wolfram, "Athanaric the Visigoth: monarchy or judgeship? A Study in comparative history," transl. Henry A. Myers, *Journal of Medieval History,* Vol. I (1975), pp. 259–78.

16. Ammianus, who refers to Frithigern many times, calls him "rex" only once, in recounting how he dispatched a Christian priest to negotiate for him: this "Christiani ritus presbyter . . . a Fritigerne legatus. . . ." is the "idem Christianus, ut conscius arcanorum et fidus, secretas alias eiusdem regis obtulerit." Op. cit., XXXI, xii, 8–9, pp. 464–65.

17. Claude, *Adel, Kirche and Königtum,* loc. cit., p. 18. His reasoning is that since Ulfilas's Gothic translation of the Bible uses "kuni" twice for the individual tribes of the Hebrews, it is likely that the Goths called their own individual tribal units by the same name; further, that the representative or personifier of such a unit would possibly have been called by a derivative of the same word, which would then have been a cognate of "cyning" (king).

18. Walter Schlesinger gives Alaric as the prime example of a warrior king (Heerkönig) of the migration period who used his victories to attain full royal dignity (Königswürde) for himself. "Über germanisches Königtum," *Königtum,* p. 138. The specific evidence that Alaric himself was called a "thiudans" is a little thin. It is known that some Visigoths thought of Roman emperors as kings from a gold medallion of Gothic origin featuring Valens and Valentinian with the inscription REGIS (sic) ROMANORUM. Herwig Wolfram, *Intitulatio I. Lateinische Königs- und Fürstentitel bis zum Ende des 8. Jahrhunderts, MIÖG, Ergänzungsband* XXI (1967), pp. 36–38. A Visigothic calendar refers to an Emperor Constantius as "Kustanteinus Thiudanis." W. Streitberg, *Die gothische Bibel,* repr. 1960, p. 472. Cited by Claude, op. cit., p. 28. Actually, the second of these items must stem not only from after Alaric's death but from after Athaulf's as well, if Constantius III, who ruled for seven months in 421, is meant; Constantius II, on the other hand, died in 361, too early for any Gothic reference to him to reflect distinctly Visigothic usage. Still, the duration of Alaric's rule over the Visigothic nation during periods of relative peace as well as war certainly make it likely that he was thought of as *thiudans* as well as *reiks.*

19. Normally, the post of "magister militum," literally "Master of the Soldiers," the rank which Stilicho held under Theodosius, which Alaric was to hold and

which Theoderic the Great was later either to hold or to refuse to allow anyone else to hold, was the highest strictly military designation, although persons holding that office did not necessarily confine themselves to military affairs. A. H. M. Jones, *The Later Roman Empire, 284–602* (Norman: University of Oklahoma Press, 1964), Vol. I, pp. 183, 247, and 256.

20. *Adversum paganos,* Book VII, ch. xliii; CSEL, Vol. V, pp. 560–61. The marriage of Galla Placidia and Athaulf was obviously a special step for the Visigothic king from the outset in view of the fact that mixed marriages were officially forbidden until the sixth century. Claude, *Geschichte der Westgoten,* loc. cit., pp. 22 and 70.

21. "Constantius was the first to be called 'patricius et magister peditum praesentalis.' This position allowed interference in civil affairs, although Constantius was primarily a military officer. Until then, 'patrician,' meaning 'father of the emperor,' was a title usually given to top civil officials. Now things had completely changed: a new superoffice came into being, which semiofficial sources called 'patriciate of the West,' and this was the antecedent and prelude to the Italian kingdoms and the Exarchate of Ravenna directly and to the Gallic kingdoms indirectly." Wolfram, ". . . Early Medieval Kingdom," loc. cit., p. 12. Cf. Jones, op. cit., Vol. I, p. 176.

22. From 425 to about 435 or 440 (the fact that no clear terminal date is recognized is significant in itself), she was regent for her son; from then until her death in 450 her influence was often decisive. (Notice that Pope Leo thought it advisable to get her backing, along with Valentinian III's and Eudoxia's, to undo the *Latrocinium Ephesium.*) On Placidia's regency, see M. Assunta Nagl, *Galla Placidia. Studien zur Geschichte und Kultur des Altertums,* Vol. II, 3, 1908 (repr. N.Y.: Johnson Repr. Corp., 1967), pp. 37–46, and Stewart I. Oost, *Galla Placidia Augusta* (Chicago: University of Chicago Press, 1968), pp. 203–9).

23. When Odoakar effectively took power in 476, he did so by deposing Romulus Augustulus as emperor; however, the young Augustulus was a figurehead put up by his father, the usurper Orestes, whom Odoakar killed. The lawful western emperor was Julius Nepos, who had fled to Dalmatia. Odoakar got the Roman Senate to ask Emperor Zeno in the East to let Odoakar administer Italian affairs and have the title of "Patrician." Zeno replied to the effect that he would be willing to confer upon him the title of "patricius," if Nepos had not already done so. The death of Nepos, who had been appointed by Emperor Leo and who sought help from Zeno to be reinstalled in Italy, made things considerably less complex for both Zeno and Odoakar.

24. Herwig Wolfram, *Intitulatio I. Lateinische Königs- und Fürstentitel bis zum Ende des 8. Jahrhunderts.* MIÖG, Ergänzungsband XXI, 1967, p. 59.

25. Ibid., pp. 57–58.

26. Ibid., p. 59.

27. Otto Höfler, "Der Sakralcharakter des germanischen Königtums," in *Königtum,* pp. 85–87.

28. William A. Chaney, *The Cult of Kingship in Anglo-Saxon England* (Berkeley

and Los Angeles: University of California Press, 1970), passim, but esp. ch. I, "The Woden-sprung kings: Germanic sacral kingship and divine descent," pp. 7–42.

29. Jordanes, op. cit., ch. lii, 269, p. 128.

30. Procopius, op. cit., Book V, ch. i, 28–29; LCL, Vol. III, p. 13. When German troops were quartered in Italy, about a third of the property in land was transferred to their control. From the ranks of these military settlers, economically independent landlords of a sort who would be seen as nobility at a later date were emerging, and the Goths, who had not had any such opportunities on the Balkan peninsula, were most eager to claim a share of what previous German settlers had received in land.

31. On the independence left the Roman Senate by Theoderic, Procopius records a speech by King Totila near the end of the Ostrogothic Kingdom in Italy. Ibid., VII, xxi, 12; LCL, IV, 339. On the exactions of Roman officials under Theoderic and other Germanic kings who used them: Jones, op. cit., Vol. I, p. 248.

32. This is the construction which must be placed on Procopius' record of a statement by Gothic emissaries to Justinian's general, Belisarius: " 'We have preserved both the laws and the form of government as strictly as any who have been Roman emperors, and there is absolutely no law, either written or unwritten, introduced by Theoderic or by any of his successors on the throne of the Goths.' " Op. cit., VI, vi, 17; LCL, III, p. 341.

33. Jones, op. cit., Vol. I, pp. 254 and 265; Vol. II, p. 1,118, n. 43.

34. Procopius, op. cit., V, i, 27–29; LCL, III, 11–12.

35. The first of these is from the anonymous *Excerpta Valesiana.* Their latter part contains a chronicle of Theoderic's reign compiled about 550. Having made their way through the Middle Ages in a single copy attached to the works of Ammianus Marcellinus, they are still published that way. "Tantae enim disciplinae fuit, ut, si quis voluit in agro suo argentum vel aurum dimittere, ac si intra muros civitatis esset ita existimaretur." Ch. xii, 72; LCL (Ammianus), Vol. III, p. 544. The second is from the *Vita S. Caesarii,* cited by Edward Gibbon, *The Decline and Fall of the Roman Empire* (1776–1788), ed. J. B. Bury, Vol. IV, p. 193, n. 87.

36. "Sic enim oblectavit vicinas gentes, ut se illi sub foedus darent aliae gentes, sibi eum regem sperantes." *Excerpta Vales.,* xii, 72, p. 552.

37. Ibid., xii, 70, p. 552. The names are given from this source with a few emendations.

38. Wenskus, op. cit., pp. 31–32.

39. Even in Spain the results were mixed, in spite of the fact that there was a greater feeling of real kinship between the houses joined by the marriage of Theoderic's daughter, Thiudigotho, to the Visigothic king than existed in the other instances. When Alaric II was killed and left a son, Amalric, too young to rule, it is true that Theoderic, as the boy's grandfather, became regent, and the Visigoths did well under his protection from 511 to 526; however, there is some evidence that Theudis, Theoderic's trusted commander in Spain, insti-

gated Amalric's death in 531. With that, the Visigothic dynasty with its royal Ostrogothic connections became extinct, and Theudis became king of the Visigoths himself until 548. E. A. Thompson, *The Goths in Spain* (Oxford: Clarendon Press, 1969), pp. 7–13.

40. Wolfram, *Intitulatio,* loc. cit., p. 56, n. 5, and pp. 60–61.

41. Op. cit. lvii, p. 134. Procopius notes that before coming to Italy, Theoderic was a "man of patrician rank and had attained the consular office in Byzantium." Op. cit., V, i, 9–10; LCL, Vol. III, p. 5.

42. Op. cit., lvii, p. 136.

43. *Excerpta Valesiana,* 59. loc. cit., ch. xii, 59, p. 544. Cf. Jones, op. cit., Vol. I, p. 247.

44. Ostrogoths after Theoderic seem to have regarded his title of *patricius* as legitimization of their subsequent kings' rights in Italy. Procopius, op. cit., VI, vi, 16; LCL, III, p. 341. Theoderic had unquestionably been given the *magister militum* rank by Zeno. The fact that the title drops from view in the West until Amalaswintha, Theoderic's daughter and regent for her young son after Theoderic's death, appointed men of equivalent rank can be taken to mean that Theoderic quietly reserved it for himself during his lifetime. Bury, op. cit., pp. 191–92.

45. Jordanes, op. cit., pp. 129–32.

46. Cassiodorus, *Variae Epistolae* (letters written in the name of Theoderic and his successors), Book I, no. xl, and V, xxiii, MGH, AA, pp. 36–37 and 157. Also Gibbon, op. cit., Vol. IV, ch. xxxix, pp. 182–83.

47. Cassiodorus, *Var. Epist.,* IV, xvii, pp. 153–54, and Bury, op cit., pp. 184–85.

48. *Excerpta Valesiana,* loc. cit., ch. xiii, 79, pp. 556–58. It is not clear whether the key phrase, "quattuor litteras," is followed by "legi" or "regis." The first would imply a stencil, LEGI, for "I have read it" the second, four letters abbreviating the king's name. Modern editors seem to agree that this would have been in Greek: ΘΕΟΔ.

49. Procopius, op. cit., V, ii, 14–15; LCL, Vol. III, p. 19.

50. "Habebit felix Thoringia quod nutrivit Italia, litteris doctam, moribus eruditam, decoram non solum genere, quantum et feminea dignitate, ut non minus patria vestra istius splendeat moribus quam suis triumphis." Cassiodorus, *Var. Epist.,* IV, i. p. 114.

51. King Theoderic was evidently articulating a Gothic prejudice in his disdain of classical schools for boys. When Amalaswintha attempted to have her son Atalaric given an elementary literary education, she set off a considerable reaction among some of her powerful subjects, who found this unfitting for a future king of the Goths: "And they asked her to reflect that her father Theoderic before he died had become master of all this territory and had invested himself with a kingdom which was his by no sort of right, although he had not so much as heard of letters." Procopius, op. cit., V, ii, 15–17.

52. Jordanes used the work of Cassiodorus for his own shorter history of the Goths, who in turn drew on the work of Ablavius, a Roman who seems to have lived under Visigothic rule in Gaul in the fifth century. Cassiodorus'

collection of letters, which survives in twelve books, is still one of the major sources for the history of the period. After retiring around 550, when the Ostrogothic kingdom was on its last legs, he spent several decades devising the trivium and quadrivium, on which the whole medieval system of higher education was ultimately based.

53. ". . . etiam a Romanis Traianus vel Valentinianus, quorum tempora sectatus est, appellaretur. . . ." *Excerpta Valesiana,* loc. cit., ch. xii, 60, p. 544.

54. Op. cit., IV, xxxix, p. 188.

55. There is a particularly intriguing contrast between the two rulers in the way Theoderic commanded the Roman inhabitants of Ravenna to rebuild synagogues burned by them. *Exc. Val.,* loc. cit, ch. xiv, 82, pp. 558–60.

56. It is not known exactly what this entailed. The phrasing, "ut reconciliatos in catholica restituat religione," sounds as if he wanted nothing more than reacceptance by the Catholic Church of those who had turned to Arianism but who wished to go back to their original faith. Whatever it was, it upset John greatly. Ibid., ch. xv, 88–89, pp. 562–64.

57. "Revertens Iohannes papa . . . , quen Theodericus cum dolo suscepit et in offensa sua eum esse iubet." Ibid., ch. xv, 93, p. 566.

58. "Se autem vivo fecit sibi monimentum ex lapide quadrato, mirae magnitudinis opus, et saxum ingens quod superponeret inquisivit." Ibid.,ch. xvi, 96, p. 568.

59. *Gesta Theoderici regis,* anonymous, ed. Bruno Krusch, MGH, *Scriptores rerum Merovingicarum,* Vol. II, §19, pp. 209–10. The ultimate source of the dialogue is Pope Gregory I in his *Dialogus* IV, 30, *De morte Theoderici regis Ariani,* PL, Vol. LXXVII, cols. 368–69.

60. The scholarly Otto of Freising and the popular *Book of Emperors,* see above, n.12, attest to the interest in King Theoderic's end six centuries later. Otto notes the passage cited from Pope Gregory's dialogue and observes: "Hinc puto fabulam illam traductam, qua vulgo dicitur Theodoricus equo sedens ad inferos descendisse." *Chron.,* V, iii; WBG, p. 380. The *Book of Emperors* had devils seize him alive at the command of Pope John and carry him off to the Volcano Island in the Liparis. L1. 14,164–14,175, p. 337. Present oral tradition in Ravenna puts it differently, but the moral of the story is the same: "It is said among the people that the crack was caused when lightning struck the [mausoleum], on the very day when Theoderic, whose death by lightning had been foretold to him, had taken refuge there during a terrible storm. But in spite of this the lightning, cleaving its way through the mighty stone, struck the Arian King and reduced his body to ashes." Giuseppe Bovini, *Ravenna: An Art City* (Ravenna: A. Longo, 1966), p. 130.

61. Jordanes, op. cit., ch. lvii, p. 136.

62. Ibid., lix, p. 139.

63. Wenskus, op. cit., p. 67.

64. ". . . . . provincia missos
expellet citius fasces quam Francia reges,
quos dederis. acie nec iam pulsare rebelles,

> sed vinculis punire licet; sub iudice nostro
> regia Romanus disquirit crimina carcer:
> Marcomeres Sunnoque docet; quorum alter Etruscum
> pertulit exilium; cum se promitteret alter
> exulis ultorem, iacuit mucrone suorum:
> res avidi concire novas odioque furentes
> pacis et ingenio scelerumque cupidine fratres."
> *De Consulatu Stilichonis,* I, 232–45; LCL. Vol. I, p. 380.

65. Sulpicius Alexander's history is lost, but Gregory of Tours incorporated chunks verbatim from his Roman history into his own *Historiarum libri decem;* WBG, Vol. I. The former's terms, "regales" and "subregolus" appear in the latter's Book II, ch. ix, p. 84.

66. Attempts to go beyond this fact have produced much acrimonious discussion and little agreement on interpretations. Jean Hoyoux cites an abundance of sources to show that long hair also distinguished the free Franks from unfree persons. "Reges criniti: chevelures, tonsures et scalps chez les Mérovingiens," *Revue Belge de philologie et d'histoire,* Vol. XXVI (1948), pp. 480–89. The explanation he cites (p. 484), which brings these facts together with the fewest contradictions, is one from A. Marignan, *Études sur la civilisation française,* Vol. I: *La société mérovingienne* (Paris, 1899), p. 134, according to which kings wore their hair shoulder length, while the nobility wore theirs at about what we would call page-boy length. Hoyoux's own thesis is that the length of hair distinguishing the king from the nobility and other free men was insignificant but that since a king had to have long hair, deposed kings or members of the royal house who were feared as possible rivals were subjected to a mild form of scalping; pp. 496–508. None of his significant examples, however, withstands the attack on them all and singly by Ekkehard Kaufmann, "Über das Scheren abgesetzter Merovingerkönige," *Zeitschrift der Savigny-Stiftung für Rechtsgeschichte,* Germ. Abt., Vol. LXXII (1955), pp. 177–85.

67. Gregory of Tours, op. cit. III, xviii, p. 172. There is every reason to assume that the Merovingians attributed some sort of magic power to their kings' long hair. Marc Bloch seems to have been the first to draw the parallel with the biblical Samson. *Les rois thaumaturges: Étude sur le caractère surnaturel attribué a la puissance royale.* . . . (Strasbourg: Librairie Istra, 1924), p. 61. In another connection, Rudolf Buchner notes that only one Merovingian child is recorded (Gregory of Tours, V, xxii, p. 330) to have been baptized with a non-Germanic name. He was weak and sickly, and his parents gave him a biblical name in the expectation that he would soon die, which he did. The name chosen was Samson. "Das merovingische Königtum," in *Königtum,* p. 147.

68. Gregory of Tours, op. cit., II, xli, p. 136.

69. The term "Salian" has been variously derived from "living near the salt-water sea," on the basis of the Latin stem "sal," and from the Saale River in Thuringia. Recent research, however, accepts neither etymology as convincing, and the habitation of the Franks before moving towards Belgium remains as

unknown as before. Erich Zöllner, *Geschichte der Franken* (München: C. H. Beck, 1970), p. 36.

70. Gregory of Tours, op. cit., II, ix, p. 90. Zöllner leaves open the possibility that the Frankish capture of Cambrai and Gaul as far as the Somme may have taken place as late as 454, after the death of Aetius, who commanded Roman and allied forces against Attila. Op. cit., p. 36. It is impossible for this to be attributed to Clodio that late and for some of the Salian Franks to have been led against the Huns by his successor Merovech, whose reign has previously been dated on the basis of scant evidence as 448 to 458. Marcomer, Sunno, Clodio, and Merovech can be shown to have been real historical personages; however, there is a great deal of conjecture in any attempts to tie down closely any Frankish kings before Childeric in chronological sequence or to relate them to each other.

71. Wallace-Hadrill, *Long-Haired Kings,* op. cit., p. 162.

72. Zöllner, op. cit., pp. 123–24, and P. E. Schramm, *Herrschaftszeichen und Staatssymbolik;* series: *Schriften der MGH,* 13, Vol. I (1954), p. 157. Gregory of Tours affirms the spear as the symbol of rule, when he records how his own contemporary, King Gunthramn, bestowed it on Childebert II in 585 as his heir with the words: " 'Hoc est indicium, quod tibi omne regnum meum tradedi.' " VII, xxxiii, p. 134.

73. Ibid., II, xii; Vol. I, p. 94.

74. Cf. Matthew 1:25.

75. Wallace-Hadrill raises the possibility, supported by material contained in a popular epic, that Childeric received support from the eastern emperor against the western Roman general who led the Franks in his absence. *Long-Haired Kings,* loc. cit., pp. 160–62 and *Early Germanic Kingship,* loc. cit., pp. 18–19.

76. Euric's successor as king of the Visigoths, Alaric II, was much less capable and feared than Euric had been. Zöllner, op. cit., p. 46.

77. Gregory of Tours, op. cit., Prologue to Book V; Vol. I, pp. 276–78.

78. Gregory uses the term "bipennis," the highly polished double-edged Roman ax, to denote this traditional Frankish weapon, but, as Professor Zöllner has pointed out in his lectures at the University of Vienna, the actual excavation of Frankish artifacts has shown these axes to resemble the weapons of American Indians considerably more than those of the Romans.

79. Gregory of Tours; op. cit. II, xxvii; Vol. I, pp. 110–12.

80. Queen Chrodechilde lived as a widow in Tours from 511 to 548. Zöllner, pp. 60 and 62. Thus Gregory had an opportunity to pick up his account of her husband's conversion and baptism from sources which had been close to her.

81. Gregory does not mention how their king died, only that his soldiers saw him dead. This has suggested the interpretation that it was their king's death which caused the Alamanni to flee in the first place, i.e., that Gregory somehow absorbed the fact that the tribe's loss of its political identity and independence upon the death of its king was the cause of its defeat, but also retained without any feeling of contradiction the traditional story of how the warriors turned

in flight as the result of Clovis's prayer and pledge. Vilhelm Grønbech, *Kultur und Religion der Germanen,* transl. Ellen Hoffmeyer; ed. and intr. O. Höfler, 6th ed. (Darmstadt: WBG, 1961), Vol. I, p. 137.

82. Popular imagination in the Middle Ages was capable of portraying Constantine's conversion of his mother in full and dramatic versions, e.g., that of the twelfth-century *Book of Emperors,* 11. 8,200–305 and 10,373–380, pp. 232–34 and 272. For the nucleus of historic fact behind this, see Ramsay Macmullen, *Constantine* (New York: Dial Press, 1969), p. 217.

83. This is included by Wenskus as one among six examples of early medieval queens or princesses from other nations attempting to make a convert of a husband and his people. Op. cit., pp. 264–65, n. 796. The Frankish princess, Ingundis, got as far as converting her husband, the Visigoth Hermenigild, to orthodox Christianity, although Hermenigild revolted against his father, King Leovigild, and was killed. Wallace-Hadrill, *Early Germanic Kingship,* loc. cit., p. 27.

84. Gregory of Tours, op. cit., II, xxxi; Vol. I, p. 118. Bernard S. Bachrach cites Acts 2:42 as Gregory's probable source and then poses the question of why Gregory picked that particular biblical model: his answer is that Gregory wanted to record a modest number, since all the Franks did not convert then. "Procopius and the Chronology of Clovis's Reign," *Viator,* Vol. I (1970), pp. 27–28. Professor Bachrach amply demonstrates from other sources that many Franks hesitated in following Clovis into orthodox Christianity; however, the more immediate source of Gregory's three thousand figure was probably the three thousand Jews who followed Constantine in conversion and baptism in the *Acts of Saint Sylvester,* since he was modeling the scene partly on the story of Constantine. Far from showing restraint in writing of the conversion of the Franks, he asserts that all the people (*omnes populus*) joined in the wondrous shout of conversion induced by the Holy Spirit.

85. Marc Bloch asserted in this connection that "the only unction which he received was that which the Gallican rite placed on catechumens. . . . [I]t was in truth nothing but a simple baptism." Op. cit., p. 68. There seems to be no disagreement among scholars concerning this; however, the totality of the scene perhaps deserves a little more consideration. There is no mention of the anointment of any of the other three thousand men who were said to have been baptized at the time. Surely the anointment of a victorious king by a bishop in front of a throng of his people must have suggested something in the way of an Old Testament parallel to Gregory. Clovis was already a king, and there was obviously no reason to entertain the thought of his being made one by Remigius. Still, as addicted as the early Middle Ages were to prefiguring and foreshadowing in history, the scene can hardly help but have exerted some influence on the Carolingians as they and clergy loyal to them pondered the most fitting consecration rite for themselves.

86. Gregory of Tours, op. cit., II, xl; Vol. I, pp. 134–36.

87. Ibid., II, xlii; Vol. I, p. 140.

88. Rudolf Buchner, "Das merovingische Königtum," in *Königtum,* pp. 153–54.

89. Samson (noted above) was one; the other was "Daniel," the clerical name assumed by an early eighth-century Merovingian in the period when the dynasty had been reduced to furnishing puppet rulers for the Carolingian major-domos. To fill a vacancy, Charles Martell had him grow his hair long and become king with a suitably Germanic and traditional name as Chilperic II. Ibid., p. 147.

90. In one of these cases, Theudebert I, on becoming king about 533, attempted to make his concubine, Deoteria, his queen by marrying her. He was forced by the Frankish nobility, however, to disown her and marry a Lombard princess. In the other, King Gunthramn seems not to have attempted to raise the low status of his Gallo-Roman concubine, Veneranda, although she bore him a son who was considered significant enough that his subsequent queen took the trouble of having him poisoned. Ibid., p. 146. Concubines of Frankish extraction could become queens, but evidently this was not possible for those of Roman extraction.

91. Gregory of Tours, op. cit., IV, xxviii; Vol. I, p. 232.

92. Wallace-Hadrill, *Long-Haired Kings,* loc. cit., pp. 203–4. On the other hand, Buchner points out that "Gregory of Tours documents as something quite new 'the fact that now, with no attention paid to the family origins of the women, all those who are sired by kings are called children of kings.' " Op. cit., p. 145. This would rule out the antiquity of any such attitude toward the royal blood. I would not argue about his translation of Gregory as such (". . . quod, praetermissis nunc generibus feminarum, regis vocitantur liberi, qui de regibus fuerant procreati." V, xx, p. 326), but any great stress upon the now may be unjustified. Gregory's *nunc* could emphasize what for him is the wrongness of the view rather than its novelty. Fritz Kern cites sources from earlier centuries and other tribes to confirm a fairly wide acceptance of bastards' royal blood. *Gottesgnadentum und Widerstandsrecht,* rev. ed. (Darmstadt: WBG, 1954), p. 38, n. 84. This acceptance seems also to have lasted later in some quarters. Even in the eleventh century, in spite of a stress by the Church on legitimate birth for legitimate rulers for centuries, the decrees of William the Conqueror could still be issued as "Decreta domini regis Willelmi bastardi . . . ," in A. J. Robertson, ed., *The Laws of the Kings of England from Edmund to Henry I* (Cambridge: University Press, 1925), p. 244.

93. Gregory of Tours, op. cit., IV, li; pp. 270–72.

94. Ibid., V, xviii; Vol. I, pp. 310 and 320–22, and VII, vii; Vol. II, pp. 98–100.

95. Ibid., V, xxxix; Vol. I, p. 352.

96. Ibid., V, xxviii; Vol. I, pp. 334–36, and xxxiv; I, pp. 342–44. Brunhilde in Austrasia also attempted to introduce taxes of a direct and Roman sort, thus evoking local resentment against her. Wallace-Hadrill, *Long-Haired Kings,* loc. cit., pp. 204–5.

97. Ibid., X, xi; Vol. II, 346.

98. Ibid., VIII, xxxi; Vol. II, pp. 202–6.

99. Ibid., IX, xxxiv; Vol. II, pp. 288–90.

100. Ibid., IV, xxv; Vol. I, p. 226.

101. Ibid., IX, iii; Vol. II, p. 230.

102. Ibid., VIII, vi; Vol. II, p. 168.

103. Ibid., IX, xxviii; Vol. II, p. 278.

104. Ibid., IV, xxx; Vol. I, p. 236.

105. Ibid., VI, xxxiii; Vol. II, p. 58.

106. It was to be revived early in the next century. King Theudebert II was defeated in battle and tonsured, fulfilling a prophecy of Saint Columbanus. Jonas of Bobbio, *Vita S. Columbani,* cited by Wallace-Hadrill, *Early Germanic Kingship,* p. 58.

107. Gregory of Tours, op. cit., VII, xxi; Vol. II, p. 114.

108. Ibid., VII, vii; Vol. II, p. 100.

109. Ibid., IX, xxi; Vol. II, p. 270.

110. Ibid., Wallace-Hadrill finds that there "is good evidence for a Burgundian cult of Gunthramn, inspired no doubt by his good works in endowing churches and his role in furthering the decisions of church councils." *Long-Haired Kings,* loc. cit., p. 200.

111. Gregory of Tours, op. cit., VIII, xxx; Vol. II, p. 200.

112. Fredegar as a source should perhaps be given with the following caveat: "The history of the Franks in the seventh century degenerates into a hodge-podge which goes under the name of 'Fredegarius.' . . . Its value lies in the fact that we have nothing else. From 593 to 614 the chronology is accurate; between 615 and 631 it is vague. The best part of the narration is for the years 631–642, where it is concise and precise and seems to be the relation of an eye-witness." James W. Thompson, *A History of Historical Writing* (New York: Macmillan, 1942), Vol. I, p. 151. Modern scholarship has shown that this work was written by at least two and possibly three authors and, further, that the name "Fredegar" was probably an error dating from the sixteenth century. Nonetheless for the sake of brevity, it seems useful to employ the name "Fredegar" to designate any of the anonymous authors of the so-called *Fredegarii Chronica.* The whole work is in the MGH *Scriptores rerum Merovingicarum* series, ed. Bruno Krusch, Vol. II. References to Book IV in this chapter are to the Latin text: *Fredegarii Chronicorum Liber Quartus,* ed. with an English translation as *The Fourth Book of the Chronicle of Fredegar with Its Continuations,* ed. J. M. Wallace-Hadrill (London: Thomas Nelson, 1960). The question of authorship is discussed at length in the introduction to that edition, esp. pp. xiv-xliii.

113. Ibid., Book IV, ch. xlii, p. 36.

114. The list furnished by Fredegar includes his young opponent, Sigebert, a brother of Sigebert named Corbus, and another brother named Childebert, who had escaped from Chlothar for the time being, but who Chlothar evidently considered as good as dead. Ibid., ch. xlii, p. 35.

115. Ibid.

116. Eugen Ewig, *Volkstum und Volksbewusstsein im Frankenreich des 7. Jahrhunderts,* 1958 (repr. Darmstadt: WBG, 1969), p. 646.

117. Ibid., p. 645. Ewig does not actually include the Alamanni in listing the latter,

possibly because it was doubtful whether many Alamanni accepted Frankish domination as permanent.

118. *Liber Historiae Francorum,* ch. li; MGH, SRM, Vol. II, p. 325. Cf. Ewig, op. cit., p. 643.

119. Fredegar, Book IV, ch. xliv, p. 37.

120. J. M. Wallace-Hadrill, *The Long-Haired Kings,* loc. cit., pp. 215–16.

121. Ibid., p. 213.

122. Ibid., p. 207.

123. Detailed descriptions and examples of the components of royal and other documents from the Merovingian period on are given by A. von Brandt, *Werkzeug des Historikers,* 3rd ed. (Stuttgart: Kohlhammer, 1963), pp. 109–12.

124. Wallace-Hadrill, *The Long-Haired Kings,* loc. cit., p. 209.

125. Fredegar, Book IV, ch. lvi, p. 47.

126. Fredegar, Book II, chs. iv-viii and III, ch. ii; MGH, SRM, Vol. II, pp. 45–47 and 95–97.

127. Fredegar, Book III, ch. ix; MGH, SRM, Vol. II, p. 95.

128. Fredegar, Book IV, ch. lviii, p. 48.

129. Ibid., Book IV, ch. lx, p. 50.

130. Wallace-Hadrill, *The Long-Haired Kings,* loc. cit., p. 212.

CHAPTER 4 NOTES

1. An exception should be made only for Childeric II, who ruled independently and reasonably effectively before being murdered in 675.

2. Heinrich Fichtenau, *The Carolingian Empire,* transl. Peter Munz (Oxford: Basil Blackwell, 1963), pp. 10–11.

3. For the reigns and numbering of Merovingian kings, the synoptic catalog arrangement of Bruno Krusch still provides a generally reliable standard in this and other instances: "Chronologica regum Francorum stirpis Merowingicae," MGH, SRM, Vol. VII, pp. 468–516 (483).

4. *Liber Historiae Francorum,* ch. xliii; MGH, SRM, Vol. II, p. 316.

5. Herwig Wolfram, "The Shaping of the Early Medieval Principality," *Viator,* Vol. II (1971), pp. 37–38.

6. J. M. Wallace-Hadrill, *The Long-Haired Kings and Other Studies in Frankish History* (New York: Barnes and Noble, 1962), p. 233.

7. The whole relationship of medieval kings to feudalism as it developed is dealt with in the first section of Chapter 5.

8. *Chronica,* Book IV, ch. lxxxvii; MGH, SRM, Vol. II, p. 165; J. M. Wallace-Hadrill, *The Fourth Book of the Chronicle of Fredegar with Its Continuators* (London: Th. Nelson, 1960), p. 74.

9. Herwig Wolfram, *Intitulatio I: Lateinische Königs- und Fürstentitel bis zum Ende des 8. Jahrhunderts;* MIÖG, *Ergänzungsband* XXI (Wien: Böhlaus Nachf., 1967), p. 145.

10. Here and probably a good many other places where English translators use the term "concubine," some other phrase is more appropriate in referring to

women joined to husbands of Frankish royal or aristocratic background in limited and temporary, as opposed to full and permanent, marriages.

11. Wallace-Hadrill, op. cit., p. 241.

12. Ibid., p. 242.

13. S. Hellmann, *Das Mittelalter bis zum Ausgange der Kreuzzüge;* series: *Weltgeschichte in gemeinverständlicher Darstellung,* ed. L. M. Hartmann (Gotha: Perthes, 1920), p. 32. It has been pointed out that the actual battle took place at Niré, about forty miles south of Tours and forty miles north of Poitiers; consequently, neither of the traditional names, "Battle of Tours" or "Battle of Poitiers," is particularly accurate. Be that as it may, it seems just as well to stick with the admittedly arbitrary designation, "Battle of Tours," rather than introduce a third one which is more exact but unfamiliar.

14. Continuator of Fredegar's *Chronicle,* ed. Wallace-Hadrill (as in n. 8 above), p. 89.

15. Wallace-Hadrill, *Long-Haired Kings* . . ., loc. cit., p. 240.

16. In MGH, *Diplomata,* no. 14, p. 106; cited in ibid., p. 241.

17. Fichtenau, op. cit., p. 16.

18. Ibid., pp. 16–17.

19. Gregory of Tours seems to have used the plural term, "principes," for secular magnates only once in his *Historiarum Libri Decem*; the reference is to a group of nobles before whom, as well as before some high clergy, a solemn protestation of innocence is made. Book V, ch. v; WBG, Vol. I, p. 288, 1. 25. After the sixth century, however, this usage became more common. In the eleventh century, Lampert of Hersfeld made repeated use of the term to denote ranking nobles of the empire, e.g., a group who wanted to intercede for Duke Godfrey of Lorraine in 1046, or to refer to the high nobility of a given political unit within the empire, e.g., the "principes Saxoniae." *Annales*; WBG, pp. 46, 1. 22 and 60, 1. 16.

20. Wolfram, *Intitulatio I*, p. 137, n. 5.

21. "Eratque Pippino principe uxor nobilissima et sapientissima nomine Plectrudis." *Liber Historiae Francorum,* loc. cit., ch. xlviii, p. 323. "Grimoaldus, Pippini principis filius iunior, in aula regis Childeberti maiorum domus effectus est." Ch. xl, p. 323. "Cedendum enim tempore, egrogante Pippino principe . . ." Ch. 1, p. 324.

22. Cited by Wolfram, *Intitulatio I*, p. 138.

23. *Diplomata maiorum domus e stirpe Arnulfingorum,* ed. Georg Heinrich Pertz, MGH, DD, Vol. I (Hannover, 1872), no. 21, p. 107.

24. Wolfram, *Intitulatio I*, p. 144.

25. Ibid., p. 123, n. 62.

26. *Vita Karoli Magni,* ch. ii; in WBG, *Quellen zur karolingischen Reichsgeschichte,* Vol. I, p. 168.

27. *Annales regni Francorum,* entry for 749; in WBG, *Quellen zur karolingischen Reichsgeschichte,* Vol. I, p. 14.

28. ". . . una cum consilio et consensu omnium Francorum missa relatione ad sede apostolica, auctoritate praecepta, praecelsus Pippinus electione totius

Francorum in sedem regni cum consecratione episcoporum et subiectione principum una cum regina Bertradane, ut antiquitus ordo deposcit, sublimatur in regno." One of Fredegar's continuators, ch. xxxiii, Wallace-Hadrill, ed., loc. cit., p. 102. Also MGH, SRM, Vol. II, p. 182.

29. Paul, the leader of a revolt against the Visigothic king Wamba, styled himself *"Flavius Paulus unctus rex orientalis"* in 673; after nominating Erwig as his successor in 681, Wamba instructed the Metropolitan of Spain to anoint him as soon as possible. E. A. Thompson, *The Goths in Spain* (Oxford: Clarendon Press, 1969), pp. 222–30. William A. Chaney traces the title "Anointed of the Lord" back to the Venerable Bede, whose use of it, to be sure, may have been a figure of speech. *The Cult of Kingship in Anglo-Saxon England* (Berkeley and Los Angeles: University of California Press, 1970), p. 251, n. 16. If there were no English precedents, the influence of Byzantine custom may have been decisive, while a direct adoption of the rite from the Old Testament can certainly not be ruled out. What we are left with, when we look for certainty concerning the anointment ceremony, is a rite with Visigothic precedents which was worked out by Anglo-Saxon monks with the advice or approval of Rome and a rite which had not previously been used among the Franks.

30. "Hildericus vero, qui false rex vocabatur, tonsoratus est et in monasterium missus." *Annales regni Francorum*, entry for 750 (751), loc. cit., p. 14. Being thus "falsely called king" is not quite the same thing as being a "rex falsus" (Wallace-Hadrill's interpretation of the passage, *Long-Haired Kings*, loc. cit., p. 245), which has in it a hint of pretense at least and of abuse more generally; it was not even theoretically Childeric's fault that he had the name but not the power of a king. The incident established an important precedent for deposing useless kings, while the deposition of immoral or tyrannical ones was based on related but still distinct theories, even when the medieval papacy was most emphatically claiming the power to depose kings for a battery of reasons. Edward Peters, *The Shadow King; "Rex Inutilis" in Medieval Law and Literature, 751–1327* (New Haven: Yale University Press, 1970), pp. 39–57.

31. "Nota de unctione Pippini," in *Quellen zur Geschichte der Entstehung des Kirchenstaates*, ed. Horst Fuhrmann (Göttingen: Vandenhoeck & Ruprecht, 1968), pp. 73–74.

32. Manfred Silber, *The Gallic Royalty of the Merovingians in Its Relationship to the "Orbis terrarum Romanus" during the 5th and 6th Centuries* (Bern: Herbert Lang, 1971), pp. 51–53.

33. Cited in Wolfram, *Intitulatio I*, loc. cit., p. 126.

34. Ernst Klebel, "Zur Geschichte des Herzogs Theodo," *Zur Geschichte der Bayern*; WGB, 1965, *Wege der Forschung* series, Vol. LX, p. 172 ff.

35. Wolfram, *Intitulatio I*, loc. cit., p. 161.

36. Ibid.

37. Ibid., pp. 167 and 181.

38. Ibid., p. 183.

39. Ibid., p. 182.

40. *Annales regni Francorum*, loc. cit., p. 70.

41. Wolfram, *Intitulatio I*, loc. cit., p. 223.

42. Ibid., p. 184.

43. *Reg.*, VI, 6, p. 384, Sept. 595; cited by Walter Ullmann, *The Carolingian Renaissance and the Idea of Kingship* (London: Methuen, 1969), p. 152.

44. "Pippinus rex per apostolicam invitationem in Italiam iter peragens, iustitiam Petri apostoli quaerendo. . . ." Entry for 755, loc. cit., p. 16.

45. Compare the tone of the passage (1) describing Charlemagne's expedition to Saxony in 772 with that (2) describing his expedition to Lombardy for the Pope the following year: 1. "Et inde [from Worms] perrexit . . . domnus Carolus mitissimus rex . . . partibus Saxoniae prima vice, Eresburgum castrum coepit, ad Ermensul usque pervenit et ipsum fanum destruxit et aurum vel argentum, quod ibi repperit, abstulit." 2. [A messenger sent by Pope Adrian] . . . ad domnum Carolum regem usque periungens, invitando scilicet supranominatum gloriosum regem una cum Francis pro Dei servitio et iustitia sancti Petri seu solatio ecclesiae super Desiderium regem et Langobardos. . . . Tunc domnus ac praecelsus Carolus rex consiliavit una cum Francis, quid perageret; et sumpto consilio, ut ita, sicut missus apostolici per verbum domni Adriani apostolici postulavit. . . . [The Lombards were eventually forced to yield by a show of force] auxiliant Domino et intercedente beato Petro apostolico." Ibid., pp. 26–28.

46. Ibid., entries under the years, 786 and 787; p. 50.

47. Ibid., entry under the year, 787; p. 52.

48. ". . . claves etiam confessionis sancti Petri et vexillum Romanae urbis. . . ." Ibid., entry for 796; p. 64.

49. Apart from the *Annales* themselves, entry for 799, there are the words of Angilbert, the assumed author of "Carmen de Karolo Magno" (see n.126 below); MGH, *Poet.*, Vol. I, pp. 366–79, and the testimony of Einhard, *Vita Karoli Magni*, ch. xxviii; op. cit., p. 198.

50. ". . . gloriosus domnus Carolus rex, ipsa Italia subiugata et ordinata. . . ." *Annales regni Francorum,* loc. cit., entry for 774, p. 30.

51. ". . . anno . . . regni autem XLVII. subactaeque Italiae XLIII. . . ." *Annales regni Francorum*, loc. cit., entry on Charlemagne's death in 814, p. 104.

52. Ibid., entry for 767; p. 22.

53. Charlemagne's Council of Frankfurt was probably also a reaction to the recent Second Council of Nicaea, convoked by Empress Irene in 787, which dealt with the worship of images. Heinrich Fichtenau, *The Carolingian Empire*, loc. cit., pp. 66–69.

54. *Annales regni Francorum*, entry for 809, p. 92.

55. Ibid., entry for 805; p. 80.

56. Ibid., entry for 808; p. 88. This certainly looks on the face of it like an instance where his imperial title gave Charlemagne added authority to adjudicate among kings who otherwise would have been his equals. Recent interpretations vary, however, concerning how much importance, if any, should be

attached to the imperial connection here. "[When Charlemagne] and the pope sent *missi* to restore a deposed Northumbrian king to his throne, his action should not be interpreted as a demonstration of hegemonial authority or a move toward acquiring it: in the circumstances, the emperor's personal prestige was apparently such that he could use diplomatic means to satisfy his sense of what was right." F. L. Ganshof, *The Carolingians and the Frankish Monarchy,* transl. Janet Sondeimer (Ithaca: Cornell University Press, 1971), p. 173. It may be, on the other hand, that Eardwulf or Eardulf, the Northumbrian king, had made himself what amounted to Charlemagne's vassal and that the subordination of a king to an emperor in return for a right to protection made it logical for him to seek and obtain Charlemagne's intervention, particularly since Charlemagne could avail himself of papal authority to supplement his own. "Eardwulf, himself an anointed king, was the *fidelis* of an emperor who exercised *imperialis defensio.*" J. M. Wallace-Hadrill, *Early Germanic Kingship in England and on the Continent* (Oxford: Clarendon Press, 1971), p. 117.

57. *Annales regni Francorum*, entry for 797; p. 66.

58. *Vita Karoli magni*, chs. xxviii-xxix, loc. cit., pp. 198–200. Cf. Herwig Wolfram, "Lateinische Herrscher- und Fürstentitel im neunten und zehnten Jahrhundert," Part 1 of *Intitulatio II,* ed. H. Wolfram (Wien: Böhlaus Nachf., 1973), p. 41.

59. Karl Heldmann, *Das Kaisertum Karls des Grossen* (Weimar, 1928), cited by Heinrich Fichtenau, *Karl der Grosse und das Kaisertum*, MIÖG, 1953 (repr. Darmstadt: WBG, 1971), pp. 322–33.

60. Ibid., intr. to reprint, pp. v–vi.

61. "Peregrina vero indumenta, quamvis pulcherimma, respuebat nec umquam eis indui patiebatur, excepto quod Romae semel Hadriano pontifice petente et iterum Leone successore eius supplicante longe tunica et clamide amictus, calceis quoque Romano more formatis induebatur." Einhard, op. cit., p. 194.

62. Fichtenau, *Karl der Grosse* . . ., loc. cit., p. 333, and F. L. Ganshof, op. cit., p. 47.

63. Fichtenau, *Karl der Grosse* . . ., loc. cit., p. 329.

64. *Annales Laureshamenses*, entry for the year, 800; cited in ibid., p. 319.

65. Helmut Beumann, "Karolus Magnus et Leo Papa: Ein Paderborner Epos vom Jahre 799," *Studien und Quellen zur westfälischen Geschichte*, 8 (1966); cited by Wolfram, *Intitulatio II,* loc. cit., p. 29, n. 40.

66. *Liber Pontificalis*, cited in ibid., p. 29, n. 40. This original form of the acclamation does not mention the Romans; however, the title of emperor was understood to have a Roman reference from the first. The Frankish author of the *Annales regni Francorum* dropped the "piisimo" in recording the acclamation and added "Romanorum" to "imperatori." Loc. cit., entry for 801, p. 74.

67. Ganshof, op. cit., p. 48.

68. Cf. Eckhard Müller-Mertens, *Regnum Teutonicum; Aufkommen und*

Verbreitung der deutschen Reichs- und Königsauffassung im frühen Mittelalter (Wien: Böhlau, 1970), pp. 381–82.

69. Maria Theresa was sometimes addressed as "Imperial Highness" at home even in the period between her father's death in 1740 and the election of her husband as Roman emperor in 1745. She refused to hand over the imperial archives to Charles VII, a rival who was elected emperor in 1742 but who died in 1745, and in other ways she treated the imperial title rather much as an inherited possession, but there was no question but that the elected emperor himself had to be a man. Robert Pick, *Empress Maria Theresa: The Earlier Years, 1717–1757* (New York: Harper and Row, 1966), pp. 9, 35, 57, 62, 68, 88, 134–35, and 148–49. This is not to imply, certainly, that the Roman imperial tradition was the only one in Europe excluding female rulers. For example, while queens ruled — on rare occasion to be sure — in Castile, England, and Sweden, in France they functioned at most as regents. The point is, instead, that the Roman imperial tradition ruled women sovereigns out of the picture firmly from the beginning, where the admissibility of female rulership was decided by a variety of factors outside the medieval empire.

70. This admittedly somewhat arbitrary assignment of dates has its basis in the theory and reality of a special segment of medieval kingship: 742 marks the first explicit and official mention of the Franks as the "people of God" and introduces the idea of religious-political regeneration of an international scope under Frankish rulers, which underlay the Carolingians' faith in their specific mission and characterized their various successes and subsequent failures. The Treaty of Verdun in 843 marks the breaking up of the Carolingian Empire in what soon became France, Germany, and territories to be disputed among their rulers. The idea of a European-wide regeneration of society under the guidance of a Frankish king and his clergy had spent most of its force. If one emphasizes general cultural achievements rather than kingship, a case can be made for placing the Carolingian Renaissance more accurately in time from the end of the eighth century through the whole of the ninth century, as does, for example, Jacques Boussard, *The Civilization of Charlemagne*, transl. Frances Partridge (New York and Toronto: McGraw-Hill, 1968), p. 118.

71. Ullmann, op. cit., p. 21. This was thus at the time that Karlomann assumed the "dux et princeps Francorum" title for himself, which in turn coincided with his backing of Saint Boniface and the introduction of sweeping papal reforms into lands controlled by the Franks through their joint efforts. There are, of course, implicit references to the Franks as the "chosen people of God" from the Merovingian period, e.g., Gregory I's evaluation of the Frankish kingdom in relation to that of other peoples (above, n. 43) and the sentiments in the "Prologue" to the *Lex Salica*.

72. The "gentes" were the nonchosen people in Latin translations of the Old Testament. By the early Middle Ages, the term, with its adjectival form, "gentiles," had come by extension to signify non-Christians. Gregory of Tours, for example, uses "gentiles" as a synonym for "heathens." The pre-

Christian Roman tradition used "populus" particularly for the Roman people, but the Christian Roman tradition, as perceived in the West, had scarcely begun to equate the Roman people with the chosen people in contrast to the "gentes" or "gentiles" when first Roman military reverses and then the end of the western empire put an end to that sort of talk for a while.

73. Einhard, op. cit., ch. xxix; p. 200.

74. Ganshof, op. cit., pp. 148–49.

75. Wolfram, *Intitulatio I*, op. cit., p. 213.

76. Einhard, op. cit., ch. xxiii, p. 194.

77. *Annales regni Francorum*, entry for 798; p. 68.

78. Ibid., under 802 and 810; pp. 76 and 94.

79. Ibid., under 814, p. 106; 817, pp. 110–12; 821, pp. 126–28; 822, p. 130; 823, pp. 134–36; 826, p. 144; 827, p. 148; and 828, p. 152. Also Thegan, *Vita Hludowici*, ch. xxxiii; in WBG, *Quellen zur karolingischen Reichsgeschichte*, Vol. I, p. 234, and the anonymous *Vita Hludowici Imperatoris*, sometimes called *The Astronomer's Life of Emperor Louis*, chs. xxiv, xxvii, and xl; in ibid., pp. 294, 298–300, and 330.

80. *Annales regni Francorum*, entry for 922, p. 130.

81. Thegan, op. cit., ch. xiv, p. 224. Cf. Fichtenau, *Carolingian Empire*, loc. cit., pp. 80–81, on the extensive Carolingian receipt of foreign tribute.

82. Ganshof, op. cit., p. 65, n. 115.

83. There is some evidence that Emperor Constantine V, who sent legates to Pippin the Short in 766–67, requested the hand of his daughter, Gisla, for his designated successor, the future Leo IV. Empress Irene definitely sought a marriage between Charlemagne's daughter, Hrotrud, and her son, Constantine VI, in the 780s. Ibid., p. 170.

84. Ibid., p. 179.

85. ". . . more suo, id est, Greca lingua, laudes ei dixerunt, imperatorem eum et basileum appelantes." *Annales Regni Francorum*, loc. cit., entry for 812, p. 100. By this time, "basileus" was understood at the Frankish court as the equivalent of "augustus" in the sense of "senior emperor"; thus the acclamation contained Charlemagne's own imperial title elements, "imperator" and "augustus". Wolfram, *Intitulatio II*, loc. cit., pp. 32 and 51 with n. 61.

86. Einhard, op. cit., ch. xvii, p. 186.

87. Fichtenau, *Carolingian Empire*, loc. cit., pp. 14 and 17. Ganshof, op. cit., p. 220. The assurance of tithe payments was at least partly the Carolingian way of compensating the Church for granting the use of Church lands to members of the nobility.

88. Ullmann, op. cit., p. 37.

89. As Ullmann puts it, there was no power in any "Establishment" to resist Carolingian reforms with an ideology of its own. Ibid., p. 23. Actually, if tradition and legitimacy are characteristic attributes of an Establishment, the Carolingians stressed in their public relations that they were the Establishment, which, of course, put them in a stronger position as innovators and reformers.

90. The Donation of Constantine discussed below is a special exception. Later it was a sign of approaching Carolingian decline that royal absolutism—the idea that "the prince is king and subject to neither laws nor to judges but only to God"—was expressed so baldly that it seemed to threaten the rights of the Church and evoked a strong clerical response. Hincmar of Rheims, *De divortio Lotharii regis et Tetbergae reginae*, PL, Vol. CXXV, col. 756.

91. "Ut pax sit et concordia et unianimitas cum omni populo christiano inter episcopos, abbates, comites, iudices et omnes ubique seu maiores seu minores personas, quia nihil Deo sine pace placet . . ." Ch. lxii of the *Admonitio Generalis*, a capitulary issued by Charlemagne in 789. MGH, *Cap.*, nos. 22–24. Ganshof describes this as the "fundamental rule of the Carolingian method of government: there must be peace and concord, that is to say, trusting collaboration between the ecclesiastical authorities and the secular agents of royal power." Op. cit., p. 144.

92. Ullmann, op. cit., p. 41.

93. "Dum prospexisset Pippinus rex, ab Haistulfo Langobardorum rege ea non esse vera, quod antea promiserat de iustitiis sancti Petri, iterum iter peragens in Italiam Papiam obsedit, Haistulfum inclusit, magis magisque de iustitiis sancti Petri confirmavit, ut stabiles permanerent, quod antea promiserat; et insuper Ravennam cum Pentapolim et omni Exarcatu conquisivit et sancto Petro tradidit." *Annales regni Francorum*, loc. cit., p. 16.

94. Eleanor Shipley Duckett, *Alcuin, Friend of Charlemagne; His World and Work* (New York: Macmillan, 1951), pp. 73–74.

95. *Codex Carolinus*, cited in ibid., p. 78.

96. Percy Ernst Schramm, *Kaiser, Rom und Renovatio*, 2nd ed. (Darmstadt: Hermann Gentner Verlag, 1957), p. 23. It was conclusively shown to be a forgery in 1440 by the Italian humanist, Lorenzo Valla, who not only showed that it was foreign to the spirit of the times which it purported to date from but identified words and phrases in it of later origin than the fourth century.

97. "Constitutio Constantini," §11 in H. Fuhrmann, ed. *Quellen zur Geschichte der Entstehung des Kirchenstaates* (Göttingen: Vandenhoeck & Ruprecht, 1968), pp. 79–83 (80).

98. Ibid., §13, p. 81.

99. Ibid., §14, p. 81.

100. Loc. cit., ch. xxix, p. 200.

101. *Capitulare* of 790, 95, ch. x; cited by Ullmann, op. cit., p. 47.

102. Ganshof, op. cit., p. 148.

103. Ibid., p. 150.

104. Ibid., p. 147, n. 30.

105. Ibid., p. 151.

106. Ibid., p. 149.

107. Ibid., pp. 91–92.

108. Ibid., p. 149.

109. Ibid., pp. 64–65.

110. Fichtenau, *Carolingian Empire*, loc. cit., pp. 107-8.

111. Ganshof, op. cit., p. 130.
112. Charlemagne's capitularies commit him clearly to the idea of free public education for at least the sons of free men. Instructions survive, given through Theodulf, bishop of Orleans, for implementing this program in the provinces as well as at the more famous palace school. "Presbyteri per villas et vicos scholas habeant et si quilibet fidelium suos parvulos ad discendas literas eis commendare vult eos suscipere ac docere non renuant, sed cum summa caritate eos doceant. . . . Cum ergo docent, nihil ab eis pretii pro hac re exigant, excepto quod eis parentes caritatis studio sua voluntate obtulerint." PL, Vol. CV, cols. 191 and 207. Cf. Andrew F. West, *Alcuin and the Rise of Christian Schools* (N. Y.: Scribner's, 1903), pp. 54–56.
113. Fichtenau, *Carolingian Empire*, loc. cit., p. 131.
114. This applied to base-born ecclesiastics as well as secular officials appointed by the king. "During the whole of his tenure of office, Archbishop Ebo of Rheims had to contend with the indignant opposition of the nobility, and no doubt he was reminded more than once that his ancestors had been goatherds and not councillors of kings. When the abbot Waldo, a relative of the Carolingians, was engaged in a feud with the Bishop of Constance, he swore an oath: 'I will not acknowledge a superior of lower birth than I am, so long as I have three fingers on my right hand.' " Ibid., p. 125.
115. Ganshof, op. cit., p. 56.
116. Ullmann, op. cit., p. 22.
117. While official cooperation flourished, and the power of the pope was even insignificant in the realm when contrasted with Charlemagne's domination of the Frankish territorial Church, ". . . the pope could at least lay claim to the position which his successors were to secure during the Investiture Controversy: overlordship over the whole ecclesiastical hierarchy and the right to be the sole judge in matters of faith." Fichtenau, *Carolingian Empire*, loc. cit., p. 61.
118. Ganshof, op. cit., p. 61. Pippin the Short had already made use of regular episcopal visitation as a measure of controlling clerics and laymen alike. Louis the Pious eventually put a capstone on the structure of Frankish royal control of the monasteries by appointing a General Abbot for the whole realm. Ullmann, op. cit., pp. 12 and 22.
119. Ganshof, op. cit., p. 68.
120. Ullmann, op. cit., p. 11.
121. Ganshof, op. cit., pp. 64–65.
122. *Vita Karoli Magni*, loc. cit., ch. xxiv, p. 196.
123. This is given in ch. 2. It is, again, doubtful whether Augustine ever thought of this sketch of the happiness of the best Christian rulers as part of a program for redeeming the earthly city, but it is equally true that a phrase like "using their power to spread the worship of God as far as they can," sounds a bit like a programmatic challenge.
124. ". . . divina nobis providentia in solium regni unxisse manifestum est." MGH, *Diplomata Karolina*, Vol. I, no. 16, p. 22. Cited by Marc Bloch, *Les*

rois thaumaturges: Étude sur le caractère surnaturel attribué a la puissance royale particulièrement en France et en Angleterre (Strasbourg: Librairie Istra, 1924), p. 69. Cf. Wolfram, *Intitulatio I,* loc. cit., p. 216.

125. Fichtenau, *Carolingian Empire*, loc. cit., pp. 71–72.

126. "Carmen de Karolo Magno" (also called "Carolus Magnus et Leo papa"), MGH, *Scriptores*, 11. 13–15; ed. Pertz (Hannover: Hahn, 1829), Vol. II, pp. 393–403; also in MGH, Poetae, Vol. I, pp. 366–77. Gaston Paris supports Pertz's identification of the author as Angilbert, particularly since Angilbert acquired the name at court of "Homer," which could easily be a reference to his authorship of such an epic poem as this. Max Manitius questions Angilbert's authorship of the poem in *Geschichte der Lateinischen Literatur im Mittelalter* (München: Oskar Beck, 1911), Vol. II, Erster Teil, pp. 546–47, but the evidence on both sides remains rather inconclusive.

127. *Vita Hludowici*, ch. iii; WBG, *Quellen zur karolingischen Reichsgeschichte*, Vol. I, pp. 216–18.

128. Ibid., ch. xvi, pp. 224–26.

129. *Anonymi vita Hludowici*, ch. lv; WBG, *Quellen zur karolingischen Reichsgeschichte*, Vol. I, p. 358. The occasion was a severe illness of Lothar, who had revolted against his father. Writers in the later Carolingian period preferred to see Louis the Pious as the image of Solomon rather than David.

130. Gregory of Tours, *Historiarum libri decem*, Book IX, chs. xxi–xxii; WBG, Vol. II, pp. 270–72. Even here we have at most a borderline case of sacerdotal kingship.

131.   "[H]aec Pius egregio rex Childebercthus amore
                      dona suo populo non moritura dedit;
                 totus in affectu divini cultus adhaerens
                 ecclesiae iuges amplificavit opes;
                      Melchisedek noster merito rex atque sacerdos
                 conplevit laicus religionis opus."
Carmina, Book II, no. 10, *"De ecclesia Parisiaca"; MGH* (Berlin: Weidmann, 1881), p. 40.

132. *Codex Carolinus*, 45; ed. Wilhelm Gundlach; MGH, *Epistolae*, Vol. III, p. 561. The quotation is from 1 Peter, 2:9.

133. Fichtenau, *Carolingian Empire*, loc. cit., p. 58.

134. Cited in ibid., from PL, Vol. CI, col. 251. According to Alcuin, Charlemagne was supposed to be able to preach like a priest, but the broader and more generally applicable sense of the passage was that the life he led was, in its exemplary nature, a sermon to his subjects.

135. The *Libri Carolini* were written for Charlemagne by Theodulf of Orleans. Citations in Fichtenau, *Carolingian Empire*, loc. cit., p. 70.

136. *Anonymi vita Hludovici*, loc. cit., ch. xix, p. 284.

137. Ibid., ch. xl, p. 338, and ch. lvi, pp. 360–62.

138. In MGH, *Epist.*, Vol. IV: *Epistolae Variorum Carolo Magno Regnante Scriptae*, 7. The same enumeration is found in Sedulius Scotus, *De Rectori-*

bus Christianis, ch. x; cited by A. J. Carlyle, *A History of Mediaeval Political Theory in the West* (repr. New York: Barnes and Noble, n. d.), Vol. I, p. 225, n. 1. On the king as God's regent (*regnator*), see Sedulius Scotus, *De Rect. Christ.,* ch. xix, Carlyle, p. 215, n. 2.

139. *De Institutione Regia,* 4; cited by Carlyle, op. cit., Vol. I, p. 225, n. 2.

140. "It displeased Samuel that the Children of Israel should say 'Let us have a king to rule us,' so he prayed to Yahweh. But Yahweh said to Samuel, 'Obey the voice of the people in all that they say to you, for it is not you they have rejected; they have rejected me from ruling over them.' " Samuel then paints before his people a grim picture of what kings, if they insist on having them, would have in store for them; however, "the people refused to listen to the words of Samuel. They said, 'No! We want a king, so that we in our turn can be like the other nations; our king shall rule us and be our leader and fight our battles.' " Still unsure, Samuel consults again with Yahweh. "Yahweh then said to Samuel, 'Obey their voice and give them a king.' " 1 Samuel, 8:6–7, 18–20, and 21–22.

141. Carlyle, op. cit., Vol. I, pp. 227–28 gives quotations from Hincmar of Rheims and Sedulius Scotus.

142. On the mystical connotation of *nomen* with particular reference to the Carolingian imperial title, see Fichtenau, *Karl der Grosse . . . ,* loc. cit., pp. 259–63.

143. Citation from address presented to Louis the Pious by his bishops and written by Jonas, MGH, *Leges,* Sect. 2, Vol. II, no. 196, "Episcoporum ad Hludovicum Imperatorem Relatio," 56; in Carlyle, op. cit., Vol. I, p. 227, n. 1.

144. "Reges a regendo vocati. Non autem regit, qui non corrigit. Recte igitur faciendo regis nomen tenetur, peccando amittitur." *Etymologiarum sive originum libri,* IX, iii, 4; cited by Wolfram, *Intitulatio I . . . ,* p. 32. Cf. also Hans Hubert Anton, *Fürstenspiegel und Herrscherethos in der Karolingerzeit.* Series: *Bonner Historische Forschungen* (Bonn: Rohrscheid, 1968), pp. 384–85. Augustine's presentation of the etymology is in the context of the Roman deposition of Tarquin and consequently thoroughly negative: ". . . cum et reges utique a regendo dicti melius videantur, ut regnum a regibus, reges autem, ut dictum est, a regendo; sed fastus regius non disciplina putata est regentis vel benevolentia consulentis, sed superbia dominantis." *De civitate Dei,* Book V, ch. xii; LCL, Vol. II, p. 192.

145. Another side of this same early phenomenon in Carolingian kingship, the identity of interests between the king and the ecclesiastical hierarchy in producing "something of a common front against the aristocracy," is stressed by Ullmann in ch. 5, "The King's Stunted Sovereignty," in his *The Carolingian Renaissance and the Idea of Kingship,* loc. cit., pp. 111–34. This was part of a necessary policy of stabilizing and balancing at the outset, but it put Carolingian kingship under additional strain with the rapid growth of aristocratic power in the ninth century.

146. *Notkeri Gesta Karoli,* ed. Reinhold Rau, in WBG series, *Quellen zur karolingischen Reichsgeschichte,* Vol. III, pp. 322–426. Subsequent references are

to this edition. The beginning and end of the work are lost, and the author describes himself only as "ego balbus et edentulus," Book, II, ch. xvii, p. 414. The final substantiation of Notker as author is comparatively recent, and many older editions of the work ascribe it simply to a "monk of Saint Gall." The superiority of Notker's *Gesta* as a mirror of princes to other Carolingian works more usually cited as the best of that class (the writings of Jonas of Orleans, Sedulius Scotus, Hincmar of Rheims, and Smaragdus, author of the *Via Regia*, a mirror of princes stressing the king's function as that of a vicar of Christ) is cautiously asserted but more than amply demonstrated by Theodor Siegrist, *Herrscherbild und Weltsicht bei Notker Balbulus: Untersuchungen zu den Gesta Karoli* (Zürich: Fretz & Wasmuth AG, 1963), pp. 72–108.

147. *Gesta Karoli*, II, xvi, p. 410.

148. Ibid., II, vi, p. 384. On the whole topic of sunlike imperial emanations, from origins in the East to Charlemagne's court via ancient Rome, see Herwig Wolfram, *Splendor Imperii: Die Epiphanie von Tugend und Heil in Herrschaft und Reich*; MIÖG, Ergänzungsband XX, Heft 3 (Graz: Böhlaus Nachf., 1963), pp. 134–44.

149. *Gesta Karoli*, II, xix, p. 420.

150. Ibid., II, xii, p. 400. Citation from 1 Kings, 12:16.

151. Under such circumstances, the parallels between Old Israel and the New Israel of the Franks "fostered the suspicion of the ninth century that bad kings were dispensable." J. M. Wallace-Hadrill, *Early Germanic Kingship in England and on the Continent* (Oxford: Clarendon Press, 1971), p. 125.

152. *Gesta Karoli*, I, v., p. 330.

153. Letter to Charlemagne, cited by Siegrist, op. cit., p. 75.

154. *Gesta Karoli*, II, xii, p. 406. This is the way the ruler's wisdom generally figures in Carolingian didactic writings, by raising him in his powers of perception and comprehension several notches above his subjects. Siegrist points out an interesting variation on this theme in Notker's work. Greek emissaries had brought musical instruments to Charlemagne's court. "[q]uae cuncta ab opificibus sagacissimi Karoli, quasi dissimulanter aspecta accuratissime sunt in opus conversa." II, vii, p. 386. Here it is the ruler's mental power which has somehow been transferred to his artisans: "The *sagitas* of the Emperor brought his engineers to the point of copying unnoticed the musical instruments which the Greek emissaries had brought along, in order to reproduce them in every detail afterwards." Op. cit., p. 78.

155. *Gesta Karoli*, II, xii, p. 408.

156. ". . . fulmineas in eum acies imperator intorquens attonitum terrae prostravit." Ibid., I, xix, p. 348.

157. Ibid., II, xiii, p. 406.

158. Ibid., I, xxv, pp. 358–60.

159. Notker, in fact, calls him "religiossimus Karolus, episcopus episcoporum," in introducing the anecdote just recounted; this again refers to an overseeing rather than a sacerdotal function. Fichtenau, *Carolingian Imperium*, pp. 58–59.

160. *Gesta Karoli*, I, xvi, p. 344.

161. Ibid., II, xii, pp. 402–4.

162. Ibid., II, xvii, p. 416.

163. Ibid., II, xviii, p. 420 and II, xv, p. 410. In a similar fashion, Thegan had given an idealized depiction of the physical appearance of Louis the Pious and made him into the best archer and lance-hurler of his people. *Vita Hludowici*, loc. cit., ch. xix, p. 226.

164. *Gesta Karoli*, II, iii, p. 378.

165. Notker calls these people simply "barbarae nationes." Scholars have reasoned that he must be thinking of Slavs from the fact that he has them coming from the north into Noricum and East Franconia. *Gesta Karoli*, II, xii, pp. 398–400. Rau as editor notes similar incidents in Merovingian sources, all in the *MGH Scriptores rerum Merovingicarum* series: *Gesta regum Francorum*, xli, Vol. II, p. 314; *Gesta Dagoberti*, xiv, Vol. II, p. 405; and *Vita Faronis*, Vol. V, p. 193.

166. Joshua 11: 11–12 and 21–23.

167. *Gesta Karoli*, I, iii, pp. 324–26. Siegrist notes that in this and similar examples Notker is assigning the ideal king the function of humbling the exalted and exalting the humble, something which is normally left to God to do. "Der Herrscher als Richter und Hirte, ein Abbild Gottes," part of ch. III in op. cit., pp. 79–89.

168. *Gesta Karoli*, I, xxx, p. 366.

169. Ibid., I, xxviii, p. 364.

170. Ibid., I, xxxi, p. 368.

171. Ibid., I, xxix, pp. 364–66.

172. Ibid., II, xiv, p. 408.

173. Manitius, op. cit., pp. 354–56, and M. O'C. Walshe, *Medieval German Literature* (Cambridge, Mass.: Harvard University Press, 1962), pp. 31–33.

CHAPTER 5 NOTES

1. Gustav Freytag, *Bilder aus der deutschen Vergangenheit*; 14. Aufl. (Leipzig: S. Hirzel, 1883), p. 320.

2. Tacitus, *Germania*, ch. xxvi; LCL, *Dialogus, Agricola, Germania*, p. 300.

3. His lament was that now royal rule would disintegrate and the rule of clerics would ensue, since real wealth was now theirs to bestow and not his: " 'Ecce pauper remansit fiscus noster, ecce divitiae noster ad eclesias sunt translatae; nulli penitus nisi soli episcopi regnant; periet honor noster et translatus est ad episcopus civitatum.' " Gregory of Tours, *Hist.* VI, xlvi; WGB, Vol. 2, p. 84.

4. F. L. Ganshof, *Feudalism*, transl. Philip Grierson (London: Longmans, Green & Co., 1952), pp. 6–7. The model charter cited by him from the *Formulae Turonensis* contains a statement that the future vassal's virtual indigence is a matter of public knowledge: "Dum et omnibus habetur percognitum, qualiter ego minime habeo, unde me pascere vel vestire debeam. . . ."

5. This is indicated by his use of the term "principes," which in another place in the same work signifies the military leaders or warrior chiefs who had "reiks" status in the Germanic tribes. See ch. I, notes 8 and 9.

6. *Germania,* chs. xiii-xiv; loc. cit., pp. 282–84.

7. Ganshof, op. cit., p. 5.

8. Ibid., p. 11.

9. Lynn White, Jr., *Medieval Technology and Social Change* (Oxford: Clarendon Press, 1962), pp. 14–28. Also David Herlihy, editor's intro. to *The History of Feudalism* (New York: Walker and Co., 1970), p. xxiii. In fact, nearly all American medievalists dealing with the subject during the 1960s, e.g., Joseph R. Strayer, Jeffery Russell, and Norman Cantor, to list only the most familiar names, accepted White's thesis that mounted shock combat, based on equipping riders to ram their weapons into opponents or knock them off their horses without getting knocked off themselves, derived from the Carolingian use of the stirrup, an invention previously unknown or disregarded in Europe, "which joined man and steed into a fighting organism." Both this theory and the related idea that bestowing land benefits in return for military service essentially began feudalism during the first part of the eighth century are attacked by Bernard S. Bachrach with a thorough reexamination of the evidence in which he finds, among other things, the use of the stirrup in Carolingian times to have been too isolated to have been decisive in warfare of the period and the earlier Merovingian exchanges of land for expected service too numerous to have led to the origin of Western feudalism in Charles Martel's time. "Charles Martel, Mounted Shock Combat, the Stirrup, and Feudalism," *Studies in Medieval and Renaissance History,* Vol. VII (Lincoln: University of Nebraska Press, 1970), pp. 47–75. Probably a rebuttal from defenders of the questioned theories is in order before firm conclusions concerning them can be drawn.

10. Ganshof, op. cit., pp. 53–54.

11. *Homo* was not, to be sure, 100 percent new in this usage. Cassiodorus recorded a letter from the Ostrogothic King Theodad in 534 as written to "his man," an otherwise unknown Theodosius: "Theodosio homini suo Theodahadus rex." *Variae Epist.,* Book X, no. v; MGH, AA, Vol. XII, p. 301. This was, however, a rare usage in documents before the Carolingian period.

12. Loc. cit., pp. 53–54.

13. Charles Petit-Dutaillis, *The Feudal Monarchy in France and England from the Tenth to the Thirteenth Century,* transl. E. D. Hunt, 1936 (repr. London: Routledge & Kegan Paul, 1964), p. 7.

14. Previously, "fief" or its cognates had meant moveable property, particularly cattle; etymologically, the word is akin to the modern German "Vieh" (cattle).

15. Cited by Austin L. Poole, *Obligations of Society in the XII and XIII Centuries* (Oxford: Clarendon Press, 1946), p. 62.

16. " '. . . ad narrandam familiam scaccarii domini regis in camera regis et ad ponendam in loculo cum dominus rex ludum suum perfecerit.' " Ibid., p. 66, n. 1.

17. *Anglo-Saxon Chronicle,* cited by David C. Douglas, *William the Conqueror* (Berkeley and Los Angeles: University of California Press, 1964), p. 355.

18. Ganshof, op. cit., citing *Leges Henrici I,* 82.5, in *Die Gesetze der Angelsachsen,* ed. F. Liebermann (Halle, 1903), p. 599.

19. There is an illustrative twelfth-century example of the multiple-vassalage contract specifying one liege lord from the *Liber Feudorum maior,* a collection of charters chiefly from Catalonia and Barcelona, in David Herlihy's documentary *History of Feudalism,* loc. cit., pp. 101–2.

20. *De moribus et actis primorum Normanniae ducum libri tres,* PL, Vol. CXLI, col. 648. Dudo, a monk and then Dean of Saint Quentin's, wrote his history between 994–1015, by which time the story of Rollo had taken on a somewhat legendary character, although much of his account has been authenticated by Henri Prentout, *Étude critique sur Dudon de Saint-Quentin et Son Histoire de premiers Ducs Normands* (Paris: A Picard, 1916).

21. Dudo, loc. cit., col. 650.

22. Ibid., col. 650–51. Prentout makes a good case for at least the rough historicity of the contract sealing incident. Op. cit., pp. 231–44. Dudo's account of Gisela as Charles's daughter fares less well in his study: King Charles was born in 879 and married in 907; although he had a daughter named Gisela, by 911 she could hardly have fit Dudo's description of her. Prentout suggests Dudo's probable confusion over two royal Giselas at the time: one, the daughter of Lothar II, was indeed given to a Norman chieftain, while a girl of a different name was given to Rollo. Ibid., pp. 176–78 and 206–7.

23. Richer, *Historiae,* Book I, ch. liii, ed. R. Latouche (Paris, 1930), p. 104; cited in Ganshof, op. cit., p. 64.

24. Petit-Dutaillis, op. cit., p. 218.

25. Ibid., p. 219. The author notes that there is no evidence of a document having been issued by Philip and his barons at this time. It was certainly widely believed at the time, however, that the barons had at least given their verbal assent to Philip's proposal that John's fiefs be forfeited, since they fought on Philip's side during the ensuing conflict.

26. Ibid., p. 291.

27. Interpretations differ concerning the extent of Raymond's involvement with the Albigensians. Sidney Painter concludes that he was no heretic himself. *The Rise of the Feudal Monarchies* (Ithaca: Cornell University Press, 1951), p. 31. Petit-Dutaillis, on the other hand, calls him "one of the heads of Catharism" (the Albigensian heresy). Op cit., p. 279. The role of north-south hostility was also of the essence in the way the crusade developed. "The northerners thought that the southerners were undisciplined, spoiled by luxury, a little soft, too much interested in social graces, too much influenced by contemptible people such as businessmen, lawyers, and Jews. The southerners thought the northerners were crude, arrogant, discourteous, uncultured, and aggressive." Joseph R. Strayer, *The Albigensian Crusade* (New York: Dial Press, 1971), pp. 9–10.

28. Ibid., p. 134.

29. Painter, op. cit., p. 47, and Douglas, op. cit., pp. 276–83.
30. "Quincunque habet foedum unius militis habeat loricam et cassidem, cly-peum et lanceam; et omnis miles habeat tot loricas et cassides, et clypeos et lanceas quot habuerit feoda militum in dominico suo." Art. I of the "Assisa de Armis habendis in Anglia"; in William Stubbs, ed., *Select Charters and Other Illustrations of English Constitutional History,* 7th ed. (Oxford: Clarendon, 1890), p. 154.
31. Douglas, op. cit., pp. 280–81.
32. Agreements cited by Ganshof, op. cit., p. 79, n. 3.
33. The key incident in this regard was Frederick's redistribution of lands taken from Henry the Lion, duke of Bavaria, who had been in revolt against him, to the territorial lords in Germany. In England or France there would have been no question but that the lands of a vassal in revolt against the king should revert to the crown. One explanation for Frederick's behavior is the absence in Germany of the 1180s of any body of imperial officials to entrust with the administration of so much recently acquired land. Peter Munz, *Frederick Barbarossa* (Ithaca: Cornell University Press, 1969), pp. 356–57, with the considerable literature on Frederick's possible motives here and the question of how binding the precedent of *Leihezwang* (requirement to regrant lands reverting to the crown) actually was. N. 2.
34. Charles H. Haskins, *Norman Institutions,* 1918 (repr. New York: F. Ungar, 1960), pp. 39 and 47–49.
35. Richard FitzNigel or Fitzneal, *Dialogus de Scaccario,* I, xi; Stubbs, op. cit., pp. 205–6.
36. "Assisa Domini Henricis regis de Foresta," Articles viii and xvi. Text in Stubbs, op. cit., pp. 158–59.
37. Loc. cit., p. 141. On the other hand, it might be noted that in spite of the selfish royal motives behind them, such laws and their continental equivalents gave environmental protection to forest areas which would otherwise have been cleared and have disappeared in England, France, and Germany.
38. Douglas, op. cit. p. 302.
39. Painter, op. cit., p. 38.
40. The idea of a lord being paid relief by his vassals suggests that the lord, far from furnishing his vassals with economic maintenance, was receiving main-tenance payments himself. Actually, the term "relevium" signified a "lifting up again" of the feudal grant which had "fallen" on the death of one of the contracting parties. The German terms for termination of the feudal con-tract, "Thronfall" or "Herrenfall," on the death of the king or other lord, and "Mannfall," on the death of the vassal, the lord's "man," reflect the concep-tion of transfer as a falling and lifting up again.
41. S. K. Mitchell, *Studies in Taxation under John and Henry III* (New Haven: Yale Historical Publications, 1914), p. 346. The total ransom was about £100,000.
42. Saint Louis felt that he was both procuring peace and reestablishing the vassal relation of the king of England to the king of France, which had disappeared

with King John's loss of his French fiefs. "[F]rom the peace I am making with the King of England, I derive the great honor of having him as my vassal, which he was not before." John de Joinville, *The Life of Saint Louis,* Book I, ch. xiv, no. 65; transl. René Hague (New York: Sheed and Ward, 1955), pp. 39–40. In the long run, however, the English king's concessions were worthless; the price to the French was immediate and high. One stipulation provided for enough silver to maintain 500 knights for two years, and records of the time show much of the assessment passed on to the French towns. Michel Gavrilovitch, *Étude sur le Traité de Paris de 1259 entre Louis IX, Roi de France, & Henry III, Roi d'Angleterre;* no. 125 in series: *Bibliothèque de l'École des Hautes Études* (Paris, 1899), pp. 54 and 64–65.

43. Ganshof, op. cit., pp. 100–101.
44. "Oration on the Tricennalia of Constantine," ii, 1–5; English text from NPNF, 2nd ser., Vol. 1, p. 583, with alterations by J. Stevenson, *A New Eusebius: Documents Illustrative of the History of the Church to A.D. 337* (London: SPCK, 1957), p. 392.
45. Fritz Kern, *Gottesgnadentum und Widerstandsrecht im früheren Mittelalter,* 2nd rev. ed. (Darmstadt: WGB, 1962), pp. 108–9.
46. *De divortio Lotharii regis et Tetbergae reginae,* "Quaestio VI"; PL, Vol. CXXV, col. 756.
47. This is the view, for example, of Wenric of Trier in an open letter written under the name of a bishop of Verdun to Gregory VII: "Novum est autem et omnibus retro seculis inauditum, pontifices regna gentium tam facile velle dividere, nomen regum, inter ipsa mundi initia repertum, a Deo postea stabilitum, repentina factione elidere, cristos Domini quotiens libuerit plebeia sorte sicut villicos mutare, regno patrum suorum decedere iussos, nisi confestim adquieverint, anathemate damnare." MGH, *Libelli de lite,* Vol. I, p. 289, ll. 30–36.
48. Marc Bloch, *Les rois thaumaturges: Étude sur le caractère surnaturel attribué a la puissance royale particulièrement en France et en Angleterre* (Strasburg: Librairie Istra, 1924), p. 60.
49. Bloch's exceptionally well-documented book just cited is still the most comprehensive treatise on the magic attributes of medieval European kingship. Bloch, however, applies "thaumaturgic" to kingship in a very strict and limited sense: his conception of miracle working through royal power excludes, in effect, both the miracles worked by kings as saints (his assumption is that their saintly rather than their royal power worked their wonders) and the divine responses to royal prayers. My own feeling is that saintly power earned in a royal role was never really separated from kingship: Saints Edward, Olaf, and Louis, for example, continued to be perceived by those who sought their aid not only as saints but also as past kings of their peoples. It is true, to be sure, that as far as the divine response to prayers was concerned living kings were perceived only as sharing the grace accorded all Christians of having their prayers answered, sometimes by miracles; but the point is that good kings' proportionately large share of this grace or, to put it clearly but

crudely, the special influence good kings were thought to have with God, made their prayers more capable of bringing about wondrous happenings than the prayers of the general run of laymen.

50. *Book of Emperors,* ll. 14,689–724. Edited by Edward Schröder as *Die Kaiserchronik eines Regensburger Geistlichen,* MGH, *Deutsche Chroniken,* Vol. 1, pp. 347–48. See below ch. VI.

51. Henry A. Myers, "The Concept of Kingship in the Book of Emperors (Kaiserchronik)," *Traditio,* Vol. XXVII (1971), pp. 224–25.

52. To achieve his victory over Arbogast, Theodosius in the account of Orosius "dehinc postquam insomen noctem precum continuatione transegit et testes propemodum quas in pretium praesidii caelestis adpenderat lacrimarum lacunas reliquit, fiducialiter arma corripuit solus, sciens, se esse non solum. Signo crucis signum proelio dedit ac se in bellum, etiamsi nemo sequeretur, victor futurus, inmisit." *Adversum paganos,* Book VII, Ch. xxxv; CSEL, Vol. V, pp. 529–30.

53. Fervent prayer brought Otto victory at the moment of the greatest Hungarian threat through new might which God suddenly bestowed on him, according to the *Saxon History* of Widukind of Corvey; cited and interpreted by Lothar Bornscheuer, *Miserae Regum: Untersuchungen zum Krisen- und Todesgedanken in den herrschaftstheologischen Vorstellungen der ottonisch-salischen Zeit* (Berlin: De Gruyter, 1968), pp. 22–25.

54. In post-Carolingian France, the royal healing touch was first attributed to Robert the Pious (r. 996–1030), who was more of a general practitioner than his successors and is recorded to have cured a variety of afflictions, including leprosy. "Nam ipsa terra multos habens infirmos et praecipue leprosos, hos vir Dei non abhorruit, quia in Scripturis sanctis legit Dominum Christum multoties in speciem leprosorum hospitio susceptum. Ad hos avida mente properans et intrans, manu propria dabat denariorum summam et ore proprio figens eorum manibus oscula, in omnibus Deum collaudabat. . . . Tantam quippe gratiam in medendis corporibus perfecto viro contulit divina virtus ut, sua piissima manu infirmis locum tangens vulneris et illis imprimens signum sanctae crucis, omnen auferret ab eis dolorem infirmitatis." Helgaud, *Epitoma Vitae Roberti Regis* [*Francorum*], PL, Vol. CXLI, col. 931. Philip I (r. 1060–1108) is the first king mentioned as having touched specifically for scrofula in France. There is some debate about the point, but it appears most likely that Henry I (r. 1100–1135) was the first king credited with analogous powers in England; he specialized in scrofula from the first. Bloch, op. cit., pp. 36–38 and 41–49.

55. Thomas Bradwardinus, *De cause Dei contra Pelagium. . .* ; cited by Bloch, op. cit., p. 99. The "present king" is Edward III, and the work dates from 1344, thus something like two and a half centuries after the custom had taken root in England.

56. John Browne, *Adenochoiradelogia,* pp. 109 and 150 ff.; cited by Bloch, op. cit., p. 375.

57. Karl Hauck presents a collection of these expressions of high religious status

accorded rulers in his *Geblütsheiligkeit;* cited by Herwig Wolfram, *Splendor Imperii: Die Epiphanie von Tugend und Heil in Herrschaft und Reich.* MIÖG, Ergänzungsband XX, Heft 3 (1963), p. 120.

58. No. IV in a series called the *Tractatus Eboracenses* (York Tracts): "De consecratione pontificum et regum"; MGH, *Libelli de lite,* Vol. III, p. 663. The association with York is no longer maintained; the author is now generally called "The Anglo-Norman Anonymous."

59. Kern, op. cit., p. 109, n. 229.

60. Boyd H. Hill, Jr., *Medieval Monarchy in Action: The German Empire from Henry I to Henry IV* (New York: Barnes and Noble, 1972), p. 29.

61. Wolfram, op. cit., p. 154.

62. Guillaume de Saint-Pathus, *Les Miracles de Saint Louis,* ed. Percival B. Fay (Paris: Librairie Ancienne Honore Champion, 1931). Miracle no. 46 is that of the royal saint's hat of white peacock feathers. Guillaume's approach to Saint Louis's miracles shows how difficult it is to separate medieval kingship and sainthood when they were perceived in the same personage. For one thing, Saint Louis had clearly earned his sainthood in utilizing the "petiz cours de ceste vie" as an exemplary "devot prince" and "defendeeur de la foi crestienne." P. 1. For another, Saint Louis, in working wonders from his tomb, remains for the author the "jadis noble roi de France," no. 11, p. 34–37 (37); "le benoiet saint Loys, roy de France," no. 13, pp. 41–45 (41); "le benoeit saint Loys, jadis roi de France," no. 19, pp. 63–67 (65); etc.

63. There is a rich background of legendary material which connects rings, epilepsy, valuables entrusted to sacred keeping, and English kingship. According to one legend, Joseph of Arimethea, who was believed in medieval England to have brought Christianity to Britain soon after the Crucifixion, instructed his new countrymen in certain eastern arts, which included curing epilepsy by means of rings. According to a twelfth-century life of King Edward the Confessor, that king was once approached by Saint John the Evangelist in the guise of a beggar. Finding his purse empty, King Edward gave him his ring. Seven years later, the saint gave the ring to two English pilgrims in the Holy Land to return to Edward with the message of his assured salvation. Bloch, op. cit., pp. 159–63.

64. *On the Sacred Disease;* transl. W. H. S. Jones, LCL, Vol. II, pp. 139–51.

65. It was the main thesis of J. N. Figgis, *The Theory of the Divine Right of Kings,* 2nd ed. (Cambridge: University Press, 1914), passim, esp. pp. 14–16 and 44–65, that the divine right of kings developed as part of the struggle to liberate secular power from Church control. Kern, on the other hand, stresses that the monarchical principle, the idea of kingship made legitimate through royal blood and heredity, the sacred character of kingship, and absolutist tendencies in general, all led in the direction of divine right, quite apart from any particular relationship of the Church to the state. Op cit., p. 208, n. 449. It is certainly of the essence here that kings such as Charlemagne and Saint Louis could work on increasing the power of the monarchy and stress, as

rulers, their personal and direct responsibility to God, while maintaining excellent relations with the Church.

66. "Neque enim populus ideo eum [a king or emperor] super se exaltat ut liberam in se exercendae tyrannidis facultatem concedat, sed ut a tyrannide ceterorum et improbitate defendat. . . . Ut enim de rebus vilioribus exemplum trahamus, si quis alicui digne mercede porcos suos pascendos committeret ipsumque postmodo eos non pascere, sed furari, mactare et perdere cognosceret, nonne . . . illum amoveret?" *Ad Gebehardum liber*: MGH, *Libelli de lite,* Vol. I, p. 365.

67. The speech is recorded by Helmold, Priest of Bosau, *Chronicle of the Slavs,* I, xxxii; transl. and ed., Francis Joseph Tschan, 1935 (repr. New York: Octagon Books, 1966). I have made some changes in the translation on the basis of the text in the MGH, SS series.

68. Kern cites Frankish royal documents from the ninth century, one of which guarantees: ". . . unumquemque secundum sui ordinis dignitatem et personam honorare et salvare. . . ; et legem . . . unicuique competentem, sicut antecessores sui tempore antecessorum meorum habuerunt in omni dignitate et ordine [conservare]." Another paraphrases the same idea, op. cit., p. 129, n. 279 and Appendix XII, pp. 294–97. Even William the Conqueror promised Londoners early in his reign that he would maintain their old inheritance rights; with some circumlocution he implied that they could keep their other laws as well. "Charter of William I to the City of London," in Stubbs, op. cit., pp. 82–83.

69. George H. Sabine provides some examples of this phenomenon in his *History of Political Theory,* 3rd ed. (New York: Holt, Rinehart and Winston, 1961), pp. 203–7. One of the more striking is an exhortation by a follower of Simon de Montfort after the Battle of Lewes in 1264: "Therefore let the community of the kingdom advise, and let it be known what the generality thinks, to whom their own laws are best known. Nor are all those of the country so ignorant that they do not know better than strangers the customs of their own kingdom which have been handed down to them by their ancestors." (P. 206).

70. Paine's political theory is eloquent testimony to the vitality of medieval tradition in England and the way that memory of a time before the solidification of monarchical power preserved a sense of popular rights against those of the king. This is all the more significant in view of Paine's typicality as an Enlightenment writer full of conscious scorn for what seemed to him the barbarous and superstitious centuries of the Middle Ages. "The hatred which the Norman invasion and tyranny begat must have been deeply rooted in the nation, to have outlived the contrivance to obliterate it. Though not a courtier will talk of the curfew-bell, not a village in England has forgotten it. . . ." *The Rights of Man,* Part Second, 1792 (Garden City, N.Y.: Doubleday, 1961), p. 404. In his hatred of monarchy in any form, Paine is, of course, unwilling to give the Norman kings any credit for strengthening the English common law. Cf. R. C. Van Caenegem, *The Birth of the English Common Law* (Cambridge University Press, 1973), pp. 90–93. On the part that folk memory

concerning William the Conqueror and the Norman Yoke played in English revolutionary thought of the seventeenth century, see Christopher Hill, *The World Turned Upside Down; Radical Ideas during the English Revolution* (New York: Viking Press, 1972), pp. 53, 107, 181–82, and 218–19.

71. Bishop Liutprand of Cremona, *Liber de rebus gestis Ottonis;* excerpted by B. Hill, op. cit., as Doc. no. 7, pp. 137–49 (143).

72. The imperial document, usually called the *Ottonianum,* bears the date, February 3, 962; in Ibid., as Doc. no. 8, pp. 149–52. There is considerable reason to assume, however, that the crucial sections giving the emperor considerable control over papal elections may have been inserted somewhat later. Walter Ullmann, "The Origins of the Ottonianum," *Cambridge Historical Journal,* Vol. XI (1953), pp. 114–28. Hill discusses different interpretations of the document in relation to its time of appearance in the introduction to his documentary collection cited above, pp. 33–35.

73. *Chronica* of Frutolf of Michelsberg, entry for 1046; in *Frutolfi et Ekkehardi Chronica.* . . . (Darmstadt: WBG, 1972), p. 64.

74. Text in Ernest F. Henderson, ed. and transl., *Select Historical Documents of the Middle Ages* (London: G. Bell and Sons, 1896), pp. 366–67. Like the "Donation of Constantine" itself, the "Dictatus Papae" is now thought to have been originally drafted with an eye to disputing Byzantine claims. There is a certain oddity in the fact that Gregory must have resorted to the "Donation" even though he never cites it among his documentary authorities. The simplest answer is perhaps that he wanted the rights which the "Donation" bestowed on the papacy but did not like the idea of acknowledging a source which showed those papal rights to have come from a secular, imperial hand. Gerhard Laehr, *Die Konstantinische Schenkung in der abendländischen Literatur* (Vaduz, 1926; Kraus Reprint, 1965), p. 37.

75. Letter dated January 24, 1076; in Henderson, op. cit., pp. 372–73.

76. Letter to Hermann, Bishop of Metz, March 15, 1081; text in Henry Bettenson, ed. *Documents of the Christian Church,* 2nd ed. (London: Oxford University Press, 1963), pp. 145–53; cited with a few changes in translation by Edgar N. Johnson, in his *Introduction to the History of the Western Tradition* (Boston: Ginn, 1959), Vol. I, p. 534.

77. Among others, Lampert of Hersfeld gives a restrained, largely factual account in his *Annales* under 1077; WBG, p. 406, while Helmold gives a rather exaggerated and embellished one; loc. cit., pp. 107–9.

78. Letter from 1079, Reg., VII, I. Cited by Z. N. Brooke, *The English Church and the Papacy from the Conquest to the Reign of King John* (Cambridge University Press, 1931), p. 137.

79. "Epist. V ad Hugonem Diensem Episcopum," PL, Vol. CXLVII, col. 610, translation by Douglas, op. cit., p. 341.

80. Text in Stubbs, op. cit., pp. 137–40 (138).

81. William of Newburgh, *History of England,* ed. and transl. Joseph Stevenson (London: S. Beeley's, 1856); excerpted in Thomas M. Jones, ed., *The Becket Controversy* (New York: John Wiley, 1970), pp. 22–30 (24).

82. Letter dated June 1165; in David C. Douglas and George Greenaway, *English Historical Documents* (Oxford: University Press, 1953), Vol. II, p. 742.

83. Roger of Hoveden, *Annales;* transl. Henry T. Riley (London: H. G. Bohn, 1853); excerpted in Jones, op. cit., pp. 16–22 (20).

84. Letter written sometime in 1166, included by Roger of Hoveden in his *Annales;* in ibid., pp. 33–35.

85. William of Newburgh, op. cit., in Jones, p. 30.

86. These were traceable to the heavy hand of Hubert Walter, Richard's man as royal justiciar and archbishop of Canterbury, who saw nothing wrong with setting fire to a church to smoke out agitators or with forcing the Church to make payments for a military campaign in Normandy. Lyon, op. cit., pp. 305–6.

87. Sidney Painter, *The Reign of King John* (Baltimore: Johns Hopkins Press, 1949), pp. 164–72.

88. Mitchell notes that the years of John's worst relations with the papacy were those in which he does not seem to have lacked money. The records of the time show King John as having taken in over £50,000 from Church revenues. A case can be made for the likelihood that his total income from Church property during the period of the Interdict was about double that amount. *Studies in Taxation under John and Henry III,* loc. cit., pp. 93–94 and 106–9.

89. Painter, *Reign of King John,* loc. cit., pp. 193–94.

90. Henry Bettenson, *Documents of the Christian Church,* 2nd ed. (London: Oxford University Press, 1963), pp. 157–59.

91. The phenomenon of thirteenth-century resentment against the papacy in the wake of lost crusades emerges clearly in Palmer Throop's *Criticism of the Crusade: A Study of Public Opinion and Crusade Propaganda* (Amsterdam: Swets & Zeitlinger, 1940), passim.

92. In H. Dupuy, *Histoire du differend d'entre le pape Boniface VIII et Philippes le Bel* (1655); cited by Thomas S. R. Boase, *Boniface VIII* (London: Constable and Co., 1933), p. 305.

93. Text in Bettenson, op. cit., pp. 159–61.

94. Fines and taxes could go profitably hand in hand for medieval kings bent on raising more revenue. When King John once levied a tax of one-thirteenth on his subjects' moveable property and income, the fines and forfeitures of property from those attempting to escape it swelled the receipts to fifteen times the amount yielded by the scutage, which was the feudal "aid" yielding the highest amount of revenue from lay subjects next to the one-thirteenth tax that year (1206). Mitchell, op. cit., pp. 91 and 127.

95. Bryce Lyon, *A Constitutional and Legal History of Medieval England* (New York: Harper, 1960), pp. 42–43 and pp. 189–90.

96. Painter, *Rise of the Feudal Monarchies,* loc. cit., pp. 20–21.

97. Richard Barber, *Henry Plantagenet* (Totowa, N.J.: Rowman and Littlefield, 1964), p. 60. This and subsequent citations from this book are given with the kind permission of the publisher.

98. Ibid., p. 58.

99. Ibid., p. 82.
100. Joinville, op. cit., ch. xi, 55, p. 37.
101. Ibid., xiii, 61–64, p. 39.
102. Ibid., xii, 59, p. 38.
103. Petit-Dutaillis, op. cit., p. 185, and Painter, *Rise of the Feudal Monarchies,* loc. cit., p. 34. The difference stemmed from the feeling that areas in need of strong garrison forces, such as those bordering on the Duchy of Aquitaine, should be commanded by men of knightly rank representing the king. Soldiers were more likely to obey a noble with the title of seneschal than a non-noble *bailli.*
104. Painter, *Feudal Monarchies,* loc. cit., p. 36.
105. Ibid., p. 37.
106. Petit-Dutaillis, op. cit.
107. Painter, *Feudal Monarchies,* loc. cit., p. 44, and Petit-Dutaillis, op. cit., p. 42.
108. Painter, *Feudal Monarchies,* p. 53.
109. Petit-Dutaillis, op. cit., pp. 135 and 186.
110. Lyon, op. cit., p. 148.
111. Ibid., p. 144.
112. Ibid., p. 250.
113. Ibid., pp. 152–54, 251–54, and 353–54; also, Petit-Dutaillis, op. cit., p. 131.
114. John E. Rodes, *Germany: A History* (New York: Holt, Rinehart and Winston, 1964), pp. 57–58.
115. Joinville, op. cit., ch. cxxxviii, 685, p. 201, and editor's notes from Guillaume de Saint-Pathus (cf. above, n. 62), p. 293.
116. *Anglo-Saxon Chronicle,* transl. and ed., G. N. Garmonsway (New York: E. P. Dutton—Everyman's Library series, 1953), pp. 220–21. Notice how the safety with which a man could transport gold continued from as early as the time of King Theoderic the Ostrogoth (ch. 3) to serve in the Middle Ages as a standard by which the effectiveness of royal peace-keeping efforts were measured.
117. Going on the principle that " 'the trunk must remain alive as witness of its crimes,' [William I] populated the country with ghastly objects whose head and trunk only remained. Blind, armless and legless, they could move only by directionless rollings. Their usually short lives were sustained by the charity of their relations and friends if they were fortunate enough to have any." John D. Potter, *The Art of Hanging* (South Brunswick: A. S. Barnes, 1965), p. 10.
118. Art. 1. "Inprimis statuit praedictus rex Henricus de consilio omnium baronum suorum, pro pace servanda et justitia tenenda, quod per singulos comitatus inquiratur, et per singulos hundredos, per xii. legaliores homines de hundredo, et per iv. legaliores homines de qualibet villata, per sacramentum quod illi verum dicent: si in hundredo suo vel villata sua sit aliquis homo qui sit rettatus vel publicatus quod ipse sit robator vel murdrator vel latro vel aliquis qui sit receptor robatorum vel murdratorum vel latronum, postquam

dominus rex fuit rex. Et hoc inquirant Justitiae coram se, et vicecomites coram se." Text in Stubbs, op. cit., pp. 143–46 (143).

119. Text in ibid., pp. 150–53.
120. Jacques Boussard, *The Civilization of Charlemagne* (New York and Toronto: McGraw-Hill, 1968), pp. 81–84.
121. The overall picture was one of alliances between towns and rulers of large areas, among whom medieval kings were only the most conspicuous, against the smaller lords in whose landholdings the new towns and growing cities were located. "The interests of the town . . . were not infrequently opposed to those of the lord holding the land. Whereas he had an interest in the autarky and compactness of his territory, the town was interested in relationships which spanned wide regions. . . . Things often culminated in a relationship of fighting-alliance and negotiated obligations like those between partners enjoying more or less equal status legally. In the dominions of great territorial lords, landgraves, dukes, kings, and in general, rulers resembling kings, both partners easily recognized each other as natural allies, united as allies to curb the gentry, i.e., the landowners and lords of smaller areas." Eugen Lemberg, *Geschichte des Nationalismus in Europa* (Stuttgart: Curt E. Schwab, 1950), p. 69.
122. Petit-Dutaillis, op. cit., p. 196.
123. Text in Joinville, op. cit., ch. cxl, pp. 203–7; some alterations are made in the translation cited.
124. Painter, *Feudal Monarchies,* loc. cit., p. 105.
125. Ibid., p. 106.
126. MGH *Diplomata,* VI, Parts 1–2, 341–43; transl. by B. Hill as Doc. no. 48 in *Medieval Monarchy in Action,* loc. cit., pp. 235–36. The wording of the original was slightly tampered with early in the thirteenth century, but not in the parts cited. Citations from this translation are made with the kind permission of Professor Hill and George Allen and Unwin, Ltd., publishers.
127. Rodes, op. cit., p. 34.
128. Ibid., p. 56.
129. S. Hellman, *Das Mittelalter bis zum Ausgange der Kreuzzüge* (Gotha: Perthes, 1920), p. 198.
130. Text in Roy C. Cave and Herbert H. Coulson, eds., *A Source Book for Medieval Economic History* (Milwaukee: Bruce Publishing Co., 1936), p. 123.
131. "Quicunque vero liber laicus habuerit in catallo vel in redditu ad valentiam de xvi. marcis, habeat loricam et cassidem et clypeum et lanceam; quicunque vero liber laicus habuerit in catallo vel redditu x. marcas habeat aubergel, et capellet ferri et lanceam." Every man of the free middle class was, in fact, ordered by the king to equip himself with at least minimal arms: "Item omnes burgenses et tota communa liberorum hominum habeant wambais et capellet ferri et lanceam." "Assisa de Armis habendis in Anglia," Art. 2–3; in Stubbs, op. cit., pp. 153–56 (154).
132. In doing so, they were actually reflecting ancient attitudes as well. Virgil, for

example, saw tribal attributes as those which distinguished at least non-Romans or newly conquered peoples from each other: "longo ordine gentes, quam variae linguis, habitu tam vestis et armis." *Aeneid,* VII, 11. 722–23; LCL, Vol. II, pp. 108–10.

133. D. A. Binchy, *Celtic and Anglo-Saxon Kingship* (Oxford: Clarendon Press, 1970), pp. 27 (Wales) and 8–12 (Ireland).

134. It seems to have survived in its Anglo-Saxon, Irish, and Welsh forms: "Tudor," for example, is held to be a derivative of "tud" and "rhi," the Welsh equivalents of "thiud" and "reiks," thus the same stems which formed Theoderic's name. Ibid., pp. 4–6. Cf. above, Ch. III.

135. *King Lear,* Act I, Scene 1. The stage directions and Lear himself call the French king simply "France." Among political theorists, there was a clear distinction between the natural body of the king, which was subject to age and infirmities, and his political body, which in personifying the government and the people's well-being, was timeless and perfect. Ernst H. Kantorowicz, *The King's Two Bodies: A Study in Mediaeval Political Theology* (Princeton University Press, 1967), passim. The distinction was of crucial importance when the living king for any reason did not seem to be filling his political role, particularly when the question arose of deposing an unfit king; however, the very fact that this difference had to be stressed on occasion implies that the norm was for an effective king to be perceived as the man who embodied the kingdom in an almost literal sense.

136. Robert Fawtier, *The Capetian Kings of France,* transl. L. Butler and R. J. Adams (London: Macmillan, 1964), p. 78.

137. Lyon, op. cit., p. 307.

138. Ibid., p. 455.

139. ". . . regis Jhesu Christi in regno suo temporalis vicarius" and "victorie minister. . . ."; text of royal document cited by Helene Wieruszowski, *Vom Imperium zum Nationalen Königtum: Vergleichende Studien über die publizistischen Kämpfe Kaiser Friedrichs II. und König Philipps des Schönen mit der Kurie;* Beiheft 30 der *Historischen Zeitschrift* (München: R. Oldenbourg, 1933), p. 144.

140. From letter dated June 29, 1312, to Emperor Henry VII; text cited in ibid., p. 148, n. 26.

141. *Miracles de Saint Louis,* loc. cit., no. xxv, pp. 83–85.

142. Bloch, op. cit., pp. 146–47. The Hundred Years War predictably heightened competitive feelings concerning such royal powers. One Jean de Lyons, for example, was imprisoned in France for counting Edward III's royal touch better than the French king's. P. S. Lewis, *Later Medieval France* (New York: Macmillan, 1968), p. 62.

143. "Igitur sinceritatis ac iustitiae eius rumore increbrescente, Germanicae matres parvulos suos in eius adventum offerendos curabant, ratae eos regio contactu perinde ac caelesti aliquo beneficio feliciora naturae incrementa sumpturos ac prosperioribus educationis auspiciis nutriendos. Nec minus superstitiosi agrestes, qui iaciendorum seminum grana, quo melius adolescerent, dexterae

eius disicienda praebebant." Saxo Grammaticus, *Gesta Danorum,* Book XIV, ch. clix, 13 (Hauniae: Levin & Munksgaard, 1931), Vol. I, p. 442.

144. Oswald Redlich, *Rudolf von Habsburg; das deutsche Reich nach dem Untergange des alten Kaisertums* (Innsbruck: Wagner, 1903), pp. 177–333, passim.

145. Decree prohibiting mixed marriages without the special consent of the emperor, cited by Ernst H. Kantorowicz, *Frederick The Second* (1931), transl. E. O. Lorimer (repr. N.Y.: Fred. Ungar, 1957), pp. 291–92. The issue of national identity is, of course, only one strand in the complex of medieval Sicilian political history. The measures applied by Emperor Frederick II were "aimed at the complete destruction of the feudal state, at the transformation of the people into a multitude destitute of will and of the means of resistance, but profitable in the utmost degree to the exchequer. He centralized in a manner hitherto unknown in the West, the whole judicial and political administration by establishing the right of appeal from the feudal courts, which he did not, however, abolish, to the imperial judges." Jacob Burckhardt, *The Civilization of the Renaissance in Italy* (1860), transl. S. G. C. Middlemore (New York: Harper, 1929), p. 24. Frederick had Mohammedan precedents for his policies of leveling and centralizing which produced in the eyes of Burckhardt and others "the first modern state structure." Wieruszowski, op. cit., pp. 38–39, presents some modifying evidence, but leaves such an assessment basically intact. The government of Sicily was efficient enough to raise revenue with a regularity well in advance of the age, but it lost all claims to a progressive character at the close of the Middle Ages; in fact, by the early nineteenth century, the "Kingdom of the Two Sicilies" (Sicily and Southern Italy, also called the "Kingdom of Naples") was a vestigial symbol of backwardness and incompetent despotism. In assessing causal factors behind this, there is no agreement on the weight properly attributable to overtaxed Norman statecraft, to Frederick's progressive but radical policies, and to other factors, such as the intervention of France and later Aragon. One recent study, however, stresses the failure of the Norman Kingdom "to develop any national tradition of its own" as a seed of its own destruction which it carried within itself from the start. John J. Norwich, *The Kingdom in the Sun, 1130–94* (N.Y. and Evanston: Harper and Row, 1970), p. 391.

146. See pp. 243–44.

147. Herwig Wolfram, *Intitulatio II. Lateinische Herrscher- und Fürstentitel im neunten und zehnten Jahrhundert;* MIÖG, Ergänzungsband XXIV (Wien: Böhlaus Nachf., 1973), p. 114.

148. Ibid., pp. 124–25.

149. Ibid., p. 556.

150. Charles T. Wood, *The French Apanages and the Capetian Monarchy* (Cambridge: Harvard University Press, 1966), pp. 3–9.

151. Ibid., p. 41.

152. Ibid., p. 31.

153. Robert Fawtier, *The Capetian Kings of France,* transl. L. Butler and R. Adam (New York: St. Martin's Press, 1960), p. 147.

154. Ibid., pp. 167–68.

155. Examples in Wood, op. cit., pp. 38–39, 40–41, and 46–47.

156. "Oath of Salisbury," see above p. 156 and n. 17.

157. Text in Stubbs, op. cit., p. 297.

158. Ibid., pp. 298 and 301.

159. Painter, *Rise of the Feudal Monarchies,* loc. cit., p. 46.

160. William A. Chaney, *The Cult of Kingship in Anglo-Saxon England* (Berkeley and Los Angeles: University of California Press, 1970), p. 152.

161. Citations in ibid., pp. 211 and 251, including one from Bede. "The Lord's anointed" is the usual translation. There is no doubt philological justification in the association of chrism (anointing oil) with *Christus Domini*, but in itself this would signify something too early or too little: anointing in the sense of anointing to kingship did not arrive in Anglo-Saxon England until some half a century after Bede's death; on the other hand, if the reference were simply to baptismal anointment, there would be nothing all that special about a king's having it. In view of subsequent references to the king as Christ's deputy, I can see no objection to understanding the phrase in terms of the king's being the divinely chosen one of his people, the image of Christ.

162. Ibid., p. 248.

163. Archbishop Wulfstan of York, *Institutes of Polity, Civil and Ecclesiastical,* cited in ibid., pp. 186–87 and 258.

164. Bede, *History of the English Church and People,* Book II, ch. ix.

165. Ibid., chs. x–xiv.

166. Chaney, op. cit., p. 248.

167. Binchy, op. cit., p. 12. Medieval Irish historiography retained the image quite concretely: in 1318 "the inauguration of a king of Connacht is described by one of the annalists as a 'wedding feast (banais)' followed by the king's 'sleeping (feis)' with the province of Connacht."

168. Ibid., pp. 162 and 166. The evidence that a Christian Anglo-Saxon king was still thought to need "Heil" for victory is clear; for good seasons, more equivocal.

169. J. M. Wallace-Hadrill, *Early Germanic Kingship in England and on the Continent* (Oxford: Clarendon Press, 1971), p. 141.

170. Ibid., pp. 147–48.

171. Cited by Chaney, op. cit., p. 246.

172. Ibid., pp. 195–96.

173. Figgis, op. cit., p. 80. Between 1154 and 1399, if an eldest son survived an English king, he succeeded his father to the English throne. Applying or not applying the principle was of greatest importance when no eldest son survived, and the question arose of whether or not to skip a generation, in following the line of the eldest son.

174. Texts of Henry I's "Charter of Liberties" or "Coronation Charter" and the Magna Carta are in Stubbs, op. cit., pp. 99–102 and 296–306; annotated

English translations in Carl Stephenson and Frederick G. Marcham, eds., *Sources of English Constitutional History* (New York: Harper and Row, 1937), pp. 46–48 and 115-26.

175. Ganshof, op. cit., p. 80.

176. *Heinrici Chronicon Livoniae,* completed in 1227 (Darmstadt: WBG, 1959), passim.

177. Rodes, op. cit., pp. 40 and 107-8.

178. Ganshof, op. cit., p. 55.

179. "The dukes . . . extended their hands to him, swore fidelity and aid to him against all his enemies and thus made him king according to their custom." Widukind of Corvey, *Res gestae Saxoniae,* II, i; transl. as *"Sächsische Geschichten"* by Paul Hirsch in series, *Geschichtsschreiber der deutschen Vorzeit,* Vol. XXXIII (Leipzig: Verlag der Dykschen Buchhandlung, 1931), p. 64.

180. The chief example is the effort of Conrad II (r. 1024-1039) to break the power of the great territorial lords by allying with their vassals and giving them the right of inheritance. Ganshof, op. cit., p. 120, and Norman Zacour, *An Introduction to Medieval Institutions* (New York: St. Martin's Press, 1969), p. 95.

181. Frederick's ambitious intentions emerge very clearly in the Constitution which he promulgated for Sicily as his kingdom in 1231. Under Title L, for example, he notes that he has established enough officials of his own to provide for peace and justice throughout his kingdom and goes on to prohibit anyone from usurping "any office or jurisdiction for himself by authority of some custom or by election of the people." A city which disobeys by attempting to choose its own officials is to "suffer perpetual desolation, and all the men of that city should be held as perpetual forced laborers." Receiving an office which is seen as part of the royal administration is then made punishable by death. *The "Liber Augustalis" or "Constitutions of Melfi,"* transl. and annotated by James M. Powell (Syracuse: Syracuse University Press, 1971), pp. 48-49.

182. Harold Livermore, *A History of Spain* (New York: Farrar, Straus and Co., 1956), pp. 81-84.

183. J. Lee Shneidman, *The Rise of the Aragonese-Catalan Empire, 1200-1300* (New York: New York University Press, 1970), Vol. I, p. 112.

184. Charles E. Chapman, *A History of Spain;* founded on the *Historia de España y de la Civilización Española* of Rafael Altamira (New York: Macmillan, 1941), p. 81.

185. Roger B. Merriman, *The Rise of the Spanish Empire* (New York: Macmillan, 1936), Vol. I, p. 452.

186. Ibid., pp. 429-30.

187. "Simon de Montfort developed his idea of a Parliament for England from the *Cortes* of Aragon with which he had come into contact as he fought under his father. . . ." George Hills, *Spain* (New York: Praeger, 1970), p. 42, n. 1.

188. Shneidman, op. cit., Vol. I, pp. 117-18.

189. Ibid., p. 116.

190. Ibid., p. 224. This and the subsequent citation from this book are reprinted by the kind permission of New York University Press.

191. Ibid., pp. 224 and 235.

192. Roger B. Merriman, "The Cortes of the Spanish Kingdom in the Later Middle Ages," *American Historical Review,* Vol. XVI (1910–1911), pp. 487–88.

193. Ralph E. Giesey, *If Not, Not: the Oath of the Aragonese and the Legendary Laws of Sobrarbe* (Princeton: Princeton University Press, 1968), p. 6.

194. Ibid., pp. 181–99.

195. Ibid., pp. 190–95.

196. Shneidman, op. cit., Vol. I, p. 127.

197. Ibid., pp. 127–28. Eventually the presence of the Justicia or one of his representatives became necessary for meetings of the Cortes. Merriman, ". . . Cortes," loc. cit., pp. 487–88.

198. Jerónimo Blancas y Tomás, *Comentarios de las cosas de Aragón* (Zaragoza: Impr. del Hospicio, 1878), pp. 359–60.

199. Shneidman, op. cit., Vol. I, pp. 119–20.

200. In fact, their Catalan court writers heightened its clarity in French translation: "Si veut le roi, si veut la loi." Ibid., Vol. I, p. 223.

201. Ibid., Vol. I, p. 227.

202. Ibid., Vol. II, pp. 355, n. 9, and 379–80.

203. Ibid., pp. 465–68.

204. Latin text and German translation in *Gesetze der Westgoten,* ed. Eugen Wohlhaupter (Weimar: Böhlaus Nachf., 1936). English edition: *The Visigothic Code,* transl. and ed. S. P. Scott (Boston: Boston Book Co., 1910). Arguments for the pervasive influence of the Visigoths on Castilian law, in spite of many Roman formulations and changes with local origins, emerge in an extensive analysis of the legal element in Sempere's *Histoire des Cortes d'Éspagne,* entitled "The Gothic Laws of Spain," by the editors of the *Edinburgh Review,* No. 61, 1818, pp. 94–132. There is, however, no agreement on the overall impact of the Visigothic Kingdom on later Spanish institutions and ideology. Américo Castro places little emphasis on Visigothic influence because of the lack of institutional continuity and because of the percentage of historic fictions which became part of the revived interest in the Visigoths. *The Spaniards: An Introduction to Their History,* transl. W. F. King and Selma Margaretten (Berkeley and Los Angeles: University of California Press, 1971), esp. pp. 179–91. Some other Spanish historians, however, emphasize that even revivals which play fast and loose with historicity show the influence of the older civilization which is being imitated and, at the least, Spanish history would have taken different turns without the Visigothic model as an ancient point of reference: this is roughly the view of Dietrich Claude, who reviews the literature and arguments on both sides in *Geschichte der Westgoten* (Stuttgart: Kohlhammer, 1970), p. 120.

205. On Visigothic influence upon nobles who offered constant resistance to

kings, see Louis Bertrand, *The History of Spain,* 2nd ed. (London: Eyre and Spottiswoode, 1952), p. 18.

206. "[Mariana's] view of the constitution of Spain was derived from, or reinforced by, his studies in Spanish history." J. W. Allen, *A History of Political Thought in the Sixteenth Century* (London: Methuen, 1928), p. 360. Mariana deals at length with the Visigoths in Book V, ch. ii, of his monumental Spanish history, *Historia de rebus Hispaniae,* first published in 1592; *Historia General de España,* in Mariana's *Obras* (Madrid: Rivadeneyra, 1864), Vol. I, pp. 119–83. In the sixteenth and seventeenth centuries, "nostalgic memory" of the fierce independence of the Goths led many Spaniards to adopt them as their family's ancestors. Carlos Claveria, "Reflejos del 'goticismo' espanol en la fraseología del Siglo de Oro," in *Homanaje a Damaso Alonso* (Madrid, 1960), pp. 358–60.

207. The Visigoths had transformed the Roman relationship of patron and freedman or client (libertus) into one which made the patron, as former master, the protector of his client in return for the performance of certain duties, including military service. The notion of reciprocal, quasi-feudal obligations were firmly fixed in Visigothic law, although the patron furnished the client often with moveable goods rather than land, while the client was allowed to change patrons far more easily than later vassals were able to change lords. *Visigothic Code,* loc. cit., Book V, Title iii, Laws 1–4, pp. 156–58. Cf. Aloysius K. Ziegler, *Church and State in Visigothic Spain* (Dissertation, Catholic University; Washington, D.C.: Catholic University Press, 1930), pp. 15–16.

208. Merriman, . . . *Spanish Empire,* loc. cit., Vol. I, p. 172.

209. William H. Prescott, *History of the Reign of Ferdinand and Isabella the Catholic* (Philadelphia: Lippincott, 1871), pp. lxxx-lxxxi.

210. Merriman, . . . *Spanish Empire,* loc. cit., Vol. I, pp. 213–14.

211. Francisco Martinez Marina, *Teoria de las Cortes,* 2nd ed. (Madrid: Collado, 1820), part 2, chs. 27–29; Vol. II, pp. 360–431.

212. Merriman, . . . *Spanish Empire,* loc. cit., pp. 213–14.

213. "The Gothic Laws of Spain," loc. cit., p. 99. The councils of Toledo had developed under the Visigothic Kingdom from purely ecclesiastical convocations to authoritative legislative bodies in secular affairs, as the monarchy grew progressively weaker prior to the Arab invasions. Charles J. Bishko, "Spanish Abbots and the Visigothic Councils of Toledo," *Humanistic Studies in Honor of John Calvin Metcalf; University of Virginia Studies,* Vol. I (1941), p. 139.

214. Saint James was eventually credited with appearing for the first time in this fashion at the legendary, ninth-century Battle of Clavijo to inspire the Christians against the Mohammedans. The story, in which Galician King Ramiro I first beheld the vision of Saint James, has many parallels to a story told of Charlemagne on his Spanish campaign. The final medieval Spanish version is recounted by John A. Crow, *Spain: The Root and the Flower* (New York and Evanston: Harper and Row, 1963), p. 84.

215. Prescott, op. cit., pp. lxix-lxx and notes 79–80.

216. Merriman, . . . *Spanish Empire,* loc. cit., pp. 206–7.

217. Marina, op. cit., part 2, chs. 2, 5, and 6; Vol. II, pp. 7–18 and 39–66.

218. Merriman, ". . . Cortes," p. 484.

219. Philipp Wolff-Windegg, *Die Gekrönten: Sinn und Sinnbilder des Königtums* (Stuttgart: Klett, 1958), p. 209.

220. The king's reaction, on being brought a child with scrofula to cure, was to correct the benighted physicians who brought her to him and then to have her cured by drinking water over a five-day period (one day for each letter of the name, Maria) from a communion chalice in which the image of the Virgin and Child had been washed. His position as king of Castile had nothing to do with the cure. The incident is recorded in the king's own 321st *Cantiga;* cited by Castro, op. cit., p. 431.

221. Marina, op. cit., part 2, chs. 21–23, Vol. II, pp. 283–315.

222. *Estracto de las Siete Partidas, Partida V, Titulo vi;* ed. Juan de la Reguera Valdelomar (Barcelona; Indar, 1847), Vol. II, pp. 101–2.

223. D. Manuel Colmeiro, *Curso de Derecho Político, segun la Historia de Leon y Castilla* (Madrid: Martinez Garcia, 1873), pp. 535–43.

224. Merriman, . . . *Spanish Empire,* loc. cit., pp. 229–30.

225. Colmeiro, op. cit., pp. 560–69.

226. Prescott, op. cit., p. lxxiv.

227. *Siete Partidas,* Part. IV, Tit. xxv, ley 2; loc. cit., Vol. II, pp. 67–68.

228. Townsend Miller, *The Castles and the Crown; Spain: 1451–1555* (New York: Coward-McCann, 1963), pp. 21–22.

229. Mary W. Williams, *Social Scandinavia in the Viking Age* (New York: Macmillan, 1920), p. 54.

230. Stewart Oakley, *A Short History of Sweden* (New York: Praeger, 1966), p. 24.

231. Halvdan Koht and Sigmund Skard, *The Voice of Norway* (New York: Columbia University Press, 1944), p. 7.

232. The appellation of Norway's first generally recognized king, Harald Haarfager, is usually translated "Harold Fairhair," but in the context of the legend from which it comes it does not signify blond or fair haired in the usual sense. Young Harold was said to have attempted to win a Norse princess named Gyda as his mistress, but Gyda refused to be his except as his lawful wife and only after he had conquered all of Norway. Harold liked the challenge and—whether to display his commitment, or to make himself keep his mind on his project, or both—swore not to cut or comb his hair until he had become master of all Norway, which in due course he did. G. Turville-Petre, *The Heroic Age of Scandinavia* (London: Hutchinson House, 1951), p. 113.

233. Williams, op. cit., p. 54.

234. Oakley, op. cit., p. 39.

235. Ibid., p. 36.

236. Ben A. Arneson, *The Democratic Monarchies of Scandinavia* (New York: Van Nostrand, 1949), pp. 21-22.

237. Oakley, op. cit. p. 27.

238. Wilhelm Keilhau, *Norway in World History* (London: McDonald & Co., 1944), p. 68. This is admittedly a minority version of his death. More frequently his murder is recounted as the result of a complex conspiracy in which Harold Bluetooth, king of Denmark, had a hand. Cf. Paul C. Sinding, *History of Scandinavia from the Early Times of the Norsemen and Vikings to the Present Day* (New York: Pudney and Russell, 1858), pp. 58–59.

239. In *Heimskringla or The Lives of the Norse Kings,* ed. Erling Monsen and transl. with A. H. Smith (Cambridge: W. Heffer & Sons, 1932), pp. 10–11.

240. Ibid., p. 32.

241. Keilhau, op. cit., p. 86. The key provision in an act adopted by one of the "Things" during his reign allowed certain high clergy and men appointed by them to select any of the sons of the previous king, in case the oldest son should be found "evil-minded" or stupid. The article was the subject of much subsequent controversy.

242. Cited in Koht and Skard, op. cit., p. 20.

243. At the grave of his foremost opponent, the powerful Earl Erling, whose son had been raised to the throne as Magnus V and who had been supported by Archbishop Eystein, Sverri made it clear that he was filling all the foremost vacancies himself: "Times are greatly changed, as you may see, and have taken a marvellous turn, when one man stands in the place of three – of King, of Earl, of Archbishop – and I am that one." Cited in *Sverrissaga: The Saga of King Sverri of Norway,* ch. 38; transl. John Sephton (London: D. Nutt, 1899), pp. 49–50. He is also referred to by a twentieth-century historian and linguist as a "priest-king." Lawrence M. Larson, "Introduction" to his translation, *The King's Mirror, (Speculum Regale – Konungs Skuggsja)* (New York: American-Scandinavian Foundation, 1917), p. 57.

244. Karen Larsen, *A History of Norway* (Princeton: Princeton University Press, 1948), pp. 136–47.

245. Andrew A. Stromberg, *A History of Sweden* (London: Allen & Unwin, 1932), pp. 146–48 and 161–62.

246. John Danstrup, *A History of Denmark* (Copenhagen: Wivels Forlag, 1947), pp. 22–24.

247. Ibid., pp. 32–35.

248. Keilhau, op. cit., p. 101.

249. Williams, op. cit., p. 272.

250. Oakley, op. cit., pp. 24–25.

251. *The King's Mirror,* loc. cit., p. 294. According to one theory, this anonymous work was written by a clergyman as a handbook on kingship for the son of Haakon Haaksonsson, later called Magnus the Law-Mender. Ingrid Semmingsen, "The King's Mirror," in Jorgen Bukdahl, et al., eds., *Scandinavia – Past and Present,* Vol. I: *From the Viking Age to Absolute Monarchy* (Odense: Arnkrone, 1959), p. 288.

252. Ibid., p. 36.

253. Danstrup, op. cit., pp. 28–30.

254. Keilhau, op. cit., pp. 88–94.

255. Oakley, op. cit., p. 42.
256. Stromberg, op. cit., p. 153.
257. Oakley, op. cit., p. 41.
258. Ibid., pp. 32–35.
259. Keilhau, op. cit., pp. 108–12 and 115–16.
260. Oakley, op. cit., pp. 31–32.
261. Snorre Sturlason, op. cit., p. 42. Enough other sagas vouch for the essentials of this story to give it a reasonable claim to historicity. Sir Henry A. Haworth, *"Harald Fairhair" and His Ancestors,* lectures published as *Saga-Book of the Viking Society for Northern Research,* Vol. IX, Part I (London: H. Williams and Son, [1919(?)], pp. 137–38.
262. Larsen, op. cit., pp. 104–5. Ingrid Semmingson, "St. Olav," in Bukdahl, et al., op. cit., pp. 165–68.
263. Stromberg, op. cit., p. 143.
264. Hal Koch, "Canute the Great and the Descendants of Sven Estridson," in Bukdahl, op. cit., p. 176.
265. Oakley, op. cit., pp. 31–32.
266. Cf. Bloch, op. cit., pp. 57–58, who labels Saxo's portrayal of Valdemar as a manifestation of "chauvinisme."
267. *Heimskringla,* loc. cit., p. 286. The Norwegian King Haakon the Good was reproved in a similar fashion. Ibid., pp. 88–89.
268. The Frostathing Law. Text transl. by Lawrence M. Larson in *The Earliest Norwegian Laws.* (New York: Columbia University Press, 1935), p. 278.
269. Danstrup, op. cit., pp. 33–35.
270. Oakley, op. cit., p. 35.
271. This is the title and substance of Ch. IX, Keilhau, op. cit., pp. 118–47.
272. Actually, Norway and Sweden were united in a federal government headed by a single king until 1905 when Norway became completely independent, but the constitutional arrangements which followed the Napoleonic Wars were agreed to by representatives of "the Kingdom of Norway," only when concessions had been made to assure that Norwegians should have virtual sovereignty in their internal affairs. Ibid., p. 156.

CHAPTER 6 NOTES

1. Otto of Freising, Book VI, chs. xxxv-xxxvi and prologue to Book VII; written about 1145–1146. *Chronica, sive historia de duabus civitatibus,* ed. A. Hofmeister and W. Lammers (Darmstadt: Wissenschaftliche Buchgesellschaft, 1961), pp. 490–96. The reasoning used is typical of the medieval historian's search for divine symmetry in history. The Church put the state firmly to its own use under Theodosius I and began divesting itself of the secular state, which had outworn its function, under Henry IV. The two excommunications thus mark the beginning and end of the usefulness of the empire to the Church.
2. This designation of the Policraticus is taken from Reginald Poole, *Illustra-*

tions of the History of Medieval Thought and Learning, 2nd ed., SPCK, 1920
(repr. New York: Dover, 1960), p. 204. It is presented without qualification
by John Dickinson in the introduction to his translation, *Policraticus or The
Statesman's Book,* New York, 1927 (repr. New York: Meridian, 1957), p.
359. It would seem advisable to question such a sweeping claim to primacy for
John of Salisbury in view of the detailed philosophical treatment of the
secular power by earlier medieval writers such as Hugh of Fleury and Jonas of
Orleans; however, the actual context of Poole's statement is limited to the
dispute over the independence of the civil state following the Investiture
Controversy, and the claim for John's being the first medieval writer to
attempt systematic political philosophy with some success is not so sweeping
after all.

3. The term *res publica* is now variously translated "state," "republic," and
"commonwealth." The morally neutral term "state" fails to convey the ethical
basis which medieval writers such as John took for granted in writing of any
true res publica; the fact that "republic" is currently used as a near synonym
for democracy, often in conscious contrast with "monarchy," makes it a bad
translation of *res publica* in writings which defend monarchy as the best
possible form of *res publica*; "commonwealth" remains the best translation,
as long as it is literally understood as "government committed to the well-
being of all."

4. *Policraticus,* V, ii, 540a–540b; Vol. I, pp. 282–83. Cited here and afterwards
from the edition of C.C.I. Webb, 1909 (repr. Frankfurt: Minerva GMBH,
1965).

5. There are bits and scraps of Plutarch's writings which can be related to this
passage, and Webb asserts that the ideas presented are "not foreign" to the
times in which the religions of antiquity flourished. Ibid., Vol. I, notes, p.
280. The notion of the priesthood as a ruling group was common enough in
the ancient Middle East, but the religious element in Greek and Roman
political theory—that political authority must respect the Good, whose
source is God; that no ruler may defy the law of God, the gods or Nature—did
not carry with it the institutional subordination of the ruler to the priesthood.
Ancient Greek and Roman authors more typically sought to use the priesthood to give the religious stamp of approval to decisions which were reached
by rulers who did their own meditating on the Good and the Eternal, or to
increase the authority of high officials by making them priests (as Plato, *The
Laws,* 945e–946e), after they had shown themselves to be worthy of ruling
functions. Hans Liebeschütz makes a plausible case for John's having virtually composed the "Institutio Trainani" himself. "John of Salisbury and
Pseudo-Plutarch," *Journal of the Warburg and Courtauld Institutes,* Vol. VI
(1943), pp. 33–39. His argumentation is reviewed and subsequent literature
on the question given by Richard H. and Mary A. Rouse, "John of Salisbury
and the Doctrine of Tyrannicide," *Speculum,* Vol. XLII (1967), p. 700, n. 44.

6. John sees in the prince's receiving his sword from "the hand of the Church" a
recognition of his acceptance of inferior duties which are unfit ones for

churchmen because of their relation to blood and violence. "Est ergo princeps sacerdotii quidem minister et qui sacrorum officiorum illam partem exercet quae sacerdotii manibus videtur indigna." Ibid., IV, iii, 516a; Vol. I, p. 239.

7. Ibid., VI, viii, 600c; Vol. II, p. 22.

8. Ibid., IV, vi, 524d; Vol. I, p. 254. John seems to feel that it was no accident that the Roman commonwealth prospered under rulers of some education and that the institution of the emperor declined in an age of neglected learning. "Romanos imperatores aut duces, dum eorum respublica viguit, illiteratos extitisse non memini. Et nescio quomodo contingit quod, ex quo in principibus virtus languit litterarum, armatae quoque militiae infirmata est manus et ipsius principatus quasi praecisa radix." IV, vi, 525c–525d; Vol. I, p. 256. There is some doubt about the authenticity of Conrad III's letter to Louis VII, which, of course, does not affect the fact that it contains what for John were quite valid sentiments.

9. Ibid., VI, ii, 592a; Vol. II, pp. 8–9.

10. To a certain extent, according to John, he can rely on provincial governors for help in keeping abreast of events; in describing the functions of these officials, John clearly has an ancient context in mind with limited relevance to the Europe of his own time. Ibid., V, xi, 567c–568c; Vol. I, pp. 330–32. Transported to twelfth-century England or France, these men seem to be high royal judges with the additional function of relaying important information to the king from the extremities of his realm. But keeping well informed about royal judges and the whole administration of justice remains a principal task of the king.

11. The heart for medieval men was the seat of the reflective faculty of the mind, rather than of the emotions, as it is for moderns. John talks about counselors providing an equivalent of the Roman Senate; in doing so, he has only that body's advisory capacity in mind. While, historically, separate legislative bodies did evolve from kings' councils, this development was still in the future when John wrote.

12. Ibid., V, ix, 562a; Vol. I, pp. 321–22.

13. "Famam namque benignitatis conciliat sermo bonus et lingua gratiosa. Amorem fidelissimum et constantissimum etiam a durioribus extorquent beneficia et, quem fecere, fovent et solidant. Et morum dignitati debetur reverentia subditorum." Ibid., IV, viii, 529c–d; Vol. I, p. 263.

14. Ibid., IV, viii, 530a; Vol. I, pp. 263–64.

15. Ibid., VIII, xxii, 807b–c; Vol. II, pp. 396–97. Although he somewhat clouds the passage with references to an ancient Roman slave's enjoyment of the annual freedom of the Saturnalia, John brings out the fact that he is availing himself of what he considers to be the ancient right of a free citizen to criticize the shortcomings of constituted authority. Ibid., VII, xxv, 710b; Vol. II, pp. 224–25.

16. Ibid., V, viii, 558d–559a; Vol. I, p. 315.

17. Ibid., VI, vi, 598c–599a; Vol. II, pp. 19–20.

18. Ibid., IV, vii, 527b; Vol. I, p. 259. It was a medieval commonplace that

human lawgivers were bound to respect a higher law in preserving old laws and enacting new ones. This concept, elaborated on in pre-Christian times by Cicero, overlapped the concept of God's eternal laws to a great extent for medieval Christians, but to scholars such as John it was still distinguishable as the basis for the just laws of all nations, whether they were Christian or not. John notes that such laws are unchangeable because they stem from "perpetual necessity"; they provide what moderns would see as the constitutional limits on a king's legislative power. John's ideal king will, of course, listen to advice on laws from the clergy and his counselors, but it is ultimately up to the king to decide which planned laws are "constitutional" and which are not.

19. Ibid., VI, viii, 600c; Vol. II, p. 23.

20. Ibid., VI, i, 591a–592a; Vol. II, pp. 6–7.

21. This possibility is noted by John Dickenson in his translation of the passage in the *Policraticus* where John remarks of King Henry: ". . . the period which marks the end of a man's youth is looked upon by some with suspicion, and may it prove that the fears of the good are groundless!" (. . . adolescentiae exitus aliquibus suspectus est, ut utinam frustra a bonis timeatur.) Dickenson, op. cit., p. 237, n. 4. VI, xviii, 616b; Vol. II, p. 54.

22. The "still quite unconquered" (adhuc invictissimum) can, of course, be read as noting the possible withdrawal of divine favor from the sovereign if this bad practice continues uncorrected.

23. John of Salisbury, *Policraticus,* VII, xx, 688c; Vol. II, p. 186.

24. Ibid., ". . . illa superna civita[s], quae sursum est mater nostra. . . ." VIII, xix, 680d; Vol. II, p. 171.

25. Ibid., VII, xxi, 691a–696c; Vol. II, pp. 190–201.

26. John's organic analogy would logically make the papacy into the highest faculty of the soul of the commonwealth, but he does not explicitly make this connection. Curiously enough, he passes on to his readers an altogether different organic analogy which illustrates the position of the papacy, by way of a parable told to him personally by Pope Adrian IV. This is the fable in which the human body's stomach is accused of parasitism by the more obviously working members of the body, until they find that their concerted action in depriving the stomach of food also damages themselves. Ibid., VI, xxiv, 625b–626a; Vol. II, pp. 71–72. In the ancient Roman version of this parable (see pages 56–57), the "stomach" was the patrician class; in Pope Adrian's version, it was the papacy. The most obvious emotion that John feels for the papacy is sympathy. He is so convinced of the depravity of the inhabitants of Rome that his discussion of the papal title, "servant of the servants of God" is ironic: "Thus the Romans serve God, too, and are at the same time tyrants whom the Roman Pontiff must serve. What is more, unless he keeps serving them, he will find himself either ex-Pontiff or ex-Roman (aut expontificem aut exromanum esse necesse sit). Who then would doubt that he is the 'servant of servants'?" Ibid., VIII, xxiii, 814b; Vol. II, p. 410.

27. ". . . pro merito principis formatur populus et ex populi merito formatur principatus. . . ." Ibid., VI, xxix, 633d; Vol. II, p. 86.

28. "Nec tamen quod litterae prima facies promittit excludo, quae et longi temporis regnum promittit patribus et eiusdem successionem protendit ad filios qui, sicut temporalis regni, ita erunt et eternae beatitudinis successores." Ibid., IV, xi, 533a; Vol. I, p. 269. Elsewhere he notes that kings have a rare opportunity to prosper in this life and the next, thus enjoying, almost literally, the best of both worlds: "Atqui et reges florere possunt et mundalium florum dulcissimos et utilissimos in eternum carpere fructus. Quid autem beatius est quam si de divitiis ad divitias, de deliciis ad delicias, de gloria ad gloriam principes transferantur, de temporalibus ad eterna?" Ibid., IV, x, 523d–533a; Vol. I, p. 268.

29. Ibid., V, vi, 549a; Vol. I, pp. 298–299. Ref. to I Kings, ix, 2.

30. Ibid., VI, xxiv, 623a–b; Vol. II, pp. 66–67. The story is from Justin's epitome (third or fourth century) of a general history by Pompeius Trogus (late first century B.C. – early first century A.D., now lost).

31. This had been a theme in the Old Testament, which saw the sins of a sovereign visited on his people, and became firmly established in Christian historiography during the fourth century. Paulus Orosius, writing in the early fifth century, made a particular point of noting how great calamities had befallen Rome after each bout of misconduct by pagan emperors, particularly their persecution of Christians. John takes a number of biographical sketches directly from the *Seven Books of History Against the Pagans* by Orosius and shares his belief in historical cause and effect concerning tyrants and diseases, implicitly in the case of Nero and explicitly in the case of both Commodus ("The King's outrages were followed by a punishment inflicted on the city, for the Capitol was struck by lightning, and the resulting fire burned a library, which the care and efforts of generations had well furnished, and rushed to consume nearby buildings with the speed of a whirlwind." Ibid., VIII, xix, 792b; Vol. II, p. 370) and Septimius Severus ("Swift, heavenly vengeance followed on the heels of this profane persecution of Christians and the Church, for civil wars broke out without delay, in which much Roman blood was shed." Ibid., VIII, xix, 792; Vol. II, p. 371). Cf. Orosius, VII, xvi-xvii; CSEL, Vol. V. pp. 472–75.

32. "Logical consistency is not Salisbury's thing," notes Fritz Kern after reviewing John's main passages on tyrannicide. *Gottesgnadentum und Widerstandsrecht,* 2nd ed. with revisions by Rudolf Buchner, 1954 (repr. Darmstadt: Wissenschaftliche Buchgesellschaft, 1962), p. 356, n. 433. See also John Dickenson, "The Mediaeval Conception of Kingship and some of its limitations as developed in the *Policraticus* of John of Salisbury," *Speculum,* Vol. I (1926), pp. 308–37, esp. 325–35, and the Rouses, op. cit., pp. 693–709, who, for somewhat different reasons, come to much the same conclusion as the present author concerning John's defense of tyrannicide.

33. John of Salisbury, op. cit., VIII, xvii, 777d–778a; Vol. II, p. 345.

34. Ibid.

35. "Hoc tamen cavendum docent historiae, ne quis illius moliatur interitum cui fidei aut sacramenti religione tenetur astrictus. . . . Sed nec veneni, licet

videam ab infidelibus aliquando usurpatam, ullo umquam iure indultam lego licentiam. Non quod tirannos de medio tollendos esse non credam sed sine religionis honestatisque dispendio." Ibid., VIII, xx, 796b-c; Vol. II, pp. 377–78.

36. Ibid., VIII, xxi, 798b-806d.
37. Henry A. Myers, "Kingship in 'The Book of Emperors' ('Kaiserchronik')," *Traditio,* Vol. XXVII (1971), pp. 206–7.
38. Ernst Friedrich Ohly, *Sage und Legende in der Kaiserchronik* (Münster, 1940; photogr. repr. Darmstadt: WGB, 1968) pp. 238–41.
39. *The Book of Emperors,* lines 1379–86 and 1397–1403. Citations here and afterwards are to Edward Schröder's edition of the Middle High German text, in Vol. I of the *Deutsche Chroniken* series of the *Monumenta Germaniae Historica* (1892); photogr. repr. (Zürich: Weidmann, 1964 and 1969). Faustinian was Saint Clement's father in a ninth-century life of that pope and martyr, based ultimately on the *Recognitiones Clementis* from the fourth century, the earliest surviving novel with a Christian theme. PG, Vol. I, cols. 1202-1454. Over the centuries, Saint Clement's father had been moved closer and closer to rulership: having been first mentioned as a relative of the Julio-Claudian family, he was later portrayed as the brother of Augustus Caesar, and in *The Book of Emperors* he is an emperor in his own right. As the living model of true kingship, he is set off against the historical figure of Emperor Claudius, whom the author assigns to Faustinian as a brother instead of Augustus Caesar and who is a full model of tyranny.
40. Ibid., ll. 1637–60.
41. Ibid., ll. 6083–90. Cf. *Policraticus,* V, viii, 559d; Vol. I, p. 317.
42. Ibid., ll. 5845–58.
43. Ibid., ll. 5873–6006. Cf. *Policraticus,* V, viii, 560a; Vol. I, pp. 317–18.
44. Ibid., ll. 5374–76.
45. Ibid., ll. 8099–105.
46. Ibid., ll. 15,148–56.
47. Ibid., ll. 15,164–75.
48. Ibid., ll. 5377–5530. The characterizing attribute of clemency for Titus can be traced all the way back to Suetonius, "Divus Titus," ch. viii: "Duos patricii generis convictos in adfectione imperii nihil amplius quam ut desisterent monuit, docens principatum fato dari, si quid praeterea desiderarent promittens se tributurum." *Lives of the Caesars;* LCL, Vol. II, p. 334.
49. *The Book of Emperors,* ll. 13,417–26.
50. Ibid., ll. 15,900–910. The quite factual historical original of this anecdote was furnished by the Byzantine emperor, Basil II, who more than lived up to his sobriquet, Basil Bulgaroctonus (Basil the Bulgar-Killer). In 1014, after killing many Bulgarians in battle and taking a larger number of them prisoner, he had the captives blinded except for one out of each hundred, who was left with one eye to guide the others back to the Bulgarian Tsar Samuel. George Ostrogorsky, *History of the Byzantine State,* transl. Joan Hussey (New Brunswick, N.J.: Rutgers University Press, 1957), p. 275.

51. *The Book of Emperors,* ll. 1331–51 and 4025–38.

52. Ibid., ll. 4667–800.

53. Ibid., ll. 6127–50. All early Christian histories name Emperor Philip the Arab, whose short reign (244–249 A.D.) antedated that of Constantine by about sixty years, as the first Christian emperor. Modern historians dismiss the supporting evidence that no persecutions of Christians are known to have taken place during his reign and that his court was less tolerant of vice than that of many other fourth-century emperors as inadequate to support this claim for Philip, in spite of the affirmations of Saint Jerome and Sulpicius Severus. Orosius reasoned that the magnificent celebration during Philip's reign in honor of the thousandth anniversary of Rome's founding showed the work of the divine hand, in reserving such a distinction for a Christian rather than a pagan ruler. *Historiarum adversum paganos libri septem,* Book VII, ch. xx; CSEL, Vol. V, pp. 478–79. Similar figurative considerations were of the greatest weight for historians in the Middle Ages, particularly since Philip served as an excellent point of contrast with his persecuting successor, Decius.

54. *The Book of Emperors,* ll. 7619 and 8006–14.

55. Ibid., ll. 14,873 and 15,005–14.

56. Friedrich Neumann, "Wann entstanden Kaiserchronik und Rolandslied?" *Zeitschrift für deutsches Altertum und deutsche Literatur,* Vol. XCL (1961/ 1962), pp. 292–95.

57. *The Book of Emperors,* ll. 839–1104.

58. Ibid., ll. 11,305.

59. Ibid., ll. 11,312 and 11,318–38.

60. Ibid., ll. 16,470–86.

61. Ibid., ll. 14,689–724.

62. Text in Erik Routley, *The English Carol* (London: Herbert Jenkins, 1958), pp. 37–38.

63. Medieval people were fully aware of the immense practical value of a duel as substitute for a battle in keeping down casualties. Gregory of Tours attributes the following pronouncement to an early fifth-century king of the Alamanni, faced with the prospect of an all-out battle between his people and the Vandals under the successor to King Gunderic: "Quousque bellum super cunctum populum commovetur? Ne pereant, quaeso populi utriusque falangae, sed procedant duo de nostris in campum cum armis bellicis, et ipse inter se confligant. Tunc ille, cuius puer vicerit, regione sine certamine obtenebit." *Historiarum libri decem,* II, ii; WBG, Vol. I, p. 60.

64. As for personal duels in lieu of battles by Holy Roman emperors, with whom the author of *The Book of Emperors* is particularly concerned, the most that is attested to from what purports to be a factual contemporary account is the following on the occasion of a sojourn of Emperor Henry III in Carignan with the French king, Henry I, ". . . a quo contumeliose atque hostiliter obiurgatus, quod multa sepe sibi mentitus fuisset, et quod partem maximam regni Francorum dolo a patribus eius occupatam reddere tamdiu distulisset, cum imperator paratum se diceret singulariter cum eo conserta manu obiecta

refellere, ille proxima nocte fuga lapsus in suos se fines recepit." Lampert of Hersfeld, *Annales,* entry under the year 1056; WBG, pp. 58–60.

65. *The Book of Emperors,* ll. 271–84.

66. These are reproduced on fourteen plates for the Hofmeister and Lammers edition of *Chronica sive historia de duabus civitatibus,* loc. cit.; plate no. 7 depicts the abdication of Diocletian and Maximian.

67. The *Annolied,* ed. M. Roediger, is included in the original Vol. I of the MGH *Deutsche Chroniken* with *The Book of Emperors* (see above, n. 39) but not in the recent reprints of *The Book of Emperors.*

68. *Annolied,* ll. 471–72.

69. Ohly, op. cit., p. 42, n. 2.

70. *The Book of Emperors,* ll. 11,060–129.

71. M. D. Chenu, *Towards Understanding Saint Thomas,* transl. A. M. Landry and D. Hughes (Chicago: Regnery, 1964), citing resumé of M. Grandclaude, "Les particularités du *De regimine principum,*" pp. 336–37.

72. Yes, king. The male chauvinism of the ancient and medieval world may have been offset by the fact that women could be queens over some peoples, where they had few citizenship rights otherwise; however, Aristotle and other ancient writers evidently could not envision such an orderly and altogether satisfactory society as that of the bees being ruled by a queen.

73. *De regimine principum,* I, viii, cited here and afterwards from A. P. D. Entreves, *Aquinas: Selected Political Writings* (Oxford: Basil Blackwell, 1954), p. 50.

74. *Summa Theologica,* Prima Secundae Partis, Quaestio XC, Art.4, in ibid., p. 112.

75. Ibid., Quaest. XCI, Art. 1, Concl., p. 112.

76. Ibid., Quaest. XVI, Art. 3, Concl., p. 114.

77. Ibid., Quaest. XCV, Art. 4, p. 130.

78. "Unde omne leges, inquantum participant de ratione recta, intantum derivantur a lege aeterna." Ibid., Quaest. XCIII, Art. 3, Concl., p. 120.

79. Ibid., Quaest. XC, Art. 3, ad tert., p. 110 and Quaest. XCVI, Art. 5, ad tert., pp. 138–40.

80. *De Reg. Princ.,* I, xv, p. 80. Aristotle devotes considerable attention to the art of maintaining an economic sufficiency as one necessary to managers of households and statesmen alike. *Politics,* I, vii-xi, esp. viii, 15. Thomas respects the expertise of the practitioner of this art (oeconomus) with a certain reservation, noting that if it were the goal of good kingship rather than a means to an end such a professional should himself be the king. "Si autem ultimus finis esset divitiarum affluentia, oeconomus rex quidam multitudinis esset." *De Reg. Princ.,* I, xiv, p. 74.

81. *De Regimine Iudaeorum* in Entrèves, op. cit., pp. 90–92.

82. Ibid., pp. 88–90.

83. *De Reg. Princ.,* I, vii, pp. 36–38 and xv, p. 78. In connection with specifically royal rewards in Heaven, we find: "Hic declarat sanctus doctor, quod praemium regum at principum tenet supremum gradum in beatitudine

coelesti. . . ." Although added by a later editor as a title (*De Reg. Princ.*, I, ch. ix), Thomas's statements and reasoning justify at this point the use of the superlative: since God rewards individual men for right living, He will reward good kings, who foster the right living of a whole realm, far more. Since earthly monarchical rule resembles God's rule of the universe, God will have special love for the king as a creature most like Him. The king is subject to the highest temptations, and God will reward him accordingly. And so it goes. By the end of the chapter, Thomas has transformed the pagan superstition that rulers became gods into a partial, figurative vision of the truth: "Hoc etiam fuit apud gentiles aliqualiter somniatum."

84. Ibid., I, xiii, p. 70.

85. Ibid., I, iv, pp. 20–22.

86. *Summa Theologica,* Prima Secundae Partis, Quaest. CV, Art. 1, p. 148.

87. Ibid. and also Quaest. XCV, Art. 4, Concl.: "Est etiam aliquod regimen ex istis [monarchy, aristocracy, and democracy] commixtum quod est optimum."

88. *De Reg. Princ.,* I, iv, pp. 20–22.

89. *Summa Theologica,* Prima Secundae Partis, Quaest. CV, Art. 1, ad secundum, p. 150.

90. *De Reg. Princ.,* I, iii, pp. 14–18.

91. *Summa Theologica,* Pars Prima, Quaest. CIII, Art. 3, p. 106: "Optima autem gubernatio est quae fit per unum."

92. *De Reg. Princ.,* I, xv, p. 78.

93. *Summa Theologica,* Secunda Secundae Partis, Quaest. 10, Art. 8, p. 152.

94. Ibid., Quaest. XI, Art. 3, p. 156.

95. Not, to be sure, with any impressive consistency. In *De Reg. Princ.*, I, vi, the single member directing the body politic — Thomas uses either heart or head for illustration — is implicitly the king. By ch. xii, the royal analogy has advanced from implicitly "heart" or "head" to explicitly "soul": "Hoc igitur officium rex suscepisse cognoscat, ut sit in regno sicut in corpore anima, et sicut Deus in mundo." But Thomas's own heart seems more in it when he cites Gregory Nazianzen: ". . . potestas saecularis subditur spirituali, sicut corpus animae," and continues, "[i]deo non est usurpatum iudicium, si spiritualis Praelatus se intromittat de temporalibus, quantum ad ea in quibus subditur ei saecularis potestas, vel quae ei a saeculari potestate reliquuntur," *Summa Theologica,* Secunda Secundae Partis, Quaest. LX, Art. 6, ad tertium.

96. *De Reg. Princ.,* I, xv, p. 78.

97. Thomas correctly relates rex to regit: ". . . in civitate vero, quae est perfecta communitas, quantum ad omnia necessaria vitae; sed adhuc magis in provincia una propter necessitatem compugnationis et mutui auxilii contra hostes. Unde qui perfectam communitatem regit, id est civitatem vel provinciam, antonomastice rex vocatur. . . ." Ibid., I, i, p. 8. The underlying idea is that the king's ruling stands out to the point that his person subsumes the whole concept of ruling and that his title is a reflection of this. It is unlikely that Thomas was thinking beyond cognates in the Romance languages, and yet

Germanic examples show how generally antonomastic in other ways, too, the royal title was.

98. "Hanc autem virtutem coactivam habet multitudo vel persona publica, ad quam pertinet poenas infligere. . . . Et ideo solius eius est leges facere." *Summa Theol.,* Prima Secundae Partis, Quaest. XC, Art. 2, Concl., p. 112.

99. "Nihil est aliud lex quoddam dictamen practicae rationis in principe qui gubernat aliquam communitatem perfectam." Ibid., Quaest. XCI, Art. 1, Concl., p. 112.

100. *De Reg. Princ.,* I, iv, p. 22.

101. Ibid., I, vi, p. 30.

102. Ibid., p. 32.

103. Book I, ch. iii, *De monarchia,* ed., with Ital. transl., Gustavo Vinay (Firenze: Sanzoni, 1950), pp. 14–28. Subsequent citations are from this edition.

104. Ibid., I, v–vi, pp. 34–42.

105. *On World Government or De Monarchia,* transl., W. Schneider (New York: Liberal Arts Press, 1949).

106. *De monarchia,* I, xi–xiii, pp. 52–86.

107. "Hinc etiam patet quod, quamvis consul sive rex respectu vie sint domini aliorum, respectu tamen termini aliorum ministri sunt, et maxime Monarcha qui minister omnium procul dubio habendus est. Hinc etiam iam innotescere potest quod Monarcha necessitatur a fine sibi prefixo in legibus ponendis." Ibid., I, xii, p. 78.

108. Ibid., I, xi, p. 62.

109. This sort of decision is to be sought ". . . ubicunque humanum iudicium deficit vel ignorantia tenebris involutum vel propter presidium iudiciis non habere." Ibid., II, ix, p. 166. The metaphor and proof is varied in the adjoining chapters: "Ille igitur populus qui cunctis athletizantibus pro imperio mundi prevaluit, de divino iudicio prevaluit." Ibid., ch. viii, pp. 158–66. "Sed Romanus populus per duellum requisivit imperium." Ch. x, pp. 172–76.

110. Ibid., II, xi, pp. 178–82.

111. Orosius, op. cit., VI, xxii, p. 428.

112. *De monarchia,* III, ch. x.

113. Later imperialist and secularist historiography was to make Henry VII into a martyr at the hands of an assassin-monk who slipped him a poisoned sacramental wafer. Among others, the sixteenth-century Protestant polemicist, Johann Fischart, found that the deed established a pattern of assassinations of kings by preaching monks, of which the murder of the French king, Henry III, in 1589, was simply the most recent manifestation. "Wohlbedenckliche Beschreibung des an dem König in Franckreich newlich verrhäterisch begangenen Meuchelmords, von einem Mönch Prediger Ordens," Fischart, *Sämtliche Dichtungen,* ed. Heinrich Kurz (Vols. VIII-X of *Deutsche Bibliothek*), Vol. X, p. 378. Voltaire uses the example as one among others for contrast with the orderly judicial manner in which the English executed King Charles: "Après tout, regardez d'un coté Charles IER vaincu en bataille rangée, prisonnier, jugé, condamné dans Westminster, et de l'autre l'Empereur

Henri VII empoisonné par son chapelain en communiant, Henri III assassiné par un Moine ministre de la rage de tout un Parti. . . ." 18th Letter, "Sur le Parlement," *Lettres philosophiques ou lettres anglaises* (1726–1730), ed. and annot. Raymond Naves (Paris: Garnier, 1964), p. 37.

114. This is true, as will be demonstrated later, only when Marsiglio discusses kingship as such. When it is a question of polemicizing against the papacy, Marsiglio shifts his ground considerably: any ruler whose career ever ran in opposition to papal claims is likely to appear as a just one for Marsiglio, and if he happened to be a sole legislator as well as ruler, this is not held against him. Even when it is a question of selecting a general council, to replace papal power in the Church, Marsiglio is not particular whether the "legislator" is one man or many.

115. "Debet autem iudicium, preceptum et execucio cuiuscumque correctionis principantis iuxta illius demeritum seu transgressionem fieri per legislatorem, vel per aliquem aut aliquos legislatoris auctoritate. . . ." I, §3, p. 222. Cited here and afterwards from: Marsilius von Padua, *Der Verteidiger des Friedens (Defensor Pacis)*, bilingual ed., with notes by Horst Kusch (Berlin: Rütten & Loening, 1958).

116. Marsiglio espoused the cause of Ludwig IV (Louis the Bavarian), who was considerably more successful than Dante's Henry VII. Ludwig invaded Italy in 1327, seized Rome, and set up his own antipope there, Nicholas V, who challenged the authority of Pope John XXII in Avignon from 1328 to 1330.

117. "[I]n te quoque respiciens singulariter, tamquam Dei ministrum huic operi finem daturum, quem extrinsecus optat inesse, inclitissime Ludovice Romanorum imperator. . . ." *Defensor Pacis,* I, i, §6, p. 22.

118. Marsiglio seems to have used not only the Latin translation of Aristotle by William of Moerbeke, but to have compared with it a translation from the Arabic. Ibid., I, xi, §3, p. 106.

119. "Bene temperatum genus" and "viciatum genus"; ibid., I, viii 2, p. 74.

120. Ibid., I, ix, §§1–4, pp. 76–84.

121. ". . . una specierum bene temperati principatus, et fortasse perfeccior, est regalis monarchia. . . . Ibid., I, ix §5, p. 84.

122. Instead of using "aequitas" here, he transliterates $\epsilon\pi\iota\epsilon\iota\kappa\epsilon\iota\alpha$ as if it were a concept previously peculiar to the ancient Greeks. Probably "aequitas" had for him too much the meaning of absolute impartiality or justice and had not yet acquired the connotation of balance and redress of legal rigor by the sovereign.

123. Ibid., I, xiv, §3, p. 146.

124. Saint Augustine of Hippo discusses this dilemma at length in *De civitate Dei*, III, xx, and finds that the lack of any good answer indicts the whole of Rome's pagan worship. He hypothesizes a Christian response only with a patently false analogy.

125. "Est ergo futuro principanti prudencia necessaria, quoniam per ipsam magnifice potest in ipsius opus proprium, iudicio videlicet conferencium et iustorum civilium." *Defensor Pacis,* I, xiv, 3, p. 146.

126. Ibid., I, xvi, §1, pp. 172–74 and §14, p. 184.

127. Ibid., I, xvi, §1, p. 174 and §15, pp. 184–88 (186).

128. Ibid., I, xvi, §2, p. 174 and §16, pp. 188–90.

129. The chief passage in question occurs when Aristotle allows the logic of acknowledging superior ability to lead him into statements on behalf of absolute monarchy which are at a variance with most of the *Politics*. "When it happens that the whole of a family, or even a single person, is of merit so outstanding as to surpass that of all the rest, it is only just that this family should be vested with kingship and absolute sovereignty, or that this single person should become king. . . . It would surely be improper to execute a man of outstanding superiority, or to banish him permanently, or to ostracize him for a period. It would be no less improper to require him to take his turn at being a subject under a system of rotation. A whole is never intended by nature to be inferior to a part; and a man so greatly superior to others stands to them in relation of a whole to its parts. The only course which remains is that he should receive obedience, and should have sovereign power without any limit of tenure—not by turn with others." *The Politics of Aristotle,* transl., Ernest Barker (Oxford University Press, 1958), III, xvii, pp. 150–52.

130. *Defensor Pacis,* I, xvi, §3, p. 176 and §17, pp. 190–92. Reference is to Aristotle's *Rhetoric,* II, xxiv, as Marsiglio cites it, xv in modern editions.

131. Ibid., I, xvi, §4, pp. 176–78 and §18, p. 192.

132. Ibid., I, xvi, §5, p. 178 and §19, pp. 192–94.

133. Ibid., I, xvi, §6, p. 178 and §20, pp. 194–98.

134. Ibid., I, xvi, §7, pp. 178–80 and §21, pp. 198–200.

135. Ibid., I, xvi, §8, p. 180 and §22, p. 200.

136. This contradicts Marsiglio's use of the term "species" for "kingly monarchy" as a whole (ibid., I, ix, §5), but since his reasoning is drawn from biological analogy anyway, the difference between species and subspecies is not very important, as long as the subspecies is a natural grouping and not an aberration from a natural one.

137. Ibid., I, xvi, §9, p. 180 and §23, pp. 200–202.

138. Ibid., I, xvi, §10, pp. 180–82 and §24, p. 202.

139. Ibid., I, xvii, §10, p. 216.

140. "[N]on enim eadem necessitas est unius yconomi numero in unica domo et in tota civitate aut provinciis pluribus, quoniam non existentes in eadem familia domestica non agent unitate numerali cuiusquam yconomi, eo quod sibi invicem cibos et reliqua victui necessaria, mansionem, accubitum et reliqua, non invicem participant, nec in tali unitate, sicut qui sunt eiusdem domestice familie insimul conversantur. Concluderet enim racio hec, pariter oportere unum numero esse yconomum in orbe universo, quod non est expedience neque verum. Sufficiunt enim ad convictum humanum quietum unitates numerales principatuum secundum provincias. . . ." Ibid., I, xxviii, §15, pp. 984–86. The context involves refutation of the idea that one world ruler is necessary for the Church.

141. Ibid., II, iii–v, passim.

142. Ibid., II, iv, §9, pp. 300–302.
143. Ibid., I, xviii, §3, p. 223. The fact that he places no check on the legislative body means that theoretically a legislative authority could exercise such powers that the people's sovereignty is destroyed. Leo Strauss makes much of this, to accuse Marsiglio of "vacillation between populism and what one may call monarchic absolutism." "Marsilius of Padua," in *History of Political Philosophy,* ed. L. Strauss and J. Cropsey (Chicago: Rand McNally, 1963), pp. 227–46 (234–35). But if one notes that Marsiglio sees the legislative authority in relation to monarchy as giving laws under which the ruler must govern and as correcting that ruler when necessary, it is difficult to accuse Marsiglio of any propensity towards putting absolute power anywhere.
144. *Defensor Pacis,* I, xviii, §§4–7, pp. 222–26.
145. [D]icamus . . . potestatem factivam institucionis principatus seu eleccionis ipsius ad legislatorem seu civium universitatem . . . pertinere. . . , principatus quoque correpcionem, quamlibet eciam deposicionem, si expediens fuerit propter commune conferens, eidem similiter convenire." Ibid., I, xv, §2, p. 156.
146. The generation after Marsiglio saw this arrangement formally decreed in the Golden Bull of Charles IV in 1356.
147. Ibid., II, xx, §2, pp. 716–18.
148. This was, of course, not true in Italy, and it is possible that Marsiglio derived the title partly from remembering the oath of the *podesti* to defend the peace of their city or even directly from the Florentine title, *Defensor artium artificum et Conservator pacis.* Kusch, "Einleitung" to cited edition of Marsiglio, p. xxiv. The point, however, is that Marsiglio's work was also aimed at people with a royal or imperial orientation elsewhere, to whom the term would most familiarly connote "king" or "emperor."
149. Alan Gewirth, *Marsilius of Padua; The Defender of Peace,* Vol. I, pp. 20–23 and Vol. II (Translation of the *Defensor Pacis*), "Introduction," pp. xix–xxii; also Kusch, op. cit., "Das Leben des Marsilius von Padua," part of "Einleitung," pp. xv–xviii.
150. A. J. Black, *Monarchy and Community: Political Ideas in the Later Conciliar Controversy, 1430–1450* (Cambridge University Press, 1970), pp. 58, 70–72 and 77–80.
151. Ibid., p. 127.
152. Fortescue's writing career began with the first deposition of Henry VI in 1461. In exile he wrote his first two major works and remained an active supporter of Henry VI. He figured prominently in the brief Lancastrian Restoration of 1470–1471, but less than a month after he returned to England in April 1471, he was taken prisoner at the Battle of Tewkesbury, although he was pardoned by the victorious Yorkists during the same year. There is some question as to whether the *Governance of England* was written with the Lancastrian Restoration in mind or with a view to the author's attempt to be better tolerated in England afterwards under Edward IV.
153. *The Governance of England: otherwise called the Difference between an*

Absolute and a Limited Monarchy, ed. Charles Plummer (Oxford University Press, 1885), p. 109. All subsequent citations refer to this edition.

154. He does not, of course, distinguish between parts of the *De Regimine Principum* done by Saint Thomas himself and those of his continuator, but the more serious objection is that Fortescue paid little attention either to how Thomas distinguished good and bad governments by their aims rather than their forms, or to how his continuator saw monarchical rule as essentially absolute and "political dominion" as essentially elective. Ibid., editor's notes to ch. 1, pp. 172–73. On the other hand, in Book II, ch. 8, of the *De Regimine Principum,* the continuator indicates that a "political dominion" (*principatus politicus*) is one in which citizens are governed "according to their own laws" in contrast with despotism (*principatus despoticus*), a form of government which is exercised "through law which is in the heart of the prince." It would seem that Fortescue accepted just this much of the distinction made between "political" and "despotical" from the *De Regimine Principum,* without feeling bound to accept his source's further distinctions and conclusions.

155. In a legend of Brittany, greatly improved on by Robert Wace and Geoffrey of Monmouth, Brute (also called Brutus or Brut) was a great-grandson of Aeneas and consequently of the line of the ancient kings of Rome. Forced to leave Italy after accidentally killing his father with an arrow, he returned to the land of his ancestors and freed the Trojans taken captive by the Greeks. Eventually he made his conquering way to Britain and after other exploits founded London and ruled from that capital to the great satisfaction of the inhabitants.

156. *Governance of England,* p. 112.

157. Ibid., p. 125.

158. Ibid., pp. 118–20.

159. Ibid., p. 133.

160. Ibid., p. 122.

161. Ibid., pp. 124–25.

162. "And trewly it were bettir, that a priuat person lakked is rewarde which he hath well deserued, then that be his rewarde the gode publike and all the lande were hurte." Ibid., p. 144.

163. Ibid., pp. 133–34.

164. Ibid., pp. 138–39.

165. Ibid., pp. 131–32.

166. Ibid., p. 140.

167. This also accounts, paradoxically, for the absence of many actual rebellions in France, since, if poverty and good cause for rebellion were the only factors, rebellions in France should be much more frequent than in England. Ibid., ch. 13, entitled "Only Lak off Harte and Cowardisse Keepen the Ffrenchmen ffrom Rysynge," pp. 141–42.

168. Ibid., p. 148.

169. "[As] the kyngis counsell was wonned to be chosen . . . what lower man was ther sytinge in that counsell, that durste say ayen the openyon off any off the grete lordis?" Ibid., p. 145.

170. Ibid.
171. Ibid., p. 146.
172. Ibid., p. 145. Concerning thirteenth-century commoners as representatives, Edward Miller, "The Origins of Parliament" (British Historical Association pamphlets, no. 44, 1960), gives a convenient summary, pp. 16–18.
173. *The Governance of England,* p. 113.
174. Ibid., p. 148.
175. The members of the council are to have tenure of office during good behavior, their "hed" or "cheeff," the Capitalis consiliarus, "at the kynges pleasur." Ibid., p. 146.
176. Ibid.
177. All this is set forth more clearly and concisely in the second of a series of "Articles" which Prince Edward of Lancaster was supposed to have sent off to the earl of Warwick in connection with the Restoration of Henry VI. This reads: "It is thought good that it shulde please the king testablysshe a counseill of Spirituel men xij, and of temporel men xij, of the mooste wise and indifferent that can be chosen in alle the londe. And that ther be chosen to theime yerly iiij lordis spirituelx, and iiij lordis temporelx, or in lasse numbre. And that the king do no grete thing towching the rewle of his reaume, nor geve lande, ffee, office, or benefice but that firste his intente therinne be communed and disputed in that counseill, and that he haue herde their advises ther upon; which may in no thing restreyne his power, libertee, or prerogatiff. And thanne shall the king not be counseled by menn of his Chambre, of his housholde, nor other which can not counsele him; but the good publique shal by wise men be condute to the prosperite and honoure of the land, to the suretie and welfare of the kyng, and to the suretie af alle theyme that shal be aboute his persone, whome the peopull haue oftyn tymes slayne for the myscounceling of theire Souraigne lorde." Printed as "Appendix B" in Plummer's ed. of the *Governance,* pp. 348–53. On the basis of both style and content, there is not much question but what Fortescue wrote these "Articles."

CHAPTER 7 NOTES

1. Sydney Herbert, *The Fall of Feudalism in France* (New York: Barnes and Noble, 1921), pp. xv–xvi.
2. *Chronicles of England, France, Spain and the Adjoining Countries* (compl. ca. 1392), Book I, ch. cxxix; transl. Thomas Johnes (London: Wm. Smith, 1844), Vol. I, p. 166.
3. Henry Thomas, *Spanish and Portuguese Romances of Chivalry* (Cambridge: University Press, 1920), p. 21.
4. Raphael Hythloday, the critic of early sixteenth-century European society returning from Utopia, notes with disgust that ". . . the most parte of all princes have more delyte in warlike matters and feates of chivalrie (the knowl-

edge whereof I neither have nor desire) than in the good feates of peace. . . ."
Sir Thomas More, *Utopia* (1516), Book I; transl. Raphe Robynson (London:
J. M. Dent, 1910), p. 19.

5. Sidney Painter, *French Chivalry,* 1940 (repr. Ithaca: Cornell University
Press, 1959), pp. 28–32 (29).

6. Ibid., p. 53.

7. *Register of Edward the Black Prince* (Rolls Series, IV, 66–77, 89), cited by
Painter, op. cit., p. 43.

8. Raymond L. Kilgour, *The Decline of Chivalry* (Gloucester, Mass.: Peter
Smith, 1966), p. 38.

9. As late as 1531, speculations about a crusade headed toward Constantinople
were current enough that Ferdinand I thought it necessary to warn his
brother, Emperor Charles V, with some fervor of their unreality; at the same
time, he presented an urgent request for active support in combating the
Turks as an indispensable measure of defense for the empire.

10. Kilgour, op. cit., pp. 21–22.

11. J. M. W. Bean, *The Decline of English Feudalism, 1215–1540* (New York:
Barnes and Noble, 1968), p. 8.

12. Robert Fawtier, *The Capetian Kings of France,* transl. L. Butler and R.
Adam (New York: St. Martin's Press, 1960), pp. 171–72.

13. *De legibus et consuetudinibus Angliae,* Book II, ch. xix, fol. 45. Text cited
and transl. by Sir Kenelm E. Digby, *An Introduction to the History of the
Law of Real Property;* 5th ed. (Oxford: Clarendon Press, 1897), pp. 159–61.

14. Bean, op. cit., pp. 40–41.

15. Ibid., pp. 79–83.

16. Ibid., pp. 101–2.

17. Cf. Joseph R. Strayer, *On the Medieval Origins of the Modern State* (Princeton University Press, 1970), p. 43, who counts the "disentangling of royal
prerogatives from feudal control of land" as a main factor related to the royal
right to tax all men and to the royal monopoly on the administration of
justice—all of which, taken together, meant that suzerainty had become
sovereignty.

18. May McKisack, *The Fourteenth Century, 1307–1399* (Oxford: Clarendon
Press, 1959), p. 141, and H. J. Hewitt, *The Organization of War under
Edward III, 1338–62* (Manchester University Press, 1966), pp. 140–53.

19. Kilgour, op. cit., pp. 29–30.

20. Arthur B. Ferguson, *The Indian Summer of English Chivalry* (Durham:
Duke University Press, 1960), p. 134.

21. Bernard and Fawn M. Brodie, *From Crossbow to H-Bomb,* rev. ed.
(Bloomington: Indiana University Press, 1973), pp. 35–36.

22. Kilgour, op. cit., p. 46, and J. F. C. Fuller, *A Military History of the Western
World* (New York: Funk and Wagnalls, 1954), Vol. I, p. 441.

23. Richard A. Preston and Sydney F. Wise, *Men in Arms; a History of Warfare
and Its Interrelationships with Western Society;* 2nd rev. ed. (New York:
Praeger, 1970), pp. 85–86.

24. Lynn Montross, *War Through the Ages* (New York: Harper and Bros., 1944), pp. 167–68. To increase its penetrating power, the actual bow section of the crossbow was made stronger and stronger, until it required a lever or a winch for cocking. It is a bit of a technological mystery why the longbow, which was simply a considerably taller version of the ancient and early medieval straight bow, should have come into use later than the more complex crossbow: it, too, could penetrate armor, and it could be fired at something like three times the rate of the crossbow.

25. Baker of Swinbrook, cited by Sir Charles Oman, *History of the Art of War in the Middle Ages,* rev. ed. (New York: Burt Franklin, 1924), Vol. I, p. 143.

26. Oliver L. Spaulding, Jr., Hoffman Nickerson, and John W. Wright, *Warfare: A Study of Military Methods From the Earliest Times* (New York: Harcourt, Brace and Co.), pp. 385–87.

27. Ibid., pp. 391–92.

28. Kilgour, op. cit., p. 52.

29. Paul M. Kendall, *Louis XI, "The Universal Spider,"* (New York: W. W. Norton, 1971), pp. 270; 280–81.

30. John B. Henneman, *Royal Taxation in Fourteenth Century France* (Princeton: Princeton University Press, 1971), pp. 20–30.

31. Spaulding, et al., op. cit., pp. 368–69.

32. Preston and Wise, op. cit., pp. 91–92.

33. J. F. C. Fuller, *Decisive Battles: Their Influence Upon History and Civilization* (New York: Scribner's, 1940), pp. 265–66.

34. Ferguson, op. cit., p. 177.

35. Preston and Wise, op. cit., p. 91.

36. D. Manuel Colmeiro, *Curso de derecho político segun la historia de Leon y Castilla* (Madrid: Martinez Garcia, 1873), p. 395.

37. Henneman, op. cit., p. 3.

38. Bryce Lyon, *A Constitutional and Legal History of Medieval England* (New York: Harper, 1960), passim.

39. The sources do not state this clearly, but it seems to be a safe inference. Town leaders took the trouble to negotiate round sums with the royal assessors, which indicates that they expected to reduce the tax below what they could expect on a per capita basis. On the other hand, there are records of tallage payments by individuals in the towns as well as in the countryside, which indicate that such negotiations were not always successful. Sydney K. Mitchell, *Studies in Taxation under John and Henry III* (New Haven: Yale University Press, 1914), pp. 68, 82, 148, and 172.

40. M. M. Knappen, *Constitutional and Legal History of England* (New York: Harcourt, Brace and Co., 1942), p. 20. This king is usually called "Ethelred the Unready" in English; the sense of "redeless," however, is more "not knowing what to say," "lacking in ideas," or "without counsel."

41. Mitchell, *Studies. . . ,* loc. cit., p. 354.

42. It was used, for example, for the Saladin Tithe of 1188. Henry II had intro-

duced this tax to England in a levy authorized but apparently not collected for the defense of the Holy Land in 1166. Lyon, op. cit., pp. 269 and 385.

43. Article 12. In France, going on a Crusade provided another regular occasion for a feudal "aid." Alphonse Callery, *Histoire du pouvoir royal d'imposer depuis la féodalité jusqu'au règne de Charles V* (Bruxelles: A. Bromant [1879?], pp. 23–24.

44. Julius Hatschek, *Englische Verfassungsgeschichte bis zum Regierungsantritt der Königin Viktoria* (München & Berlin: R. Oldenbourg, 1913), p. 142.

45. "The basis of this levy was that on which the great taxes of the future were to be taken; the amount which it yielded was very large; the assessment was quite generally carried out; and the plea for its levy was ingenious and unanswerable at the time. These facts combine to make the thirteenth of 1207 the most important single levy of the reign." Mitchell, *Studies. . . ,* loc. cit., p. 84. At the same time, the requirement of aids for the three traditional occasions noted above was not affected by this and remained in force.

46. Henneman, op. cit., p. 4.

47. Ibid., pp. 157–58.

48. Henneman, op. cit., p. 307.

49. Gaines Post traces the origins and development of the principle *Quod omnes tangit. . . .* in Ch. IV of his *Studies in Medieval Legal Thought: Public Law and the State* (Princeton: Princeton University Press, 1964), pp. 163–238.

50. Helen Maud Cam, "The Theory and Practice of Representation in Medieval England," in *Lordship and Community in Medieval Europe,* ed. Frederic L. Cheyette (New York: Holt, Rinehart and Winston, 1967), pp. 425–30.

51. Sydney K. Mitchell, *Taxation in Medieval England,* ed. Sidney Painter (New Haven: Yale University Press), p. 227.

52. Antonio Marongiu, "The Theory of Democracy and Consent in the Fourteenth Century," transl. Giuseppe Galigani, in *Lordship and Community. . .* (as in n. 50), pp. 404–21.

53. Lyon, op. cit., p. 162.

54. Callery, op. cit., pp. 28–29.

55. Henneman, op. cit., p. 37.

56. Mitchell, *Studies in Taxation . . . ,* loc. cit., p. 378.

57. "Deinde, rege iubente capti sunt Iudaei per totam Angliam utriusque sexus et incarcerati poenisque gravissimis afflicti, ut de pecunia sua regis facerent voluntatem, quorum quidam graviter torti dederunt omnia quae habebant et plura promittebant, ut sic possent evadere tot genera tormentorum; inter quos unus apud Bristollum variis dilaceratus tormentis, cum se redimere nec finem facere voluisset, iussit rex tortoribus suis, ut diebus singulis unum ex molaribus excuterent dentibus, donec regi decem millia marcas argenti persollvisset; cumque tandem per dies septem tot dentes cum intolerabili cruciatu excussissent, et die octavo simile opus agere tortores iam incepissent Iudaeus ille utilium tardus provisor dedit pecuniam memoratam, ut, septem dentibus evulsis, octavum sibi salvare licet." *Flores historiarum,* entry for 1210; ed.

Henry G. Hewlett, Rolls series (London: Eyre and Spottiswoode, 1886–1889), Vol. II, pp. 54–55.

58. *Chronique Parisienne anonyme de 1316 a 1339,* ed. M. A. Hellot, in *Mémoires de la Société de l'Histoire de Paris,* Vol. XI (1884), pp. 57–59.

59. The whole thing was presented as an act of "grant desloialté et cruelle malice" or, in the official phrasing of Philip's decree, a "crimen lese majestatis nostrae ac contra rem publicam." It ended, however, according to the anonymous chronicler, with all the Jews in the kingdom held captive and their goods "saisis et inventoriés." Ibid., including editor's note 4.

60. Henneman, op. cit., pp. 32–33 and 305.

61. Summerfield Baldwin, *Business in the Middle Ages* (New York: Henry Holt, 1937), p. 86.

62. J. R. Tanner, *English Constitutional Conflicts of the Seventeenth Century, 1603–1689* (Cambridge: University Press, 1928), pp. 76–79.

63. Henneman, op. cit., pp. 34–35 and 321.

64. Henneman, op. cit., pp. 16 and 310–13.

65. "This usefulness—in fact, the indispensable position—of the Jews in trade and commerce had the result that rulers acting in their own interest and that of the community would seek to encourage Jews to settle permanently and would protect and further them in their occupations by issuing special privileges to relieve them of the consequences of living in alien status and offer them a substitute for the legal protection which they did not have otherwise." J. E. Scherer, *Die Rechtsverhältnisse der Juden in den deutsch-österreichischen Ländern* (Leipzig: Duncker & Humblot, 1901), p. 73.

66. North of the Alps there were great differences in timing. The basic change in France, for example, seems to have come around the end of the twelfth century. Louis VII had rejected charges of ritual murder made against the Jews, but his son, Philip II, professed belief in them: he punished the Jews by such measures as taking for himself their 20 percent interest due on loans to Christians and confiscating their lands and buildings. Rigord, *Gesta Philippi Augusti,* sections 6 and 12–17; *Oeuvres de Rigord et de Guillaume le Breton* (Paris: Société de l'Histoire de France, 1882), Vol. I, pp. 14–16 and 24–31. Some half a century later in Austria, however, Duke Frederick the Belligerent was still attempting, in accordance with what was basically the earlier outlook, to protect the money-lending activities of Jews with a charter guaranteeing the Jewish communities a great deal of independence and self-government and the Jewish merchants fair treatment in his courts in disputes involving loans and pledges. Latin text in Scherer, op. cit., pp. 179–84.

67. *Summa Theologica,* Part II, Question 78, articles 1 and 2.

68. Jacob R. Marcus, *The Jew in the Medieval World* (Cincinnati: Union of American Hebrew Congregations, 1948), p. 66.

69. There was, to be sure, considerable disagreement between Clement and Philip concerning how the goods of the order should be divided, since Philip seems fully to have intended keeping the property of the dissolved order for the

crown to dispose of. Heinrich Finke, *Papsttum und Untergang des Templerordens* (Münster: Aschendorff, 1907), Vol. I, pp. 370–86.

70. They were allowed to sell their property beforehand but not to take gold or silver out of the country, which meant, in effect, that they could convert their property only into bills of exchange, which did not enjoy much faith and credit outside of Spain. William H. Prescott, *History of the Reign of Ferdinand and Isabella* (Philadelphia: J. B. Lippincott, 1872), Vol. II, pp. 137–42.

71. Summary of decrees for Castile with commentary in ibid., pp. 446–56.

72. S. B. Chrimes, *Henry VII* (Berkeley and Los Angeles: University of California Press, 1972), pp. 137–44.

73. Ibid., p. 203.

74. Bryce Lyon, *A Constitutional and Legal History of Medieval England* (New York: Harper, 1960), pp. 398–99.

75. Ibid., p. 624.

76. Chrimes, op. cit., p. 166.

77. Quotation in Froissart, op. cit., Vol. I, p. 166. Cf. Fuller, op. cit., p. 464.

78. "Quel besoin avons-nous de ces boutinquiers?" cited by the "Religieux de Saint-Denis" in Edgard Boutaric, *Institutions militaires de la France* (Paris: Henri Plon, 1863), p. 212.

79. Paul Vinogradoff, *Roman Law in Medieval Europe* (Cambridge: Speculum Historiale, 1929), p. 67, and George W. Keeton, *The Norman Conquest and the Common Law* (New York: Barnes and Noble, 1966), pp. 63 and 71–72. Vacarius had support from opponents of King Stephen, who seems to have had no idea of the benefits which a ruler could gain from Roman legal doctrines and who attempted in vain to prevent Vacarius from teaching either civil or canon law. The succeeding Plantagenet dynasty, however, was much more positively inclined to the study of Roman law.

80. Vinogradoff, op. cit., p. 67.

81. P. S. Lewis gives recent literature on formulae making the French king emperor or *princeps* in his own kingdom in his *Later Medieval France: the Polity* (New York: St. Martin's Press, 1968), pp. 84–85, n. 9.

82. Fawtier, op. cit., pp. 46–47 and 188.

83. Ibid., pp. 86–87. The reasons for English King Stephen's opposition to the teaching of Roman law by Vacarius—or why Vacarius should have been supported by his opponents—are not known. It seems at least likely, however, that Stephen may have felt that his opponent, Empress Matilda, would use imperial associations based on Roman law at his expense.

84. Vinogradoff, op. cit., p. 139.

85. Lewis, op. cit., pp. 84–87.

86. See above, ch. VI, pp. 281–87.

87. One theory of the origin of corporate representation in medieval assemblies convoked by kings is that the Roman usage of proctors was adopted by the Church—as in having an agent who represented an abbey litigate or take oaths in court in a manner not suited to monks and abbots—and this fur-

nished kings with a model for group commitment. Gaines Post, "Roman Law and Early Representation in Spain and Italy," *Speculum,* Vol. XVIII (1943), p. 215. This study attempts to demolish the claim made for the king of Aragon as having had the first national assembly with corporate representatives in 1163. The reasoning used, however, rests on a false premise of mutual exclusiveness. Post shows that the Roman law concept of proctor or syndic was legally airtight in medieval Italy, then finds that in Aragon ". . . the representatives of the municipalities . . . were so numerous from each city that they bear only a faint resemblance to the proctors and syndics of Roman and Canon Law." This amounts to asserting that, since the Roman law concept of proctors as representatives was unchallenged where it was used in the twelfth century, representatives who did not have the same standing could not make commitments for the bodies which sent them, which simply does not follow.

88. F. W. Maitland, *The Constitutional History of England* (repr., Cambridge: University Press, 1961), p. 14.

89. Vinogradoff, op. cit., p. 98.

90. The American teacher of political science, for example, is very hard pressed to find examples of unwritten common law prevailing against codified law. In Virginia, for example, it was at least widely believed that, when a man and woman cohabited for seven years, they were to be considered as man and wife under a valid provision of the unwritten common law. Whether a modern court of law would uphold the rights of such a "common-law wife" or "common-law husband" seems increasingly doubtful.

91. This is done repeatedly and apparently almost unconsciously, for example, by Sir Matthew Hale (1609–1676), which would indicate that during the later Middle Ages it had become common practice in England. See his *History of the Common Law of England,* publ. posth. 1713, ed. and intr., Charles M. Gray (Chicago: University of Chicago Press, 1971), pp. 133–39, esp. 136–37.

92. W. S. Holdsworth, *Sources and Literature of English Law* (Oxford: Clarendon Press, 1925), p. 29.

93. Post, "Roman Law . . . ," loc. cit., p. 225.

94. René A. Wormser, *The Law* (New York: Simon and Schuster, 1949), pp. 268–69.

95. William E. Brynteson, "Roman Law and Legislation in the Middle Ages," *Speculum,* Vol. XLI (1966), pp. 422–23.

96. A recent two-volume world history text, for example, having given very short shrift to national pride in the Middle Ages, excuses the statesmen who drew up the Vienna settlement for their ignorance of nationalism since "[o]nly the eye of hindsight could have discerned nationalism as an emergent principle in 1815." John Roberts, et al., *Civilization* (Del Mar, Cal.: CRM Books, 1973), Vol. I, *The Emergence of Man in Society,* p. 398, and Vol. II, *Journey to the Modern World,* p. 281. Another textbook finds it in the ancient world in the ". . . Chosen People belief of the Hebrews and the racial exclusiveness of the Greeks. Nevertheless, nationalism did not really become an all-pervading

force until after the French Revolution." Its medieval manifestations are evidently beside the point. Edward McNall Burns and Philip L. Ralph, *World Civilizations: Their History and Their Culture*, 5th ed. (New York: W. W. Norton, 1974), Vol. II, p. 754. In neither better nor worse fashion, most beginning political science textbooks stress the importance of nationalism since the French Revolution and let its origins go at that: e.g., Stephen L. Wasby, *Political Science — The Discipline and Its Dimensions; An Introduction* (New York: Scribner's, 1970), p. 540. There is, however, a good, although largely ignored account of medieval nationalism linked with sectarianism: Salo W. Baron, *Modern Nationalism and Religion* (New York: Harper and Bros., 1947), pp. 10-17.

97. "At present the concept [nation] usually means at least some unit of territory, a people with a common past and some common cultural characteristics as a common language, and an independent government (actual or hoped for). The devotion to this territory, these characteristics, this history, this government, we call nationalism." Boyd C. Shafer, *Nationalism: Interpreters and Interpretations* (Washington, D.C.: American Historical Association Service Center for Teachers of History, 1959), pp. 3-4. This definition does not claim to be authoritative, but what it includes is sufficiently common in books dealing with the subject to be noncontroversial.

98. Eugen Lemberg, *Die Geschichte des Nationalismus in Europa* (Stuttgart: Curt Schwab, 1950), p. 103.

99. Anonymous troubadour cited by Léon Gautier, *Chivalry*, transl. Henry Frith (London: George Routledge, 1891), p. 50.

100. Abbot Adso of Montierender, *Libellus de Antichristo*; PL, Vol. CI, col. 1295.

101. Ewart Lewis, *Medieval Political Ideas* (New York: Knopf, 1954), Vol. II, p. 452.

102. *De Recuperatione Terrae Sanctae*; cited by G. G. Coulton, "Nationalism in the Middle Ages," *Cambridge Historical Journal*, Vol. V (1935), p. 36. There is no denying the frank nationalism in Dubois' chain of reasoning: "Certainly the French make far surer use of reasonable judgment than any other nations whatsoever, nor are they moved by disorderly impulses; seldom or never do they fight against true reason, a quality which we see not among other folk." Coulton's article is, incidentally, one of the few studies to take nationalism as a pervasive factor in the intellectual life of the Middle Ages.

103. "When Britain first at Heaven's command
Arose from out the azure main,
This was the charter, the charter of the land,
And guardian angels sang this strain:
'Rule Britannia! Britannia rules the waves!
Britons never shall be slaves!' "
The objection can be made that such verses self-consciously display archaic imagery, not at all to be taken seriously in their author's time, but it is precisely the display of archaic (often Roman or biblical) imagery which has

characterized literary reflections of universal monarchy since the tenth century. In fact, such works consistently display at least an esthetic balance by having their unreal ideas couched in unreal phraseology, a redeeming attribute not found in the sober, factual sounding pronouncements of nations committed to universal ideas they have no genuine possibility of living by, as, say, those of the Atlantic Charter or the United Nations Charter.

104. Chivalry was inherently international as a set of ideals, and attempts to graft patriotic sentiments onto it necessarily met with limited success and diminishing returns particularly after the crusading era when other European nations rather than the infidel world became obvious points of contrast with the home country. Cf. Kilgour, op. cit., pp. 180–81. English kings could still resort to it, however, as one element among others as late as the fifteenth century, as illustrated, for example, in the *Agincourt Carol.*

105. Kilgour, op. cit., pp. 222–23.

106. James G. Greenlee, "French Royal Propaganda from Philip the Fair to Louis XI (1300–1485)." Master's thesis, McMaster University, 1969, pp. 1, 10, and passim.

107. At Constance, the English advocated this principle from two sides: (1) to expand English representational jurisdiction to include Scotland, since the Scots "cum Anglicis eandem habent linguam," and (2) to support the English right to representation for five nations on the basis of five languages spoken within Britain, while limiting the French to one because of the common language understood by all Frenchmen. Heinrich Finke, *Weltimperialismus und nationale Regungen im späteren Mittelalter* (Freiburg i. B.: Speyer & Kaerner, 1916), pp. 60–61, n. 83.

108. The courtly poets and singers in Germany used a highly standardized national language, which was understood from the Rhineland to Bohemia. This gave way to the influence of local dialects on the written language in the later thirteenth century. The twelfth-century *Book of Emperors* is permeated with the spirit of German national mission, as is some of the early thirteenth-century poetry of Walther von der Vogelweide, for example, his "Diu krône ist elter danne der künec Philippes sî," "Ir fürsten, die des küneges gerne waeren âne," and "Bot, sage dem keiser sînes armen mannes rât," in his *Gedichte,* ed. Hans Böhm (Berlin: Walther de Gruyter, 1955), pp. 22, 240–42, and 248.

109. Anonymous troubadour cited by Gautier, op. cit., p. 50. The author of the lines on France as the source of all other nations also wrote in the vernacular.

110. Greenlee, op. cit., pp. 2–4.

111. G. E. Woodbine, "The Language of the English Law," *Speculum,* Vol. XVIII (1943), p. 399.

112. All the summonses to the Parliament were, to be sure, in Latin. References to the language threat do not appear in the shorter, less desperate sounding summonses to nobles and representatives of the shires and towns. Texts in William Stubbs, ed., *Select Charters of English Constitutional History,* 7th ed. (Oxford: Clarendon Press, 1980), pp. 484–86.

113. Thomas B. Costain, *The Three Edwards* (Garden City, N. Y.: Doubleday, 1958), p. 43.

114. Geoffrey Chaucer, *Treatise on the Astrolabe*, preface; in *Works*, ed. Alfred W. Pollard (London: Macmillan, 1932), p. 639.

115. In Pierre Mathieu's *Histoire de Henry IV* (1631); cited here from Boyd C. Shafer, *Nationalism: Myth and Reality* (New York: Harcourt, Brace and Co.), p. 80.

116. P. S. Lewis, "Two Pieces of Fifteenth-Century Political Iconography. (a.) Clovis touches for the King's Evil," *Journal of the Warburg and Courtauld Institutes*," Vol. XXVII (1964), pp. 317–19. On these later modifications of the Clovis legend generally, see the same author's *Later Medieval France*, loc. cit., pp. 82–83.

117. Cited in ibid., pp. 83–84.

118. ". . . quo maior nostri patet excellentia regni dignior ut vere rex noster sit omni." Guillaume le Breton, cited here from Joseph R. Strayer, "France, the Holy Land, the Chosen People, and the Most Christian King," in T. K. Rabb and J. E. Siegel, eds., *Action and Conviction in Medieval Europe* (Princeton University Press, 1969), pp. 5–6, and n. 5.

119. Finke, *Weltimperialismus und nationale Regungen. . .,* loc. cit., pp. 39–40.

120. Wenceslaus had bursts of enthusiasm but tended to abandon difficult projects; also, while many medieval kings drank heavily, Wenceslaus was one of the few full-fledged alcoholics among them. Theodor Lindner, *Geschichte des deutschen Reiches unter König Wenzel* (Braunschweig: Schwetzschke, 1880), Vol. II, pp. 170–77 and 469–72.

121. Cited as the appeal circularized throughout Bohemia by the Hussite leaders after their victory at Vysehrad (November 5, 1420). Salo W. Baron, *Modern Nationalism and Religion* (New York: Harper and Bros., 1947), p. 11.

122. Henri Guillemin, *Joan, Maid of Orleans*, transl. Harold J. Salemson (New York: Saturday Review Press, 1973), pp. 8–9.

123. Cited by Lucien Fabre, *Joan of Arc*, transl. Gerard Hopkins (New York: McGraw-Hill, 1954), p. 77.

124. At her trial, Joan acknowledged the contents of this letter as her own, except for insisting that she had demanded that the English surrender to the king rather than to her and that it was the king rather than she who would drive the English "body for body" out of France. Text and contemporary notes in W. P. Barrett, transl., *The Trial of Jeanne d'Arc . . . from the Original Latin and French Documents* (New York: Gotham House, 1932), pp. 177–78.

125. Fabre, op. cit., pp. 136–37.

126. Of the Great Peers who were ecclesiastics, only three were present: the archbishop of Rheims, the bishop of Laon, and the bishop of Châlon. None of the great lords temporal appeared: three had been declared enemies of the crown, two were vassals of the outlawed peers, and one simply chose not to incite to enmity the English, who occupied lands near his own. Nine substitutes were chosen for those absent, however, to assure the validity of the ceremony. Fabre, op. cit., p. 199.

127. Cited by Guy Endore, *The Sword of God: Jeanne d'Arc* (Garden City, N.Y.: Garden City Publishing Co., 1931), p. 143.

128. Pierre Sala, *Hardiesses des grand rois et empereurs* (1516) and an anonymous compiler and editor of documents and chronicles concerning Joan (1500); cited by Endore, op. cit., pp. 352–56; also Fabre, op. cit., pp. 115–16 and 244.

129. Guillemin, op. cit., pp. 164–65. There is, on the other hand, a persistent theory that Charles attempted to ransom Joan but did so in utmost secrecy ". . . because of the heresy issue which had been raised." Charles W. Lightbody, *The Judgments of Joan; Joan of Arc: A Study in Cultural History* (Cambridge, Mass.: Harvard University Press, 1961), pp. 96–97. The evidence to support such a conjecture is rather slender.

130. E. Thornton Cook, *The Royal Line of France* (New York: E. P. Dutton, 1934), p. 6.

131. Its leaders rather ingloriously ". . . agreed to retire with honour and an income." Antony Black, *Monarchy and Community: Political Ideas in the Later Conciliar Controversy* (Cambridge: University Press, 1970), p. 125.

132. P. S. Lewis, *Later Medieval France*, loc. cit., p. 65.

133. P. S. Lewis, "War Propaganda and Historiography in Fifteenth-Century France and England," *Transactions of the Royal Historical Society*, Series 5, Vol. XV (1965), p. 9.

134. "Such parodies could only have convinced the most ignorant or the willfully blind, but reference to them in the current letters of the dispute make it clear they were put in circulation, and the court's followers eagerly took up the cry. 'A pope who writes thus,' exclaims Peter Dubois, 'must be considered a heretic,' " Thomas S. Boase, *Boniface VIII* (London: Constable & Co., 1933), p. 305.

135. Helene Wieruszowski, *Vom Imperium zum nationalen Königtum, Beiheft 30 der Historischen Zeitschrift* (München and Berlin: R. Oldenbourg, 1933). pp. 122–24.

136. Cited by Greenlee, op. cit., p. 18.

BIBLIOGRAPHY

Primary Sources

Adso, Abbot of Montierender. *Libellus de Antichristo;* PL, Vol. CI, cols. 1295ff.

Saint Ambrose (Ambrosius), Bishop of Milan. Sermons and letters in PL, Vol. XVI, cols. 849–1286: "Sermo contra Auxentium de basilicis tradendis," cols. 1007–18; and "Epistolae XXIV, XL, and XLI," cols. 1035–39, 1101–13 and 1113–22.

Ammianus Marcellinus. *Rerum gestarum libri qui supersunt;* ed. and transl. John C. Rolfe, LCL. 3 vols. Cambridge, Mass.: Harvard University Press, 1939. (Vol. III includes the anonymous *Excerpta Valesiana.*)

Anonymous. *The Anglo-Saxon Chronicle,* transl. and ed. G. N. Garmonsway. New York: E. P. Dutton, 1953.

—————. *Annales regni Francorum;* in series: *Quellen zur karolingischen Reichsgeschichte,* ed. Reinhold Rau. Darmstadt: WBG, 1968. Vol. I, pp. 10–154.

—————. *Das Annolied,* ed. M. Roediger, in MGH, *Deutsche Chroniken,* Vol. I. Hannover: Hahn, 1892. Not included in subsequent reprints of that volume.

—————. *Book of Emperors,* ed. and ann. Edward Schröder as *Die Kaiserchronik eines Regensburger Geistlichen,* in MGH, *Deutsche Chroniken,* Vol. I. Hannover: Hahn, 1892. (Printed alone in subsequent reprints dividing that work in *Erster Band, 1. Abteilung.* Zürich: Weidmann, 1964 and 1969.)

—————. *Chronique Parisienne de 1316 à 1339,* ed. M. A. Hellot, *Mémoires de la Sociéte de l'Histoire de Paris,* Vol. XI (1884), pp. 1–207.

—————. "De consecratione pontificum et regum," no. iv in series *Tractatus Eboracenses;* MGH, *Libelli de lite,* Vol. III, pp. 662–79.

—————. *Excerpta Valesiana:* see Ammianus Marcellinus.

—————. *Gesta Theoderici regis,* ed. Bruno Krusch, MGH, *Scriptores rerum Merovingicarum.* Hannover: Hahn, 1888. Vol. II, pp. 200–214.

—————. *The King's Mirror (Speculum Regale—Konungs Skuggsja),* transl. and ann. Laurence M. Larson. New York: American-Scandinavian Foundation, 1917.

—————. *Liber Historiae Francorum,* ed. Bruno Krusch, MGH, *Scriptores rerum Merovingicarum.* Hannover: Hahn, 1888. Vol. II, pp. 215–329.

—————. "Nota de unctione Pippini," in *Quellen zur Entstehung des Kirchenstaates,* ed. Horst Fuhrmann. Göttingen: Vandenhoeck & Ruprecht, 1968. Pp. 73–74.

————. *Sverrissaga — The Saga of King Sverri of Norway,* transl. John Sephton. London: David Nutt, 1899.

————. *Vita Hludowici Imperatoris,* sometimes called *"The Astronomer's Life of Emperor Louis,"* ed. Reinhold Rau in series: *Quellen zur karolingischen Reichsgeschichte.* Darmstadt: WBG, 1968. Vol. I, pp. 255–380.

Aristotle. *The Politics,* transl. and ed. Sir Ernest Barker. Oxford University Press, 1958.

Saint Athanasius, Anastasius Alexandrinus. Works cited from NPNF (2), Vol. IV: *Apologia contra Arianos,* pp. 100–147; *Historia Arianorum,* pp. 266–302; *De Synodis,* pp. 451–80.

Saint Augustine (Augustinus Aurelius), Bishop of Hippo. *De Bono coniugali;* in PL, Vol. XL, cols. 374–95.

————. *De civitate Dei;* LCL, Vols. I and II (6 vols.)

————. *Enarrationes in Psalmos,* CXXIV; CCSL, Vol. XL, pp. 1835–44.

————. "Epistola XCIII"; CSEL, Vol. XXXIV, part 2, pp. 445–96.

Bede (Venerabilis Baedae). *Historia ecclesiastica gentis Anglorum,* with other works, ed. Charles Plummer. Oxford: Clarendon Press, 1896.

Bracton, Henry de. *De legibus et consuetudinibus Angliae libri quinque,* ed. George E. Woodbine. 2 vols. New Haven: Yale University Press, 1922.

Cassiodorus, Magnus Aurelius. *Variae Epistolae,* ed. Theodore Mommsen, MGH, *Auctores Antiquissimi,* Vol. XII. Berlin: Weidmann, 1894.

Chaucer, Geoffrey. *Treatise on the Astrolabe,* in *Works,* ed. Alfred W. Pollard. London: Macmillan, 1932. Pp. 638–58.

Claudianus, Claudius. *De Consulatu Stilichonis,* transl. and ann. Maurice Platnauer, in *Claudian,* LCL. London: Heinemann, 1922. Vol. I, pp. 366–92; Vol. II, pp. 2–66.

————. *Panegyricus de quarto consulatu Honorii Augusti,* LCL (as above), Vol. I, pp. 286–334.

Codex Carolinus; MGH, *Epistolae,* Vol. III: *Epistolae Merowingici et Karolini Aevi,* Part (*Tomus*) I, pp. 468–657.

Codex Iustinianus, ed. Paul Krueger as Vol. II of *Corpus Iuris Civilis.* Berlin: Weidmann, 1915.

Codex Theodosianus, ed. Gustavus Haenel. Bonn: A. Marcus, 1842.

Constantine I, Roman Emperor. Letters known almost entirely from historical works, particularly those of Eusebius of Caesarea, but collected in PL, Vol. VIII, cols. 477–566: "Epistola II ad Anulinum," col. 481; "Epistola ad Caecilianum," cols. 481–84; and "Epistola ad Celsum," cols. 489–92. Also "Epistola Constantini de basilica catholicis erepta," CSEL, Vol. XXVI, Appendix IX, p. 213.

pseudo-Constantine. "Constitutio Constantini" ("Donation of Constantine") in Horst Fuhrmann, ed., *Quellen zur Geschichte der Entstehung des Kirchenstaates.* Göttingen: Vandenhoeck & Ruprecht, 1968. Pp. 79–83.

Council of Chalcedon. Letter to Pope Leo I (in collection of Leo's letters as no. 98); NPNF (2), Vol. XII, pp. 72–73.

Council of Rome (4th century). "Epistola Romani Concilii sub Damaso Habiti ad Gratianum et Valentinianum Imperatores"; PL, Vol. XIII, cols. 575–83.

Dante. *De monarchia,* ed. with Ital. transl., Gustavo Vinay. Firenze: Sanzoni, 1950.

Dudo, Dean of Saint Quentin. *De moribus et actis primorum Normanniae ducum libri tres;* PL, Vol. CXLI, cols. 605–758.

Einhard. *Vita Karoli Magni,* in series: *Quellen zur karolingischen Reichsgeschichte,* ed, Reinhold Rau. Darmstadt: WBG, 1968. Vol. I, pp. 157–210.

Eusebius Pamphili, Bishop of Caesarea. Works in NPNF (2), Vol. I: *Church History,* pp. 73–403; *Life of Constantine the Great,* pp. 481–559; and *Oration in Praise of Constantine,* pp. 580–610. New York: Christian Literature Company, 1890.

Firmicus Maternus, Julius. *De errore profanorum religionum,* ed. Karl Halm; CSEL, Vol. II. Vienna, 1867.

FitzNigel (or Fitzneal), Richard. *Dialogus de Scaccario,* in William Stubbs, ed., *Select Charters and Other Illustrations of English Constitutional History,* 7th ed. Oxford: Clarendon, 1890. Pp. 168–248.

Fortescue, Sir John. *The Governance of England: Otherwise called The Difference between an Absolute and a Limited Monarchy,* ed. and ann. Charles Plummer. Oxford: University Press, 1885; photogr. repr. London: Muston Co., 1926.

Fortunatus, Venantius. "De ecclesia Parisiaca," *Carmina,* Book II, no. 10. Berlin: MGH, Weidmann, 1881. Pp. 39–40.

Frederick the Belligerent, Duke of Austria. Statute fixing the legal position of Jews (1244); Latin text in J. E. Scherer, *Die Rechtsverhältnisse der Juden in den deutsch-österreichischen Ländern.* Leipzig: Duncker & Humblot, 1901. Pp. 179–84.

"Fredegar." *Chronicarum quae dicuntur Fredegarii Scholastici libri IV cum continuationibus,* ed. Bruno Krusch, MGH, *Scriptores rerum Merovingicarum.* Hannover: Hahn, 1888. Vol. II, pp. 1–193.

————. *The Fourth Book of the Chronicle of Fredegar with its continuations,* transl. and ed. J. M. Wallace-Hadrill. London: Thomas Nelson, 1960.

Froissart, Sir John. *Chronicles of England, France, Spain and the Adjoining Countries,* transl. Thomas Johnes. London: William Smith, 1844.

Frutolf and Ekkehard. *Chronica,* ed. with anonymous imperial chronicle Franz-Josef Schmale and Irene Schmale-Ott. Darmstadt: WBG, 1972.

Galla Placidia, Roman Empress. Letter to Theodosius II; written on behalf of Pope Leo I and included among his letters in NPNF (2), Vol. XII, as no. 56, pp. 57–58.

Gebehard, Archbishop of Salzburg. "Epistola ad Herimannum Mettensem episcopum"; MGH, *Libelli de lite,* Vol. I, pp. 261–79.

Gelasius I, Pope. "Epistolae IV, VII and XIV" in A. Thiel, ed., *Epistolae Romanorum Pontificum Genuinae a. S. Hilaro usque ad S. Hormisdam.* Brunsbergae: Peter, 1868. "Vol. I" (intended to be first of a series extending to Pelagius II, although no further volumes followed), pp. 350–568.

Gregory VII, Pope. Letter to Hermann, Bishop of Metz, March 15, 1081, in Henry

Bettenson, ed., *Documents Illustrative of the Christian Church,* 2nd ed. London: Oxford University Press, 1963.

Gregory Nazianzen. "First Invective against Julian," in *Julian the Emperor, containing Gregory Nazianzen's two invectives and Libanius' monody,* ed. and transl. C. W. King. London: George Bell & Sons, 1888. Pp. 1–85.

————. "De vita sua (Περὶ τον εαυτοῦ βιον)" in his *Poemata de seipso,* PG, Vol. XXXVII, cols. 1029–1166.

Gregory, Bishop of Tours. *Historiarum libri decem,* ed. Rudolf Buchner. 2 vols. Darmstadt: WBG, 1967.

Guillaume le Breton. *Philippidos libri XII,* ed., H. F. Delaborde, Vol. II of *Oevres de Rigord et de Guillaume le Breton.* Paris: Société de l'Histoire de France, 1885.

Guillaume de Saint-Pathus. *Les Miracles de Saint Louis,* ed. Percival B. Fay. Paris: Librairie Ancienne Honoré Champion, 1931.

Helgaud. *Epitoma Vitae Roberti Regis Francorum,* in PL, Vol. CSLI, cols. 903–35.

Helmold, Priest of Bosau. *Chronicle of the Slavs,* transl. and ed. Francis Joseph Tschan. New York: Octogon Books, 1966.

Henry II, King of England. Decrees in W. Stubbs, ed., *Select Charters and Other Illustrations of English Constitutional History,* 7th ed. Oxford: Clarendon Press, 1890: "Assisa de armis habendis in Anglia," pp. 153–56, and "Assisa . . . de Foresta," pp. 158–59.

Henry of Livonia. *Chronicon Livoniae* (1227), ed. L. Arbusow and Albert Bauer. Darmstadt: WBG, 1959.

Hilary (Hilarius) of Poitiers. Works in PL, Vol. X: *Contra Auxentium,* cols. 610–18; *Contra Constantium Imperatorem,* cols. 578–610; and *ex Opere Historico, Fragmentum II,* cols. 632–58; *VI,* cols. 686–95; *VII,* 695–99; and *IX,* cols. 703–5.

Hincmar of Rheims. Works in PL, Vol. CXXV: *De cavendis vitiis et virtutibus exercendis,* cols. 857–930; *De divortio Lotharii regis et Tetbergae reginae,* cols. 619–771; and *De regis persona et regio ministerio. . . ,* cols. 833–56.

Hippocrates of Cos. *On the Sacred Disease* (epilepsy); transl. W. H. S. Jones in *Works,* LCL, Vol. II, pp. 139–51.

Hydatius (or Idatius). *Chronicon,* in PL, Vol. LI, cols. 873–90.

Joinville, Jean de. *The Life of Saint Louis,* transl. René Hague. New York: Shred and Ward, 1955.

John of Salisbury (Ioannes Saresberiensis). *Historia Pontificalis — Memoirs of the Papal Court,* transl. and ed. Marjorie Chibnall. London and New York: Thomas Nelson and Sons, 1956.

————. *Policratici sive de Nugis Curialium et Vestigiis Philosophorum libri VII,* ed. Clemens C. I. Webb. 2 vols. London; 1909; repr. Frankfurt am Main: Minerva GMBH, 1965.

————. *Policraticus or The Statesman's Book,* transl. John Dickinson. New York, 1927; repr. New York: Russell Publishing Co., 1963.

Jonas of Orleans (Ionas Aurelianensis). "Episcoporum ad Hludovicum Imperatorem Relatio," in MGH, *Leges,* Sect. 2, Vol. II, no. 196, pp. 26–27.

_____. *De institutione laicali;* in PL, Vol. CVI, cols. 121–279.

_____. *Opusculum de institutione regia;* in PL, Vol. CVI, cols. 280–306.

Jordanes. *The Gothic History,* transl. and ed. Charles C. Mierow. Cambridge: Speculum Historiale and New York: Barnes and Noble, 2nd ed., 1915; photogr. repr. 1960.

Lactantius, Firmianus. *De mortibus persecutorum;* CSEL, Vol. XXVI, part 2.

Lampert of Hersfeld. *Annales,* ed. O. Holder-Egger and W. D. Fritz. Darmstadt: WBG, 1962.

Leo I, Pope. Works in NPNF (2), Vol. XII: "Letters 27–28," pp. 38–43; "nos. 43–44," pp. 53–54; "no. 59," pp. 58–61; "no. 156," pp. 90–101; and "no. 162," p. 104; also "Sermon III," pp. 116–18.

Liberatus. *Breviarum causae Nestorianorum et Eutychianorum";* PL, Vol. LXVII, cols. 968–1051.

Manegold of Lautenbach. *Ad Gebehardum liber;* MGH, *Libelli de lite,* Vol. I, pp. 300–430.

Marsiglio of Padua. *Defensor Pacis — Der Verteidiger des Friedens,* bilingual ed., annot. Horst Kusch. Berlin: Rütten & Loening, 1958.

_____. *The Defender of Peace,* transl. and annot. Alan Gewirth. 2 vols. New York: Columbia University Press, 1956. (Vol. I is an introduction, Vol. II an English translation of the text.)

More, Sir Thomas. *Utopia,* transl. Raphe Robynson. London: J. M. Dent, 1910.

Norway, Laws. *The Frostathing Law,* in Laurence M. Larson, transl. and annot., *The Earliest Norwegian Laws.* New York: Columbia University Press, 1935.

Notker Balbulus. *Gesta Karoli,* ed. Reinhold Rau, in series: *Quellen zur karolingischen Reichsgeschichte.* Darmstadt: WBG, 1966. Vol. III, pp. 322–426.

Optatus Milevitanus. *Libri VII de schismate Donatistarum;* CSEL, Vol. XXVI.

Orosius Paulus. *Historiarum adversus paganos libri VII;* CSEL, Vol. V.

Ossius (or Hosius), Bishop of Cordova. "Epistola ad Constantium Augustum"; in PL, Vol. VIII, cols. 1328–32.

Otto, Bishop of Freising. *Chronica, sive Historia de duabus civitatibus,* ed. Walther Lammers. Darmstadt: WBG, 1961.

Paulinus, Deacon of Milan. *Vita Sancti Ambrosii;* included as an introduction to works of Saint Ambrose in PL, Vol. XIV, cols. 28–50.

Plutarch. "Tiberius Gracchus," in *Lives of Illustrious Men,* transl. John Dryden. Chicago: Belford, Clark & Co., n.d. Vol. III, pp. 104–22.

Polybius. *The Histories,* transl. Mortimer Chambers, ed. E. Badian. New York: Washington Square Press, 1966.

Priscus Panites. *Historia Byzantina or Historia Gothica,* ed. C. Muller, in *Fragmenta Historicorum Graecorum.* Paris: Didot, 1851. Pp. 77–95.

_____. His report of his journey to the court of Attila the Hun is given in a free translation by J. B. Bury, *History of the Later Roman Empire from the Death of Theodosius I to the Death of Justinian.* London and New York: Macmillan, 1923. Vol. I, pp. 279–88.

Procopius. *The Gothic War,* Vols. III–V of *History of the Wars,* transl. H. B. Dewing; LCL, 7 vols.

Prosper of Aquitaine. *Chronicon;* in PL, Vol. LI, cols. 535-606.

Rigord. *Gesta Philippi Augusti,* ed. H. F. Delaborde, Vol. I of *Oevres de Rigord et de Guillaume le Breton.* Paris: Société de l'Histoire de France, 1882.

Roger of Hoveden. *Annales,* transl. Henry T. Riley. London: H. G. Bohn, 1853.

Roger of Wendover. *Liber qui dicitur Flores historiarum. . . ,* ed. Henry G. Hewlett; Rolls series. 3 vols. London: Eyre & Spottiswoode, 1886-1889.

Rufinus, Priest of Aquileia. *Historiae Ecclesiasticae libri duo*; PL, Vol. XXI, cols. 463-540.

Saxo Grammaticus. *Gesta Danorum,* ed. J. Olrik and H. Raeder. Hauniae: Levin & Munksgaard, 1931.

Sedulius Scotus (or Scottus). *Liber de rectoribus christianis;* in PL, Vol. CIII, cols. 291-332.

Severus, Sulpicius. Works ed. C. Halm in CSEL, Vol. I (1866): *Chronicon,* pp. 1-105; *Dialogus* II (III), pp. 198-216.

Sicily, Laws. *The Liber Augustalis, or Constitutions of Melfi, Promulgated by the Emperor Frederick II for the Kingdom of Sicily in 1231,* transl. James M. Powell. Syracuse, N.Y.: Syracuse University Press, 1971.

Smaragdus. *Via regia;* in PL, Vol. CII, cols. 931-70.

Socrates Scholasticus. *Church History from A.D. 305-439;* NPNF (2), Vol. II, pp. 1-178.

Sozomen, Salaminius Hermias. *Church History from A.D. 323 to A.D. 425;* NPNF (2), Vol. II, pp. 179-427.

Spain, Laws. *Estracto de las Siete Partidas,* ed. Juan de la Reguera Valdelomar. 2 vols. Barcelona: Inder, 1847.

_____. *Libro de los fueros de Castilla,* ed. Galo Sanchez. Barcelona: Universidad de Barcelona, Facultad de Derecho, 1924.

Sturlason, Snorre. *Heimskringla* or *The Lives of the Norse Kings,* ed. Erling Monsen, transl. with assistance of A. H. Smith. Cambridge: W. Heffer & Sons, 1932.

Suetonius Tranquillus, Gaius. *De vita caesarum;* LCL, 2 vols.

Symmachus, Quintus Aurelius. "Relatio III," in *Opera quae supersunt,* ed. Otto Seeck; MGH, *Auctorum Antiquissimorum,* Vol. VI, Part I, pp. 280-83.

Tactitus. *Germania,* in *Dialogus, Agricola, Germania;* LCL, 1946, pp. 264-332.

_____. *Historiarum liber IV;* LCL, *Histories,* Vol. II, pp. 2-170.

Tertullian. *Apologeticum;* in CCSL, Vol. I, pp. 85-171.

Thegan. *Vita Hludowici,* in series: *Quellen zur karolingischen Reichsgeschichte,* ed. Reinhold Rau. Darmstadt: WBG, 1968. Vol. I, pp. 215-52.

Theodoret. *The Ecclesiastical History and Letters,* transl. and ann. Bloomfield Jackson in *Historical Writings, Etc. of Theodoret, Jerome, Gennadius, and Rufinus;* NPNF (2), Vol. III, 34-159.

Theodosius II, Roman Emperor. Letters (answers to Pope Leo's letters and numbered with them); NPNF (2), Vol. XII, pp. 52-54 and 63-64.

Saint Thomas Aquinas. *On Kingship, to the King of Cyprus.* transl. Gerald B. Phelan. Toronto: Pontifical Institute of Medieval Studies, 1949.

_____. *Selected Political Writings,* ed. with intr. A. P. D'Entreves. Oxford: Basil Blackwell, 1954.

_____. *Summa Theologica;* PL, Vols. CXCI–CXCII.

Titus Livy. *Ab urbe condita,* Books I–II; LCL, Vol. I.

Valentinian III, Roman Emperor. Edict against the Manichaeans; text in PL, Vol. LIV, cols. 622–23.

Visigoths, Laws. *Gesetze der Westgoten — Codex Euricanus & Lex Visigothorum,* ed. Eugen Wohlhaupter; series: *Germanenrechte: Texte und Übersetzungen,* Vol. XI. Weimar: Böhlaus Nachf., 1936.

_____. *The Visigothic Code — Forum Judicium,* transl. and ed. S. P. Scott. Boston: Boston Book Co., 1910.

Walther von der Vogelweide. "Bot, sage dem keiser sînes armen mannes rât," "Ir fürsten, die des küneges gerne waeren âne," and "Diu krône ist elter danne der künec Philippes sî." in *Gedichte,* ed. Hans Böhm. Berlin: Walther de Gruyter, 1955. Pp. 248, 240–42, and 22.

Wenric, Scholastic of Trier. Open letter written under the name of "Theoderic, Bishop of Verdun," to Gregory VII, ed. Kuno Franke; MGH, *Libelli de lite.* Hannover: Hahn, 1891. Vol. I, pp. 280–99.

Widukind. *Res Gestae Saxonicae,* ed. Reinhold Rau et al. in *Quellen zur Geschichte der Sächsischen Kaiserzeit.* Darmstadt: WBG, 1971. Pp. 3–182.

William of Newburgh. *History of England,* ed. and transl. Joseph Stevenson. London: S. Beeley's, 1856.

Zosimus. *Historia nova — New History,* transl. James J. Buchanan and T. Davis. San Antonio: Trinity University Press, 1967.

SECONDARY SOURCES

Adams, John. Letter to Roger Sherman, July 18, 1789. *Works,* ed. Charles F. Adams. Freeport, N.Y.: Books for Libraries reprint, 1969. Vol. VI, pp. 429–32.

Alföldi, A. *The Conversion of Constantine and Pagan Rome,* transl. Harold Mattingly. Oxford: Clarendon Press, 1948.

Allen, J. W. *A History of Political Thought in the Sixteenth Century.* London: Methuen, 1928.

Anton, Hans H. *Fürstenspiegel und Herrscherethos in der Karolingerzeit; Bonner Historische Forschungen,* no. 32. Bonn: Röhrscheidt, 1968.

Arneson, Ben A. *The Democratic Monarchies of Scandinavia,* 2nd ed. Toronto and New York: D. Van Nostrand Co., 1942.

Bachrach, Bernard S. "Charles Martel, Mounted Shock Combat, the Stirrup, and Feudalism," in *Studies in Medieval and Renaissance History.* Lincoln: University of Nebraska Press, 1970. Vol. VII, pp. 49–75.

Baldwin, Summerfield. *Business in the Middle Ages.* New York: Henry Holt, 1937.

Barber, Richard. *Henry Plantagenet.* Totowa, N.J.: Rowman and Littlefield, 1964.

Barker, Ernest. *Social and Political Thought in Byzantium.* London: Oxford University Press, 1957.

Baron, Salo W. *Modern Nationalism and Religion*. New York: Harper and Bros., 1947.

Barrett, W. P. *The Trial of Jeanne d'Arc Translated into English from the Original Latin and French Documents*. New York: Gotham House, 1932.

Bean. J. M. W. *The Decline of English Feudalism, 1215-1540*. Manchester: Manchester University Press, 1968; New York: Barnes and Noble, 1968.

Bertrand, Louis. *The History of Spain*, 2nd ed. London: Eyre and Spottiswoode, 1952.

Bettenson, Henry, ed. *Documents of the Christian Church*, 2nd ed. London: Oxford University Press, 1963.

Beumann, Helmut. "Zur Entwicklung transpersonaler Staatsvorstellungen," in *Königtum*, pp. 185-224.

Binchy, D. A. *Celtic and Anglo-Saxon Kingship*. O'Donnell Lectures, 1967-1968. Oxford: Clarendon Press, 1970.

Bishko, Charles J. "Spanish Abbots and the Visigothic Councils of Toledo," in *Humanistic Studies in Honor of John Calvin Metcalf; University of Virginia Studies*, Charlottesville: University Press, 1941, Vol. I, pp. 139-50.

Black, A. J. *Monarchy and Community: Political Ideas in the Later Conciliar Controversy, 1430-1450*. Cambridge: University Press, 1970.

Blancas y Tomas, Jeronimo. *Comentarios de las cosas de Aragón*. Zaragoza: Imprenta del Hospicio, 1878.

Bloch, Marc. *Les rois thaumaturges: Étude sur le caractère surnaturel attribué a la puissance royale particulièrement en France et en Angleterre*. Strasbourg: Librairie Istra, 1924.

Bloch, Herbert. "A New Document of the Last Pagan Revival in the West." *Harvard Theological Review*, Vol. XXXVIII (1945), pp. 199-244.

Boase, Thomas S. *Boniface VIII*. London: Constable & Co., 1933.

Bornscheuer, Lothar. *Miserae Regum: Untersuchungen zum Krisen- und Todesgedanken in den herrschaftstheologischen Vorstellungen der ottonisch-salischen Zeit*. Berlin: De Gruyter, 1968.

Boussard, Jacques. *The Civilization of Charlemagne*, transl. Frances Partridge. New York and Toronto: McGraw-Hill, 1968.

Boutaric, Edgard. *Institutions militaires de la France avant les armées permanentes*. Paris: Henri Plon, 1863.

Bovini, Guiseppe. *Ravenna: An Art City*. Ravenna: A. Longo, 1966.

Brodie, Bernard and Fawn M. *From Crossbow to H-Bomb*, rev. ed. Bloomington: Indiana University Press, 1973.

Brooke, Zachary N. *The English Church and the Papacy*. Cambridge: University Press, 1931.

von Brandt, A. *Werkzeug des Historikers*, 3rd ed. Stuttgart: Kohlhammer, 1963.

Brynteson, William E. "Roman Law and Legislation in the Middle Ages." *Speculum*, Vol. XLI (1966), pp. 420-37.

Buchner, Rudolf. "Das merowingische Königtum," in *Königtum*, pp. 143-67.

Burckhardt, Jacob. *The Age of Constantine the Great*, transl. Moses Hadas. New York: Pantheon Books, 1949.

_____. *The Civilization of the Renaissance in Italy,* transl. S. G. C. Middlemor. New York: Harper, 1929.

Burns, Edward McNall and Philip L. Ralph. *World Civilizations: Their History and Their Culture,* 5th ed. 2 vols. New York: W. W. Norton, 1974.

Bury, J. B. *The Invasion of Europe by the Barbarians.* N.p., 1928; repr. New York: Russell and Russell, 1963.

_____. *History of the Later Roman Empire from the Death of Theodosius I to the Death of Justinian.* 2 vols. London and New York: Macmillan, 1923.

Callery, Alphonse. *Histoire du pouvoir royal d'imposer depuis la féodalité jusque'au regne de Charles V.* Bruxelles: A. Vromant, 1879.

Cam, Helen Maud. "The Theory and Practice of Representation in Medieval England," in *Lordship and Community in Medieval Europe,* ed. Frederick L. Cheyette. New York: Holt, Rinehart and Winston, 1967. Pp. 256–67.

Carlyle, Sir R. W. and A. J. *A History of Medieval Political Theory in the West.* Edinburgh and London: W. Blackwood, 1903–1936; repr. New York: Barnes and Noble, n.d.

Carlyle, Thomas. *The Early Kings of Norway.* New York: Harper and Bros., 1875.

Castro, Americo. *The Spaniards: An Introduction to Their History,* transl. Willard F. King and Selma Margaretten. Berkeley and Los Angeles: University of California Press, 1971.

Cave, Roy C. and Herbert H. Coulson, eds. *A Source Book for Medieval Economic History.* Milwaukee: Bruce Publishing Co., 1936.

Chaney, William A. *The Cult of Kingship in Anglo-Saxon England.* Berkeley and Los Angeles: University of California Press, 1970.

Chapman, Charles E. *A History of Spain; Founded on the Historia de España y de la Civilización española of Rafael Altamira.* New York: Macmillan, 1941.

Chenu, M. D., O. P. *Toward Understanding Saint Thomas,* transl. with additions A. M. Landry, O. P., and D. Hughes, O. P. Chicago: Henry Regnery, 1964.

Chrimes, S. B. *Henry VII.* Berkeley and Los Angeles: University of California Press, 1972.

Claveria, Carlos. "Reflejos del 'goticismo' español en la fraseología del Siglo de Oro," in *Homenaja ofrecido a Damaso Alonso.* Madrid: Editorial Gredes, 1960. Pp. 357–72.

Claude, Dietrich. *Adel, Kirche und Königtum im Westgotenreich;* series: *Vorträge und Forschungen,* Sonderband 8. Sigmaringen: Jan Thorbecke-Verlag, 1971.

_____. *Geschichte der Westgoten;* Urban-Taschenbücher 128. Stuttgart: Kohlhammer, 1970.

Colmeiro, D. Manuel. *Curso de Derecho Politico segun la Historia de Leon y Castilla.* Madrid: Martinez Garcia, 1873.

Cook, E. Thornton. *The Royal Line of France.* New York: E. P. Dutton, 1934.

Costain, Thomas B. *The Three Edwards.* Garden City, N.Y.: Doubleday, 1958.

Coulton, G. G. "Nationalism in the Middle Ages." *Cambridge Historical Journal,* Vol. V (1935), pp. 15–40.

Crow, John A. *Spain: The Root and the Flower.* New York and Evanston: Harper and Row, 1963.

Danstrup, John. *A History of Denmark*. Copenhagen: Wivels Forlag, 1947.

Deane, Herbert A. *The Political and Social Ideas of Saint Augustine*. New York: Columbia University Press, 1963.

Dickinson, John. "The Medieval Conception of Kingship and Some of its Limitations as Developed in the *Policraticus* of John of Salisbury." *Speculum,* Vol. I (1926), pp. 308–37.

Digby, Sir Kenelm Edward. *An Introduction to the History of the Law of Real Property,* 5th ed. Oxford: Clarendon Press, 1897.

Doerries, Hermann. *Constantine and Religious Liberty,* transl. Roland H. Bainton. New Haven: Yale University Press, 1960.

————. *Das Selbstzeugnis Kaiser Konstantins*. Series: *Abhandlungen der Akademie der Wissenschaften in Göttingen, Philologisch-Historische Klasse;* Dritte Folge, 34. Göttingen: Vandenhoeck & Ruprecht, 1954.

Douglas, David C. and George Greenaway. *English Historical Documents*. Oxford University Press, 1953. Vol. II.

Douglas, David Charles. *William the Conqueror*. Berkeley and Los Angeles: University of California Press, 1964.

Duchesne, Msgr. Louis. *The Early History of the Christian Church from Its Foundation to the End of the Fifth Century,* transl. Claude Jenkins. 3 vols. London: John Murray, 1924.

Duckett, Eleanor Shipley. *Alcuin, Friend of Charlemagne; His World and Work*. New York: Macmillan, 1951.

Dudden, Frederick H. *The Life and Times of Saint Ambrose*. Oxford: Clarendon Press, 1935.

Dvornik, Francis. *Early Christian and Byzantine Political Philosophy*. Washington: Dumbarton Oaks Center for Byzantine Studies, 1966.

Edinburgh Review, Editors. "The Gothic Laws of Spain," No. 61, 1818, pp. 94–132.

Elliott, J. H. *Imperial Spain, 1469–1716*. New York: St. Martin's Press, 1964.

Endore, Guy. *The Sword of God: Jeanne d'Arc*. Garden City, N.Y.: Garden City Publishing Co., 1931.

England, Laws. *Select Pleas of the Forest,* ed. G. J. Turner. London: Selden Society, 1901.

Ensslin, Wilhelm. *Theoderich der Grosse*. München: Verlag F. Bruckmann, 1947.

Ewig, Eugen. *Volkstum und Volksbewusstsein im Frankenreich des 7. Jahrhunderts*. N.p., 1958; repr. Darmstadt: WBG, 1969.

————. "Zum christlichen Königsgedanken im Frühmittelalter," in *Königtum,* pp. 7–73.

Fabre, Lucien. *Joan of Arc,* transl. Gerard Hopkins. New York: McGraw-Hill, 1954.

Fawtier, Robert. *The Capetian Kings of France,* transl. L. Butler and R. Adam. New York: Saint Martin's Press, 1960.

Ferguson, Arthur B. *The Indian Summer of English Chivalry*. Durham: Duke University Press, 1960.

Fichtenau, Heinrich. *The Carolingian Imperium,* transl. Peter Munz. Oxford: Basil Blackwell, 1957.

————. *Karl der Grosse und das Kaisertum.* MIÖG, 1953; repr. Darmstadt: WBG, 1971.

Figgis, J. N. *The Theory of the Divine Right of Kings,* 2nd ed. Cambridge: University Press, 1914.

Finke, Heinrich. *Papsttum und Untergang des Templerordens.* Münster: Aschendorff, 1907.

————. *Weltimperialismus und nationale Regungen im späteren Mittelalter.* Freiburg i. B.; Speyer & Kaerner, 1916.

Fischart, Johann. "Wohlbedenckliche Beschreibung des an dem König in Franckreich newlich verrhäterisch begangenen Meuchelmords. . . ," 1589, in *Sämtliche Dichtungen,* ed. Heinrich Kurz (Vols. VIII-X of *Deutsche Bibliothek*). Leipzig: J. J. Weber, 1866/1867. Vol. X, pp. 377-80.

Frend, W. H. C. *The Donatist Church; A Movement of Protest in Roman North Africa.* Oxford: Clarendon Press, 1952.

Freytag, Gustav. *Bilder aus der deutschen Vergangenheit,* 14th ed. Leipzig: S. Hirzel, 1883.

Fuhrmann, Horst, ed. *Quellen zur Geschichte der Entstehung des Kirchenstaates.* Göttingen: Vandenhoeck & Ruprecht, 1968.

Fuller, J. F. C. *Decisive Battles: Their Influence upon History and Civilization.* New York: Scribner's, 1940.

————. *A Military History of the Western World,* Vol. I: *From the Earliest Times to the Battle of Lepanto.* New York: Funk and Wagnalls, 1954.

Ganshof, F. L. *The Carolingians and the Frankish Monarchy,* transl. Janet Sondeimer. Ithaca: Cornell University Press, 1971.

————. *Feudalism,* transl. Philip Grierson. London: Longmans, Green and Co., 1952.

Gautier, Leon. *Chivalry,* transl. Henry Frith. London: George Routledge, 1891.

Gavrilovitch, Michel. *Étude sur le Traité de Paris de 1259 entre Louis IX, Roi de France & Henry III, Roi d'Angleterre.* Paris: Bibliothèque de l'École des Hautes Études, fasc. CXXV, 1899.

Gewirth, Alan. *Marsilius of Padua, The Defender of Peace.* 2 vols. New York: Columbia University Press, 1956. (Vol. I is an introduction to, Vol. II a translation of, the *Defensor Pacis.*)

Gibbon, Edward. *The Decline and Fall of the Roman Empire,* ed. J. B. Bury. London: Methuen, 1901. Vols. III-IV.

Giesey, Falph E. *If Not, Not: The Oath of the Aragonese and the Legendary Laws of Sobrarbe.* Princeton, N.J.: Princeton University Press, 1968.

Greenlee, James G. "French Royal Propaganda from Philip the Fair to Louis XI (1300-1483)." Unpublished master's thesis, McMaster University, Hamilton, 1969.

Grønbech, Vilhelm. *Kultur und Religion der Germanen,* transl. Ellen Hoffmeyer, ed. and intr. O. Höfler, 6th ed. Darmstadt: WBG, 1961. Vol. I.

Guellemin, Henri. *Joan, Maid of Orleans,* transl. Harold J. Salemson. New York: Saturday Review Press, 1973.

Hale, Sir Matthew. *The History of the Common Law of England;* publ. post. 1713; ed. and intr. Charles M. Gray. Chicago: University of Chicago Press, 1971.

Hammond, Mason. *The Augustan Principate in Theory and Practice during the Julio-Claudian Period,* enlarged ed. New York: Russell and Russell, 1968.

Haskins, Charles H. *Norman Institutions.* N.p., 1918; repr. New York: F. Ungar, 1960.

————. *The Renaissance of the Twelfth Century.* N.p., 1927; repr. New York: Meridian, 1957.

Hatschek, Julius. *Englische Verfassungsgeschichte bis zum Regierungsantritt der Königin Viktoria.* München: R. Oldenbourg, 1913.

Heisenberg, August. *Grabeskirche und Apostelkirche, zwei Basiliken Konstantins.* Leipzig: J. C. Hinrichs, 1908.

Hellman, Sigmund. *Das Mittelalter bis zum Ausgange der Kreuzzüge.* Gotha: Perthes, 1920.

Henderson, Ernest F. *Select Historical Documents of the Middle Ages.* London: G. Bell & Sons, 1896.

Henneman, John Bell. *Royal Taxation in Fourteenth Century France: The Development of War Financing, 1322-1356.* Princeton, N.J.: Princeton University Press, 1971.

Herbert, Sydney. *The Fall of Feudalism in France.* New York: Barnes and Noble, 1921.

Herlihy, David, ed. *The History of Feudalism.* New York: Walker and Co., 1970.

Hewitt, H. J. *The Organization of War under Edward III, 1338-1362.* Manchester: University Press, 1966.

Hill, Boyd H., Jr. *Medieval Monarchy in Action: the German Empire from Henry I to Henry IV.* New York: Barnes and Noble, 1972.

Hill, George. *Spain.* New York: Praeger, 1970.

Höfler, Otto. "Der Sakralcharacter des germanischen Königtums," in *Königtum,* pp. 75-104.

Holdsworth, W. S. *Sources and Literature of English Law.* Oxford: Clarendon Press, 1925.

Howorth, Sir Henry H. *"Harald Fairhair" and His Ancestors,* Vol. IX, Part I, *Saga-Book of the Viking Society.* London: Viking Society for Northern Research, n.d.

Hoyoux, Jean. "Reges criniti: chevelures, tonsures et scalps chez les Mérovingiens." *Revue Belge de philologie et d'histoire,* Vol. XXVI (1948), pp. 479-508.

Hutchins, Robert M. *Saint Thomas and the World State.* Milwaukee: Marquette University Press, 1949.

Johnson, Edgar N. *An Introduction to the History of the Western Tradition,* vol. I. Boston: Ginn and Co., 1959.

Jones, A. H. M. *Constantine and the Conversion of Europe.* London: English Universities Press, Ltd., 1948.

_____. *The Later Roman Empire, 284–602; A Social, Economic, and Administrative Survey.* 2 vols. Norman: University of Oklahoma Press, 1964.

Kantorowicz, Ernst H. *Frederick the Second, 1194–1250,* transl. E. O. Lorrimer. N.p., 1931; repr. N.Y.: Frederick Ungar, 1957.

_____. *The King's Two Bodies: A Study in Mediaeval Political Theology.* Princeton, N.J.: Princeton University Press, 1967.

Kaufmann, E. "Über das Scheren abgesetzter Merowinger," *Zeitschrift der Savigny-Stiftung fur Rechtsgeschichte,* Germ. Abt., Vol. LXXII (1955), pp. 177–85.

Keeton, George W. *The Norman Conquest and the Common Law.* New York: Barnes and Noble, 1966.

Keilhau, Wilhelm. *Norway in World History.* London: MacDonald & Co., 1944.

Kendall, Paul M. *Louis XI, "The Universal Spider."* New York: W. W. Norton, 1971.

Kern, Fritz. *Gottesgnadentum und Widerstandsrecht im früheren Mittelalter,* rev. ed. Rudolf Buchner. N.p., 1954; repr. Darmstadt: WBG, 1962.

Kilgour, Raymond L. *The Decline of Chivalry as Shown in the French Literature of the Later Middle Ages.* Gloucester, Mass.: Peter Smith, 1966.

King, Noel Quinton. *The Emperor Theodosius and the Establishment of Christianity.* Philadelphia: Westminster Press, 1960.

Klein, Richard. *Tertullian und das römische Reich.* Heidelberg: C. Winter, 1968.

Knappen, M. M. *Constitutional and Legal History of England.* New York: Harcourt Brace and Co., 1942.

Koch, Hal. "Canute the Great and the Descendants of Sven Estridsøn," in Jørgen Bukdahl, et al., eds., *Scandinavia Past and Present,* Vol. I: *From the Viking Age to Absolute Monarchy.* Odense: Arnkrone, 1959. Pp. 175–78.

Koht, Halvdan, and Sigmund Skard. *The Voice of Norway.* New York: Columbia University Press, 1944.

Krusch, Bruno. "Chronologica regum Francorum stirpis Merowingicae," MGH, SRM, Vol. VII, pp. 468–516.

Laehr, Gerhard. *Die Konstantinische Schenkung in der abendländischen Literatur des Mittelalters bis zur Mitte des 14. Jahrhunderts.* Berlin, 1926; Vaduz: Kraus Reprints, 1965.

Larsen, Karen. *A History of Norway.* Princeton, N.J.: Princeton University Press, 1948.

Larson, Laurence M. "The Household of the Norwegian Kings in the Thirteenth Century." *American Historical Review,* Vol. XIII (1908), pp. 459–79.

Lemberg, Eugen. *Die Geschichte des Nationalismus in Europa.* Stuttgart: Curt E. Schwab, 1950.

Lewis, Ewart. *Medieval Political Ideas.* 2 vols. New York: Knopf, 1954.

Lewis, P. S. *Later Medieval France: The Polity.* London and New York: Macmillan and St. Martin's Press, 1968.

_____. "Two Pieces of Fifteenth-Century Political Iconography: (a) Clovis touches for the King's Evil; (b) The English Kill Their Kings." *Journal of the Warburg and Courtault Institutes,* Vol. XXVII (1964), pp. 317–20.

————, ed. *The Recovery of France in the Fifteenth Century,* transl. G. F. Martin. New York: Harper and Row, 1971.

————. "War Propaganda and Historiography in Fifteenth-Century France and England." *Transactions of the Royal Historical Society,* Series 5, Vol. XV (1965), pp. 1-21.

Liebeschütz, Hans. "John of Salisbury and Pseudo-Plutarch," *Journal of the Warburg and Courtault Institutes,* Vol. VI (1943), pp. 33-39.

Lindner, Theodor. *Geschichte des deutschen Reiches unter König Wenzel.* 2 vols. Braunschweig: Schwetschke und Sohn, 1880.

Livermore, Harold. *A History of Spain.* New York: Ferrar, Straus and Co., 1956.

Lowe, Walter I. "The Considerations which Induced Edward III to Assume the Title, 'King of France.' " *Annual Report of the American Historical Association for 1900,* Vol. I, pp. 537-73.

Lyon, Bryce. *A Constitutional and Legal History of Medieval England.* New York: Harper, 1960.

Macmullen, Ramsey. *Constantine.* New York: Dial Press, 1969.

Maitland, Frederic W. *The Constitutional History of England.* Cambridge: University Press, 1908; repr. 1961.

Manitius, Max. *Geschichte der Lateinischen Literatur des Mittelalters,* Vol. II, Part 1: *Von Justinian bis zur Mitte des zehnten Jahrhunderts.* München: Beck, 1911.

Marcus, Jacob R. *The Jew in the Medieval World; a Source Book, 315-1791.* Cincinnati: Union of American Hebrew Congregations, 1938.

Mariana, Juan de. *Historia de rebus Hispaniae, 1592; in Obras.* 2 vols. Madrid: Rivadeneyra, 1864-1872.

Marignan, A. *Études sur la civilisation française,* Vol. I: *La société mérovingienne.* Paris: É. Bouillon, 1899.

Marongiu, Antonio. "The Theory of Democracy and Consent in the Fourteenth Century," transl., Guiseppe Galigani in *Lordship and Community in Medieval Europe,* ed. Frederic L. Cheyette. New York: Holt, Rinehart and Winston, 1967. Pp. 404-21.

McFayden, Donald. *The History of the Title* Imperator *Under the Roman Empire.* Chicago: University of Chicago Press, 1920. Vol. IV of series *Ancient History Pamphlets.* Menasha, Wisc.: Banta Publ. Co., 1915-1923.

McGuire, Martin R. P. "A New Study on the Political Role of Saint Ambrose." *Catholic Historical Review,* Vol. XXII (1936-1937), pp. 304-18.

McKisack, May. *The Fourteenth Century.* Oxford: Clarendon Press, 1959.

Martínex Marina, Francisco. *Teoria le las Cortes.* 3 vols. Madrid: Collado; Villalpando, 1820.

Merriman, Roger B. "The Cortes of the Spanish Kingdoms in the Later Middle Ages." *American Historical Review,* Vol. XVI (1910-1911), pp. 476-95.

————. *The Rise of the Spanish Empire.* New York: Macmillan, 1936. Vol. I.

Miller, Townsend. *The Castles and the Crown; Spain: 1451-1555.* New York: Coward-McCann, 1936.

Mitchell, Sydney K. *Studies in Taxation under John and Henry III.* New Haven: Yale Historical Publications, 1914.

————. *Taxation in Medieval England,* posthum. ed. Sidney Painter. New Haven: Yale University Press, 1951.

Mommsen, Theodor. *Römisches Staatsrecht,* 3rd ed. 3 vols. Leipzig: Hirzel, 1887.

Montross, Lynn. *War Through the Ages.* New York: Harper and Bros., 1944.

Muller-Mertens, Eckhard. *Regnum Teutonicum; Aufkommen und Verbreitung der deutschen Reichs- und Königsauffassung im frühen Mittelalter.* Wien: Böhlau, 1970.

Munz, Peter. *Frederick Barbarossa.* Ithaca: Cornell University Press, 1969.

Myers, Henry A. "The Concept of Kingship in the *Book of Emperors (Kaiserchronik)." Traditio,* Vol. XXVII (1971), pp. 205-30.

Nagl, M. Assunta. *Galla Placidia,* Vol. II, no. 3 of series: *Studien zur Geschichte und Kultur des Altertums.* N.p., 1908; repr. N.Y.: Johnson Reprint Corp., 1967.

Neumann, Freidrich. "Wann entstanden Kaiserchronik und Rolandslied?" *Zeitschrift für deutsches Altertum und deutsche Literatur,* Vol. XCI (1961/1962), pp. 263-329.

Oakley, Stewart. *A Short History of Sweden.* New York: Praeger, 1966.

Ohly, Ernst Friedrich. *Sage und Legende in der Kaiserchronik.* Münster, 1940; repr. Darmstadt: WBG, 1968.

Oman, Sir Charles. *A History of the Art of War in the Middle Ages,* rev. ed. 2 vols. New York: Burt Franklin, 1924.

Oost, Stewart Irvin. *Galla Placidia Augusta; a Biographical Essay.* Chicago: University of Chicago Press, 1968.

Ostrogorsky, George. *History of the Byzantine State,* transl. Joan Hussey. New Brunswick, N.J.: Rutgers University Press, 1957.

Paine, Thomas. *The Rights of Man.* 1792; repr. Garden City, N.Y.: Doubleday, 1961. Published in one volume with Edmund Burke's *Reflections on the Revolution in France.*

Painter, Sidney. *French Chivalry.* N.p., 1940; repr. Ithaca: Cornell University Press, 1957.

————. *The Reign of King John.* Baltimore: Johns Hopkins Press, 1949.

————. *The Rise of the Feudal Monarchies.* Ithaca: Cornell University Press, 1951.

Paredi, Angelo. *Saint Ambrose; His Life and Times,* transl. M. Joseph Costelloe, S. J. Notre Dame, Ind.: University of Notre Dame Press, 1964.

Perroy, Edouard. *The Hundred Years War,* transl. W. B. Wells, intro. David C. Douglas. New York: Oxford University Press, 1951.

Peters, Edward. *The Shadow King:* Rex Inutilis *in Medieval Law and Literature, 751-1327.* New Haven: Yale University Press, 1970.

Petit-Dutaillis. Charles Edmond, *The Feudal Monarchy in France and England from the Tenth to the Thirteenth Century.* London: K. Paul, Trench, Trubner & Co., 1936.

Pick, Robert. *Empress Maria Theresa: The Earlier Years, 1717-1757.* New York: Harper and Row, 1966.

Poole, Austin L. *Obligations of Society in the XII and XIII Centuries.* Oxford: Clarendon Press, 1946.

Poole, Reginald L. *Illustrations of the History of Medieval Thought and Learning,* 2nd ed. SPCK, 1920; repr. New York: Dover, 1960.

Post, Gaines. "Roman Law and Early Representation in Spain and Italy." *Speculum,* Vol. XVIII (1943), pp. 211–32.

_____. "Status, id est, magistratus; l'état, c'est moi; and status regis, the "estate royal" (1100–1322)," in *Studies in Medieval and Renaissance History.* Lincoln: University of Nebraska Press, 1964. Vol. I, pp. 3–103.

_____. *Studies in Medieval Legal Thought: Public Law and the State, 1100–1322.* Princeton, N.J.: Princeton University Press, 1964.

Potter, John D. *The Art of Hanging.* South Brunswick: A. S. Barnes, 1965.

Prentout, Henri, *Étude critique sur Dudon de Saint-Quentin et son Histoire des premiers Ducs Normands.* Paris: Auguste Picard, 1916.

Prescott, William H. *History of the Reign of Ferdinand and Isabella the Catholic.* Philadelphia: J. B. Lippincott, 1871–1872. Vols. I–II.

Preston, Richard A. and Sydney F. Wise. *Men in Arms: A History of Warfare and Its Interrelationships with Western Society,* 2nd rev. ed. New York and Washington: Praeger, 1970.

Ramsey, Sir James H. *The Angevin Empire; or The Three Reigns of Henry II, Richard I, and John (A.D. 1154–1216).* London: S. Sonnenschein & Co., 1903.

Redlich, Oswald. *Rudolf von Habsburg; das deutsche Reich nach dem Untergange des alten Kaisertums.* Innsbruck: Wagner, 1903.

Roberts, John, et al. *Civilization.* 2 vols. DelMar, Cal.: CRM Books, 1973.

Robertson, A. J. ed. and transl., *The Laws of the Kings of England from Edmund to Henry I;* bilingual ed. Cambridge: University Press, 1925.

Rodes, John E. *Germany: A History.* New York: Holt, Rinehart and Winston, 1964.

Rouse, Richard H. and Mary A. "John of Salisbury and the Doctrine of Tyrannicide." *Speculum,* Vol. XLII (1967), pp. 693–709.

Routley, Erik. *The English Carol.* London: Herbert Jenkins, 1958.

Sabine, George H. *History of Political Theory,* 3rd ed. New York: Holt, Rinehart and Winston, 1961.

Scherer, J. E. *Die Rechtsverhältnisse der Juden in den deutschösterreichischen Ländern.* Leipzig: Duncker & Humblot, 1901.

Schlesinger, Walter. "Über germanisches Heerkönigtum," in *Königtum,* pp. 105–41.

Schneider, Reinhard. *Königswahl und Königserhebung im Frühmittelalter: Untersuchungen zur Herrschaftsnachfolge bei den Langobarden und Merowingern.* Stuttgart: A. Hiersemann, 1970.

Schramm, Percy Ernst. *Herrschaftszeichen und Staatssymbolik;* series: *Schriften der MGH,* 13, Vol. I (1954).

_____. *Kaiser, Rom und Renovatio,* 2nd ed. Darmstadt: Hermann Gentner Verlag, 1957.

_____. *Der König von Frankreich: Das Wesen der Monarchie vom 9. zum 16.*

Jahrhundert, 2nd ed. Weimar: Böhlaus Nachf., 1960.

Semmingsen, Ingrid. "St. Olav," in Jorgen Bukdahl, et al., eds., *Scandinavia Past and Present;* Vol. I: *From the Viking Age to Absolute Monarchy.* Odense: Arnkrone, 1959. Pp. 165–68.

Sergeant, Lewis. *The Franks from Their Origin as a Confederacy to the Establishment of the Kingdom of France and the German Empire.* New York: G. P. Putnam, 1898.

Shafer, Boyd C. *Nationalism: Interpreters and Interpretations.* Washington, D.C.: American Historical Association Service Center for Teachers of History, 1959.

_____. *Nationalism; Myth and Reality.* New York: Harcourt Brace and Co., 1955.

Shneidman, J. Lee. *The Rise of the Aragonese-Catalan Empire, 1200–1350.* 2 vols. New York: New York University Press, 1970.

Siegrist, Theodor. *Herrscherbild und Weltsicht bei Notker Balbulus: Untersuchungen zu den Gesta Karoli.* Dissertation, University of Zürich. Zürich: Fretz & Wasmuth, 1963.

Silber, Manfred. *The Gallic Royalty of the Merovingians in its Relationship to the "Orbis Terrarum Romanus" during the 5th and 6th Centuries, A.D.* Bern and Frankfurt: Herbert Lang & Cie AG, 1971.

Sinding, Paul C. *History of Scandinavia from the Early Times of the Norsemen and Vikings to the Present Day.* New York: Pudney and Russell, 1858.

Spaulding, Oliver L., Hoffman Nickerson, and John W. Wright, *Warfare: A Study of Military Methods from the Earliest Times.* N.p., 1925; repr. New York: Arno Press, 1972.

Stevenson, J., ed. *Creeds, Councils and Controversies; Documents Illustrative of the History of the Church A.D. 337–461.* New York: Seabury Press, 1966.

_____, ed. *A New Eusebius: Documents Illustrative of the History of the Church to A.D. 337.* London: SPCK, 1957.

Strauss, Leo. "Marsilius of Padua," in *History of Political Philosophy,* ed. L. Strauss and J. Cropsey. Chicago: Rand McNally, 1963. Pp. 227–45.

Strayer, Joseph. *The Albigensian Crusades.* New York: Dial Press, 1971.

_____. "France: the Holy Land, the Chosen People, and the Most Christian King," in *Action and Conviction in Early Modern Europe,* ed. T. Rabb and J. Siegel. Princeton, N.J.: Princeton University Press, 1969. Pp. 3–16.

_____. *Medieval Statecraft and the Perspectives of History,* ed. Gaines Post. Princeton, N.J.: Princeton University Press, 1971.

_____. *On the Medieval Origins of the Modern State.* Princeton, N.J.: Princeton University Press, 1970.

Stromberg, Andrew A. *A History of Sweden.* London: George Allen and Unwin, 1932.

Stubbs, William. *Select Charters and Other Illustrations of English Constitutional History,* 7th ed. Oxford: Clarendon, 1890.

Tanner, J. R. *English Constitutional Conflicts of the Seventeenth Century, 1603–1689.* Cambridge: University Press, 1928.

Van Caenegem, R. C. *The Birth of the English Common Law.* Cambridge: University Press, 1973.

Walshe, M. O'C. *Medieval German Literature.* Cambridge, Mass.: Harvard University Press, 1962.

Wasby, Stephen L. *Political Science — the Discipline and Its Dimensions; an Introduction.* New York: Scribner's, 1970.

Wenskus, Reinhard. *Stammesbildung und Verfassung.* Köln: Böhlau Verlag, 1961.

West, Andrew F. *Alcuin and the Rise of Christian Schools.* New York: Scribner's, 1903.

White, Lynn, Jr. *Medieval Technology and Social Change.* Oxford: Clarendon Press, 1962.

Wieruszowski, Helene. *Vom Imperium zum nationalen Königtum: Vergleichende Studien über die publizistischen Kämpfe Kaiser Friedrichs II und König Philipps des Schönen mit der Kurie;* Beiheft 30 der Historischen Zeitschrift. München & Berlin: R. Oldenbourg, 1933.

Williams, Mary W. *Social Scandinavia in the Viking Age.* New York: Macmillan, 1920.

Wolfram, Herwig. *Intitulatio I. Lateinische Königs- und Fürstentitel bis zum Ende des 8. Jahrhunderts.* MIÖG, Ergänzungsband XXI, 1967. Graz: Böhlaus Nachf., 1967.

————. *Lateinische Herrscher- und Fürstentitel im neunten Jahrhundert,* in Part 1 of *Intitulatio II,* ed. H. Wolfram. Wien: Böhlaus Nachf., 1973, pp. 19–178 and "Schlusswort" to the same work, pp. 549–56.

————. "The Shaping of the Early Medieval Kingdom." *Viator,* Vol. I (1970), pp. 1–20.

————. "The Shaping of the Early Medieval Principality as a type of Non-Royal Rulership." *Viator,* Vol. II (1971), pp. 33–51.

————. *Splendor Imperii: Die Epiphanie von Tugend und Heil in Herrschaft und Reich.* MIÖG, Ergänzungsband XX, Heft 3. Graz: Böhlaus Nachf., 1963.

Woloch, G. Michael. "A Survey of Scholarship on Ostrogothic Italy, A.D. 489–552." *Classical Folia* 25 (1971), pp. 320–31.

Wolff-Windegg, Philipp. *Die Gekrönten: Sinn und Sinnbilder des Königtums.* Stuttgart: Klett, 1958.

Wood, Charles T. *The French Apanages and the Capetian Monarchy, 1224–1328.* Cambridge, Mass.: Harvard University Press, 1966.

Woodbine, G. E. "The Language of the English Law." *Speculum,* Vol. XVIII (1943), pp. 395–436.

Wormser, Rene A. *The Law.* New York: Simon and Schuster, 1949.

Zacour, Norman. *An Introduction to Medieval Institutions.* New York: St. Martin's Press, 1969.

Ziegler, Aloysius K. *Church and State in Visigothic Spain.* Dissertation. Washington, D.C.: Catholic University, 1930.

Zöllner, Erich. *Geschichte der Franken bis zur Mitte des sechsten Jahrhunderts.* München: C. H. Beck, 1970.

INDEX